Understanding Social Psychology

Understanding Social Psychology

Stephen Worchel
Texas A&M University

Joel Cooper
Princeton University

George R. Goethals
Williams College

Fourth Edition

The Dorsey Press

Chicago, Illinois 60604

Cover art: "5:05" by Giancarlo Impiglia. © Giancarlo Impiglia 1980. Acrylic on canvas, 40" × 48", from the private collection of Harriet Levin, New York.

Giancarlo Impiglia was born in Rome, Italy. He received his art training there at the Liceo Artistico and Accademia Di Belle Arti. His works have appeared in numerous exhibitions in Europe and America, and they are included in both public and private collections. He lives and works in New York City.

ISBN 0-256-03400-1

Library of Congress Catalog Card No. 86–72564

Printed in the United States of America

1 2 3 4 5 6 7 8 9 0 DO 5 4 3 2 1 0 9 8

To our parents,
who were our first teachers
of psychology;
to Jack W. Brehm and Edward E. Jones,
who imparted to us a respect
for the field of social psychology;
to our children, Leah, Jessica,
        Jason, Aaron, Grant, Jefferson, and Andrew,
who have shown us how much more
psychology we still have to learn;
and to our wives, Frances, Barbara, and Marion,
who have worked so hard
at creating the type of environment
that allows us to continue our own learning.

PREFACE

There are two approaches to revising textbooks. One is the "fine tuning" approach where the author(s) keep the book basically as it was but update and add areas they overlooked in the earlier edition. This approach works if a field has not experienced significant changes over the three or four years between revisions. The other type of revision calls for more radical surgery. It involves taking a broader look at the discipline by asking, "If I were to write a new book, how would I present the field?"

After three editions, we decided that it was time to attempt a more radical revision. The previous editions each presented roughly the same outline of social psychology. Further, each edition was longer than its predecessor as we attempted to retain the cherished tidbits while adding new material. Eliminating sections or topics felt like giving away our old baseball cards. Too often we soothed our pain by keeping the old section and simply added on a new section or chapter.

To overcome our reluctance to eliminate old material, we decided to bring in a new co-author, someone familiar with our purposes and the course who could help us revise the text with a fresh and knowing eye. The perfect choice was our long-time colleague, George R. Goethals, who knew our approach but was not constrained by a previous association with the book. We hoped he could see the shortcomings that we had previously overlooked, and one of his appointed tasks was to point out these lapses, omissions, and excesses. We also requested reviewers to point out sections that could be deleted or covered more concisely, as well as to suggest material that we needed to add. Thus, with a new mission and a new co-author, who seemed to delight in his role as devil's advocate and inquisitor, we began the fourth edition of *Understanding Social Psychology*.

It was clear from the reviews of the third edition and our own discussions that the first principle in any presentation of social psychology was to include both the classical and the new. New material would be included, not only because it was new, but also because it helped define or integrate key areas of study. A second principle that guided us was to present a balanced coverage of both theory and research in social psychology. The field was built on solid theory and methodology, and these basics must form the foundation of the text. The third principle was that we must show both the basic scientific and applied sides of social psychology. These two sides do not represent unrelated approaches; rather, they are two sides of the same coin. They support and draw from each other. We resisted the temptation to add a number of "applied" chapters at the end of the book. To do so would give the students the impression that research and application were unrelated. We decided instead to blend the basic and applied work into the appropriate chapters to show their kinship. (In our own class testing, we found that this approach greatly enhances students' ability to remember theories and to see the value of applications.) Finally, new developments in the discipline made it imperative to expand coverage of both the motivational and cognitive approaches to social psychology. While the two approaches are often presented as competing explanations for social behavior, they in fact complement one another and add important pieces to the puzzle of human behavior.

With these principles in mind we set out to rework the text so that it would instruct without being encyclopedic. The result is a somewhat shorter volume, but one that more fairly represents cognition and motivation, classical and new areas, and basic and applied social psychology. We retained our structure of focusing first on individuals (cognitions, attribution, and attitudes), next examining dyadic interactions (attraction, altruism, and aggression), and then studying group and intergroup behavior. In concert with the field, there is a greater emphasis in this edition on social cognition and the self. There is a new chapter on social cognition (Chapter 2) and a new chapter on the self in social interaction (Chapter 3). At the other end of the continuum, there is more material on intergroup relations (Chapters 9 and 11). We have worked in new material on applied areas such as health, law, sports, and organizations throughout the text.

We also retained our approach of showing how social psychology can be used to better understand situations and events that are encountered in everyday life. Each chapter begins with an incident that raises questions central to the chapter's themes. We then refer to the incident throughout the chapter. The incidents should not only serve as a heuristic device for learning the material, but we hope that they will challenge readers to apply social psychology to their own experiences. The glossary has been expanded and, as in the previous edition, we have included suggested readings at the end of each chapter. We might describe the end product by stating that the heart of the old edition beats strongly in the new.

A Student Study Guide, prepared by Frederick Rhodewalt of the University of Utah is available separately. The Study Guide will help students place the information in the text into theoretical frameworks enabling them to understand and integrate the research areas.

Many people contributed to this new edition. First, we would like to thank the surprisingly large number of students and faculty members who wrote us with suggestions for a revised edition. We tried to include as much of your input as possible. Please continue to send us your comments.

We would like to thank our brave band of reviewers, whose creative suggestions and sensitivity to the frazzled state of the authors managed to help us overcome our biases and expand our coverage. We appreciate the help of Richard L. Archer, Southwest State University; Roy F. Baumeister, Case Western Reserve University; Sharon S. Brehm, University of Kansas; John T. Cacioppo, University of Iowa; Jerome M. Chertkoff, Indiana University; Keith E. Davis, University of South Carolina; E. Tory Higgins, New York University; Douglas T. Kenrick, Arizona State University; Eric Knowles, University of Arkansas; Diane M. Mackie, University of California, Santa Barbara; Richard L. Moreland, University of Pittsburgh; Miles L. Patterson, University of Missouri; and Daniel M. Wegner, Trinity University.

We would also like to thank Brian Mullen, Fred Rhodewalt, and Bill Webb for additional, and much needed, comments and support. Within each of our respective schools, an army of students and staff helped prepare the manuscript, track down material, and offer suggestions. More importantly, these people had to put up with our ranting and raving during the revision period. The following contributors to the book and to our mental health are: Dink Asano, Sandy Camp, Vicky Corrington, John Fleming, Linda Ginzel, Angie Giusti, Therese Marcellin, Kerry Marsh, Susie Marten, Sarah McFarland, DiAnne Poehl, Steven Scher, Alan Singh, and Vera Sohl. We would also like to thank O. K. (Buddy) Davis of the *Ruston* (L.A.) *Daily Leader* for his help in providing information on Eddie Robinson.

Finally, we'd like to thank the people at Dorsey Press who rallied for yet another revision. As the number of authors increased, so did the number and scope of diabolical plots we could hatch on the Dorsey staff. Your support, good humor, and professionalism made the project possible. We will long remember Paul O'Connell's stoic smile as yet another deadline passed, Ann Knowles's cheerful telephone calls to ask whether Joel Cooper really existed, Charlotte Green's letters asking what type of book this really was, Jane Lightell who orchestrated the works of the three authors who often had nonoverlapping styles, and Keith McPherson who put the final bow on the package through his design. Thanks also to Waivah Clement who skillfully coordinated our schedule with Dorsey's schedule and guided the text to completion.

Stephen Worchel
Joel Cooper
George R. Goethals

CONTENTS

LIST OF FIGURES

LIST OF TABLES

ONE

SOCIAL PSYCHOLOGY: WHAT, WHY, AND HOW

On Halloween eve, 1938, a radio program of Spanish music was interrupted by a "newscast" reporting explosions on Mars. Sometime later, "Roman Raquello" and his orchestra were again interrupted, this time with the information that a huge flaming object had landed in the small town of Grover's Mill, near Princeton, New Jersey. The radio network sent reporter "Carl Phillips" to the scene. This is part of the report heard by millions of listeners on the CBS network:

> [Phillips] Well, I . . . I hardly know where to begin, to paint for you a word picture of the strange scene before my eyes, like something out of a modern *Arabian Nights*. Well, I just got here. I haven't had a chance to look around yet. I guess that's it. Yes, I guess that's the . . . thing, directly in front of me, half buried in a vast pit. Must have struck with terrific force. The ground is covered with splinters of a tree it must have struck on its way down. What I can see of the . . . object itself doesn't look very much like a meteor, at least not the meteors I've seen. It looks more like a huge cylinder. . . . The metal on the sheath is . . . well, I've never seen anything like it. The color is sort of yellowish-white. Curious spectators now are pressing close to the object in spite of the efforts of the police to keep them back. (Hadley Cantril in *The Panic Broadcast: Portrait of an Event* by Howard Koch [copyright 1940 by Princeton University Press, © renewed 1968 by Howard Koch], reprinted by permission of International Creative Management, Inc.)

After a short period of time in which Phillips goes into a more detailed description, he gasps:

> [Phillips] Just a minute! Something's happening! Ladies and gentlemen, this is terrific! This end of the thing is beginning to flake off! The top is beginning to rotate like a screw! The thing must be hollow! . . . Ladies and gentlemen, this is the most terrifying thing I have ever witnessed. . . . Wait a minute! Someone's crawling out of the hollow top. Someone or . . . something. I can see peering out of that black hole two luminous disks . . . are they eyes? It might be a face. It might be . . . Good heavens, something's wriggling out of the shadow like a gray snake. Now it's another one, and another. They look like tentacles to me. There, I can see the thing's body. It's large as a bear and it glistens like wet leather. But that face. It . . . it's indescribable. I can hardly force myself to keep looking at it. The eyes are black and gleam like a serpent. The mouth is V-shaped with saliva dripping from its rimless lips that seem to quiver and pulsate. The monster or whatever it is can hardly move. It seems weighed down by . . . possibly gravity or something. The thing's raising up. The crowd falls back. (Koch, 1968)

Phillips then moves to find a better position from which to view the strange happenings. Once in position, he reports:

> [Phillips] A humped shape is rising out of the pit. I can make out a small beam of light against a mirror. What's that? There's a jet of flame springing

Over six million people heard Orson Welles's "Mercury Theater," and over one million people believed the newscast that Earth was being invaded by Martians. Before the program ended, thousands began to flee "the Martians" and many others sought out friends and loved ones. *(Top, The Bettmann Archive; bottom, United Press International Photo)* from that mirror, and it leaps right at the advancing men. It strikes them head on! Good Lord, they're turning into flame! Now the whole field's caught fire. [Explosion] The woods . . . the barns . . . the gas tanks of automobiles . . . it's spreading everywhere. It's coming this way. About 20 yards to my right. . . .

[Announcer Two] Ladies and gentlemen, due to circumstances beyond our control, we are unable to continue the broadcast from Grover's Mill. Evidently there's some difficulty with our field transmission. (Koch, 1968)

Within minutes, events began to happen that terrified many of the listeners. When communication with the scene was restored, forty people, including six troopers, were reported dead, burned beyond all recognition. Martial law was declared in central New Jersey. Captain Lansing of the armed forces took to the air to announce that the feared object was surrounded by eight infantry battalions. In his words, "All cause for alarm is now entirely unjustified."

As the "invasion" continued, listeners learned that Martians had been sighted from New York to Virginia and in Chicago and St. Louis. A tidal wave of terror swept the nation. Some people even readied themselves for battle. (*United Press International Photo*)

A few seconds later, the radio audience was exposed to sounds of gunfire, the shouting of orders, and general pandemonium. Silence fell, only to be broken by a bulletin read by a newsman in the New York studio:

> [Announcer Two] Ladies and gentlemen, I have a grave announcement to make. Incredible as it may seem, both the observations of science and the evidence of our eyes lead to the inescapable assumption that those strange beings who landed in the Jersey farmlands tonight are the vanguard of an invading army from the planet Mars. The battle which took place tonight at Grover's Mill has ended in one of the most startling defeats ever suffered by an army in modern times; seven thousand men armed with rifles and machine guns pitted against a single fighting machine of the invaders from Mars. One hundred and twenty known survivors. The rest strewn over the battle area from Grover's Mill to Plainsboro, crushed and trampled to death under the metal feet of the monster, or burned to cinders by its heat ray. The monster is now in control of the middle section of New Jersey and has effectively cut the state through its center. (Koch, 1968)

More Martian landings were said to have been made in Virginia. As the drama continued, the listeners were addressed by the U.S. Secretary of the Interior, whose advice to the worried citizens was that they should place their faith in God.

After this encouragement, residents of New York were urged to evacuate and were told which routes to take and which to avoid. It was reported that communication with New Jersey had been broken and that the smoke was descending upon New York as reports were being received of Martian landings in Buffalo, Chicago, and St. Louis. "This is the end now," exclaimed the reporter. "People are trying to run from it, but it's no use. They're falling like flies. Now the smoke's crossing Sixth Avenue . . . Fifth Avenue . . . 100 yards away . . . it's 50 feet. . . ."

It is estimated that at least six million people heard Orson Welles's Mercury Theater broadcast based on H. G. Wells's *War of the Worlds* and that well over one million people believed that it was a legitimate newscast and that the Earth was being invaded by Martians. Before the hour-long program had ended, hundreds of thousands of Americans were seized with panic as they tried to flee the monsters from the planet Mars. The newspapers were to say on Sunday morning, "A tidal wave of terror swept the nation."

The general panic was not confined to any educational, economic, or geographic group. People cried, screamed, gathered loved ones, huddled together, or drove to flee the attacking onslaught. A male college student reported:

> One of the first things I did was to try to phone my girl but the lines were all busy, so that just confirmed my impression that the thing was true. We

just started driving. We had heard that Princeton was wiped out and gas was spreading over New Jersey . . . we figured our friends and families were all dead. I made the 45 miles in 35 minutes and didn't even realize it. I drove right through [the city of] Newburgh and never even knew I went through it. . . . My roommate was crying and praying. (*The Invasion from Mars: A Study in the Psychology of Panic* by Hadley Cantril [copyright 1940 © 1968 by Princeton University Press], p. 52. Reprinted by permission of Princeton University Press)

The "invasion from Mars" stimulated a variety of responses and created a fertile ground for the study of numerous social phenomena. Hadley Cantril, a Princeton social psychologist, conducted 135 interviews in an effort to catalog people's reactions. One that occurred with regularity was the tendency of people to gather together when confronted by the stress of the situation. People huddled in stores, storm cellars, apartments, and houses, and groups crowded into cars. One hysterical New Jersey woman phoned her local police department, which informed her that the danger was probably not "immediate." "We all kissed one another," she reported, "and felt we would all die. When I heard the gas was in the streets of Newark, I called my brother and his wife and told them to get in their car and come right over so we could all be together." Another of Cantril's respondents spoke of "gathering her friends and driving as far as she could," and coeds recalled that "the girls in the sorority houses and dormitories huddled around their radios, trembling and weeping in each other's arms."

DEFINING SOCIAL PSYCHOLOGY

The *War of the Worlds* broadcast had a profound and far-reaching effect on the people who turned on their radios on Halloween eve. Assume for the moment that you are part of a group whose class project is to describe and explain the effects of the broadcast. This is clearly a mammoth task; six million people heard the broadcast. How would your group go about working on this project?

One way would be for each group member to take a slightly different approach in examining the audience and its reactions. For example, you could examine the impact on individuals who heard the broadcast and on those who did not. You could then compare the attitudes, behaviors, and emotions of the people in these two categories. Another member of your group could focus on the effects of the broadcast on groups. This person could study how families or social groups were influenced by the events of that evening. Still a third member of your group might focus on specific individuals. This student might identify four people who heard the broadcast and compare each person's reaction to the reactions of the other three. Each of these perspectives would add to our understanding of the event by taking a slightly different approach.

In laying out these approaches, we have roughly identified the focuses of social psychology, sociology, and personality psychology. *Social psychology* can be defined as a discipline that uses scientific methods to "understand and explain how the thought, feeling, and behavior of individuals are influenced by the actual, imagined, or implied presence, of others" (Allport, 1985, p. 3). Social psychology is interested in how *most* people react to a particular social situation. Taking this approach to your class project might lead you to ask whether most people were frightened by the broadcast (emotions), whether most people tried to be with others or stayed alone (behavior), and whether most people believed the Martians were coming to their area (attitudes). Carrying your role as a social psychologist further, you would be interested in explaining why people reacted as they did: Was it fear that caused people to want to be with others, and if so, why? And you might conclude your presentation with predictions about how people would respond in other similar situations.

Your classmate who was interested in the effects of the broadcast on groups would be taking the sociological perspective. In general, sociologists are interested in the structure and functioning of groups. The groups can be small (a family), moderately sized (a sorority or fraternity), or large (a society). The focus here might be on the rules that the group has developed to deal with the crisis created by the *War of the Worlds*; or on what groups (social or work) were most strongly affected by the broadcast.

The third student who researched a single individual represents the approach of personality psychologists. The interest here is in identifying *individual differences* that guide behavior. In this case, we would be concerned with how a single individual (Mary) reacted to different situations and how Mary's response differed from that of another person (John). To illustrate this approach, consider Table 1–1. The personality psychologist, who is primarily interested in identifying consistencies within people, will be most concerned with the horizontal axis: How does Mary (John, Sue, or George) act across situations? The social psychologist, who considers the effects of situations on persons, is interested in investigating the vertical consistencies in Table 1–1. We know that Mary, John, Sue, and George are different in many ways. They will react to situations with some differences, and we may come to recognize them as having different personalities. But personality differences are not what concern the social psychologist; he or she is interested in determining the way in which *most* people react.

Social psychologists are concerned with how most people act in a situation. This approach acknowledges that not everyone will act the same. (© *Peter Menzel*)

Table 1–1
Reactions of people to various social situations

	Meeting a friend at dinner	Listening to a frightening broadcast	Encountering two friends arguing
Mary	Ignores him	Seeks a friend	Ignores them
John	Acts politely	Seeks a friend	Breaks up argument
Sue	Gets into argument	Seeks a friend to argue with	Joins argument
George	Races to cafeteria line	Seeks a friend	Listens to argument

From the table, it appears that being frightened causes most people to affiliate—to seek other persons. Though Mary generally seems to be more reclusive than John and less argumentative than Sue, this does not alter the fact that all of the individuals in the sample react to the social situation of the frightening broadcast by wanting to affiliate. As social psychologists, we know that if we continue to sample individuals, we will find someone who will not affiliate when afraid; differences among people will lead some to behave differently from the way the majority act.

Having examined these differences, it is important to point out that we are referring to the *emphasis* of the fields and not to clear disciplinary boundaries: while these distinctions may help us understand the focus of social psychology, personality, and sociology, they do not exclude the fact of considerable overlap. No sharp boundaries separate these fields; instead, interest and approach overlap among these and other fields (Figure 1–1). As we will see, social psychologists do study group behavior and they are deeply interested in the effects of personal factors on social behavior. In fact, a close historical relationship exists among social psychology, personality, and sociology. Hence, rather than being neighbors on the social science block, these fields are actually close cousins.

THE HISTORY OF SOCIAL PSYCHOLOGY

Now that we have identified social psychology's next of kin, let us take a quick look at its roots. This is actually a rather easy task since social psychology is really a child of the twentieth century. In fact, it has been estimated that 90 percent of all social psychologists who ever lived are alive today (Cartwright, 1979)! Further, social psychology is largely a product of the United States; it began in the United States and until recently, it has remained a U.S. phenomenon (Jones, 1985).

Figure 1–1
Social psychology and its relatives

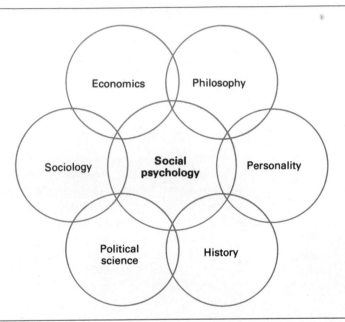

In addition to these disciplines, social psychology is developing close relationships with business, education, architecture, medicine, and law.

As we read the history of the field, let us keep one interesting point in mind. Possibly more than any other science, social psychology has been shaped by world events and social issues. Important events of the day have been the impetus for many of its themes and areas of study. And, of equal importance, the findings of this young science can be used to influence the course of social events.

The year 1897 is generally celebrated as the year of the first social psychology experiment. Norman Triplett (1897; see Chapter Eleven) examined official records of bicycle races and noticed that a rider's maximum speed was approximately 20 percent faster when he raced in the presence of other riders than when he raced alone. Triplett then devised a laboratory study to further demonstrate this effect. In that study, children were given the task of winding line on a fishing reel either alone or in the presence of other children performing the same task. The effect of the presence of others on individual task performance was essentially the only issue studied experimentally for the first three decades of social psychology (Allport, 1985).

Soon after the turn of the century, two social psychology textbooks were written. One titled *Social Psychology* was authored by E. A. Ross (1908), a sociologist who argued that social behavior was caused by imitation or suggestion. A second text, written by William McDougall (1908), suggested that much of human behavior resulted from instincts. *Instincts* are innate, unlearned, behavior tendencies that are common to members of a species. Hence, McDougall viewed much of human social behavior as internally derived or motivated. Although the two decades following McDougall's book were a time of growth for social psychology, it remained a discipline devoid of its own theoretical approach.

The behavior of many species of animals is guided by instincts. Some early attempts to explain human social behavior relied heavily on the concept of instinct. *(Jaye R. Phillips/ The Picture Cube)*

Its methodology was also derivative, with techniques borrowed from the study of memory, learning, and education.

In 1929, Thurstone and Chave published *The Measurement of Attitudes.* With this work, an entire new field was born. As we shall see in Chapter Five, Thurstone and Chave's work meant that attitudes could be conceptualized and measured. Soon, new techniques were added (e.g., Likert, 1932) and the 1930s became an era for measuring and studying the functions of attitudes. The first public opinion polling institute was founded in 1934 and spawned the giant industry that today tells us what we think about everything from tubes of toothpaste to presidential candidates.

Research in social psychology was still very different from what it is today until Kurt Lewin came on the scene. Lewin, who emigrated from Hitler's Germany in 1933, introduced theory into social psychology. He was an unabashed proponent of the deductive method in science who believed that general propositions that linked human behavior with social situations could and should be developed (Lewin, 1935). Moreover, he felt that these general propositions could be tested with the aid of experimentation. Under the influence of Lewin and his colleagues, social psychology began to view research not just as investigations into separate and unconnected phenomena, but also as a way of testing general theories on human behavior (Lewin, 1935). With this new outlook, social psychology entered its modern age.

Lewin was also noteworthy because he set the tone for social psychology to be a science that investigated social phenomena of the time and could, in turn, use its data to influence those social issues. For example, the beginning of World War II raised the issue of how people in the United States could be persuaded to conserve materials and food that were needed for the war effort. Lewin (1943) conducted a study on the effectiveness of different methods of social influence (see Chapter Ten) in getting homemakers to serve different and readily available foods. The war also created increased interest in the United States about what type of government was most effective: dictatorship or democracy. Lewin (Lewin, Lippit, & White, 1939) used the war climate to conduct a study comparing different styles of leadership on group performance and dynamics (see Chapter Ten). Lewin and his students also initiated a series of studies on group dynamics that served as one of the foundations for industrial/organizational psychology. In an effort to closely study group development, Lewin developed the participant-observation method, which gave rise to the use of T-groups in research and industry.

World War II was also the stimulus for the development of the Yale Communication Research Program. National leaders' concerns with the effects of propaganda and their desire to construct effective, persuasive

An important issue during World War II was how to develop effective propaganda to influence citizens to aid the war effort. This situation contributed to social psychologists' interests in attitude change. Investigators conducted numerous studies examining how the source and message affect persuasion. *(Thopam/The Image Works)*

propaganda campaigns led this group of researchers to apply learning theory to the area of attitude change (Lott & Lott, 1985). These investigators conducted dozens of studies to answer the question of who should say what and how to persuade an audience to believe and/or adopt a position (see Chapter Five).

The period of the 1950s and early 1960s saw social psychology leave the starting gate and enter the race with a vengeance. The atrocities of the war created concerns about the extent to which people would obey the orders of authority figures and conform to group patterns. Social psychologists initiated studies on conformity (Asch, 1956; see Chapter Ten) and obedience (Milgram, 1965; see Chapter Ten). Growing world tension, the arms race, and a war of words and nerve between Eastern and Western powers that was known as the cold war focused attention on the issues of conflict and conflict resolution. Social psychologists combined their talents with those of sociologists, mathematicians, political scientists, and economists to develop theories and research methodologies for the study of conflict and decision making (Deutsch & Krauss, 1960; see Chapter Nine).

While these efforts focused on the *relationship* between individuals, the theory that fanned the glowing embers of social psychology into a blaze emphasized the effect of *social situations* on individuals. Leon Festinger began his work by questioning how people evaluate themselves, including their efforts, attitudes, appearances, and behavior. He argued that in the absence of objective measures, people compare themselves with others (Festinger, 1954; see Chapter Three). The concern with the evaluation process led Festinger to examine what happened when people were faced with inconsistencies between their behaviors, their attitudes and behaviors, and their attitudes. He proposed the theory of cognitive dissonance (Festinger, 1957; see Chapter Six) in which he argued that people strive for consistency between their cognitions (beliefs, attitudes, and information about their behaviors and those of others). The discovery of inconsistency creates a state of cognitive dissonance and motivates individuals to restore consistency. Research on cognitive dissonance filled the social psychology journals for the next fifteen years and the theory was used to better understand such issues as consumer behavior, interpersonal attraction, school desegregation, and learning.

The ten years from the mid 1960s to the mid 1970s found social psychology increasingly concerned with the way in which the individual perceived and interpreted social events. The attribution process (Kelley, 1967; Jones & Davis, 1965; see Chapter Two) captured the imagination of social psychologists and was applied to further explain emotions, self-evaluation, and the perception of other people. This period also witnessed another change in emphasis in social psychology. If the field was to truly be taken seriously as a science, it had to develop study methods that could be replicated, reported, and stand the rigor demanded by other sciences. Hence, social psychologists turned their attention to refining their methods, embracing new techniques for recording and observing human behavior, and applying more advanced statistical tools for analyzing and interpreting their data (Kenny, 1985). Technological advances allowed researchers to incorporate physiological measures and precise video recordings into their studies and to use increasingly sophisticated computer software to conduct research and analyze data. In addition to refining their methodology, social scientists were able to refine their theories thanks to the new vistas that the technological advances gave them.

This concern with housekeeping was viewed with alarm by some (Elms, 1975). Was social psychology losing its dedication to social issues and was it destined to become a science preoccupied with minutiae and irrelevant details? Indeed, this was not a new concern; it was expressed by J. F. Brown, one of Lewin's students, in the early 1930s (Minton,

1984). The alarm was, however, unfounded as the 1970s saw social psychology incorporate its more sophisticated methodologies and theories into the study of women's issues (see Chapter Three), the environment (see Chapter Twelve), the law and legal process (see Chapter Eleven), and peace and conflict resolution (see Chapter Nine). And with their unique training in behavioral theories and methodology, social psychologists have been sought for positions in applied settings by government, law firms, and industry.

The last decade has also seen a change in the emphasis of social psychological theory and research. There is an increasing fascination with the way in which people perceive and process social information (cognition). Emphasis on the cognitive approach (Markus & Zajonc, 1985; see Chapter Two) has shown that people are not merely passive pawns who react to their social environment; rather, they organize and interpret events. The work on social cognition is directed at identifying how people process this information, and at making more precise predictions about the relationship between people and their social world.

Thus, present-day social psychology is neither myopically focused on applied issues nor solely concerned with basic theoretical ones. Rather, the social psychology of today represents the coexistence of the applied and basic approaches—and a new excitement characterizes both. Although debates—sometimes heated—rage about which approach is the true social psychology, a new, more vigorous field may grow out of this philosophical conflict. The basic research is gleaning new ideas and areas of study from the virgin territory being opened by investigators in the applied area. And conversely, the applied psychologist whose interest is carrying the torch of social psychology into the arena of social issues is able to draw on a rapidly expanding store of knowledge. As we will see throughout this text, social psychology today is represented by a diversity of concerns, approaches, and methods, each with the potential to complement and strengthen the other.

METHODS OF SOCIAL PSYCHOLOGY

Now that we have clearly identified the field of social psychology, let us turn from the question of what to that of how. We can begin by returning to the panic created by the *War of the Worlds* broadcast.

Cantril's account of the events following the broadcast provides us with detailed illustrations of human behavior during a crisis. However, our first response to the 135 interviews might be one of dismay and confusion. We would find that some people screamed, some wept, some gathered their families together, and some ran to be with friends. We would find that some people panicked while others calmly stood their ground and waited for the Martian onslaught. Still others did not believe the broadcast and went on with their normal routine. This is quite an array of events, and we would be hard pressed to give an accurate description of human behavior in crisis from a cursory glance at Cantril's interviews.

Investigators in almost every field of knowledge are often faced with similarly imposing tasks: they must make sense of vast amounts of data and be able to communicate their conclusions to other investigators. In an effort to achieve consistency in the investigating and reporting of events, researchers develop a standardized set of rules governing these procedures. It is this set of rules for inquiry that constitutes a *science*. Whether we talk about the study of chemistry, physics, or social behavior, the common ground that leads each of these to be labeled a science is adherence to the scientific method—a standardized set of rules for investigating events and communicating findings.

The goals of any science involve (*a*) the description of events, (*b*) the prediction of events, and (*c*) an explanation or understanding of why events occur. A clear understanding of why events occur allows the scientist to control conditions so that the desired events can be produced. Control can be used in the laboratory to demonstrate the understanding of the event, or it can be applied to the mastery of problems that exist in everyday life. Such control enabled the Salk vaccine to virtually eliminate polio.

In an effort to expedite these goals and to guide inquiry, scientists develop theories and hypotheses. A *theory* is a systematic statement that seeks to explain *why* two or more events are related. Theories may be of broad scope, such as Copernicus's theory of the heliocentric motion of the planets, or they may be more focused in scope, seeking to explain, for example, why people become fearful in a given situation, why particular attitudes are formed, or why people act aggressively toward others.

Scientists also develop *hypotheses,* which express educated guesses about the relationship between events. Unlike theories, hypotheses do not attempt to explain why two events are related; they express *what* the relationship between two events will be. Hypotheses can be derived from theories, or they can be formed by looking at existing data. For example, one hypothesis that is suggested by Cantril's interview data is that people tend to affiliate when they are anxious, nervous, or afraid. This statement is a hypothesis rather than a theory because it simply states a relationship and does not attempt to explain why this relationship exists. The hypothesis may be correct or incorrect; testing hypotheses is a major task of science. Social psychology, like other sciences, is involved in explaining, predicting, understanding, and verifying the relationships between events.

In using the scientific method, the social psychologist becomes a detective. The social psychologist may have a theory or a hypothesis about a certain type of human behavior, just as a detective may have a hunch about the perpetrator of a certain crime. The task of both is to track down information that will verify or refute the theory or hunch. Just as a detective must collect information that is clear enough to convince a judge or a jury that a hunch is correct "beyond all reasonable doubt," so too must the social psychologist obtain enough clear support for a theory to convince critics and other social psychologists of its correctness. Carrying the analogy one step farther, just as detectives have developed methods for tracking down leads, so too have social psychologists devised procedures for following through on their hunches and testing their theories.

Social psychologists use a number of different methods in testing theories and "tracking down leads." Hence, part of the social psychologist's detective work involves selecting the best strategy for investigating a particular problem. With this point in mind, we will examine the methodologies of social psychology. In order to illustrate their use, we will focus on the reactions of people to the *War of the Worlds* broadcast. If we want to pursue the hypothesis that fear, such as that aroused by the broadcast, causes people to affiliate with others, how can we go about obtaining evidence to support the hypothesis?

The Case History   One method of testing hypotheses, the *case history*, utilizes a few respondents and analyzes their reactions in depth. In one part of Cantril's work, for example, people who admitted that they had been scared by the broadcast were interviewed at length about their reactions; several excerpts from those interviews have been presented in this chapter. Such testimony is valuable, but are we certain that we have learned much that is reliable about the way most people behave? We do not know whether the reports are representative of the population at large or are unique to the few individuals whose statements were recorded. For example, most of Cantril's reports were gathered in the state of New Jersey, the reputed site of the Martians' landing. The imminent disaster may have led people there to behave very differently from people in more distant areas. Other case histories were obtained from people who learned of Cantril's investigation and took the trouble to write to him. Such reports are interesting, but they represent a very select portion of the population, those who felt the desire or need to relate their stories. Consequently, we tend to use case histories as ways of generating, not testing, hypotheses.

The social psychologist works much like a detective. He or she develops theories and then works to collect evidence (data) to support or refute the theory. *(Thopam/The Image Works)*

The Survey   Another way we can gather evidence is to devise a questionnaire; select a large sample that represents the geographic, socioeconomic, and educational background of the population; and ask questions of persons in the sample about their fear and their desire to affiliate. This is the *survey* method (Schuman & Kaulton, 1985).

The survey is useful because it attempts to uncover how people react to a real situation. In addition, a representative sample of respondents can be chosen to participate. A survey is used to describe people's attitudes, feelings, and reported behaviors as regards a particular event. There are problems with a survey, however. First, a person often does not remember exactly what he or she did in a particular situation. Second, respondents may try to slant their answers to a survey in order to appear in a better light. A man who panicked and ran screaming from his house when he heard that the Martians were coming may tell the interviewer that he quickly ran outside to see whether he could help his neighbors. In short, the responses on a survey questionnaire may not be completely accurate. Finally, some people are not willing to be interviewed.

When we obtain information through a survey, we are usually looking to see whether two variables are correlated. A *correlation* is a measure of association or relationship. If we have two variables that we are interested in (for example, fear and affiliation) and we notice that people who have a high degree of one variable also tend to have a high degree of the second variable, then the two variables are said to be positively correlated.

Knowing the degree of relationship between two variables gives us a valuable piece of information. If we know that two events are positively correlated, we know that when one of the two events occurs, the other is also likely to occur. However, we probably also want to know which event *caused* the other; that is, does fear *cause* people to

Interviews and surveys allow investigators to collect a large amount of information from many people. However, data obtained from surveys must be examined with correlations because the experimenter does not control the independent variables and subjects are not randomly assigned to conditions. *(Owen Franken/Stock, Boston)*

affiliate, or does affiliation *cause* people to become fearful? A correlation does not provide this answer. A correlation between two variables can have one of three meanings:

1. A difference in the first variable causes a difference in the second variable.
2. A difference in the second variable causes a difference in the first variable.
3. A third, unspecified variable causes differences in both the first and the second variable.

For example, suppose that Cantril found the following data:

1. Seventy-five percent of the people who reported feeling a great deal of fear after hearing the broadcast spent time with other people after the broadcast.
2. Fifteen percent of the people who reported feeling little fear after hearing the broadcast spent time with other people after the broadcast.

What do these data mean with regard to the hypothesis that fear causes people to affiliate? One possible meaning is the one suggested by the hypothesis—fear causes people to affiliate. However, a second possible interpretation is that affiliation leads to fear. This is a plausible explanation, since we can easily imagine that people may have congregated and discussed the *War of the Worlds* program and that this discussion may have generated fear. Finally, it is also possible that a third variable that is not even measured in the correlation could be responsible for the results. For example, we might find that individuals who score high on some personality dimension, say gregariousness, are motivated to be with other people and also tend to frighten easily. Thus, the correlation may not be the result of fear leading to affiliation or of affiliation leading to fear. It may simply result from the fact that the third variable, the personality trait, was responsible for both fear and affiliation.

Thus, survey research can be utilized to achieve the aim of prediction since it tells how related two variables are. In most cases, however, it does not enable the researcher to achieve the second scientific goal of understanding or explanation. That is, it does not enable the researcher to uncover a cause-and-effect relationship between variables.

The Experiment To examine cause-and-effect relationships, the researcher must have some control over the variables he or she wishes to study and must be able to eliminate the possibility that some unspecified variable is systematically affecting the results. The method that is designed to allow the necessary control so that cause-and-effect relationships can be uncovered is the *experiment*.

The experiment is a procedure for testing the validity or correctness of a hypothesis. The basic design of an experiment is quite simple. The experimenter manipulates the *independent variable* and studies the effects of the manipulation on the *dependent variable*. The independent variable gets its name from the fact that it is independent (not under the control) of the subject. The experimenter determines which level of the independent variable the subject will receive. The dependent variable is the subject's response. The hypothesis is stated in terms of the independent variable causing the dependent variable (fear causes affiliation). Thus the aim of the experiment is to investigate the causal relationship between the independent variable and the dependent variable.

To be able to say that a particular independent variable did cause the dependent variable, the experimenter must be sure that no *extraneous variables* were present in the experiment. An extraneous variable is a factor that may influence people's reactions in a systematic way, although it has nothing to do with the relationship between the independent and dependent variables. As an illustration, let us assume that you set up an experiment to test whether fear causes people to affiliate. You decided to use two levels of fear (high and low). You manipulate high fear by running into a room and telling people that their building is on fire. In the low-fear condition, you would run into a room and tell people that a building in the next town is on fire. Hence, the degree of fear is your independent variable and you have control over it. Your dependent variable is affiliation, and this is measured by how often people in the room talk to one another after they hear the news. So far, so good. You run the experiment, and you find that high fear leads to greater affiliation than does low fear. Can you be confident that you have obtained evidence that fear causes affiliation?

It is possible that in reviewing your procedure you might find that all of your efforts were for naught. Even though you manipulated and controlled your independent variable and carefully observed your dependent variable, extraneous variables may have affected your results. For example, you might discover that the people who happened to be in the rooms where you manipulated high fear were all friends, whereas the people in the low-fear rooms were strangers to one another. Thus, the extraneous variable of prior acquaintance may have "caused" your affiliation results. Further, you may find that all of your high-fear conditions were run after lunch, when people naturally wanted to affiliate, whereas the low-fear conditions were run just before lunch, when people tended to be grumpy and wished isolation. Thus, even though you manipulated your independent variable and found the predicted results, the existence of these extraneous variables would not allow you to believe that your study demonstrated that fear causes affiliation.

An experiment involves manipulating the *independent variables* and studying the effects on the *dependent variables*. The experimenter's goal is to be able to say that the independent variables *caused* the dependent variables. In order to achieve this he or she must eliminate or control any *extraneous variables* that could affect the results.

A "clean" experiment must eliminate or control the extraneous variables. To ensure that the extraneous variable of preexisting subject characteristics is not the cause of the results in an experiment, subjects are randomly assigned to the various conditions. By *random assignment* we mean that each subject has an equal opportunity of being in each experimental condition. Through random assignment, the experimenter ensures that the characteristics of the subjects assigned to any particular experimental condition are the same as those of subjects in the other experimental conditions. One way to illustrate the procedure of random assignment is to imagine a blindfolded individual whose task is to divide 100 pennies, half of which are colored red and half green, into two equal piles. The chances are that when the task is finished, each pile will have a similar distribution of red and green pennies. Thus, the reason for randomly assigning subjects to conditions is to get similar groups of subjects into the different experimental conditions so that preexisting subject characteristics cannot be the cause of differences in the results. In addition to randomly assigning subjects to conditions, we can eliminate other extraneous variables by randomly assigning the order of conditions. In the earlier example, we could eliminate the alternative explanation based on hunger by not running all high-fear conditions after lunch and all low-fear conditions just before lunch. This can be done by randomly choosing a condition to run at a particular time.

As you can see, much of experimentation involves exercising control. We must have control to determine when and how the independent variable will be manipulated, and we must have control to eliminate extraneous variables. Campbell and Stanley (1963) have used the term *internal validity* to describe an experimental design that is free from contamination by extraneous variables. As they phrase it, "Internal validity is the basic ingredient without which an experiment is uninterpretable" (p. 5). Making certain that an experimental design is internally valid is ascertaining that it is the experimental treatment (independent variable) that is responsible for affecting the dependent variable.

To summarize, an experiment involves varying the levels of the independent variable and studying the effects of this manipulation on the dependent variable. The aim of the experiment is to say that the independent variable caused the dependent variable results. To say this, the experimenter must ensure internal validity by eliminating extraneous variables from his or her experiment.

Constructing an experiment. An illustrative example. We have discussed the aims and some of the possible pitfalls of experimentation. You may be able to think of a way to conduct an experiment to test the hypothesis that fear leads to affiliation. The important points to remember are:

1. You must create at least two levels of the independent variable (that is, conditions of high fear and low fear).
2. Participants must be randomly assigned to the conditions (that is, you would not want to assign all smart people, or all poor people, or all Northerners to one condition).
3. The dependent variable (affiliation) must be measured.

An example of an experiment that was designed to demonstrate that high fear causes people to affiliate is reported in Schachter (1959). Suppose that you are a volunteer who has been randomly assigned to the high-fear condition. You would encounter a serious-looking man in horn-rimmed glasses who is intent on giving you a good scare. For effect, he is dressed in a white lab coat with a stethoscope dribbling conspicuously from his pocket, and he is standing in front of an array of elaborate-looking electrical equipment. He introduces himself to you as Dr. Gregor Zilstein,

Random assignment is similar to a game of chance. Through random assignment, the experimenter ensures that each subject has an equal opportunity of being in each experimental condition. *(Ellis Herwig, 1980/Stock, Boston)*

and he informs you that you are in an experiment that is concerned with the effects of electric shock. Pausing slightly, so that his words will have maximum impact, Zilstein says:

> What we will ask each of you to do is very simple. We would like to give each of you a series of electric shocks. Now, I feel I must be completely honest with you and tell you exactly what you are in for. These shocks will hurt, they will be painful. As you can guess, it is necessary that our shocks be intense. What we will do is put an electrode on your hand, hook you into apparatus such as this, give you a series of shocks, and take various measures. . . . Again, I do want to be honest with you and tell you that these shocks will be quite painful but, of course, they will do no permanent damage. (Schachter, 1959, p. 13)

You probably would have been more fortunate, or at least less frightened, if you had been randomly assigned to the low-fear condition. You would still have been greeted by Dr. Zilstein, but the pile of electrical equipment would not have been displayed. With a much more pleasant demeanor, Dr. Zilstein would tell you (as he does in the high-fear condition) that this is an experiment involving the effects of electric shock. But this time he would qualify this statement by saying, "I hasten to add, do not let the word *shock* trouble you; I am sure that you will enjoy this experiment." He would continue:

> What we will ask each of you to do is very simple. We would like to give each of you a series of very mild electric shocks. I assure you that what you will feel will not in any way be painful. It will resemble more a tickle than anything unpleasant. We will put an electrode on your hand, give you a series of very mild shocks and measure such things as your pulse rate . . . which I am sure you are all familiar with from visits to your family doctor. (pp. 13–14)

In this manner Schachter manipulated the independent variable into two levels: low fear and high fear. Did he successfully create two levels of fear in the minds and feelings of his subjects? One way to find out is to ask. So Schachter gave each participant a printed form to be filled out that asked: "How do you feel about taking part in this experiment and being shocked?" The participant was asked to respond along a five-point scale ranging from "I dislike the idea very much" to "I enjoy the idea very much." When the questionnaires were examined, subjects who had met the stern Dr. Zilstein in the high-fear condition were much less inclined to be shocked than were those who had met the benign and reassuring Dr. Zilstein. This procedure, which is known as a "check on the manipulation" allows investigators to feel secure that the variable they thought they were manipulating with elaborate staging was accurately perceived in the minds of the participants.

Schachter's experiment was trying to test the hypothesis that fear leads to affiliation. Once he had successfully induced two levels of fear, the next step was to get a measure of the desire to affiliate (dependent variable). Schachter decided to solve this problem by giving the participants a choice of waiting together or alone for the shock portion of the study. In both fear conditions, Dr. Zilstein stated:

> Before we begin with the shocking proper there will be about a 10-minute delay while we get this room in order. We have several pieces of equipment to bring in and get set up. . . . Here is what we will ask you to do for this 10-minute period of waiting. We have on this floor a number of additional

Schachter's hypothesis was that people seek out others in high-fear situations. He tested this hypothesis by designing a laboratory study where subjects experienced high or low fear. Unlike real-life situations, Schachter was able to control the level of fear in the laboratory. *(Alon Reininger/Contact)*

rooms so that each of you, if you would like, can wait alone in your own room. These rooms are comfortable and spacious; they all have armchairs and there are books and magazines in each room. It did occur to us, however, that some of you might want to wait for these 10 minutes together with some of the other girls here. If you would prefer this, of course, just let us know. We'll take one of the empty classrooms on the floor and you can wait together with some of the other girls there. (pp. 13–14)

Participants were then given a chance to state whether they preferred waiting alone or waiting with others or had no preference. This constituted the measurement of the dependent variable. What Schachter hoped to find was that women assigned to the high-fear condition would want to wait together more than women in the low-fear condition. Schachter's results are presented in Table 1–2.

The table makes it quite clear that subjects in the high-anxiety condition wanted to wait together much more than subjects in the low-anxiety condition did. Thus, the hypothesis was supported by the data.

Table 1–2
Relationship of fear to the affiliative tendency

	Number choosing		
	Waiting together	*Don't care*	*Waiting alone*
High fear	20	9	3
Low fear	10	18	2

Source: Adapted from Schachter (1959).

THE ADVANTAGES OF EXPERIMENTS

As you can see, Schachter went to a great deal of time and effort to test the rather simple hypothesis that fear leads to affiliation. Was it worth it? Why go to such lengths to set up an experiment? The answer is that there are many important advantages to experiments that justify their use. In fact, the vast majority of data collected in social psychology come from laboratory research.

A number of advantages of experimentation should be clear. First and most important, experimentation provides a way of determining the direction of causation. Because the experimenter controls the independent variable and randomly assigns people to different levels of that variable on a random basis, the question of which variable is cause and which is effect can be answered.

Another advantage of experimentation is that extraneous elements that might otherwise influence the results can be well controlled. For example, some of the people in Cantril's survey may have listened during a thunderstorm, tuned in late, or heard the program on a crackling radio. It is unknown whether any of these factors could have influenced fear or affiliation. We do know, though, that such factors are extraneous to the relationship in question. Some individuals were exposed to one or more of them; others to none. The factors remain uncontrolled. By contrast, the experiment controls for such events. The variables are usually manipulated in the confines of a small unit of space and time. All subjects are generally treated identically, with the exception of the one event that serves as the independent variable. This variable gives us more confidence that the effect we found is due to that independent variable rather than to a series of fortuitous and extraneous factors.

Yet another advantage of experimentation is that the experimenter can devise *numerous levels* of an independent variable and study trends in the data. For example, Schachter used only two levels of fear arousal (high and low). The experimenter might hold the hypothesis that very fearful subjects would not want to affiliate. An experiment could then be developed so that there were three conditions of fear (low, high, and very high). Such systematic variation of the fear variable would present a clear relationship between fear and affiliation.

Thus, there are a number of important reasons for using the experiment as a method of investigation. The experiment is a vital tool for science because it allows the researcher to seek and uncover cause-and-effect relationships between variables.

ISSUES OF CONCERN IN EXPERIMENTATION

Mark Twain once remarked that a common characteristic of everything developed by humans is imperfection. This statement clearly describes experimentation: While the experiment represents an excellent method for collecting data and determining cause-and-effect, it is not perfect. You have probably already identified many of the problems with the experimental method.

One of the basic problems that plagues research is *generalization* beyond the laboratory: How far can we go in applying the results we collect in an experiment? For example, we would like to be able to argue that the Schachter study supported the position that *fear* causes *people* to *affiliate*. This desire to generalize raises a number of questions. One is that we want to describe the behavior of people in general, while the study used only college students as subjects. In raising this issue, we do not wish to imply that college students are not people; rather, college students may be special people in that they possess characteristics that are not common to the population as a whole. For example, Schachter's subjects were white, female, mostly from the Northeast, most probably from middle-class families, and had some years of college education. Would respondents from different backgrounds or educational levels behave as Schachter's subjects did? We can take this question of generalization further by asking whether studies of (1) females can predict males' behavior, (2) studies of whites can predict the behavior of blacks or Hispanics, (3) studies of eighteen to twenty-two-year-olds can predict behavior of older or younger people, (4) studies of college students can predict behavior of less educated people—and so on. To make these generalizations with some degree of confidence, additional experiments with different subjects must be conducted. As we find similarities across groups with different characteristics, we can expand the application of our results. And, when

An important question in experimentation involves generalization. Can results obtained with a group of students (left) be used to predict and understand the behavior of a broader group of people (right)? *(Left, © Ellis Herwig/The Picture Cube; right, Alan Carey/The Image Works)*

we find differences, as is sometimes the case in comparing the behavior of males and females, we must alter and expand our theories to take these differences into account.

Another generalization question concerns the setting and specific manipulations that we use in the experiment. In Schachter's study, for example, the data indicated that people who expected Dr. Zilstein to shock them would rather wait together while people who expected Dr. Zilstein to tickle them would rather wait alone. However, it is still a leap of faith to say that fear leads to affiliation. Are people who are afraid of having a university scientist place electrodes on them experiencing the same kind of fear that people experience in a natural ongoing situation? Is the fear of Schachter's laboratory the same as the fear that is experienced when encountering a burglar in one's house, a lion in the jungle, or a Martian in the New Jersey meadowland? When we raise these questions, we are referring to the *external validity* of an experiment (Carlsmith, Ellsworth, & Aronson, 1976).

The best way to deal with questions of external validity is to test the relationship in a series of similar but not identical ways. If Schachter's participants were "really" scared and if they "really" felt that waiting with another participant was an opportunity to affiliate, then other studies using different fear manipulations and different types of affiliation possibilities should yield the same result. Indeed, several other studies that use different methods of fear arousal and affiliation measurement have produced very similar results (e.g., Darley & Aronson, 1966; Gerard,

1963). This fact makes us more confident that we can generalize from our experimental results to fear and affiliation as they occur in the natural environment.

Another concern with experimentation is that of realism. We must actually consider two types of realism. The first, *experimental realism*, involves the impact the experiment has on subjects. "An experiment is realistic if the situation is involving to the subjects, if they are forced to take it seriously, if it has impact on them" (Aronson, Brewer, & Carlsmith, 1985, p. 482). In most experiments, we strive to achieve a high degree of experimental realism because we want to maximize subjects' involvement in the study. It is not hard to see that Schachter's study had a high degree of experimental realism; the ominous-looking Dr. Zilstein who gravely explained the painful shocks certainly captured the subjects' attention. The second type of realism is *mundane realism*. An experiment is high in mundane realism to the extent that the situation subjects encounter is similar to that which they face in the normal course of their lives. While having a high degree of mundane realism may increase a study's impact, its presence is not a necessary research requirement. For example, Schachter's study was quite low in mundane realism. (How often are we approached in our everyday lives by a Dr. Zilstein who threatens to shock us?) Yet Schachter's study did manipulate the fear that subjects experienced, as well as allowing him to study the relationship between fear and affiliation.

THE PSYCHOLOGY OF THE SUBJECT AND EXPERIMENTER

Thus far, our concern has been the design and manipulation of the experimental setting. Experiments, however, involve more than just a setting; they are also the stage for the interaction of the subjects and the experimenter. Let us quickly examine how the psychology of subject and experimenter can influence the results of a study. The subject's role in a study is a unique one. Martin Orne (1962) has demonstrated people's willingness to do the "right thing" when in an experiment, that is, to do what you think the experimenter wants you to do. You do not want to appear silly, obstinate, or recalcitrant. You want to be cooperative and to be seen as a "good subject." In some of his demonstrations, Orne showed that people will use a variety of bizarre behaviors to be good subjects. For example, Orne asked people whether they would be willing to copy numbers in the school library, although he told them that doing so would not be very useful to anyone. Not only were subjects willing to comply with the request, but they stayed after the investigator and librarian had left and after the library was closed and locked!

Experimental realism involves the degree to which the situation is involving to the subject. Mundane realism concerns the extent to which the subject is likely to encounter the situation in everyday life. An experiment involving the pictured situation would be high in experimental realism, but may not have high mundane realism. *(Chris Brown/ Stock, Boston)*

The significant implication of such behavior is clear. If people who want to be good subjects can know the purpose of an experiment or if they have a notion about what the experimenter wants them to do, they are likely to cooperate. If the subjects in Schachter's study had known that he hoped they would affiliate in the high-fear condition and remain alone in the low-fear condition, they might have cooperated. When people act in a particular way, not because it is their typical reaction to the situation but because they are trying to do what the experimenter desires, we say that they are acting in accord with the experiment's *demand characteristics*.

There are a number of methods that can be used to guard against demand characteristics in an experiment (Aronson et al., 1985). A popular method, though not necessarily the most effective one, is *deception*. In this case, the experimenter gives the subject a false but plausible hypothesis so that, if the subject's behavior is affected by this hypothesis, it will not be done in a systematic way. Further, through this deception or cover story the experimenter prevents subjects from discovering the true hypothesis. Schachter used deception in his study. He told subjects that he was interested in studying the effects of subjects receiving actual electric shocks, when in fact he was only interested in how fear would affect affiliation.

Another way to reduce the problem of demand characteristics is to measure the dependent variable in a context apart from the independent variable and to use *unobtrusive measures*. For example, after telling a subject that she would be shocked, Schacter could have followed through with the story he gave the subject. He might have told his subject that he would not be able to run her immediately and that she should wait in the experimental waiting room until the study was ready. When the subject arrived at the waiting room, she could find two or three other subjects who had been given similar instructions. Unknown to the subjects, an experimenter could be observing through a one-way mirror whether or not the subjects affiliated and interacted with one another. This method would have the advantage of the dependent measure being examined away from (in time and place) the independent manipulation. Further, the measure would be unobtrusive; the subjects would not know that their responses were being studied. Thus, precautions can be taken to reduce the role of demand characteristics in an experiment.

A final problem involves the unique psychology of the experimenter in a research effort. Experimenters have hypotheses: they think that they *know* what a subject will do; they know what they *want* a subject to do to confirm their hypotheses. Robert Rosenthal and his colleagues have shown that such expectations may actually influence the behavior of subjects in experiments. In one study, Rosenthal and Fode

(1963) used photographs of faces that had previously been rated as neutral with regard to success and failure. They gave these pictures to students who were serving as assistant experimenters and asked the students to obtain ratings from subjects as to whether the faces appeared successful or unsuccessful. Rosenthal and Fode told half of the assistant experimenters that they were trying to duplicate a "well-established" finding that people generally rated the persons photographed as successful. The other half of the experimenters were told that the "well-established" finding was that people generally rated the persons photographed as unsuccessful.

Armed with identical photographs, two sets of assistant experimenters set out to collect evidence. They were instructed about what to say and how to collect the ratings. Both groups were supposed to behave in precisely the same fashion. Yet the results were dramatically different. Every experimenter who was led to expect that people generally rated the persons photographed as successful obtained higher success ratings than

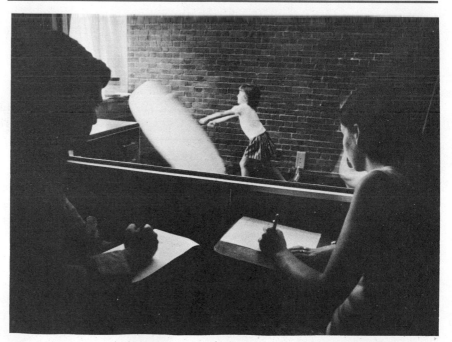

One way to reduce the probability of experimenter demand is to take unobtrusive measures. One such method involves observing subjects without their knowledge that they are being studied. *(Stock/Boston)*

the experimenters who expected to obtain failure ratings. Most assuredly, the experimenter's influence on the subject's rating was unintentional, yet his expectation was somehow communicated to the subject, who behaved accordingly. The influence of a subject's performance as a function of an investigator's expectation has been called *experimenter bias*.

The problem of experimenter bias is a troublesome one, and investigators are now more careful to make certain that their hypotheses do not become self-fulfilling because of bias. The best way to eliminate an experimenter's expectancy from influencing people's behavior on a dependent variable is to keep the experimenter unaware of the experimental treatment to which the subject has been exposed. This is often done by using two experimenters. For example, in Schachter's research, any possibility of experimenter bias could have been eliminated if someone other than Dr. Zilstein had asked the subjects whether they wished to wait together or alone. Only Zilstein would know whether a particular participant had been subjected to a high-fear or a low-fear treatment. Therefore, only his expectations could affect the final measure. If someone else had collected that final measure, he would not have known what to expect on the measure of affiliation.

THE FIELD EXPERIMENT

One common criticism of laboratory experiments is that because the setting is unlike that experienced in the real world, it is difficult to create an impactful experience for subjects. While we could successfully argue that the Schachter study was highly impactful, a counterposition would be that the manipulation was not as successful as it could have been because the subjects knew they were in a experiment; they may have reduced their fear by telling themselves that Dr. Zilstein couldn't really do anything too terrible because this was only an experiment. To achieve a real-world effect, we might want to run a field experiment.

In theory, the *field experiment* is similar to the laboratory experiment except that the location has changed. The field experiment is run in a natural setting, and subjects often do not know that they are in an experiment. The experimenter varies the independent variables and examines the effects of the manipulation on the dependent variable. This added realism of setting should allow greater generalization of results from the field experiment.

Earlier in this chapter, we discussed one way in which the fear-affiliation hypothesis can be tested as a field experiment. The experimenter can randomly select people in a building and tell them either that their building

Field experiments involve manipulating the independent variables in a natural setting and examining people's responses. However, for ethical and practical reasons many studies cannot be run in a field setting. *(Cary Wolinsky/Stock, Boston)*

is on fire or that a building in another town is on fire. The experimenter can then record the behavior of the subjects.

This method includes the randomization of subjects to conditions, and it has control over the independent variable. It also has the advantage of studying subjects in their natural habitat. These advantages are responsible for the increasing popularity of the field experiment in social psychology.

However, before adopting field experimentation as the "best" method, it is important to examine the potential weaknesses of the method. First, control over some types of extraneous variables is more difficult to obtain in the field than in the laboratory. In the laboratory, we can ensure that the setting is the same for each subject; we cannot do this in the field. For example, if we were to run our "building on fire" experiment, we might find that some of our subjects were run when other people were in sight, whereas other subjects were run when no other people were around. Some subjects may have been run when there was a lot of distracting noise, such as elevators opening or airplanes flying overhead, whereas other subjects may have been run without these distractions. Although such extraneous variables may not influence the results of our study in any systematic manner, they do reduce the precision of our experiment. Hence, the laboratory setting permits a more precise test of our hypothesis because of the increased control that this setting makes possible.

Another drawback to field experimentation is that in the field it is often difficult to manipulate complex variables or to manipulate a number of variables simultaneously. For example, it would be difficult to conduct a field experiment that tests the hypothesis that tired people have a stronger desire to affiliate when fearful than do well-rested people. To test this hypothesis we would have to manipulate both fear and tiredness. In the field it would be nearly impossible to randomly assign people to a restful or tired condition. We could, however, do this in the laboratory where before manipulating fear we could have some subjects go one night without sleep while providing other subjects with a restful night.

Hence, the field experiment has the advantage of generalization of results, but often achieves this advantage at the sacrifice of control over extraneous variables. Further, some hypotheses are difficult to test in the field setting because of the complexity of the required manipulations.

Choosing a Method   At the beginning of this section we pointed out that social psychology often requires a great deal of detective work. Not only must social psychologists observe behavior and develop theories to explain that behavior; they must also determine the best method for testing their theories. As you can see, there is no single right or wrong method; each method offers both advantages and disadvantages. The researcher must determine the goal of his or her investigation and select the method that will best fit that goal. In most cases, the social psychologist is interested in establishing a cause-and-effect relationship and therefore uses the laboratory experiment.

The ideal modus operandi, however, would be to use a number of methods to study a problem. That is, the same hypothesis could be tested by means of a survey, a laboratory experiment, and a field experiment. If the hypothesis were tested and supported by each of these methods, a great deal more confidence could be placed in its correctness than if it were tested and supported by only one method. This multiple-method approach requires considerable time, and it is rarely used by a single investigator. However, later in this book we will examine instances in which certain hypotheses have been tested by different investigators using a number of different methods.

One other point should be made clear: an experiment, whether it is carried out in the laboratory or field, can only be as good as the idea it is testing. As Festinger (1980) points out: "Precision of measurement and precision of experimental control are a means to an end—the discovery of new knowledge. Too much emphasis on precision can lead to research which is barren" (p. 252). Like a hammer used to build a house, experimental methods are only tools used to expand knowledge. The success of an experiment is not so much measured by how precisely it is conducted, but rather in the knowledge that results. Therefore, careful planning and thought about the idea to be tested are vital steps to be taken before a method is chosen.

BEYOND REASONABLE DOUBT: STATISTICAL SIGNIFICANCE

To obtain a guilty verdict from a jury, a prosecuting attorney must convince the members of the jury that a defendant is guilty beyond reasonable doubt. This does not mean that the prosecutor must positively "prove" guilt—it only means that the jury must believe it highly probable that the defendant is guilty. The social psychologist, too, works with probabilities. The aim of an experiment is not to prove that a hypothesis is correct. Rather, the aim is to demonstrate that it is highly probable that the hypothesis is correct. Hence, social psychology, like most other sciences, deals with probabilities rather than absolutes.

As a means of demonstrating this point, let us reexamine the Schachter experiment. Schachter found that approximately 63 percent of the high-fear subjects wanted to wait together, whereas only 33 percent of the low-fear subjects wanted to do so. What does this difference mean? Is it reliable, or is it simply a chance finding? With the Schachter study we must ask whether highly fearful people really want to affiliate more than do low-fear people. Is the difference large enough to make us believe that if more and more people participated in the study, the same connection between fear and affiliation would be found? Or would we find that the difference was only a chance finding and that the addition of more people "washes" the difference out?

To answer these questions, investigators apply statistical tests that are designed to estimate the likelihood that a difference that exists in the data would continue to be manifested if everyone in the population participated in the study. By convention, we agree that we will accept a difference as *statistically significant* (reliable) if the likelihood of its having occurred by chance (that is, the likelihood that the difference would disappear if the entire population were tested) is less than one in twenty. In other words, the result could have occurred by chance less than 5 percent of the time. The difference reported in the Schachter

Although many students are often confused and frightened by statistics, statistical formulas tell psychologists whether they are looking at "real" differences.

study was tested with one statistical procedure, and it was found that the likelihood that the difference had occurred by chance was less than one in twenty. We therefore refer to the result as statistically significant. Thus, social psychologists assume that an event that could have occurred by chance less than 5 percent of the time is beyond reasonable doubt.

QUESTIONS OF ETHICS

We have discussed some of the methods that are used in social psychology and have examined how the hypothesis that fear leads to affiliation could be tested. You may have become uncomfortable at the suggestion that the hypothesis could be tested by telling people that the building they are in is burning. You may even have winced as you thought about the fear experienced by the subjects in Schachter's high-fear condition. Finally, you may have felt that we were a little callous when we suggested that the method used in a study should be chosen on the grounds of how well it fits the goals of the experimenter. In all of these cases we seem to have been overlooking one important ingredient in the experiment—the subject.

Shouldn't some concern be shown for the subject who is terribly frightened? Shouldn't some attention be given to choosing a method that will protect the subject? The answer to both of these questions is an emphatic yes. Almost from the time social psychologists began conducting experiments, they expressed deep concern for the physical and psychological safety of their subjects. Before our newspapers reported secret CIA experiments with LSD and before the Kennedy Committee on Human Experimentation began its hearings, social psychologists were discussing the problems of ethics in research and developing guidelines to protect subjects in psychological experimentation. The American Psychological Association (1982) published a comprehensive guideline outlining ethical precautions that should be taken when research is conducted.

Let us review quickly some of the ethical problems that social psychologists have identified. The first problem involves the *invasion of privacy*. Although this may not have been a serious problem in the Schachter study because little "sensitive" information was asked from the subject, it does become a problem when sensitive information is requested. Some studies ask subjects questions about their sex life or about criminal activity that they may have participated in. Other studies give subjects personality and intelligence tests. In all of these cases, the experimenter is obtaining private information from the subject. Is this ethical? That is a difficult question to answer. Psychologists have attempted to safeguard the privacy of subjects by keeping responses anonymous or by letting no one but the experimenter have access to them. Further, they attempt to follow the principle of *informed consent:* subjects are given the choice of participating or not participating in an experiment after they have been told of the procedures that will be used. In practice, however, this principle is often difficult to follow because in some cases deception is used so that the subject will not be aware of what is really being studied in the experiment.

A second problem is the use of *deception*. Deception involves having the experimenter tell subjects something other than the truth. In the Schachter study, the subjects were deceived about the purpose of the study and they were told that they would receive an electric shock even though they were never actually shocked. Such deception is often necessary to prevent the subjects from focusing on the true nature of the interaction being studied. In an effort to make the deception only temporary, experimenters carry out elaborate debriefing sessions at the conclusion of studies. At these sessions, subjects are told exactly what did happen in the study, what problem was being investigated, and why deception was used. In this way, the experiment and debriefing become an educational experience for the subjects.

A third problem involves the *harmful consequences* that the subject may suffer in the study. Subjects may be given drugs that have unpleasant side effects or may have to suffer painful shocks. Other harmful consequences may be psychological rather than physical. In the Schachter study, the subject suffered stress and fear. In other studies, the subject may be degraded or insulted and suffer depression. Again, the question can be asked: Is this ethical? There has been a great deal of discussion about this matter. The answer is to try to find procedures that do not create negative consequences for the subject.

Another ethical problem is that *subjects may be taught something about themselves that they may not wish to know.* For example, a subject in the Schachter study could become so fearful that she cries and begs to be let out of the study. In this case, the subject is being shown that she has little tolerance for stress. One might argue that the experimenter is only showing the subject something true about herself. However, the subject did not come to the experiment asking to learn about herself. She came to be a subject in an experiment.

The question of ethics is a difficult and controversial one; what is ethical to one person may not be ethical to another. And while it is important to consider ethical issues in every experiment, it is also important not to become paralyzed by these issues. Festinger (1980) argues that a valuable experiment must be both impactful and involving for the subject and considerate of ethical issues. An experiment that slights either of these concerns in favor of the other loses value for the subject, the experimenter, and our store of knowledge on human behavior.

Social psychologists are well aware of the ethical problems connected with research and have spent a great deal of time pondering those problems. Despite the value of social psychological research, such research will have a bitter taste if it is achieved at the expense of the subjects involved in it. In an effort to protect the rights of subjects, many universities and many psychology departments have set up peer review committees in which a cross section of professionals considers the risks and benefits to participants of research. Usually, these committees operate in accordance with guidelines established by the U.S. federal government's Office of Protection from Research Risks (*U.S. Federal Register,* 1981). In addition, increasing concern over the ethical issues of experimentation has led psychologists to use less stressful manipulations in their research (Aronson et al., 1985). The bottom line then is that there are actually three principles that guide research: the desire for maximum control, the desire to create impactful situations, and the desire to protect the subjects in the study. As you read the remainder of this text, you will see how these three guidelines have been skillfully combined to create settings that yield valuable knowledge about human social behavior.

SUMMARY

Social psychology is defined as a discipline that employs scientific methods to understand and explain how the thoughts, feelings, and behaviors of individuals are influenced by the actual, imagined, or implied presence of others. Social psychologists are interested in studying how most people behave most of the time. Sociologists generally focus on the structure and functioning of groups, while personality psychologists are most concerned with differences between individuals.

Social psychology is a twentieth-century science that is largely confined to the United States. World and social events have played a major role in influencing the themes and issues studied by its practitioners. The first social psychology study in 1897 examined the effects of performing alone and performing in front of a group. The first social psychology textbooks were published in 1908. In the 1930s, social psychology was concerned with measuring and studying the functions of attitudes. During that decade, Kurt Lewin (1935) presented his field theory and demonstrated the importance of conducting controlled research on social phenomena. World War II influenced the direction of Lewin's research; Lewin examined social influence, leadership, and group dynamics. The war also gave rise to the study of attitude and attitude change by the Yale Communication Research Program. The postwar period of the 1950s and 1960s found social psychologists studying conformity, obedience, and conflict. Leon Festinger introduced the theory of cognitive dissonance in 1957; this theory captured the attention of social psychologists for the next fifteen years. In the late 1960s and early 1970s, attribution theory was a much researched topic. In addition, social psychologists developed new methods for gathering and analyzing data. Social cognition has been the field's major focus in recent years.

Science is a set of rules for investigating events and communicating findings. The goals of any science include (*a*) the description of events, (*b*) the prediction of events, and (*c*) the explanation of why events occur. Scientists generally work with *theories* that explain why events are related and with *hypotheses* that are educated guesses about the nature of the relationship between events.

Social psychologists use numerous methods in conducting their inquiry into human behavior. The *case history* and the *survey* are correlational methods for making predictions about the relationship between events. The *laboratory experiment* and the *field experiment* are methods for determining cause-and-effect relationships. In an experiment, the experimenter controls the *independent variable* and examines changes in the *dependent* variable. *Extraneous variables* must be eliminated if the experimenter is to be able to determine that the manipulation of the independent variable caused the observed changes in the dependent variable. The experiment is a valuable scientific tool because it allows the experimenter to randomly assign subjects to conditions and hence to arrive at the cause-and-effect relationship between variables. Laboratory experiments are often criticized because it is sometimes difficult to generalize beyond the laboratory, because they may lack *external validity* and *mundane realism*, and because they may allow *demand characteristics* and *experimenter bias* to affect the results. The field experiment is used because it generally has more external validity and mundane realism than the laboratory experiment. The field experiment's major drawback is that the experimenter loses some control over the extraneous variable.

Statistical tests are used to determine whether the results obtained in a study are reliable. Social psychologists have adopted the 5 percent chance level as the acceptable measure of significance of results. An important consideration in all research is the protection of subjects' psychological and physical safety. *Ethical concerns* in research center on the invasion of privacy, the use of deception, potential harmful consequences, and the fact that subjects are often the unwilling students of a lesson about themselves. Strict guidelines have been developed to protect human subjects in social psychology research studies.

KEY WORDS

case history
cause-and-effect
correlation
deception
demand characteristics
dependent variable
ethics
experiment
experimental realism
experimenter bias
external validity
extraneous variable
field experiment

hypothesis
independent variable
informed consent
instinct
internal validity
mundane realism
random assignment of subjects
science
social psychology
statistically significant
survey
theory
unobtrusive measure

SUGGESTED READINGS

Allport, G. W. (1985). The historical background of social psychology. In G. Lindzey and E. Aronson (Eds.), *Handbook of social psychology* (Vol. 1, 3rd ed.). New York: Random House, 1–46.

Aronson, E., Brewer, M., & Carlsmith, S. M. (1985). Experimentation in social psychology. In G. Lindzey and E. Aronson (Eds.), *Handbook of social psychology* (Vol. 1, pp. 441–486). New York: Random House.

Campbell, D. T., & Stanley, J. C. (1963). *Experimental and quasi-experimental designs for research.* Skokie, IL: Rand McNally.

Carlsmith, J. M., Ellsworth, P. C., & Aronson, E. (1976). *Methods of research in social psychology.* Reading, MA: Addison-Wesley Publishing.

Deutsch, M., & Krauss, R. M. (1965). *Theories of social psychology.* New York: Basic Books.

Festinger, L. (1980). *Retrospections on social psychology.* New York: Basic Books.

Hendrick, C., & Jones, R. A. (1972). *The nature of theory and research in social psychology.* New York: Academic Press.

Lindzey, G., & Aronson, E. (1985). *Handbook of social psychology* (Vol. 1, 3rd ed.). New York: Random House.

Selltiz, C., Wrightsman, L. S., & Cook, S. W. (1976). *Research methods in social relations.* New York: Holt, Rinehart & Winston.

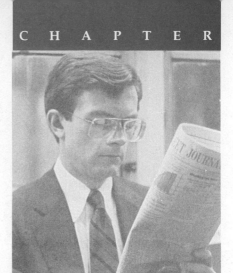

TWO

SOCIAL COGNITION

Finally someone popped the question. Henry Trewhitt of *The Baltimore Sun* addressed Ronald Reagan:

> Mr. President, I want to raise an issue that I think has been lurking out there for two or three weeks, and cast it specifically in national security terms. You are already the oldest President in history, and some of your staff say you were tired after your most recent encounter with Mr. Mondale. I recall, yet, that President Kennedy . . . had to go for days on end with very little sleep during the Cuban missile crisis. Is there any doubt in your mind that you would be able to function in such circumstances?

For two weeks, beginning with Reagan's surprisingly lackluster performance in the first presidential debate with Walter Mondale, there had been hushed talk about the president's age. Although it was being discussed widely in the press, the subject had something of a forbidden quality. The media handled it very gently, knowing perhaps how explosive it would be to raise openly and directly the issue of the president's advanced age, seventy-three, and the possibility that there had been a serious decline in his mental faculties. There was also the possibility that in times of stress or fatigue his capacity to think clearly might be worse than usual, or might come unhinged completely. Even the people in the opposing camp seemed reluctant to suggest that the president was experiencing a decline in mental acuity. But Trewhitt's question finally brought the matter out into the open in a nationally televised debate.

Ronald Reagan looked intense—like all candidates when "under the gun" in a debate—as he listened to the beginning of Trewhitt's question. When it was clear, however, that the question concerned his age and mental capacities, a smile came over his face. It was clear that he felt in control. Newspaper accounts indicate that before the debate Reagan refused to discuss the age issue with his staff, only indicating that he would be able to handle the matter.

And handle it he did. Reagan began, "Not at all, Mr. Trewhitt." Then looking very serious he added, "And I want you to know that also I will not make age an issue in this campaign. I am not going to exploit, for partisan political purposes, my opponent's youth and inexperience." The response was almost immediate. There followed a distinctly audible "whoop" and loud laughter and applause. Mr. Trewhitt laughed while visibly conceding that he had lost a big point in the struggle between press and politician for the upper hand. Walter Mondale could not hide his amusement; his smile was broad and his laugh loud. During the commotion, Ronald Reagan coolly sipped from the glass of water at the podium and relished the biggest score anyone was to run up in the series of 1984 presidential debates. What Reagan had done was to use a planned humorous response, a one-liner, to dodge a vitally important

As voters watched the 1984 debates between Ronald Reagan and Walter Mondale, they had to make inferences about each man's personal qualities and which one would make the better president. *(Georges Pierre/Sygma)*

and potentially devastating issue in the campaign. Critics have argued that debates are too much style and too little substance. Ronald Reagan's performance seemed to prove that. What he did is probably the most important thing a politician can do in such a situation: he conveyed mastery. He refused to let himself be taken by surprise or caught unprepared. By deflecting the age issue with one good joke, and showing everyone a good time during the sometimes tiresome ninety-minute debate, Ronald Reagan regained control of the headlines and the campaign. From that point on, he sailed home to his forty-nine state victory without a hitch.

The 1984 presidential and vice-presidential debates produced more drama than anyone expected. Ronald Reagan entered the campaign with what appeared to be an insurmountable lead in the polls, while his opponent floundered. Most people had an image of Reagan as forceful, in charge, somewhat lazy, but decent and likable. Their view of Mondale was that he was competent, dedicated, somewhat shrill, and less warm than Reagan. Mondale desperately wanted to debate Reagan, both to show his own command of issues and information and to expose the president's shallow understanding of the difficulties facing our country. Though Reagan had proved a skilled debater over the years, Mondale felt he could best him, and debating was his only chance.

The first debate on October 7, 1984, was a big surprise and a big plus for Walter Mondale. Mondale seemed finally to be hitting his stride in the campaign, and he looked relaxed, youthful, and commanding; he answered questions with clarity and force. Reagan, in contrast, looked unprepared and ill at ease; his answers seemed labored and full of uninformative detail. At several points in the debate he was unable to finish a sentence, and there were moments of marked tension while people waited to see if Reagan would be able to break the silence, and continue, and clarify his response. It felt like blessed relief when the host, Barbara Walters, began speaking again. Nowhere was Mondale's confidence and command and Reagan's seeming confusion and ineptness more apparent than when Reagan attempted to score by using the phrase that had worked for him so well in 1980—"There you go again." In his 1980 debate with the then incumbent, President Jimmy Carter, Reagan frequently poked fun at supposed Carter factual errors by using that phrase. Reagan had been warned by his advisers not to try it again, that Mondale would be ready, but the president couldn't resist the temptation. When he said it, Mondale was indeed ready. He smiled, looked directly at Reagan, took a threatening step toward him, and crisply articulated the ways in which Reagan had been wrong when he had used the phrase in the past. Reagan was thrown off-balance and became frustrated. He couldn't seem to gather his thoughts and he ended his reply in mid-sentence. That particular event, and Reagan's

In our everyday lives we encounter many different kinds of people. We actively strive to understand why they perform the behaviors they do and to make inferences about their personal characteristics. *(Alan Carey/The Image Works)*

generally weak performance made that first debate among the most one-sided in debating history. It led to muted speculations in the press that perhaps the "age issue," which had lain dormant during the whole campaign, should be raised. Clearly, if Reagan did not do better in the second debate (two weeks after the first), the age issue could become explosive, and create a stunning Mondale upset in the election.

Reagan's poor performance in the first debate and the consequent change in the tide of the campaign made the debate between the vice-presidential candidates, George Bush and Geraldine Ferraro, far more important than it would otherwise have been. It took place just four days after the first presidential debate. If Ferraro won, the shift in the Democrats' favor might accelerate and change the complexion of the whole campaign. Thus, Bush felt he had to at least hold his own to prevent further damage. The debate was a spirited one, with neither candidate clearly dominating. Ferraro impressed many voters with her skillful use of the sex discrimination issue. At one point she responded, "Let me just say, first of all, that I almost resent, Vice-President Bush, your patronizing attitude that you have to teach me about foreign policy." Many in the audience cheered loudly at this thinly veiled charge of vice-presidential sexism.

The struggle continued as Mondale and Reagan met for a second time on October 21. Mondale looked surprisingly tired and listless despite the fact that since the first debate the campaign had been going his way, while Reagan appeared more relaxed and in control. The president scored with a comment about one of Mondale's television ads in which he was seen standing on the aircraft carrier *Nimitz* watching a jet test flight. Reagan remarked: "If he had had his way when the *Nimitz* was being planned, he would have been deep in the water out there, because there wouldn't have been any *Nimitz* to stand on. He was against it." In the battle to win the voters' perception that one man was better qualified to be president than the other, Reagan edged ahead. But the clincher, in a debate in which Reagan still made several bad slips, was his one-liner about the age issue.

SOCIAL COGNITION: MAKING SENSE OF PEOPLE

Throughout a presidential campaign, citizens try to understand and make sense of the candidates' behavior. They try to understand specific behaviors, remember who said and did what, and form general impressions of each candidate's character and qualifications. This whole social understanding process goes into high gear during a presidential debate. We watch the candidates behave, we hear what they say, and we form opinions about their competence, their decisiveness, their drive and energy, and other important leadership traits. While debates may have more to do with personality than with issues, this doesn't mean that they are all style and no substance: they give voters a chance to see the candidates in action in a competitive stressful setting, which enables people to make important inferences about whether the candidates will be good presidents. In this chapter, we will consider just how people form impressions and make inferences about others. In the next chapter, we will consider the closely related topics of self-perception and self-understanding.

We call the process of understanding or making sense of people *social cognition*. Two key components of social cognition are making attributions about why people acted as they did, and interpreting their behavior in light of our general knowledge of them as individuals and as members of groups. We will consider these two aspects of social cognition: making attributions and using general knowledge, or *schemata*, in the first part of the chapter. In the remainder of the chapter, we will look more closely at how we make inferences about people and how powerful these inferences can be.

MAKING ATTRIBUTIONS: UNDERSTANDING WHY

In our everyday experience, we attempt to decide what other people are like. We want to know whether a person is kind or cruel, warm or cold, generous or stingy. We do not have access to people's innermost thoughts and feelings; we can only make judgments based on their behavior. So we must *infer* what they are really like from the behavior that we observe.

This section will consider three related views of the processes in which a person engages when examining the behavior of another to make decisions about what he or she is like. First, we will look at Jones's theory of correspondent inferences (Jones & Davis, 1965; Jones & McGillis, 1976), then at Kelley's (1967, 1972) model of attribution processes, and finally at Weiner, Freize, Kukla, Reed, Rest, and Rosenbaum's (1972) model of attributions for success and failure. Although the three models approach phenomena from slightly different points of view, they all ask the basic question, "How do you know what someone is like from his or her observed behavior?" Each approach seeks to determine rules for attributing stable characteristics to a person after knowing of his or her actions.

The Theory of Correspondent Inferences   When Walter Mondale took an aggressive step toward Ronald Reagan after Reagan's "there you go again" comment in their first debate, what could be said about Mondale the person? Was he an aggressive individual whose behavior reflected his underlying character or disposition accurately? To the extent that a viewer decided that Mondale's aggressive behavior was caused by an underlying aggressive disposition, he or she has made a correspondent inference. That is, the person has attributed the aggressive behavior to a corresponding personally aggressive disposition.

More formally, we may say that an inference is correspondent to the extent that the observer infers that the behavior corresponds to or was caused by a personal disposition that is similar to the behavior. The *degree* of correspondence relates to the confidence with which one makes such an attribution. It is evident that an observer attempts to make correspondent inferences for the purpose of attributing enduring dispositions to others. Hence, some voters may have made the attribution, or *correspondent inference,* that Walter Mondale was aggressive.

The meaning of an act depends on the context: In certain contexts, carrying a balloon is perfectly appropriate or "socially desirable." The act tells us little about the actor's underlying dispositions. However, in the context of a solemn ceremony, carrying a balloon is not socially desirable and should enable us to make a correspondent inference. *(William S. Nawrocki)*

Three major factors determine the degree to which we make a correspondent inference. The first is the number of effects or consequences of the behavior that the actor had in mind when he or she performed it. The fewer the number of effects, the more likely that we can make a correspondent inference. If the only effect of Mondale's act was to threaten Reagan, we might be likely to make the correspondent inference that Mondale is aggressive. However, if we felt that another effect was to impress the debate's viewers with his confidence and assertiveness, we experience ambiguity about why Mondale was aggressive. In the last case, a correspondent inference would be less likely. Research has shown that judges make more correspondent inferences each time an effect is eliminated as a possible explanation for a particular behavior (Newtson, 1974). Thus, the fewer the number of effects that remain to be considered, the greater the correspondence.

The second important factor in determining the degree to which we make a correspondent inference is the *social desirability* of the behavior. If you do something that "everybody" does because it is the accepted thing to do in a given situation, your act does not give us information about your disposition. We come to expect certain behaviors from certain people; their occurrence tells us little about the dispositions of the people who perform them. Geraldine Ferraro shook hands with George Bush after their debate. Perhaps she did so because she is a friendly person, but it is more likely that she was just doing the accepted thing. In short, we cannot make a correspondent inference solely on the basis of a socially desirable behavior.

The third factor in determining the degree of correspondence is *expectancy*. Just as we can't make correspondent inferences on the basis

Often people do the expected or "socially desirable" thing. When Geraldine Ferraro shakes a policeman's hand we don't know whether her behavior means that she is friendly or just that she is doing what is expected. *(A. Tannenbaum/Sygma)*

of socially desirable and therefore "expected" behavior, we typically make weak correspondent inferences from other behaviors that we expect from people. Whether we expect something from a person based on the group to which he or she belongs (category-based expectancy) or based on the knowledge we have of the person as an individual (target-based expectancy), we tend to make weaker correspondent inferences when a behavior is expected (Miller, 1976).

The concepts of social desirability and number of effects have been integrated into a general attributional principle that Harold Kelley (1971) has called the *discounting principle.* In his words, "The role of a given cause in producing a given effect is discounted if other plausible causes are also present" (p. 8). Both social desirability and an increasing number of effects provide "other plausible causes" and therefore serve to discount any particular cause.

An early study by Thibaut and Riecken (1955) demonstrated the degree to which multiple possible effects — and therefore multiple plausible causes — can lead to the discounting of a particular attribution. Each subject participated in a project with two other students who were both confederates of the experimenter. One of the confederates was always of higher status than the subject, and one was of lower status. At one point in the session, it became necessary for the subject to ask the two confederates for help. Both complied. At the end of the session, the subject was asked to rate the two other students in terms of how much their actions had been internally or externally motivated. That is, the subject had to decide whether he had been done a favor by a friendly person "who wanted to" or by a person who had been constrained by the situation to do so. The results were clear. Although the behavior in each case was identical, higher status compliers were seen as behaving because they wanted to, whereas lower status compliers were seen as behaving because they had to. Thus, an inference about the internal disposition and intention of an actor was made only when there was no other effect to discount the attribution of friendliness. The lower status person was only doing what almost anyone would do — he was doing a favor for a higher status person.

Another interesting study that provides evidence for the discounting principle was conducted by Jones, Davis, and Gergen (1961). They examined the effect of behavior that was consistent with a role that a person was playing versus behavior that was inconsistent. In general, they argued that behavior that is contrary to a person's role is more informative about the internal disposition of that person than behavior that is inherent in the role. When a person does something that is part of his or her role, there are multiple causes and multiple effects. If politicians shake your hand at a rally, does it really mean that you are their bosom buddy? Very few of us would make that interpretation. Rather, we see the behavior as part of the game that politicians play, and we discount the disposition of friendliness as an explanation. (Remember, however, that "discount" does not mean eliminate.)

In the Jones et al. study, subjects listened to a person applying for a job. Half of the subjects believed that the applicant was applying for a job as an astronaut, and the other half thought that he was applying for a job as a member of a submarine crew. In the second case, the subjects heard the job interviewer describe the ideal candidate as one who was outgoing, friendly, and cooperative—in short, outer-directed. Subjects who listened to the astronaut job interview heard the ideal candidate described as one who was inner-directed. As the interview proceeded, the subjects heard the job candidate act either consistently or inconsistently with his role requirement. Half of the astronaut candidates and half of the submariner candidates acted in a friendly and outer-directed fashion. The other half of them acted in an introverted, inner-directed manner. The inner-directed astronauts and the outer-directed submariners were acting consistently with their role requirements; the inner-directed submariners and the outer-directed astronauts were acting in an out-of-role fashion. The conditions are summarized in Table 2–1.

After listening to the tape-recorded interview, the subjects were asked to judge the way they thought the candidate *really* was. That is, they were asked to make inferences about the true dispositions of the job candidates. The result showed that the two in-role candidates were rated near the neutral point of all personality dimensions and that the degree of confidence that subjects had in these ratings was quite low. On the other hand, the outer-directed astronaut was seen as being outgoing, friendly, and so on, whereas the inner-directed submariner was seen as being truly quiet and reserved. Moreover, subjects were quite confident about their

Table 2–1
Summary of conditions in experiment on behavior and role conformity

Behavior	Job	Role conformity
Inner-directed	Submariner	Out of role
Outer-directed	Submariner	In role
Inner-directed	Astronaut	In role
Outer-directed	Astronaut	Out of role

Source: Jones, Davis, and Gergen (1961).

judgment of the out-of-role job candidates. As in the Thibaut and Riecken study, providing more than one plausible effect reduces an observer's confidence in being able to infer a stable disposition in the actor.

Kelley's Model of Causal Attribution   Harold Kelley (1967, 1971) has proposed a system of attributing dispositions to people that is based upon the idea that we, as perceivers, are like naive scientists. We sift through the events in our environment to find the causes of the phenomena we see. Our goal is to eliminate the "noise" or variance from the multitude of possible causes for an event and ultimately to try to locate the event's cause either within a person (internal causality) or in properties of the environment (external causality). To use one of Kelley's examples, suppose that we observe a man laughing at a particular motion picture. We wish to decide whether the laughter tells us something unique about the person (he laughs easily, he has a good sense of humor) or whether it simply tells us something about the environmental entity (the movie) that evoked the behavior. Kelley discussed three basic factors that must be considered if we are to make an inference as to the meaning of a behavioral act. These factors are described below.

Distinctiveness of the response. Does the man respond this way to all entities, or is his laughter distinctive to this particular movie? The more the laughter is specific to this one entity, the less likely it is that the behavior tells us something unique about the person. *High distinctiveness leads to external or entity attributions*. In the particular case in point, high distinctiveness makes us believe that the movie is funny.

Consensus. Do all people respond this way to the entity? That is, are all people in the movie theater laughing at the film? If they are (i.e., if the response is a consensus response), then it is more likely that the man's behavior is due to the entity than to anything unique about him. On the other hand, if he is the only one laughing, we are more confident that the laughter tells us something unique about the person. It may be that we judge him to have a heightened sense of humor or, if the movie is *War and Peace*, for example, we may judge him to be crazy. In either case, we are more likely to make an attribution to the person than to the movie. *High consensus, then, leads to external attributions, whereas high uniqueness leads to internal attributions*.

Consistency. Will the man act this way over time and modality? That is, will he always find the movie funny (time), and will he find it funny whether he sees it in the movie theater or on television (modality)?

High consistency is essential for either internal or external attributions. If the person finds the movie funny on Tuesday but not on Wednesday or Friday, and if he only finds it funny while seeing it at the RKO but not at the Paramount, then we are less confident that the movie was the source of the original laughter. We are also less confident that some *stable* property of the person was responsible (for example, his sense of humor). Rather, we are likely to suspect that some momentary circumstance led to the laughter. In this case, the man may have had a very tense day, and the movie may have served as a release, or he may have had a particularly ticklish toenail. The fact is that low consistency makes it difficult to make a stable attribution to the environment or the person, and thus circumstance is more often held to be accountable.

Kelley's model has provided an extremely provocative approach to understanding the causes of behavior. It has been a productive approach in part because of its ability to take "naive psychology"—the psychology we use informally in everyday life—and to systematize it in a way that enables precise predictions. In addition, the model has been intriguing because of its suggestion that it is equally applicable in making judgments about oneself. In principle, we may see ourselves as observers of our own behavior. Did *we* laugh because we have a good sense of humor or because the movie was funny? A simple substitution of ourselves for the person in the example above would enable us to follow the same rules in understanding our own actions. Chapter Three will discuss this question in some detail.

McArthur (1972) put the predictions drawn from Kelley's model to an experimental test. Participants in her study were given information about a fictitious other person. They were told about a particular behavior and then read three pieces of information designed to manipulate the degrees of (1) consensus, (2) distinctiveness, and (3) consistency. For example, subjects may have learned that "John laughed at the comedian." They were then told that *either*:

Consensus

a. Almost everyone (who hears the comedian) laughs at him; *or*

b. Hardly anyone (who hears the comedian) laughs at him.

Distinctiveness

a. John does not laugh at almost any other comedian; *or*

b. John also laughs at almost any other comedian.

Consistency

a. In the past, John has almost always laughed at the same comedian; *or*

b. In the past, John has almost never laughed at the same comedian.

In this way, either high- or low-consensus information could be combined with either high- or low-distinctiveness information and with either high- or low-consistency information to allow subjects to form an impression of John's behavior. In the end, subjects were asked to attribute the source of John's laughter either to (1) something about John, (2) something about the comedian, (3) something about the particular circumstances, or (4) some combination of factors.

The results of such a study are bound to be complex, due in large part to the eight possible combinations produced by the three informational factors. However, the results of McArthur's study were generally supportive of Kelley's model. Internal attributions (something about John) were facilitated by low distinctiveness, low consensus, and high consistency. External attributions (something about the comedian) were facilitated by high distinctiveness, high consensus, and high consistency. Of the three types of information, distinctiveness played the most important role in determining whether the attribution should be internal or external. Finally, attribution to fleeting circumstances was created by low consistency (and also by high distinctiveness). When John laughed only at this comedian but had almost never laughed at him in the past, the attribution was neither to John nor to the comedian, but rather to the circumstances. The results showed that the consistency information played by far the most important role in attributions to circumstances.

Surprisingly, consensus played a smaller role in determining attributions than might have been expected from Kelley's model. Although high consensus did facilitate entity or external attributions and low consensus generally facilitated attributions to the person, the effect was rather small. In subsequent studies, McArthur (1976), Nisbett and Borgida (1975), and Borgida and Nisbett (1977) have continued to find that consensus, particularly when it is presented in an abstract or statistical fashion, has less effect on a person's attributions than Kelley's model would predict.

New emphasis on the importance of consensus has been provided by a recent analysis by Pruitt and Insko (1980). These investigators have shown that the use of consensus information may be somewhat more complex. More information is needed before people can make adequate use of consensus information. Specifically, we need to know how John, in our previous example, reacts to other comedians compared to the way other people react to the other comedian. That is, when John attends a different nightclub and hears another comedian, is there consensus between his reaction and that of the audience? If there is, then consensus information will be used by observers in the above example. In the context of high consensus toward other relevant stimulus persons, consensus information toward the comedian will be used to make the entity attribution: the comedian is indeed funny.

Other studies have also helped to identify the conditions that accentuate the usefulness of consensus information. These studies, reviewed by Kassin (1979), suggest that information about the behavior of others (consensus) is important in making attributions: (*a*) when information about consensus is presented last in a sequence (Ruble & Feldman, 1976); (*b*) when such information is presented concretely rather than abstractly (Nisbett & Borgida, 1975); (*c*) when people do not have their own private impressions of the situation (Feldman, Higgins, Karlovac, & Ruble, 1976; Hansen & Donoghue, 1977; Tyler, 1980); (*d*) when individuals are making attributions about others rather than themselves (Hansen & Donoghue, 1977). In summary, then, consensus does play an important role in the attribution process, but the conditions necessary for its operation appear to be more exacting than the conditions for the utilization of distinctiveness and consistency information.

Attributions for Success and Failure A special type of attribution is that which is involved in success and failure experiences. We turn on the television set on a Sunday in November and see a football player diving to make a catch in the end zone. "Lucky!" shouts someone in the room. "What d'ya mean?" another responds angrily, "He's the best pass catcher in the league." A third, more intellectual-looking viewer (perhaps with a Harvard book bag) explains that the success was not due to the player's luck or skill but to the unusual amount of effort that he expended for this particular catch. To which the fourth person in the room responds, "Aw, it was easy anyway."

These four participants in America's favorite Sunday afternoon pastime are expressing each of the four possible attributions that Weiner, Frieze, Kukla, Reed, Rest, and Rosenbaum (1971) have suggested can follow success and failure. Weiner et al. suggested a two-step process. First, an observer must decide whether the attribution is to be internal or external; presumably, Kelley's (1967, 1971) model would serve as the basis for such a judgment. After that attribution is made, the observer must decide whether the success or failure is a stable or unstable occurrence. Could the football player make that kind of a catch again, or is making a good catch something that he does very infrequently? Only when attributions of internality-externality *and* attributions of stability-instability are made can a final attribution for the success or failure be made.

Table 2–2 summarizes the Weiner et al. view of how the factors are combined to form a final attribution. We can judge that the football player made his catch because he is good (a stable, internal attribution), because making such a catch is easy (a stable, external attribution—he could do it again and again; anyone could; it has to do with the kind of catch, not his ability), because he tried hard (an unstable, internal attribution—he

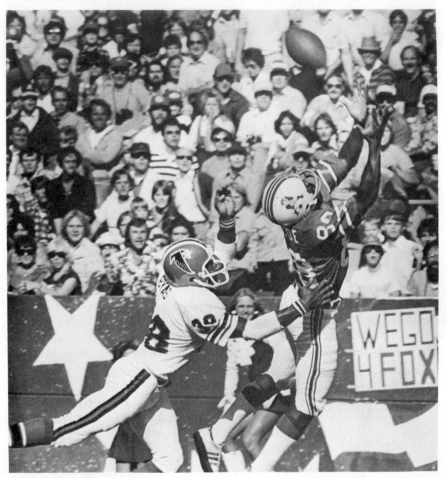

When a football player makes a clutch catch we try to decide why he succeeded. Does he have lots of ability? Was the pass an easy one to catch? Did he try very hard? Or was he just lucky? *(Anestis Diakopoulos Photography/Stock, Boston)*

couldn't do that again and again; it was his tremendous effort), or because of luck (an unstable, external attribution—he couldn't do that many times; it was lucky that his hands and the ball happened to wind up in the same place).

An interesting study that provides data relevant to the football player situation was conducted by Frieze and Weiner (1971). They told subjects of the success or failure that a hypothetical person had experienced at a task. They then told the subjects of the success or failure that that person had

Table 2–2
Classification scheme for the perceived determinants of achievement behavior

Stability \ *Locus of control*	*Internal*	*External*
Stable	**Ability**	**Task difficulty**
Unstable	**Effort**	**Luck**

Source: Weiner, Frieze, Kukla, Reed, Rest, and Rosenbaum (1971).

had at similar tasks and the percentage of other people who had succeeded or failed at that task. In this way, Frieze and Weiner established the
basic conditions that would enable attribution of internality or externality
(recall Kelley's model). Then the subjects were informed that the actor had
done the task one more time, and some subjects were told that he had succeeded, whereas other subjects were told that he had failed.

To what did subjects attribute the most recent success or failure? The
answers generally confirmed the predictions of the Weiner et al. model.
Performance that was inconsistent with the person's past performance
(whether it was success or failure) and different from the performance of
other persons was attributed to effort (he tried extra hard in the case of success; he didn't try very hard in the case of failure). Performance that was
consistent with the person's past performance and similar to the performance of other persons was attributed to task difficulty (success = easy
task; failure = hard task). Performance that was consistent with the person's past performance and different from the performance of other persons was attributed to ability (success = high ability; failure = low ability).

Thus, the questions we would have to ask about the football player in
order to make an attribution from the success we observed on TV become
clear. First, was it a catch that anyone could make—that is, was consensus high or low? Second, was the success a stable attribution—that is,
was it something that was consistent or inconsistent with the player's
past behavior as a pass catcher? We would conclude that he is a player of
high ability if we rated the pass catching to be internal and his success in
catching passes to be stable.

More recently, Weiner (1979) has expanded his model of achievement
attribution by adding an additional dimension. In his revised view, three

decisions rather than two need to be made. The dimension of "locus of control," he contends, needs to be broken into two independent elements. One is the locus of causality (internal versus external) and the other is whether the attribute is or is not controllable. Ability, according to the revised model, is an internal attribution that is stable but not controllable. (We cannot control how much ability we have to catch a football.) The expanded model deals not only with attributions of ability, effort, task difficulty, and luck, but also with such dimensions as mood and the distinction between typical and unusual degrees of effort.

Whether the revised model is useful will undoubtedly be the subject of considerable research. Weiner reports work by Meyer that suggests that it is. But Weiner also cautions that the kinds of attributions that any model should seek to explain are very much dependent on the goal of the investigator and the culture in which the participants are enmeshed. More dimensions, or different dimensions, may be necessary if the culture determines that other kinds of attributes are important. For example, Triandis (1971) found that in Japan and in Greece patience is considered an important component of success, while in India tact and unity are perceived as causes of success. In those cultures, models would be needed that helped to explain the conditions under which those explanations (attributions) for success or failure will be made.

MAKING BIASED ATTRIBUTIONS: MISUNDERSTANDING WHY

We have seen that the attribution models view people as scientists who are identifying the causes of behavior. The processes that have been developed in the various models are logical in form and make the assumption that human beings have the ability to weigh rationally and without bias all of the factors involved. As we have observed, studies such as McArthur's (1972) demonstrate that if people are given the relevant information, they are capable of combining it in a logical way that fits the attributional analysis.

But *will* they? Knowing that people can process information in the manner suggested by attributional models does not mean that they will do so in the complex environment.

Consider, for example, voters trying to decide why Ronald Reagan fared so poorly in his first debate with Walter Mondale. They might try to apply correspondent inference theory principles and determine whether Reagan's confused behavior corresponded to a confused disposition. They might have thought about Kelley's criteria of consensus, distinctiveness, and consistency in deciding whether to attribute Reagan's behavior to the president himself or to something external—that is,

Mondale. Or they might try using Weiner's model to attribute Reagan's failure to ability, bad luck, low effort, or mood. While in theory, people might use these attribution models, in practice, they do not always act like scientists; in many instances their attributions are faulty. We will now consider errors in the attribution process.

It may seem peculiar for psychologists to say that people make errors in the attribution process. If people deviate from the rational models, it is not clear whether the error belongs to the people or to the psychologists. Thus, we caution the reader that, when we use the word *error*, we do not mean blame. Rather we are referring to occasions in which the model and the perceiver do not arrive at the same attribution. Errors may be made for a variety of reasons. Some of these will be unique to the person who is perceiving the target's behavior. A child, for example, may not be able to use all of the information that is available. A person may fail to pay attention for a moment and miss an important bit of information. However, some of the errors people make are *not* random or unique, but are consistent and predictable. Deviations from the "rational baseline models" (as Jones & McGillis, 1976, refer to attribution models) may be created systematically by fundamental cognitive or motivational processes. We shall use the term *error* then to refer to unique unpredictable deviations. We shall use the term *bias* to refer to a systematic, consistent, and predictable departure of person perception processes or outcomes from processes or outcomes prescribed by a particular model (Schneider, Hastorf, & Ellsworth, 1979, p. 226).

The Correspondence Bias   The social psychologist who first wrote about attribution processes was Fritz Heider (1944, 1958). Although Heider did not develop an attribution model similar to the ones we have discussed, he did develop a number of key hypotheses about both basic attribution processes and errors in using them. One of Heider's important insights was that our perceptions of other people often rely too much on behavior and too little on the environmental context in which behavior occurs. Thus, we tend to make attributions that weigh internal dispositional causes too heavily, and external environmental causes too lightly. For example, a viewer of the Bush-Ferraro debate may have attributed Geraldine Ferraro's slow deliberate manner to her personality rather than to her campaign manager's instructions that she not appear shrill or overly excitable. Because this error involves making correspondent inferences (i.e., dispositional attributions) more than we should, we refer to it as the correspondence bias (Gilbert & Jones, 1986). Because it is such a pervasive and important phenomenon, it is also known as the fundamental attribution error (Ross, 1977).

The correspondence bias is illustrated in an interesting experiment by

Jones and Harris (1967). The study was conducted at a time when Fidel Castro was still a controversial and relatively unpopular figure in the eyes of most Americans. College student subjects were asked to judge the attitudes of a particular stimulus person regarding Castro after reading a speech that the stimulus person had just written. Half of the subjects read a speech that was highly favorable to Castro and the other half read one that was highly critical. In addition, the subjects were led to believe that the writer of the speech was a member of a neighboring university's debate team. Half of the subjects who read the pro-Castro speech and half of those who read the anti-Castro speech were told that the debater had been assigned the position that he had taken in the speech. The other half in each group was told that the position taken on the Castro issue was of the debater's own choosing.

The conclusions that the subjects drew about the speech writer's true opinion can be seen in Table 2–3. The subjects were logical in their view of the writer's position in the choice conditions. The most pro-Castro attitudes were attributed to those who chose to write pro-Castro speeches, and the most anti-Castro attitudes were attributed to those who chose to write anti-Castro speeches. That finding certainly makes sense from the correspondent inference model, but look at the findings for the no-choice condition. First, note that the "average student" was moderately unfavorable toward Castro (with a rating of 31.7, where 40 represented the midpoint). In attributing an attitude to the stimulus person, his speech should have been completely discounted by the knowledge that he was forced to take his position by his debate coach. Thus, an attribution near the attitude of the average student would have been logical. But the subjects were not logical. The no-choice, anti-Castro speech writers were seen to be very nearly as anti-Castro as those

Table 2–3
Attribution of attitudes to speech writer

	Essay	
Choice condition	*Pro-Castro*	*Anti-Castro*
Choice	**59.62**	**17.38**
No Choice	**44.10**	**22.87**

Note: Higher numbers indicate more favorable attitudes toward Castro. The possible range of scores was from ten (extremely anti-Castro) to seventy (extremely pro-Castro). The subjects' own attitude toward Castro = 32.23. The rating of the "average student" = 31.70.
Source: Adapted from Jones and Harris (1967).

who chose to write the anti-Castro speech. And the no-choice, pro-Castro speech writers were seen to be slightly pro-Castro—nearly ten scale points above the average subject's attitude.

A logical attributional analysis would not have produced the inferences made in the no-choice condition. But, as Heider said, *behavior engulfs the field*. The fact that the actors wrote what they did produced an effect—albeit an illogical one—that caused the observer to make attributions in line with the behavior.

What causes the correspondence bias? While there is not an agreed-upon answer, Jones (1979) has suggested that we are too ready to assume that any single observed behavior is representative of the actor's entire repertoire of behaviors. This is particularly true if the behavior is something we are not sure that we would do in a similar circumstance. The behavior then particularly stands out as what we assume to be a representative sample of that actor's behavior—something the actor might have done even if he or she had not been constrained by the environment. An alternate explanation suggests that the correspondence bias stems from shared norms in our culture favoring internal attributions over external attributions (Fincham & Jaspars, 1980; Jellison & Green, 1981). A third explanation holds that when we judge a peer's behavior, we recognize that different individuals act differently in the same situation, so we assume that any particular individual's behavior reflects his or her own personal disposition (Higgins & Bryant, 1982). While the reason for the correspondence bias is still unclear, the pervasiveness of the phenomenon is quite clear (Jones, Worchel, Goethals, & Grumet, 1971; Schneider & Miller, 1975; see also Harvey, Town, & Yarkin, 1981 for a different point of view). Despite our knowledge of situational constraints, the behavior of the actor plays a far greater role in how we arrive at an attribution than our rational models suggest it should.

The Saliency Bias   When Heider wrote that behavior engulfs the field, he implied that we may fall prey to the correspondence bias simply because behavior is so salient and vivid compared to subtle environmental pressures. Taking this idea one step further, Taylor and Fiske (1975) argued that any stimulus that is vivid or salient in a situation will be seen as the cause of behavior in that situation. They showed that if the attention of perceivers was focused on a particular member of a dyad during a conversation, that member was perceived as more central and causative in directing the course of the conversation. McArthur and Post (1977) demonstrated that making an actor's environment salient increased the number of attributions that were made to the environment. Taylor, Fiske, Etcoff, and Ruderman (1978) showed that a novel member of a group, by being more salient, was perceived as greatly influential. Being the only

We often perceive whatever or whoever is salient in the situation as the key causal factor. We might, for example, view this highly conspicuous man as responsible for the direction a conversation takes. *(Tim Carlson/Stock, Boston)*

black in a group of whites, for example, made perceivers rate the black member as having talked more frequently and as having been more influential in affecting the discussion. His salience affected his availability in perceivers' memories, which in turn affected their memory of how frequently he contributed to the group.

Pryor and Kriss (1977) used a procedure very much like that used by McArthur (1972) to determine the way in which Kelley's attributional model might be affected by the salience of the particular elements. Much the same information about consensus, consistency, and distinctiveness was presented to the participants. However, by varying the structure of the sentences that provided the information, Pryor and Kriss made either the person or the situational variable salient for the perceiver. An example of a person-salient sentence was, "Sue likes the restaurant." On the other hand, "The restaurant was liked by Sue" provides the same information but makes the environment stimulus (the restaurant) the salient element. The results indicated that the availability of the item that was highlighted in the sentence caused it to become a more important source for the final disposition. Does Sue like the restaurant because of something about Sue or because of something about the restaurant? Although consensus, consistency, and distinctiveness were important, the answer was found to be affected fundamentally by the factor's salience.

Defensive Attribution   In his debates with Ronald Reagan, Walter Mondale tried as hard as he could to prove that Reagan was responsible for everything that had gone wrong during his tenure as president. A major issue was whether Reagan should be held responsible for more than two hundred U.S. Marine deaths at the Beirut, Lebanon, airport that resulted from a suicide attack by terrorists. Mondale may have felt that he could blame this tragedy on Reagan based on research in social psychology indicating that we often blame people more when they are associated with accidents that have serious consequences.

The first experiment studying this question required subjects to decide how responsible a person was for causing an automobile accident (Walster, 1966). Surprisingly, the victim of an accident was seen as being more responsible as the consequences of the accident became more severe. In her study, Walster described the saga of Lennie, who left his car parked at the top of a hill. Unfortunately, the brake cable came loose, and the car rolled down the hill and was damaged. The more damage there was to the car and other people, the more Lennie was held responsible.

Why should Lennie be held virtually blameless when the damage to the car and others was minimal and held responsible when the car and/or others were harmed more severely? Why was Lennie negligent about checking his brake cable in the second case but not in the first? In short, why were observers less than rational in deciding on Lennie's blame?

Research has shown that rational, controllable factors, such as driving speed and previous driving record, will be used in a rational way if they are available (Arkkelin, Oakley, & Mynatt, 1979). However, it has been suggested that we become much less the rational scientist when we feel that an unfortunate accident *might happen to us*. In these situations we become emotionally aroused and we tend to try to reduce our arousal by making a defensive attribution; we hold the victim of an act responsible for his or her fate. For example, in one study female subjects who became emotionally aroused when reading about a rape held the woman who was raped responsible for the assault (Thornton, Hogate, Moirs, Pinette, & Presby, 1986). Returning to Lennie, if we all have cars and if we can see ourselves as potentially in the same predicament as Lennie, then it is safer to attribute responsibility to Lennie as a person. As the consequences become more severe, we would rather think that Lennie's fate was caused because he was a bad or negligent person. Clearly, *we* are not bad or negligent and the accident would not have happened to us.

In conclusion, the point can be made that although we typically act as impartial scientists, there are situations in which we have definite preferences for how we would like the results of our scientific search to turn out. In the case of defensive attribution, we are motivated to perceive the

People make attributions of responsibility for accidents. Often they make defensive attributions so that they can feel assured that the accident could not happen to them. *(Jerry Howard ©/Stock, Boston)*

causes of events in a way that makes us feel that we would not become the unfortunate victims of undesirable situations. If accidents occur because of chance, luck, fate, or properties of the environment, then it is possible for the same unfortunate events to happen to us. Therefore, we may be motivated to distort events that would lead us to make an external entity or circumstance attribution so that we can arrive at an internal or person attribution instead. All we have to believe, then, is that we are not as evil or as negligent as the victim of the undesired event, for such events only happen to negligent people (cf. Lerner & Matthews, 1967).

In summary, many biases in attributional processes have been identified. Indeed, the quest for such biases has been central in attribution research (Ross, 1977). The biases may result from cognitive distortions in the processing of information, or they may be motivated by the unique needs and desires of the perceiver. Jones and McGillis (1976) have referred to attribution models as rational baseline models. They present a system for drawing accurate inferences based on a logical combination of all relevant information. Differences between what people do and what they might be predicted to do, according to the models, do not invalidate the models. Far from it, such differences or biases open new avenues for understanding the motivations and information-processing capacities of people in their social environment.

THE IMPACT OF SCHEMATA: USING WHAT WE KNOW

One of the most important concepts in social cognition is that of *schema* (plural, *schemata*). A schema is our general knowledge about any person, object, or event. We have many different kinds of schemata stored in memory, including social schemata, which contain our knowledge of particular individuals and our knowledge of certain kinds of people. The word *schema* is derived from the Greek word for "form" so that it refers to the form or general outline of what we know about somebody or something (Crider, Goethals, Kavanaugh, & Solomon, 1986). Because we use what we know to make guesses about what will happen in the future, our schemata can also be thought of as general expectations or preconceptions (Myers, 1983) about other people. For example, in the 1984 presidential debates, many people were generally aware that Ronald Reagan was a good debater. This schema (or general image) of Reagan led to the expectation that he would do well in debating Walter Mondale.

There are two concepts that are closely related to schemata—the ideas of *prototypes* and *scripts*. Prototypes are our knowledge of particular kinds of people such as extroverts or firefighters (Cantor & Mischel, 1979). The key difference between a prototype and a schema is that prototypes are more specific than schemata. For example, our schema of an extrovert will consist simply of our general knowledge of extroverted people. Our prototype, however, includes an idea of the ideal or typical extrovert. Our prototype of a "jock" might, for instance, include an image of a muscular, fun-loving male with short hair wearing blue jeans and a T-shirt. We realize that not all jocks are large, have short hair, or are men, but nevertheless we have the prototype. Prototypes are useful in thinking about the similarities and differences between various kinds of people. Because schemata and prototypes are so similar and work in the same way, for the most part we will simply refer to schemata from this point on.

A *script* is our knowledge of a particular situation and the way events in that situation unfold (Abelson, 1981; Schank & Abelson, 1977); it can be thought of as an event schema. For example, we know that when people go into a restaurant, they will be seated, given a menu, asked if they would like a cocktail, and so on. Similarly, there was a script that Reagan and Mondale followed at the end of both of their two presidential debates. They walked over and shook each other's hands, turned to kiss their wives, chatted with their advisers, and so on. The most distinctive characteristic of a script is that it includes knowledge of the sequence of events that characterize situations.

How do schemata work? Generally, they provide us with expectations or preconceptions about how people will behave. Consequently, we notice

We all have ideas about the way situations will unfold. These ideas are called scripts. We know that the waiter in a restaurant will show us to a table, give us the menu, and take our orders. *(© Gale Zucker/Stock, Boston)*

information that is consistent with our schemata, we interpret information that may be ambiguous as fitting our schemata, and we recall information that is related to our schemata better than information that is unrelated to it. Futhermore, we tend to recall information that we interpreted as fitting a schema as being even more consistent with that schema as time passes (Higgins & McCann, 1984). In the following two sections, we will consider how schemata work with respect to specific individuals and groups of people respectively.

Schemata about Individuals   Schemata provide us with expectations and a tendency to perceive people's behavior as fitting those expectations. The impact of expectations on our perception of people can be seen in a classic experiment known as the "warm-cold" study (Kelley, 1950). The subjects in this study were undergraduates taking an introductory economics course at MIT. They were all told that they were to have a guest instructor for a specific class and were then given a little bit of information about the visitor. Students in half the sections were told that the visitor was twenty-nine years old, married, and that people considered him "a rather cold person, industrious, critical, practical, and determined." Students in the other sections were given the same information except that they were told he was said to be "a rather warm person, industrious, critical, practical, and determined" (Kelley, 1950). In short, the only difference was that one-half of the subjects were told that the guest lecturer was cold and the other half were told that he was warm. Because warm versus cold is an important "central trait" (Asch, 1946) in the perception of a person, this one-word difference created strong expectancy differences in the two subject groups. The impact of this expectancy difference was dramatic. The subjects who were told that the guest was warm had much more positive impressions of him that those who were told the opposite. Both groups of subjects saw the same guest giving the same lecture. And both groups spent a full class period with him. Yet their impressions of him, based on that hour of instruction, were strongly affected by the one-word difference: they interpreted the man's behavior according to their "knowledge" that he was warm or cold.

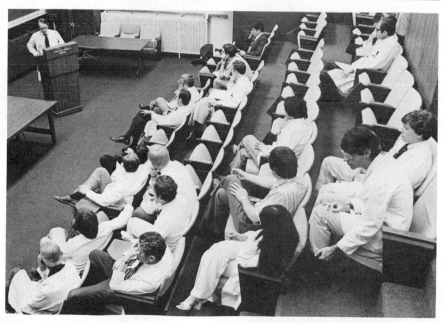

Our expectations can have a large effect on what we perceive. If we expect that a teacher will be warm and friendly, we will probably perceive him that way, and react to him as if he were. (© Fredrik D. Bodin/Stock, Boston)

How can a schema have such a strong effect? We interpret information that is ambiguous to fit our schemata. For example, when subjects were told that the guest lecturer was a determined person, they probably envisioned his determination as ruthlessness if they thought he was cold but as dedication when they thought he was warm. Second, we remember information that fits our schemata better than information that is unrelated to them. In short, we see things as fitting our schemata and we remember these things.

Although it is clear that we recall information that fits our schemata much better than information that is unrelated to them, there is also research that suggests that our attention is drawn to novel and incongruent stimuli, and that these stimuli may be remembered very clearly (Hastie, 1981). The key factor in determining whether we recall incongruent information is whether we take the time and make the effort to understand it. For example, voters who expected Reagan to do well in the presidential debate might not bother to consider the incongruous lapses in his first meeting with Mondale; they might simply overlook and forget them. On the other hand, if those voters really want to understand what is going on, they may spend time and effort in explaining Reagan's performance. Depending on the explanation, they might change their schema about Reagan's skill in debating, and perhaps, more generally, about his competence.

One clear demonstration that attributions made about incongruent information can affect whether the information is remembered and whether remembering such information changes our schemata comes from a study by Crocker, Hannah, and Weber (1983). Subjects were led to form a schema that someone named John was friendly. They were then given the incongruent information that John had cut in front of a line at the bank. The subjects were also given information that indicated that John's unexpected behavior was attributable to something external (John was being paged for an emergency) or that it was attributable to John's personal characteristics (he didn't care what the other people in line thought about his behavior). When subjects attributed John's incongruous behavior to the emergency, they forgot about it and didn't change their opinion of John. However, if they attributed his rude behavior to his personality, they remembered it well and the better they remembered it the more they thought badly of John.

In short, we typically interpret information as consistent with our schemata or expectations; we also recall information that is consistent with them. However, we sometimes recall highly incongruent information if we think about its meaning. When we do this recalling, we change our schemata to accommodate the new information.

Schemata about Groups   Every day we interact with lots of people; we see still others as we go about our daily lives; and we are exposed to infinitely more when we watch television or read newspapers. Although it is impossible to form schemata about each of these people as individuals, we do have some general knowledge about many of them based on our schemata about the groups to which they belong. One of the basic human cognitive processes is that of categorizing (Anderson, 1982). We categorize objects and experiences and we categorize people. Just as we categorize objects by groups such as animal, mineral, or vegetable, and then make many more finer gradations and groupings, we categorize people according to gender, age, race, occupation, and many other criteria. For example, we categorize politicians, and sometimes ordinary citizens as well, as either Republicans or Democrats. Thus, in judging Mondale and Reagan in the presidential debates, our knowledge about their party affiliations may have told us as much as our knowledge about each of them as individuals. Our group schemata in many instances are essentially stereotypes. In fact, we can think of stereotypes as a kind of group schema (Fiske & Taylor, 1984).

When we categorize people into groups, there are some immediate and important cognitive consequences. The first is that we magnify or accentuate the differences among people belonging to the different groups (Eiser, 1984). First, we see people belonging to two different groups as very different from each other. Second, we minimize differences between individuals belonging to the same group. However, just how much we minimize those in-group differences depends greatly on the group. Our perceptions of the groups to which we belong—the in-group—differ from our perceptions of members of groups to which we do not belong—out-groups. The biggest difference is that we minimize differences between members of the out-group much more than we minimize differences between members of our own group (Rothbart, Dawes, & Park, 1984). We tend to see "them" as all alike, while we see "us" as considerably more variable (Quattrone, 1986). We especially like to see the group of people that shares our opinions as diverse and heterogeneous. This outlook allows us to believe that our opinions are well considered and not just a reflection of narrow biases (Goethals, Allison, & Frost, 1979; Goethals, 1986).

Another difference between our in- and out-group schemata is that the out-group schema is less complex: we know less about the out-group than about the in-group. One consequence of this lowered schematic complexity is that we often have extreme reactions to information about out-group members, as we don't have as much general knowledge with which to combine and moderate the new specific information. These extreme reactions are known as the out-group polarization effect (Linville, 1982). For example, one study showed that white members of admissions committees formed a more favorable impression of a strong black applicant than a similarly qualified white applicant. On the other hand, they assessed a weak applicant described as black more negatively than the same applicant described as white. In other words, the evaluations of the out-group member, the black applicant, were polarized: positive information led to a more favorable impression and negative information led to a less favorable impression than the impressions that were formed based on equally polarized information about the white applicant (Linville & Jones, 1980).

We noted earlier that schemata can affect the way we interpret information about people. One particularly interesting demonstration of our social-class stereotypes that subtly affects our interpretation of information about a child comes from a study by Darley and Gross (1983). Subjects were shown slides about a young girl that showed where she lived and played, what her parents' backgrounds were, and so on. This information clearly told the subjects that the girl had either an upper- or lower-class background. When asked to make predictions about how well the girl would do in school, subjects seemed to resist their stereotypes. They did not make different predictions based on social-class information. However, when subjects were shown a videotape of the girl taking some tests in school, those who knew she was lower class perceived her actual performance as worse than those who thought she was upper class. Thus, sometimes we can resist making gross inferences about a person from stereotypes, but it is extremely hard to resist perceiving and understanding what we actually see the person doing from the perspective of our schemata and stereotypes.

Do group schemata affect what we remember as much as what we perceive? When we discussed schemata about individuals, we noted that we tend to remember information that is consistent with our schemata about those individuals. Something similar happens with group schemata. For example, in one study subjects were given information about an extrovert; they were told that terms such as *energetic* and *entertaining* described the person. These words are moderately related to our prototype of the extrovert. Later, subjects were asked whether certain words had been used to describe the person. They tended to remember that highly prototypic descriptions of extroverts, such as outgoing, had been used when in fact they had not (Cantor & Mischel, 1977). Thus, this study offers an interesting twist on the tendency to recall schema-consistent information: we remember schema-consistent facts about members of groups even when those "facts" never existed. We could also perceive an individual in this way. For example, somebody might recall Ronald Reagan as having smiled, nodded his head, and said "gosh" in the presidential debate even though he did none of these. We often associate Reagan with these behaviors that we might recall him as having used them when he did not.

Knowing that a person belongs to a certain occupational group can affect our memory of her behavior as much as our knowledge of what personality type she is. In one study subjects watched a videotape of a woman having a birthday dinner with her husband. Where the woman was described as a waitress, subjects remembered that she drank beer and had a television set. Where she was described as a librarian, they remembered that she wore glasses and listened to classical music (Cohen, 1981). In short, we remember information about people that fits our schemata and our stereotypes about them, and we remember it whether it is true or false.

PERSON MEMORY AND SOCIAL INFERENCE

As voters left their television sets after watching Walter Mondale and Ronald Reagan debate, their impressions of both candidates were strongly affected by the attributions they made about the candidates' performances and the schemata they used to interpret the way the two men behaved. But their thinking about the candidates probably didn't stop there. As time went on they had to rely more and more on their memory of what had happened, their recollections of who said and did what, and how the audience and reporters reacted. For example, their memory of Henry Trewhitt laughing at Reagan's comment about his opponent's youth and inexperience may have loomed large in viewers' recall of how relaxed Reagan had been. Finally, as election day approached people had to make inferences about which candidate, Reagan or Mondale, would best lead the country. They had to do so based on what they remembered and what inferences they finally made about each candidate's leadership qualities. In this section, we will consider the determinants of what people remember about others and how well they remember it, and the factors that affect the way in which we make social inferences.

Person Memory: Recalling Social Behavior   What determines how well we remember information about a person? Can we use what we know about the way people remember to improve memory? The area of social cognition that explores these issues is called *person memory*. Research in this area indicates that both the goals and particular thoughts that we have in mind as we receive information about a person affect how much we recall and how positively or negatively we recall it.

You might think that trying hard to remember what a person does as you receive information about him or her is the best way to accurately recall the information. However, research has shown that trying to remember another person's behavior is one of the worst ways to do so accurately. If, on the other hand people are asked to form an *impression* of the person rather than to remember what they learn, they actually recall better. Having to form an impression motivates people to organize and synthesize the information into a coherent whole that helps them remember specifics. In forming their impression, people build a schema and information related to this schema is more easily recalled. The superiority of recall derived from forming an impression over recall that derives from solely trying to remember is shown in a study where subjects were given a list of behaviors about a person. The list included statements such as "wrote an articulate letter to his congressman" and "helped a woman fix her bicycle." Subjects recalled more of the items if they were trying to form an impression of the person than if they were simply asked to memorize the words (Hamilton, Katz, & Leirer, 1980).

Other frames of mind aid recall as well. Recent research suggests that expecting to interact with someone leads to better memory about that person. The expectation of interaction may generate more thought about the person and more thorough processing of the information (Srull & Brand, 1983). Furthermore, if people are asked to empathize with someone else, they remember even better than if they are forming an impression. Fiske and Taylor (1984) suggest that trying to memorize your roommate's morning routine so that you will know when you can slip into the shower results in inferior memory compared to trying to decide whether your roommate is a fun-loving person, and that forming the latter kind of impression results in inferior memory compared to trying to understand how your roommate might feel about the death of a parent. Because being empathetic requires more cognitive work than either memorizing or forming an impression, this frame of mind results in more thorough information processing and better memory than either of the other two. Finally, you might expect that people will think about another person longest and hardest if they are comparing that person to themselves. Indeed, research suggests that thinking through information about a person based on how that person compares to you does lead to superior recall (Kuiper & Rogers, 1979).

In addition to the individual's frame of mind, that is, whether he or she is trying to memorize, form an impression, empathize, or compare, what is actually on a person's mind when he or she receives social

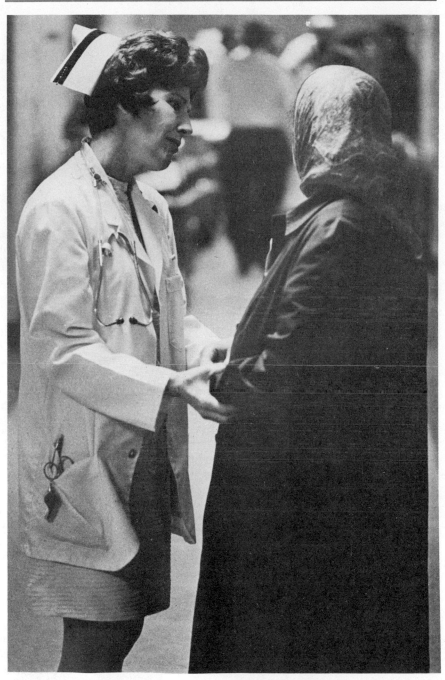

There are many ways of thinking about another person. Research suggests that if we empathize with someone we are likely to remember more about how they behave than if we actually set out to remember. *(Cary Wolinsky/Stock, Boston)*

information can have an important impact on memory. For example, someone who had been reading about mental disorders associated with old age may have interpreted Ronald Reagan's slips in the first Reagan-Mondale debate with much more alarm than someone who had been thinking about an absent-minded professor: the first person might remember Reagan's stumbles as much more serious than the second person. Exactly this kind of phenomenon has been shown in memory studies dealing with *priming*. Priming refers to the activation of certain ideas by thinking about or paying attention to them. Primed ideas, like schemata, can have an influence on incoming information that might be related to them. In one experiment, subjects read a list of dispositional labels and were urged to hold those labels in memory as part of a study on "information processing." Next, as part of what the subjects thought was a second study, they were asked to read descriptions of behavior that could be interpreted either positively or negatively. If subjects had been primed with a positive label for example, adventurous, they recalled a related behavior, shooting rapids, more positively than if they had been primed with a negative label, reckless (Higgins, Rholes, & Jones, 1977). In short, what we are thinking about when we receive information about someone can have a dramatic effect on what we remember about them and how we evaluate them.

Social Inference: Making Judgments about People   Millions of people watch the nationally televised presidential debates. For many, these debates are their major source of information about the candidates and the issues. Based on what they perceive and remember from the debates and any other sources of information, people must decide for whom to vote. How do they put together the various bits and pieces of information they have and arrive at a judgment about the two candidates? Social cognition research that focuses on inferences attempts to understand these judgment processes. What we have learned from this research is that human beings are not perfect in their judgments and inferences. Whether this imperfection means that people are basically irrational and thus make flawed judgments or that they are pretty sound in their thinking given the difficulties of meeting perfect standards, has been a matter of considerable debate in psychology (Nisbett & Ross, 1980; Markus & Zajonc, 1985). Most of the research that we will describe below illustrates people's mistakes and the shortcuts they take in making inferences. These mistakes result from following modes of thinking that work well in most instances; unfortunately, sometimes these modes are inappropriate, and then the results can be serious.

Underusing base-rate information. Imagine an individual, Bob, deciding what kind of car to buy. Since reliability is important to him, Bob has carefully gone through all the data on frequency of repair in consumer magazines and decides that he will buy a Toyota; it has the best repair record. Shortly before Bob makes a final decision, a friend tells him about his neighbor's cousin who bought a 1980, four-door Toyota Tercel that was always in the shop. Bob is impressed with this story and decides he better not get tangled up with a Toyota. In this situation, a person ignores the available base-rate information on auto repairs and makes a judgment about the most reliable car based on a single, albeit impressive, example.

Studies suggest that people make this error frequently. They ignore available general information and pay attention to concrete instances. In one study, for example, subjects were told about a taxi that was involved in a nighttime accident. One of the eyewitnesses said the cab could have been blue. Subjects were also told that 85 percent of the cabs in the city

In trying to make decisions about what kind of car to buy we may ignore important "base-rate" information such as its frequency of repair record. *(© Joel Gordon)*

were green and 15 percent were blue. Most subjects went with the eye-witness's testimony and guessed that the cab was blue, thereby ignoring the base-rate information, which indicated that the cab was probably green. On the other hand, when the subjects were told that 85 percent of the cars involved in the city's accidents were green, they did use that base-rate information (Ginosar & Trope, 1980). Furthermore, another study shows that people use base-rate information if they are induced to think scientifically or if they realize the relevance of such information to their goals (Zukier & Pepitone, 1984). Thus, people will use base-rate information if they think it is relevant; in many cases, they seem to make the mistake of ignoring its relevance.

The dilution effect. Suppose that you missed the first 1984 debate between Ronald Reagan and Walter Mondale but were told that Reagan seemed confused and uneasy all night. What prediction would you make about how well Reagan would do in the second debate? You might infer that he is losing his touch and therefore will do poorly. Now suppose that you were told not only that Reagan seemed confused and uneasy, but also that the debate was in Louisville, that Reagan wore a blue suit, and that he had eaten his usual Sunday night supper. Would your prediction be any different? Perhaps you think not, but several studies have shown that your prediction can be diluted if relevant information (in this case about Reagan's actual performance) is *diluted* with irrelevant information (such as what Reagan had for supper or what Nancy was wearing). You might actually make a less pessimistic prediction for Reagan in the second case (Zukier, 1982). Being influenced or distracted by such irrelevant information is called the dilution effect. Politicians seem to understand it; they often give out cheerful but irrelevant information to soften the impact of bad news.

Illusory correlation. Another of the errors that we make in perceiving the world around us is to conclude that a relationship exists between two things when that conclusion simply isn't supported by the available data. For example, a person might believe that "politicians are dishonest" when the available data actually show otherwise. To accurately conclude that there is a unique association between dishonesty and politicians, the person would have to list honest and dishonest politicians and honest and dishonest physicians, bankers, and college professors and then show that dishonesty occurs more frequently among politicians than among other occupational groups. Holding a belief even when the data right in front of you don't support that belief is called *illusory correlation*. People seem to make this error because confirming instances (in this case, examples of dishonest politicians) can be highly salient and can obscure all the data that show numerous honest politicians and crooked bankers.

Some important research demonstrates that illusory correlations can have a strong impact on stereotypes (Hamilton & Trollier, in press). In one study subjects were told about positive and negative behaviors by members of Group A and Group B. For instance, subjects heard that John, a member of Group A, visited a sick friend in the hospital. While Group A always had more members than Group B, the proportion of positive and negative behaviors performed by the members of the two groups was constant. Sometimes both groups performed more desirable behaviors and sometimes they performed more undesirable behaviors. However, the results showed that group B members, who were always in the minority, were recalled to have performed more desirable behaviors than they actually did when desirable behaviors were performed less and more undesirable behaviors when undesirable behaviors were preformed less (Hamilton & Gifford, 1976). See Figure 2-1. It seems that a person from an underrepresented group performing an unusual behavior is especially salient and memorable. The tendency to remember an unusual combination can lead us to see an illusory correlation between a certain

Figure 2-1

Comparison of statements describing and later attributed to groups in Hamilton & Gifford's study of stereotyping

Groups and types of behaviors	Number of statements describing each type of behavior	Number of statements attributed to each group
Variation I		
Group A		
Desirable behaviors	8	5.87
Undesirable behaviors	16	15.71
Group B (minority)		
Desirable behaviors	4	6.13
Undesirable behaviors	8	8.29
Variation II		
Group A		
Desirable behaviors	18	17.52
Undesirable behaviors	8	5.79
Group B (minority)		
Desirable behaviors	9	9.48
Undesirable behaviors	4	6.21

Source: After Hamilton & Gifford (1976). Copyright 1976 by the American Psychological Association. Adapted by permission of the author.

group of people and a certain kind of behavior. For example, to a white person being raised in the suburbs and attending predominantly white schools, blacks may be uncommon. Further, displays of aggressive behavior in either the community or the school may be unusual. In these circumstances, a black person behaving aggressively would be especially unusual and salient and therefore overrecalled, leading to the illusory correlation that blacks are aggressive. In short, noticeable and salient instances of a relationship can lead us to overlook the other relevant data and infer an illusory correlation.

The availability bias. Suppose a friend of yours asked you how President Reagan had done in his second debate with Walter Mondale. What comes to mind most readily are the two times Reagan cracked facile jokes, one about Mondale standing in the water instead of on the aircraft carrier and the other about Mondale's youth and inexperience. Because these events are available you might recall Reagan doing well as the dominant tone of the debate. Making judgments about the frequency or probability of events based on the instances that come easily or quickly to mind is called the *availability bias* (Tversky & Kahneman, 1973). If you think back to illusory correlations, you can see that the availability bias is implicated there as well. Watergate and other instances of political corruption are available to you so that you overestimate the frequency of dishonest politicians, thereby inferring the illusory correlation.

The representativeness heuristic. Sometimes people deliberately use certain shortcuts or rules of thumb to make inferences. When they do so we speak of *heuristics* rather than biases. For example, a person might deliberately use the ease of recalling Reagan being facile as a tool to infer how well the president did. In this case we would say that the person used the availability heuristic rather than bias. But calling the inference a heuristic doesn't make it any more accurate. A heuristic is simply a special kind of bias, one that is used deliberately (Markus & Zajonc, 1985). A heuristic that is used quite commonly is called the *representativeness heuristic*. It refers to judging whether a person belongs to a group based on how similar he or she is to typical members of that group. For example, people reading that Tom is intelligent but not creative, that he is orderly with a corny sense of humor, and that he has little interest in interacting with others are likely to see him as an engineer or computer scientist, even if they knew that engineers and computer scientists are rare (Kahneman & Tversky, 1973). He seems representative of the category. Using the representativeness heuristic to make this judgment when engineers and computer scientists are rare involves the error of underusing the base-rate information that we discussed earlier. Thus, as you can see from the last two examples, errors in inference often work together.

ORDER EFFECTS IN PERSON PERCEPTION: "THE FIRST TIME EVER I SAW YOUR FACE"

A friend of yours is going on a job interview tomorrow. He has spent hours choosing the right suit to wear and deciding what brand of after-shave to use. Standing in front of a mirror, he rehearses the words "Hello, it's good to meet you" over and over again. You ask him why he is going through these torturous procedures. He reminds you of the conventional wisdom that first impressions are what count. So, instead of thinking about all the things that he should know for his interview, he is concentrating on what happens up to the time he says hello. You remind him that there is also a popular wisdom that urges the importance of leaving a favorable impression; the last impression that the interviewer will get about him is based on what happens at the end of the interview. You remind him how, on a recent blind date, he was obsessed with the way he said goodbye, not hello!

Primacy Effects: The Importance of First Impressions   Social psychologists are extremely interested in how impressions of people are formed. In addition to outlining the rules that a person uses to infer dispositions about people from their behavior, social psychologists are interested in the effect of the order in which the impressions are formed. Whenever there are opposing conventional wisdoms about a social phenomenon, we should not be surprised to find evidence supporting both points of view. As we shall see, there is evidence to support the importance that your friend attaches to first impressions, and there is also evidence to support the conventional wisdom of "recency."

In the pioneering investigation in this area, Solomon Asch (1946) used a very simple procedure. Subjects were shown a list of six adjectives that described a hypothetical person. Each of the adjectives was related to a stable disposition of that person, so the subjects did not have to infer dispositions from behavior. The hypothetical person was described as (1) intelligent, (2) industrious, (3) impulsive, (4) critical, (5) stubborn, and (6) envious. You might try to do what half of the subjects were asked to do—form an impression of this hypothetical person. The other half of Asch's subjects also had to form an impression of the person, but they were given the list of six adjectives in the *reverse* order: (1) envious, (2) stubborn, (3) critical, (4) impulsive, (5) industrious, and (6) intelligent. Do you see a difference between a person who is described with adjectives that run from good to bad and a person who is described with

The impressions we form of someone when we first meet can have a lasting influence. When we base our impressions on that early information, the result is called a primacy effect. *(Copyright © Ken Robert Buck 1980/The Picture Cube)*

adjectives that run from bad to good? Asch's subjects did. The order of presentation made an important difference in the impression that the subjects formed of the hypothetical person. The subjects who read the intelligent → envious list rated the person as more sociable, humorous, and happy than did the subjects who read the envious → intelligent order.

The results were evidence for a *primacy effect* in forming impressions. The adjectives read first seemed to have more weight than the adjectives that came later. Why should this be? Typically, we remember more recent events better than earlier ones. So why should adjectives that are read first be more influential than those that come later? Asch provided an interesting hypothesis. He contended that the order of trait adjectives is important because the meaning of the later adjectives is changed by that of the earlier adjectives. We might call this the *assimilation of meaning* hypothesis. According to this reasoning, an impression is formed by virtue of the early trait descriptions. As soon as we say that a person is intelligent, we are forming a general impression of that person. The later terms *stubborn* and *envious* take on a meaning that is consistent with that first impression. So

This woman is "intelligent, industrious, impulsive, critical, stubborn, and envious."

This woman is "envious, stubborn, critical, impulsive, industrious, and intelligent."

Do you get a different impression of this woman depending on which caption you read?

the intelligent person who is later described as stubborn may be seen as persevering. However, the stubborn person who is later described as intelligent may be viewed more as a spoiled brat than as a persevering intellectual. Again, it is the meaning of the later information that is assimilated to (changed toward) the meaning of the earlier information.

Because Asch's study provided subjects with a list of adjectives, it might be viewed as a rather artificial situation that has as much to do with linguistic memory as with the perception of persons. A later study of Luchins (1975b) provided further support for a primacy effect in a different type of situation. Subjects read a story that described the behavior of a boy named Jim. In one paragraph, Jim was described as an outgoing, affable person. For example:

Jim left the house to get some stationery. He walked out into the sun-filled street with two of his friends. . . . Jim entered the stationery store, which was full of people. Jim talked with an acquaintance while he waited for the clerk to catch his eye. On his way out, he met the girl to whom he had been introduced the night before. They talked for a short while, and then Jim left for school.

Another paragraph described Jim somewhat differently.

After school, Jim left the classroom alone. . . . The street was brilliantly filled with sunshine. Jim walked down the street on the shady side. Coming down the street toward him, he saw the pretty girl whom he had met the previous evening. Jim crossed the street and entered a candy store. . . . Jim waited quietly until the counterman caught his eye and then gave his order. Taking his drink, he sat down at a side table. When he had finished his drink, he went home.

Subjects who read only the first paragraph saw Jim as a highly extroverted sociable person. Those who read only the second paragraph saw him as a quiet introverted person. The interesting question was how subjects who read *both* paragraphs would rate him. As we might expect from Asch's (1946) study, the order in which the paragraphs were read made the critical difference. Subjects who read the extroverted paragraph and then the introverted paragraph saw Jim as much more outgoing and sociable than did subjects who read the paragraphs in the reverse order.

Luchins believed that the first paragraph does produce a set that affects the reading of the second paragraph. For example, if we form the first impression that Jim is gregarious, then we might interpret the events of the second paragraph as having more to do with a temporary state of Jim's health (he had a headache) than with Jim's stable disposition.

Primacy in Success and Failure   An interesting experiment that was less abstract than either Asch's or Luchins's was conducted by Jones, Rock, Shaver, Goethals, and Ward (1968). In their experiment, subjects observed a stimulus person performing a test of intellectual ability. The test that this person was taking looked much like a standard college aptitude test (such as the SAT) and contained thirty multiple-choice items. In all conditions, the stimulus person answered fifteen questions correctly. But in one condition, after starting off like the proverbial "house on fire" on the first few items, she trailed off into mediocrity. In another condition, the stimulus person started poorly but then improved considerably. The patterning of correct responses in the latter (ascending) condition was the mirror image of the patterning in the former (descending) condition.

At the end of the study, the subjects were asked to predict how well the stimulus person would do on the next series of thirty problems, and to rate the person's intelligence. Although both the ascending and the descending overall performances were the same, the stimulus person in the descending condition (who started well and then trailed off) was rated as more intelligent than the stimulus person in the ascending condition. In addition, subjects predicted that the person with the descending performance would do better on the next set of items than the person with the ascending performance.

The Jones et al. study offers strong evidence of a primacy effect and also indicates the potentially insidious manner in which primacy effects can influence our judgments of people. In this study, both test takers were equal in their overall performance, yet one was seen as brighter than the other. The only difference between them was the way in which the observer processed the information received—that is, by giving more weight to earlier information. Consider the consequences that such a primacy effect might have in a classroom. Students who start poorly at the beginning of a semester but show improvement at the end of the semester may still be rated as less intelligent than students who start well. And consider the implications for a student for whom first impressions are formed before he enters the classroom. Suppose that he is a student from a minority group and that the commonly held stereotype is that members of his group are not intelligent and cannot learn. Suppose, too, that despite the growing evidence that they unfairly discriminate against minority cultures (see Kamin, 1974), standardized test scores are used that show that the minority group student has less ability than do other students in the class. The results of the Jones et al. study indicate that it is very difficult for the student to do anything to rectify fully the impression that the teacher may already have. If the student succeeds, to what will the success be attributed? Combining the Jones et al. finding with the attribution model of Weiner et al. (1971), we can predict that the success, which is inconsistent with the first impression, may be seen as unstable and then attributed either to an unusual expenditure of effort or to luck.

Other Explanations of Primacy   Asch's assimilation of meaning hypothesis is not the only explanation of why earlier information is more important than later information in producing a final impression. Anderson and his colleagues have proposed a system of *averaging* the various trait characteristics. Making extensive use of the adjective-listing paradigm developed by Asch, Anderson concluded that people form impressions by averaging the favorableness of the various adjectives presented to them and that the meaning of one adjective does not change as a function of earlier or later adjectives in the list. Rather, in the averaging explanation, later adjectives are said to be discounted relative to earlier adjectives. In Anderson's terms, "the net influence of an adjective decreases linearly with its ordinal position in the set" (Anderson, 1965). That is, each adjective has less weight as it is presented farther down on the list of adjectives that supposedly describe a person. At least two mechanisms might cause later descriptive terms to lose relative weight in this way. One is that people may tend to "tune out" later information. Once they feel that they have enough information to make a judgment, they may become less attentive to subsequent information. Evidence for the loss of attention can be found in an experiment by Hendrick and Constantini (1970). An alternative, which Anderson (1968) supports, is that later information is *discounted*. In the mind of the perceiver, later information is simply not worth as much as earlier information. At this point, the evidence is not conclusive regarding the role of the attention loss versus discounting processes in accounting for the primacy effect.

Moreover, the basic controversy between Asch's change of meaning hypothesis and Anderson's weighted averaging of trait descriptions has been the subject of active research (Hamilton & Zanna, 1974; Wyer, 1974; Kaplan, 1975). Higgins and Rholes (1976) attempted to demonstrate that words used in a particular context or in particular combinations do not always convey the same meaning that they do in isolation. They argued that the connotative or emotional value of a word is not a fixed part of the word itself, but is derived from what the word refers to in the world. They suggested that the function of words in forming impressions is mainly to single out or refer to a person or thing. It is the "thing," or referent, that is being evaluated, and not the words. Thus, if a set of words refers to a person or thing that is evaluatively different from the kind of person or thing that the words in isolation usually refer to, the "meaning" of the words will change. In a demonstration of this point, Higgins and Rholes had people rate their impressions of such word combinations as *aged wine* and *mature wine*. Though in isolation *aged* is rated negatively and *mature* is rated positively, *aged wine* and *mature wine* mean the same thing, and were therefore rated as giving the same (positive) impression. Since this study demonstrates a change of word meaning in context, it has been taken as supporting Asch's perspective on impression formation.

Some Evidence for Recency   It would defy common experience if we did not have evidence that supported the importance of last impressions. There are occasions in which the powerful effect of primacy can be broken and even reversed. If there is merit to the idea that later information is tuned out, then asking subjects to recall all of the descriptive traits about a person before forming a final impression should reduce the primacy effect. In one study, Anderson and Hubert (1963) had some subjects believe that their memory for the traits listed would be tested. They found evidence that, under this condition, the more recent traits were more important in forming a final impression. In another study, Stewart (1965) showed that, by asking people to form a separate judgment about a stimulus person after each presentation of a trait adjective, the effect of the undue weight of the early information was eliminated.

In addition, Luchins (1957a) found that a simple instruction (warning of the dangers of first impressions) weakened the primacy effect that had been obtained with the two paragraphs about Jim that we reprinted above. Even more effective in reducing the primacy effect in the story of Jim was increasing the time between the presentation of the two paragraphs. Luchins found that the greater the time that elapsed between the presentation of the two paragraphs the more the final judgment of Jim depended on the second and not the first paragraph. This was probably due to increased forgetting of the material presented in the first paragraph.

In general, though, the bulk of the evidence appears to be on the side of your friend who was concerned with his first impression in an upcoming job interview. At present, it is not clear whether the assimilation of meaning hypothesis or the various weighted averaging hypotheses explain more of the available data (see Anderson & Jacobson, 1965). It is certainly not true that later information has no effect on the final impression formed, but the evidence does appear to favor the position that early attributions influence total judgments more than later attributions do.

SOME CONSEQUENCES OF FORMING IMPRESSIONS: THE SELF-FULFILLING PROPHECY

When we form impressions of people, we tend to act in ways that perpetuate those impressions. In Kelley's (1950) study of warm and cold guest lecturers, students tended to act in a distant fashion to the instructor who they believed would be cold. Undoubtedly, in a situation in which the instructor was not a confederate, the distant approach of the student would have encouraged behaviors in the teacher that would confirm the student's impression that the teacher was a cold person.

There has been some interesting research on the consequences of believing information about others. In a famous study, Rosenthal and Jacobson (1968) told elementary school teachers that some of the children in their classrooms could be expected to show dramatic spurts in academic performance during the school year. It was alleged that such information was based on the reliable Harvard Test of Inflected Acquisition. In truth, there was no such test, and approximately one-third of the students were chosen at random to be designated as spurters. At the end of the school year, the children's IQs were measured. Figure 2–2 depicts the results for the children in the first and second grades. Those students who had been

Figure 2–2

Gains in total IQ for children in first and second grades

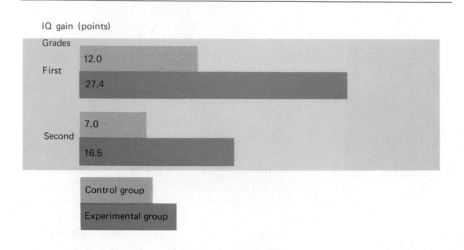

Source: Rosenthal and Jacobson (1968).

designated as spurters actually showed a marked gain in their IQ scores over the year—even though their designation as spurters bore no relation to any legitimate test.

Like Pygmalion in George Bernard Shaw's play, the teachers apparently created the person whom they expected to find. The possible implications of this research were startling. Is long-term academic achievement largely a function of biased expectations? The Rosenthal and Jacobson study thus drew the attention of many social psychologists and policymakers.

It is important to realize that Rosenthal and Jacobson's work has been the subject of considerable criticism. Questions have been directed at the intelligence instrument that was used (Flemming & Anttonen, 1971; Snow, 1969), at the way in which it was used (Jensen, 1969); and at the analyses of the data that were obtained (Elashoff & Snow, 1971). In addition, differences between boys and girls in the various grades and differences between different subtests of the intelligence scale have been embarrassing for the study's major conclusion.

Despite all of these very important problems, the main result found by Rosenthal and Jacobson has withstood the test of time. Over one hundred studies have examined the effects of teacher expectation (Brophy, 1982). Systematic expectancy effects were found in middle-class schools in the

East and West (Conn, Edwards, Rosenthal & Crowne, 1968; Rosenthal & Evans, 1968). Anderson and Rosenthal (1968) observed the expectancy effect in a class of mentally retarded boys, and Michenbaum, Bowers, and Ross (1969) reported it in a study that systematically varied behavioral and academic expectancies in an Ontario training school for female offenders.

The problem of expectations producing changes in behavior is an important one, for both theoretical and practical reasons (Cooper & Croyle, 1982). Problems for basic research include discovering the process by which our perceptions and expectations are communicated to the targets of those expectations (Adair & Epstein, 1968; Jones & Cooper, 1971). Research has indicated, for example, that teachers provide low-expectation students with less time to answer (Taylor, 1979; Allington, 1980), more criticism for failure (Cooper & Baron, 1977), and less eye contact (Chaiken, Sigler, & Derlega, 1974). Problems for applied research include the determination of how classroom and other situations can be structured to maximize the communication of positive constructive expectations while reducing the communication of negative perceptions and expectations. Based on the research findings currently available, educators have begun to develop teacher training programs to achieve these goals (Kerman, 1979)

The pervasiveness of the self-fulfilling prophecy extends past the classroom and affects a wide array of social interactions. Evidence that extends the applicability of the self-fulfilling prophecy and that examines the way in which it operates has been provided by Word, Zanna, and Cooper (1974) and by Snyder and Swann (1978). Word et al. took note of the fact that black job applicants are often reported to perform less well on job interviews than white applicants. Using the analysis of the self-fulfilling prophecy, Word et al. designed a study in two stages. In the first stage, white subjects took the role of a job interviewer. They interviewed both white and black applicants. Unknown to the subjects, the applicants were carefully trained confederates who had rehearsed their answers to all the questions of the forthcoming interview. When the interview took place, therefore, there was no objective difference between the black and white applicants on their verbal and nonverbal performance.

The investigators were actually observing the behavior of the *interviewers*. It was found that their interviews with white applicants lasted longer and that in those interviews there was a significant increase in the behaviors that Mehrabian (1968) has labeled "immediacy." White applicants received greater eye contact, greater forward body lean, and other responses that are usually associated with positive interactions.

In the second phase of the study, white subjects served as applicants and carefully trained confederates served as interviewers. The trained interviewers responded to half of the applicants with precisely the

Research suggests that the expectancies we have about people can become self-fulfilling prophecies. If teachers treat students as if they are bright, they may live up to those expectations. (© *Elizabeth Crews/Stock, Boston*)

behaviors that had been afforded to the black applicants in the first stage of the study. That is, they responded with low-immediacy behaviors. The other half of the applicants received the high-immediacy behaviors that had been afforded to the white applicants in the first stage.

At the end of the second-stage interview, independent judges rated the performance of the applicants. Those applicants who were treated as the black applicants had been treated in the first stage (low-immediacy behaviors) performed considerably worse in the second-stage interview. And those applicants also reported feeling worse about themselves at the end of the interview. Thus, starting with some assumptions about the way in which blacks would perform on a job interview, the interviewers had acted in a way (with low-immediacy behaviors) that was sufficient to produce poor performance in such an interview.

Snyder and Swann (1978) led one member of a dyad to believe that a second member—the target—was either hostile or nonhostile, depending on the condition to which that member was assigned. In fact, these labels had no necessary relationship to what the target was really like. During the discussion that followed, members who had been led to believe that the target would be hostile acted differently from members who thought that the target would not be hostile. The loudness with which the first member talked to the target, for example, was greater if the target was believed to be hostile. An analysis of the conversation also showed that the target whom the first member expected to be hostile actually began to act with greater hostility during the interview.

In a second stage of Snyder and Swann's experiment, the target was brought into a conversation with a new partner who had no particular expectations about him. The target person who was expected to have a hostile disposition in the first stage of the experiment actually acted hostile in the second stage of the experiment. Thus, a chain of events resulted from an expectation. When a person expected a target to be hostile, the target became hostile. Having behaved with hostility in the first setting, the target continued to act hostile even when he was no longer expected to do so.

As Darley and Fazio (1980) have noted, the self-fulfilling prophecy is just one of the possible outcomes of our day-to-day social interactions. It is a particularly intriguing phenomenon, however, because the individuals involved are seldom aware that the expectancy of one has substantially influenced the behavior of the other. As the research discussed above illustrates, the potential for misunderstanding and perpetuation of bias among social participants is great.

SUMMARY

Attribution theory is a name given to models that attempt to infer causation for behavior either to stable dispositions of persons or to stable properties of the environment. One such theory is *correspondent inference theory*. An inference is said to be *correspondent* to the extent that the same term may be used to describe both an actor's behavior and his disposition. The *degree of correspondence* refers to the confidence with which such inferences can be made. Correspondent inferences are a function of the *number of effects*, the *social desirability* of a behavior, and whether the behavior is expected.

Kelley's *model of causal attribution* considers the factors necessary for making *internal* (person) or *external* (entity) attributions for behaviors. Observers of other people's behavior consider (1) the distinctiveness, (2) the consensus, and (3) the consistency of that behavior. Low distinctiveness, low consensus, and high consistency lead to internal attributions.

Weiner and his colleagues have considered the factors that affect *attributions for success and failure*. Attributions may be made to (1) ability, (2) luck, (3) effort, or (4) task difficulty. In Weiner's view, attributions of internality-externality and of stability-instability of the performance are the crucial determinants in attributions of causation for success and failure. In Weiner's revised model, the dimension of *controllability* plays a significant role.

Although each attribution perspective views human beings as impartial scientists, objectively sifting through the stimuli in their environment, it has also been suggested that various *biases*—or systematic deviations from the attribution models—also exist. The *correspondence bias* is the tendency to attribute behavior to corresponding internal dispositions rather than external factors. The *saliency bias* is the tendency to attribute behavior to salient or easily noticeable possible causes. *Defensive attribution* occurs when an observer feels threatened by a misfortune that befalls another person and blames that person for his or her misfortune.

Schemata are our general knowledge about people, objects, or events. Closely related concepts are *prototypes* and *scripts*. Our schemata about individuals and our schemata or stereotypes about groups lead us to interpret information consistently with our schemata and to recall information that is consistent with them. Incongruent information is also well recalled when people take the time to think about its meaning.

People remember information about others better if they are trying to form an impression of them, trying to empathize with them, comparing them with the self, or anticipating interacting with them. *Priming* occurs when specific ideas are activated through recent or frequent use. Information that has been primed and is on our minds can affect our memory for people's behavior. In making inferences about other people, individuals make many errors. These include *underusing* or *ignoring base-rate data*, letting irrelevant information affect an inference (*dilution effect*), and perceiving *illusory correlations*. In addition, people show biases of availability, judging the likelihood of events based on the ease with which they come to mind; and the *representativeness heuristic*, judging people as belonging to a group based on their similarity to typical members of the group.

Research on first impressions shows that we are often most affected by the early information we get about other people, thereby showing a primacy effect. Other research shows that recency effects, where impressions are more affected by later information, can occur when subjects are cautioned about jumping to conclusions or are required to think about and remember all the information.

The impressions that people form of others have implications for the way in which those others act. Rosenthal and Jacobson are among those who have demonstrated the effect of the *self-fulfilling prophecy*. In their research, elementary school children whose teachers expected them to perform well actually performed better than did students for whom teachers had no favorable expectation. Applications of this phenomenon to interpersonal hostility and to racial differences in job interviews were also discussed in the chapter.

KEY WORDS

availability bias
base-rate information
bias
category-based expectancy
consensus
consistency
controllability
correspondence bias
correspondent inference
defensive attribution
dilution effect
discounting principle
disposition
error
external causality
fundamental attribution error
heuristic
illusory correlation

impression formation
internal causality
person memory
primacy effects
prototype
rational baseline models
recency effects
representativeness heuristic
saliency
schema
script
self-fulfilling prophecies
social cognition
social desirability
social inference
stability
target-based expectancy

SUGGESTED READINGS

Fiske, S. T., & Taylor, S. E. *Social cognition.* (1984). Reading, MA: Addison-Wesley Publishing.

Heider, F. (1958). *The psychology of interpersonal relations.* New York: John Wiley & Sons.

Higgins, E. T., Herman, C. P., & Zanna, M. P. (1981). *Social cognition. The Ontario Symposium, Volume 1.* Hillsdale, NJ: Erlbaum, 1981.

Jones, E. E., & Davis, K. E. (1965). "From acts to dispositions: The attribution process in person perception." In L. Berkowitz (Ed.), *Advances in experimental social psychology* (Vol. 2, pp. 219–266). New York: Academic Press.

Kelley, H. H. "Attribution theory in social psychology." (1967). *Nebraska Symposium on Motivation, 15,* pp. 192–238.

Markus, H., & Zajonc, R. B. (1985). The cognitive perspective in social psychology. In G. Lindzey and E. Aronson (Eds.), *The handbook of social psychology* (Vol. 1, pp. 137–230). New York: Random House.

Nisbett, R., & Ross, L. (1980). *Human inference: Strategies and shortcomings of human judgments.* Englewood Cliffs, NJ: Prentice-Hall.

Ross, M., & Fletcher, G. J. O. (1985). Attribution and social perception. In G. Lindzey and E. Aronson (Eds.), *The handbook of social psychology* (Vol. 2, pp. 73–122). New York: Random House.

Schneider, D., Hastorf, A., & Ellsworth, P. (1979). *Person perception* (2nd ed.). Reading, MA: Addison-Wesley Publishing.

THREE

SELF-PERCEPTION

On October 5, 1985, the Grambling Tigers football team won its fourth straight game of the season, beating Prairie View in Dallas, Texas. It was not unusual for the Tigers to win a football game, but this one was special. It was the 324th victory of Coach Eddie Robinson's career. Number 324 broke coach Paul "Bear" Bryant's 323-game record and made Eddie Robinson the most winning college football coach in history. Four weeks later, Grambling won its seventh game of the season. Victory number 327 broke the all-time winning record of a single football coach at *any* level, a record set in the pros by George "Papa Bear" Halas of the Chicago Bears. The man who guided Grambling to all these victories has been widely known to most American sports fans for only a few years, but he has been coaching football—and educating young men and women—for more than forty-five years (Davis, 1983, 1985).

Grambling State University is a predominantly black college in northern Louisiana. Over the years it has sent dozens of exceptional players—and exceptional human beings—to the pro football ranks. Eddie Robinson has been its coach since 1941; he may be its coach for several more years. He will reach mandatory retirement age in 1989 but he has the health, spirit, and energy to stay at Grambling after that. There is obviously something special about Eddie Robinson: he is a black man from Louisiana who is revered in Alabama for being the person to break Bear Bryant's record. Only an individual with extraordinary character could have such a profound impact.

Eddie Robinson's beginnings were not especially impressive. He was born in 1919 and grew up in Baton Rouge, Louisiana. Before he became a teenager he was small, frail, slow, and uncoordinated. Other boys laughed at him. But he believed in himself, and once he was given the chance to play he was never sidelined again. He was an outstanding pitcher in baseball and quarterback in football. Robinson played quarterback for McKinley High School and then Leland College near Baton Rouge; from these experiences, he learned to become part of a winning tradition. During his last two years at Leland, he became an assistant coach who took over when the head coach was away. He worked himself and his teammates strenuously, but they succeeded, losing only one game in two championship seasons.

The summer after graduating from college, Eddie Robinson went to work. He had married and his wife was expecting their first child. There were hard times in Louisiana and Eddie had to take whatever work he could find. To make enough money to support his family, Eddie took two jobs—one at a feed mill, the other driving a truck. He earned twenty-five cents an hour. Later that summer he heard about the coaching job at Grambling and he applied for it. He was hired for sixty-four dollars a

Eddie Robinson holds the record for most wins by a football coach at any level, college or professional. Eddie is a strong leader whose clear sense of who he is has enabled him to help others find out who they are. *(AP/Wide World Photos)*

month and his duties included coaching basketball and teaching physical education classes.

Grambling did not have a winning tradition but Eddie Robinson changed that quickly. After going three and five in 1941, Eddie's first year, Grambling won all eight games in 1942. In the war years of 1943 and 1944, there was no football, but Eddie has coached for forty-one straight seasons since then. Between 1945 and 1985, he had only had two losing seasons. Overall, through 1985, he had won 329 games and lost only 109. Eddie Robinson's record is a remarkable one. What is even more remarkable is how much he is respected and even loved by other coaches, former players, parents of students at Grambling, and anyone else who has come in contact with him. He has received numerous awards and the Louisiana state legislature has named Grambling's new football stadium (Robinson Stadium) after Eddie. What manner of man is this enormously successful and admired individual?

Eddie Robinson demands a great deal from his players but he gives a great deal in return. He demands a lot on the practice field. Eddie believes in hard work and perfecting plays until he knows they will work. He strongly believes that hard work pays off and that there are no excuses for failure. But he cares about more than winning football games. He insists that his players go to classes, that they graduate, and they always dress with coats and ties when they travel, and that they take classes in social living to learn proper behavior. He wants his young men to have the skills and knowledge to succeed in the world, not just in football. And he enforces these standards. The first thing he does every morning at 6:00 A.M. is go to the dorms where his players live and wake them up with an old-fashioned school bell to make sure they are all ready to go to class. One of his best known former pro players was Willie Davis of the Green Bay Packers. Davis illustrates Robinson's strength and character with this story: he says that Robinson persuaded his mother to send him to Grambling by promising her that he would make sure Davis was in church every Sunday morning. He did.

It is clear to Grambling players that in demanding a great deal of them, Robinson cares about and wants the best for them. Robinson said that he loves best seeing his players in their homes as fathers, and seeing that their lives are successful. He says "Coaching is a profession of love. You can't coach people unless you love them" (Callahan, 1982). Obviously, his players return Eddie Robinson's caring. They feel that they are a special breed to have had the chance to work with Robinson, and they return to Grambling frequently to help the young players develop their skills and their lives.

Eddie Robinson feels that he owes his success to the many people who have played for and worked with him over the years. But he knows the value of hard work and love, and he has clearly used both to become one of the most successful and respected sportsmen in the country.

SELF-PERCEPTION

Eddie Robinson has had a clear idea of who he is, what he wants, and what he can accomplish since his earliest boyhood years. A strong sense of value and purpose has guided his coaching for nearly fifty years. Where does an individual acquire a sense of self? How do we know what we believe, how well we can perform, and, generally speaking, what kind of person we are? In this chapter on self-perception, we will start answering these questions. Social psychologists have discovered a great deal about the ways we know ourselves and how we evaluate ourselves. We will begin by considering how our self-concept emerges from our interactions with other people. Then we will consider the way we make attributions about ourselves based on our behavior. We will also consider important applications of research on self-perception and the ways in which self-perception can be biased.

SOCIAL INTERACTION AND SELF-CONCEPTION

We learn who we are based on all our experience in the world, especially our interactions with other people. One of the founders of psychology, William James (1890) wrote nearly a century ago of the fact that our sense of who we are, of "me," is derived from our experiences with others. For example, we learn that we are polite when an uncle or aunt compliments our behavior; or that we are a good speller by finding out that we got the highest score in the class. One way we learn about ourselves from social interaction is by finding out what other people think of us. Throughout our lives, we are influenced by other people's opinions about everything from how cold it is outside to whether our national government should allow prayer in the schools. Our self-concepts are no exception. We are impressed with what other people think of us. The process of perceiving what we are like, and whether we are good or bad based on what other people think of us has been called reflected appraisal (Gergen, 1971). It is one of the most important processes affecting our self-concept.

Reflected Appraisal   The term *reflected appraisal* refers to the idea that how we appraise ourself reflects, or mirrors, how others appraise us. Charles Horton Cooley (1902) talked about this concept many years ago; he called it the looking-glass self. Cooley said that we always imagine

All of us, children especially, partially base our self-conceptions on what other peopie think of us. Parents often convey their evaluation of their children by the way they treat them. *(Peter Vandermark/Stock, Boston)*

what others think of us, and what we think they think about us affects our own self-evaluation. A few years later, George Herbert Mead (1934) used the same idea. He said that we pay close attention to the opinion of us that is implied in the behavior of "significant others," that is, important other people such as parents and friends. Furthermore, we come to think of ourselves in terms of the opinion that their behavior implies. Again, our self-concept reflects what others seem to think of us.

Several studies indicate that our self-evaluations reflect other people's appraisals of us. Videbeck (1960) showed that when students in a speech class received appraisals from experts on various aspects of the way they delivered a speech, their self-evaluations were affected by that feedback: students hearing that they had performed well rated their performances higher than those who were told they had done poorly. What seems surprising—and important—is that subjects' self-evaluations in areas that *weren't* evaluated by the expert were also affected. For example, subjects' opinions of their speech techniques that were not appraised were affected (though not as much as their opinions of the techniques that were evaluated). Furthermore, subjects' ratings of general characteristics such as their adequacy in social conversations were affected by the feedback—even though the feedback was specific and limited. It seems that the various parts of our self-evaluation are connected, which isn't so surprising: when we find out something—good or bad—about ourselves, it can affect our overall, or global, sense of worth.

Another important study shows that other people's appraisals of us affect our behavior as well as our self-concept. In this study, schoolchildren who were told that they were tidy actually littered less on the school grounds than students who were told nothing or than those who were told that they *should* be neat. Thus, people made to feel neat actually *acted* that way. The results were even more impressive when littering was measured after two weeks had passed (Miller, Brickman, & Bolen, 1975).

These two studies and other research on reflected appraisal show how much we can be affected by our social interactions with others. Perhaps, though, we would do well to remember that we know a great deal about ourselves that others do not know, and that we shouldn't let ourselves be too affected by what others think. Eddie Robinson was impressive in not letting other people's negative opinions affect his own self-concept. Because he had learned pride from his strong and well-respected family, he continued to believe that he could be a top athlete even when his peers laughed at him. Reflected appraisal is powerful, but not all-powerful.

Social Comparison   Another way we learn about ourselves during social interaction is through the social comparison process. For example, we can evaluate our ability in math or tennis by comparing our performances with those of other people, and we can evaluate our opinion of a movie or a presidential candidate by comparing our opinions with those of other people. Eddie Robinson has to evaluate his coaching ability by seeing how his win-loss record compares to that of other coaches. Leon Festinger, one of our most distinguished social psychologists, developed a theory of social comparison processes that outlines how comparison with other people affects our self-evaluations (Festinger, 1954). Inspired by Festinger's original theory, other researchers have illustrated social comparsion in detail (Goethals & Darley, 1986; Latané, 1966; Suls & Miller, 1977).

Research on the way people describe themselves illustrates the importance of social comparison. When they are asked to respond to the question "who am I," people answer by mentioning ways in which they differ from others, ways in which they are unique. For example, fourth-grade children who were asked to describe themselves mentioned whether they were male or female more often if they came from homes where their gender was in the minority (McGuire & McGuire, 1981). So, if you are the only boy in your family, being male makes you distinctive and becomes part of your self-concept. Similarly, people are likely to mention their race or ethnicity if that characteristic makes them distinct; or they are apt to mention being tall or heavy if those qualities are distinctive (McGuire,

People's self-conceptions are affected by social comparison. If we find that we have performed well in comparison to similar others, we will believe that we are intelligent. *(Owen Franken/Stock, Boston)*

McGuire, Child, & Fijioka, 1978; McGuire & Padawar-Singer, 1976). In short, people's sense of who they are depends on the ways they are distinct in comparison to others.

Another study shows that our overall self-evaluation (i.e., our self-esteem) is affected by social comparison (Morse & Gergen, 1970). Subjects who came to apply for a job as a research assistant in a college research center encountered someone, actually a confederate of the experiment, who posed as another job applicant: the confederate presented himself as either Mr. Clean or Mr. Dirty. Mr. Clean was immaculately dressed, seemed serious and well prepared, and acted sophisticated and well read. Mr. Dirty seemed sloppy, confused, and disinterested. Subjects filled out questionnaires that measured their self-esteem both before and after meeting Mr. Clean or Mr. Dirty. The results showed that people evaluated themselves in comparison to the other applicant. Their self-esteem rose when the other was Mr. Dirty, who seemed less qualified, and it fell if the other was Mr. Clean, who seemed more qualified. Both the traits or characteristics that we feel define us and how favorably we evaluate ourselves are affected by comparison with other people.

The similarity and related attributes hypotheses. One of the central hypotheses of social comparison theory is that we choose to compare ourselves with people who are similar to us. For example, if we want to evaluate our tennis-playing ability, we need to compete against other people whose performance level is about the same as our own to find out just how good we are. Research shows that we usually compare with either similar others or with people who are slightly better than we are. We strive to become better and better (Festinger called this the *unidirectional drive upward*), so we want to see how well we compare with others whose level of performance is slightly above ours (Wheeler, 1966; Wheeler, Koestner, & Driver, 1982). Eddie Robinson compared himself with Bear Bryant as he got closer and closer to Bear's record, until he finally beat it.

The *related attributes hypothesis* means that we not only compare with others whose performance is similar, but also with people whose performance level *should* be similar to ours given their standing on performance related attributes (Goethals & Darley, 1977). By comparing with people who are similar on related attributes, we can most accurately assess our ability. For example, if you wanted to compare your basketball-playing ability, you would learn the most by comparing with others of the same sex, roughly the same age, and about the same amount of recent practice. In that way, if your performance is better, you know that the reason is your greater ability rather than the fact that you are in better shape or have been working like mad to improve your game. Similarly, Eddie Robinson would compare his coaching record with that of coaches who had the same recruiting budget, the same college admissions policies, and so on.

The related attributes hypothesis also applies to opinion evaluation. We should compare our opinion about President Reagan's performance in office with the opinions of other Americans rather than those of Russians, and with Americans who share our political philosophy. Knowing that you disagree with a Russian only tells you that the two of you have dissimilar points of view. You need to know how your opinion compares with someone whose opinions should be similar.

There is a great deal of research supporting the related attributes hypothesis (Suls, Gaes, & Gastorf, 1979; Wheeler & Koestner, 1984). One study, for example, showed that when people felt that sex was related to performance on a test, they wanted to compare with other people of the same sex (Zanna, Goethals, & Hill, 1975). Men sought to learn the scores of men to assess the adequacy of their performance while women wanted to compare with women. Research shows that we sometimes want to compare with people who are similar on salient attributes such as physical attractiveness or sex, even when those characteristics are not specifically related to the ability or opinion being evaluated, but this tendency is generally stronger when the characteristic is related to performance (Miller, 1982, 1984).

Downward comparison and self-evaluation maintenance. While we generally compare with people who are similar or with people who are slightly superior, there are times when we engage in *downward comparison* by comparing with people who are inferior. In one study, subjects who thought they had moderately high degrees of an undesirable trait—hostility to parents—wanted to compare with people who had the greatest degree of hostility toward their parents (Hakmiller, 1966). Downward comparison is defensive. It makes us feel better about ourselves because it allows us to feel that even if we have negative traits, there are others who have them to a far greater degree (Wills, 1981).

The principle of downward comparison shows that not all of our social comparison choices are designed for objective self-evaluation: often, we compare to validate ourselves as well (Gruder, 1977). Trying to show that we are as good as people who are superior, or very different from people who are inferior are examples of self-validating, or self-serving, social comparisons. They reflect our desire to evaluate ourselves positively. Sometimes that desire leads to "active" downward comparison, actually denigrating or harming others so that we can feel good in comparison to them (Wills, 1981).

Our desire to evaluate ourselves positively sometimes leads to more constructive behavior than downward comparison. A recent theory of *self-evaluation maintenance* suggests that people often put extra effort into tasks that are important to their self-definitions if they compare unfavorably to people around them (Tesser, 1984, 1985). If your piano-playing ability is less than that of a friend and you pride yourself on that ability, you may try to improve your performance level to maintain your self-evaluation. On the other hand, if piano playing isn't important to your self-definition, you will maintain your self-evaluation by closely associating with your talented friend and basking in her reflected glory. Consistent with the principles of downward comparison, studies on self-evaluation maintenance also show that people don't always try to improve their performance level to maintain their self-evaluation. Sometimes they denigrate the other person's performance or actually try to interfere with it. Thus, the desire to compare favorably can lead to both constructive efforts at self-improvement and destructive efforts to undermine others.

False consensus estimates. Another way that social comparison is self-serving is that we sometimes make estimates about how other people's opinions or behaviors compare with our own in ways that make us feel good about ourselves, and we then ignore social comparison information that shows that perhaps we are wrong. For example, several studies show what are known as *false consensus effects*. False consensus refers to overestimating the number of people that agrees with our opinions or behaves as we do (Ross, 1977; Mullen, Atkins, Champion, Edwards, Hardy, Story, and Vanderklok, 1985). If we overestimate how many people agree with us, we can evaluate our opinion as correct. And if we overestimate the number of people who do what we do, we can feel that our actions are appropriate. One study of false consensus judgments asked college students whether they would be willing to walk around campus wearing a sign that said Eat at Joe's. Those who agreed to wear the sign thought that most other people would wear it, specifically, 62 percent of the others. Those who said no thought that only 33 percent would wear the sign and that 67 percent would say no (Ross, Greene, & House, 1977). Each group felt that it had made the appropriate choice and assumed that others had done the same. Other research shows that when people are given comparison information showing that their consensus estimates are wrong, that other people don't agree as much as they thought, they ignore this information unless it is very clear and simple (Goethals, 1986).

Not all self-serving consensus estimates inflate the number of people who act as we do. If we do something that isn't clearly good or bad, like wearing a sign saying Eat at Joe's, we may be prompted to believe that most other people will do the same. Further, if we do something negative, we may want to think that most others will do the same so that we can feel that we aren't so bad. On the other hand, if we do something positive, we may want to think that our good behavior is distinctive. Hence we may underestimate how many other people would do the same thing, showing a *false uniqueness* or false idiosyncrasy effect. Several recent studies show that if people make a desirable choice, such as helping someone in trouble, giving blood, or leaving the larger piece of pizza for their friend, they underestimate the number of others who would do the same. When they refuse to help or take the big piece of pizza for themselves, they show

Both men and women may enjoy succeeding, but they often interpret their successes differently. Men are more likely to attribute their successes to ability. *(Fredrik D. Bodin/ Stock, Boston)*

the typical false consensus overestimates (Goethals, 1986). Similarly, we overestimate the number of people who share our opinions but underestimate the number with ability levels as high as our own (Campbell, 1986; Marks, 1984).

Role Internalization: The Case of Gender Expectations   Another way that social interaction helps us discover ourselves is by leading us to perform various social roles (Gergen, 1971). Associated with each of the roles we play, such as son or daughter, sister or brother, soccer player, musician, or college student, are a set of expectations about the proper forms of behavior. In general, people use the behaviors associated with their various roles, and for the most part they internalize those behaviors so that they see the roles as part of who they are. When Eddie Robinson took the head-coaching position at Grambling, he began to view himself as teacher, authority figure, and disciplinarian; the role became part of him. Similarly, when scholars act introverted, when politicians act extroverted, or when psychotherapists act helpful, they often internalize the role and assume the disposition associated with the behavior. In this section, we will consider some of the consequences of men and women behaving according to expectations or stereotypes about the masculine or feminine role.

For many years, a key aspect of the female role in our society has been the belief that women should not strive to succeed. Many scholars have noted that there are numerous ways in which women are discouraged from achieving success (Frieze, Parsons, Johnson, Ruble, & Zellman, 1978). As a consequence, women are underrepresented in high-status occupations and tend to earn significantly lower salaries than their male counterparts. Part of this state of affairs is caused by pure and simple discrimination, but part may also be explained by the fact that women conform to and internalize society's expectations that they should not or cannot succeed. Several studies illustrate the various factors that lead to achievement differences between men and women.

The fear of success. Some influential studies by Matina Horner suggest that sex differences in achievement may be due to women learning to *fear success* and thus acquiring a reason to avoid it. Horner (1970, 1972) asked female and male students to write a story that took the following fact into account: "After first-term finals, Anne (John) finds her (him) self at the top of her (his) medical school class." Such a task is known as a projective test. Here, rather than merely writing a fictional story about Anne (for females) or John (for males), respondents are seen as revealing something about themselves in the story. How do you think you might respond to such a task? If you were a male in Horner's study, it is likely that you would have written an all-American-boy tale such as the following:

> John is a conscientious young man who worked hard. He is pleased with himself. John has always wanted to go into medicine and is very dedicated. His hard work paid off. He is thinking that he must not let up now, but must work even harder than he did before. His good marks have encouraged him. . . . He eventually graduates at the top of his class.

On the other hand, if you were a female in this study, you might have dealt with the situation as this excerpt from Horner implies:

Anne has a boy friend in the same class and they are quite serious. Anne met Carl at college and they started dating. . . . Anne is rather upset and so is Carl. She wants him to be higher in school than she is. Anne will deliberately lower her academic standing next term, while she does all she subtly can to help Carl. His grades come up and Anne soon drops out of medical school. They marry and he goes on in school while she raises their family.

In Horner's view, the motive to avoid success forms a stable portion of the personality of most females. Reinforcements in early childhood are thought to have shaped an attitude or a fear that characterizes the adult female in her interaction with the opportunities in her life.

Attributions for success and failure. Regardless of whether women fear success or want to avoid it, they sometimes succeed and they sometimes fail—just like men: when they do either, they often think about the causes of their performances and make attributions about them. In Chapter Two, we considered how people make attributions about the causes of other people's behavior. In similar ways they make self-attributions, that is, attributions about the causes of their own behavior. We will discuss self-attribution in detail in the next section. For now, we will simply note that studies of self-attribution show that men and women make very different attributions about their successes and failures, attributions that reflect society's stereotypes and expectations. In the typical pattern, men attribute their successes to high ability while women attribute theirs to high effort or good luck (Deaux, 1976; Deaux & Farris, 1977; Fiske & Taylor, 1984). Not surprisingly, these are the same attributions that men and women typically (but not always) make about how other men and women succeed (McHugh, Frieze, & Hanusa, 1982). Conversely, men attribute their failures to bad luck or lack of effort while women attribute their failures to low ability.

These attributions also affect future performance (Weiner, et al., 1972). Men attribute success to a stable factor, ability, so that they are likely to expect to succeed in the future. Because men believe that their ability will enable them to succeed again, they will try. Women believe that their success is due to unstable factors, trying hard or good luck, that may not exist in the future. Thus, they have lower expectations for future success, with the result that they may not bother to try.

Gender schemata. In Chapter Two, we discussed the concept of schemata. A social schema is our general knowledge about a person, group, or event that helps us to make sense of behavior. Sandra Bem (1981) has recently proposed a gender schema theory to account for some of the differences in attributions that men and women make.

Bem sees women's self-concepts, including their reluctance to strive for success, as a natural outgrowth of the way in which schemata develop. Bem points out that gender is a salient and ubiquitous concept during our childhood. Male and female symbols help to organize a child's world. In school, boys may line up on one side, girls on another. Little paper dolls in the form of boys and girls may alternately be placed on the monthly calendar in kindergarten to help children keep track of the days of the week. The constant focusing on gender forces children to organize the world in terms of what is appropriate for each gender.

No one defines for a child what must be in the schema of boyness and girlness. But numerous characteristics are associated with each gender. Not only are terms like *strong* applied to boys and *nurturant* applied to girls, but they are studiously not applied to the other sex. For example, adults rarely associate the concept of nurturant with boys. So children, by dint of the constant reference to gender differences, form a gender schema. Depending on the child's gender, he or she begins to organize the social world into what is appropriate for that gender. Bem's point is that all schemata are generated this way, and the gender schema is but one important example.

The process of forming a gender schema is universal, but the schema's content may vary culture by culture. Opportunities for success and failure will be interpreted in terms of the male or female schema. Since, in our culture, success is part of the male schema, males (particularly those who have strong gender schemata) will seize the opportunity for success. Females, on the other hand, will be likely to bring such situations into their schema for failure. Consequently, males and females will show great differences in their approach to achievement related situations. When given a chance to succeed, males are more likely to strive for success while women may strive for failure.

Situational demands. Another explanation for women's lack of success focuses on the demands of the immediate situation that lead men and women to choose the best or most appropriate behavior (Darley, 1976). As we have noted, people want to see themselves as good, correct, and appropriate. They are likely to get positive feedback from others about these traits if they conform to others' expectations, including expectations about whether it is appropriate to succeed. For women, success is not seen as particularly appropriate; thus, women do not get positive feedback when they violate these expectations. In a recent study, for example, females who failed at a task were regarded favorably by other females, whereas successful females were downgraded by their female peers (Feather & Simon, 1975). It is not surprising then that we may go out of our way to conform to the sex-role expectations held by others.

The impact on achievement of these tendencies to conform may be rather subtle. For example, consider the ability to perform well on an anagrams task (forming words from scrambled letters). If men and women are placed in competition, who should want to succeed and who should want to fail? The answer will probably depend on the demands of the situation and on other people's expectations about appropriate behavior. If solving anagrams is defined as a reasoning skill, men may think that it is good to succeed, whereas females may believe that they are expected to fail. On the other hand, if verbal aptitude is required, women may feel that it is appropriate to succeed, whereas men may feel that it would be best to fail.

Howe and Zanna (1975) conducted an experiment with similar characteristics. Two males and two females came to a session to perform an anagrams task. In each group, one male and one female were led to believe that success at anagrams "correlates highly with masculine interests and abilities," whereas the other male and female were told that success correlates with feminine interests and abilities. At one point in the study, the subjects were given feedback about their performance. Some found that they had done quite well, others that they had done poorly. They were then asked to complete the rest of the anagrams.

The results indicated that males who were succeeding at a task that they thought was feminine "adjusted" their performance to do less well the next time, but they improved when they regarded success at the task as appropriate for males. And females who were led to believe that success at the task was appropriate for females increased their performance in the second part of the study, whereas they "took a dive" and decreased their performance if they thought that success was the province of the male sex.

The results of the study indicate that sex-role behavior is tuned in to the demands and expectations of a situation. When we hear that certain types of activities are reserved for males, we react accordingly. We wish to receive good feedback from others and thereby to think of ourselves as good. Conforming to what we have been told to expect is the surest way of receiving the feedback we seek.

SELF-ATTRIBUTION

In the previous section we considered the way our self-concept is affected by reflected appraisal, social comparison, and role internalization. We also touched on the role of self-attribution. In this section, we will consider further the important role that attribution processes play in self-knowledge and self-perception. The basic notion behind theories of

People may adjust their performances on a test according to whether it measures an ability that is masculine or feminine. They may perform poorly if they believe that the test measures an ability of the opposite sex. (© *Susan Lapides 1981/design conceptions*)

self-attribution is that we can make attributions about our own behavior in the same ways that we can make them about other people's behavior. For example, a person might use Kelley's covariation principle (see Chapter Two) to decide whether his roommate's interest in chemistry is attributable to the roommate's personality or to chemistry itself. Similarly, you could use the same principle to decide whether the fun you had watching *Young Sherlock Holmes* is attributable to your own unique tastes and interests (maybe you're a Holmes buff) or to the fact that the movie was really good. You would use the same criteria of distinctiveness (Do you like other movies?), consistency (Did you like it as much the second time?), and consensus (Did other people enjoy the movie?).

Another attribution theory that can be applied to your own behavior as well as that of other people is Weiner's theory of attributions about success and failure. In the previous section on internalizing sex roles, we saw that people make attributions about their own successes and failures just as they do for others. They decide that their success is due to high ability, extra effort, or good luck. Eddie Robinson was often asked to make attributions about his success at Grambling. Typically modest, he refused to attribute his success to ability, even though almost everyone else does. Robinson attributed his success to help from other people, which, he has stated, made his task easier: "Any success that Eddie Robinson has enjoyed has been only because of the support I have received from Grambling fans, administrators, friends, players, assistant coaches and others" (Davis, 1985). It is also clear that he believes his success is attributable to high effort and that other people can succeed if they try. Eddie recently said, "The things that have happened to me couldn't have happened in any other country than America. Nobody is going to give you anything here, but you sure receive a lot when you work for it" (Davis, 1985).

Although the attribution theories we considered earlier can generally be applied to self-attribution, there are several attribution theories that apply *only* to the self. We will consider them below.

Self-Perception Theory   One of the most provocative theories of self-attribution is known as self-perception theory (Bem, 1972). Self-perception theory considers the way we perceive our own attitudes and preferences. It argues that just as we would infer that our friend likes rock music because he listens to it whenever he has a chance, so we infer that we like country music from our own behavior. We notice that when we are in the car we are most likely to push the button that brings in the local country station. All this sounds reasonable enough—but isn't something missing? Don't we just *know* whether we like country music? Must we infer that we do? Self-perception theory says we don't "just know," that we don't have a very good idea of how we feel about things based on feelings alone. We *really* learn what we like or dislike from our behavior.

The basic principles of self-perception theory follow. First, self-perception is simply the special case of perceiving people in general where we rather than others are the objects of perception. That is, we perceive ourselves in exactly the same way as we perceive others. Second, we learn about our attitudes, preferences, and feelings by considering two things: our behavior and the situation in which it took place. The most important aspect of the situation that must be taken into account is whether there were situational constraints that explain the behavior. For example, if you listen to the country station because your sister begs you to turn it on, you would not infer that you like country music; your sister's pressure explains your behavior. From the perspective of the discounting principle discussed in Chapter Two, you would discount your own attitude as a cause of your behavior since your sister's begging explains why you listened. Only when our behavior is freely chosen do we infer that it reflects our attitudes or feelings. But the basic idea is the most important one. We infer our attitudes and feelings, internal characteristics, based on external information, our behavior, that we consider along with the forces in the situation. As the British novelist

If we see ourselves engaging in some activity, do we infer that we like it? Self-perception theory suggests that often we do infer our attitudes from our behaviors. *(Alan Carey/ The Image Works)*

E. M. Forster said many years ago, "How can I tell what I think 'til I see what I say?"

Considerable evidence exists in support of self-perception theory. First, the fact that we *do* internalize roles, as discussed in the previous section, supports the theory. People define themselves according to the behavior specified by their roles. Second, several experiments illustrate important aspects of inferring attitudes and feelings from behavior. For example, in one experiment subjects had to summarize a description of one individual's personality for a second person who either liked or disliked that individual. Not surprisingly, people responded to the second person's expectations and made their summary more positive or more negative depending on that person's feelings about the first individual. What is surprising is that subjects reported liking the person more if they had described him positively than if they had described him negatively (Higgins & Rholes, 1978). Further, they felt that they had freely chosen to describe the person somewhat positively or negatively and they perceived their attitudes by inferring them from their behavior.

There is also evidence that our descriptions of ourselves can be a basis for inferring what we actually think of ourselves. In one study subjects were induced to describe themselves to an interviewer in either very modest or very flattering terms. On a later test of self-esteem, subjects who had described themselves positively actually felt more positively about themselves while those who had been modest felt more negatively. Consistent with self-perception theory, these effects on self-esteem were stronger when subjects felt they had freely chosen the way they described themselves (Jones, Rhodewalt, Berglas, & Skelton, 1981).

Two other studies show fascinating self-perception effects. In one, subjects were asked to smile or frown. They felt angry when they frowned and happy when they smiled (Laird, 1974). In another, subjects were asked to nod their heads up and down or from side to side to test their headphones while they listened to a speech. Those who nodded up and down (the usual yes gesture), agreed with the speech they had heard more than those who shook their head in the usual negative fashion (Wells & Petty, 1980).

Even though self-perception effects are remarkably strong and remarkably pervasive, they are not without limits. For example, when people have clearly defined internal attitudes about an issue, they are less likely to infer how they feel about the issue from a single instance of a particular behavior (Chaiken & Baldwin, 1981). Still, self-perception theory has shown interesting and impressive effects. In the remainder of the book, we will see that it has wide applicability. One particularly important application is in the area of what are called "overjustification effects," which we will consider in the next section.

Overjustification: Killing a Good Thing   We are deluged by offers of bonuses for buying a particular brand of popcorn, extra Green Stamps for shopping at a particular supermarket, and so on. In the advertising trade these are known as "come-ons"; their purpose is to get you to come into the store or to try a product. But if you already like the product and do not need the come-on to enter the store, what effect will the added inducement have on your attitude toward the store or the product? An attributional analysis suggests that the come-ons, or the "overjustification," may have the reverse effect of the one intended.

After behavior is committed, the actor asks himself why he behaved that way. A review of the stimuli surrounding the behavior suggests an answer: "I bought Poppy brand popcorn because they offered me a Mickey Mouse ring inside the package." In other words, the behavior is attributed *not* to the actor's preference for that kind of popcorn, but rather to the bonus—or overjustification. Now, popcorn brands outlive the bonus come-ons that are offered inside. When the actor who has already bought Poppy popcorn returns to the supermarket to restock his popcorn supply, he recalls that he purchased that particular brand *because of the extra bonus*. With the bonus removed, there is no reason to purchase the brand anymore. Indeed, in a recent study that examined consumer behavior in the city of Chicago, Dodson, Tybout, and Sternthal (1978) concluded that advertisements featuring come-ons actually resulted in reduced loyalty to the brand offering the come-on.

The last laugh may be on Madison Avenue's advertising and gimmick men in this instance. But a moment's reflection will conjure up less laughable situations in which needless overjustifications can ruin the intrinsic value that an important behavior might hold. In a first-grade classroom, children know that they will receive one gold star for picking up a book and two gold stars for reading it. In a mental hospital, patients know that they will receive better food if they successfully make their beds and put on their clothing (cf. Ayllon & Azrin, 1968). But adding an attractive inducement may cause the behavior to be attributed not to an interest in reading or in taking care of oneself, but rather to the gold stars and other external rewards. When the rewards no longer exist, when the children are no longer being awarded stars, when the mental patients leave the hospital and try to return to their natural environment, the overjustifications for their original behaviors may result in a lack of interest in continuing those behaviors.

A fascinating study was conducted at Horizon House, a psychiatric rehabilitation center in Philadelphia (Bogart, Loeb, & Rittman, 1969). To achieve better attendance at group therapy sessions, the institution established a reward system in which prizes were offered for good monthly attendance. In one condition, the value of the prizes could reach approximately $8. In a second condition, patients were offered prizes that could reach only $2 in value. During the month in which prizes were offered, attendance increased. In the $8 condition, it rose from 90 percent before the reward period to 95 percent during the reward period. After a month, the reward was withdrawn and attendance fell sharply—to 75 percent. In the small-reward condition, attendance improved from 82 percent to 88 percent during the reward period and stayed about there after the reward period ended (90 percent). A number of technical difficulties with the Bogart et al. study make it less than definitive in demonstrating the detrimental effect of overjustification. Nonetheless, it suggests that the effects of large rewards may often be counterproductive.

Lepper, Greene, and Nisbett (1973) undertook a direct test of the overjustification hypothesis with nursery school children in California. The children were asked to play with new drawing equipment that was so attractive that any child would welcome the opportunity to play with it. Some of the children were told that they were drawing to obtain a "Good Player award," which included a certificate with colored ribbons. Two other groups of children were offered no extrinsic reward for playing with the equipment. Of the last groups, one served as an "unexpected reward" treatment in which a Good Player award was given at the end, although it had not been anticipated. The other group served as a control, with no reward given or anticipated. Several days later, the children from all groups were allowed to use the drawing materials if they wished, or to play with a variety of other toys. Observers watched from behind a one-way mirror. Consistent with the findings of Bogart et al., they noticed that the children who had originally anticipated and received an external reward for playing with the drawing material played with it only about half as much as the children from the other two groups: it appeared that their interest in the art activity had been diminished by the award offer.

Because of its theoretical and practical implications, the concept of overjustification has received considerable attention in recent years (Fazio, 1981). It has been both extended and qualified by recent research. One interesting extension shows that if people are asked not to cheat in an exam situation, and are given "superfluous deterrence," that is, more pressure not to cheat than they need, they attribute their noncheating to the deterrence rather than their own honesty. Hence, they are not afforded the opportunity to see themselves as behaving with voluntary honesty. Consequently, they are more likely to cheat in the future (Wilson & Lassiter, 1982).

Qualifications of the overjustification effect derive from research showing that extrinsic rewards can sometimes actually increase rather than decrease the intrinsic motivation for various activities. If rewards are made contingent on good performance and are seen as signs of competence rather than efforts to control behavior, they can increase intrinsic interest (Rosenfield, Folger, & Adelman, 1980; Ryan, 1982). A child who is given extra money for bringing home a good report card might lose interest in studying if she interprets the reward as an effort to control her behavior. But if the child views the extra money as a reward for her intelligence, it can increase her interest in performing well.

The Attribution of Emotions   The research on self-perception and over-justification suggests that people often infer their attitudes, their feelings, and even why they didn't cheat from looking at their behavior and the situation in which it took place. There is also important research suggesting that we infer our emotions, for example, whether we are feeling happy or angry, from external information. This research suggests that we are often unsure about how we feel and when this is the case, we make attributions about our emotions rather than just experiencing them directly.

Considerable thought about the attribution of emotions has grown out of the work of Stanley Schachter. His classic studies of anxiety and affiliation (see Chapter One) demonstrated that anxious subjects who had been threatened with electric shock wanted to wait with other people (Schachter, 1959). Follow-up research has shown that they wanted to wait with other people only when those people were also waiting to be shocked. The threatened subjects were somewhat unsure about their own reactions and wanted help from others in understanding and interpreting what they were feeling. They needed to compare their emotions with those of people who were in the same threatening situation as they were.

Schachter (1964) took this insight and ran with it. He proposed that if people are emotionally aroused but aren't sure what they are feeling, they will look for cues in the environment, including the behavior of other people, in an effort to find the correct interpretation for their ambiguous feelings. It should be noted that Schachter's theory emphasizes not only self-attribution, but also social comparison. We clarify emotions by comparing our reactions with those of others, specifically, with reactions of people who are similar on related attributes in that they face the same situation as we do. We then attribute the same emotions to ourselves that the others are feeling.

What evidence is there that people experience emotions based on the reactions of other people? In a classic experiment, Schachter and Singer (1962) were the first to demonstrate this phenomenon. Subjects were given injections of epinephrine, or adrenalin, which makes people feel highly physiologically aroused. Some subjects were informed of the drug's effects. They were told that they would experience an increase in heart rate, a

Schachter and Singer's study shows that we sometimes feel happy when we see that someone else in the same situation is happy. We take our cue about the appropriate feeling from the other person. *(Owen Franken/Stock, Boston)*

flushed face, and occasional trembling. Since they had an explanation or attribution for the arousal they would experience later, they should not have had to compare with others to figure out what they were feeling. Other subjects were misinformed; they were told that they would experience headaches or numb feet. These subjects would need an explanation for the unexpected effects of the epinephrine. And still other subjects were uninformed; they too would need an explanation for their arousal. Finally, for control purposes, some subjects were given a placebo, which does not cause arousal. None of the subjects who received the placebo should have had to compare with others because they would not have had any arousal to explain.

After the subjects were given the injection and were informed, misinformed, or given no information, they were asked to wait with another person who presumably had had the same injection. The other person was a confederate of the experiment who acted in one of two ways during the waiting period. In some cases, he acted euphoric, throwing paper airplanes, shooting crumpled balls of paper into the wastebasket, and twirling a hula hoop. In other cases, the confederate became angry. He

Figure 3–1
Conditions of Schachter and Singer experiment

	Confederate's behavior	
Arousal information	*Angry*	*Euphoric*
Subjects informed	Subjects should not become angry	Subjects should not become euphoric
Subjects uninformed	Subjects should become angry	Subjects should become euphoric
Subjects misinformed	Subjects should become angry	Subjects should become euphoric
No arousal control (placebo)	Subjects should not become angry	Subjects should not become angry

and the subject had to complete a questionnaire that asked extremely intimate and inappropriate questions (With how many men, other than your father, has your mother had extramarital affairs? Four and under, five to nine; or ten and over?); the confederate became angrier and angrier and finally ripped up his questionnaire in a fit of rage. After a few moments, the experimenter returned and asked the subjects to complete a questionnaire about their feelings.

Figure 3–1 summarizes the conditions of the Schachter and Singer experiment and the predictions for each condition. Basically, the results were consistent with the predictions. Subjects took on the mood of the confederate when they had received an injection of epinephrine and were either misinformed or uninformed of its effects. The informed subjects, who already had an explanation of the drug's effects, and subjects who had received the placebo and were thus not aroused, did not experience the confederate's emotions to the same degree.

Based on these findings, Schachter and Singer developed a "two-factor" theory of emotion that postulates that our emotions are based on two components: physiological arousal and cognitions about what that arousal means. Stated as a formula, E (emotion) $= A$ (arousal) $\times C$ (cognition). Both the arousal and the interpretation or cognition are necessary for a specific emotion to be experienced. In their experiment, Schachter and Singer gave subjects the arousal, but in some cases (uninformed and misinformed conditions), they gave them no cognitions to explain the arousal. The subjects who did not have an explanation for their arousal compared with other people in the situation who were experiencing the same arousal and attributed the emotion the other person was obviously experiencing to themselves.

Schachter and Singer's provocative research has not gone unchallenged. First, several critics have pointed out that while the results are generally supportive, they are not as strong as they should be to give the theory unequivocal support. Other attempts to replicate Schachter and Singer have failed. They have shown that people who experience unexplained arousal do not attribute to themselves whatever emotion others are feeling in the situation. They typically feel uncomfortable and interpret the arousal negatively (Marshall and Zimbardo, 1979; Maslach, 1979). Reviews of the research on Schachter and Singer's theory caution us that the support for the theory is still "soft" (Cotton, 1981). On the other hand, there is enough evidence for us to conclude that in many situations where feelings are ambiguous, people will use the information in a situation, especially the reactions of other people, to attribute emotions to themselves.

Excitation transfer: From one emotion to another. Schachter and Singer's theory and later work by Schachter (1964; 1971) shows that arousal needs to be understood before we can experience an emotion. If there is ambiguity about the arousal we look to the environment, including other people's feelings, for an explanation. A more recent theory extends Schachter's work and shows that arousal generated by one emotion or experience can be transferred or channeled into another emotion (Zillman, 1978, 1983, 1984). For example, if you became aroused because you ran to the top of a hill, your arousal could be interpreted as romantic feelings if you had met someone really attractive at the top; or it could be interpreted as anger if a passing motorist had honked at you. In the latter case, for instance, your anger could have been fueled by the arousal from running and might therefore have been more intense than otherwise. This theory of excitation transfer holds that emotions consist of an excitatory component in which arousal occurs, and an experiential component in which the excitation is interpreted and an emotion is attributed. Arousal can be transferred if a person makes a misattribution. In the example above, if you attribute your arousal from running to the beautiful person you have just met, or to the motorist you have just cursed, that arousal increases your emotional reaction of romance or anger respectively. In later chapters, we will see how arousal from sexual feelings can be transferred to aggression and how arousal from fearful feelings can be transferred to sexual attraction. In short, Zillman's theory illustrates how we attribute and sometimes misattribute feelings to ourselves in ways suggested by Schachter and Singer.

Imagined arousal and emotions. Both Schachter and Zillman have considered the way in which we interpret genuine physiological arousal and

Excitation transfer theory says that arousal from one source, for example, jogging, can be channeled into another, for example, attraction to a pretty young woman. (© *Jim Anderson 1983/Woodfin Camp & Associates*)

the way in which our interpretations lead to the self-attribution of emotions. Some interesting related research suggests that we sometimes attribute emotions when we only *think* we are aroused. We infer that we are responding emotionally to whatever it is we *falsely* believe is arousing us. This kind of self-attribution was seen in a study where male college students were shown several centerfold pictures of nude women from *Playboy* magazine. Fake electrodes were placed on the subjects that allegedly measured their heart rates as they looked at the pictures. In addition, the subjects were allowed to "overhear their heart rates" as they looked through the pictures. At various intervals, the subjects heard what they believed were their real heart beats markedly increase or decrease. At the end of the experiment, the subjects were told that they could take home any of the nude pictures that they wanted to. Most of the pictures they chose were ones where they had had a "change of heart rate" during the experiment (Valins, 1966).

The key point here is that the changes in heart rate that the subjects heard were not real; all were preprogrammed by the experimenter. Yet subjects inferred that they were responding emotionally to pictures where their heart rates seemed to change, and those were the pictures they decided they liked. In a follow-up study, Valins (1972) repeated the procedure but after giving the subjects the bogus heart-rate feedback, he carefully debriefed them, informing them that the heart-rate change was not real. Even after the debriefing, subjects remained more attracted to the nudes that they had initially believed caused their heart rates to change. Apparently, the combination of perception of arousal and an inferred attraction created a liking that a simple debriefing could not undo.

Additional recent research suggests that we make attributions about our likes and dislikes based on false arousal feedback only in situations where we don't have to give much thought to our feelings. In one study, after rating photographs of men, college women were given false feedback about their attraction to those men. They were than asked to rerate the photographs. If they expected to meet the men, their second ratings were based more on their first ratings than on the false feedback; if they didn't expect to meet the men, their second ratings were based more on the false feedback. It is in the first situation, where the subjects expected to meet the men, that they had to think harder about who they really liked. In that case they didn't let themselves be misled by the false arousal feedback (Taylor, 1975).

Attributions for Outcomes and Feelings of Control   We have seen that people make many self-attributions, including attributions about why they succeeded or failed. Generally, they attribute their actions or the outcomes of their actions to either internal or external causes. For example, Eddie Robinson has been asked repeatedly why he is so successful. He has pointed to both internal (hard work) and external (help from friends) causes. We think a good deal about what causes our successes and failures, and more generally, what causes the outcomes, both good and bad, that we experience in day-to-day living.

Research has shown that different people have consistently different perceptions of the causes of their outcomes (Rotter, 1966; Phares, 1984; Lefcourt, 1982). Some individuals perceive an internal locus of control; they believe that they are the masters of their own destiny and are in control of their own fates. Others believe that their outcomes are determined by external factors—by luck, fate, or chance. Rotter argued that, based on their experience, people develop generalized expectancies that their outcomes are internally or externally controlled. He went on to develop a scale that measures whether people perceive an internal or external locus of control (see Figure 3–2). You might want to answer the questions in Figure 3–2 to see if you tend to perceive an internal or external locus of control.

Figure 3-2
Sample items from an early version of Rotter's test of internal-external locus of control

I more strongly believe that:

1. a. Many people can be described as victims of circumstance.
   b. What happens to other people is pretty much of their own making.
2. a. The world is so complicated that I just cannot figure things out.
   b. The world is really complicated alright, but I can usually work things out by effort and persistence.
3. a. Most students would be amazed at how much grades are determined by capricious events.
   b. The marks I get in class are completely my own responsibility.
4. a. Promotions are earned through hard work and persistence.
   b. Making a lot of money is largely a matter of getting the right breaks.
5. a. In my case the grades I make are the results of my own efforts; luck has little or nothing to do with it.
   b. Sometimes I feel that I have little to do with the grades I get.
6. a. Getting along with people is a skill that must be practiced.
   b. It is almost impossible to figure out how to please some people.

Source: Adapted from Rotter (1971)

People who perceive an internal locus of control, referred to as "internals," are like Eddie Robinson. They believe that what happens to them in this world depends on how hard they work, that nobody is going to give them anything, but anything is within their reach if they exert the effort. Thus internals work hard. They can be characterized by the slogan "We try harder." Externals, on the other hand, perceive their fate as controlled by factors outside themselves. Since they believe that they have no control over what happens to them, they don't put much effort into their lives. In one study, for example, hospitalized tuberculosis patients' attitudes differed dramatically depending on their perceived locus of control. Internals made efforts to find out what caused their disease and what they could do about it while externals were more passive (Seeman & Evans, 1962). Langer (1981) has argued that elderly people are passive not because they are senile, but because their life difficulties cause them to perceive an external locus of control.

Recent research on learned helplessness shows that you don't have to be elderly to begin perceiving that your outcomes are beyond your control and thus to become passive and helpless. It also shows that whether people become helpless or not after they have had difficult life experiences depends on the attributions they make about the causes of their difficulties. Martin Seligman and his colleagues (Overmier & Seligman, 1967; Maier, Seligman, & Solomon, 1969) have demonstrated that animals, after being exposed to inescapable shock when they are learning a task, later fail to learn a second task. Not only do animals in this situation fail to learn the second task; they usually cease behaving entirely. Seligman has labeled this state learned helplessness because the animal is learning that there is no relationship between its responding and its reinforcement, and thus it simply stops responding.

The state of learned helplessness has been experimentally produced in humans as well as animals by employing inescapable adversive stimuli (electric shocks and loud noise) or insoluble problems in the first task, or the "helplessness pretraining task" (Hiroto & Seligman, 1975; Thornton & Jacobs, 1971; Roth & Kubal, 1975). In all of these studies, prior experience with uncontrollability produced later deficits in learning, regardless of whether the later task was learning to make an avoidance response or solving a cognitive problem. The common occurrence is that subjects with helplessness pretraining make significantly fewer attempts to respond, and adopt a general state of passivity resembling depression.

People strive to succeed if they perceive an internal locus of control of their reinforcements. If they believe that their successes or failures reflect their own efforts, they try harder. (© *Frank Siteman 1982/The Picture Cube*)

In what way do attributions relate to this research? The attributions people make about the causes of their failure on the first task are extremely important. If people attribute failure to their inability to cope with difficult situations, then there is little reason for them to try again in the future. However, if people attribute failure to the task, then that failure may not lead to the state of helplessness and hence their unwillingness to try again.

The importance of attributions was shown in a study by Tennen and Eller (1977). Subjects thought that they were participating in two separate experiments. In the first experiment (the pretreatment stage), they were given either ability (self) or task difficulty (external) explanations for their apparent inability to solve a discrimination problem. The subjects in one insoluble condition were told that the task was becoming more difficult, whereas the subjects in another insoluble condition were told that the task was becoming easier. As you can see, the potential was created for the subjects in one group to attribute failure to task difficulty (the task-harder condition), whereas the subjects in the other group should have attributed failure to their own lack of ability (the task-easier condition). The measure of helplessness was the subject's success at solving anagrams in the second experiment. Subjects in the ability attribution condition solved significantly fewer anagrams than did either subjects without prior helplessness training or subjects who could attribute their previous poor performance to task difficulty. This finding provides strong support for the role of self-attribution in learned helplessness. It is not simply the expectation that responding is unrelated to outcome that is critical. Rather, it is the self-attribution that failure reflects the lack of a stable ability or trait that causes people to carry the helplessness expectation into other situations.

Consider finally a study by Dweck (1975) that has intriguing implications for the "cure" of learned helplessness and perhaps depression. In her study, Dweck wanted to investigate possible ways of reducing learned helplessness in children. She chose as her subjects children who showed extreme negative reactions to failure. These children expected to fail, and in the face of failure they would simply stop performing and give up. Dweck reasoned that this failure expectation stemmed from the fact that these children typically attributed their failure either to their own lack of ability or to the fact that they had no control over their environment—both of which were enduring stable causes that should not be expected to change from one situation to the next. Dweck proposed that if these helpless children could be retrained to take responsibility for failure and to simultaneously attribute it to a more temporary self-attribution, such as the lack of effort, then the learned helplessness could be alleviated.

Dweck's reasoning turned out to be correct. Helpless children in her study received either reattribution training or extensive training with only success experiences. Children in the reattribution training condition were told that they had failed on a certain number of the math problems that they had attempted. However, each time they failed they were told that they had done so because they had not tried hard enough. In the success-only condition, the children simply worked on the same number of math problems, but they were never made to fail or confronted with failure. Each child received five weeks of training. The results provided strong support for Dweck's proposal. Only the children who received reattribution training could experience later failures in other situations without again giving up and becoming helpless. These are provocative findings that attest not only to the role of self-attribution in the learning and maintenance of helplessness, but also to the possibility of treating people who have expectations of helplessness.

As a result of a large number of investigations such as those we have discussed, Seligman and his colleagues (Abramson, Seligman, & Teasdale, 1978) have concluded that the learned helplessness phenomenon is intrinsically involved with the attribution process. In their view, people first learn that certain outcomes and responses are independent —that is, their behaviors do not control those outcomes. They then seek to make attributions along three independent dimensions. As we have noted in the research by Dweck and by Tennen and Eller (1977), attributions of stability-instability and attributions of internality-externality are made. Abramson et al. suggest that attributions along a global-specific dimension are also made. The more global the attribution, the more likely that the learned helplessness effect will generalize to a wide array of situations.

Abramson, Seligman, and Teasdale's view of the attribution process in learned helplessness has been applied to the psychological illness of depression. They contend that depressed individuals are those who are more likely to view their situation wth a bias toward internal, stable, and global attribution. When asked to indicate reasons why certain negative events occurred, depressed college students were more likely than non-depressed students to attribute the events to stable, internal, and global dispositions (Seligman, Abramson, Semmel, & Von Baeyer, 1979). Sweeney, Shaeffer, and Golin (1982) added further credibility for the learned helplessness view of depression. They argued that the set of attributions identified by Abramson et al. should relate specifically to attributions that depressed persons make about themselves. It should not necessarily reflect a general attributional style. Sweeney et al. asked depressed and nondepressed persons to infer the causes of a variety of negative outcomes. But the subjects were to make two sets of attributions —one as though the incident happened to them and one as though it happened to someone else. The results showed that depressed and nondepressed subjects did not differ in their attributions when making them for someone else's outcomes. However, when attributing the outcomes to themselves, depressed subjects were much more likely than nondepressed patients to use the stable, internal, and global set of attributions that characterize helplessness.

If depression is characterized by learned helplessness, then adult patients, consistent with Dweck's analysis of children's behavior, ought to feel better if they are provided with experiences that alleviate the helplessness and add a sense of personal control. A series of studies conducted in nursing homes for the elderly (Langer & Rodin, 1976; Rodin & Langer, 1977; also see Schulz, 1976) suggest that control-enhancing interventions are both psychologically and physically beneficial to patients. When patients were encouraged and provided with the means to exercise greater personal control, they felt happier and were more active, sociable, and alert. Staff rated such patients as showing physical and psychological improvement (Langer & Rodin), and as being in generally better health (Rodin & Langer) than patients who did not receive the control-enhancing intervention. Even more startling, there appears to be a tendency for the mortality rates of control-enhanced patients to be lower than those among other patients (Rodin & Langer, 1977), although this tendency may reflect only chance fluctuations.

The research we have discussed thus far makes it clear that attributions are crucial in determining feelings of helplessness. There is some controversy, however, about just what those attributions are (Wortman & Dintzer, 1978). Further, it is clear that there are subtle connections between attributions and feelings of helplessness. For example, we have seen that if people make internal, ability-based attributions for failure, they are likely to become helpless but that, overall, perceptions of internal locus of control counteract helplessness feelings. In Dweck's study, an internal effort attribution counteracted feelings of helplessness. Thus, we see again how individuals who learn Eddie Robinson's view of life will persevere. People like Eddie believe that what you get, including success or failure, depends on how much effort you expend—how hard you try. To such people, the answer to setbacks and failure isn't becoming passive and helpless; rather, it is putting on the internals' "We try harder" button and making a greater effort. Recent research shows that people with high self-esteem, like Eddie Robinson, are more likely to react to failure with sustained effort (Brockner, Mahan, Thomas, Weiss, Winters, & Mitchell, 1983). High self-esteem and perceptions of internal locus of control go hand in hand (Phares, 1984).

Attributions to Self and Others: The Actor-Observer Bias   We began this section on self-attribution by noting that attribution theories discussed in Chapter Two, such as those of Kelley and Weiner, could be applied to the self. At times we make attributions about the self just as we make them about other people. Bem's (1972) self-perception theory makes an even stronger claim. He argues that self-perception is just like other-people perception; it's simply the special case where the actor and the perceiver are the same person. In contrast to this emphasis on the similarity of self-attribution and attributing to others is a theory that holds that actors and observers view the world quite differently.

Let us consider the following clinical case. Betty and George Barnes seek psychotherapy for problems in their marriage. Both of them agree that Betty often flies into fits of rage, throws dishes, and makes life very difficult for the two of them. Betty claims that her actions are caused by her husband's stupidity. She asserts that she becomes enraged when George forgets to put enough money into the checking account, loses his keys, is unable to get a raise. George asserts that his wife becomes enraged because she is unpleasant, illogical, and irascible.

No doubt there is motivation to this madness. Betty's behavior is attributed to George's actions by Betty, and attributed to Betty by George. He blames her; she blames him. But the analysis must go deeper. Betty, the actor, blames the *situations* that George allegedly causes. George, the observer, blames Betty's *disposition*. Jones and Nisbett (1971) have argued that this is a common occurrence in attribution. In their terms, "there is a pervasive tendency for actors to attribute their actions to situational requirements whereas observers tend to attribute the actions to stable dispositions" (p. 80).

A study reported by McArthur (1972) supports this proposition. The procedure was elegantly simple. She asked subjects to volunteer for a survey about interpersonal relationships and then asked the subjects why they had agreed to participate. Written accounts of the request and the consent were given to observers. Like the involved subjects, the observers were asked why they thought the subjects had agreed to participate. The results showed that the involved subjects attributed their participation to the importance of the survey (situational attribution). The observers, on the other hand, attributed the actors' participation to a disposition to take part in surveys. Similar differences between actors and observers have been obtained by Nisbett, Caputo, Legant, and Marecek (1973).

Actors and observers: Why are they different? Jones and Nisbett contend that there are at least two explanations for the difference between actor and observer attributions. The first is that the actor has access to a greater *history* of behaviors than the observer. The actor knows that he behaved in one way today, in a different way yesterday, and in yet another way last week. Therefore, the actor looks to the environment for an explanation. The observer, on the other hand, has but one act of behavior with which to judge the actor. The observer is apt to generalize and to assume that the actor's behavior would be consistent across situations. Consequently, the observer is more prepared to attribute the cause of a behavior to the disposition of the actor.

Second, Jones and Nisbett reason that the actor and the observer approach an act from different perspectives. Each has a different focus and different information is salient to each. As we noted in Chapter Two, people tend to attribute causality to whatever is salient in their environment or whatever they are focusing their attention on (Taylor & Fiske, 1978). Since the actor's attention is focused on the environment, he or she is more likely to attribute causality to things in the environment. The observer's attention is focused on the actor, an important aspect of his or her environment, so he or she is likely to attribute causality to the actor. Therefore, the observer will make more internal dispositional attributions for the actor's behavior than the actor will.

There is considerable support for this differential focus-of-attention explanation of the actor-observer bias (Ross & Fletcher, 1985). For example, one study showed that attributions to internal versus external causes made by actors and observers could be changed by giving each of them a different perspective. Two actors, A and B, had a conversation and were watched by two observers, one looking at each actor. After the conversation, A and B and the two observers made attributions consistent with the focus-of-attention explanation. Each actor attributed his own behavior to the situation and the other actor's behavior to his dispositions, while each observer attributed the behavior of the actor he watched to that actor and the behavior of the other actor to the situation. That is, all four subjects attributed causality to the person on whom they were focused. Later in the experiment, the subjects were shown a videotape of actor A participating in the conversation. The subjects who had not paid attention to actor A before, that is, actor A himself and the observer watching actor B, now made more dispositional attributions to actor A; they saw him more as the locus of causality. The subjects who had been paying attention to actor A previously, that is, actor B and the observer watching A, did not change their attributions. As before (see Figure 3–3), they made dispositional attributions for the behavior of actor A (Storms, 1973).

APPLYING SELF-ATTRIBUTION: MISATTRIBUTION THERAPY

One of the major problems that confronts psychotherapists is the problem of anxiety. Complaints may range from the relatively trivial anxiety associated with insects or snakes to extremely debilitating fears of flying in airplanes, taking tests, or performing in public. The research on self-attribution suggests a unique approach to dealing with such fears. This approach entails accomplishing therapy by having patients misattribute the source of their arousal. If people are given an opportunity to attribute their arousal to an external source rather than to anxiety, perhaps their symptoms can be reduced. For example, telling someone who is afraid of flying that her anxiety attack is due to an airsickness pill could provide a

Figure 3–3
Testing the perceptual explanation for the actor-observer effect

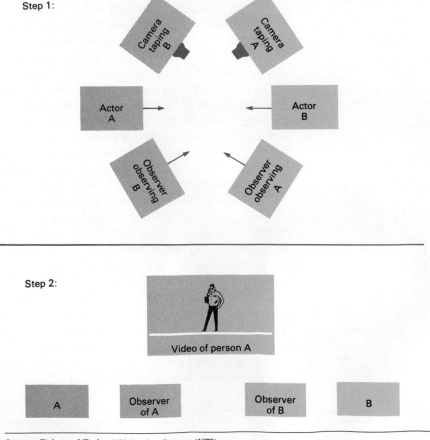

Source: Fiske and Taylor (1984), after Storms (1973).

credible explanation for her anxious feelings and might lead her to actually experience less anxiety. Her arousal can be misattributed to the pill.

Several studies show exactly this kind of symptom reduction due to misattribution of arousal. In one study (Ross, Rodin, & Zimbardo, 1969), subjects were made anxious by being told that they would be given painful electric shocks. However, half of the subjects were exposed to a very loud noise piped over a headset and were led to believe that their arousal was due to the loud noise. Subjects were then given a chance to work on two puzzles. Solving one puzzle would enable them to escape the forthcoming shock; solving the other would bring them a cash reward. Ross et al. found that the subjects who attributed their arousal to the noise abandoned work on the escape-the-shock puzzle and worked significantly more for the cash reward. That is, their behavior indicated less fear of the shock.

The implication of the Ross et al. study is that the psychological disorder known as the *phobia*, or irrational fear, is amenable to an attribution approach. In their study, Ross et al. were able to lessen subjects' fear of shock so that they could pursue more positive and productive goals. Presumably, such common phobias as fear of height and fear of closed or open spaces can be alleviated if patients can be convinced to attribute their emotional arousal (falsely) to other external stimuli.

Another important study of misattribution therapy (Storms & Nisbett, 1970) used the emotional relabeling approach to alleviate a common but sometimes debilitating symptom: insomnia. Under the guise of a drug and fantasy experiment, subjects known to be insomniacs were given a pill (actually a placebo sugar pill with no real physiological effects) to take before going to bed. Since it was assumed that people suffering from insomnia experience a considerable amount of physiological arousal at bedtime, it was predicted that being able to attribute the arousal to a pill would help insomniacs fall asleep.

Subjects in an arousal condition were told that the pill would increase their bodily activity and make them tense and uneasy (in using this explanation of the side effects of the pill, the experimenters were mapping the reports of insomniac victims about how they felt at bedtime). In the relaxation condition, subjects were told that the pill would reduce their heart rates, calm and relax them. In the placebo condition, subjects were told that the pill would have no side effects.

Subjects were then asked to record how long it took them to fall asleep (see Figure 3–4). The subjects in the arousal condition reported that on the nights when they took the pill, they fell asleep almost twelve minutes sooner than on the nights when they did not take the pill. By contrast, the subjects who experienced their normal insomniac arousal but thought that they were supposed to be calmed by the pill took over fifteen

Figure 3–4
Reported speed of falling asleep as a function of misattribution to a pill

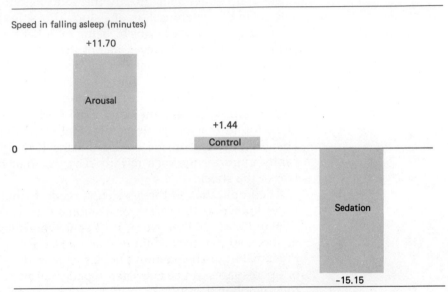

Note: Positive numbers indicate greater speed than usual in falling asleep.
Source: Adapted from Storms and Nisbett (1970).

minutes longer to fall asleep on the nights that they took the pill. The arousal subjects apparently were able to relabel their insomniac arousal on the nights that they took the pill. Thinking that the arousal was attributable to a pill and not to their own psyche, they fell asleep. On the other hand, the subjects who felt that they should be calm (because of the pill), yet still experienced arousal, may have become more worried and upset over the tremendous amount of insomniac arousal that they believed they were suffering.

Not only is Storms and Nisbett's approach an interesting one in the alleviation of insomnia; it also sheds doubt on what we normally think of as the "placebo effect." We can all conjure up situations in which a physician is tempted to prescribe a sugar pill to a nervous and upset patient while convincing the patient that the pill will effect a cure. The placebo effect implies that patients' symptoms will abate if they believe that the treatment will be of help.

Medical evidence has been accumulating that placebo treatments often have deleterious effects (Rickels & Downing, 1967). The data provided by

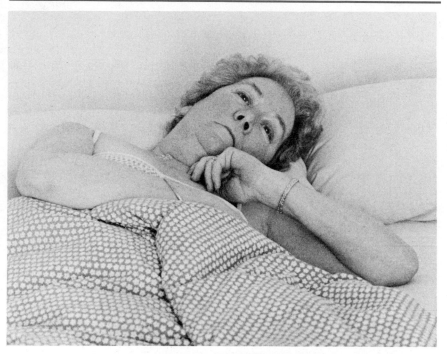

Psychologists have studied cures for insomnia based on principles of attribution. If we believe that a pill is keeping us awake, we might forget our anxieties and fall asleep. *(Nancy Durrel McKenna from* Woman's Experience of Sex *by Sheila Kitzinger, published by Dorling Kindersley U.K. 1983/Photo Researchers, Inc.)*

Storms and Nisbett support this evidence, for it can be said that their procedure produced a "negative placebo effect." In their study, the subjects who believed that the pill would calm them had more, not less, difficulty in falling asleep. In attributional terms, the fact that arousal existed even though an environmental force (the pill) was working against it caused an even greater attribution to a personal disposition ("I must really be a grade A insomniac"). Therefore, it would seem that if a patient's problem persists in the face of a reason for it not to exist, a greater personal attribution will be made—the patient will feel that he has more of the problem than he originally thought he had.

The provocative results of Storms and Nisbett's study, if taken by themselves, would indicate that placebo treatments must be run in reverse. The placebo should always be introduced as causing the symptoms that the patient wants alleviated. Then the patient's feeling that his disposition (neurosis) is the cause of the problem can be *discounted* (recall the discussion of Kelley, 1971, in Chapter Two) and the arousal can be misattributed to an external source. However, the research picture is somewhat more complex.

Several studies show that there are often direct placebo effects, that is, people seem to accept the direct suggestion that a placebo pill will alleviate their symptoms, and they got better (Kellogg & Baron, 1975; Bootzin, Herman, & Nicassio, 1976). It may be that direct suggestion works in situations where people do not have clear internal standards for the way they are feeling and can accept the suggestion that they are experiencing less arousal (Snyder, Schultz, & Jones, 1974). There is ongoing controversy about when direct placebo suggestions work and when they produce negative placebo effects (Ross & Olson, 1981). Additional research will be needed to clarify the situation.

Another experiment on misattribution therapy (Wilson & Linville, 1982) shows how widely it can be applied—in this case to improving academic performance. College freshmen who had done less well than they had expected and were worried about their grades were given information that allowed them to attribute their problems to temporary factors that would eventually go away. Specifically, they were told that grades improve after freshman year and they saw videotapes of juniors and seniors testifying that their grades had improved over time. Subjects who received this information showed improved academic performance compared to subjects who did not. They scored higher a week later on a test of academic performance, they got higher grades during the next year, and they were less likely to drop out of school. Clearly, misattribution therapy has great potential. It remains a promising and intriguing extension of experimentation on the attribution of arousal.

BIASES IN SELF-PERCEPTION: THE TOTALITARIAN EGO

In Chapter Two, we discussed several biases (e.g., the correspondence bias) that affect our perceptions of other people. What biases exist, if any, in our perceptions of ourselves? Jones and Nisbett's actor-observer concept shows that we don't make attributions about ourselves in exactly the same way that we make them about others. It's not surprising, then, to learn that there are several biases that are unique to self-perception. Taken together, they comprise what is known as the totalitarian ego (Greenwald, 1980).

The totalitarian ego or self is described as an organization of knowledge characterized by cognitive biases. These biases function to preserve our organization of social information and our positive views of ourselves. The ego's control and biasing of information is similar to the ways that information is controlled and biased in totalitarian countries, which led Greenwald to characterize it as totalitarian. The totalitarian ego manages information by using three biases: egocentricity, beneffectance, and cognitive conservatism. We will consider each of these biases in turn.

Egocentricity: Self as the Focus of Knowledge and Attribution   Much of our knowledge about the world around us is autobiographical in nature —we remember people and events based on our role in interacting with them and in influencing them or being influenced by them. Our memory of a city that we visited, for example, centers around where we went and what we saw. Our memory of what happened when we participated in a softball game centers around hits that we made and balls that we caught. This tendency to recall information better if it is related to the self is called *egocentricity*.

One of the consequences of egocentricity is the tendency for individuals to exaggerate the importance of their role in shaping events. Ross (1981) provides numerous examples of this. Those people who have collaborated on a research project, a newspaper story, or a music composition may try to recall their perceptions of what their contributions were to the joint product. Where order of authorship implies level of contribution, there are many collaborators who sit in disbelief as their partners indicate that they believe they should come first in that order. Each person, however, tends to remember events through his or her own eyes. A meeting that the authors may have had will be remembered differently by each participant, because each views it with egocentricity. None of the participants may be lying when they each claim that they were the primary contributor to the meeting. Each recalls that part of the event to which he or she contributed, and remembers less well those parts to which others contributed.

Consider, for example, husbands and wives who are asked how much they contributed to various household chores. Ross and Sicoly (1979) interviewed married couples and asked them how much each contributed to cleaning house, caring for children, making important decisions, and causing conflicts. Both husbands and wives claimed to have made the major contribution about 70 percent of the time. Of course, it is impossible for an activity to be the wife's responsibility 70 percent of the time and the husband's responsibility 70 percent of the time. It is not that the partners wish to lie about their role. The fact is, their judgments of responsibility for everyday activities are self-centered: the bias in processing and recalling information results in the egocentric judgment.

Another aspect of the egocentricity bias refers to the "self as locus of cause and effect." That is, we see ourselves as generating behavior. For example, we think of other people's actions in terms of the effects those

We tend to remember our contributions to group tasks egocentrically. For example, husbands and wives both tend to take more than half the credit for completing household tasks. *(© Peter Menzel)*

actions have on us and we assume they acted to produce those effects. We can see these tendencies in international affairs. Americans tend to see what the Soviet Union does as being caused by our actions. Similarly, we see the Soviets' behaviors as designed to have some effect on us. We may think that they are trying to cooperate with us or to compete with us. The key fact here is that we see ourselves as central in their behavior.

Beneffectance: the Self-Serving Bias   People are motivated to see themselves in a good light. We tend to take credit for success and deny responsibility for failure. This bias is referred to as *beneffectance.* The term comes from the fact that we tend to view ourselves positively in two ways: (1) we see ourselves as beneficent, that is, helpful and moral, and as competent, that is, as having "effectance." Beneffectance combines beneficence with effectance. Although this bias is not inconsistent with the actor-observer bias, it does qualify it. While we generally attribute our behavior to the environment, this tendency is much greater when our negative actions are at issue than when our positive actions are under consideration. The beneffectance bias is illustrated in a study on interpersonal competition (Streufert & Streufert, 1969). Pairs of subjects were led to believe that they were competing against other pairs. Some of the subjects were made to believe that they were winning, whereas the other subjects believed that they were losing. The losing subjects attributed their losses to the play of the winning subjects, whereas the winning subjects were convinced that their good fortune was due to their own skillful play.

Observers are not likely to share the actor's bias. Johnson, Feigenbaum, and Weiby (1964) asked women taking educational psychology classes to participate in an experiment in teaching mathematics to nine-year-old boys. Each teacher taught two boys. During the first part of the learning sequence, boy A did well and boy B did poorly. During the second half, A continued to do well. For half of the teachers, B showed improvement so that he was doing as well as A; for the other half, B continued to do poorly. When the teachers were asked how they attributed the performance of the students, teachers who had an improving B saw themselves as responsible for the performance. The teachers whose B continued to do poorly blamed the performance on the student (see Figure 3–5). In a replication of this study, Beckman (1970) found precisely the same effect. However, she also asked observers in an interpersonal replication how they attributed the students' performance. In marked contrast to the teachers, the observers saw the teachers as more responsible for B's poor performance and saw B as more responsible for his own good performance.

Reviews of the literature on the self-serving bias generally support it (Fiske & Taylor, 1984; Riess, Rosenfeld, Melburg, & Tedeschi, 1981; Ross & Fletcher, 1985). One review by Bradley (1978) specified that both beneffectance biases—taking credit for success and denying responsibility for failure—are most likely to occur under the following conditions: (a) when the actor is highly *involved* in an activity, (b) when the actor has *choice* in engaging in the activity, and (c) when the actor's performance in the activity is *public*.

In recent research, this last condition has been explored carefully. Is the beneffectance effect simply a public claim or do people really believe in private that they are responsible for their success but not their failure? Several studies seem to suggest that people genuinely believe in their own beneffectance. For example, in one study (Greenberg, Pyszczynski, & Solomon, 1982), subjects took what they believed to be a test of intelligence. In half of the cases, the test results were private. Subjects graded their own test, they did not put names on their answer sheets, and they were told the tests would not be collected. The other subjects had their tests scored by the instructor with their names attached. All of the subjects learned that they had answered twelve of twenty items correctly,

Figure 3–5
Teachers' attributions for the success and failure of students

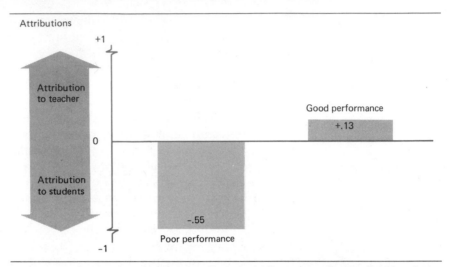

Note: A score of +1 equals total attribution to the teacher's effort; a score of −1 equals total attribution to the student.
Source: Johnson, Feigenbaum, and Weiby (1964).

but half were led to believe this was a good score; the other half believed this was a bad score.

After receiving their scores, the subjects were asked to attribute their performance to their ability, their effort, or to luck. Consistent with the self-serving bias, subjects who believed they had done well indicated that their performance was due to their effort and ability, while subjects who thought they had done poorly attributed their results to bad luck. And it made no difference whether the test performance was public or private.

Riess, Rosenfeld, Melburg, and Tedeschi (1981) also explored whether beneffectance was a private, self-serving bias designed to bolster self-esteem or a public display of impression management. They used a technique known as the bogus pipeline to measure attributions. With this technique, subjects are convinced that their true attributions are being measured by the electronic gadgetry of an electromyograph. Their job is to predict what the machine is saying about their real attributions. These predictions are taken as the subjects' attributions. The results showed that the self-serving bias held up under the scrutiny of the bogus pipeline. Subjects took credit for good performance and avoided blame for poor performance, even if they believed that their private perceptions were being measured accurately by the machinery.

Research has also shown what is known as vicarious beneffectance. Married people evidence the beneffectance bias when explaining their spouse's behavior (Hall & Taylor, 1976). People also evidence this bias when explaining poor debate performances by their preferred presidential candidates (Winkler & Taylor, 1979). Similarly, people strengthen their identification with groups to which they belong when a group is doing well. For example, people are more likely to wear their college's sweatshirts following a football victory than after a football loss; they report "We won" and "They lost" after victory and defeat (Cialdini, Borden, Thorne, Walker, Freeman, and Sloan, 1976).

In summary, beneffectance seems to be a distortion of information that is designed to protect self-esteem. We protect ourselves and those with whom we identify, although we may identify with people or groups less after they fail.

Cognitive Conservatism: Resisting Changes in Thinking   The egocentricity bias considered above implies that our information about ourselves is plentiful and highly organized. Recent evidence indicates that our self-conceptions also are resistant to change. Swann and Read (1981) conducted three experiments that demonstrated that people use social interactions to verify their previously held beliefs about themselves. That is, they prefer to seek information that is consistent with a hypothesis about themselves and avoid situations where they might discover inconsistent information. When people choose interaction partners, when they choose the topics to converse with their partners about, when they choose the topics to avoid, they do so with the goal of confirming their self-concept. As a result, it is difficult for self-concepts to change. If attribution processes result in the formation of ideas about the self, then we would normally predict that people would be fluid in their self-concept development. But the conservatism bias suggests that we "stack the deck." We tend to put ourselves into social situations in which our behavior leads to attributions consistent with our self-image and in which the information we receive further confirms our view of ourselves.

While we may try hard to resist change, we aren't always successful. When we do change, we try to maintain the belief that our knowledge about ourselves and the world has not actually changed much. We do this through the "rewriting of personal history." For example, when we are given information that we didn't know before, we tend to feel that perhaps we actually did know it. This is called the "I knew it all along effect" (Fischoff, 1975). Furthermore, when we change our attitudes or beliefs about the world, we tend to misrecall our earlier attitudes. We

When our own school or college wins a football game we are more likely to identify with it by wearing a school T-shirt. This way we can bask in the reflected glory of the team's success. *(David S. Strickler/The Picture Cube)*

remember those earlier attitudes as being essentially the same as our new ones. Thus, we perceive our attitudes as consistent over time, and we keep ourselves unaware of having changed them (Goethals & Reckman, 1973).

SELF-SCHEMATA: KNOWLEDGE ABOUT OURSELVES

In Chapter Two, we considered the influence of schemata on perception and memory. Not surprisingly, we have schemata about ourselves as well as about other individuals and groups. Research on self-schemata has explored the way our beliefs about ourselves affect the way we perceive and recall our behavior and our personal characteristics (Markus, 1977; Markus & Sentis, 1982; Markus, Smith, & Moreland, 1983).

Individuals are regarded as having a schema about a personal characteristic, such as honesty or dependability, if they feel that that trait is important, that they possess it to an extreme degree, and that the trait's opposite is not applicable to them. People who have schemata about particular characteristics are referred to as *schematic* with respect to that trait. A person who perceives herself as highly and importantly assertive is schematic for assertiveness. A person who does not believe that she is extremely assertive, or who doesn't feel that assertiveness is important, is *aschematic* on assertiveness. Eddie Robinson has certain beliefs about himself that indicate the characteristics for which he is schematic. He believes himself to be hardworking, religious, perfectionistic, a disciplinarian, stoutly American, and persistent. For example, he believes in sticking to tried and true ways of getting ahead, describing his philosophy as "dancing with the girl you brought to the dance." He also admits, "I'm a crier. I can't hold it back" (Wiley, 1982).

When people are schematic on certain traits, they know a lot about themselves based on those traits. Eddie Robinson could tell you a great deal about his beliefs in America and how he has persisted in ways of working that have brought him success. Furthermore, schematics make rapid judgments about whether or not they possess characteristics for which they are schematic. Eddie Robinson knows he is a crier and can thus immediately mention times when he has wept with emotion. Research also shows that we notice characteristics in other people for which we ourselves are schematic. For example, people who are schematic for weight notice when other people are dieting or gaining weight; they are acutely aware of their own and other people's weight (Fiske & Taylor, 1984). Eddie Robinson saw Bear Bryant as sharing his belief in hard work, and he admired Bryant for that.

Consistent with the cognitive conservatism bias, we are highly resistant to information that contradicts our self-schemata, but we easily recall

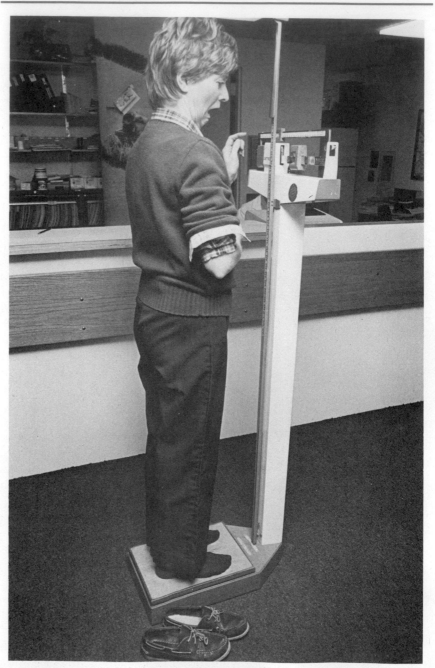

People who have self-schemata about being heavy or thin are able to make quick judgments about their own weight and other people's as well. *(Copyright © by J. Berndt 1983/Stock, Boston)*

information that fits them. Consistent with the egocentricity bias, our knowledge about ourselves is more readily at hand than our knowledge about others (Rogers, 1981). Although we have schemata for other people as well as for ourselves, our memory makes knowledge about ourselves more accessible. Finally, consistent with the beneffectance bias, we have strong emotional reactions to information about ourselves, and we tend to view that information in the most positive possible light (Greenwald, 1980; Greenwald & Pratkanis, 1984). In short, social psychologists are doing more and more research on self-schemata. That research is consistent in interesting ways with research about the theory of the totalitarian ego. Self-schemata allow people to think about themselves and recall their behavior quickly and efficiently; they also contribute to enduring and vivid perceptions of self.

SUMMARY

As a result of social interaction, we learn a great deal about ourselves. Our view of self is affected by both reflected appraisal—what others think of us—and social comparison—the ways in which we appraise ourselves in comparison to others. Usually, we compare with other people who are similar on related attributes, though we may compare with people who are worse (or more negative) than we are to enhance our feelings of well-being. Sometimes people "make up" social comparison information in self-serving ways: they overestimate consensus for many behaviors but underestimate consensus for socially desirable behaviors. People also form self-concepts based on role internalization. Men and women must respond to different expectations about how much they should strive for success. Fear of success, attributions about success and failure, gender schema, and situational pressures can all contribute to women's lower success rates.

Bem's theory of self-perception argues that we make attributions about ourselves just as we do for others; that is, we consider our own behavior and the situation in which it takes place. We do not attribute attitudes to ourselves from behaviors we were forced or pressured to perform. One application of self-perception theory is understanding the overjustification effect in which high external justification leads to the possibly mistaken attribution that a behavior was engaged in not for its own intrinsic merit, but rather for its high external reward.

Schachter and Singer have suggested that emotions are subject to a type of attribution process. In their view, emotions are a function of physiological arousal and cognitive labeling. Schachter and Singer demonstrated that people who were physiologically aroused by a drug, but who had no adequate explanation for their arousal used the behavior of another person in the same situation to infer their emotion. Zillman has shown that arousal from one source can be transferred to another emotion and make that emotion more intense.

Different individuals perceive different loci of control for their outcomes. Internals perceive their outcomes as being a result of their own behavior and they generally "try harder." Externals believe that chance controls their outcomes and they are more passive. Learned helplessness is a phenomenon whereby people cease to behave adaptively after experiencing uncontrollable events. Learned helplessness is a function of the attributions people make about their failures as well as a function of their perceptions about their degree of control over their outcomes in general.

Jones and Nisbett have shown that we do not make attributions about ourselves in exactly the same way as we make them about others. As actors, we attribute our own behavior to external causes while as observers, we attribute other people's behavior to internal personal causes.

Studies have shown that if automatic arousal is misattributed, people's anxieties can be lowered. Misattribution can take on therapeutic aspects if people's troublesome fears can be attributed to external agents. Using misattribution, Ross, Rodin, and Zimbardo were able to reduce subjects' fears and enable them to work on productive pursuits, and Storms and Nisbett were able to use misattribution to enable insomniacs to fall asleep. Wilson and Linville used misattribution to increase academic performance.

A number of biases affect our perceptions of ourselves. They operate much like the biases encountered in our discussion of attributions to others. However, the operation of biases in self-perception leads to different outcomes than that of biases in perceiving others. Many of the biases that affect the self have been characterized as part of the totalitarian ego—the organization of information in a manner that enables us to form a favorable impression of ourselves. Included in these biases are egocentricity, the tendency to process and recall information that is self-relevant; beneffectance, the tendency to see ourselves as responsible for good rather than bad outcomes; and cognitive conservatism, the resistance of self-perceptions to change and the tendency to deny that actual change has taken place.

Research on self-schemata indicates that people who have a schema for particular personal characteristics process information about themselves that is related to those characteristics rapidly and efficiently. We also tend to process information about other people on characteristics on which we are schematic.

KEY WORDS

beneffectance	misattribution
cognitive conservatism	negative placebo effect
defensive attribution	overjustification
egocentricity	reflected appraisal
excitation transfer	related attributes hypothesis
external locus of control	self-perception theory
false consensus effect	self-schemata
false uniqueness effect	similarity hypothesis
fear of success	social comparison process
gender schema	totalitarian ego
internal locus of control	two-factor theory of emotions
learned helplessness	

SUGGESTED READINGS

Bem, S. L. (1981). Gender schema theory: A cognitive account of sex typing. *Psychological Review, 88,* 354–364.

Cotton, J. L. (1981). A review of research on Schachter's theory of emotion and the misattribution of arousal. *European Journal of Social Psychology, 11,* 365–397.

Festinger, L. (1954). A theory of social comparison processes. *Human Relations, 7,* 117–140.

Frieze, I. H., et al., Eds. (1978). *Women and sex roles: A social psychological perspective.* New York: W. W. Norton.

Gergen, K. J. (1971). *The concept of self.* New York: Holt, Rinehart & Winston.

Jones, E. E., & Nisbett, R. (1971). *The actor and the observer: Divergent perceptions of the causes of behavior.* Morristown, NJ: General Learning Press.

Nisbett, R., & Ross, L. (1980). *Human inference: Strategies and shortcomings of social judgment.* Englewood Cliffs, NJ: Prentice-Hall.

Schachter, S., & Singer, J. E. (1962). Cognitive, social, and physiological determinants of emotional state. *Psychological Review, 69,* 379–399.

Suls, J., & Miller, R. J. (Eds.), (1977). *Social comparison processes: Theoretical and empirical perspectives.* Washington, DC: Hemisphere/Halsted.

Wegner, D. M., and Vallacher, R. R. (1980). *The self in social psychology.* New York: Oxford University Press.

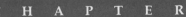

FOUR

Early in Meryl Streep's film career, the actress had to give her best performances at home. The man she loved and lived with, actor John Cazale, was dying of bone cancer. Although Meryl knew he was near death, she threw herself into the role of being optimistic, cheerful, and supportive. In cheering John up, in behaving as if she had hope and faith, Meryl actually came to believe in his recovery. Not only did she "perform" well enough to keep despair away from Cazale, she kept it from herself as well. Meryl nursed him until his death, eventually moving into the hospital with him for his last two weeks of life. A nurse at the hospital said that Meryl "became his mother, his lover, his buddy. It was the kind of love you read about in poetry books" (Maychick, 1984). Cazale died on March 12, 1978.

Since Cazale's death, Meryl Streep has become known as one of the finest actresses in the world. She has been nominated for six Academy Awards, most recently in 1986 for her stirring and powerful performance in *Out of Africa,* and she has been the winner twice. Her success is unprecedented but it has created predictable difficulties. Meryl has lost much of her privacy. She longs for the simple anonymous life. But she also works with utmost devotion to be the consummate actress. Most critics believe that this is what she has become.

Meryl Streep was born in 1949 in suburban New Jersey. She was a happy child who concentrated on boys and cheerleading during her high school years. She was voted homecoming queen in her senior year. She was admitted to Vassar College in New York based on her excellent high school record (except in math), a record that reflected superior intelligence more than hard work. Vassar was to have a profound influence on Meryl Streep's life. It was there that she became serious about acting. Her impact as an actress was so stunning that the head of the Drama department was persuaded to do a play that he originally thought too difficult for college students after watching Meryl read the part. He saw that she was special, and that the power of her ability alone could carry the most difficult theatrical production. At Vassar, Meryl also learned something that would shape the way she portrayed many of her film characters: she learned that she could have significant intellectual and personal relationships with her women peers. Vassar certainly wasn't all cheerleading.

After college, Meryl pursued her acting career. She worked in summer theaters and spent three years studying at the Yale Drama School. After her graduation from Yale in 1974, she headed for New York to work in the theater and—if the opportunity presented itself—the movies. Her first film role was a small part in the movie *Julia* with Jane Fonda and Vanessa Redgrave. Few people remembered her in that role, but they began to take notice after her performance in the television miniseries

Meryl Streep has had an outstanding acting career. She has been nominated for six Academy Awards and she has won two Oscars. *(Simon Pietri/ Sygma)*

"Holocaust," and her subsequent stunning portrayal of Linda, a young woman from a steel manufacturing town in the movie *The Deer Hunter*. She was nominated for her first Oscar for her performance in that film.

It was while she was in New York that Meryl met and fell in love with her leading man in Shakespeare's *Measure for Measure*. The man was John Cazale and Meryl began living with him shortly after they fell in love. They starred in *The Deer Hunter* together, but that was to be Cazale's last role; he died before the film was released. Meryl was devastated and exhausted by the effort to keep her acting career moving and Cazale smiling. Despite being emotionally drained after Cazale's death Meryl kept working. It was not long before she got a key role in the movie *Kramer vs. Kramer* and her first Academy Award. Much of the power of her performance was due to her own rewriting of the script to make her character, who finally chose to relinquish custody of her child, both believable and sympathetic.

Not long after John Cazale's death, Meryl became involved with and soon married a sculptor named Donald Gummer. Like Meryl, Gummer is a devoted artist who prefers a private existence. Although the Gummers are busy raising a family and avoid publicity as much as possible, Meryl's devotion to her craft means that she must be a public figure. In the last five years, she has won another Oscar for her role in the film *Sophie's Choice*, and has been nominated for her performances in *The French Lieutenant's Woman*, *Silkwood*, and *Out of Africa*.

The amount of effort and sacrifice that Streep puts into her work is considerably greater than the general public realizes. For example, Meryl had to learn German and Polish for *Sophie's Choice*. Learning a language or an accent for a part demands such immersion in a role that it becomes part of a performer's identity during the whole filming period. When Streep was making *The French Lieutenant's Woman*, a lifelong friend couldn't recognize Meryl's voice on the phone. And while she was making *Sophie's Choice*, Meryl's baby son couldn't recognize his mother's voice and cried when she approached him. Meryl must also deal with problems beyond being unrecognizable to close friends and family. For example, in a studio ad for *The French Lieutenant's Woman*, her character was referred to as the "French Lieutenant's Whore," a description she knew would be upsetting to her family.

When Meryl gave the commencement address at Vassar in 1983, she spoke of "the intrusion of extreme self-consciousness" that is intrinsic to life as a public figure, but at the same time she encouraged the graduates to "take your heart to work, and ask the best of everybody else too." Fortunately for those of us who enjoy her work, Meryl Streep gives the best to her craft and, we will enjoy it for years to come.

THE SELF AND INTERPERSONAL BEHAVIOR

In his famous play *As You Like It*, William Shakespeare wrote "All the world's a stage," implying that the way people behave in everyday life is like playing different parts in the theater. Meryl Streep's life—and our own lives as well—shows that there is a big difference between private life and life on the stage. At the same time, however, the *real* optimism that Streep's optimistic acting gave her when John Cazale was dying demonstrates the degree to which we become the way we act. Much of the way we interact with our fellow human beings involves presenting ourselves in ways that we hope will make a certain impression on them, just as actors and actresses do. In fact, as we shall see, many have argued that Shakespeare's comparison of life and the stage is highly instructive, and that we need to understand how much of our everyday behavior involves presenting ourselves as people in the theater do. In this chapter, we will consider how people present themselves, and how concerns with the self affect the way they behave in face-to-face interaction.

THE PRESENTATION OF SELF IN EVERYDAY LIFE

Sociologist Erving Goffman (1959, 1967) was one of the keenest observers of human interaction in general and of self-presentation in particular. His approach is often referred to as the *dramaturgical approach* because he compared the way we present ourselves to the way people on the stage present themselves. In this section, we will discuss Goffman's work and some closely related concepts.

Goffman's Dramaturgical Approach   Goffman wrote that when people interact, each person acts out a *line*, much like a part in a play. By a line, Goffman meant all the verbal and nonverbal expressions that people use to convey their view of the situation, the people they are interacting with, and themselves. An important part of the individual's line is what Goffman called his or her *face*, which he defined as the positive social value one claims about him- or herself when interacting with others. For example, when a person walks into a party, her line may convey that she thinks that this is a good place to have a good time, that the people are friendly and interesting, and that she is looking forward to the evening. The face she presents is that of one who enjoys a good time and knows how to have one. Acting out certain lines and claiming a certain face are the heart of self-presentation.

One important way that people claim face is through the acting out of what Goffman calls *idealized performances*. When we give an ideal performance, we act as though we support and live up to ideal social values and behavioral standards more than in fact we do. For example, we may act as though we have more interest in culture and education than we really do by letting people see our copy of *War and Peace* (largely unread though it is), but keeping our *People* magazine hidden. This idealized performance is part of our line that claims *face*, that is positive social value, in the realm of history and literature.

Goffman makes it very clear why people act out lines and present certain faces. One of the realities of social life that we saw in Chapter Two is that people are constantly forming impressions of each other and making attributions. We need to understand our world, particularly our fellow human beings. In so doing, we quickly realize that just as we are judging others, they are judging us. It then becomes apparent that it is in our interest to control, if we can, other people's impressions so that they will treat us as we would like them to. Thus, the basic reason for engaging in self-presentation is to control other people's impressions of us. Trying to control these impressions is referred to as *impression management*. As we shall

People in formal settings often follow the interaction rituals that specify how one should behave. They may, for example, give "idealized performances." *(T. R. Hollard/Stock, Boston)*

see, more must be said about the motives behind self-presentation, but the heart of the phenomenon is trying to control what others think of us.

Once an individual has claimed a certain face by acting out a line, how do other people respond? For example, when someone drops hints that he is experienced in dancing and is pretty good at it, what is the reaction from others likely to be? Goffman argues that at least publicly people go along with other people's claims of face, thereby achieving a working consensus or the "veneer of consensus." Thus, we would act as though we were impressed by and interested in the person's dancing experience. The agreement may not be genuine but it is carefully maintained by everyone. Goffman also suggests that others expect that we will claim good things about ourselves, just as they expect we will openly agree with the good things they claim about themselves. Furthermore, not only do we initially support other people's faces, but we do all we can to help them when subsequent events embarrass or contradict their claims. For example, if one of your classmates who has presented herself as good in biology gets a poor grade on a test, we will not only go along with *her* excuses, but we are also likely to offer our own (e.g., "You really didn't have enough time to study properly with all the noise in the dorm the night before the exam"). In fact, if we think our friend did poorly, we will avoid even asking about her grade to prevent embarrassing her. And similarly, we expect the same treatment from other people. These efforts to either prevent embarrassment, or to correct it and restore face when someone has lost it, are referred to as *face work*.

Why are we so often expected to present ourselves positively and to put so much effort into maintaining faces—our own and others? Goffman thinks that face work, and other "interaction rituals" such as the "How are you-Fine, thanks" exchange are necessary conditions for social life to work. They allow people to interact smoothly, if somewhat superficially, and to avoid having to worry about hurt feelings or discomfort. Interaction rituals allow us to transact our business with people in a relatively safe and predictable environment. If something is lost in honesty and authenticity, something is gained in security, simplicity, and efficiency. As you might imagine, psychologists and sociologists have argued at length about whether face work is desirable; but there is considerable agreement that it is necessary, and even more agreement that it is pervasive.

Audience Pleasing, Self-Construction, and Situated Identities   Goffman's theories have inspired much thinking and research about how and why people engage in self-presentation. One recent general theory of self-presentation by Baumeister (Baumeister, 1982; Baumeister & Hutton, 1987) suggests two major self-presentation motives. The first is *audience pleasing*. We want to please other people, either because we have a generally high need for approval (Crowne & Marlow, 1964) or because *we* want *them* to behave in certain ways (Arkin, 1980). Thus, in general, we try to conform to their expectations and preferences. The second important motive in self-presentation is called *self-construction*. Here we have an ideal image of the kind of person we would like to be, and we want to come as close to the ideal in our actual behavior as we can: in many respects, however, we are unsure about how close we really come. Therefore, we act as if we have certain desired traits and then see if others view our behavior as supporting our self-image. When others validate our self-presentation, the process of self-construction has occurred. For example, a person may want to see herself as effective in leading a group. In a review session for an exam, she takes the initiative in organizing the discussion. When others go along, she has advanced the construction of her identity as a leader.

An important distinction between audience pleasing and self-construction rests on *whose* ideas and preferences determine self-presentation—the audience's or the actor's. Oftentimes these preferences can conflict, as when a student back home from college on vacation doesn't know if he should reveal his new values and tastes—in the hope that they will be accepted—or conform to his parents' expectations.

When we engage in self-construction, we may do so in particular settings. For instance, the young woman mentioned above may want to be identified as a leader by her peers, an aspiring musician by her parents, and a witty humorist by her boyfriend. We attempt to get others to accept our view of ourselves in each of these settings, thereby "negotiating" a *situated identity* for each (Alexander & Rudd, 1981). Meryl Streep would like to maintain an identity as an outstanding actress in her professional life and as the quiet and private Mrs. Gummer, wife and mother, in her private life. We try to negotiate the most positive and satisfying situated identity we can in each different setting that is important to us.

An interesting study of the difficulties of achieving desired identities indicates that professional sports teams on the verge of winning a championship are more likely to choke if they have to win at home (Baumeister, 1985; Baumeister & Steinhilber, 1984). Data from seventh games played in baseball's World Series and basketball's NBA Finals show that the home team often loses in the final game. The pressure of achieving the desired identity plus the pressure and distraction of supportive home-town fans can lead to more fielding errors and missed free throws for the home team. Ironically, home-town support acts to distract players from concentrating on effective performance.

Self-Presentation and the Self-Concept   We saw earlier that when Meryl Streep acted cheerful and optimistic while she was caring for John Cazale, she actually began to feel better. Do our self-presentations often lead to changes in attitude or feeling? Goffman (1959) argued that we are often "taken in by our own act" and hence begin to feel like the person we are portraying. Further, recent research suggests that self-presentation can cause us to adopt attitudes consistent with the way we have presented ourselves (Baumeister & Tice, 1984). That is, once we act as though we believe or feel something, we often internalize our behavior and come to genuinely feel the way we act. Thus, Meryl Streep's experience is a common one. Just as we internalize the roles we play (recall Chapter Three), we internalize many of our self-presentations (Baumeister, 1986).

POWER AND INGRATIATION

Implicit in Goffman's self-presentation theory is the idea that in everyday life, power is important. We want to be able to control other people's impressions of us and, ultimately, the way they treat us, which is why we engage in various forms of impression management. The idea that power is important in social life is much more *explicit* in two recent self-presentation theories, both influenced by Goffman, that we will now consider.

Impression Management Theory Impression management theory (Tedeschi, Schlenker, & Bonoma, 1971; Tedeschi, 1981) holds that people try to obtain power in large part because power is important to effective interaction with others. One of the consequences of the desire to have power is that we strive to ensure that we have credibility. That is, if we can't be believed, if people can't depend on us, we rapidly lose power. And to be credible, it is important that other people regard us as consistent in our attitudes and beliefs. Some observers of the presidency in the United States say that former President Jimmy Carter lost his credibility and power due to his inconsistency in formulating policy: because he sometimes changed his policies and couldn't be depended on, he wasn't always believed. As a result, his power to influence events quickly eroded. Thus, according to impression management theory, one major aspect of self-presentation is that we try to appear consistent in the interest of maintaining our credibility and power.

Strategic Self-Presentation Theory

The principles of ingratiation. Power is also important in another theory of self-presentation; Edward E. Jones's theory of ingratiation and strategic self-presentation (Jones, 1964; Jones & Wortman, 1973; Jones & Pittman, 1982). Jones's theory begins by considering the plight of the person in a low-power position. Power is one person's ability to reward or punish, help or hurt, another person. The person in the low-power position in a relationship is the one who has less power to reward or punish the other. A factory foreman, for example, may have the power to give a worker a raise or to fire her. The worker, on the other hand, has relatively little ability to affect the actions of the foreman, and thus has less power. In contrast, an actress like Meryl Streep has considerable power in negotiating her salary: she can affect potential employers' profits by making a film with one company or by taking her services elsewhere. Assuming the perspective of the low-power individual, Jones suggests that this person will be motivated to modify the power relationship.

How can a person in a low-power position modify the relationship and thereby reduce the power differential? The answer: If the low-power person can ingratiate himself with the higher power person and induce that person to like him, the power differential can be reduced. What does liking have to do with relative power? Let us consider a student and a professor. Assume that the professor, by virtue of her ability to give grades, has more power than the student who, whether friendly or unfriendly, has little real impact. If the student can make the professor like him, two things will happen. First, the professor will be less likely to punish the student by giving him a bad grade, which reduces her power over him. Second, the professor will be more affected by the student's friendliness or unfriendliness and will care more about what the student thinks of her teaching, which increases the student's ability to reward or punish the professor. In these two ways, the professor's power advantage is reduced —though she can still flunk the student if she has to!

Based on this analysis, Jones (1964) predicts that low-power people will try to "curry favor" or attempt to ingratiate themselves with those in power and make themselves liked. A great deal of research has been conducted on the various ways in which people try to ingratiate themselves. Most of this research recognizes the difficulty of successful ingratiation and how those difficulties can be overcome. Some of these difficulties are summarized in the concept of "the ingratiator's dilemma," which has two aspects. The first is that the less power one person has in a relationship, the more he or she will want to ingratiate. At the same time, the more powerful person will be increasingly alert to possible ingratiation attempts. Thus, the less powerful person's attempts to win the approval of the more powerful person may be seen as ingratiating and thus backfire. For example, the manager of a fast-food restaurant may be aware that certain employees act friendly in an effort to influence their chances for promotion. The dilemma for the employee is that the less power he has, the more he wants to ingratiate, which makes it harder for him to succeed because of the manager's awareness of his ingratiating behavior.

A person in a lower status position may attempt to curry favor with a superior so as reduce the power differential between them. Such behavior is called ingratiation. (© *Michel Heron 1983/Woodfin Camp & Associates*)

The second aspect of the ingratiator's dilemma is that low-power persons, such as an employee interacting with a manager or a local manager interacting with a regional manager, do not want to view themselves as ingratiating. Ingratiation is considered somewhat demeaning behavior. Ideal behavioral standards dictate they we don't try to get someone to like us for ulterior motives, so we typically give "idealized performances," indicating that we concur with that standard. But, as in the case with other idealized performances, we sometimes violate the standard; that is, we ingratiate more than we admit. But the fact remains that people don't like to see themselves as ingratiating, as being a "brownie," and this too is part of the ingratiator's dilemma.

One phenomenon that lessens the ingratiator's dilemma is known as the *autistic conspiracy.* As mentioned above, the potential ingratiator, the low-power individual, does not want to view himself as such. Further, the target person, the more powerful person toward whom ingratiating behavior is directed, does not want to view the low-power person as an ingratiator either. For example, the manager doesn't want to think that the employee is being nice for ulterior motives. She prefers to see the ingratiator's behavior as genuine. If the employee compliments the manager's decision, the manager wants to believe that her decision is really a good one and that the employee's compliment is therefore well deserved.

Similarly, if a student agrees with a professor's point in class, the professor wants to believe that she was really persuasive and insightful, not that the student was "brownnosing." In short, both persons, the high- and low-power individuals, prefer to look the other way and believe that ingratiation is not taking place. This mutual self-deception about what's really happening is what is meant by autistic conspiracy, a phenomenon that not only lessens the ingratiator's dilemma, but also makes it much easier for ingratiation to be successful.

Another way that people try to cope with the ingratiator's dilemma is by being subtle. While there are a variety of ingratiation tactics, the general subtlety principle applies to all of them. Since they want their behavior to be believed, ingratiation can't be so blatant that it arouses suspicions about whether it derives from ulterior motives. We will discuss three different behaviors that can be ingratiation tactics, all of which require subtlety.

Ingratiation tactics. One ingratiation tactic is conformity to the opinions and values of the high-power person. You can easily imagine a student nodding his head and saying yes when the professor makes a point. You have probably also heard of presidential aides doing the same thing when talking to the chief executive. Several studies of conformity by Jones and his colleagues indicate how frequently and subtly people conform in experiments where they have an opportunity to agree or disagree with the opinions of a high-power person who can control their outcomes. These studies show that lower power leads to both more conformity and more subtlety—just as the ingratiator's dilemma would lead us to predict.

In one study, naval ROTC freshmen conformed a good deal to the opinions expressed by high-status ROTC seniors. However, they seemed to "pick their spots." That is, they would conform on issues that concerned the ROTC program, but they maintained independence on issues like music or the movies, things having nothing to do with ROTC. In this way, they showed that they could think for themselves without challenging the authority of their senior officers (Jones, Gergen, & Jones, 1964). In another study, low-power subjects who conformed indicated that they were extremely confident about their opinions, as if to show that the views they were mirroring were their own. When they disagreed, they qualified what they said by indicating that they were not very confident about their opinions (Jones & Jones, 1963). In still another study, subjects who were low in power showed a tendency to conform more on the target person's basic values than on his specific opinions (Davis & Florquist, 1964). In all cases, people tried to indicate that their conformity was not total and that they really meant it when they agreed.

Sometimes conformity is nonverbal. In one study, women subjects who came to interview for a job were given information about the opinions of the male interviewer. Some were told that the interviewer valued the traditional emotional and deferential female, while others were told that the interviewer preferred more "liberated" women. Depending on what they had been told about the interviewer, when the subjects came to the interview they actually dressed and behaved differently, in addition to saying the things they thought the interviewer wanted to hear. When the interviewer allegedly preferred traditional women, the subjects wore more makeup and a lot of feminine jewelry; they also behaved more passively in general. The women who were interviewed by the man who allegedly preferred liberated women talked more and made more eye contact with the interviewer, and generally acted more assertively (Von Baeyer, Sherk, & Zanna, 1981). In short, ingratiating conformity can be both verbal and nonverbal and it is usually highly subtle.

Another ingratiation tactic is flattery, or other-enhancement. If we say nice things to other people, indicating that we like or admire them, there is a good chance that they will like us in return. As with other ingratiation tactics, subtlety is important here as well. Our flattery or building up of the other person must be perceived as sincere and credible. For example, research indicates that we like other people who like us—especially if they appear discerning and discriminating in their judgments. People who are *always* positive aren't liked as much; their enhancing comments about us aren't perceived as especially significant (Mettee & Arsonson, 1974). Other research shows that it is important that the person who says nice things about us doesn't seem to have anything to gain. In general, the more people like us, the more we like them but this isn't true if the other person has an ulterior motive and is obviously ingratiating (Jones & Wortman, 1973).

There are a number of interesting ways to flatter others. In his famous book *How to Win Friends and Influence People,* Dale Carnegie (1936) talked about ways to show that others are significant to you. One way is simply to call them by name. Army officers sometimes find that soldiers generally respond more favorably when they are called by name. As Carnegie said, our names are the "sweetest sound" we can hear.

We noted earlier that the behavior of "self-construction" (Baumeister & Hutton, 1986) often occurs around personal characteristics that we value highly but are unsure that we possess. For example, a person who values being athletic will see if he can impress others in a game of volleyball. Gaining others' approval results in self-construction. Not surprisingly, flattery often works best when we flatter other people in areas where they are unsure of themselves (Schlenker, 1980). Complimenting a statistics professor on her facility with mathematical expressions won't have much impact; she already knows she's good with numbers. But telling her that you like witty examples, which she is very insecure about, should lead her to appreciate your discerning appraisal.

Meryl Streep works in a highly competitive profession—acting—where, as we can imagine, conformity and flattery are used frequently, along with a host of other ingratiation tactics designed to get people roles in plays, top billing in a film, and so on. Meryl's remarkable career shows that a third form of ingratiation is often successful—simply presenting oneself as positively as possible. Often this means using *self-enhancement*, revealing positive information about ourselves. In Meryl's case, it typically means just showing what she can do in reading a role. Meryl is neither overly modest nor self-congratulatory; she is simply direct about how she thinks parts should be played and what she believes she can bring to them. Research shows, however, that people often present themselves very positively, or sometimes modestly, depending on what they consider is appropriate to the occasion (Gergen & Taylor, 1969). In short, self-presentation, either in the direction of modesty or self-enhancement, is a third ingratiation tactic, along with conformity and flattery.

Other self-presentation strategies. Thus far, we have considered self-presentation tactics designed for ingratiation—making other people like us. Making others like us gives us more power in our relationships. However, there are several other important self-presentation strategies (Jones & Pittman, 1982), all of which are used to try to control how other people view and treat us. While ingratiation aims at getting people to like us, the other strategies are designed to elicit somewhat different perceptions in others, and to induce them to act accordingly. The four we will consider—intimidation, self-promotion, exemplification, and supplication—are used to induce others to fear us, respect our abilities, respect our morals, or feel sorry for us, respectively.

In the case of *intimidation*, a person tries to influence someone else's behavior through fear. The intimidator attempts to appear powerful and willing to use power, and often uses threats of punishment. Jones and Pittman give street robbers or muggers as examples of intimidators who use threats and fear to gain compliance, for example, to force their victims to hand over money. Intimidation is frequently seen in sports. During the introductions and instructions before a boxing match, the fighters glare at each other as menacingly as possible, each trying to strike fear into the other. In football games, the players frequently shout in threatening ways at each other, especially at quarterbacks who have just been tackled. One former football player, Jack Tatum of the Oakland Raiders, wrote a book called *They Call Me Assassin* to discuss the intimidating

One self-presentation strategy is intimidation. We try to convey to other people the idea that we are dangerous and that we should be feared. *(J. Pavlovsky/Sygma)*

reputation he had while playing for the NFL, a reputation he carefully cultivated to frighten his opponents and disrupt their play. The word *intimidation* is now used frequently to describe a tactic for dominating other players in hockey and basketball, as well as in football.

Intimidation can also be used in other domains. When Lyndon Johnson was president of the United States, he would often intimidate members of Congress and aides to gain their compliance. Jones and Pittman note that self-presentation strategies can be combined and Johnson provides a good example of such mixing. Often, he would mix the intimidating use of fear with sweet cajolery and ingratiation. He wanted to be liked as well as feared, so he presented himself as both likable and formidable.

The person who uses *self-promotion* wants to be respected more than liked. Specifically, self-promoters want to be respected for their intelligence and competence. To enhance the credibility of claims that they make about their abilities, self-promoters may acknowledge certain of their minor flaws or shortcomings (Baumeister & Jones, 1978). In so doing, they acknowledge that they have both strengths and weaknesses, but are generally confident about their competencies. Meryl Streep frequently worried that she was not as pretty as she needed to be for romantic parts. After one of her few unsuccessful films, a critic wrote of Meryl and her costar, Roy Scheider, "You can't strike a flame with two metallic matches" (Maychick, 1984). The respect that critics have for Streep's ability and competence is all the more impressive in light of the fact they do not view her as exceptionally beautiful. Having and admitting a flaw can enhance our claims of competence.

Related to the idea of enhancing the credibility of competence claims by admitting weaknesses is the notion of enhancements (Schlenker, 1980). When we have done something competently, we may try to enhance the amount of ability that went into our successful performance by emphasizing how difficult it was (Quattrone & Jones, 1978). Some of Meryl Streep's performances seem even more impressive when we realize the emotional strain she was under due to John Cazale's fatal illness when she gave them. Self-promoters might try to take advantage of the enhancement phenomenon by suggesting, for example, that their performance would have been more effective had they not been ill when they gave it.

Another method of self-promotion is "basking in reflected glory" (Cialdini, Borden, Thorne, Walker, Freeman, and Sloan, 1976), which is similar to the idea of vicarious beneffectance discussed in the previous chapter. One way of basking in reflected glory is to wear college sweatshirts after the school's football team has won. We operate on the "principle of association" (Schlenker, 1980), meaning that we present ourselves as a part of what is successful or competent. For example, a president of the United States will visit or telephone the locker room of a championship team to enjoy the feeling of being associated to some degree with the team's victory. In general, people probably want to be respected for their abilities as much as they want to be liked. Therefore, self-promotion is as common as ingratiation. Further, the two can be combined, as when we flatter both ourselves (self-promotion) and others (ingratiation) and try to be both liked *and* respected.

A third self-presentation strategy is termed *exemplification*. Here individuals try to present themselves as being moral and worthy, and as having integrity. The person who works late at the office or gives a great deal to charity is being "exemplary" in ways that might influence other people to behave in the same manner. Such individuals provide a clear and worthy model for others to follow. As with other self-presentation strategies, exemplification is used to influence both other people's impressions and their behavior.

A final self-presentation strategy, which can be viewed almost as a last resort, is one that Jones and Pittman term *supplication*. In this case, people play on others' sympathies by acting weak and helpless. The goal of

Drinking too much may be a form of self-handicapping. When we deliberately put obstacles in the way of successful performance, we provide ourselves with an excuse for failure. *(Alan Carey/The Image Works)*

the supplicator, quite simply, is to get help. Children who want to stay home from school may act ill or otherwise helpless to get their parents to relent and allow them to stay home. Supplication works best when people convey the fact that their helpless or weak position is not their fault. For example, college students faced with accumulating paper deadlines may ask for help from professors or deans by pleading the overwhelming pressures of assignments that are beyond their control. In short, we often present ourselves as being likable. But we also try to appear threatening, competent, morally exemplary, and needy, all of which can affect people's behavior as effectively as ingratiation.

THE PSYCHOLOGY OF SELF-HANDICAPPING

Others often judge us by the way we perform. For this reason, people use the self-promotion strategy discussed in the previous section. They convey as much information as possible about their competence. Of course, what people claim about their abilities eventually must be put to the test. Surprisingly, it has been observed that people often do things that put obstacles in the way of giving effective performances. For example, those in Meryl Streep's profession have been known to skip key rehearsals or to be drunk on opening night. And college students frequently stay up all night before exams, sometimes studying, but often partying. Sometimes they lose their notebooks or forget to take care of themselves so that they become ill. (At least, on occasion, that is what students have told us at exam time.) Why would people, college students included, put obstacles in the way of successful performance? Why would they engage in what has come to be known as *self-handicapping?*

Self-Handicapping: Discounting Failure   Self-handicapping can easily be seen as a self-presentational strategy that makes clever use of some of the basic principles of attribution. It is premised on the idea that putting obstacles in our own way provides an excuse for failure (Jones & Berglas, 1978). If we fail in the face of obstacles, an attribution of low ability can be discounted. The failure can be attributed to the obstacles; they provide the excuse. For example, the student who fails after partying can blame the poor grade on being unprepared, not on low ability. Research on self-handicapping suggest that drinking and underachieving are specific strategies that people use to give themselves and others excuses for failure. Thus, having a problem with alcohol and having trouble working to capacity are personal problems that can explain poor performance (Jones & Berglas, 1978).

Studies of self-handicapping have helped to make us aware of the circumstances in which it is most likely to be used. One such circumstance is when people do not have confidence in their abilities: they are therefore likely to be worried about failure and are more apt to engage in excuse-generating self-handicapping. In a study designed to support this hypothesis, subjects participated in an experiment described as a study of the effects of various drugs on performance. One of the drugs was expected to lower performance and the other was expected to raise it. Before taking the drug, one group of subjects was given a form of an intelligence test. For some, the test was easy and they were told that they did well. Other subjects were given insoluble problems but they too were told that they had done well. The first group felt that they had performed well, were told that they had, and felt confident about future success. The second group did well but didn't know why. They were *not* confident about doing well in the future, as they did not feel that they had been in control of the situation.

After receiving the feedback, subjects had the option of taking one of the two drugs before another of the same intelligence test was administered. As predicted by the researchers, those subjects who did not feel they had been in control of the situation, those who were told that they had answered the insoluble questions correctly, chose the drug that lowered performance; that is, they self-handicapped. Those who were confident tried to do even better on the second part of the test; they took the performance-enhancing drug (Jones & Berglas, 1978). These findings suggests that people are likely to self-handicap when they are unsure of their abilities because then at least they can avoid being *blamed* for failure should it occur.

There are many forms of self-handicapping. One of the most interesting is presenting oneself as ill, or actually feeling ill (Smith, Snyder, & Perkins, 1983). A study similar to the one described above shows that people will use—and possibly abuse—alcohol to self-handicap. Students at Vanderbilt University in Nashville were told that they would be taking part in a study of the effects of self-determined quantities of alcohol on intellectual performance. Some subjects were given insoluble problems and either told or not told that they had done well. Subjects who were told that they had done well on the insoluble problems drank more alcohol before taking a second test than subjects who were not told that they had done well. Thus, in a situation where people succeeded but didn't have confidence about future success, they used drinking as a means of self-handicapping (Tucker, Vucinish, & Sobell, 1981).

Self-handicapping strategies are not only ways of managing impressions that others form of you. They also provide solutions for the attributions that you make about yourself. Self-handicappers never have to face their own negative attributions about themselves. By self-handicapping, they can always discount the possibility that their abilities are too limited (Smith, Snyder, & Handelsman, 1982). Even though self-handicapping can be done for oneself as well as others, research suggests that it is primarily a self-presentational tactic (Baumeister & Tice, 1985; Baumeister & Hutton, 1987). Self-handicapping is particularly likely to be used when other people expect future success from you based on your past success, and it is less likely to occur when people can't observe your self-handicapping actions (Kolditz & Arkin, 1982).

Individual Differences in Self-Handicapping   A final example of self-handicapping shows that individual college athletes differ in the degree to which they actually use the strategy. Social psychologists at Princeton

University developed a scale to measure how much different people are likely to self-handicap. They gave the scale to members of the swimming team, then observed attendance at team practices and asked the coaches to rate how hard individual swimmers worked at each practice. The psychologists predicted that the tendency to self-handicap might be greatest just before a big important meet, at which time swimmers might want an excuse for failure. The results showed that before unimportant meets, the high and low self-handicapping swimmers did not differ in their behavior at practice. However, the low self-handicappers increased their attendance at practices and worked harder before *important* meets, while the high self-handicappers did not. The combination of an individual's tendency to self-handicap and a difficult situation produced self-handicapping behavior. Similar results were found for professional golfers (Rhodewalt, Saltzman, & Wittmer, 1982).

Self-handicapping gives people an excuse for failure. But it also has another effect, one that is related to our earlier concept of enhancements. If a person succeeds after setting up self-handicapping obstacles, he or she can enhance that success. That is, the success looks even more impressive if it occurs *in spite of* obstacles. Thus, self-handicapping can be used as a self-promotion tactic if people succeed in spite of it.

SELF-AWARENESS

Much of our everyday behavior is fairly routine and automatic. We get up, get dressed, eat breakfast, and read the newspaper in a fairly habitual manner, without giving a lot of thought to what we are doing. Some of this behavior is referred to as *mindless* (Palmerino, Langer, & McGillis, 1984). Generally, we do not think about ourselves very much when we are performing automatic behaviors, nor do we think about what others may be thinking of us (Wicklund & Frey, 1980): we just go about our business. On the other hand, events in the environment can make us self-conscious and self-aware. As we shall see, when this happens we can behave with a great deal of deliberation and thought. We will also see that self-awareness is often unpleasant. Meryl Streep makes plain that one of the most difficult parts of her career is losing her anonymity and dealing with the "intrusion of extreme self-consciousness" that is part of the celebrity role. Like others, Meryl Streep does not enjoy being the focus of attention, even though she understands that in her profession being in the spotlight in inevitable. What happens when people become self-aware, and why is self-awareness so often unpleasant?

Self-Awareness and Comparing to Standards   Recent theories of self-awareness, or what is also known as self-focused attention, suggest that people can become self-aware whenever they are asked to talk about themselves, when they are in unfamiliar or unstructured settings, when they can see themselves in the mirror or hear themselves on a tape recorder, when television cameras are pointing at them or people are looking at them, or when they are in a minority status in a group and thus stand out. Obviously, being on stage or performing before movie cameras produces self-awareness, so self-awareness must be a large part of Meryl Streep's life. But it is something we *all* deal with at times, so what are its consequences?

Self-awareness theorists (Duval & Wicklund, 1972; Carver & Scheier, 1981; Wicklund & Frey, 1980) argue that when people become self-focused they compare their behavior with rules, norms, or other behavioral standards. For example, suppose we see ourselves in the mirror. We

People experience self-awareness when they see themselves in a mirror or hear a recording of their own voice. Usually they find self-awareness unpleasant. (*Anna Kaufman/Stock, Boston*)

are likely to compare the way we look or the way we are acting with ideal standards of appearance or conduct. When we make this comparison, we often find that our behavior falls short of what we perceive as ideal. We may feel that our performance is not as good as we would like it to be, that our appearance isn't as pleasing as that of attractive people we see on television, or that we aren't being as helpful or cooperative as we feel we ought to be. In other words, comparing behavior to standards is apt to be an unpleasant and painful experience because in all likelihood we will discover that we fall short of *our ideal standards*. What happens when people experience the unpleasant feelings that accompany the self-aware state of mind?

Escaping from Self-Awareness   One obvious method of dealing with an unpleasant situation is to simply try getting out of it. For example, Meryl Streep and other celebrities try to avoid or escape from self-focused attention by wearing inconspicuous clothes and attempting to blend into the crowd. What coping methods do people in psychological experiments on self-awareness use? If they face the unpleasant combination of self-awareness and falling short of standards they too will escape as soon as they feel they can. In one study, subjects took a test that measured "cleverness," a combination of intelligence and creativity. Some subjects were told that they had done very well (in the upper 10 percent), and others were told that they had scored very poorly (in the bottom 10 percent). The subjects were then told to wait in another room for a different experimenter to arrive but that if, after waiting for five minutes, the experimenter did not arrive, they should leave. For some subjects, the other room had a mirror and a television camera pointed at them, which, of course, induced self-awareness. Others went to a room that had no mirror or camera. According to self-awareness theory, the subjects who were not made self-focused by the mirror and camera should not have wanted to escape; they didn't need to think about themselves or their performance. But the situation was different for subjects who *were* made self-aware. Those who had scored at the top on the cleverness scale should not have minded being self-aware since they would have felt that they had done well in meeting ideal standards. The subjects who scored poorly, however, should have felt extremely unpleasant when they were self-aware and would have compared their performance with ideal standards; they should have wanted to get out of the situation, to escape. And they did! Subjects in the low-performance/self-aware condition stopped waiting for the absent experimenter and left significantly sooner than subjects in the other three conditions (Duval, Wicklund, & Fine, in Duval & Wicklund, 1972).

Although people typically avoid self-focused attention, several studies indicate that there are exceptions. If we expect to compare well to standards and to achieve a desired identity, we may welcome self-focused attention; we may even seek it out (Greenberg & Musham, 1981).

Matching to Standards   Sometimes people cannot run away from self-awareness; escape is impossible. What typically happens here is that people try to change their behavior so that it more nearly meets ideal standards. These attempts are referred to as matching to standards (Carver & Scheier, 1981; Mullen, 1983). However, whether or not people attempt to match to standards is influenced by their sense of whether they will be successful, their *outcome expectancy*. If people have a positive outcome expectancy, if they think they will succeed in matching to standards, they will attempt to do so. This process is called *self-regulation*. For example, people who are self-aware are more likely to be helpful. In one study, subjects who had seen a videotape about a venereal disease epidemic and were made self-aware were more likely to volunteer their services in a prevention program than control-group subjects. The self-aware group attempted to match to social responsibility standards (Duval, Duval, & Neely, 1979). Another interesting instance of self-regulation occurred in a study of Halloween trick or treaters (Beaman, Klentz, Diener, & Svanum, 1979). The trick or treaters were told by the owner of a house (actually an experimenter) not to take more than one piece of candy. The candy was put in a bowl and the children were left alone to take what they wanted. Self-awareness was created with a mirror behind the candy bowl. The results showed that without the mirror, well over half the children took more than one piece of candy. But when the mirror stood behind the bowl and the children watched themselves taking candy, the cheating (taking more than one piece of candy) dropped to less than 10 percent. In general, when people are made self-aware, their efforts to match to standards lead them to perform socially desirable behavior that matches to social standards.

There are other interesting instances of self-regulation. For example, self-aware individuals are more likely to behave according to their own personal values. College women who were either high or low on guilt about sex were required to read pornographic passages and to rate how much they enjoyed them. Some of the subjects were made self-aware when participating in the experiment and some were not. For self-aware subjects, there was a much higher correlation between sex-guilt scores and dislike of the passages. That is, when made self-aware, the subjects thought about the extent to which they had negative feelings about sex and reacted to the pornography accordingly (Gibbons, 1978).

While self-regulation or matching to standards is a common response to self-awareness or self-focused attention, people will not self-regulate if they have a low outcome expectancy. If they *expect to fail*, they will simply demonstrate *withdrawal*, a breakdown of normal self-regulation and matching to standards.

A Self-Attention Perspective on Group Behavior   We noted earlier that having a minority status in a group can generate self-awareness (Wicklund & Frey, 1980). A recent theory has taken this insight and considered the consequences of being self-attentive in a group setting (Mullen, 1983, 1987). The application of self-attention theory to groups holds that self-attention and matching to standards increases in a group as the individual and his or her subgroup become outnumbered by people belonging to another subgroup. For example, when performing in a play, Meryl Streep will tend to become more self-attentive as the size of the audience (the other subgroup) increases but less self-attentive as the size of the cast (her own subgroup) increases. More specifically, self-attention is proportional to what is known as the *Other-Total ratio*. In Meryl Streep's case, this ratio translates to the number of people in the audience (Other subgroup) divided by the Total number of people in the group—both cast and audience. Mullen (1983) has shown that self-attention and self-regulation increase precisely according to increases in the Other-Total ratio. Stated simply, the more you feel that you or your group is outnumbered, the more self-attentive you become.

A number of interesting studies demonstrate this effect. For example, in classrooms students are more likely to participate in discussions (matching standards for classroom behavior) as the ratio of teachers (Other subgroup) to the teacher plus student Total increases. As the number of students increases and the above ratio decreases, students spend less time participating. Similarly, reports of lynchings in the South show that when the lynching mob is large, the atrocity of the lynching, as measured by shooting, burning, dismembering the victim, and so on increases. Engaging in these kinds of behaviors represents an absence of self-regulation, which is what self-awareness theory predicts will occur when self-attention is low. When mob members vastly outnumber victims, the Other-Total ratio (number of victims divided by number of victims plus mob members) is low and the predicted absence of self-regulation occurs (Mullen, 1986).

Self-awareness theory is like a theory of the superego or conscience in that people who constitute a majority in a group have a low Other-Total ratio, are less self-aware, and show less evidence of being regulated by a conscience. Individuals in a large mob provide an excellent example of lack of self-regulation. Fortunately, self-awareness is generally a civilizing state (Wicklund & Frey, 1980).

The Effects of Public Self-Consciousness   We just saw some of the situational factors that can make people self-aware or self-conscious, for example, mirrors, television cameras, or being outnumbered by people belonging to a different subgroup. However, situational factors are not the only ones that affect self-awareness. Some individuals have greater tendencies to be self-aware than others. Research has shown that people differ in both *private self-consciousness* and *public self-consciousness* (Fenigstein, Scheier, & Buss, 1975). Items from the self-consciousness scale are shown in Table 4–1. Answer the questions and see how *you* score on them. People who are high on private self-consciousness tend to be more aware of their own internal states and feelings and their own attitudes and opinions. People who are high on public self-consciousness are more aware of themselves as social objects and are very concerned with their appearance and how other people perceive them. The second group is interesting in terms of self-presentation because their concern with making a good impression, with audience pleasing, can lead them to change their behavior to conform to other people's attitudes and expectations (Froming & Carver, 1981; Scheier, 1980).

People who are high on public self-consciousness tend to be more interested in clothing and fashion; this difference between high and low

---

Table 4–1
Private self-consciousness and public self-consciousness

Items measuring private self-consciousness:

I reflect about myself a lot.
I'm generally attentive to my inner feelings.
I'm constantly examining my motives.
I'm alert to changes in my mood.
I'm aware of the way my mind works when I work through a problem.

Items measuring public self-consciousness:

I'm concerned about what other people think of me.
I usually worry about making a good impression.
I'm concerned about the way I present myself.
I'm usually aware of my appearance.
One of the last things I do before leaving my house is look in the mirror.

Source: From Arnold H. Buss, *Self-Consciousness and Social Anxiety.* Copyright © 1980, W. H. Freeman. Used by permission.

People who are high on public self-consciousness are interested in pleasing their audiences. They are also concerned with their appearance and the ways others perceive them. *(© Joel Gordon 1984)*

individuals is especially marked among men (Solomon & Schopler, 1982). Perhaps the degree of difference here is due to the fact that women are *typically* interested in fashion, regardless of their degree of public self-consciousness, a phenomenon that does not hold for men. High public self-consciousness individuals are also more sensitive to others in that they can predict how others will react to them (Tobey & Tunnel, 1981). One study of public self-consciousness clearly shows how sensitive people who are high on this characteristic can be to other people's reactions to them. Subjects had to wait for an experiment to begin with two confederates posing as fellow subjects who talked to each other and ignored the subject. Shortly thereafter, the subjects had a chance to indicate whether they wanted to work with the pair they had waited with or another pair. How did the subjects react to being ignored? Those who were low on public self-consciousness chose to work with another pair 50 percent of the time. Those who were high on public self-consciousness chose to work with another pair 85 percent of the time: These subjects were very concerned with their shabby treatment by the two confederates (Fenigstein, 1979).

It is important to remember that people can become self-aware either as a result of situational factors such as mirrors or voice recordings or as a result of personal factors such as a high degree of public or private self-consciousness. A study of juror behavior in mock trials shows that individuals who are low in public self-consciousness behave much like high self-consciousness jurors when they are in the presence of a television camera (Kassin, 1985).

SELF-MONITORING

In addition to self-consciousness, there is another personality difference that has important implications for the way people present themselves. Individuals differ greatly in the extent to which they engage in self-monitoring (Snyder, 1974, 1979). *Self-monitoring* is adjusting your own behavior to situational norms or to the expectations of others. It entails controlling both your verbal and nonverbal self-presentation so that you can respond to those expectations. Being a high self-monitor is similar to being high in public self-consciousness, but self-monitoring is more complete. People who are high on public self-consciousness are concerned about and aware of how others react to them. The high self-monitoring individual is more marked by actively and effectively changing his or her behavior to adjust to others' reactions and expectations.

Snyder has developed a scale to measure the extent to which people self-monitor. It contains items such as "I may deceive people by being friendly when I really dislike them"; and "When I am uncertain how to act in social situations, I look at the behavior of others for clues." (See Table 4–2 for other self-monitoring scale items.) High self-monitors have been shown to have the following characteristics: (1) a concern for the appropriateness of behavior; (2) giving careful attention to others for cues as to what is appropriate; (3) skill in presenting many different behaviors in different situations; and (4) the ability to change the manner of self-presentation (Gabrenya & Arkin, 1980). In short, high self-monitors are interested in adapting to the situation, they are skillful in sensing others' wishes and expectations, and they are able to modify

---

Table 4–2
Sample items measuring self-monitoring

Answer the following items, true or false.

1. I find it hard to imitate the behavior of other people.   T F
2. In a group of people, I am rarely the center of attention.   T F
3. I may deceive people by being friendly when I really dislike them.   T F
4. I can only argue for ideas which I already believe.   T F
5. I can make impromptu speeches even on topics about which I have almost no information.   T F
6. I am not always the person I appear to be.   T F
7. In different situations and with different people, I often act like very different persons.   T F

Source: Adapted from Snyder (1974).

---

their behavior to meet others' expectations. One interesting example of adapting behavior to the situation is shown in a study where subjects either did or did not anticipate future interaction with a fellow subject. When they anticipated future interaction, high self-monitors were more cooperative than when they didn't. Low self-monitors were equally cooperative whether they anticipated future interaction or not (Danheiser & Graziano, 1982).

As implied above, low self-monitors are marked by consistency in behavior across situations. They have a clearer self-image and are truer to that self-image than high self-monitors. They are more likely to enter situations that are consistent with their self-image and they behave in ways that are consistent with their attitudes (Snyder & Gangestad, 1982). For example, in one study, low self-monitors supported a woman suing a university for sex discrimination to a degree that was predictable from their attitudes about affirmative action. The support of high self-monitors was not consistent with their affirmative action attitudes (Snyder & Swann, 1976). High self-monitors show their adaptability and flexibility regarding consistency by acting in accordance with their attitude more often in a situation where the importance of being consistent is made salient (Snyder & Kendzierski, 1982). That is, they can demonstrate the consistency of low self-monitors if that's what's expected.

There are some interesting differences between the ways high and low self-monitors process social information. High self-monitors remember more information about other people and make more confident and extreme inferences about them (Berscheid, Graziano, Monson, & Dermer, 1976). Highs also attribute their behavior primarily to the environment since they are aware of how much they respond to the expectations of different situations. Lows attribute their behavior more to internal factors, that is, their own character (Snyder, 1976). These attributions make sense in light of the situational variability in the behavior of high self-monitors and the consistency of the behavior of low self-monitors.

Finally, a field study of people in organizations shows that high self-monitoring individuals function better in what are known as boundary-spanning positions. Boundary spanning means working at the intersection between organizations or with people in several different organizations outside one's own. Such behavior requires flexibility and being open to other people's desires and expectations. This is where the high self-monitor excels.

Nearly a century ago, William James (1890) wrote about the many different social selves an individual shows to different audiences: "Many a youth who is demure enough before his parents and teachers, swears and swaggers like a pirate among his 'tough' friends. We do not show ourselves to our children as to our club-companions, to our customers as to the laborers we employ, to our own masters and employers as to our intimate friends" (p. 282). The kind of variability in behavior that James suggests is truer for some individuals than others. The high self-monitor has the ability and inclination to behave differently with different people in different situations. Low self-monitors are on a straighter track: they know who they are and they act that way without being unduly influenced by the social situation.

NONVERBAL COMMUNICATION

In his book on the presentation of self in everyday life, Erving Goffman (1959) noted that self-presentation involves both verbal and nonverbal behavior. He distinguished expression "given," or verbal expression, from expression "given off," or nonverbal expression, and he suggested that the latter is less controllable than the former. Nonverbal behavior or expression is especially powerful in conveying emotion, and because it is less controllable, it conveys our true feelings even when we wish we could hide them. The feelings that nonverbal behavior expresses are shown with unusual power in one of Meryl Streep's most stirring roles: Sophie in *Sophie's Choice*. In the climactic scene, Sophie is ordered by a guard at a Nazi concentration camp to choose which of her two children will be sent to immediate death and which will survive. The horror of the situation and the emotional wrenching it causes are portrayed with genius. Meryl Streep must control her nonverbal expressions to make it look like Sophie's feelings are spilling out despite her attempts to contain them. It's a stunning performance.

Nonverbal behavior communicates a great deal of information about feelings, moods, and attitudes. Information about these internal states comes from voice quality, eye contact, facial expressions, gestures, body movements, and touching (Brown, 1986). Nonverbal expression is often called the language of emotion and many studies report that verbal behavior, by comparison, contributes relatively little to our inferences about a person's feelings (e.g., Archer & Akert, 1977). Brown (1986) has pointed out, however, that words certainly can convey a lot of what we feel. Meryl Streep's moving courtroom speech in *Kramer vs. Kramer* in which she describes the difficulty of holding her life together shows the power of words to convey feelings. Nonetheless, nonverbal behavior communicates feelings with great force.

Some Elements of Nonverbal Communication   As noted above, there are many nonverbal behaviors that communicate. We will now briefly consider the significance of several of these behaviors. We shall discuss gaze, which is often referred to as eye contact, facial expression, and gestures and body movements.

The effects of gaze. The way we look at a person says a great deal about our feelings, and it can significantly affect the quality of social interaction. People in love spend a lot of time looking at each other (Rubin, 1970) and looking at another person generally conveys positive feelings and leads to positive reactions (Imada & Hakel, 1977). In addition, gaze is associated with status. Lower status people tend to gaze more at upper status people (Exline, Ellyson, & Long, 1975). One important exception here is staring or *visual dominance behavior.* Staring or looking at someone while speaking is assertive, dominating behavior. It can be an effective aspect of leadership behavior (Exline et al., 1975). But staring can also generate uncomfortable feelings (Strom & Buck, 1979). In short, looking into someone's eyes can convey extremely warm feelings, but *staring* conveys feelings of dominance. Thus, high degrees of eye contact can intensify any feeling, positive or negative (Ellsworth & Carlsmith, 1968).

Facial expressions. Scientists have been studying facial expression for more than a century. In 1872, Charles Darwin argued in *The Expression of the Emotions in Man and Animals* that particular facial expressions may convey the same emotions in all human societies and in animals as well as people. Recent research provides support for the idea that the same facial expressions are distinguished across cultures and that people in one culture can identify the videotaped emotions of a person in a culture with

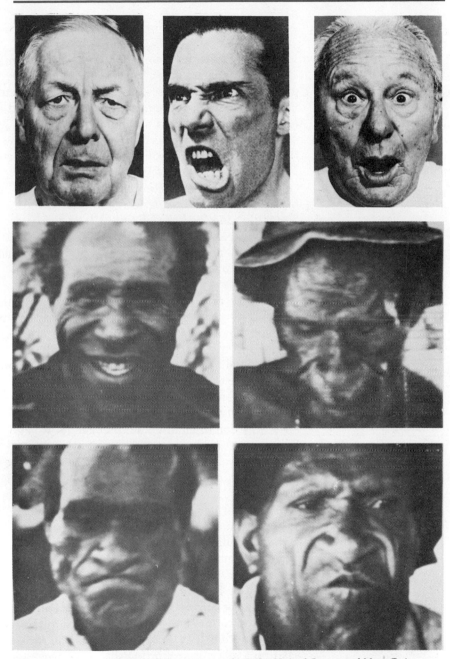

Above are some of the photos shown to people in the United States and New Guinea. People in one society were able to accurately identify the emotions of people in the other. These results suggest that there may be universal emotions and universal ways of expressing them. *(Copyright Dr. Paul Ekman. From Friesen, W. V., and Ekman, P., Pictures of facial affect. [1970]. Palo Alto, CA: Consulting Psychologist Press.)*

which they have had no visual contact (Ekman, Friesen, & Ellsworth, 1982). Six separate emotions can be reliably identified: fear, anger, disgust, happiness, sadness, and surprise. For example, members of the Fore society in New Guinea who had never had contact with the Western media and had had almost no contact with any white people were shown pictures of westerners expressing these six emotions: they made the same judgments about the feelings as subjects in the United States. Then the expressions of the New Guinea subjects in various hypothetical situations such as "Your child has died and you are sad" were videotaped and shown to American subjects. The American subjects, in turn, generally identified the emotions being expressed accurately. In short, the face expresses the same emotions in different cultures and the emotions felt by people in one culture can be identified via facial expression by those in another.

Gestures and body movements. Even though there appears to be some universality in human emotions and their nonverbal expressions, social psychologists recognize that there are also marked cultural differences in the expression of emotions. Ekman and Friesen (1969) have discussed different *display rules* or norms about what emotions are appropriate to express in different situations in different cultures. One interesting study of the way feelings are expressed in different cultures showed that people looking at silent films of Mayor Fiorello LaGuardia of New York could tell in what language he was giving a speech—English, Italian, or Yiddish—because of the typical gesturing pattern that is associated with speaking in each of those languages (Birdwhistell, 1952). What are some of the feelings expressed through gestures and body movements in Western culture?

Some gestures are referred to as *emblems* (Johnson, Ekman, & Friesen, 1975): they are commonly used in a particular culture or group to express certain feelings or ideas. In our culture, waves convey a warm greeting and a thumbs up gesture conveys happiness. Other hand gestures, euphemistically termed *uncomplimentary*, convey aggressive contempt; you may be familiar with some of them. Body movements convey not only how positively we feel about someone else, but also how much relative power or status we feel we have in the relationship. People who like each other lean toward one another, face each other directly, and assume a relaxed position. Dislike is conveyed by leaning away, looking away, and visible tenseness. High status or dominance is conveyed by relaxing and leaning back; low status is shown by physical rigidity—arms drawn in, feet together, and standing or sitting straight, more less as if at attention (Mehrabian, 1972).

Deception and Detection   Earlier in this chapter, we noted that self-presentation and ingratiation can be somewhat demeaning. Ingratiation, for example, may involve flattering someone when you don't mean it, or pretending to agree with his or her opinions. Goffman (1959) recognized the exaggerated or downright deceitful side of self-presentation and suggested that people constantly try to check up on others' self-presentations by observing whether the less controllable aspects of self-presentation, the nonverbal, are congruent with what is being said. In recent years, a good deal of research has been done on the nonverbal aspects of deception and its detection (Zuckerman, DePaulo, & Rosenthal, 1981).

Central to this research are studies that deal with nonverbal sensitivity (Hall, 1984; Rosenthal & Benowitz, 1985). These studies show that in making judgments about people's emotions from videotaped nonverbal behavior, with voice quality but not actual words preserved, viewers come to the most accurate conclusions when they pay attention to those aspects or *channels* of nonverbal behavior that are the most controllable.

One of the sex differences in nonverbal behavior is the tendency of women to gaze at men while men speak. Men are less likely to give women this degree of attention.

The most controllable *nonverbal* channel is facial expression, which is followed by body movement; the least controllable is voice quality. Words, that is, *verbal* expressions, are the most controllable channel and, if added to the videotapes, convey the most information as long as they are congruent or consistent with the nonverbal behaviors and the nonverbal behaviors are congruent with each other (Blanck & Rosenthal, 1982).

The nonverbal behaviors that are the *least* controllable, voice quality and body movement, have the most "leakage"; that is, they reveal or leak the individual's real feelings, feelings that he or she may be trying to conceal. Therefore, these are the behaviors that are important to note in attempting to detect deception. One can construct a controllability-leakage continuum, with controllable behaviors on one end and uncontrollable leaky behaviors on the other (Brown, 1986; Ekman & Friesen, 1969; see Figure 4–1). As noted above, when the various verbal and nonverbal channels of expression are congruent, the controllable behaviors generally convey the most precise information. Thus, when we are being truthful, words followed by facial expression say the most about our feelings. However, when one person is deceiving another, incongruent messages are likely to be coming through the other channels. This incongruity can alert the target to the deception. Or the person toward whom deception is aimed may be alerted by specific cues associated with deception such as slow speech, speech slips, and avoidance of eye contact (Zuckerman et al., 1981).

When deception is occurring, it is the leakier rather than the more controllable nonverbal channels that are apt to be most informative, and those are the channels to which people look when trying to detect the deceiver's real thoughts or feelings. Parents can often tell, for example, if their child is lying about a mess in the kitchen by paying attention to voice quality and body movement, as those channels can leak the truth

Figure 4–1
The controllability-leakage continuum

Controllable channels of communication
> **Verbal Expression, Words**
> **Facial Expression**
> **Body Movement**
> **Voice Quality**

Leaky channels of communication

Note: The communication channels at the top of this list are relatively controllable. The ones at the bottom are relatively leaky.
Source: Adapted with permission of The Free Press, a division of Macmillan, Inc., from *Social Psychology*, 2nd edition, by Roger Brown. Copyright © 1986 by The Free Press.

and disconfirm the child's denial. Thus, when deception is being practiced, the controllable and generally informative verbal and facial expressions must be taken with a grain of salt. Although the less controllable channels, voice quality and body movement, are less precise and informative when they are congruent with the other channels, because they leak what is being hidden, they are crucial in detecting deception.

Gender Differences in Nonverbal Communication   Throughout the history of research on nonverbal communication, a number of gender differences have been observed. Since these differences are important in helping us to understand the ways in which men and women differ and the relationships between the sexes, we will consider them here.

Gender differences in nonverbal behavior. One difference between men and women is that their nonverbal behaviors are not the same (Henley, 1977). Women typically gaze when someone else is speaking, especially a man while men typically do not look at women speaking. Women are generally apt to be more tense and formal in their posture and demeanor while men are generally relaxed and informal in these areas. Women are more likely to smile. Henley (1977) has argued that these differences between men and women are associated with the high-status, high-power position of men in our society and the lower status and power of women. Men's nonverbal behaviors are those that are performed by people and animals with power. Women's nonverbal behaviors are those of the submissive. Henley argues that by engaging in these inconspicuous, small behaviors many times each day, the power difference between men and women is maintained. For example, although women may behave ingratiatingly, their behavior is so clearly a product of the power difference that it reinforces that difference.

Another particularly pervasive difference between men and women has to do with touching. Men touch but do not generally like being touched (Whitcher & Fisher, 1979). Women generally respond positively to touch, but do not usually initiate touching. In short, in day-to-day interactions, men touch women but women do not touch men (Henley, 1977; Major, 1981). In noting that men assert the right to touch and women acknowledge that right but do not claim it for themselves, we see another example of differences in nonverbal behavior that perpetuate power differences between the sexes.

Gender differences in expressiveness and sensitivity. The difference between men and women in nonverbal expressiveness and sensitivity can be stated succinctly: women are superior both in accurately sending and in understanding nonverbal communication (Hall, 1984; Mayo &

A person with a friendly-dominant style of interpersonal behavior is likely to lead others in a relaxed and friendly manner. (© *John Maher 1980/EKM — Nepenthe*)

Henley, 1981; Rosenthal & Benowitz, 1985). Some recent research suggests that women's superiority in conveying nonverbal messages may, in fact, be related more to the masculinity versus femininity phenomenon than to their actual gender. The term *masculinity* versus *femininity* refers to people's psychological tendencies (measured by a questionnaire) to behave in either a typically masculine or typically feminine manner. Subjects higher on femininity, whether male or female, were superior in using both facial expressions and tone of voice to convey their feelings (Zuckerman, Amidon, Bishop, & Pomerantz, 1982). Women's superiority in understanding nonverbal communication is especially evident in their ability to identify negative feelings. This heightened ability may be a function of women being in a less powerful position than men and thus developing more sensitivity to the leakage of negative feelings (Brown, 1986).

Nonverbal communication of feelings, whether regarding affection, dominance, or temporary moods, is important in relationships. Research has shown that such communication is important in marriage, an obviously special relationship between a man and a woman. One study showed that the nonverbal skill of the wife, both in conveying and interpreting nonverbal information, was significantly related to marital satisfaction (Sabatelli, Buck, & Dreyer, 1983). Another study showed again that women's nonverbal skills were superior to men's and that both the husbands' and wives' ability to communicate with each other nonverbally was related to marital adjustment (Noller, 1980). Nonverbal communication is an important element of both self-presentation and mutual understanding. Its subtlety and pervasiveness makes it a subject worthy of continued research.

CLASSIFICATIONS OF INTERPERSONAL BEHAVIORS AND STYLES

Goffman (1955) noted that during self-presentation an individual acts out a line, a total pattern of verbal and nonverbal expression that conveys his or her definition of the situation, other people in the situation, and him- or herself. It might seem that there is an endless set of lines that different people could enact and that the varieties of interpersonal behavior would be infinite. Certainly, if you imagine how different people are, or even the wide range of characters and styles of interpersonal behavior that Meryl Streep has acted out in her film career, you are impressed with the great variety in human behavior. However, psychologists who have studied the varieties and classifications of interpersonal behavior have found that they fall into a surprisingly small number of categories (Bales, 1958; Carson, 1969; Leary, 1957).

Leary's research showed that if the correlations between diverse sets of ratings of interpersonal behavior were subjected to factor analysis (a statistical technique for determining the basic dimensions that describe the ratings) that the basic dimensions numbered only two. One was a positive versus negative or friendly versus hostile dimension and the other a dominant versus submissive dimension. That is, even though people can be rated along numerous different scales, many of the ratings correlated with each other. There seemed to be only two basic sets of correlations, one indicating that behavior was classified according to how friendly or hostile it was and the other indicating that it was classified according to how dominant or submissive it was. From these findings, Leary developed the *circumplex*, the depiction of the varieties of interpersonal behavior shown in Figure 4–2. Each variety differs from others in terms of how friendly it is—anywhere from very friendly to very hostile— and how dominant or submissive it is—from highly dominant through partly dominant and partly submissive to highly submissive.

Since people tend to behave consistently within and to some extent across situations, we can talk about interpersonal styles in terms of whether people's characteristic interpersonal behaviors are of the friendly versus unfriendly variety and of the dominant versus submissive variety.

Figure 4–2
Leary Interpersonal Behavior Classification System

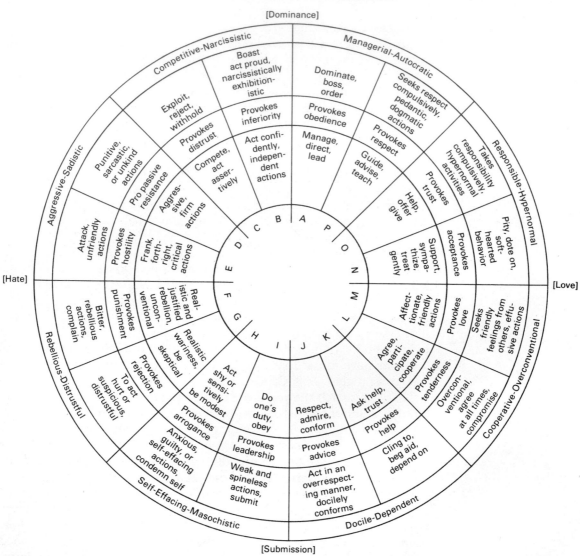

Leary Interpersonal Behavior Classification System

Classification of Interpersonal Behavior into Sixteen Mechanisms or Reflexes. Each of the sixteen interpersonal variables is illustrated by sample behaviors. The inner circle presents illustrations of adaptive reflexes, e.g., for the variable *A*, *manage*. The center ring indicates the type of behavior that this interpersonal reflex tends to "pull" from the other one. Thus we see that the person who uses the reflex *A* tends to provoke others to *obedience*, etc. These findings involve two-way interpersonal phenomena (what the subject does and what the "Other" does back) and are therefore less reliable than the other interpersonal codes presented in this figure. The next circle illustrates extreme or rigid reflexes, e.g., *dominates*. The perimeter of the circle is divided into eight general categories employed in *interpersonal diagnosis*. Each category has a moderate (adaptive) and an extreme (pathological) intensity, e.g., *Managerial-Autocratic.*

On stage or in front of the camera, Meryl Streep can adopt any interpersonal style. Off camera, however, her style seems friendly but not exceptionally dominant, though it is certainly not submissive: she can be assertive and has thus held leadership positions, but she is not domineering.

Research on interpersonal behavior in groups working on tasks and trying to resolve problems indicates that there is a third important dimension of interpersonal behavior that occurs in those group settings (Bales, 1970). People can be classified as task and authority oriented (forward) or as rebellious and oriented away from tasks and toward emotional involvement and fantasy (backward). Thus, people can be described as friendly, neutral, or unfriendly; as dominant, submissive, or in between; and as task oriented, feeling oriented, or in between. One person may be what Bales calls an upward-positive type (UP), someone who is dominant and friendly but in the middle on task orientation, while another person might be downward, positive, and forward (DPF), which means submissive, friendly, and task oriented. Since people can be high, moderate, or low on all three dimensions, there are twenty-seven possible types, including the average type who is in the middle on all three dimensions. These types are listed in Table 4–3.

Table 4–3
Bales's twenty-seven types

Average	Negative
Upward	Negative-backward
Upward-positive	Backward
Upward-positive-forward	Positive-backward
Upward-forward	Downward-positive
Upward-negative-forward	Downward-positive-forward
Upward-negative	Downward-forward
Upward-negative-backward	Downward-negative-forward
Upward-backward	Downward-negative
Upward-positive-backward	Downward-negative-backward
Positive	Downward-backward
Positive-forward	Downward-positive-backward
Forward	Backward
Negative-forward	

Upward = dominant; downward = submissive; positive = friendly; negative = unfriendly; forward = task oriented; backward = emotion oriented.

Source: From *Personality and Interpersonal Behavior* by Robert Freed Bales. Copyright © 1970 by Holt, Rinehart & Winston, Inc. Reprinted by permission of Holt, Rinehart & Winston, Inc.

Bales terms these types *group roles* rather than *interpersonal styles*. The difference between the two terms is that interpersonal style implies a characteristic mode of behavior that is largely a function of internal personality dispositions, while group role recognizes that a person's behavior in a group is affected by the situation and other people as well as by his or her personality. For example, Meryl Streep may be consistently friendly and warm regardless of the situation or who's in it, but she may be quite variable in whether she is dominant or submissive in different situations. In one group, her role may be upward-positive (UP) while in another it may simply be positive (P). In general, people's friendliness is probably consistent across situations but their power and dominance can vary considerably as can their degree of task orientation.

The idea of interpersonal styles is helpful in understanding the different lines that people act out in self-presentation. Although there are many different kinds of lines, all of them can be classified according to one of the interpersonal styles. Thus, in acting out a line a person behaves in a way that is—both verbally and nonverbally—to some degree friendly or hostile and to some degree dominant or submissive. In this way the person conveys what she thinks of herself and how she feels about her relationship to the other person. By acting friendly, she indicates that she sees the relationship as a friendly one. By acting submissive, she indicates that she sees the relationship as one of unequal status in which the other person is dominant. The two basic dimensions of a relationship are whether it is characterized by friendliness, warmth, and "solidarity," and whether it is one of equal or unequal status (Brown, 1965). These two dimensions are essentially the same as the friendliness and dominance dimensions of interpersonal behavior. The quality of interpersonal behavior that we enact in our lines conveys how we see the quality of our relationship with the other person.

Finally, it should be pointed out that interpersonal behavior can be classified according to Leary's circumplex or Bales's types because those are the ways that observers categorize behavior. In reality, interpersonal behavior is extremely varied, just as we thought at the beginning of this section. However, as perceivers and interactors, we impose order on behavior and classify people ourselves. Thus, the classifications reflect our own perceptions and categorizations rather than divinely given sets of behaviors or styles.

SELF-DISCLOSURE

Self-presentation, especially of the audience-pleasing variety, has a somewhat distasteful quality. It is pervasive, but as we saw when we

Self-disclosure involves talking about private matters. When we self-disclose we tell about our dreams and aspirations and our anxieties and fears. *(© Henry C. Esatwood/ Southern Light)*

discussed the autistic conspiracy earlier in the chapter, no one likes to admit that it happens. We can distinguish audience pleasing from self-construction (Baumeister, 1982; Baumeister & Hutton, 1987) and realize that sometimes when we present ourselves we are being true to the person we would like to be and hope we are, and that at such times we would like the other person to accept that definition of who we are. One of the kinds of behavior involved in self-construction is *self-disclosure.*

Self-disclosure can be defined as talking to another person about private matters, for example, your needs, values, attitudes, background, worries, and aspirations (Archer, 1980). Several items from a scale measuring self-disclosure are shown in Table 4–4 in which people are asked to indicate how much they have talked to their parents, their male and female friends, and their spouses about each topic.

People generally find self-disclosure highly rewarding: it offers the possibility of both self-construction and self-realization. It also often leads to intimacy with the person to whom we disclose (Jourard, 1971; Rubin & Schlenker, 1978). In intimate relationships, including marriage, mutual self-disclosure enhances the quality of the relationship (Hendrick, 1981). One important determinant of self-disclosure is *reciprocity* (Cohn & Strassberg, 1983; Cozby, 1972). The more someone discloses to us, the more we disclose to him or her. We don't always like a person who discloses a great deal to us—sometimes it's too much too soon—but even here we follow the reciprocity principle and disclose more in return (Kleinke & Kahn, 1980). We might not match the other's degree of self-disclosure exactly if it doesn't seem appropriate to do so in the situation; instead, we will compromise between the reciprocity principle and a desire to follow the situational norms for appropriate self-disclosure.

Table 4–4
Sample items from Jourard's Self-Disclosure Questionnaire

Instructions: The answer sheet you have been given has columns with the headings "Mother," "Father," "Male Friend," "Female Friend," and "Spouse." You are to read each item on the questionnaire and then indicate on the answer sheet the extent that you have talked about that item to each person; that is, the extent that you have made yourself known to that person. Use the rating scale that you see on the answer sheet to describe the extent that you have talked about each item.

1. My personal views on sexual morality—how I feel that I and others ought to behave in sexual matters.
2. What I would appreciate most for a present.
3. What I enjoy most, and get the most satisfaction from in my present work.
4. How I really feel about the people that I work for, or work with.
5. All of my present sources of income—wages, fees, allowance, dividends, etc.
6. The facts of my present sex life—including knowledge of how I get sexual gratification; any problems that I might have; with whom I have relations, if anybody.
7. Things in the past or present that I feel guilty or ashamed and guilty about.
8. My present physical measurements, for example, height, weight, waist, etc.

Source: From S. M. Jourard, *The Transparent Self*, 1971. New York: Van Nostrand Reinhold. Reprinted by permission.

If mutual self-disclosure often leads to intimacy but sometimes, if it happens too soon, produces negative reactions, what *is* the right amount at the right time? We prefer people who warm up to us slowly in that their self-disclosures come at the end of a conversation (Jones & Gordon, 1972; Jones & Archer, 1976). One exception to this rule is that we like being told very early in our interaction with someone about a negative event for which that person was responsible (Archer & Burleson, 1980): this seems to clear the air and lead to greater liking. Also, we like it when someone who is ordinarily reserved opens up to us and discloses something that seems to signify that he or she feels unusually open with us (Taylor, Gould, & Brounstein, 1981).

Research on self-disclosure shows consistent differences between men and women in the degree of self-disclosure and our reactions to self-disclosures from men and women. Women generally disclose more than men, especially about relationships and other personal matters (Cozby, 1972; Davidson & Duberman, 1982). This may be changing, but recent research shows that men are still evaluated more negatively than women for personal self-disclosure, perhaps because men see disclosing as a sign of weakness (Cunningham, 1981). If this is the case, no wonder men don't self-disclose as much! Jourard (1971) has argued that men's lack of self-disclosure, their tendency to hold everything in, adds stress to their lives. Henley (1977) has argued that men only disclose to women with whom they are intimate, which puts the woman in the position of being an "emotional service station." She argues that such a pattern is not good for either men or women. Given the satisfaction that comes from intimate self-disclosure, it seems regrettable that it should be so difficult for men to take part in it.

SUMMARY

Erving Goffman argued that self-presentation is pervasive in everyday life because we try to control other people's impressions of us by presenting ourselves positively. We do this by claiming face. When we claim face, other people generally go along with our claim to form a working consensus that facilitates efficient social interaction. We try to support each other's faces by preventing or ignoring embarrassments or explaining them in a positive way. These mutually supportive behaviors are called face work.

Jones's theory of ingratiation and strategic self-presentation holds that we ingratiate, or try to get other people to like us, to enhance our power in a relationship. We must do this subtly to avoid alerting the other person to our attempts to ingratiate. We can ingratiate by conforming, flattering the other person, or presenting ourselves positively. Besides ingratiation, other self-presentation strategies include intimidation, self-promotion, exemplification, and supplication.

Sometimes individuals put obstacles to successful performance in their own way. This behavior is known as self-handicapping. Self-handicapping is most likely to happen when people are unsure of their abilities in an area. They self-handicap so that they can have an excuse for failure and so that failure cannot be attributed to low ability.

When people are not self-aware, their behavior is generally fairly routine and automatic. People can be made self-aware by a variety of external stimuli such as tape recordings of their own voices and mirrors. Self-aware people compare their behavior with ideal standards and generally find themselves falling short. Therefore, self-awareness is usually unpleasant and people will escape it if they can. If they cannot escape, people will respond to self-awareness by attempting to match their behavior to salient standards. In a group, people become more self-attentive if there is a proportionally large number of people in subgroups *other than* their own. Some individuals are more self-aware than others. People who are high on public self-consciousness are especially concerned with how they appear to others and how others evaluate them.

People who are high self-monitors are extremely sensitive to other people's expectations and are skilled in modifying their behavior to respond to those expectations. Low self-monitors are consistent across situations and their behavior reflects their clear self-concept.

Nonverbal behaviors convey a great deal about our emotions and our feelings about others. Channels of nonverbal communication include gaze or eye contact, facial expression, body movements and gestures, touch, and voice quality. Much of our nonverbal communication conveys our liking for other people and our feelings of relative power or status in relation to them. Facial expression conveys six different emotions and the way people express these emotions—joy, sadness, anger, surprise, disgust, and fear—seems to be universal. Nonverbal channels vary along a controllability-leakage continuum, with facial expression the most controllable and voice quality the most leaky. Men and women differ in their nonverbal behaviors and abilities. In general, men assert their power in nonverbal behavior while women are submissive in theirs. Women are superior to men in conveying feelings nonverbally and in interpreting nonverbal communications.

Interpersonal behaviors can be classified along the dimensions of friendliness versus hostility and dominance versus submissiveness. Individuals' *interpersonal* styles vary along these same two dimensions; their *group* roles vary along these dimensions and a third, task orientation versus emotion orientation.

Self-disclosure is extremely rewarding and can lead to the forming of intimate relationships. While people generally like others who self-disclose, self-disclosure must be timed and limited carefully. Self-disclosure follows a reciprocity principle; that is, we generally disclose as much as others disclose, although we also observe norms about the appropriate degree of self-disclosure in different situations. Women disclose more than men. Men are evaluated less positively when they self-disclose.

KEY WORDS

audience pleasing	matching to standards
autistic conspiracy	nonverbal channels
circumplex	private self-consciousness
display rules	public self-consciousness
emblems	reciprocity
exemplification	self-awareness
idealized performance	self-construction
impression management	self-disclosure
ingratiation	self-handicapping
ingratiator's dilemma	self-monitoring
interpersonal style	self-promotion
intimidation	situated identity
leakage	supplication
line-face	veneer of consensus
face work	visual dominance behavior

SUGGESTED READINGS

Bales, R. F. (1970). *Personality and interpersonal behavior.* New York: Holt, Rinehart & Winston.

Chaikin, A. L., & Derlega, V. L. (1974). *Self-disclosure.* Morristown, NJ: General Learning Press.

Duval, S., & Wicklund, R. A. (1972). *A theory of objective self-awareness.* New York: Academic Press.

Ekman, P. (Ed.). (1982). *Emotion in the human face* (2nd ed.). Cambridge, England: Cambridge University Press.

Goffman, E. (1959). *The presentation of self in everyday life.* Garden City, NY: Doubleday Publishing.

Jones, E. E. (1964). *Ingratiation: A social psychological analysis.* New York: Appleton-Century-Crofts.

Schlenker, B. R. (1980). *Impression management: The self-concept, social identity, and interpersonal behavior.* Monterey, CA: Brooks/Cole Publishing.

Tedeschi, J. T. (Ed.). (1981). *Impression management theory and social psychological research.* New York: Academic Press.

FIVE

ATTITUDE AND ATTITUDE CHANGE

"After 87 years of going it eyeball-to-eyeball, the other guy just blinked," or so touted the newspaper ads. The advertiser? Pepsi-Cola. The "other guy"? Coca-Cola, of course. In a controversial change from Dr. John S. Pemberton's original ninety-nine-year-old "7X" formula, the Coca-Cola Company altered its recipe for Coke. The emergent preference for decaffeinated, sugar-free, and "natural" beverages (in keeping with America's obsession with fitness and health) had cut deeply into Coke's share of the market. Coke's response was to introduce a product that would appeal to a larger segment of the consuming public.

It was not that these two beverage giants were engaged in a new struggle: the race to be the biggest and the best has a long tradition in the soft-drink industry (Louis & Yazijian, 1980), just as it does in most businesses. Ever since its inception in 1898, Pepsi-Cola had been the thorn in Coca-Cola's side. This new turn signaled the Coca-Cola Company's growing awareness of how quickly Pepsi was catching up.

Within twenty-four hours of the announcement, Coke's advertising agency, McCann-Erickson, claimed that nearly two-thirds of the country had heard about the change—"a level of recognition," as *Newsweek* (Coke tampers, 1985) aptly noted, "that many national politicians spend a lifetime failing to achieve." Odd as it may seem, Coke was on everyone's mind. For several nights during the summer of 1985, the new "Cola Wars" was the lead story on all three network evening newscasts (rivaled only by Humphrey, the wayward whale, whose antics in California competed for coverage).

The announcement produced near hysteria among diehard Coke drinkers. Citizen action groups sprang up in response. In Seattle, one such group was the Old Cola Drinkers of America (OCDA), headed by "soft-drink activist" Gay Mullins, who spent $45,000 of his own money to produce "anti-New Coke" T-shirts and to set up an Old Coke hotline. By June 24, 1985, a month-and-a-half after the announcement, the hotline had claimed over sixty thousand protest calls. Reactions among afficionados of "The Real Thing" were varied. Some began stockpiling supplies of Old Coke; others began the arduous task of trying to get Coca-Cola to change its mind; and still others switched to Pepsi in protest, claiming that "Coke had ceased to exist" (Morgenthau, Smith, Josephs, & Leslie, 1985).

Meanwhile, the power brokers at Pepsi were contenting themselves with a not-so-minor victory over "The Giant." Apparently, Coke had succumbed to the fickle fortunes of the fast-paced marketplace. In an attempt to appeal to those who preferred the "taste of a new generation," Coca-Cola had inadvertently provided Pepsi with a marketing windfall. Not even Bill Cosby, New Coke's master of ceremonies, could convince Americans to accept the new product.

Old Coke versus New Coke: The battle for winning over public opinion to a new taste cost millions of dollars. But was it effective in changing attitudes or behaviors? (© Trune/Waldman 1986)

In May of 1985, following a remarkable 14 percent increase in sales, Pepsi dispatched a flurry of anti-Coke persuasion attempts that enlisted the talents of celebrity endorsers and high-tech graphics experts to take advantage of Coke's *faux pas*. In what has been referred to as an example of comedic genius in advertising, Pepsi declared all-out war on Coca-Cola. In referring to Coke's marketing strategy as the "Cola-of-the-Month Club," and by calling New Coke the "Edsel of the '80s," Pepsi sought to capitalize on Coke's vulnerability.

In mid-July, Coke had sufficiently regrouped its forces to mount a counterattack. In what was called by some a stroke of marketing genius and by others a backdoor, last-ditch attempt to polish its tarnished image, Coca-Cola responded by reintroducing the old Coke formula under the moniker of "Coca-Cola Classic." As it turned out, sales of the New Coke had not been all that bad, but the Coca-Cola Company decided that they could not afford to lose the support of their Old Coke clientele. The clamors of discord had won out over some of the best minds in consumer marketing (*Newsweek*, 1985c). America could now have its Coke and drink it too.

Was Coke's decision to change its formula a marketing nightmare or a well-planned advertising tour de force? We may never know for sure, but a number of results are clear from the so-called Coke two-step. Only rarely does a product receive so much free and widespread publicity. So extensive was the media hype surrounding the Coca-Cola move that by July of 1985 virtually every American had heard about the switch. If it had not been one before, Coke surely became a household word (but then so had Pepsi). And having two products (Coca-Cola Classic and New Coke) with which to compete with Pepsi-Cola, Coke could now please two segments of the market—young soft-drink consumers to whom Pepsi strongly appealed, and the stalwart Old Coke adherents.

Why did Coke raise all the fuss in the first place? They could have slipped New Coke onto the market quietly and without much ado; instead, they chose to make the switch a media event. Was this an unwise strategy? Why did marketing research steer Coke so far afield? Results from two hundred thousand taste tests had demonstrated to Coca-Cola's satisfaction that New Coke was preferred two to one over the old formula. Why were New Coke's celebrity endorsers unable to sell the product despite the fact that most people couldn't tell the difference between the two varieties? (Gay Mullins, head and founder of OCDA repeatedly failed to identify or prefer Old Coke in taste tests.) Was the image provided by Bill Cosby the wrong one to use? If so, who and what would have been better? (Some [*Newsweek*, 1985c] have suggested Walter Cronkite!) Did Coca-Cola tamper with something that to Middle America had come to symbolize, along with mom, baseball, the flag, and apple pie, the essence of America? Or was the problem something more subtle? We may never know the answers, but these generic questions are certainly some of the key questions in the social-psychological work on attitude and attitude change.

The year 1985 marked perhaps the major skirmish in the great cola wars. Each side pulled out all the stops in trying to persuade the public to like and buy its product. Appeals to facts, emotions, and images were all used. So too were humor, drama, and association with celebrities. How effective are such appeals? What have social psychologists been able to tell us about the attitude determinants and the process of attitude change? It is to these questions that the present chapter is addressed.

DEFINING THE ATTITUDE

What is an attitude? People have attitudes about a wide variety of items: presidential politics, Pepsi and Coke, our friends, our teachers, and so forth. Yet the precise definition of *attitude* has remained elusive. A friend of yours, Suzanne, may tell you that she *believes* that Coke is better than Pepsi. You may have every reason to think that you know Suzanne's attitude. But wait! She may then tell you that she *likes* Pepsi better. Amazed at this twist of events, you press her further. She tells you that, although Coke has won her taste test, her sentiments are with Pepsi. Which statement do you take as her attitude? Is she Pro-Pepsi or Pro-Coke? Before you decide, you should know that Suzanne is drinking an RC.

Put another way, your friend has a belief about cola drinks, a sentiment, and a behavior. Although there may be many occasions where these three indicators of an attitude are consistent, in this case they are not. Which one represents Suzanne's *true* attitude?

Not all social psychologists agree on a definition of the term *attitude*. Some view attitudes exclusively as sentiments, statements of feeling or affect. "I like Coca-Cola, I feel terrible about war," are examples of sentiment or affect statements. Others include beliefs in their definition. "War kills many people; President Reagan is the oldest man to serve as President; Coca-Cola is made with caffeine." And still others include behaviors as part of their definition. William McGuire (1985), in his extensive search of the attitude-change literature, reported that more than five hundred definitions of attitude have been used by social psychologists in their research on the subject.

Despite the plethora of definitions, most research has considered the sentiment, or affect, to be the most important attitude dimension. Therefore, we will adopt a definition of attitudes offered originally by Thurstone that will serve us well through this book.

> Attitudes: The intensity of positive or negative affect for or against a psychological object.

A "psychological object," in this definition, "is any symbol, person, phrase, slogan or idea toward which people can differ as regards positive or negative affect" (Thurstone, 1946, p. 39). That is, an attitude is one's liking or disliking for any object, person, idea, and so on.

MEASURING ATTITUDES

Imagine that the board of directors of PepsiCo has hired you in your capacity as a social psychologist to study the attitudes of college students toward the major cola alternatives. You recall that our definition of an attitude had us considering the sentiment or affect of people toward an attitude object. You will want to have students respond to questions such as "Do you like or dislike Pepsi Cola?" "How much do you like or dislike Pepsi Cola?" The first question assesses the *direction* of affect while the second measures its *intensity*. A good attitude scale will provide answers to both of these questions. Although investigators are free to create their own ways of asking questions about attitudes, some standard types of scales can be used.

One widely used measurement device is the Likert scale. In this technique, subjects are presented with a list of statements concerning the object of the attitude, for example, one such item might be, "Coca-Cola is the best soft drink available." Another might be, "Coca-Cola pales by contrast to Pepsi." The respondents' task is to indicate whether they agree or disagree with the various statements (the direction of affect) and to indicate the intensity with which they agree or disagree. A typical Likert scale consists of five possible positions—two levels of agreement (strongly and slightly), two levels of disagreement, and a neutral position.

Helping the Pencil: The Bogus Pipeline   Occasionally, it is difficult to get people to tell us what their true attitudes are on a given question. It is difficult for subjects in an experiment to express negative attitudes about a colleague; it is difficult for subjects to express unpopular political opinions; it is difficult for subjects to admit to bigoted or other socially unacceptable attitudes. If social scientists are to study problems involving attitudes toward others, however, techniques are needed that can overcome the understandable hesitancy of respondents to express opinions that they feel they ought not express.

Jones and Sigall (1971) have reviewed a number of studies that used a form of deception to get people to state honest, even if unpopular, attitudes. They have called this technique the "bogus pipeline." The essential feature of the technique is to convince participants that the investigators already know their true attitudes. Typically, elaborate-looking machinery is attached to subjects, who are told that it is capable of measuring their attitudes toward an object. Using an appropriate rationale, the investigators ask subjects to indicate verbally or in writing what they believe the machine has discovered. In this way, subjects tend to disclose their true attitudes, for they believe that those attitudes have already been recorded by the electronic gadgetry.

Sigall and Page (1971) were among the first to use the bogus pipeline in their study of racial stereotyping. In an earlier report, Karlin, Coffman, and Walters (1969) found that in the years leading up to their study, white students had adopted more favorable stereotypes of blacks in this country. Although not questioning the notion that stereotypical attitudes had changed over time, Sigall and Page wondered whether some of the changes might be due to a reluctance on the part of white students to admit that they held some negatively stereotyped racial attitudes. Consequently, the researchers asked half of their subjects to rate on a questionnaire the degree to which various stereotypical terms applied to black Americans. The other half of the subjects were attached to a bogus pipeline and asked the same questions. Some of the results were dramatic. For example, white students using the pencil-and-paper approach indicated that they did not think that the term *lazy* really characterized blacks. However

An example of the bogus pipeline measurement of attitudes, as used by Sigall and Page (1971). A subject is wired to the apparatus and made to believe that his attitudes are being measured. This often encourages respondents to provide more honest attitudes. *(Harold Sigall, University of Maryland)*

subjects who believed that the investigator was getting an accurate reading of their opinion by means of the bogus pipeline admitted that, to a degree, they did think the term applied to blacks.

As another example, consider the situation that student-subjects found themselves in during an experiment conducted by Quigley-Fernandez and Tedeschi (1978). They were given secret illicit information as to how to succeed at a test. They were then given an opportunity to use that information—that is, to cheat while taking the test. Later, the subjects were asked if they had indeed cheated. Subjects who responded while connected to a bogus pipeline were more likely to confess than were those who responded via a paper-and-pencil technique.

Physiological Recordings   There is often a desire to reduce complex attitudes to the most microscopic form of measurement. To this end, attempts have been made to assess attitudes toward stimuli by using physiological recordings. If a person's truest and most private attitudes can be recorded on the surface of the skin or by the pounding of the heart or the constriction of the pupils, then investigators would have an ideal measure, devoid of many of the problems we have been discussing. There are reports of skin resistance being used to assess attitudes toward people of different races (Rankin & Campbell, 1955). Pupil size (Hess, 1965) and heart rate (Katz, Cadoret, Hughes & Abbey, 1965) have also been used as measurement techniques.

Recently, great advancements have been made using physiological recordings to measure attitudes. It had been known for some time that the strength of an attitude might be related to the intensity of various bodily responses. For example, a person's heart might start beating more rapidly as he considers the psychological object "final examination." The more he dislikes the final, the faster the heart rate. But are we sure that the faster heart rate signals dislike? Might it be signaling a positive attitude? Might the person instead be relishing the idea of the final exam as his chance to overcome his poor performance?

Cacioppo and Petty (1979, 1981, 1986) are among those who have been advocating greater reliance on physiological techniques. They pointed out (1981) that portions of our faces show greater electrical activity when we are happy and other parts of the face show electrical activity when we are unhappy. Different muscle groups in the face respond during different mood states. These groupings are shown in Figure 5–1. A piece of equipment that can directly measure electrical activity in the facial muscles is the electromyograph (EMG).

Cacioppo, Petty, Losch, and Kim (1986) showed that the EMG can be used to measure both the direction and intensity of attitudes by having subjects view slides that produced either moderately positive or

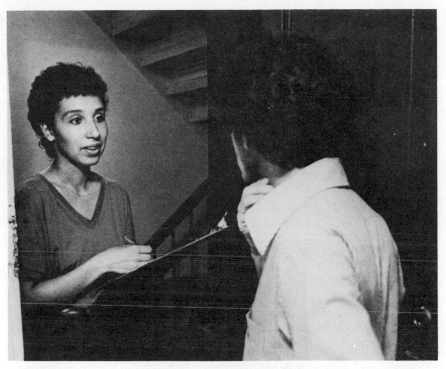

Attitudes can be measured in many ways. In an opinion poll, attitudes are measured by the pencil-and-paper technique of an attitude scale. (© *Teri Leigh Stratford 1981/ Photo Researchers, Inc.*)

moderately negative responses. As the subjects watched the slides, their facial muscles were monitored with the EMG. The machine was not only able to determine whether the subjects had a favorable or unfavorable attitude toward the slides, but also how favorable or unfavorable their responses were. More importantly, the EMG was able to detect differences that were not noticeable to the naked eye—emotional responses too subtle or fleeting to be discerned by just looking at the participants' faces.

GROWING UP WITH ATTITUDES

Two children grow up in the same town. One becomes a physician, marries, settles in suburbia and opposes socialized medicine, tax reform, and nuclear disarmament negotiations. The other becomes a political

Figure 5–1
Major facial muscles and recording sites for electrode placement

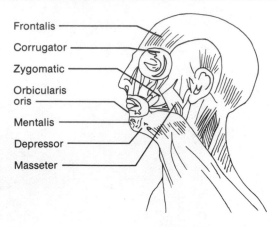

Frontalis
Corrugator
Zygomatic
Orbicularis oris
Mentalis
Depressor
Masseter

Source: Cacioppo and Petty (1981).

activist for the Peace-Now movement, supports disarmament, tax reform, environmental groups, and so forth.

What accounts for the development of different attitudes? The specific roles of heredity and environment are not entirely clear; heredity may play a part—perhaps through differences in physical characteristics and intelligence. Heredity may also interact in interesting and complex ways to affect attitudes (Scarr & McCartney, 1983; Goldsmith, 1983). Despite the importance of these issues, definitive answers about the role of heredity in attitude formation remain elusive (Cavalli-Sforza, Feldman, Chen, & Dornbusch, 1982). For our purposes, we will confine ourselves to the role played by the environment, for it is in this area that social psychologists have sought to find answers.

The Parents: Getting There First with the Most   Parents, of course, are exceedingly important forces in development, and it would be surprising if they were not among the most important determinants in the development of our attitudes and values. The issue is not so much whether parents influence the development of attitudes in children, but rather *how* they do so.

In our early years, parents—or other persons who raise us—have control over two important aspects of our lives. First, they control most of our *rewards* and *punishments*. They can permit access to the things we like; they can force us to do things that we do not want to do. They control access to the candy and the ice cream. Their smiles of approval and their frowns of disappointment are of paramount importance to us. In addition, they control a sizable portion of the *information* that reaches us. If we wanted to know why the sky is blue, the stars are bright, or the sun is hot, we asked our parents. As many of us realize when we leave the protection of childhood, our parents do not always (and in some cases, not even often) have the correct answers. But they do begin the information flow that results in our forming beliefs and attitudes about things.

Categories are formed in our heads on the basis of early information. For example, a child may form a rudimentary category of "witch" from stories his parents told him. He knows that a witch is old, ugly, and mean, but drives a wicked broomstick. Subsequently he hears that in *The Wizard of Oz* the Witch of the North is young, beautiful, and not at all mean. What happens to the child's original category?

Almost all theorists agree that the new information about the Witch of the North will be *assimilated* to the already existing category. That is, it will be distorted to some degree to fit into the established category. At the same time, the category will be *accommodated* to the new information (see Piaget, 1932). The child's category of "witch" will show some expansion to incorporate the new information.

So far, so good. The extraordinary influence of the parents in forming attitudes, beliefs, or values arises from the fact that they establish the initial categories and that those categories are *resistant to change*. That is, the result of the clash between the existing category and any new information is usually resolved more in the direction of assimilation than of accommodation. This may be due to two factors. First, parents are particularly credible sources of information for a young child. Subsequent information, if provided by a different source, may not weigh as heavily because the source of the communication may not be as credible as the parents. Second, there is some good evidence that preexisting categories exert more influence on stimuli than the stimuli do on the categories.

For example, Bruner, Busiek, and Minturn (1952) had subjects look at line drawings that were quickly flashed upon a screen (Figure 5–2). Some subjects were first told that they would see a drawing of a pine tree. Others were told that they would see a drawing of a trowel. When the subjects were asked to reproduce faithfully the pictures that they had seen, the pictures were distorted in the direction of the category that had previously been established by the experimenter's suggestion.

We can imagine how this phenomenon might work in the case of a social attitude. If a child's parents believe in a set of attitudes and communicate those attitudes to their child, the child will establish categories.

Figure 5–2
Stimulus figures used in study of preexisting categories

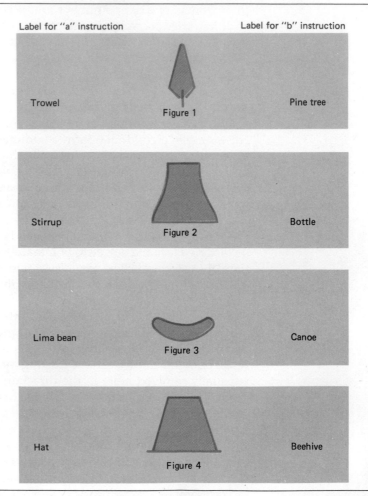

Source: Bruner, Busiek, and Minturn (1952).

For example, suppose a parent believes that all soft drinks are bad and the child comes to share this attitude. Then, if the child hears a classmate extol the wonders of drinking soda pop, it is more likely that the child will see the classmate as unworthy, evil, or just incorrect rather than adopt the classmate's attitude. That is, the preexisting category

will shape the subsequent information more than it will be modified by
that information.

Indeed, Lord, Ross, and Lepper (1979) showed arguments both in favor
of and against capital punishment to subjects who were already committed
to a procapital-punishment stance. These subjects considered the weight
of the evidence to be overwhelmingly in favor of capital punishment—so
much so that they became even more polarized in their procapital-
punishment attitudes. Lord et al. also used the identical arguments with
anticapital-punishment subjects. These subjects considered the weight of
the very same evidence to be anticapital-punishment and they became still
more militant on that side of the issue. As our analysis would suggest, the
preexisting category regarding the attitude toward capital punishment
clearly had more influence on the new information than that same information had on the cognitive category.

In a different context, the eminent psychiatrist and personality theorist
Harry Stack Sullivan has observed that the information provided by
parents in the earliest stages of life is very difficult to undo. Erroneous and
maladaptive attitudes molded from parental feedback have tremendous
implications for future personality development. This is precisely because
the early categories formed from this information alter a child's view of the
events around him more than those events alter his early categories. It remains the extremely difficult task of subsequent stages of development to
open the child's horizons to new information about himself or herself, the
environment, and the people therein (Sullivan, 1950).

Expanding Horizons: The Influence of Reference Groups   As we grow,
the number of influences on our lives increases. Instead of viewing parents
as the exclusive bearers of information, we begin to realize that the teacher
at school, the police officer on the corner, and the counselor at camp all
have information to transmit. Sometimes they agree with parents, and
sometimes they do not. One of the most important influences with which
we come into contact is that of our peers, who often serve as a *reference
group* against which our attitudes and values can be compared. A reference group is a group toward which an individual orients him- or herself. A person may or may not actually hold membership in the group
but nevertheless it forms the basis of comparison for attitudes, values,
and behaviors. A classic study by Newcomb (1943) demonstrated the
power of reference groups in affecting our attitudes.

In 1935, Newcomb conducted extensive interviews with the incoming
class at Bennington College. Bennington had not yet earned the reputation
of being an extremely liberal campus, although the prevailing attitudes of
the upperclasspeople and the faculty were quite liberal. Consequently,
families from the upper crust of conservative New England were willing

to send their daughters there. To attest to the conservatism of the parents of Bennington's incoming class, attitudes were collected about the upcoming election between the liberal Franklin D. Roosevelt and the conservative Alfred M. Landon. Although Roosevelt won the election by a remarkable landslide, carrying over 62 percent of the popular vote, 60 percent of the families of the Bennington students favored Landon. The students of the incoming class seemed to echo their parents' attitudes, with 62 percent of them favoring Landon's election.

What influence would Bennington's peer group structure have on the attitudes of students? One way to study this question would be to compare the attitudes of the incoming freshmen with the attitudes of students in the other classes. In this comparison, it was found that only 43 percent of the sophomore class favored Landon and that the percentage dropped to 15 percent for juniors and seniors. However, it was conceivable that the members of the incoming class were in fact different from the members of the upper classes in some important ways and would hold onto their original beliefs until graduation day. So Newcomb traced an incoming class for four years. He found a conclusive shift toward liberalism among the women in the class of 1939 as they proceeded through Bennington. Moreover, the degree of liberalism that a coed expressed was highly correlated with her popularity and prestige on campus. One way to interpret the shift toward liberalism is to see it as an attitude approved of by the important people in the reference group. Since the seniors in the class of 1935 were far more liberal than the incoming freshmen that year, it is likely that interactions with the more prestigious seniors encouraged the incoming freshmen's attitudes toward political and social issues to shift in the direction of those peers. An apparent benefit of the shift toward agreement with the more prestigious peers was that students' prestige and popularity increased accordingly.

What of the women who did not adopt the attitudes of their reference group? They were less popular with their classmates and less influential on the campus. In addition, Newcomb reported two different subgroups of "un-influenced" (that is, conservative) coeds. One subgroup appeared unaware that their attitudes were at variance with the Bennington norm. Their friendship groups tended to be quite small and generally included only women who shared their conservative beliefs. We do not know whether these coeds chose friends because of their conservatism or whether they remained conservative because of the friends they chose. Newcomb's data suggest the second proposition more strongly than the first. In other words, this subgroup was uninfluenced by the Bennington liberalism because they had less opportunity or occasion to interact with a wide cross section of Bennington students.

Newcomb's study showed that reference groups influenced people's choices between presidential candidates Alf Landon and Franklin D. Roosevelt in 1936 *and* the choice between Richard Nixon and John F. Kennedy 24 years later. *(Top left, courtesy Franklin Delano Roosevelt Library; others, Wide World Photos)*

Another subgroup of uninfluenced students might be called the *"family"* group. These were women who were well aware of the disparity between their own attitudes and those of the Bennington College community, but they expressed very strong attachment to their families. They either stated that they felt attached to their families or expressed an awareness of the difficulty that they would experience at home if they were to adopt the prevailing attitudes on campus. We might say that for these women, the family rather than the campus of peers served as the relevant reference group.

How long lasting are attitudes that are formed by close attachments to reference groups? Two follow-up studies conducted by Newcomb and his colleagues are exceedingly interesting. First, recall the power of parental influence before the women entered college. The incoming class in 1935 very closely resembled their parents in their attitudes, despite roughly eighteen years of being subjected to all types of external influences. However, as most of you will attest, living in a residential college community is a powerful experience. Contacts and relationships that have survived for a long time are abruptly pushed into the background, and a large number of strangers have to be relied on for social, physical, and mental support. So it is not surprising that reference-group pressures on a college campus are strong and, as Newcomb was able to demonstrate, often long lasting.

In 1960, twenty-five years after interviewing the Bennington freshmen, Newcomb (1963) reinterviewed the entire class of 1939. The Bennington group was found to be much more liberal than a comparable group of women from the identical social and economic class. In addition, it was found that the Bennington women had married men who were considerably more liberal than a comparable group of men of equal socioeconomic status. Newcomb, Koenig, Flacks, and Warwick (1967) reported that, whereas only 30 percent of the women in a similar socioeconomic class supported John Kennedy over Richard Nixon in the 1960 election, 60 percent of the Bennington graduates supported Kennedy. As for the uninfluenced conservatives, Newcomb et al. reported that they had not changed much either. Of the college conservatives, 67 percent were married to men who had voted for Nixon rather than Kennedy.

The Influence of Reference Groups on Sex, Childbearing, and Drugs
The importance of reference groups in influencing attitudes and behaviors is enormous. Walsh, Ferrell, and Tolone (1976) studied the effect of peer reference groups on attitudes and behaviors regarding sexual permissiveness. Working with the class of 1971 and the class of 1974 at a midwestern university, the investigators examined changing attitudes and behaviors from the students' freshman to senior years. Like the students in

Reference groups provide support for attitudes and behaviors. Attitudes about drugs, alcohol, and so forth, which may be deviant in the general culture, often find support and encouragement in people's reference groups. (© *Joel Gordon 1983*)

Newcomb's study, the investigators found that attitudes and behaviors from the beginning of college until the senior year were very much affected by the students' reference groups. Sexual attitudes and behaviors became much more permissive provided that the student's reference group was a group of peers. Students who were still oriented toward their parents did not show this shift.

People need reference groups to anchor their opinions and behaviors, even if those behaviors are different from the attitudes of the general culture. Houseknecht (1977) took this approach in her study of voluntary childlessness. Several investigators (e.g., Griffith, 1973) had shown that a decision not to have any children in marriage is an attitude not shared by the general population—that is, it is deviant to take such a position. Houseknecht asked introductory sociology students at Penn State University to respond to a questionnaire. They were asked to specify the people and groups who served as their reference groups, the attitudes of the reference groups, and their own attitudes toward having children after they were married. The results showed that, although it was statistically unusual to decide to have no children, these attitudes had the strong support of the respondents' reference groups. In fact, those people who had decided to have no children had reference group support far beyond that of the respondents who did desire children. Thus, while the former group had deviant attitudes with regard to the general society, it appeared that they were in conformity with the attitudes held by their reference groups.

Finally, the important question of directionality of influence was addressed by Kandel's (1978) study of marijuana use. As we noted in Newcomb's study, it is difficult to assess whether people of similar attitudes come together to form reference groups or whether reference groups cause people's attitudes to become similar. Kandel conducted initial and follow-up interviews with a large group of high school students in New York State. He found convincing evidence that both effects are true: students with similar marijuana-use patterns tended to form reference groups for each other and those groups caused attitudes and behavior to become more similar once the reference groups had formed. Given some discrepancy in the attitudes held by different members of a reference group, Kandel's results showed that people either conformed to the other members of a reference group or the group was likely to break apart. Although Kandel also found some support for this phenomenon with regard to attitudes toward educational and political issues as well, it was most striking when the issue was of present and immediate concern: the smoking of marijuana.

FORMING ATTITUDES BY BALANCE

A very popular group of theories concerning the way in which attitudes are formed are known as balance theories (Cartwright & Harary, 1956; Heider, 1946, 1958; Newcomb, 1953, 1968). The earliest of these, Heider's theory of psychological balance, was created more as an explanation of the way in which we come to like or dislike other persons. However, it has had equally important use in the study of attitudes of all kinds.

According to Heider, two kinds of relationships wed people to objects or to other people. One of these is the *unit* relationship. An example is the statement that Peter works for Coca-Cola. The statement relates Peter to Coca-Cola but does not express an emotion. It does not tell us whether Peter likes or dislikes his company. The other type of relationship is known as a *sentiment*. An example is the statement that Peter is ecstatic about The Coca-Cola Company. Love, hate, agreement and disagreement are all typical statements used in sentiment relationships.

Heider's system is essentially an uncomplicated one that involves the relationship of two people and an attitude object. The people, P and O, are related to each other and to the attitude object, X, usually by sentiment relationships. Heider was a psychologist in the gestalt tradition, which holds that people prefer relationships that "fit well" to relationships that are discordant. Therefore, he felt, people prefer that their relationships be

Figure 5-3
Balanced and imbalanced triadic relationships

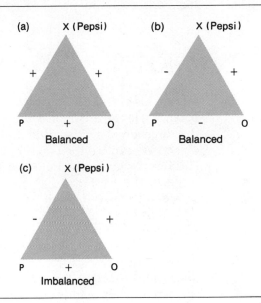

balanced rather than imbalanced. An example should make this clear. Suppose that P has a girlfriend whom he likes very much. Suppose too that she very strongly favors bringing Pepsi Cola to picnics they share together. Figure 5-3 puts these relationships in one of Heider's P−O−X triads. The figure shows three possible sentiment relationships among an actor (P), his girlfriend (O), and the attitude object Pepsi (X). The question is, What will P's attitudes be toward Pepsi? It should be evident that P's relationships will be balanced if he too feels positively about Pepsi. What if P secretly feels negatively toward his girlfriend and has concluded that she and he are not to be? Figure 5-3(b) shows a balanced state in that situation; P must come to feel negatively about Pepsi.

There is a relatively simple way to determine when a triadic relationship is balanced or imbalanced (Cartwright & Harary, 1956). In Figure 5-3, a simple algebraic multiplication of the affective signs on the three sides of the triangle should produce the result. If the product is positive, the triangle is balanced. If it is negative, the triangle is imbalanced. Therefore, when P likes O (+) and O likes X (+), it would follow that P should come to like X (+):

$$(+) \times (+) \times (+) = +.$$

This is a balanced state. On the other hand, had P decided that he did not like Pepsi even though his loved one did, as in figure 5-3(c),

$$(+) \times (+) \times (-) = -.$$

This is an imbalanced state.

What happens if there is imbalance in a relationship? According to Heider, there will be a "strain" to restore balance. In Figure 5-3(c), where P loves his girlfriend but dislikes Pepsi, he experiences a strain to restore balance. He can accomplish the restoration of balance by changing either the direction of sentiment toward his girlfriend or his attitude about the object. We can see the power of balance to produce the effect Newcomb (1943) reported for the influence of peer reference groups at Bennington College. If a freshman has not yet formed an opinion about the 1936 presidential election, but knows that someone she likes or respects endorses Roosevelt, balance theory predicts that she will like Roosevelt. Alternatively, if because of her upbringing, the freshman enters college feeling negatively about Roosevelt, there will be a strain in the system—a strain to restore balance. She can retain her negative attitude toward Roosevelt and adopt a negative attitude toward the group. Alternatively, she can do as most girls did and change her attitude toward Roosevelt to a positive one. Then, as Figure 5-4 shows, the positive attitude toward the Bennington coeds, the positive attitude between the coeds and

Figure 5–4
Balance theory representation of Bennington students' attitudes toward Franklin Roosevelt

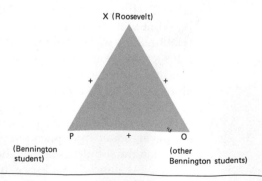

Roosevelt, and the positive attitude she has now adopted toward Roosevelt would form a balanced relationship.

Finally, P in Figure 5–3 can restore balance by *misperceiving* O's sentiment toward X. He can selectively attend to information that O really *does not* like Pepsi, or he can distort his girlfriend's behavior so that it *appears* she does not like Pepsi. In any of these ways, P can achieve balance—a state he very much prefers.

THE CONDITIONING OF ATTITUDES

Operant or Instrumental Conditioning   People (and other organisms) seek to increase their pleasure and decrease their pain. When we behave in a way that increases our pleasure, we are likely to behave that way again. For example, if we order a roast beef dinner in a particular restaurant and it turns out to be superb, there is every likelihood that we will come back to that restaurant and order roast beef. Skinner (1938) called this type of learning *operant conditioning*. A behavior (or response) that is emitted in the presence of a situational stimulus (that is, in a particular situation), and is followed by a reinforcing stimulus is more likely to be repeated.

In the example of the good roast beef dinner, the restaurant serves as the situational stimulus or location. The response is ordering a roast beef dinner, and the reinforcing stimulus is the delectable taste of the food. That reward reinforces the behavior in the sense that it increases the probability that the behavior will occur again in the same situation.

Now consider the child who is raised in a household in which the parents believe that premarital sex is bad. Let us say that the topic becomes relevant because a television program that has just concluded touched on the topic in some way. Perhaps the child says, "Gee, I think what they were doing is immoral." This precocious statement might be met with smiles from mommy and daddy followed by a hug and a kiss. The attitudinal statement, a response made in the presence of a particular stimulus, is reinforced by smiles, hugs, and kisses. Looked at in another way, we could say that the attitude statement was *instrumental* in obtaining a reward. Thus, this type of learning has been called instrumental, as well as *operant conditioning*. In either case, an attitude has been learned through rewards administered by the parents.

Since parents hold a full house of rewards early in a child's life, it is likely that they make the most ready use of conditioning techniques in shaping the child's attitudes. But the model of operant conditioning is silent as to who would be most effective in administering the rewards. Presumably, attitudes can be conditioned at any time by virtually anyone who is in a position to bestow rewards.

Being rewarded by the succulent taste of a good dinner increases the likelihood that the dinner will be ordered on other occasions in this hotel. This is an illustration of the principles of operant conditioning. (© *Joel Gordon 1976*)

For example, Insko (1965) conducted an interesting study that showed the persistence of conditioned attitudes over time. He called students at the University of North Carolina by telephone and used a verbal conditioning technique to alter some of their attitudes. Approximately one week later, an instructor handed out an attitude survey in class. Some of the items on the survey were identical with those that had been reinforced with a "Good" on the telephone a week earlier. The students did not realize that all students in the class had been called and that the survey was connected to those phone calls. The results indicated that even in a different context, and after a week's delay, the attitude that had been conditioned on the phone remained conditioned on the survey.

Attitudes by Association: Classical Conditioning   A little boy is sitting in a high chair near a window. As his mother begins to bring chopped meat to his mouth, a tremendous clap of thunder is heard. To the mother's astonishment, the child subsequently throws temper tantrums every time meat is put on his tray. In another room, a little girl is about to eat her vegetables when her mother, delighted with some news about

Classical conditioning . . . of the experimenter. *(By permission of John Hart and Field Enterprises, Inc.)*

her husband, breaks into a smile. From that point on, the child wants vegetables. Both of these children have been *classically conditioned*. They have learned behaviors based on a different kind of conditioning, one that stresses the association between a neutral stimulus, such as chopped meat, and a stimulus that produces an emotional response, such as the thunderclap.

Perhaps the first organisms to be studied while being classically conditioned were the dogs of Ivan Pavlov (1927). Pavlov reasoned that some responses are inherently connected to certain stimuli. For example, when a hungry dog sees food, it salivates. Such a connection is called an *unconditioned reflex*, for it links an unconditioned stimulus (food) with an unconditioned response (salivation) in a biologically determined way. What would happen if the stimulus that produces the reflex response were associated with a neutral stimulus? Pavlov sought the answer to this question by sounding a bell just before offering meat powder to a hungry dog. After a few pairings, the dog began to salivate at the bell, though the bell bore no logical connection to the powder. The bell was neither a reward for eating nor instrumental in the dog's receiving a reward; it was associated with the meat powder simply because it was contiguous in time with it. Such contiguity with a stimulus that necessarily evokes a reflexive response invests the new stimulus with the capacity to bring about the same response. In Pavlov's case, the bell came to produce the salivation response. In the first example in this section, the little boy had a reflexive reaction of fear to the stimulus of the thunderclap. The chopped meat was paired contiguously in time with the thunderclap and thus took on the capacity of bringing fear to the child. In the other example, the little girl's vegetables were paired in time with her mother's smile. Since the smile

Figure 5–5
The classical conditioning paradigm

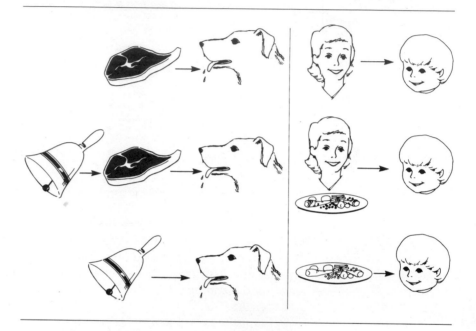

usually evoked pleasure in the girl, the vegetables took on the power to produce pleasure in her. Figure 5–5 demonstrates the pairings of the neutral stimuli with the unconditioned reflexes that lead the dog to salivate at the bell and the little girl to like vegetables.

In the present context, we are not so much concerned with dogs that salivate as with people who form positive and negative attitudes. As the examples above have shown, classical conditioning—by focusing on the pairing of a neutral attitude object with a stimulus that evokes an emotional reaction—can account for a number of attitudes. For example, in one experiment, Staats and Staats (1958) showed that words that have acquired affective meaning can create positive or negative attitudes about a neutral stimulus if they are merely paired with that stimulus. They chose the names of two nationalities (*Swedish* and *Dutch*) as the neutral words. The affective words were either positive (*happy, gifted*) or negative (*bitter, ugly*). Half of the subjects always had the positive words associated with Dutch and the negative words with Swedish; the other half had the pairings reversed.

Table 5–1
Means of conditioned attitude scores in "neutral stimulus" rating

Name positively reinforced	Names	
	Dutch	Swedish
Swedish	2.67	3.42
Dutch	2.67	1.00

Note: Higher numbers indicate greater liking.
Source: Adapted from Staats and Staats (1958).

At the end of the study, subjects were asked to rate the pleasantness of the two nationalities. The results are presented in Table 5–1. Even though the experimenter was not indicating that the word pairings had any logical connection—he was not saying that bitter was attached to Dutch because the Dutch are bitter—subjects still rated the nationality that had been paired with positive words more positively than the nationality that had been paired with negative words. Positive and negative attitudes were apparently formed through the association of classical conditioning.

PERSUASION: THE PSYCHOLOGY OF ATTITUDE CHANGE

Perhaps no other area of social psychology has generated as much interest as that of attitude change. William McGuire (1985), in his chapter on attitude change in the most recent edition of the *Handbook of Social Psychology*, points out that interest in the phenomenon has had its peaks and valleys. In the 1930s, social psychologists made attitude change their major area of interest; their concentration was on measurement. During the 1940s, interest declined, only to peak again in a more comprehensive way at the end of the 1950s and in the early 1960s. The 1970s showed another valley in the progression of attitude-change research (Kiesler & Munson, 1975), but McGuire sees the present decade, the 1980s, as one in which the preeminence of attitude change as social psychologists' focus of study has been regained. And even during the supposedly fallow period of the 1970s, Dawes and Smith (1985) counted 20,209 articles and books on the topic from 1970 to 1979.

If you are trying to convince a friend that he should abandon his Sunday football game and go to the movies, an employer that she should promote you rather than her son, or a teacher that your unpreparedness for class is really a virtue, then you are actively engaged in the persuasion or attitude-change process. The stakes may be politically high, as in persuading the populace to elect your candidate president of the United States; or they may be financially high, as in convincing people that Coke is it! rather than the Pepsi Generation.

In trying to persuade people, what factors would you consider important? You would probably have a great deal of concern about *what* you say: Do you have the facts? Is there a well-reasoned argument? You would also have some regard for *who* is going to deliver the message: a sexy voice, a politician, an actor? Finally, you would have some regard for your *audience*; you would not want to waste your time selling Pepsi to the chairman of the board of Coca-Cola.

Aristotle was one of the first to construct the basic skeleton of attitude-change inquiries, although modern research has added numerous facets and modifications. In his *Rhetoric*, Aristotle states: "Of the modes of persuasion furnished by the spoken word, there are three kinds. The first depends on the personal character of the speaker; the second on putting the audience into a certain frame of mind; the third on the proof . . . provided by the words of the speech itself." For Aristotle, then, the analysis of communication involved an analysis of the *speaker*, the *message*, and the *audience*.

In more modern times, Carl Hovland and his associates at the Yale Communication and Attitude Change Program (Hovland, Janis, & Kelley, 1953) began a systematic inquiry into attitude-change processes. To paraphrase the Yale group's paradigm, the study of attitudes basically involves studying "who says what to whom and with what effect" (Lasswell, 1948).

In this chapter, we will examine the research on attitude change, focusing on these factors. We will consider the aspects of the persuasion process that exist apart from the target of the communication; that is, the communicator and the message *(who says what)*. In so doing, we will pay particular attention to the way in which facets of the communicator and the message affect persuasion. Then we will consider factors involving the audience or target of the influence attempt *(to whom)*. In all of the research, the dependent variable—the object of the study—is the result of the influence attempt *(with what effect)*. Was the message delivered by a particular communicator to a particular audience successful in producing attitude change? First, we will consider a general theoretical orientation that will help to tie many of the research ideas together.

AN OVERARCHING VIEW: THE E.L.M.

Suppose we knew a great deal about the effects of attitude change. For example, suppose we knew that a carefully constructed message led to greater change than a sloppily worded, poorly organized message.

Persuasion takes many forms. People attempt to sway public opinion by organizing demonstrations, others are persuaded to enjoy Coca-Cola by messages carried on a billboard, while an individual here resorts to personal persuasion to convince a city policeman. *(Top left, © Lapides 1979; top right, Arthur Tress, Photo Researchers, Inc.; lower left, © Jim Anderson 1978/Woodfin Camp & Associates)*

Suppose we knew that a Ph.D. in physics was more persuasive about the likelihood of nuclear destruction than the first baseman for a minor league ball club? And what if we knew that the first baseman was more persuasive about the quality of a shortstop than the physicist? We would probably still be dissatisfied unless we were able to move toward a setting of overarching principles to help us understand why a particular factor led to attitude change while another did not. We would want some guidance about why a factor that is influential on some occasions is ineffective on others.

As a way of dealing with the overarching questions, investigators have been working with models that help to explain the process by which persuasive attempts lead to attitude change (Eagly, Chaiken, & Wood, 1981; Petty & Cacioppo, 1986). Petty and Cacioppo (1986) have proposed the Elaboration Likelihood Model (E.L.M.) of persuasion. They point out that there are at least two routes to persuasion: sometimes we are convinced via a *central route*, and sometimes by a *peripheral route*. The central route involves the scrutinizing and processing of the arguments that are actually contained in a message. How strong are the arguments? How consistent are they? How reliable are the facts? The more we scrutinize the message, the more persuasive it will be—if and only if the arguments are strong. Petty and Cacioppo use the term *elaboration* to refer to the scrutiny with which a person examines a message's content. To understand attitude change, it will be important for us to consider those conditions that make a person more likely to use elaboration—that is, the conditions that will motivate someone to make more use of the central information-processing route.

Contrasted to the central route is the peripheral route. Here the targets of a persuasive message do not pay much attention to the message's content; they may be more influenced by the mood they're in or by some other factor besides the message itself. As we shall soon see, the personal characteristics of the source (i.e., the communicator) play an important role, one that is independent of the message that he or she is delivering. The communicator's expertise, trustworthiness, likability, and similarity to the audience all share in determining the message's impact. Since these factors require no elaboration of the message, they are regarded as forming the peripheral route to persuasion.

We return then to the "who says what to whom" question that characterized Aristotle's *Rhetoric* and that provided the organizing theme for modern persuasion research. As we do so, we will pay attention to the central and peripheral-processing routes that can help us understand how persuasion occurs.

THE COMMUNICATOR: ATTITUDE CHANGE BY THE PERIPHERAL ROUTE

Tens of billions of dollars are spent each year on persuasion attempts in the mass media. From the salaries that various communicators receive to appear on radio and television, we can assume that persuasion is, at the least, *thought* to be affected by the communicator's characteristics. Pepsi-Cola has spent millions attracting well-known celebrities (Michael Jackson, Michael J. Fox, Lionel Richie) and public figures (Geraldine Ferraro) to extol the virtues of its product. Campaigning political figures compete for endorsements from entertainers, scientists, and other political figures. Although the characteristics of the communicator may be related to the communicator's message, they nonetheless attempt to persuade via the peripheral route. Therefore, we will now examine some of the qualities of the communicator that basic research has proven effective in creating attitude change.

Credibility   In most persuasion attempts, a highly credible communicator is preferable to one with low credibility. Someone who ought to know what he or she is talking about is preferable to someone who is not qualified. When Reagan ran for the presidency in 1980, he relied on help from the highly credible former president, Gerald Ford. Who could know better and with more authority that Reagan was the right man for the White House? Newspaper editorials that endorse a candidate are (appropriately or inappropriately) adopting the role of the expert in telling us what to do. Countless TV commercials implore us to buy a product because "doctors recommend . . ." or "the American Dental Association recommends. . . ." Presumably, doctors know the facts and therefore should be effective at changing our attitudes.

I'm Not a Doctor But I Play One on TV: Incredible Credibility   Credibility can also be invested in individuals who do not have it in any *real* sense. Several examples spring to mind. The actor Robert Young who played Marcus Welby, M.D., on television made several advertisements for Sanka decaffeinated coffee. Apparently, his role as a warm and friendly general practitioner was sufficient for people to attribute credibility and knowledge to him—even though they knew logically that he had no such credibility (Cialdini, 1985).

Ronald Reagan sought to influence opinion by associating himself with the highly credible former president. *(M. Evans/Sygma)*

Credibility over Time: The Sleeper Effect   Hovland and Weiss (1952) were among the first to study the effect of the communicator's credibility on persuasion attempts. Subjects received communications on several topics. The source of the communication was made to seem of either high or suspect credibility. For example, a communication on the advisability of selling antihistamine drugs without a prescription was attributed either to *The New England Journal of Biology and Medicine* or to a mass-circulation pictorial magazine; a persuasive communication on the effect of television on the motion-picture industry was attributed either to *Fortune* magazine or to a gossip columnist; a message on the practicality of building atomic submarines was attributed either to the eminent scientist J. Robert Oppenheimer or to *Pravda*. In each case, the communication extolled the virtues of one side of an issue. The communications were identical, regardless of the alleged source. At the left of Figure 5–6 it can be seen that on an immediate basis, the highly credible source was significantly more effective in altering opinions than was the communicator with low credibility. When compared to the attitudes of the same subjects as measured one week before the experiment, the highly credible source produced far more attitude change than did the source with low credibility.

Figure 5–6
Immediate and long-term effects of communicators with low and high credibility

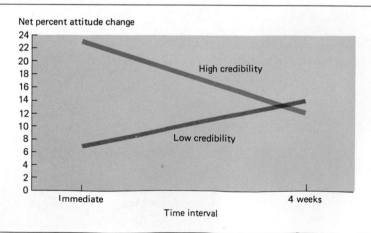

Source: Hovland and Weiss (1952).

What will happen over time, however? Will the words spoken by a believable source continue to be respected and will the same words spoken by a less credible source continue to be derogated? The more complete story told at the right of Figure 5–6 indicates that the immediate effect of the communicator's credibility does not appear to last very long. When subjects were asked what their opinions were on the various issues after four weeks had elapsed, the credibility of the communicator ceased to make a significant difference. Not only did the large amount of attitude change induced by the highly credible communicators decrease over time, but the degree of attitude change that the message produced actually *increased* in the low-credibility condition. The increase in the strength of a communication's persuasiveness over time has been called the *sleeper effect*.

What accounts for the sleeper effect? One way to think about the situation is that people tend to dissociate the communication from the communicator as time goes by. In other words, subjects in the high-credibility condition, immediately after hearing the communication, were influenced in part by the content of what they had heard and in part by the fact that the author was an expert. As time elapsed, that part of the persuasion process attributable to the communicator's expert and trustworthy status tended to disappear, since the subjects had dissociated the speech from the speaker. Similarly, subjects in the low-credibility condition indicated an attitude that reflected the content of the message *minus* the effect due to the communicator's low credibility. As dissociation set in, the inhibitory effect of the speaker's low prestige tended to disappear.

To test this idea, Kelman and Hovland (1953) had subjects listen to a communication about the treatment of juvenile delinquents. One group of subjects was informed that the speaker was a juvenile court judge (high credibility). In another condition, the speaker was introduced as someone who had recently been picked up for peddling dope (low credibility). As in the Hovland and Weiss study, opinion measures were taken before, immediately following, and three weeks after the communication. However, half of the subjects in each credibility condition were reminded of the identity of the communicator after the three-week interval, before they filled out the final questionnaire. No such reminder or reinstatement of the association was made for the other half of the subjects.

The results of Kelman and Hovland's study are depicted in Figure 5–7. Figure 5–7(a) shows the results for subjects who had been treated similarly to Hovland and Weiss's subjects. Their attitude-change scores are similar to those of the earlier study; that is, the sleeper effect was replicated. Figure 5–7(b) shows what happened to the sleeper effect when the subjects were reminded of the source of the communication after the three-week interval. In that case, although there was a slight decay of attitude change over time, it was not nearly as great as the loss in attitude

Figure 5-7
Immediate and delayed attitude change with and without reinstatement of the communicator's credibility

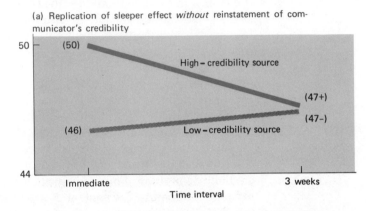

(a) Replication of sleeper effect *without* reinstatement of communicator's credibility

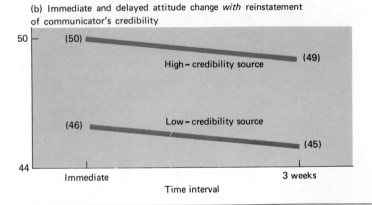

(b) Immediate and delayed attitude change *with* reinstatement of communicator's credibility

Source: Kelman and Hovland (1953).

change for the high-credibility nonreinstatement subjects. Moreover, there was no increase in attitude change on the part of the low-credibility subjects. The sleeper effect was eliminated by reinstating the association between communicator and communication.

The robustness of the sleeper effect has been controversial. Some subsequent studies have found evidence for the sleeper effect (Cook, Gruder, Hennigan, & Flay, 1979) while others have not (Gillig & Greenwald, 1974; Pratkanis & Greenwald, 1982). Petty and Cacioppo have commented that the crucial element here may be the identification of the low-credibility source of a communication *after* the presentation of the message. In this condition, the message is still taken into memory accurately and thought about impartially before it is denigrated by association with the source. If the communicator's low credibility is presented *before* the message, the meaning of the message may be changed or little attention may be paid to it. Thus, for the sleeper effect to occur, it may be necessary to identify the source after the message has been conveyed.

Expertise and trustworthiness. Credibility is a multifaceted concept. Is someone more believable because she is an expert or because she has no ulterior motives for the opinion she offers? In Hovland and Weiss's study, we cannot be certain. Is *Pravda* less credible than Oppenheimer because it is less expert about atomic submarines or because it is perceived as less trustworthy? The two factors often go together. The fact that a doctor endorses a particular laxative on television is effective both because the doctor supposedly knows what he is talking about and because he is perceived as having nothing to gain by promoting the product.

It is probably true that both factors are necessary to make a source highly credible. Reviews by Eagly (1983) and Hass (1981) have made it abundantly clear that the communicator's expertise affects persuasion. Hass (1981) has shown that such cues as level of education, intelligence, social status, and professional attainment all function to enhance expertise and, ultimately, attitude change, even though these cues can be very subtle indeed (Hastie, Penrod, & Pennington, 1984).

Our analysis of central and peripheral routes to persuasion suggests how the role of expertise may operate. Expertise, like other communicator variables, operates in the peripheral mode. That is, it absolves the recipient from having to pay too close attention to the message that is actually used in the communication. It should follow then that any factor that increases a person's involvement in the issue being presented will decrease the role of communicator variables such as expertise. The degree to which a person is involved in the issue raises his or her motivation to process the arguments in the message and therefore to rely less heavily on the source of the communication.

The role of personal involvement in persuasion has been a recurrent theme in recent research (e.g., Leippe and Elkin, 1987; Petty, Cacioppo and Goldman, 1981; Petty, Cacioppo, and Heesacker, 1981; Sivacek and Crano, 1982). Consider the study conducted by Petty, Cacioppo, and Goldman (1981). They had senior undergraduates listen to a communication advocating a policy of compulsory comprehensive examinations to graduate from college. Half of the students were highly involved in the issue, since the college in question was their own and the timing was

Figure 5–8

Interactive effect of involvement and source expertise on postcommunication attitudes

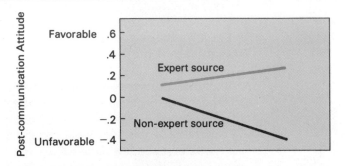

immediate. The other half believed that the exam policy, if put into effect, would take place in ten years and therefore was not highly relevant. The expertise of the communicator and the strength of the message were also varied. Sometimes the arguments themselves were strong and cogent; other times they were weak and unconvincing. Finally, the communicator was described as either a professor of education from Princeton University (expert source) or as a junior from a local high school (nonexpert).

Who was convinced by the message they read? Who underwent attitude change? The results showed that the expertise of the source made all the difference if, and only if, the students were not personally involved. When they thought the exam policy was ten years away, they were persuaded that it was a good idea *when the communicator was from Princeton*. The strength of his arguments was irrelevant. It was his expert status that created the attitude change. This, as we have discussed, is attitude change along the *peripheral* route.

When subjects were highly involved because of the possibility of an imminent change, the cogency of the arguments created attitude change and the characteristics of the communicator became irrelevant. In this circumstance, strong arguments caused persuasion. This was an example of attitude change along the *central* route. The relevance created a motivation for elaboration (i.e., critical examination) of the arguments.

Trustworthiness is a bit more difficult to test. Some gimmicks of the advertising trade may provide a clue about testing this factor. In the days following the introduction of Coca-Cola Classic, Pepsi-Cola ran a series of TV ads that featured a group of elderly farmers chatting on the front porch. As the camera zooms in, some of the men are discussing soft drinks and are feigning disbelief that New Coke is now Old Coke and Old Coke is now a classic. In discussing their enthusiasm for Pepsi, they convince remaining members of their little group to drink it. Why is this ad convincing? It is designed to show that the communicators were not intending to convince *us*; we just happened on the men in conversation. Thus, their credibility increases because they do not appear to be purposefully trying to persuade us.

Walster and Festinger (1962) conducted two studies to assess the effectiveness of "overheard" as opposed to "regular" communications. In one of their studies, students overheard speakers discussing the link between cigarette smoking and cancer: these communicators always took the position that the view of a causal link between the two was a misconception. In the study's regular condition, it was made clear that the communicators were aware that the subjects were listening to them. In its overheard condition, the subjects believed that their presence was completely unknown to the speakers. Several days later, the subjects (college students) were given a health survey in their classrooms. One question asked how certain they were that cigarette smoking leads to lung cancer. The results showed that for subjects who smoked, the link between smoking and cancer was doubted more strongly (i.e., attitudes were changed) when the communication was overheard than when it was supposed to be heard.

We might also expect communicators to be seen as more credible when they take stands that are at odds with the position we might expect them to take given their background, race, religion, or other group affiliations. In other words, communicators who take unexpected stands should generally be seen as more trustworthy. To examine this question, Wood and Chaiken (1981) directly manipulated a person's expectation regarding the position that a communicator was likely to take. The issue was the support of pornography. Jim, the communicator, was described to subjects as a member of the Catholic church, as against abortion, and as knowledgeable on the topic of free speech. In an interview he was heard to say, "I very definitely do not think that everyone should have unlimited free speech. There are basic human principles—like the right not to be exploited . . . which are a lot more important than a concept like freedom of speech." From this background, Wood and Chaiken established the expectation that Jim would be against pornography. In one experimental condition, this expectation was confirmed. In another condition, the expectation was disconfirmed, with Jim citing his belief that

Jimmy Carter was an effective communicator when he urged amnesty for draft evaders at the American Legion convention in August 1976. *(United Press International Photo)*

pornography was cathartic and led to a reduction of sex related crimes. Jim's speech in support of pornography was extremely effective when it stood in contrast with what would have been expected, given his background.

In summary, we can say that a high-credibility communicator is more effective than a low-credibility communicator in producing attitude changes. Credibility seems to be a function of at least expertise and trustworthiness, and seems to be effective along the peripheral route to persuasion. However, research on the sleeper effect has shown that the effect of credibility may be shortlived. The enhancing effect of the high-credibility source may diminish over time and the attitude change produced by the low-credibility source may increase over time. If we wish to preserve the effectiveness of the high-credibility source, reinstating the connection between the message and its communicator is necessary.

Similarity. Instead of relying on an expert communicator, some influence attempts find success with a message that is carried by someone who is just like the communication's target. If you want to sell an automobile to a homemaker, it may be better to get the endorsement of another homemaker rather than that of an automotive expert.

In a paint store in Ohio, Brock (1965) found evidence for the persuasiveness of a similar communicator. Salespeople tried to persuade potential customers to purchase a particular brand of paint. In one condition, a salesman let it be known that he knew very little about paint except that he had purchased a quantity of paint similar to that wanted by the customer a short time before. In another condition, the salesman established himself as a paint expert, but the information he provided about his own paint purchase made him quite dissimilar from the customer. The customer's own purchase was the study's dependent measure. It was found that the customer purchased a lot more of the paint brand being extolled if the communication was delivered by the similar nonexpert salesman.

Why should a communicator who is *not* an expert be effective in changing our attitudes? Chapter Seven will present research that indicates that similar others are liked better than dissimilar others. In brief, similarity often leads to attraction. Further, several studies have shown that well-liked communicators are more persuasive than disliked ones. Chaiken (1980), for example, showed that college students were persuaded more by a likable communicator who presented only one strong argument in favor of his position than by an unlikable communicator who presented as many as eight cogent arguments. Consistent with our reasoning about the peripheral route to persuasion, this was the result when the personal relevance of the situation to the subject was low rather than high.

Likability provides only a partial answer to our question, however. We know that it does lead to greater persuasion and that it occurs along the peripheral route. But we are still left wondering *why* people we like should be more convincing than people we do not like.

Balance theory, which we introduced earlier, provides one answer. Figure 5–9 shows that if a famous entertainer whom we like and admire endorses Pepsi-Cola, there is a strain toward balance that pushes us in the direction of a positive attitude toward Pepsi. For example, if Lionel Richie feels positively toward Pepsi and we aspire to be like that star singer, balance principles will push our attitudes more positively toward Pepsi.

THE COMMUNICATION: FACTORS AFFECTING CENTRAL AND PERIPHERAL PERSUASION

It might be expected that a well-reasoned communication, delivered in an eloquent and organized fashion, would be the most persuasive of all possible communications. Although there is truth to this, many other factors must also be considered. First, the arguments contained in a communication can only be persuasive if the target is motivated to use the

Figure 5–9
A balance theory look at a person's (P) attitude toward Pepsi-Cola

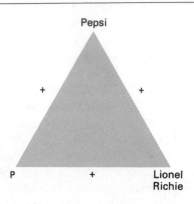

central route to persuasion. Why should I bother to think about the relative merits of Coke over Pepsi if I am not partial to cola drinks in general? Elaborating or scrutinizing the message takes effort, and will only be done if the target has good reason to spend that effort. As we have seen, personal involvement or importance are reasons that motivate central processing. Second, attitudes are not always shaped or changed by reason. As we indicated earlier, some attitudes are formed by association.

When attitudes are changed by reasoned arguments, many questions can be raised: Should a reasoned argument contain a consideration of two sides of an issue, or just one? If two, which side should be presented first? Should the communication draw its own conclusion, or should that be left to the recipient? Should it ask rhetorical questions? In this section, we will consider what is known about the various aspects that come together to make a communication effective in producing attitude change.

Creating an Image: Appeals to Emotions   "He says such incredible pap," stated one of the major figures in Richard Nixon's 1968 presidential campaign about the man whose candidacy he was selling. "In fact, the radicalness of this [campaign] is in the fact of creating an image without actually saying anything" (McGinniss, 1969). And such was the Nixon campaign precedent that became the hallmark of many campaigns to come.

What made the 1968 election of Richard Nixon so important in the history of electoral politics was not its use of advertising agencies, mass

Why is Joe DiMaggio effective in persuading consumers to use Mr. Coffee or Lionel Richie effective in getting people to drink Pepsi? No one believes that the Yankee centerfielder is a coffee expert or that the popular recording star is an expert on soft drinks. Their effectiveness lies in our positive feelings toward them and, as Figure 5-9 shows, toward their product. (© *Paul Sequeira/Photo Researchers, Inc.*)

media, and gimmicks. Rather, it was important because it set the stage for campaigns of the future to rely almost totally on the emotional value-laden "image" nature of the influence process.

Feeling Good   There seems to be no greater persuasion appeal in the selling of a soft drink than creating an atmosphere of good feeling. People playing volleyball on a sunny beach drink Coke. People having a great time at a rock concert drink Pepsi. Attitudes can be formed and changed by simple associations with good feelings.

Persuasiveness can be increased by positive feelings that are induced by factors that would seem to bear little relation to the persuasion attempt. Consider eating, for example. Janis, Kaye, and Kirschner (1965) asked subjects to read persuasive messages about a number of controversial topics, such as the wisdom of reducing the size of the armed forces. Some of the participants merely read the messages in a typical laboratory room. Others were provided with a snack and soda while they read the messages. At the conclusion of the study, it was found that the people who were snacking while reading were more persuaded by the messages than the people who merely read the messages (Figure 5–10).

Biggers and Pryor (1982) had subjects listen to a speaker giving a presentation on automobile safety. The slides that were presented with the speech were selected to create either a very pleasant, neutral, or unpleasant feeling in the listener. When attitudes were later assessed, it was found that participants who had been put in a pleasant mood were more persuaded by the speech than those who had been put in a neutral mood. Participants who had been placed in an unpleasant mood actually showed negative change—that is, they came to adopt a position opposite to the one taken in the speech.

Finally, Ross Norman (1976) showed that people can be diverted from central processing by pleasant associations. He had female students at the University of Western Ontario read a statement arguing that people should get less sleep at night than they usually do. The students were provided with a photograph of the communicator and with some information about his background. Half of the subjects saw a picture of a young attractive male. The other half had the speech associated with an unattractive middle-aged male whose background made clear that he was an expert. The communication was presented either as a single statement or as a statement buttressed by several reasoned arguments. Norman predicted that the unattractive expert would allow central processing to occur. Targets of his communication would be persuaded as a function of the number of strong arguments presented. On the other hand, the attractive male was predicted to be persuasive along a peripheral route—that is, because of the association of his position with the pleasant feeling aroused by his attractiveness. Thus, the number of arguments was not expected to affect the convincingness of the attractive communicator. The results showed these predictions to be accurate. Only the unattractive expert's persuasiveness was determined by the number of arguments. The attractive communicator

Figure 5-10
Effects of eating while reading on the persuasiveness of various messages

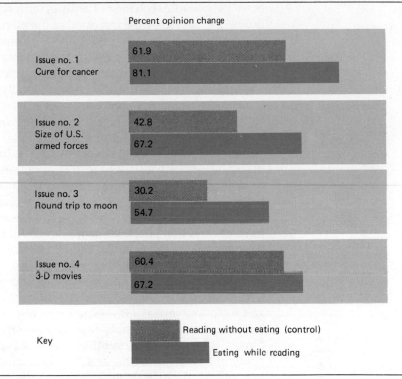

Source: Janis, Kaye, and Kirschner (1965).

was effective regardless of the number of arguments he used (cf. Snyder & deBono, 1985).

Feeling Bad: The Arousal of Fear In the standard "protection" racket, a storekeeper is asked whether he would like to take out insurance against accidents occurring to his property. When a naive storekeeper replies that he does not need such insurance since accidents do not happen to his property, the "salesmen" turn over cartons, break windows, ruin stock, and perhaps injure the storekeeper. Now protection *is* called for and for a fee, the salesmen provide it. This is, and has been, an effective "sales technique."

Arousing an undesired emotion that could be reduced by an appropriate change of attitude was the subject of a study by Janis and Feshbach

(1953). Their purpose was to study the relationship between fear and attitude change, and they chose to try to persuade people to brush their teeth more carefully and to use better oral hygiene practices. Could they scare people into a change of attitude and behavior? In the low-fear condition, the subjects were informed of the painful consequences of diseased gums and teeth. Recommendations about improved dental hygiene were offered. In the moderate-fear condition, the pain and diseases were made slightly more vivid, and the same recommendations were made. In the high-fear condition, the investigators really turned it on. The hygiene recommendations were preceded with such comments as "These [gum] infections can spread to your eyes, or your heart, or your joints, and cause paralysis, kidney damage, or total blindness." The messages were accompanied by relevant visual slides that, in the high-fear condition, portrayed disgustingly decayed teeth, results of oral infections, and so on.

Contrary to expectations, the study showed that the old protection racket did not produce significant attitude change. The results can be seen in Table 5–2. Subjects were asked to state their attitudes regarding hygiene practices and to report their own practices in the week following the study. As can be seen in the table, only 8 percent of the subjects who had received a message producing high fear followed the recommendations.

Subsequent research has tended to find a different pattern of results. Leventhal and his colleagues have found that the protection racket is alive and well. In a series of investigations, they found greater influence when subjects were made highly fearful (Leventhal & Niles, 1965; Leventhal, Singer, & Jones, 1965; Leventhal, Watts, & Pagano, 1967). For example, the study by Leventhal, Watts, and Pagano examined the relationship between fear and the desire to stop smoking. In the moderate-fear condition, subjects saw a lecturer point to charts that demonstrated the relationship between the number of cigarettes sold and the incidence of death from lung

---

Table 5–2
Effect of illustrated talk on conformity to dental hygiene recommendations

Type of change	High-fear group (N = 50)	Moderate-fear group (N = 50)	Low-fear group (N = 50)
Increased conformity	28%	44%	50%
Decreased conformity	20	22	14
No change	52	34	36
Net change in conformity	+ 8	+22	+36

Source: Adapted from Janis and Feshbach (1953).

cancer. In the high-fear condition, subjects viewed the identical information but also saw a vivid, gory version of a lung operation on a patient suffering from lung cancer. After the films, the subjects were asked about their desire to stop smoking cigarettes. In this study, unlike Janis and Feshbach's study, the subjects in the high-fear group indicated a much greater desire to stop smoking than the subjects in the moderate-fear group.

How can the differences in this research be reconciled? It is difficult to compare conditions between two studies, even if they are both labeled "high fear." It may be that the amount of fear created by Janis and Feshbach's gory pictures was much greater than than inspired by the film in the Leventhal, Watts, and Pagano study. It may then be true that attitude change increases with greater fear—but only up to a point. At some magnitude of fear arousal, we may simply refuse or be unable to cope with the information we receive.

We know from studies such as that of Leventhal, Singer, and Jones (1965) that attitude change will follow a fear-arousing communication only if people know what to do to reduce their fear. If an intense degree of fear is aroused by a communication, the panic that is experienced may interfere with people's ability to take action to make certain that the dreaded event (lung cancer, oral infection) will not happen to them. In that case, attitude change might not be expected to occur.

A graphical depiction of the actual relationship between fear and attitude change may resemble an inverted U (see Figure 5–11). In this view, attitude change increases as fear increases from low to moderate. Arousal may make comprehension of a persuasive attempt more likely to occur. Arousal may facilitate both comprehension and yielding. However, as fear becomes so intense as to interfere with individuals' ability to cope with the problem, their response is to avoid or deny the information. They may still comprehend what is presented, but they refuse to believe that it applies to them. Thus, attitude change diminishes.

Central Processing: Organizing the Communication   Having considered some of the ways in which our emotions are used to change our attitudes, we will discuss attempts to change our attitudes through rational argument. There are many questions that must be considered. Are the clarity and comprehensibility of a message really important? Are we going to present only our side of the argument, or shall we present and perhaps respond to the arguments of another side? If we decide to present two sides, which should be presented first? And when we are finished with our well-reasoned argument, do we need to spell out the conclusion to our audience, or is it better to let our audience reach that conclusion by itself?

Figure 5–11
Inverted-U relationship between fear and opinion change

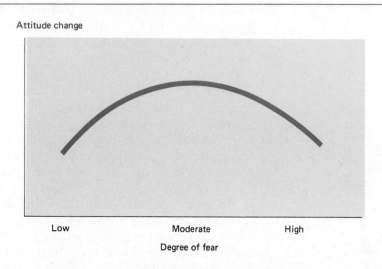

Attitude change

Low   Moderate   High

Degree of fear

The argument: How many sides? Let us consider a case from the political arena. Imagine that the year is 1984 and Ronald Reagan is running for a second term as president. His opponent is Walter Mondale. Imagine, too, a newspaper editor who would like to endorse Reagan for president. The editor knows that some people favor Mondale and he is aware of the arguments on Mondale's behalf—but his job is to convince his readers to vote for Reagan. There are at least two options available to him: (1) he can present a strong one-sided argument that Reagan should be elected president, ignoring the fact that he knows there are reasons why people should not vote for Reagan; (2) he can present some anti-Reagan arguments and explain why they are not as valid as the pro-Reagan arguments.

The relative effectiveness of one-sided and two-sided communications was one of the first questions investigated by Carl Hovland's Yale Communication and Attitude Change Program (Hovland, Lumsdaine, & Sheffield, 1949). The study used soldiers in the U.S. Army after the fall of Germany in World War II. The government wanted to motivate the soldiers to pursue the war against Japan and to convince them that it would not end quickly or easily. Several hundred soldiers took part in the study. One group was presented with a fifteen-minute radio broadcast arguing that it would take at least two more years to conclude the war with Japan.

"No thanks, I'd rather have an apple."

American Cancer Society

(MAT #5010.01)

Mark Waters was a chain smoker. Wonder who'll get his office?

Too bad about Mark. Kept hearing the same thing everyone does about lung cancer. But, like so many people, he kept right on smoking cigarettes. Must have thought,

"been smoking all my life... what good'll it do to stop now?" Fact is, once you've stopped smoking, no matter how long you've smoked, the body begins to reverse the damage done by cigarettes, provided cancer or emphysema have

not developed. Next time you reach for a cigarette, think of Mark. Then think of your office—and your home.

American Cancer Society

High- and low-fear communications. A high magnitude of fear *may* lead to a reduced effectiveness of the message . . . *if* the fear is not too high and *if* the message instructs people about how to reduce their fear. *(Both photos courtesy the American Cancer Society)*

A second group heard the identical communication except that a few minutes of contradictory arguments were woven into the broadcast. In the last group, for example, the commentator reminded the soldiers of the superiority of the U.S. Navy and the relative ease of fighting a one-front rather than a two-front war. Nonetheless, the broadcast strongly concluded that the war would take a few more years.

At the end of the study, the attitudes of both groups and those of a control group (whose members did not hear the communication) were assessed. Since the attitudes of the subjects had also been measured one week before the session, an index of attitude change was available. When the data obtained from the men were compared, it was found (1) that the experimental groups believed more strongly that the war would last at least two more years than did the control group; but (2) that there was virtually no difference in attitude change between the group that had heard the one-sided communication and the group that had heard the two-sided communication.

Interesting data emerged when the investigators took the soldiers' *initial attitude* into consideration. The one-sided communication was far more effective in strengthening the belief of those who had initially agreed with the communication. However, the two-sided communication held the advantage among those who had initially opposed the point of view of the communication.

Subsequently, Jones and Brehm (1970) refined the analysis of one-sided and two-sided communications. These investigators argued that two-sided communications are effective only to the extent that the audience realizes that there are two tenable positions. This is a reasonable interpretation of the Hovland et al. experiment. Jones and Brehm said that one-sided communications are generally more forceful and convincing since, by definition, they do not raise contradictory issues. On the other hand, individuals who realize that there is a second side to an issue may feel that their freedom to adopt a position is threatened by a communication that insists that there is only one correct stance. To maintain their freedom and independence, such individuals will resist persuasion. (The motivational aspect of restrictions of freedom will be discussed in the following chapter.)

To test this notion, Jones and Brehm devised a courtroom analogue in which subjects were asked to play the role of jurors. They were informed that they would hear the prosecution summary in the case, and half of the subjects were informed that it was not an open-and-shut case. Then, half of the subjects were presented with a one-sided prosecution argument and the other half read a two-sided statement. The jurors were then asked to rate the guilt of the defendant (i.e., whether or not they agreed with the prosecutor) on an opinion scale. The results indicated that, at least in this situation, one-sided presentations had an advantage over two-sided communications. But more important, the advantage of the one-sided communication was greatly diminished when subjects were made aware that there was a different, yet tenable, point of view.

The order of presenting arguments may dramatically affect the persuasiveness of each side. Miller and Campbell's study demonstrated that both primacy and recency effects occur in situations like courtroom trials. *(© Bill Bachman 1981/Photo Researchers, Inc.)*

For the newspaper editor, the decision about which type of communication he should use to persuade his audience to vote for Reagan would depend on his assessment of the audience. The evidence indicates that one-sided communications may have the advantage over two-sided communications, but only if the audience is not aware that a tenable case could be made for the other candidate. Thus, the editor of an arch-conservative tabloid might try the one-sided approach, since it is entirely possible that the audience has never heard of Walter Mondale or any other Democrat. However, if the audience is likely to know that there is another candidate whom respectable people are supporting, then the two-sided approach would be more effective.

Which side first? The order of presenting arguments. If you are going to present both sides of an argument, you have to know just how to use the various pro and con statements so that you will be convincing. You might begin with a list of arguments supporting your point of view, develop them fully, and then discuss and perhaps refute the arguments supporting the opposing candidate.

If we consider this approach for a moment, we can think of conventional wisdom, which suggests that everything is not so simple. A good political rally always leaves the audience singing the name of the good guy—not the opposition candidate. And some of the earliest data collected by psychologists (Ebbinghaus, 1885) demonstrate that people do forget what you tell them rather rapidly. Wouldn't we prefer to have people remember the arguments we presented about our candidate rather than the arguments supported by the opposition?

Miller and Campbell (1959) presented a carefully controlled study to clarify the matter. They argued that presenting your case first is generally more effective. However, our rate of forgetting is very fast, and if conditions are such that they allow our message to be forgotten while the other message is remembered, the second message will prevail. Since the rate of forgetting is rapid at first and then tapers off, it follows that, if two messages are presented contiguously in time and a long delay follows, there will not be much difference in the amount of each message that is forgotten when attitudes are assessed. But if a long time elapses between messages and attitudes are assessed immediately following the second message, our memory will be greater for the second message.

This type of situation happens most frequently in a courtroom where the prosecution and the defense or, in civil suits, the plaintiff and the defendant have the chance to give summations to the jury. The prosecution or plaintiff always presents the first summation. What does vary from trial to trial, however, are the frequency and the duration of recesses in the proceedings. Miller and Campbell (1959) provided subjects with transcripts of an actual court case involving negligence. In one condition, the summation for the plaintiff was followed immediately by the summation for the defense. After one week, the jury was asked to decide the case. In this condition (which we refer to as "Sum_1 Sum_2 . . . Decision"), the argument for the plaintiff was most effective—that is, a *primacy* effect prevailed—that is, the first information, the summation for the plaintiff, was more influential. In another condition, the summation for the plaintiff was followed by a week's recess. At that point, the defense summarized its case and the jury was asked to decide (Sum_1 . . . Sum_2 Decision). In this condition, a *recency* effect occurred—that is, the jury was more in favor of the defense.

Two additional conditions were also run. In one, the first summation was immediately followed by the summation for the other side, which was followed closely by the jurors' decision. In the second, a long time delay followed the first summation and the second summation. No advantage was found for the order of presentation in these conditions. The effects found in each of Miller and Campbell's conditions are summarized in Table 5–3.

Table 5-3

Conditions and findings of study on primacy and recency effects

Condition	Effect
Summation 1, Summation 2 . . . Decision	Primacy
Summation 1 . . . Summation 2, Decision	Recency
Summation 1, Summation 2, Decision	None
Summation 1 . . . Summation 2 . . . Decision	None

Note: . . . indicates a time delay.
Source: Adapted from Miller and Campbell (1959).

Adapting Miller and Campbell's results to the editor's problem, it would appear best for him to present his endorsement first *and then* deal with the arguments favoring the other candidate, since his situation is most akin to Miller and Campbell's "Sum$_1$ Sum$_2$ . . . Decision" condition.

When is more better? The multiple source effect. We've already seen conditions under which one- and two-sided communications are most effective. But factors other than the number of sides, or the order of the arguments, can affect the extent to which a communication is effective in producing attitude change. One of these other factors is the number of sources that present the persuasive arguments. To put it simply, the multiple source effect is the tendency for information presented by multiple sources to receive greater scrutiny than the same information presented by a single source (Harkins and Petty, 1981a, 1981b, 1983, 1987).

When the information is strong, increasing the number of sources tends to increase favorable issue-relevant thinking and elicits more agreement with the information than when it is weak (Harkins and Petty, 1981a). Recalling the E.L.M. model of persuasion, multiple sources apparently increase the likelihood of processing the message via the central route. When the information is strong, this increased processing produces greater agreement and persuasion. As would be predicted by the central processing route of the E.L.M., when information from multiple sources is weak, less agreement and less persuasion result (Harkins and Petty, 1987).

Television, Radio, and Print: The Effect of Mode of Communication
It is widely believed that a communication will be most effective if it is presented in "living color" on a television screen. Each year, an estimated $10 billion is spent on advertising designed to come into our living rooms on the TV. (Frank & Greenberg, 1980; McGuire, 1985). It is

We are subjected to communications in many different ways. Messages bombard us by TV, radio, and print. Which is more effective? Research shows that it depends upon the complexity of the message. *(Top left, © Ira Berger 1982/Woodfin Camp & Associates; top right, © Barbara Rios/Photo Researchers, Inc.; bottom, Marc & Evelyn Bernheim 1984/Woodfin Camp & Associates)*

assumed that people are attracted to television ads, exposure is increased, liking is increased, and purchasing will increase. Research shows that at least some of these assumptions are true.

It is certainly true that more people are exposed to persuasive communications (i.e., advertisements) on television than through the other media (Bogart, 1981). It is also true that people pay more attention to television messages and like them more than they like radio or printed messages (Andreoli & Worchel, 1978). The degree of exposure and the degree of attention certainly contributed to advertisers' paying $550,000 for thirty seconds of television time during the 1986 Super Bowl. Exposure and attention do not always lead to greater persuasion, however. Wilson (1974) showed that messages could be understood best if they were in print, and McGuire (1985) reports that both information that a person has and the attitudes he or she forms are more closely related to the duller print medium than to the more attention-receiving visual medium (TV).

Chaiken and Eagly (1976, 1983) have suggested that the difficulty or complexity of a message may actually determine which medium is most persuasive. Simple messages can be understood in any medium. For example, you do not have to pore over the pages of the *New York Times* to understand the message Coke Is It! In this case, the appeal of television may well make the simple message more persuasive in influencing viewers' attitudes. On the other hand, complex messages may miss their mark on television because they cannot easily be understood. Here the appeal of TV is of no use because the message cannot be comprehended.

Chaiken and Eagly (1976) asked students to read, listen to, or watch a persuasive communication. Half of the students in each condition found that the communication was very simple; the other half found the message complex. The results of the study showed that, when the communication was complex, printed messages were more convincing than televised messages. However, when the message was simple, the televised message produced more attitude change. These results are presented in Table 5–4.

It is no wonder then that television advertisements have almost no complex content. On television, urging people to join the Pepsi Generation may be about all the complexity that will be effective whereas in print, the message can say more. It is also little wonder that so little complexity is presented in persuasive political advertisements that are aired on television. Wrestling with the more difficult issues is usually relegated to a "position paper" that is read at a later date. Chaiken and Eagly's (1976) research supports this operating principle.

Table 5–4

Opinion change as a function of mode of presentation and message difficulty

	Simple message	Complex message
Written	2.94	4.73
Audiotape	3.75	2.32
Videotape	4.78	3.02

Note: Higher numbers indicate greater opinion change.
Source: Adapted from Chaiken and Eagly (1976).

"For Reasons of National Security . . .": Censorship   There has been much research that looks at how message content affects attitude change. There is also some recent research that suggests that *not* being allowed to listen to a communication can influence attitudes. Ashmore, Ramchandra, and Jones (1971) told subjects that they would hear a speech taking one of two positions: police should be allowed on university campuses, or they should not. Some subjects were then told that the dean had censored the speech and that they would not hear the communication. Subjects' attitudes were then measured and the results showed that censorship led subjects to change their attitude in the direction of the communication that had been censored.

Worchel and Arnold (1973) also investigated the effects of censorship on attitude change. In their study, the characteristics of the censor were varied (positive or negative). They too found that censorship of a communication created attitude change in the direction of that communication and that this occurred regardless of the subjects' initial attraction for the censor. In addition to creating attitude change, censoring a communication increased subjects' desires to obtain the communication. In a follow-up study, Worchel, Arnold, and Baker (1975) found that even when the censor was viewed as an expert, prohibiting the airing of a communication increased subjects' desires to hear it and caused attitude change in the direction of the communication.

These results suggest that a censor's actions are likely to backfire; not allowing a communication to be made may cause people to change their attitudes in the direction of the censored communication. This effect was evident in 1970 when President Nixon refused to allow the public access to the reports of the National Commission on Obscenity and Pornography (Weaver, 1970). The result of this censorship was that people who had never been interested in the report suddenly demanded to see it. The public clamor was so great that Nixon eventually released the report.

"TO WHOM? . . .": CHARACTERISTICS OF THE TARGET

The most effective communication delivered or written by an effective communicator will not achieve its maximum impact if the characteristics of the audience have not been taken into account. We do not want to say exactly the same thing in the same way to everyone. A bright audience may respond to different types of arguments than those to which a less intelligent audience would respond. An audience with one type of attitude will respond differently from an audience with another type of attitude.

Some of the factors that are basically located in the recipient of the communication will be considered in this section. These factors include the attitudes, intelligence, and personality of the audience, as well as more transient factors such as the audience's attention, mind-set, and commitment.

The Attitudes of the Audience   To some extent, communications should be tailored to the already existing attitudes of the audience. Richard Nixon, in his successful 1968 presidential campaign, created a unique set of advertisements that may help us make this point. He held a series of seemingly impromptu televised question-and-answer sessions. It was decided beforehand by his campaign staff that all such panel programs would be local; for example, the programs taped in Chicago would not be shown in Atlanta, and those taped in southern California would not be shown in New York City. Thus, it made no difference if the answer Nixon gave to a panel member's question varied from state to state. Since no one would hear any statement but the one that was designed for him to hear, a question about law and order might evoke one response in New England and a different one in the South (McGinniss, 1969).

This is not to suggest that all communications should be as unprincipled as some political campaigns are. But there is something to be said for tailoring a communication to the initial attitude of the target. On almost every issue, all of us would find some points of view unacceptable. We might listen politely to such viewpoints, but we would be absolutely uninfluenced by them. We might, however, be somewhat influenced by an opinion that is not quite as extreme as the one we found unacceptable. Research that considered the range of opinions that might be acceptable to an audience with a particular attitude was conducted by Hovland, Harvey, and Sherif (1957).

Wets and Drys in Oklahoma: Assimilation and Contrast of Attitudes
At the time of the research by Hovland et al., Oklahoma was still a dry state with Prohibition statutes. But a move to repeal Prohibition was

underway and strong feelings had been aroused on both sides of the question. The researchers wished to show (1) that when people feel very strongly about an issue they will find fewer positions other than their own to be acceptable, and (2) that people will distort opinions other than their own, such that *(a)* opinions that are unacceptable are made to appear more extremist than they really are (contrasted); and *(b)* opinions that are acceptable are made to appear more similar to their own than they really are (assimilated).

The range of opinions in which assimilation would occur was labeled as the *latitude of acceptance,* and contrast was said to occur in the *latitude of rejection.* The latitude of acceptance consists of those opinions that the individual finds tolerable—those that he or she could consider adopting—and the latitude of rejection consists of all items that the individual could not consider adopting. The investigators also predicted that as some people staked out more extreme opinions about Prohibition in Oklahoma, their latitude of acceptance would become smaller and their latitude of rejection would become larger. On the other hand, people with less extreme attitudes would have a relatively larger latitude of acceptance and a narrower latitude of rejection.

A wide cross section of Oklahoma residents served as subjects. Some held relatively moderate opinions, whereas others, such as members of the Women's Christian Temperance Union, held extreme views. All participants were shown a list of nine opinion statements about prohibition, ranging from "extreme wet" to "extreme dry." They were asked to indicate the statement with which they agreed most, all statements that they did not really object to, and all statements that they found objectionable. In this way, the participant's own attitude as well as his or her latitudes of acceptance and rejection were measured.

A week later, all participants returned and were exposed to a communication about Prohibition. In some cases, they heard an "extreme wet" statement, in other cases an "extreme dry" statement, and in still other cases, a moderate statement. Then subjects were again asked for their attitudes and their acceptance-rejection latitudes on the nine opinion statements. They were also asked to rate just how wet or dry they considered the communication that they had heard to be. The results showed that (1) extreme wet and extreme dry subjects had much narrower latitudes of acceptance and much wider latitudes of rejection that did more moderate subjects, and (2) assimilation and contrast occurred, especially for subjects exposed to the moderate communication. Extreme wets and extreme drys found the moderate position to be in their latitude of rejection. The extreme wets judged the statement to be a much more pro-dry statement than it really was, whereas the extreme drys judged it to be pro-wet (the contrast effect). Moderate subjects, for whom the statement

Strongly held attitudes for and against Prohibition formed the basis of a study by Hovland, Harvey, and Sherif. The more highly involved people are in an issue, the less accepting they are of other points of view. *(Left, The Bettmann Archive; right, Wide World Photos)*

was within the latitude of acceptance, distorted the message to make it more nearly coincide with their own opinion (the assimilation effect).

In summary, three people can hear the same politician and arrive at three different opinions about what was said. Although the talk might truly be moderately liberal, an extremely conservative person might come away shouting "Radical!"; an extreme left-winger might come away muttering "Fascist!"; and a middle-of-the-roader might think, "That's what I like, neither liberal nor conservative." Positions that are too extreme (as we shall see shortly) are less effective in altering opinions than positions that are more mildly discrepant with those of the audience. Hovland, Harvey, and Sherif's study demonstrates that not only is the extremity of a position a function of the spoken or written word, it is also dependent on the judgmental processes of the audience—processes that distort the message's content, depending on the individuals' latitudes of acceptance and rejection.

Discrepancy from the Opinion of the Audience   Regardless of the opinion we express or of how we express it, what we say is bound to be moderately deviant from the opinion of some and extremely deviant from the opinion of others. Just how far can we stray from the initial opinion of the target of our communication before we lose him? Or will we lose him at all?

Studies have shown that the relationship between the degree of discrepancy and attitude change is, in fact, a function of discrepancy *and* the perceived expertise of the communicator. In one study, Aronson, Turner, and Carlsmith (1963) asked subjects to rate stanzas of relatively

Figure 5–12

Opinion change as a function of credibility and the extent of discrepancy (theoretical and observed curves)

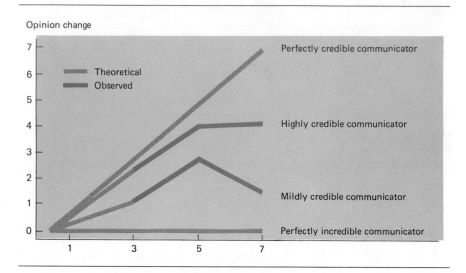

obscure poetry. They then presented the subjects with a communication that advocated ratings that were either widely, moderately, or narrowly discrepant from the subjects' ratings. The communications were attributed to either the famous poet T. S. Eliot, or Miss Agnes Sterns, from a local teachers college. Subjects were then given an opportunity to rerate the stanzas, and this served as the measure of the degree to which they were influenced by the communication. The results, shown in Figure 5–12, indicate that subjects were more influenced by a discrepant communication as a direct function of the size of the discrepancy—but only when the communicator was perceived as a credible expert. Influence peaked at a moderate level of discrepancy size when the communicator was lacking in expertise.

In interpreting these findings, it could be said that it is difficult for people to cope with the fact that their opinions are not shared by all. The wider the discrepancy, the greater the distress we have about the difference in our opinions. As discrepancy grows (perhaps into the latitude of rejection), one easy way to deal with it is to maintain our own opinion and decide that the communicator does not know whereof he or she speaks. We deal with the discrepancy by derogating the source: "Only an idiot could take such a far-out position." However, if the source is an expert, such as T. S. Eliot on poetry, then his wide discrepancy from the target of communication will still be effective in producing opinion change.

Committing the Audience: Making It Public   Attitudes that are kept private are more susceptible to change than those that are made public. For example, if during the 1985 advertising blitz for colas, a woman had preferred New Coke to all other soft drinks, that attitude would have been most resistant to change if she had expressed it publicly to her friends. Keeping the attitude to herself may have made it more amenable to Pepsi's persuasion campaigns.

To test this idea, Kiesler, Mathog, Pool, and Hovenstine (1971) had women who favored the dissemination of birth control information to high school students sign a public petition to that effect. The following day, these women—and a control group of women with similar attitudes who had not been asked to sign the petition—were exposed to literature advocating that birth control literature not be distributed. When the attitudes of all the women were assessed following the attack on their position, the committed women were much more extreme in their support of distributing the birth control literature. Moreover, by a margin of approximately 40 percent to 10 percent, the committed women were willing to do volunteer work in support of their position.

Taking Action: The Foot-in-the-Door   Anyone who has tried to sell products door-to-door or has had a salesperson appear at the door is probably aware of the "foot-in-the-door" technique. The major aspect of this approach is to have a potential customer commit himself to a very small task or favor. For example, a potential customer might be asked to thumb through an encyclopedia and give his opinion about its new format. After that, he might be given the opportunity to keep the first volume in his home for a mere fraction of the cost. Before he knows it, he could find himself signing on the dotted line for the entire set. The salesperson has put a foot in the door by committing the customer to a position in small gradations. Once the customer goes so far, it is easy for him to take the next step, and then the next, and then the next. . . .

In an attempt to see whether the foot-in-the-door method or a more straightforward request would be more successful in eliciting compliance, Freedman and Fraser (1966) devised a study that was conducted among residents of Palo Alto, California (105 women and 7 men). They were interested in seeing how many residents would comply with a request to place a large unattractive Drive Carefully sign in their front yard. In the straightforward condition, an experimenter who identified himself as being from a citizen's group for safe driving approached the subjects at their homes and asked them whether they would allow the large sign to be installed in their yards.

Several types of foot-in-the-door techniques were employed. In one, an experimenter who said he was from a traffic safety group asked the subjects to place a small sign that read Be a Safe Driver in a window of their homes. In another, the experimenter asked subjects to sign a petition promoting safe driving. Two weeks after the foot-in-the-door subjects had been approached by the first experimenter, a second experimenter came to their homes and asked them to place large Drive Carefully signs in their front yards. The experimenters were interested in seeing how many subjects would comply with this later request.

The results showed that the foot-in-the-door technique was successful in influencing others. Subjects were more likely to agree to the large request if they had already agreed to comply with a smaller request than if they had not. On the average, 55.7 percent of the foot-in-the-door subjects agreed, whereas only 16.7 percent of the subjects who had received a straightforward request agreed.

In a recent study, De Jong (1981) contacted residents from two suburban Massachusetts communities and asked them to participate in a short survey about what it is like to live near Boston. Nearly 80 percent of those contacted agreed to participate. Two nights later, different researchers, calling from a different civic organization, phoned the same residents and asked them to participate in a time-consuming survey concerning the public's use of state parks. A separate group of subjects, who had not been asked to participate in the Boston survey, were asked to be interviewed for the parks survey. Only 37 percent of this group agreed. However, more than 55 percent of the group who had taken the small step of agreeing to participate in the Boston survey agreed to participate.

De Jong (1979) reviewed several dozen studies related to the foot-in-the-door procedure. In general, De Jong concluded that evoking a small behavioral commitment does reliably increase the likelihood of gaining a larger commitment in a wide variety of settings. He concluded that the effect existed especially when (1) the original request was not so small as to be trivial, and (2) when no compelling extrinsic reason existed (e.g., a large financial reward) for engaging in the original behavior.

Why does the foot-in-the-door lead to greater compliance? De Jong's review essentially supports Freedman and Fraser (1966). These researchers speculated that by getting a subject to agree with the small request, they had caused the subject to see himself as a "person who agrees to requests made by strangers, who takes action on things he believes in, who cooperates with good causes." Because the subject had changed his self-concept to this "action posture," it was easier to get him to comply with the larger request.

One influence technique is to have people commit themselves to small requests as a way of building up to a larger request. This technique is often used by salesmen. Social psychologists have found it effective in creating attitude change. (© *Myron Wood 1973/ Photo Researchers, Inc.*)

The Door-in-the-Face   A reversal on the foot-in-the-door technique has also been suggested. Cialdini and his colleagues (Cialdini et al., 1975) reasoned that compliance could also be increased by a door-in-the-face approach. They suggested that one way to get an individual to agree to perform a moderately large task is by first asking her to perform a very difficult task. Once she refuses to carry out the very large task, *then* ask her to comply with the smaller request: "OK, if you won't do that, will you at least do this?" Cialdini and his colleagues conducted a number of studies showing that subjects were more likely to carry out a moderately large request if they had previously refused to comply with a very large request than if they had not been previously asked to comply with the very large request.

Cann, Sherman, and Elkes (1975) tested the door-in-the-face technique and the foot-in-the-door technique in the same experimental design. Subjects were randomly assigned to conditions in which they would either reject a large request or comply with a small request. In addition, Cann et al. varied the amount of time between that request and the subsequent moderate request. In one set of conditions, the moderate request was made immediately after the initial request; in another set of conditions, it was made seven to ten days later. The results showed that in the immediate condition, both the door-in-the-face and the foot-in-the-door were effective in producing compliance with the moderate request. However, in the event of a delay, the bargaining posture of the door-in-the-face was ineffective. The results of the study are depicted in Figure 5–13.

Figure 5–13
The proportion of subjects agreeing to a second request as a function of the time delay and the size of the initial request

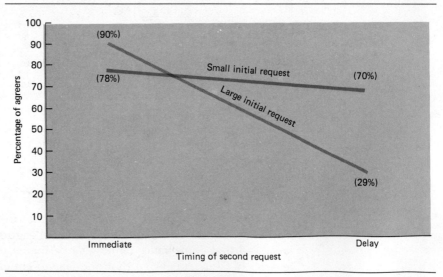

Source: Adapted from Cann, Sherman, and Elkes (1975), p. 777.

The Low Ball In a maneuver that is similar to the foot-in-the-door, there is a persuasion technique that establishes commitment by "throwing a low ball." This technique, which has been reported in many consumer magazines, such as *Consumer Reports* (1974), induces a person to make an active decision to engage in a particular action such as making a purchase. The "low ball" refers to the cost incurred in engaging in the action: it is an understatement of the true cost. When the consumer agrees to pay this cost, he or she is told that the cost has actually risen. However, the consumer is so committed to the decision that he or she is likely to bear the increased cost.

The low-ball technique is, unfortunately, very prevalent in the sale of a new car. A salesperson gets you very interested in a snappy sports car. He extols all of the good features; you really want to buy it. The good news is that he will offer you $1,000 for your 1967 Chevy. Since the net price of the sports car is now low, you make a decision to purchase the car. The salesperson then disappears into the sales manager's office for a signature. Now comes the bad news. The sales manager will not agree to the trade-in. Your Chevy is only worth $135. But you really want the car. You dig deeper into your pockets and pay the added price. You have been low-balled into a behavior that, when you walked into the showroom, you would never have considered.

Cialdini, Cacioppo, Bassett, and Miller (1978) demonstrated the low-ball effect experimentally. Subjects were contacted by phone and asked if they wished to volunteer for an experiment on thinking processes. In the control condition, subjects were informed that the experiment would require them to arrive at the laboratory at 7:00 A.M. This was the "cost" that the student had to incur to participate in the research: it was put to the control subjects in a straightforward fashion. The subjects in the low-ball condition were first asked if they wished to participate. If the subject said yes, the experimenter then revealed the true cost—that it would take place at 7:00 A.M. "Can I put you down for an appointment?" she inquired. The results showed that only 24 percent of the subjects participated who were informed before their decision of the 7:00 A.M. contingency. Of the subjects who had been low-balled, 53 percent agreed to participate.

The similarity between the foot-in-the-door technique and the low-ball procedure is that each attempts to gain compliance with a request by first obtaining compliance with a less costly version. But the difference is that the foot-in-the-door technique first obtains compliance with a harmless request, leaving the real request hidden. The low-ball technique obtains compliance with the real request; only the costs are hidden. Presumably, the low-ball procedure obtains its strength from one of two possible sources. First, it may come from the commitment the individual has made to the decision to engage in an activity. Alternatively, its strength may reside in the participant's feeling of an unfulfilled obligation to the person who made the initial request. Does the customer in the car showroom feel committed to the new sports car or to the salesman to whom he made a commitment to purchase a car? Cialdini et al. argue the first position, while Burger and Petty (1981) have presented evidence supporting the latter. Either way, the commitment implied by the low ball has a powerful influence on inducing more costly behavioral commitments.

The Sneak Attack: Resistance Due to Forewarning   Some of the most effective messages are those whose purpose is disguised until virtually the last minute. When we say "I didn't realize this was an advertisement for Coca-Cola—I thought it was another hit song," then the ad has a head start in changing our attitudes. Indeed, one of the difficulties with political advertisements is that a television viewer can find out from the local newspaper that at 10:25 there will be a five-minute spot for a political candidate. Such advance notice or forewarning can allow the potential target to build his defenses, to think of the myriad of reasons why he does not like that candidate or her commercials, or even to move toward the refrigerator for a cold beer.

What do people do during the period of forewarning? As we suggested earlier, one of the things that they may do is forearm themselves with arguments that can counter the arguments they know they will hear in the communication (Hass & Grady, 1975). We might see this as a form of inoculation or immunization. With the added time to ready arguments contrary to the message, it may be possible to fight off the communication, much as the body fights off a disease. An audience that is distracted or is not forewarned has a more difficult time gathering the necessary counterarguments. A body of literature has grown up around the question of whether it is possible to resist attitude change by immunizing the potential target against attacking arguments. This literature is discussed below.

The Medical Model: Resistance Due to Inoculation   When Hawaii was a separate nation, it kept itself considerably apart from trade, commerce, or interaction with Western nations. King Kamehameha II decided to become the first of its monarchs (and among the first of its people) to travel abroad. The king and his wife traveled to London, where they contracted measles and died. People who are raised in an environment that does not contain a particular type of germ or virus are extremely susceptible to disease from that germ or virus if they are ever placed in contact with it. People who are raised in an environment that contains a germ or virus tend to build up an immunity to it, so that the

King Kamehameha of Hawaii. His family was raised in an environment that did not contain measles virus, leaving them vulnerable to the disease. Can vulnerability to persuasion be thought of in the same terms? *(L.L.T. Rhodes/Tarus Photos)*

consequences are not as severe. Thus, the king of Hawaii, who had never been in contact with the measles (since it had never existed on the island), was unable to withstand the attack of the virus.

William McGuire and his colleagues have taken the position that the human mind can be immunized against attempted persuasion in much the same way that the body resists attack by disease. Certain of our attitudes, they argued, exist in a relative "germfree" environment. These are our cultural truisms, which are rarely if ever exposed to attack. For example, we all know that going to bed early is good, that catching a chill is bad, that brushing one's teeth after every meal is advisable. We rarely hear arguments to the contrary. Arguing from the disease analogy, it could be said that these attitudes would be extremely susceptible to attack from arguments that took contrary positions.

How could such attitudes be protected against change? One way would be to strengthen the already prevalent attitudes by providing additional reasons for holding those beliefs. This would be analogous to providing bed rest, orange juice, or chicken soup to make a person strong enough to resist a particular virus. On the other hand, we could expose him or her to a weak form of the contrary position by providing a few reasons for believing that going to bed early decays the body, that brushing teeth removes their enamel, and so on. As the body builds resistances to a weak form of virus that it receives in an inoculation, the mind can build defenses against the arguments that it may ultimately be exposed to in an attack.

In the first study to test the effectiveness of inoculation on resistance to persuasion, McGuire and Papageorgis (1961) collected a set of cultural truisms (mental illness is not contagious; it is good to brush your teeth after every meal). As has been suggested, McGuire and Papageorgis reasoned that such truisms are vulnerable to attack precisely because they are usually considered unassailable and we therefore have virtually no defense against an attack. Subjects were given two types of defenses to resist potential attacks against the truisms. For one truism, they were given a "supportive defense" in the form of arguments that upheld the truism followed by a paragraph in which the arguments were combined. The same subjects received a "refutational defense" for a second truism. Here they were exposed to arguments against the seemingly unassailable truism followed by a paragraph that refuted those arguments. The refutational defense, of course, was the inoculation analogue. Ostensibly, it aided in generating the kinds of arguments that could fight off future attacks.

Two days after the defenses were provided, the subjects heard three counterattitudinal messages. One attacked the truism that had received the supportive defense, one attacked the truism that had received the refutational defense, and one attacked a truism that had received no defense at all. After the attacks, the subjects' attitudes on all three issues (plus one truism for which there had been neither a defense nor an attack) were measured.

The results of the study are presented in Table 5–5. It can be seen that either of the two defenses was helpful in resisting the effects of an attacking message, but that the refutational defense was far more effective than the supportive defense in building resistance to persuasion.

Table 5–5
Beliefs after both immunization and exposure to strong counterarguments

Strong counterarguments only	
(no immunization)	6.64
Immunization condition	
Supportive	7.47
Refutational	11.51
Control (no immunization or counterarguments)	12.62

Note: 15 = absolute agreement; 1 = absolute disagreement.
Source: Adapted from McGuire and Papageorgis (1961).

THE FUTURE OF ATTITUDE RESEARCH: WHERE WE ARE GOING

The 1980s has been a very active decade for attitude research. William McGuire (1985) predicts that the renewed interest in this area will persist well into the 1990s.

What accounts for this enthusiasm? One answer is that attitude change has become more theoretically oriented in the past few years. Petty and Cacioppo's E.L.M. model, for example, provides one conceptual framework that helps to integrate the diverse findings in attitude research. Eagly and Chaiken (1986) offer a slightly different perspective in their attributional approach: they focus primarily on the ways in which individuals process the information they receive from persuasive communications. Regardless of the particular model chosen, conceptual models consolidate existing research and lead researchers to new predictions and therefore to investigations directed toward testing aspects of the model.

A second cause for enthusiasm is a new tendency for attitude researchers to consider the *interplay* among the many variables that lead to persuasion. For a long time, social psychologists would ask a direct question about persuasion but receive no direct answer. Sometimes, for example, research would favor one-sided communications and sometimes it would favor two-sided messages; sometimes evidence might support the effectiveness of an expert communicator and sometimes it would favor a similar communicator; sometimes it would favor television as the most persuasive medium and sometimes it would favor print.

More recently, researchers have permitted themselves to take what McGuire (1985) refers to as a "systems" approach. In this approach, the system is thought of as many interlocking variables and the researcher can

Figure 5–14
An input/output analysis of the communication persuasion process that underlies the chapter's analysis of the directive aspects of attitude change

	Input factors (independent variables)				
Output steps (mediating and dependent variables)	*Source Credibility Attractiveness Power*	*Message Appeals Styles Inclusiveness*	*Channel*	*Receiver*	*Target*
1. Tuning in that produces exposure to the communication					
2. Attending to it					
3. Liking, interest in it					
4. Comprehending its content (learning what)					
5. Generating related cognitions					
6. Acquiring relevant skills (learning how)					
7. Agreeing with the communication position (attitude change)					
8. Storing the change in memory					
9. Retrieving the relevant material from memory					
10. Decision making on the basis of the retrieved material					
11. Acting in accord with the decision made					
12. Postaction consolidating of the new pattern					

Source: Adapted from McGuire in *The Handbook of Social Psychology,* edited by G. Lindsey and E. Aronson, 1985, New York: Random House. Reprinted by permission.

consider the many paths that might connect those variables. Consider the chart in Figure 5–14. Communicator, message and audience variables are listed horizontally; the effects of those variables are listed vertically. We can see that these variables can have numerous effects. The message can affect exposure, attention, liking, comprehension, memory, and so on, as well as attitude change. In turn, these variables are related to each other as well as to the message. The "systems stylist" goes after all of these variables in his or her research design. Rather than finding the many variables a source of confusion, the systems researcher is excited about the possibilities that exist in finding the paths that connect all of the variables. Thus, research moves toward the next decade with new principles and methods and with a sense of new excitement.

SUMMARY

Attitudes are defined as the intensity of positive or negative affect for or against a psychological object. In other words, an attitude is a person's liking or disliking for any object, person, idea, and so forth. Attitudes are learned during the growing-up process. Some attitudes are learned by operant and classical conditioning; others may be adopted via the principles of balance theory.

Attitudes can be measured in a variety of ways—by paper-and-pencil scales such as the Likert, by physiological measurements such as the EMG, and by behavioral observations.

Theoretical models try to explain the way in which persuasion occurs. The Elaboration Likelihood Model (ELM) accounts for attitude change by focusing on the distinction between the central and the peripheral routes. The central route involves scrutinizing the content of a message. The peripheral route involves persuasion by other means, such as the attractiveness of the communicator and so forth.

Research on attitude change has focused upon those aspects of the *communicator*, the *communication*, and the *audience* that influence attitudes. Hovland and Weiss showed that highly credible communicators are more effective in changing attitudes than communicators with low credibility. However, they also found that with the passage of time, the effectiveness of the highly credible communicator decreases whereas the effectiveness of a communication delivered by a low-credibility communicator increases. They termed the latter phenomenon the *sleeper effect*. Kelman and Hovland showed that the sleeper effect was caused by dissociation between the message and its source. *Reinstatement* of the source eliminates the sleeper effect.

Expert and *trustworthy* communicators are more effective in producing opinion change than communicators whose expertise and motivations are suspect. Arguing against one's best interests or having a communication unintentionally *overheard* increases its trustworthiness. Communicators who are similar to the target of a persuasive message are more effective in producing changes in value oriented attitudes whereas *experts* are more effective in changing beliefs about facts.

Communications that advocate a point of view are more effective when they present *both sides* of an argument if the target of the message was initially opposed to the point of view advocated. A one-sided message is more effective for those who were initially in favor of the position advocated. Miller and Campbell showed that the *order of processing arguments* in a two-sided message is important. That is, presenting your side first will be to your advantage if there is a delay between the presentations and the attitude measurement. However, a delay between the two presentations will favor the second side if the attitude measurement is taken immediately following its presentation. Allowing an audience to *draw its own conclusion* from a persuasive message is effective provided that the audience is motivated to reach the conclusion. Communications associated with a *pleasurable emotion* can have enhanced effectiveness. Communications associated with fear can be effective if (1) they also provide a way to reduce the fear, and (2) the fear does not reach a debilitating level. It was suggested that the relationship between fear and attitude change may be of an *inverted U*-type.

The audience's attitudes are important in determining opinion change from a persuasive message. The work of Hovland, Harvey, and Sherif suggests that messages falling within a target's latitude of acceptance will be assimilated to the target's position whereas messages falling within the target's latitude of rejection will be contrasted so that they will appear more discrepant than they really are. Aronson, Turner, and Carlsmith showed that increased discrepancy from a target's position is effective in changing attitudes only if the communicator is highly credible. Committing the audience by having it agree to positions in small steps (the foot-in-the-door technique) has proven to be an effective technique for attitude change, as has asking the audience to publicly commit to a position. Related techniques such as the door-in-the-face and the low ball have also proven effective forms of persuasion. McGuire and his colleagues have shown that an audience can be helped to resist persuasion by being inoculated with small dosages of potential counterarguments. A communication topic for which an audience has no counterarguments is subject to successful counterattack from the opposite point of view. Research has also shown that *forewarning* an audience about the topic of a speech reduces its effectiveness, probably due to the audience's ability to think of counterarguments.

The development of conceptual models to account for the diversity of attitude-change findings and the new systems approach for looking at the totality of ways in which variables can interact has given attitude-change research new energy for the 1990s.

KEY WORDS

accommodation
assimilation
attitude
audience effects
balance theory
belief
bogus pipeline
classical conditioning
communication effects
communicator effects
comprehension
contrast
credibility
door-in-the-face effect
expertise
foot-in-the-door effect

forewarning
inoculation
inverted-U relationship
latitude of acceptance
latitude of rejection
Likert Scale
operant conditioning
order effects
reference group
reinstatement
secondary reinforcement
sleeper effect
socialization
triangulation
trustworthiness
value

SUGGESTED READINGS

Cooper, J., & Croyle, R. T. (1984). Attitudes and attitude change. *Annual review of psychology, 35,* 395–426.

Eagly, A. H., & Chaiken, S. (1984). Cognitive theories of persuasion. In L. Berkowitz (Ed.), *Advances in experimental social psychology* (Vol 17). New York: Academic Press.

Heider, F. (1946). "Attitudes and cognitive organization." *Journal of Psychology,* (1964). 107–12.

Hovland, C., Harvey, O., & Sherif, M. (1957). "Assimilation and contrast effects in communication and attitude change." *Journal of Abnormal and Social Psychology, 55,* 242–52.

Hovland, C., Janis, I., & Kelley, H. (1953). *Communication and persuasion.* New Haven: Yale University Press.

Hovland, C., Lumsdaine, A., & Sheffield, F. (1949). *Experiments on mass communication.* Princeton, NJ: Princeton University Press.

McGuire, W. J. (1985). Attitudes and attitude change. In G. Lundzey & E. Aronson (Eds.), *The handbook of social psychology* (Vol. 2). New York: Random House.

Newcomb, T. S. (1943). *Personality and social change.* New York: Dryden Press.

Newcomb, T. S., Koenig, K., Flacks, R., & Warwick, D. (1967). *Persistence and change: Bennington College and its students after 25 years.* New York: Wiley.

Petty, R. E., & Cacioppo, J. T. (1981). *Attitudes and persuasion: Classic and contemporary approaches.* Dubuque, IA: Brown.

Petty, R. E., & Cacioppo, J. T. (1986). The elaboration likelihood model of persuasion. In L. Berkowitz (Ed.), *Advances in experimental social psychology* (Vol. 19, pp. 123–205). New York: Academic Press.

C H A P T E R

SIX

ACTIONS AND ATTITUDES

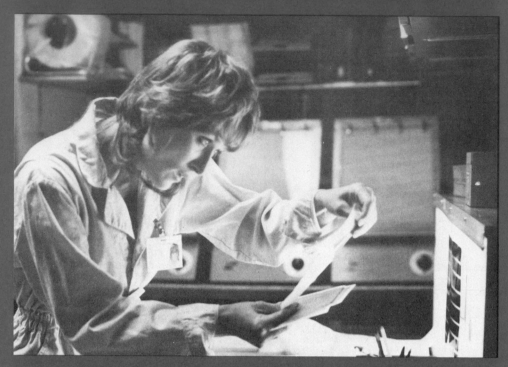

The headlights from the little white Honda were almost the only ones on Oklahoma's Highway 74 heading toward Oklahoma City. The driver was late for her meeting, but because she was a careful driver, she kept her speed at fifty-five miles per hour. Suddenly, whether by accident or by someone's design, the car crossed over to the left side of the highway, and went almost one hundred yards along the grass shoulder; it flew over one side of a culvert, smashed into the opposite side, and flipped onto its side. Karen G. Silkwood was dead.

Karen was on her way to meet with a representative of the Oil, Chemical, and Atomic Workers Union (OCAW) and a reporter from the *New York Times*. She had with her evidence that the Kerr-McGee plutonium plant where she worked had been falsifying quality-control information and sending out defective plutonium rods. Silkwood had been collecting this evidence secretly for several months, and now, in the middle of contract negotiations between the union and the company, she felt it was time to release the story. It had been dangerous for Karen to acquire the evidence but she believed in the union, so she had acted.

Karen hadn't always been so involved with OCAW. Three months after she was hired by Kerr-McGee in 1972, the union went on strike. Karen had joined the union for the same reason that many others had—out of an interest in protecting her salary and as a defense against one of the largest energy conglomerates in the country. When her local went on strike for higher wages and better working conditions, Karen had joined them—not out of any strong belief in the labor movement, but because she knew it was her responsibility as a union member to do so. Karen had begun the strike feeling somewhat apathetic. But by the time the long and bitter strike ended, Karen was one of a few workers who had stayed away from Kerr-McGee for the duration of the strike. Although she had started out apathetically, she knew at the time of her death that her relationship with the company would never be the same.

In August of 1974, with the OCAW local facing a decertification election and new contract negotiations, Karen, though still no union activist, accepted election to the union bargaining committee. She knew that the union had to negotiate a contract with the company that would call for more stringent safety standards. Plutonium contamination could cause cancer and it could produce genetic defects in the offspring of those who had been contaminated—and more and more Kerr-McGee employees were being contaminated.

However, before they could negotiate a new contract, the local had to survive the decertification election. If a majority of the workers voted against the union, Kerr-McGee would have a free hand in drawing up the new contract. Karen and the two other members of the union negotiating committee took time off from work and went to Washington to meet with

Karen Silkwood (played by Meryl Streep in the 1983 film) involved herself in union activities at the Kerr-McGee plutonium plant. Each activity led to greater involvement and finally to an investigation of safety standards at the plant. Her activities ended suddenly on Oklahoma Route 74, when her car swerved off the road and crashed . . . no one knows for sure whether by accident or design. *(Top, Movie Star News; bottom, UPI/Bettmann Newsphotos)* union officials to plan for the election and the contract negotiations. Her involvement in union activities was growing deeper.

The union officials told Karen to collect as much evidence as she could on the quality-control violations and safety problems at the plutonium plant. In the middle of the contract negotiations, the union planned to give the information to the *New York Times* as a way of putting pressure on Kerr-McGee. Karen began devoting herself to spying on the company. She was becoming increasingly convinced that the union was the only way.

Between the time of her trip to Washington and the beginning of contract negotiations in November, Silkwood's life was busy. She actively tried to convince workers to support the union in the decertification election, talking to co-workers about the union's importance. The union won. Karen carried around a little notebook and wrote down any safety-standard violations that she noticed. And she secretly made copies of quality-control documents and of touched-up X rays of faulty plutonium rods to prove her claims to the newspapers.

This union work took its toll on Karen. Management began to harass her, charging her with neglecting her work and conducting union business on company time. She was getting tired and weak. But Karen worked still harder. Her boyfriend urged her to stop working at the plant. Their relationship was growing more and more difficult as Karen devoted more time to the contract negotiations. But Karen chose to stay on. The union had won the decertification election but contract negotiations were still ahead, so Karen continued to collect her evidence.

On November 5, 1974, the day before contract negotiations were to begin, Karen Silkwood discovered that she had been contaminated by plutonium. Readings showed that some parts of her skin had over twenty times the amount of exposure to plutonium than was deemed permissible by the Atomic Energy Commission (AEC). After scrubbing herself with a mixture of Tide and Clorox, she was able to bring the plutonium levels down. The next day, Karen spent only a few hours in the plant; most of her day was spent at the contract negotiations. But again, she found that she was contaminated.

The following morning, Karen had a urine sample tested, and learned that the contamination levels had shot up overnight. She was not being contaminated at the plant! A team of technicians from Kerr-McGee was sent to Karen's apartment; they found high levels of plutonium in the bathroom and the kitchen. Everything in the apartment was taken and sealed in lead drums and Karen was sent to an AEC hospital in Los Alamos, New Mexico, for more tests. These tests revealed that somehow Karen had swallowed plutonium.

When she got back to Oklahoma, Karen put all of her evidence together. It was time to let the world know about conditions in the Kerr-McGee plant. She believed that she had to do everything she could to help the union, and she knew that this story would do just that. But she never made it to Oklahoma City, and the information about quality control in the Kerr- McGee plutonium plant disappeared.

Who, if anyone, killed Karen Silkwood? The answer has never been found. Was her death planned by Kerr-McGee, the company against whom Karen was going to testify? Was the OCAW in search of a martyr? Or did Karen fall asleep at the wheel of her Honda? The one thing that can be said with certainty is that Karen Silkwood gave her life to the union cause. Whether her union activities caused the fatigue that sent her to a fatal accident or whether she was murdered for what she had allegedly uncovered about Kerr-McGee, her devotion and dedication to the union cause had been complete—and final.

Who could have predicted Karen's dedication to the OCAW? Nothing in her past gave any indication. She had not been involved in union activities before going to work at Kerr-McGee, nor had she ever expressed pro-union sentiments. She hadn't even been particularly liberal in her political attitudes. Yet there was a marked discrepancy between her behaviors and her attitudes. Her relative indifference toward the union seemed inconsistent with her becoming a member of the negotiating team. Her initial apathy toward union activity did not lead anyone to expect that she would devote herself so thoroughly to the union during the decertification election. Nor could anyone have anticipated her behaviors in obtaining evidence about the company's alleged cover-up of their quality-control procedures. All of these behaviors were performed at great personal risk and few of them could have been predicted given what was known about Karen Silkwood's earlier attitudes.

In this chapter, we will discuss the relationship between actions and attitudes. We will deal with the way in which people's attitudes help to shape or guide their behaviors and vice-versa. In the case that we have been considering, did Karen Silkwood's attitudes lead to her significant political behavior? Or did her behavior on behalf of the union help to shape her political attitudes? The relationship between attitudes and behaviors has been a major area of study for social psychologists and it is to this relationship that we now turn.

ON THE CONSISTENCY OF ATTITUDES AND BEHAVIORS

It is a commonsense assumption that people who evaluate an object favorably will behave in a positive way toward that object and, conversely, that a negative attitude will lead to negative behaviors. This may be common sense, but it is not always the case. Consider a fascinating

Public statements of discrimination may or may not be related to actual behaviors, as La Pière's study illustrated. La Pière escorted an Asian couple to hundreds of hotels and restaurants and found that people's behavior rarely matched their stated attitudes. *(The Bettmann Archive)*

study that was conducted several decades ago. La Pière (1934) investigated the relationship between attitudes and beliefs at a time when anti-Chinese feelings were prevalent in this country. He took a Chinese couple on an automobile tour of the United States, covering more than ten thousand miles and stopping at over two hundred-fifty hotels and restaurants. In only one case did the couple receive anything but full service and courteous treatment. After their travels, La Pière wrote to all of the two hundred-fifty proprietors who had given service to the couple and asked them whether they would accept members of the Chinese race in their establishments. Despite their behavior (the fact that they had already served the couple), more than 90 percent of the proprietors who replied stated that they were against serving Chinese.

Other studies tended to corroborate La Pière's findings. Wrightsman (1969) observed the automobiles in a Tennessee parking lot during the 1968 presidential campaign. George Wallace was campaigning for the presidency on a platform arguing for stricter enforcement of the law. Owners of cars that bore bumper stickers promoting Wallace's candidacy were *less* likely to comply with a law that required them to purchase an automobile-tax stamp than supporters of the other candidates. Once again, the correlation between what appeared to be people's attitudes about the law and their actual behavior regarding a specific law was low. Wicker (1969) reviewed the relevant literature at the time and concluded that despite some evidence to the contrary, the relationship between what people say they believe in and what they actually do is not very strong.

Three Generations of Questions: Is, When, and How   In reviewing the several years of research since Wicker's review, Zanna and Fazio (1982) note that the research in attitude-behavior consistency has crossed through three classes or generations of questions. First, is there consistency between attitudes and behaviors? The answer, as numerous commentators have made clear based on studies such as La Pière's, is "a resounding sometimes." Clearly, Karen Silkwood's behavior supports this conclusion. Although certain of her behaviors followed straightforwardly from her attitudes, her activities on behalf of her union certainly did not seem to follow from the generally apathetic attitude that she initially had when she walked into the Kerr-McGee plant.

If we know that attitudes sometimes do and sometimes do not lead to consistent behaviors, then the more subtle second generation question for research is *when* do attitudes predict behavior? When—under what conditions—is it likely that a person's behavior will be predictable from his or her attitude? Research has found several such "whens"—that is, conditions that increase the likelihood of consistency between behaviors and previous attitudes.

Direct experience. Attitudes are formed in a variety of ways. You may have an attitude about the value of labor unions to a society that was formed by reading newspaper articles and by a general political orientation toward society. Alternatively, you may form an attitude about labor unions because, as Karen Silkwood did, you worked directly in a labor market in which unions were both salient and controversial. We would refer to the last as an attitude formed through direct experience with the attitude object. Attitudes that derive from direct experience are more likely to lead to behaviors that are consistent with those attitudes.

We can see what this means more clearly by looking at a study by Regan and Fazio (1977). They asked students at Cornell University to state their attitudes about a crisis in student housing that had developed at the school. Some of the students had had direct experience with the housing crisis. In fact, because of the housing situation, they were currently sleeping on temporary beds in temporary quarters. Other students had been assigned to permanent housing and therefore had had no direct experience with the housing crisis. Nonetheless, all students expressed similar attitudes; they were critical of the university's handling of the housing shortage.

All the students in the study were asked if they wished to take some action to help alleviate the crisis. Those who had had direct experience with the crisis were more likely to volunteer to behave in ways consistent with their attitude than those who had had no direct experience. Similarly, Sherman and his colleagues (Sherman, Presson, Chassin, Bensenberg, Corty, & Olshavsky, 1982) found that students who had had direct experience with cigarette smoking were more apt to act consistently with their attitudes than students who had not had any direct experience.

Relevance of attitudes to behaviors. How many attitudes does an ordinary person have? We know that there are too many to be able to keep in awareness at any one time. For attitudes to bear greatly on behavior, they would have to be accessed before the behavior. Somehow, the attitude would have to be taken from its storage in memory and then made to appear relevant to the behavior in question.

Suppose that you are participating in a social psychology experiment. Suppose too that you have a favorable attitude toward being an experimental subject in psychological research. While you are participating, you notice a sign imploring people to volunteer for yet another study. Again, you have a favorable attitude, but studies do take time and effort. What will you do?

This is a situation arranged by Snyder and Kendzierski (1982a) in their study of the role of relevance on attitude-behavioral consistency. Experimental subjects, in a situation like the one just described, read a notice inviting them to donate more of their time to a study that would give them no extra credit for participating. Half of the subjects' attitudes were made relevant to their behavior. They heard another student (actually a confederate of the experiment) say, "Well, I guess that whether you do or whether you don't is really a question of how worthwhile you think experiments are." In another condition, the confederate merely stated, "Beats me. It's up to you."

The results of the research are described in Table 6-1. Clearly, participation was related to whether or not the confederate emphasized the relevance of a person's attitude to the particular behavior. Students were much more likely to behave consistently with their attitudes by

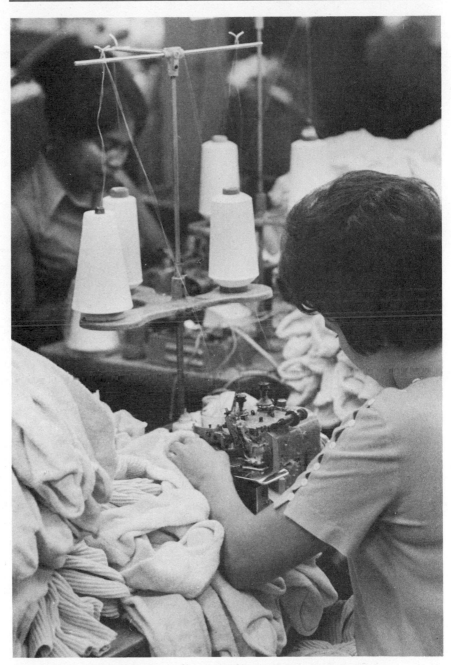

People who have *direct experience* with an attitude object are more likely to behave consistently with their attitudes. People who have worked in sweatshop conditions, such as those depicted above, are more likely to be pro-union and behave consistently with that attitude. *(Al Stephenson 1980/Woodfin Camp & Associates)*

Table 6–1

Proportions of participants volunteering for extra sessions: Investigation 2

	Relevance strategy condition	Comparison condition
Mean attitude toward psychological research	26.65	26.40
Proportion volunteering for extra sessions	.60	.25
n	10	10

Source: Adapted from Snyder and Kendzierski (1982a). Copyright 1982 by the American Psychological Association. Adapted by permission of the author.

volunteering for the research when it had been made relevant by the confederate.

Matching of attitudes to behaviors. Attitudes can exist at all levels of abstraction. Karen Silkwood had attitudes about industry, factories, plutonium factories, and the Kerr-McGee plutonium factory. Similarly, Karen had attitudes about men in general and about Drew Stephens, her boyfriend. In each case, attitudes can range from general and abstract to concrete and specific. Several investigators (Ajzen, 1982; Fishbein & Ajzen, 1975) have taken the position that if attitudes are to predict behavior, each must be measured at the same level of specificity. That is, we would not have tried to predict Karen Silkwood's behavior at her local labor union based on her attitude toward unions in general; rather, her behavior at the local union level could best be predicted from her attitude toward her OCAW local.

A study by Davidson and Jaccard (1979) provided evidence for the necessity of matching a specific attitude with specific behaviors. The investigators were interested in predicting whether women would or would not use birth control pills during a two-year period following the date of an attitude survey. Attitudes relevant to the behavior were assessed in a series of questions ranging from the very general to the very specific. When asked the general question about their attitudes toward birth control, the answers were not useful in predicting the women's behavior. As Table 6–2 illustrates, the correlation between that general attitude and the specific behavior was near zero. However, more consistency between attitudes and behavior was found as the attitude became more specific to the behavior in question. As "birth control" became more specifically "birth control pills," as the question was more directly about the "use" of

Table 6–2
Correlations between selected attitudinal variables and behavior

Attitudinal variable
Use of birth control pills during the 2-year period*
Attitude toward birth control	.083
Attitude toward birth control pills	.323‡
Attitude toward using birth control pills	.525‡
Attitude toward using birth control pills during the next 2 years	.572‡

*N = 244.
‡$p < .01$.

Source: Davidson and Jaccard (1979).

the pills, and as it became set in a relevant time frame, the attitudes and the behavior did become consistent.

The other side of the coin may be equally important. Most research up to this point, like that of Jaccard and Davidson, has examined the degree to which the atittude is sufficiently specific to be consistent with the behavior toward the attitude object. Lord, Lepper, and Mackie (1984) have suggested that we look at matters from the other side. How specific is the attitude object toward which we are behaving? Perhaps the consistency between attitudes and behaviors can be increased as we make the object more specific to the attitude. Let us return for a moment to La Pière's study. Recall that he took a well-dressed Chinese couple on a tour of the United States. They were served in all but one of the 250 establishments despite the proprietors' biases against serving Chinese. Lord et al. raise the question of whether the objects of the specific behavior (in this case, the Chinese couple) were at all similar to the proprietors' concept of "typical members of the Chinese race." Perhaps a typical Chinese was conceptualized in 1934 as "a barefoot coolie tracking mud across their lobbies" (Lord et al., 1984, p. 1256). The particular Chinese couple that entered their establishment may not have matched their prototype at all. The point here is that people have a *prototype* in mind when a general attitude is evoked; they have a prototype of a Chinese, a black, an American, a labor union, and so forth. A prototype is a standard that incorporates the essential and most characteristic features of a class (Rosch, 1978). Therefore, when we ask a person what his or her attitudes are toward the Chinese, a particular prototype is evoked and the person responds according to that prototype. It follows then that if the person has a chance to behave toward a member of the general class, but that member is not like the person's prototype, the person's behavior may indeed be different from what was expected based on his or her attitude. Thus, La Pière's respondents may have acted in a prejudiced manner had the couple matched their prototype. However, because the attitude object (the well-dressed, middle-class Chinese couple in question) did not match the prototype, the behavior and the attitude did not match. Lord, Lepper, and Mackie demonstrated that college students' attitudes toward people described as homosexuals predicted their behavior toward homosexuals only if the homosexual fit the students' prototype of the typical homosexual. Thus, to the extent that the homosexual differed from the prototype, behavior was no longer consistent with attitudes toward homosexuals.

We can conclude, then, that attitudes and behaviors will be more consistent if (1) the attitudes are specific to the behavior in question and (2) the behavioral object is a good prototype of the class of objects toward which the person has an attitude.

Individual differences. There has been a flurry of research activity that examines the kind of personality that expresses greater attitude-behavior consistency. The recent emphasis has centered on a concept known as self-monitoring that was first discussed by Mark Snyder (1979). People who are high self-monitors tend to be sensitive to situational cues; that is, they tend to make decisions based on what the outside world seems to demand. Low self-monitors, on the other hand, tend to rely on their inner states and dispositions when making behavioral decisions. Research has shown that this variable makes an important difference in predicting behaviors from attitudes. When allowed to choose, low self-monitors select situations in which they can fully express their attitudes (Snyder & Kendzierski, 1982a). And it is the low self-monitors whose behaviors follow most consistently from their expressed attitudes.

Other differences among people that have been shown to affect the consistency between attitudes and behaviors include people's conceptions of themselves as a "doer," their level of self-consciousness (Scheier, Buss, & Buss, 1978), and their level of moral reasoning (Rholes & Bailey, 1983; Gorsuch & Ortberg, 1983).

In summary, the second generation of questions on the consistency of attitudes and behaviors has received considerable attention from social psychologists. Rather than asking the general question of whether an overall relationship exists, the research has focused on the "when" of the relationship—that is, can we specify when attitudes and behaviors are consistent? As we have seen, the answer is yes. We now have a growing catalog of social situations and personality characteristics that let us know when attitude-behavior consistency is likely to occur. The ability to find the situations in which reliability leads to consistency led two investigators who surveyed a great deal of the literature to conclude that "the view that attitudes essentially have no effects on behavior can be rejected with a high degree of confidence" (Bentler & Speckart, 1981, p. 236).

The Third Generation: Asking How   How does it happen that attitudes lead to consistent behaviors? We now have some idea that under the circumstances an attitude does produce behavior that is consistent with it. However, we have been left with a catalog or list of such instances without having much of a conceptual basis for understanding the processes that make them happen (see, for example, the review of this literature by Cooper & Croyle, 1984). Fazio and Zanna (1982) predicted that research in attitude-behavior consistency would begin to approach a third generation of questions—questions designed to ask how attitudes affect behaviors. Recently, social psychology has begun to address this question.

   The theory of reasoned action. Ajzen and Fishbein (1980) suggest that a carefully reasoned or controlled process links attitudes and behaviors. According to these authors, people consider two basic factors in deciding whether to behave in a certain way. First, they consider their *attitude toward the behavior*. Did Karen Silkwood, for example, like gathering evidence for the OCAW labor union in its fight with management? Or, in a voting situation, did a person in the 1984 presidential election wish to pull the lever for Ronald Reagan? The second factor is an analysis of the subjective norms that existed in the situation. *Subjective norms* refer to what we think others want us to do. For Karen Silkwood, significant others in her environment included her boyfriend, who was vehemently opposed to her union activity, those co-workers who were also opposed to her activity, and the people at the OCAW who advocated that she perform the behaviors. For a voter, the subjective norms could include what people in his or her town might like, what the family might like, and so forth. After analyzing her subjective norms, the individual must determine her *motivation* for complying with them. If Karen Silkwood had been motivated to please her boyfriend or her co-workers, her behavior may have gone in one direction, while pleasing her union colleagues might have pushed her in another direction. Assume that we are considering Karen at a point in time at which she did have avid prounion attitudes. When she determined that she was not motivated to listen to the implied social norms expressed by her co-workers and her boyfriend, she was free to form a *behavioral intention* to copy classified documents for her union. Behavioral intentions are formed before behaviors, and are the immediate precursors to actions themselves. Schematically,

Figure 6-1
A diagram of the Theory of Reasoned Action

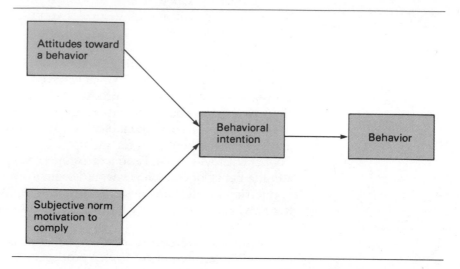

a theory involving such controlled thinking might look like that depicted in Figure 6-1.

An automatic processing model. Not all behavior is as carefully thought out as that described above. Tying your shoes, saying hello to your family, and reaching for the morning paper are all behaviors that take place rather automatically. If we did not have such automatic social behaviors, we would find the world a very difficult place to navigate. Having to expend conscious mental effort for all social behavior would be dysfunctional indeed (Langer, 1978). Fazio (1986) has proposed that behaviors follow from attitudes in much the same automatic way. He suggests that people respond relatively automatically to situations—once they interpret what that situation is.

One factor that affects our interpretation of events is attitude. Having an attitude that labor unions are good, for example, may help us to interpret an otherwise ambiguous event as one calling for prounion actions. Therefore, attitudes help lead directly and automatically to behavior because they act on our perceptions of the situation. On the other hand, we know from much of the research that we have cited thus far that attitudes do not always lead to consistent behaviors. What then is the critical factor in interpreting our behavior? The automatic processing concept holds that it is the *accessibility* of the attitude that is critical here. Recall that, as we mentioned earlier in the chapter, not all of our myriad of attitudes could possibly be brought into consciousness at the same time. Some are retrieved quickly from their storage in memory; others are retrieved with more difficulty. Anything that encourages an attitude to be more accessible (i.e., to come more quickly into consciousness) will lead to behaviors that are consistent with that attitude. Some factors that make an attitude accessible might include the strength of the attitude (Powell & Fazio, 1984; Fazio & Williams, 1985), being reminded of the attitude, and having a personality that makes you more reliant on your attitudes (recall our discussion of low self-monitors earlier in this chapter).

Research will undoubtedly continue on the third generation of questions. Reasoned actions and automatic processing, or some combination of the two (Fazio, 1986), are intriguing views of the "how" questions. (There are other models as well, including that of Abelson, 1982). At this point, we can say that attitudes sometimes do and sometimes don't lead to behaviors that are consistent with them. In the past decade, research has made great headway in determining some of the factors that make attitudes and actions more consistent. Further, research during the next era will be directed at determining the social and cognitive processes that lead to consistency and inconsistency.

BEHAVIOR LEADS TO ATTITUDES

Karen Silkwood was a person who, at the outset of her work at Kerr-McGee, did not believe in the labor movement. She described herself as apathetic toward unions. Yet, as we have seen, she became so committed to the movement and to her union that she endured great personal tragedy and eventually death. As she went through the final years of her life, she became an increasingly avid believer in her union. Her behavior seemed to precede her change in attitudes. It seemed that she acted on behalf of the union—first, by joining the OCAW, then by striking, then by remaining on strike despite company harassment that led other workers to end their participation, then by working in the decertification election, and finally by obtaining secret company documents. At every turn, her attitudes toward the union and toward her task of exposing cover-ups at the plant seemed to become more positive after she had already taken action.

Is it possible that people's behavior causes their attitudes to change at least as often as attitudes cause behavior to change? One of the social psychological theories that relates changes in attitudes to changes in actions or behaviors is the theory of cognitive dissonance. That theory is the topic of the following section.

THE THEORY OF COGNITIVE DISSONANCE

Cognitive dissonance theory, developed by Leon Festinger (1957), is concerned with the relationships among cognitions. A cognition, for the purpose of this theory, may be thought of as a "piece of knowledge." The knowledge may be about an attitude, an emotion, a behavior, a value, and so on. For example, the knowledge that you like the color red is a cognition; the knowledge that you caught a touchdown pass is a cognition; the knowledge that Karen Silkwood died in an automobile crash is a cognition. People hold a multitude of cognitions simultaneously, and these cognitions form irrelevant, consonant, or dissonant relationships with one another.

Cognitive Irrelevance   Cognitive irrelevance probably describes the bulk of the relationships among a person's cognitions. Irrelevance simply means that two cognitions have nothing to do with each other. You know that it is raining outside today, and you know that it over three thousand miles from New York to Paris. These two cognitions exist simultaneously in your head, but neither one has any implication for the other. You have no intention of jumping on a plane to Paris every time it rains in New York, and the rain does not fall because you know the distance between two cities on opposite sides of the Atlantic. Therefore, we may say that two cognitions are irrelevant if holding one cognition has no psychological bearing on the other cognition.

Consonance   Two cognitions are consonant if one cognition follows from, or fits with, the other. The cognition that it is three thousand miles from New York to Paris fits with the cognition that you choose to take an airplane to get there. The fact that the Kerr-McGee plutonium plant did not like labor unions fits with the cognition that they fought for the decertification of the OCAW. The fact that you support consumer interests is consonant with the cognition that you contributed to Common Cause.

People like consonance among their cognitions. We do not know whether this inclination stems from the nature of the human organism or whether it is learned during the growing-up process; but we do know that people appear to prefer cognitions that fit together to those that do not, as we saw in Chapter Five. This simple observation gives the theory of cognitive dissonance its interesting form.

Dissonance   Two cognitions are said to be dissonant if one cognition follows from the opposite of the other. Consider these three examples: (1) a person who is apathetic toward labor unions devoted her life to the union; (2) a man who believes in busing to achieve racial integration makes a speech opposing it; and (3) a child who dislikes chocolate ice cream purchases a chocolate ice-cream cone. In each of these situations, the cognitions about behavior follow not from the actors' cognitions about their beliefs, but rather from the opposites of those cognitions. Dissonance is aroused in each case.

Inside the Head   A person who has dissonant or discrepant cognitions is said to be in a psychological state of dissonance that is *experienced as unpleasant psychological tension.* This tension state has drivelike properties that are much like those of hunger and thirst. When a person has been deprived of food for several hours, he experiences unpleasant tension and is thus driven to reduce that tension (i.e., he eats). Similarly, when a person discovers dissonant cognitions, she is driven to reduce the unpleasant tension state that results. Reducing the psychological state of dissonance is not as simple as eating or drinking, however.

The Magnitude of Dissonance   To understand the alternatives open to an individual who is in a state of dissonance, we must understand the factors that affect the magnitude of dissonance arousal.

First, in its simplest form, *dissonance increases as the degree of discrepancy among cognitions increases.* The man who delivers a speech that is critical of school busing experiences more discrepancy between his cognitions if his attitude is extremely favorable to busing than if it is only marginally favorable.

Second, *dissonance increases as the number of discrepant cognitions increases.* A child who purchases a chocolate ice-cream cone experiences some dissonance if he knows that he does not care for chocolate as a flavor. But he experiences greater dissonance if he also has the following cognitions: (1) he is allergic to chocolate; (2) he does not like cones; and (3) he once vowed never to go to this particular store again. Moreover, other discrepancies in the situation may further increase the psychologically tense state of dissonance. For example, the child may have homework to do, but instead of doing it, he is wasting his time purchasing ice cream, an activity that is not consistent with getting the work done. Thus, dissonance is directly proportional to the number of discrepant cognitions and to the degree of discrepancy among them. As degree and number increase, so does dissonance.

Third, dissonance is inversely proportional to the number of consonant cognitions held by an individual. In most life situations, people have cognitions that support certain aspects of an otherwise discrepant situation. The child who eats chocolate ice cream despite the fact that he dislikes it may also know that (1) it is the only flavor in the store, or (2) it is the least expensive ice cream that the store sells. The greater the number of such consonant cognitions, the less the dissonance.

Fourth, to estimate the magnitude of dissonance from the factors listed above, *the importance of the various cognitions must be taken into consideration.* Glaring discrepancies among trivial cognitions would not create much dissonance in the individual. Let us say that the public library on a particular Sunday is giving away hundreds of dollars worth of free books to people who arrive before 8:00 A.M. Normally, you do not like to get up early on Sunday. However, you do it this time to get the books, which you very much want to have. We can consider this situation in terms of dissonance. Your early arisal is a cognition that is discrepant with your cognition that you like to sleep late. Your cognition that you will receive free books is consonant with your cognition that you want the books very much. Here the first cognition is trivial compared to the last. The magnitude of dissonance would therefore be low since the relative weights given to the consonant and dissonant cognitions must be adjusted based on their importance in the individual's mind.

You should be aware that precise predictions about magnitude are rarely made. Most often only global judgments as to the magnitude of dissonance are made.

Reducing the Tension   If dissonance is experienced as an unpleasant drive state, the individual is motivated to reduce it. Now that the factors that affect the magnitude of this unpleasant condition have been identified, it should be possible to predict what we can do to reduce the tension associated with it. The factors will be described here, and the evidence will be presented throughout the chapter.

1.   Changing cognitions.   If two cognitions are discrepant, we can simply change one to make it consistent with the other. Karen Silkwood could have come to believe, after engaging in prounion activities, that she really was enthusiastic about the union. She might also have believed that her behavior was not as prounion as it seemed. Either way, changes of cognitions reduce the inconsistency.

2.   Adding cognitions.   If two discrepant cognitions cause a certain magnitude of dissonance, that magnitude can be reduced by adding one or more consonant cognitions. The probusing person who delivers an antibusing speech can reduce his dissonance if he can come to believe that he made the speech only because he inadvertently found himself at a secret meeting of the Ku Klux Klan. If he can convince himself that he saved his life by making the antibusing speech, an important consonant cognition can be added to his internal formula and the magnitude of his dissonance can be reduced.

3. *Altering importance.* Since the discrepant and consonant cognitions must be weighted by importance, it may be advantageous to alter the importance of the various cognitions. The boy with the ice-cream cone might come to believe that his allergy to and dislike of chocolate are trivial compared to the exhilaration he receives when he can purchase something on sale. The importance of the consonant cognition (the one-day sale) can be magnified and the importance of the discrepant cognitions (allergy, and so forth) can be minimized. When these changes in importance are made, the overall magnitude of dissonance can be reduced.

Paradigms Used in Studying the Effects of Dissonant Cognitions   There are, of course, a multitude of situations in which people find themselves with some inconsistency among their cognitions. Social psychologists have come to use a few familiar paradigms to study the effects of inconsistent or dissonant cognitions. Their studies have often been provocative and not always in line with everyday intuition about the topics studied. The paradigms used in studying cognitive dissonance are discussed in the sections below.

The paradigm of induced compliance. In the induced compliance paradigm, individuals are persuaded to behave in ways that are inconsistent with their private attitudes. Cognitive dissonance is established by a discrepancy between one's behavioral and attitudinal cognitions. The man whose private attitude is in support of school busing is an illustration of a person in an induced compliance paradigm. For some unspecified reason, he is induced to make an attitude-discrepant speech opposed to busing. His belief is at variance with his expressed attitude. What could he do to reduce his uncomfortable tension state?

As noted above, a change of cognition is a leading possibility. What cognitions could be expected to change? Those about behaviors are very difficult to change. The behavior is often public, the actor is identified with it, and it is extremely difficult to deny that one has behaved in a certain way. People who heard the man make his antibusing speech would have been quite confused if the speechmaker had denied that he had made it. But private attitudes can be changed more easily. The man can convince himself that he is really not strongly in favor of busing. Therefore, in the psychology of induced compliance, researchers have generally looked for changes of attitudes as evidence of dissonance reduction.

In Karen Silkwood's story, Karen seemed to engage in behaviors that were discrepant from her attitudes. Her prounion behavior far exceeded her belief in the union—and each of her behaviors seemed to lead to more attitude change. It may well be that dissonance was aroused in

Karen from her counterattitudinal behavior and was reduced by a change of attitude toward the union.

The best way to get a feel for the psychology of induced compliance is to put yourself in the situation of a college student who has walked into what has become a classic experiment in dissonance research conducted by Festinger and Carlsmith (1959). As you enter the room, you are greeted by an experimenter who introduces the experiment, saying that it involves "measures of performance." You are shown a large board on which there are several rows of square pegs, and you are asked to turn each peg a quarter turn to the left and then a quarter turn to the right. You continue with this task until you are thoroughly bored, and you begin to wonder whether the experimenter is simply teasing you or has a sadistic sense of humor. No, you decide, he is serious. Then, just before you think you will fall asleep on the job, the experimenter stops you and instructs you about your next assignment. This time you have the responsibility of taking spools of thread off a large pegboard, after which you are to replace them on the pegboard. You continue this on-again, off-again project until you can barely stand it.

When you are finished, the experimenter lets you in on a secret that you have probably already guessed. He admits that he has not told you the full design of the experiment and that you really served in a control condition. If you had been assigned to the experimental condition, a paid confederate of the experimenter would have joined you in the outer office as you were waiting for this study and would have tried to convince you that the experiment would be exciting, exhilarating, and fun. Then, the experimenter continues, the performance results of subjects in the experimental condition would have been compared with those of control subjects such as yourself.

At this point, you feel fully informed about the experiment, although you may still be scratching your head, wondering why anyone would be interested in the results. What you do not know is that the experimenter has been setting you up for the most important portion of the study, which is still to come. First, he laments that the person who usually plays the role of the confederate was not able to come to the lab and that there is another subject who is supposed to be in the experimental (that is, "exciting and fun") condition in the waiting room. But all is not lost; the experimenter has a brainstorm. How would *you* like to play the role of the confederate? All you would have to do, he tells you, is enter the waiting room and convince the student that this experiment is going to be fun. If you do this, you will be paid one dollar. Would you be willing?

If you agree, you have done what the experimenter was hoping you would do, for your role in the dissonance portion of the experiment is about to begin. You have formed the belief that certain experimental procedures are dull and boring. However, you are about to make a public statement to the effect that they are interesting and fun. Those cognitions do not follow from each other, so the psychological state of dissonance will ensue. What you say to the waiting subject is not very relevant, since it is this person who is *really* the confederate of the experimenter. She is instructed to listen to your information and to accept what you have to say.

How will you reduce your dissonance in this situation? Can you deny that you stated that the tasks were interesting? That is not a likely possibility. If you really believed that they were interesting and not at all dull, however, your cognitions would be consistent and your dissonance would be reduced.

Now suppose that you are in the identical experimental situation, except that instead of offering you one dollar to make an attitude-discrepant statement, the experimenter offers you twenty dollars. How, then, would you reduce your dissonance? We noted earlier that attitude change requires work and effort and that, if there is a convenient cognition that is consistent with one of the cognitions creating the dissonance, it can be added to reduce the total magnitude of dissonance. Accepting twenty dollars is a nice juicy cognition that is consistent with performing the attitude-discrepant behavior. In this condition, it is likely that you will reduce your dissonance by recourse to the twenty dollar incentive and that you will have less need to convince yourself that the task was really interesting.

In all, Festinger and Carlsmith had three conditions in their study. In addition to the two incentive conditions (one dollar and twenty dollars),

In the induced compliance paradigm, a subject is asked to perform a boring task, such as turning pegs on a peg board. Later, he will be asked to tell someone else that he had an exciting, marvelous time. What is the effect on his attitude? *(Glenn Hausfater)*

Figure 6–2
Attitude change following induced compliance

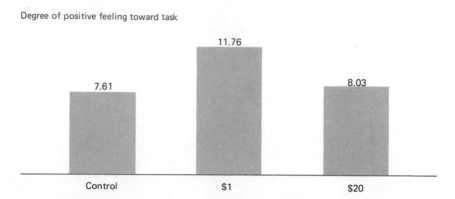

Degree of positive feeling toward task

| | 11.76 | |
| | 7.61 | | 8.03 |

Control $1 $20

Source: Festinger and Carlsmith (1959).

a control group was run in which subjects performed the boring tasks but were not asked to tell the waiting subject that the task was enjoyable.

After an appropriate explanation, all subjects were asked to tell a psychology department secretary how interesting the spool-sorting and peg-turning tasks had been. The results are illustrated in Figure 6–2. The subjects who served in the control condition did indeed think that the tasks were boring, as did the subjects who participated in the experiment for twenty dollars. But the subjects who performed the counterattitudinal behavior for only one dollar told the secretary that the task was fun and enjoyable. Thus, agreeing to make a counterattitudinal statement for a small incentive led to the greatest degree of attitude change in the Festinger and Carlsmith study.

This study provided astounding support for predictions derived from cognitive dissonance theory. It showed, first, that attitudes could be affected by behavior, such that statements made contrary to one's attitude could produce changes in attitude. Second, it demonstrated that an inverse relationship exists between the incentive that is offered for the behavior and the degree of attitude change that will take place. As incentive increases, attitude change (and presumably the internal state of dissonance) decreases.

A study conducted at Yale University by Cohen (1962) provides further support for Festinger and Carlsmith's hypothesis. Yale is situated in New Haven, Connecticut, and it was not uncommon for students to

Figure 6–3
Mean attitudes toward police actions

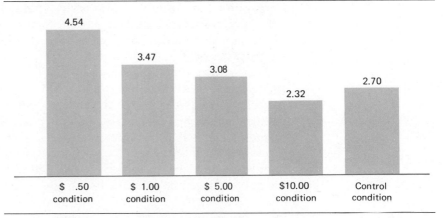

Note: The higher the mean, the more positive the attitudes toward the New Haven police. The highest value equals 7.00; the lowest value equals 1.00.
Source: Adapted from Cohen (1962).

become entangled in controversy with the New Haven police department. After one altercation, in which it was alleged that the police had acted with unnecessary aggression in handling a student melee, Cohen realized that he had the right ingredients for a dissonance study. He contacted Yale students in their dormitories and told them that an important research institute wanted them to write forceful essays taking the police side of the question. Further, the students were offered an incentive for writing the essay. Depending on the condition to which the student was assigned, he was offered fifty cents, one dollar, five dollars, or ten dollars. After the essay was completed, the subject's attitude toward the police was assessed.[1]

The results of Cohen's study are presented in Figure 6–3. As incentive increased from fifty cents to ten dollars, attitude change decreased. In fact, the ten dollar condition can be seen to be slightly less favorable to

---

[1]It should be noted that this study, like Festinger and Carlsmith's, is known as an after-only design. Subjects' attitudes are measured only once. In these studies, when a statement is made regarding attitude change, the difference between subjects in a particular condition and subjects under control conditions is being assessed. Since subjects are randomly assigned to the various conditions, it can be assumed that any difference between an experimental group and the control group must be due to a change in the experimental group, as a result of the independent variables of the experiment

the New Haven police than the control condition, although that difference was not reliable.

In summary, the major points to be abstracted from Festinger and Carlsmith's and Cohen's studies are (1) that behavior that is discrepant with one's attitudes can produce changes in those attitudes, and (2) that the amount of attitude change increases as the justification or the inducement for performing the behavior decreases.

Money isn't everything.   Induced compliance produces attitude change as an inverse function of justification. Money is not the only justification that can serve as a cognition consonant with behavior. Other forms of justification ought to serve the same purpose. For example, if an experimenter asks a subject to do something that is attitude discrepant, the experimenter is likely to get considerable compliance if he lies on the floor, sobs, and tells the subject that he will suffer a mental breakdown if the subject does not deliver a strong and forceful speech. However, the crying act may also serve as a justification, much like the twenty dollar incentive of the Festinger and Carlsmith study. It may be a large consonant cognition that reduces the magnitude of dissonance and lessens attitude change.

Rabbie, Brehm, and Cohen (1959) conducted a study similar to our hypothetical example. They asked students to deliver speeches contrary to their attitudes. Students in a high-justification condition were told how valuable the results would be for science and how much the experimenter would appreciate their cooperation. In a low-justification condition, students were asked to deliver a speech, but were given no song and dance about the value of the study for science, and so on. The results indicated that the students who made their counterattitudinal statements with no special justification became more favorable to the position expressed in their speech than the students who made their statements with the extra justifications provided by the experimenter.

The justification for committing an act that is discrepant with one's attitudes can be more subtle than the explicitly stated justification of the Rabbie et al. study. It might even depend on the likability of the person inducing one to comply. Zimbardo, Weisenberg, Firestone, and Levy (1965) had an experimenter try to persuade subjects to eat grasshoppers. In one condition, the experimenter who made this somewhat bizarre request was friendly and affable. In another condition, he was cold, unfriendly, and generally unlikable. As might be predicted from dissonance theory, the subjects who agreed to eat the grasshoppers for the aloof and unfriendly experimenter rated themselves as being more in favor of eating grasshoppers than the subjects who agreed to eat the grasshoppers for the friendly experimenter. Apparently, trying to please a friendly and likable person served as a justification for engaging in

During the Vietnam War, people sought to avoid the draft in a variety of ways. The likelihood of being drafted into the army was based on a lottery system. The lottery system and the attempts to avoid it formed the basis for dissonance study by Staw (1974). *(Bob Combs 1977/Photo Researchers, Inc.)*

grasshopper eating, whereas changing private attitudes toward eating grasshoppers was necessary for reducing dissonance when the experimenter was unfriendly.

In the natural environment outside of the laboratory, people often get involved in situations that are discrepant from their attitudes and that have less than sufficient justification. As the war in Vietnam heated up during the late 1960s, President Nixon introduced the concept of the "draft lottery." Depending on the date of their birth, young men would be given a number at random that indicated the priority with which they would be drafted into the army. By and large, people who received numbers 1–122 could be confident that they be drafted; people with numbers 245–365 could be confident that they would avoid the draft.

Many male students rushed to join a campus ROTC as a way of avoiding being drafted into the war. To be exempt from the draft, it was necessary to join ROTC before receiving a lottery number. Some signed long-term commitments; others joined for one-year intervals. Staw (1974) studied the effect on ROTC membership and attitudes of people once they learned what their draft priority was. For students who had signed short-term contracts and who received numbers in the 245–365 range, there was a high dropout rate from the ROTC program. This indicates that ROTC membership was counterattitudinal for a substantial number of students. For students who had signed long-term contracts, what justification existed for their behavior? Those who received draft numbers from 1 to 122 had sufficient justification: their ROTC membership was keeping them away from Vietnam. But students who had joined ROTC and then received numbers in the 245 to 365 range had no such justification. They probably would not have gone to Vietnam regardless of the ROTC.

Dissonance theory would predict that the low justification for ROTC membership among students with 245+ draft numbers would result in attitude change. These students would become more favorable to the ROTC. On the other hand, students with high justification (draft number lower than 122) need not change their attitudes about ROTC to make them consistent with their behavior. Staw interviewed the ROTC members and found that the long-term volunteers with the 245+ draft numbers were more favorable toward ROTC and performed better at ROTC drills than people with numbers lower than 122. Since the draft number a person received was totally random and occurred after all of the students had decided whether or not to join ROTC, the results found by Staw are compelling. Apparently, dissonance was created by receiving the high draft number (i.e., low justification) and was reduced by attitude change toward ROTC.

Critical factors in induced compliance. In the years since Festinger and Carlsmith (1959) introduced the paradigm, research has shown that the world of induced compliance has grown more complex. Reviewing twenty years in the evolution of research in dissonance theory, Greenwald and Ronis (1978) commented, "Perhaps the only victim of the evolutionary process is the original version of dissonance theory, which has effectively been discarded" (p. 56). It may be more accurate to say that more than twenty years of research has allowed the theory to become more specific, more accurate, and consequently, more qualified. It can still be said that behavior discrepant with private attitudes will produce attitude change when the justification is low—if the word *sometimes* is added. We shall now consider the factors that comprise the "sometimes" —that is, the factors that have proven necessary if induced compliance is to lead to dissonance-produced attitude change.

1. Choice. One of the most widely investigated factors in induced compliance has been the perception of the individual's freedom to act in a discrepant fashion. If I hold a gun to your head and "request" that you make certan discrepant statements, you will probably have fear—but will you have dissonance? Most likely, your magnitude of dissonance will be

Figure 6–4

Changes of attitudes toward speaker ban as a function of choice and incentive

Attitude change

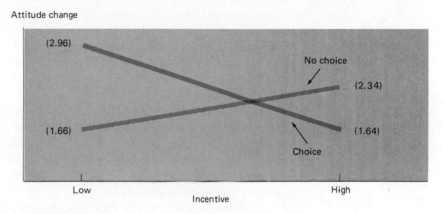

Source: Adapted from Linder, Cooper, and Jones (1967).

quite low since the gun serves as the ultimate justification for your attitude-discrepant behavior. *In general terms, coercion, because of its high justification properties, will eliminate any further need for dissonance reduction.*

To see the dramatic difference that perceived freedom makes in creating changes in attitudes, consider an experiment conducted by Linder, Cooper, and Jones (1967). Students were induced to write essays taking a very unpopular position—that controversial speakers should be banned from the university. Half of the students were *required* to write their attitude-discrepant essays and were then paid either a small or a large amount of money for their participation. The other half of the students were *asked* whether they would be willing to write their essays and were promised either the small or the large incentive for their efforts. It was emphasized that the decision to write the essay was completely up to the student.

The results of the study show the dramatic effect of the perception of freedom in determining dissonance-produced attitude change. Figure 6–4 shows that when subjects freely chose to write an attitude-discrepant essay, their attitude change (and presumably their dissonance) decreased as the incentive value increased. This is consistent with the Cohen (1962) and Festinger and Carlsmith (1959) studies reported earlier. But when choice was eliminated, so was cognitive dissonance; only then did some other process begin to operate. In this case we can call the no-choice line in Figure 6–4 a *reinforcement effect.* The more money received, the more positive the affect for the task. The process may be akin to serendipi-tously finding money on a street corner; the person who does so may go back to that spot agan and again and come to like that part of town. The more money (the more reinforcement), the more the liking. But the importance of the Linder, Cooper, and Jones study lies in its demonstra-tion that the relationship between justification and eventual attitude change that we have been discussing in the induced compliance para-digm exists only when the individual feels free to comply or not to com-ply with a request for attitude-discrepant behavior.

The illusion of choice.   The way in which the concept of freedom is applied in dissonance research is somewhat unusual. Typically, a choice is expected to be sometimes accepted and sometimes refused. However, students who serve as subjects in dissonance experiments rarely turn down an experimenter's request. Subjects have been known to undergo undue physical effort (Wicklund, Cooper, & Linder, 1967), to eat grasshop-pers (Zimbardo, Weisenberg, Firestone, & Levy, 1965), and to shock fellow students (Brock & Buss, 1962), in addition to making counterattitudinal statements, even though they had been offered a "choice" for compliance. Rarely do more than 5 to 10 percent of the subjects reject the experimenter's request. Kelley (1967) has characterized the choice offered to subjects in induced compliance experiments as an "illusion of freedom." What is important, it can be argued, is not whether the subject has the audacity to refuse the experimenter's request, but whether she feels that she could have refused. As long as people have the illusion that they are free to choose, then induced compliance can lead to dissonance arousal and to attitude change.

2.   Commitment.   Intuitively, it seems likely that we would suffer more dissonance from making a counterattitudinal statement to a group of friends than we would from merely thinking of some statements that are attitude discrepant. One of the reasons this is so may be the degree of *com-mitment* to the disliked position (Carlsmith, Collins, & Helmreich, 1966). When you are thinking to yourself, no one is a witness to your behavior. Unlike the examples in the preceding section, if you merely think a posi-tion you *can* "take it back." You are not publicly identified with your attitude-discrepant position, and you can deny to yourself that you ever thought those evil thoughts. When you are speaking to your friends, it is much harder to deny what you said, as you have been clearly and publicly identified with your statements.

An important experiment by Davis and Jones (1960) demonstrates the combined effect of commitment and perceived freedom. Each student subject was asked to serve as an ally of the experimenter and to deliver an untrue evaluation of another student. The experimenter explained that he needed someone to make a hostile and derogatory evaluation of the other student. In half of the cases, the student was told that it was her obligation as an experimental subject to deliver the negative evaluation. In the other half of the cases, the student was merely requested to do so.

In addition to the variation of perceived freedom, the experimenters gave half of the subjects reason to believe that they would meet the other student after the experiment and would have a chance to reveal to her the circumstances behind the negative evaluation. That is, half of the subjects felt that they would be able to "take back" their evaluation, whereas the other half anticipated no such opportunity.

If a lack of commitment reduces the magnitude of dissonance, and if a lack of perceived freedom reduces dissonance, then only one of the conditions of the experiment could be expected to show a difference in attitude. Subjects who delivered their evaluation under high-choice and high-commitment conditions were expected to change their evaluations of the other student in the direction of the negative statements that they had made. The results supported that prediction (see Table 6–3).

3.   **Aversive consequences.**   Not every attitude-discrepant act produces dissonance. Suppose that a Democrat is induced to make a statement urging a Republican victory in his congressional district. Cooper and Worchel (1970) and Collins and Hoyt (1972) have produced findings that imply that the Democrat would be in a state of dissonance only if he felt that he might have convinced someone to vote Republican. However, if the speech were made in front of the bathroom mirror with no possibility of persuading anyone of its contents, then it would not arouse dissonance. *In general, attitude-discrepant behavior arouses dissonance only if it can lead to an unwanted or aversive event.*

In Cooper and Worchel's study, subjects participated in the dull, peg-turning task of Festinger and Carlsmith's study and were also asked, in return for either a low or a high inducement, to mislead a waiting confederate into thinking that the task was exciting. However, after trying to

---

Table 6–3

Changes in the evaluations of the target person

	Choice	No choice
Commitment	−7.7	−1.7
No commitment	−1.8	−2.2

Source: Adapted from Davis and Jones (1960).

convince the confederate, half of the subjects in Cooper and Worchel's study heard him say, "You are entitled to your opinion, but every experiment I have ever been in has been dull, and I expect this one to be dull too." The other half of the subjects saw the confederate become enthusiastic and quite excited about participating in an interesting study. In other words, the second group had the unwanted consequence of convincing a fellow student to become excited about a study that he would soon find dull. For the first group, there was no aversive consequence since in this case the confederate remained unconvinced.

The results of the study (depicted in Figure 6–5) made it clear that the only subjects who came to believe that the task was interesting were those whose attitude-discrepant behavior was performed for a low inducement *and* who brought about the aversive consequence of misleading a fellow student. Thus, attitude-discrepant behavior that has the possibility of bringing about an unwanted event may arouse cognitive dissonance.

4. Personal responsibility. Wicklund and Brehm (1976) surveyed the entire gamut of research in dissonance theory and concluded that

Figure 6–5
Mean ratings of enjoyableness

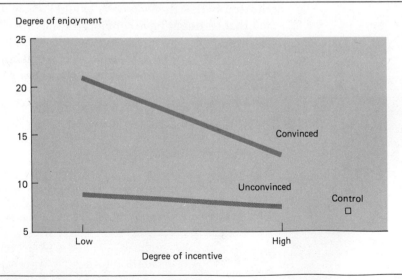

Note: Higher numbers represent greater enjoyableness.
Source: Cooper and Worchel (1970).

"dissonance as we know it takes place only when the dissonant elements have been brought together through the personal responsibility of the individual who experiences dissonance" (p. 7). Cooper (1971) has characterized personal responsibility as the blending of the already introduced concept of *choice* with the concept of *foreseeability.*

As an example, consider a hypothetical person who sees a geographic guide to the United States in a bookstore, purchases it, and then finds out that the proceeds of the book are to go to the United Klans of America. Since he despises the KKK and he has just donated money to it, does he experience dissonance? According to the viewpoint that emphasizes personal responsibility, the answer would be no. This viewpoint argues that dissonance results from counterattitudinal behavior only when (a) the behavior was freely chosen and (b) the aversive consequence that follows from that behavior could have been foreseen at the time of the commitment. In the hypothetical example, the book purchase was freely made but the aversive consequence was not foreseeable. If the book purchaser can add the cognition, "But I couldn't have known that the money would be used in that way," he can avoid personal responsibility for the inconsistency caused by despising the Klan but contributing money to it.

Goethals, Cooper, and Naficy (1979) conducted research to test the specific prediction that an aversive consequence has to be foreseeable for cognitive dissonance to be aroused. Subjects volunteered for what they believed was a study of psycholinguistics. The experimenter explained that the purpose of the study was to assess linguistic devices used in oral communications. This explanation was not exactly accurate but did serve to offer a reason to ask the students to write a counterattitudinal speech—in this case, to advocate doubling the undergraduate enrollment at the university.

Not only was the speech contrary to the subjects' attitudes, but there was also an unwanted consequence that might occur as a result of the speech. Recall that the study by Cooper and Worchel (1970) indicated that it was necessary for people to feel that some unwanted event might be caused by the speech. The unwanted consequence in the study by Goethals et al. was that the speech was going to be shown to the Board of Admissions, which was considering a change of policy to allow for the doubling of the student enrollment. Subjects in an *unforeseeable* condition were kept unaware of this consequence. They were not told that the speech would or might be sent to the Board of Admissions. Subjects in this condition, then, thought the speech was for the sole use of the psycholinguistic experiment. Subjects in a *foreseen* condition were told explicitly, before deciding to give their speech, that the Board of Admissions might be sent a copy of the speech. Finally, a *foreseeable* condition was run in which the possibility of "other interested groups" hearing the speech was

Table 6–4
Mean attitudes toward increasing the size of the freshman class

Condition	Foreseen	Foreseeable	Unforeseeable
Informed	7.1	7.4	9.6
Not informed	7.4	10.2	10.1

Note: Higher numbers indicate less favorable attitudes toward increasing class size. Low numbers are in the direction of the speech and imply greater attitude change.
Source: Goethals, Cooper, and Naficy (1979).

mentioned but the Board of Admissions was never explicitly named. When the speech was concluded, the experimenter made it clear to half of the subjects in each condition that their speeches were, in fact, going to be sent to the Board of Admissions. No mention was made to the other half of the subjects of where, if anywhere, the speech was to be sent.

Subjects' attitudes about doubling the size of the freshman class were assessed at the conclusion of the experiment. The results are presented in Table 6–4. They showed that when an aversive event was foreseen before deciding to engage in the counterattitudinal behavior, attitude change occurred. People who freely wrote essays favoring increasing the size of the student body changed their attitudes in that direction if they knew about the consequence beforehand. Apparently, they experienced personal responsibility for their actions and therefore experienced dissonance. Changing their attitudes was their way of reducing that dissonance. However, subjects who had no way of knowing the aversive use to which their essay might be put (unforeseen condition) did not experience dissonance: their ability to use an "I couldn't have known . . ." cognition eliminated their personal responsibility.

The middle column of Table 6–4 presents the interesting case of people who did not know of the ill use of their essay—but they might have been able to realize it had they thought about it. After all, the Board of Admissions certainly is an "interested group" that might want to hear students' speeches. The results showed that when the subjects were not informed that the Board of Admissions would hear their speech, they did not experience dissonance. But when they were informed, the concept that they *could* have known if they had thought about it was sufficient to invoke personal responsibility and led to the attitude change shown by the low score in the foreseeable-informed condition.

The effort justification paradigm: To suffer is to love. Closely akin to the psychology of induced compliance is a paradigm that can be called "effort justification." The observation that people love what they suffer for adequately summarizes this dissonance effect. Normally, we do not like to expend undue effort; we do not like to suffer. But we sometimes find ourselves in a position in which we are volunteering to do just that. The result may be the arousal of dissonance and the need to find a justification for having chosen to suffer.

Aronson and Mills (1959) invited women students to participate in a sexual discussion group. Before the students could join the group, it was necessary that they undergo a screening test to be certain that they would be able to contribute openly to the discussion. It was implied that the test might be embarrassing because of the words that the subject would have to say aloud. Of course, the subject could refuse to undergo the test, but she then would not be allowed to become a member of the group.

Some of the subjects who agreed to take the screening test were assigned to a severe condition in which they were given a list of obscene words and lurid descriptions of sexual activity to read aloud. Other subjects were assigned to the mild condition in which they read ordinary words such as *petting* and *prostitute* for their screening test.

After their initiations, all subjects (plus a control group that received no screening test) were asked to listen to a discussion being held by the group. It was explained that since the subjects had not done the reading for the week's discussion, it would be better if they did not actually join the group now but instead listened to the week's discussion over earphones. The discussion that the girls listened to was dreadful. As Aronson and Mills described it, the discussion concerned "secondary sex behavior in the lower animals. [The participants] inadvertently contradicted themselves and one another, mumbled several non sequiturs, started sentences that they never finished, hemmed, hawed, and in general conducted one of the most worthless and uninteresting discussions imaginable" (p. 179). In fact, the discussion that the subjects were overhearing was actually a tape recording that had been designed to be as boring as possible. At the close of the discussion, the new initiates (the subjects) were asked to rate how interesting they felt the discussion had been.

Now, assume that you were a subject in the severe condition and that you had been embarrassed by the words you had read. Why would you choose to suffer embarrassment? The cognition that you do not like to be embarrassed is dissonant with the cognition that you have chosen to be embarrassed. According to dissonance theory, this arouses an uncomfortable tension that must be reduced. What cognitive changes are possible? You could deny that the embarrassment was severe, but assume that the

Figure 6-6
The effort justification sequence

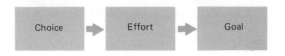

words and passages were so chosen that this is not a viable alternative. You could decide that you like to suffer. This too is not a likely possibility. Finally, *you could come to like what you suffered for.*

Consider Figure 6-6, which depicts the effort justification sequence. If you could come to like the goal for which you suffered, then you will have added a cognition that is consonant with your suffering. In the Aronson and Mills experiment, the goal (the discussion group) was dull. But if you convince yourself that the group is really worth joining, then your dissonance can be reduced.

The results of the Aronson and Mills experiment are presented in Table 6-5. It can be seen that the control group and the mild group rated the discussion and the participants as considerably more boring and less interesting than the group that suffered more severely.

The Aronson and Mills study has been supported by subsequent findings of Schopler and Bateson (1962), who used a very similar procedure, and of Gerard and Mathewson (1966), who conducted a very carefully controlled conceptual replication in a situation involving electric shock rather than embarrassment.

Table 6-5
Means of the sum of ratings for the different experimental conditions

	Experimental conditions		
Rating scales	*Control*	*Mild*	*Severe*
Discussion	**80.2**	**81.8**	**97.6**
Participants	**89.9**	**89.3**	**97.7**

Source: Adapted from Aronson and Mills (1959).

Applications of effort justification. In the effort justification paradigm, the concept of effort is taken in its most generic sense to apply to any situation that an individual would ordinarily prefer to avoid. Thus, such noxious events as electric shock (Gerard & Mathewson), embarrassment (Aronson & Mills), physical exertion (Wicklund, Cooper, & Linder, 1967), and exposure to delayed auditory feedback (Zimbardo, 1965) have all been used as ways to induce effort. Given this broad concept of effort, we can imagine that people may find themselves in many situations that they would ordinarily prefer to avoid. To the extent that they voluntarily place themselves in those situations, dissonance should be aroused. This, in turn, may lead to some interesting and practical consequences.

First, let us consider Karen Silkwood herself. At each turn, she was placed under great emotional hardship for her decision to become involved with the union. Her boyfriend pressured her and Karen became more prounion; the company harassed her and she became more prounion; she was poisoned with plutonium and she became even more adamantly prounion. Under extremely effortful conditions, Karen's attitudes seemed to change, evolve, and become stronger. Might Silkwood have been engaged in an effort justification process, continuing to reduce dissonance by changing her attitudes to justify her suffering?

Second, let us turn our effort justification approach to an activity in which many people are involved—the process of psychotherapy. We begin with a hypothetical example.

Mary has trouble losing weight. She cannot seem to sustain a diet or an exercise program. She wishes to obtain psychotherapeutic help. She can choose from a myriad of therapists and a variety of therapeutic procedures. She can settle on a psychodynamic approach, which emphasizes the hidden or repressed roots of her phobia. In this way, she can devote several years of her life, spend a considerable amount of money, and dredge up a number of unpleasant traumatic memories to arrive at an understanding of her problem. Alternatively, she can choose a learning approach to therapy. These approaches take less time and are sometimes less of a financial burden than psychodynamic approaches, but they too involve a degree of unpleasant emotional arousal.

Let us assume that Mary decides to enter into a therapeutic situation that is time consuming, costly, and emotionally draining to achieve her goal: losing weight. Let us also assume that after several sessions, the therapy pays off: Mary begins to reduce. Why has improvement been made? Naturally, Mary's therapist can talk about teaching her to avoid anxiety or about discovering the hidden meaning of her problem. That is, the therapist has a theory of therapy that may account for Mary's improvement. However, a social psychologist will realize that the therapeutic setting has caused Mary to expend *effort* in the broad sense of the term.

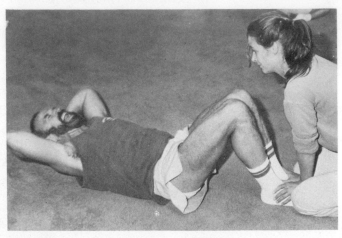

Deciding to suffer for something results in the tension state of cognitive dissonance. People can change their attitudes and behaviors about such important goals as weight loss if they are induced to suffer in order to achieve their goal. *(Left, Alan Carey/The Image Works; right, © 1981/S. Oristaglio/Photo Researchers, Inc.)*

Whatever the therapist's theoretical bent, Mary has spent money and time and has experienced unpleasant emotions. Consistent with Aronson and Mills's study, Mary should have experienced dissonance and therefore to reduce the dissonance, sought to raise her evaluation of the goal state making the cognitions more consonant. In this example, Mary's goal state was to be able to lose weight. It could be predicted that she would come to like dieting, exercising, and so forth much as Aronson and Mills's subjects came to like the boring discussion group. "Why did I expend so much effort?" Mary may have asked herself. "Because I really like to diet," may have been the response.

Cooper and Axsom (1982) conducted a study with overweight women who wanted some assistance in losing weight. Each subject participated in the experiment separately. Upon arriving at the first session, the participant was weighed by the experimenter, then informed about the "new experimental procedure" that was being developed to aid weight loss. Using an appropriate rationale, the subject was told about a series of tasks she was to perform. It was clear that each would require a great deal of effort. One task, for example, involved reading tongue twisters and nursery rhymes into a microphone while the subject heard her own voice fed back to her on earphones with a .3 second delay. None of the tasks involved any physical exercise, but each was extremely effortful. The tasks lasted about forty minutes.

Two additional conditions were run. In a low-effort condition, the same tasks were introduced to the participants, but each one was easier and shorter than the parallel tasks in the high-effort condition. Finally, there was a control group that consisted of women who had volunteered for the study, were weighed during the initial session, but were not contacted again until it was time to collect the dependent measure. Subjects in the high- and low-effort groups returned to the laboratory for a total of five sessions during a three-week period for the purpose of performing the experimental tasks. At the end of the fifth session, they returned to the scale and were weighed.

The prediction of the research was that subjects who had been in the high-effort condition would lose more weight during the three weeks than either the low-effort or control-group subjects. The first column of Table 6–6 shows that this did occur. After the three-week period, high-effort subjects lost an average of 1.76 pounds compared to the .82 pounds lost by the low-effort group and the .17 pounds that were gained by the control subjects.

How long lasting was the weight loss? Without having mentioned this to the participants at the outset of the research, each participant was called in to be weighed after an interval of six months. The results after the six-month interval were far more impressive than they were for the earlier weight measure. High-effort subjects lost nearly nine pounds. In addition, 94 percent of all subjects in the high-effort condition had lost weight after six months, while only 39 percent of the low-effort subjects had sustained any weight loss.

The free-choice paradigm. Another common way to study cognitive dissonance is called the free-choice paradigm. Consider Helen, a woman

---

Table 6–6

Weight changes in weight control experiment (in pounds)

Effort condition	Time of measurement		
	After 3 weeks	After 6 months	After 1 year
High	−1.76	−8.55	−6.70
Low	− .82	− .07	− .34
Control	+ .17	+ .94	+1.86

Source: From "Effort Justification in Psychotherapy" by J. Cooper & D. Axsom in *Integrations of Clinical and Social Psychology* edited by G. Weary and H. Mirels, 1982. New York: Oxford University Press. Reprinted by permission.

who has a week's spring vacation. There are a wide variety of vacation spots available to her, but she has narrowed the choice to two: she can spend the week tanning her body on the beach at Ft. Lauderdale, Florida, or she can schuss down the ski slopes at Whistler Ski Resort, in British Columbia, Canada. Each vacation choice has elements that are very attractive; yet each has drawbacks as well. Since Helen is an ultra-organized soul, she decides to make a list like the one below.

Ft. Lauderdale Beach

Good	*Bad*
sunny	too hot
relax	possibly boring
get tanned	possibly burned
meet men	

Whistler Ski Resort

Good	*Bad*
exercise	exhausting
invigorating	expensive
sharpen skills	might break leg

If Helen decides to go to Ft. Lauderdale, all of the good features of her ski vacation in British Columbia stand in a dissonant relationship with her decision. The same is true for all of the bad features of a trip to the beach. It doesn't make sense for Helen to go to Ft. Lauderdale if the weather may be too hot. Nor does it make sense for her to go to Ft. Lauderdale if she has to give up an invigorating time on the slopes. On the other hand, a decision to go skiing would evoke dissonance from the positive features of a potential Ft. Lauderdale trip and the negative features of skiing. From the list, it appears that Helen will have to forego meeting men if she schusses down the slopes of the Canadian Rockies.

In this example, assume that all elements are of equal importance. It follows that our subject will go to Florida since there were more positive elements involved in that choice than there were for the ski vacation. But what will she do with the dissonance? The inconsistency created by all of Florida's unwanted features and all of Canada's beautiful but rejected features creates the tension state of dissonance. Our subject has the same alternatives available to her as we have seen in other dissonance situations. She can change her cognitions, alter their importance, or add new ones that she had not thought of previously. In the present case, she can change her cognitions about skiing and sun bathing. She can peruse her list of good and bad features and decide that she really did

Making a difficult choice between going skiing or going sunbathing for spring vacation may induce cognitive dissonance. Whatever decision is made, that alternative will seem relatively more attractive as a way to reduce dissonance. *(Left,* © *Bill Bachman 1983/Photo Researchers, Inc.; right,* © *Photo by David Cain 1972/Photo Researchers, Inc.)*

not want to sharpen her skills after all (i.e., change what used to be a positive feature of the rejected alternative), or she can decide that she genuinely likes sweltering heat (i.e., change what used to be a negative feature of the chosen alternative). She can alter the importance of cognitions by deciding that her fourth cognition, meeting men, is of such importance that all the others pale by comparison. Finally, she can add a new cognition: traveling to the West at that time of year is so dreadfully dangerous that she might not want to risk life and limb by doing so.

The result of making these changes is that the chosen action is much more appealing after the decision than it was when Helen drew up the list. Postdecisionally, the two alternatives are further apart than they were predecisionally (Festinger, 1964). That is, the chosen alternative is seen as increasingly attractive; the rejected alternative is seen as increasingly unattractive. In the process, the magnitude of the dissonance is reduced.

The first study to provide data to this effect was conducted by Brehm (1956). Women college students were asked to help a marketing firm to evaluate a number of consumer items, such as a toaster, an electric coffeepot, and a silk-screen print. The women were to rate each item on a scale, and they would then be allowed to choose an item to take home with them in appreciation for their having participated in the study.

In the high-dissonance condition, the subjects were allowed to choose between two items that were rated very closely on the rating scale. In the low-dissonance condition, the two items from which the subjects were to choose were rated quite far apart on the scale. Clearly, there is less dissonance when the chosen alternative is far more attractive than the non-chosen alternative from the start. In the control condition, one of the items was selected by the experimenter and given to the women as a gift.

After having chosen one of the items (or, in the control condition, after having been given one of the items), the women were asked to read some research reports written by the manufacturers of the items and then to rerate all of the items. The measure of interest to Brehm was the degree to which the two items involved in the dissonance-producing decision were spread apart after the decision was made.

Table 6–7 presents the results, which strongly support dissonance theory. First, it is clear that the item given as a gift did not change in perceived value (there was no change in the control condition). Second, in the high-dissonance condition, the two items were spread apart more in value than they were in the low-dissonance condition.

Free choice at the racetrack and the fair. Knox and Inkster (1968) took to the racetrack to find evidence for free-choice dissonance reduction in a field situation. They reasoned that people who have already placed a bet at the track have made a choice among decision alternatives. However, potential bettors who are on line at the two dollar window have declared their intention to bet but have not yet committed themselves irrevocably to a choice. These two classes of people at the track, then, should be at different stages of the decision process. The first should be more motivated to spread the choice alternatives than the second. Knox

---

Table 6–7
The reduction of postdecision dissonance by changing the attractiveness of items

	Changes from 1st to 2nd rating for		
Condition	Chosen item	Nonchosen item	Net change
Low dissonance (items of disparate value)	+0.11	0.00	+0.11
High dissonance (items of close value)	+0.38	−0.41	+0.79
Gift (control)	0.00		

Note: A positive sign indicates an increase in attractiveness; a negative sign indicates a decrease. The "net change" represents the degree of "spreading apart" of the alternatives following a choice.
Source: Adapted from Brehm (1956).

Betting at the track: Dissonance theory predicts greater certainty *after* the bet has been placed. *(Owen Franken/Stock, Boston)*

and Inkster interviewed people who were returning from the window and people on line at the window. As predicted, the people who had already placed their bet were more confident in their selection and in the outcome of the race than the people who had not yet bet.

Younger, Walker, and Arrowood (1977) replicated the basic design of Knox and Inkster's study at the midway of the Canadian National Exposition. They interviewed as many people as possible who had just placed twenty-five cent bets on various games of chance (for example, a wheel of fortune and bingo) and who were on their way to place bets. The interviewers asked the respondents how confident they were that they would win and how lucky they felt that day. Consistent with Knox and

Figure 6–7
The degree of confidence in winning before and after placing bet

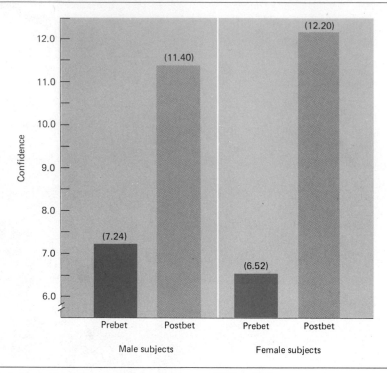

Source: Adapted from Younger, Walker, and Arrowood (1977), p. 286.

Inkster's study, the people who had already placed their bets felt luckier and more confident than the people who were on their way to bet. Figure 6–7 presents the results of the confidence measure for the subjects in the Younger et al. study.

A case study in dissonance: Prophecies about the end of the world. Just before the publication of Festinger's cognitive dissonance theory, Festinger, Riecken, and Schachter (1956) read an interesting item in their local newspaper headlined "PROPHECY FROM PLANET CLARION CALL TO CITY: FLEE THAT FLOOD." It went on to say that a suburban housewife, Mrs. Marion Keech, had received messages in the form of "automatic writing" from beings on the planet Clarion who had told her

that the world would end in a great cataclysm before dawn on December 21. A clear and definitive prediction had been made by Mrs. Keech and her followers. Moreover, the group of believers headed by Mrs. Keech had taken strong behavioral steps to indicate their degree of commitment to the belief. Some left their jobs, some left college, some left their spouses—all to prepare for the cataclysm and for the flying saucer that was to provide a safe escape for the group of true believers.

Festinger et al. saw Mrs. Keech's situation as one that would lead to the arousal of dissonance. Assuming that December 21 would come and go without an end to the world, that knowledge would induce a painful and important dissonance in the group of believers. What could they do to reduce the tension? They could not come to deny the disconfirmation of their prophecy. With any luck, the existence of the world on the 21st and for some time thereafter would be an undeniable fact. Changing the belief structure that gave rise to the particular prediction would be possible, but difficult. That is, Mrs. Keech could admit that she had been mistaken about the automatic writing and that the cataclysmic prophecy had been only a delusion. However, Mrs. Keech and the group were highly committed to their beliefs and had already endured considerable cost to maintain their belief system. A third possibility would be to seek social support for their original belief system. As Festinger et al. put it, "If more and more people can be persuaded that the system of belief is correct, then clearly it must after all be correct." As in the formulation of the magnitude of dissonance that was suggested earlier, the magnitude would decrease when cognitions that were consonant with a particular element were increased. In Mrs. Keech's case, if she could add consonant elements by convincing others that the basic premises under which she had been operating were correct, then the magnitude of her dissonance following disconfirmation would be lessened. In short,

Festinger et al. predicted that the inevitable disconfirmation would be followed by a wholehearted effort at proselytizing.

Festinger and his colleagues infiltrated Mrs. Keech's group and reported the following sequence of events:

1. *Before December 20.* The group shuns publicity. Interviews are given only grudgingly. Access to Mrs. Keech's house is only provided to those who can convince the group that they are true believers. The group evolves a belief system—provided by the automatic writing from the planet Clarion—to explain the details of the cataclysm, the reason for its occurrence, and the manner in which the group would be saved from the disaster.

2. *December 20.* The group expects a visitor from outer space to call upon them at midnight and to escort them to a waiting spacecraft. As instructed, the group goes to great lengths to remove all metallic items from their persons. As midnight approaches, zippers, bra straps, and other objects are discarded. The group waits.

3. *12:05 A.M., December 21.* No visitor. Someone in the group notices that another clock in the room shows 11:55. The group agrees that it is not yet midnight.

4. *12:10 A.M.* The second clock strikes midnight. Still no visitor. The group sits in stunned silence. The cataclysm itself is no more than seven hours away.

5. *4:00 A.M.* The group has been sitting in stunned silence. A few attempts at finding explanations have failed. Mrs. Keech begins to cry.

6. *4:45 A.M.* Another message by automatic writing is sent to Mrs. Keech. It states, in effect, that the God of Earth has decided to spare the planet from destruction. The cataclysm has been called off: "The little group, sitting all night long, had spread so much light that God had saved the world from destruction."

7. *Afternoon, December 21.* Newspapers are called; interviews are sought. In a reversal of its previous distaste for publicity, the group begins an urgent campaign to spread its message to as broad an audience as possible.

In summary, the disconfirmation of the prophecy hit Mrs. Keech's group hard. But they could neither deny its occurrence nor belittle the preparations that they had undertaken in support of their strongly held belief. Their disconfirmed prophecy probably resulted in a state of heightened unpleasant arousal as Russell and Jones (1980) later found in their study of a different group who had their expectations disconfirmed. Mrs. Keech's group's answer for reducing the arousal and making sense of their plight was to seek social support following the disconfirmation.

By persuading others that their central belief system had been correct, they could minimize the pain caused by the dissonant information.

The Arousal Properties of Dissonance   The crucial tenet of Festinger's original theory was that inconsistency led to an uncomfortable state of tension that sought reduction. Most of the research that we have considered assumed that this motivational property was present and derived hypotheses based on that assumption. In general, research has used an "as if" strategy—acting as if the motivation were there. However, some attempts have been made to measure whether dissonance is arousing.

   Indirect measurements. In 1967, Waterman and Katkin reasoned that if dissonance were arousing, it ought to produce effects similar to those of other states that we are certain are arousing. The literature from other fields of psychology has established that such physiological drives as hunger and thirst have specific consequences for the way in which people learn (Spence, Farber, & McFann, 1956). Those arousal states cause interference with complex learning tasks but facilitate simple learning tasks. When students are hungry, for example, they will not be able to learn a complex lesson, but will perform exceptionally well on a simple task. Therefore, Waterman and Katkin put participants through a counterattitudinal essay-writing procedure and then examined the way in which that activity affected their learning. The results were partially supportive of the arousal point of view. Simple learning tasks were performed better after subjects participated in the induced compliance situation, as would be predicted from the arousal point of view. However, inconsistent with that point of view, complex learning was not affected. Pallack and Pittman (1972) reviewed the several studies that sought evidence for dissonance arousal in this way (Cottrell & Wack, 1967; Waterman, 1969) and concluded that the evidence was at best equivocal.
   Zanna and Cooper (1974) took a different approach. They argued that if attitude change following induced compliance were due to arousal, then it should be possible to eliminate attitude change by misleading subjects about the source of that arousal. If people who write attitude-discrepant communications believe that any arousal they experience is due to a drug that they have taken, they should hardly be motivated to change their attitudes to eliminate their arousal. If the source of the arousal is perceived to be a drug, attitude change should be viewed as irrelevant to reducing the arousal and should not occur.
   To test this hypothesis, Zanna and Cooper had volunteers participate in a study that the volunteers believed was related to the effects of various drugs on memory. The volunteers ingested a pill that, unknown to them, was actually milk powder. But some of the subjects were led to

If people believe their arousal is due to an external source such as drugs, they are less likely to change their attitudes following a counterattitudinal essay. *(T. C. Fitzgerald/ The Picture Cube)*

believe that there was a side effect to the pill—that they would become aroused and tense within the next few moments. Other subjects were led to believe that the pill would relax them, and still other subjects were led to believe that the pill would have no side effects at all. After taking the pill, the subjects were asked to participate in "another experiment unrelated to the memory project." They wrote an essay advocating a ban on controversial speakers at their college—a position that was known to be discrepant from their true attitudes. Half of the subjects wrote their essays under high-choice conditions so that dissonance should have been aroused. The other half wrote their essays without having a choice, and thus dissonance should have been eliminated (recall Linder et al., 1967).

After writing their essays, participants had their attitudes assessed. Zanna and Cooper predicted that a typical induced compliance effect would occur in conditions in which no side effects were expected from the drug. More favorable attitudes in the direction of the essay under high- rather than low-choice conditions would be consistent with much of the research that we have considered. The middle panel of Figure 6–8 supports this prediction. More important, it was predicted that if subjects believed that they were aroused because of a pill that they had taken,

Figure 6–8

Attitude change following induced compliance as a function of choice and alleged pill side effects

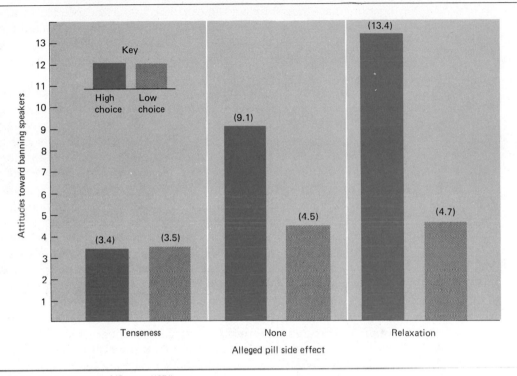

Source: Adapted from Zanna and Cooper (1974).

they should not have been motivated to change their attitudes. Consequently, no difference between high- and low-choice essay conditions was expected among this group, and as the left-hand panel of Figure 6–8 demonstrates, none was found. In contrast, Zanna and Cooper predicted that if subjects believed that they should be relaxed by the pill, then any arousal that they did experience (presumably caused by the writing of the essay) would amplify attitude change. It is as though subjects were to argue: "If I ingested a pill to relax me, but I still feel aroused, I *really* must be upset by the inconsistency between my attitude and my behavior." The right-hand side of Figure 6–8 demonstrates that high-choice subjects in the relaxation condition did, in fact, change their attitudes more than any other group in the experiment.

The results found by Zanna and Cooper and supported in further studies reviewed by Kiesler and Pallack (1976) and by Zanna and Cooper (1976) support the view originally suggested by Festinger. Recent investigations have been directed toward specifying the precise form of the arousal and toward making careful distinctions between related concepts such as tension and arousal (e.g., Comer & Rhodewalt, 1979; Cooper, Zanna, & Taves, 1978; Higgins, Rhodewalt, & Zanna, 1979).

Direct measurements. Croyle and Cooper (1983) have shown direct physiological arousal accompanying the dissonance process. Subjects participated in a study in which they were to write counterattitudinal essays. They wrote persuasive essays on the desirability of having 7:00 A.M. classes at their university, although their own attitudes disagreed with this position. Some of the subjects wrote after freely agreeing to do so. Other subjects were told to write their essays. You undoubtedly recognize this paradigm as the induced compliance paradigm and can predict that dissonance should be experienced under conditions of high choice. What Croyle added to this study was a direct physiological measurement of skin conductance. This measure is related to the degree of perspiration carried on the surface of the skin and can be used as an indicant of physiological arousal. The results indicated that subjects in the high-dissonance (i.e., high-choice) condition showed greater skin conductance activity than subjects in the low-choice condition and greater skin conductance than another group of subjects who wrote a statement that was consistent with their attitudes.

Taken as a whole, these results make explanations of dissonance phenomena that do not rely on the concept of arousal (for example, impression management and self-perception) less likely to be accurate accounts of the process that is occurring.

SOME IMPLICATIONS OF DISSONANCE AND AROUSAL: ON THE EFFECT OF ALCOHOL AND OTHER AGENTS

We have seen in this chapter that attitudes change; cognitions are added, eliminated, or changed; and attitudes are altered when dissonance is aroused by such techniques as induced compliance, free choice, effort justification, and so on. If it is true that these cognitive changes come about as a means of reducing the unpleasant tension state, then it may also be true that *any* means of reducing the tension may satisfactorily reduce the dissonance. By and large, the research we have discussed focuses on the way in which people operate on inconsistent cognitions to restore consistency. But it is possible that other stimuli, which have nothing to do with the cognitions involved in the inconsistency, may serve to eliminate the tension. This, in turn, may obviate any need to change or bolster the originally inconsistent cognitions.

A striking example of this reasoning was provided in a study by Steele, Southwick, and Critchlow (1981). They argued that alcoholic beverages may be useful in reducing dissonance. There is ample research to support the intuitive belief that, at least during the initial phases of ingestion, small amounts of alcohol lead to positive emotional experiences (e.g., McCollam, Burish, Maisto, & Sobell, 1980). "If drinking alcohol . . . eliminates the unpleasantness of dissonance," they argued, "it could also be expected to eliminate dissonance-reducing attitude change" (Steele et al., 1981, p. 833).

In one of the experiments conducted by Steele et al., subjects were run in one of three conditions. In the dissonance-alcohol condition, subjects were asked to write a counterattitudinal essay advocating a tuition increase at their university. Then, under the guise of performing a taste discrimination test between different brands of vodka, the subjects were permitted to sip the vodka (with mixers) for a period of ten minutes. After indicating their preferences, subjects were given a questionnaire to assess their attitude on increasing the tuition fee at their university. Other subjects were run in a dissonance-water condition. The procedure was identical, except that these subjects were given ten minutes to sip various kinds of water rather than vodka. Finally, some subjects were run in a base-rate control condition. These subjects sipped vodka for ten

Alcoholic beverages may help to alleviate dissonance. (*Abigail Heyman/Archive Pictures, Inc.*)

minutes, then responded to the questionnaire. They did not, however, write the counterattitudinal essay.

The results of the study are presented in Figure 6–9. It can be seen that only subjects in the dissonance-water condition showed attitude change. Subjects in the dissonance-alcohol condition indicated attitudes that were virtually identical to the base-rate control group. The results, then, confirmed the prediction that the drinking of alcohol was successful in reducing any need to change discrepant cognitions.

Steele et al. speculate on the meaning of their research by raising the possibility that normal social psychological processes such as dissonance arousal may actually lead to substance abuse. Inconsistency among cognitions, as we have pointed out at various points throughout

Figure 6–9
Postattitudes by condition and drinking habits

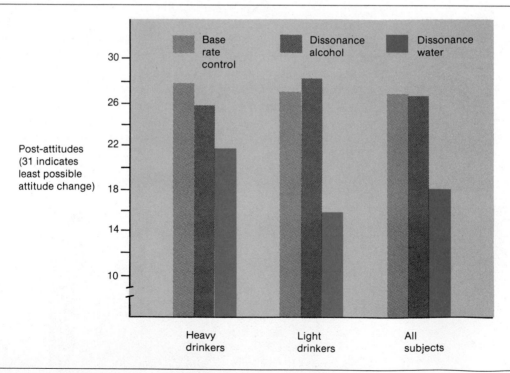

Source: Adapted from Steele, Southwick, and Critchlow (1981).

the present chapter, is a commonplace feature of daily lives. If the appropriate conditions for dissonance are present, the result may be the unpleasant tension state that Festinger (1957) originally proposed. Cognitive changes can reduce the tension; most of our laboratory research demonstrates this. But so too may alcohol. By consuming alcohol, even in small quantities, we may experience the positively reinforcing phenomenon of having that unpleasant tension removed. Alcohol use that accomplishes this function, Steele et al. suggest, may become alcohol abuse.

Revisions and Alternatives to Dissonance   Not everyone agrees that the need to maintain internal consistency is a driving factor in human behavior. In the thirty years since dissonance theory was first proposed (Festinger, 1957), several revisions and alternative explanations for the dissonance phenomena have been made.

Self-concept. An early revisionist view was proposed by Aronson (1969b). He noticed that in most experimental tests of cognitive dissonance, what was dissonant was not just *any* two cognitions, but cognitions about behavior and the self-concept. For example, in the induced compliance experiments, the original explanation for attitude change after the subject had lied to a waiting confederate about a dull task (Festinger & Carlsmith, 1959) was that he had to reduce the dissonance between the cognitions "I believe the task is dull" and "I told someone that the task is interesting." According to Aronson, however, the dissonance is between the cognitions "I am an honest person" and "I have misled someone." This revision implies that if a person does not think that he is honest and he lies to someone, no dissonance will occur and therefore he will not change his attitude about the boring task.

Self-affirmation. A related view has been proposed by Steele and Liu (1981, 1983). They claim that any inconsistency in behavior is a threat to the self. Following their logic, when self-esteem is threatened in this way, it can be protected by anything that casts the self in a positive light. Therefore, if, after performing an inconsistent behavior, subjects are allowed to do something that will affirm their beliefs or values (e.g., helping someone in need or publicly stating their beliefs), any dissonance that they may feel will be reduced. Further, this will be the case even if the affirming behavior has nothing to do with the original inconsistency.

Responsibility and dissonance motivation. Over the years, many critics of dissonance theory have claimed that the addition of so many qualifying conditions (e.g., choice, aversive consequences, foreseeability) has turned the theory into a waterlogged explanation of behavior (e.g., Greenwald & Ronis, 1978). However, Cooper and Fazio (1984) attempted to put the preconditions for cognitive dissonance into a coherent framework. They noticed that choice and foreseeability are the necessary conditions to ascribe responsibility for some outcome to an individual (Shaver, 1985). Therefore, they reasoned, dissonance arousal may not result from inconsistencies, but rather from feeling personally responsible for producing some aversive consequences. If this arousal is not misattributed to some other source, it will be converted to dissonance motivation, and attitude change will occur. Thus, by changing his or her attitude, a person makes the consequences less aversive and thereby reduces the dissonance.

The three revisions of dissonance discussed above (self-concept, self-affirmation, and responsibility and motivation) derived directly from Festinger's (1957) original concepts about the theory. They took these concepts and tried to incorporate subsequent findings into them. Some alternative explanations propose more dramatic differences in their explanations of the findings of dissonance experiments.

Self-perception. The earliest of these explanations was offered by Darryl Bem (1965, 1972), who claimed that people have no "privileged knowledge" about their attitudes. When pressed to tell someone what your attitude is, according to Bem, you merely look at your own behavior and infer your attitude, using the same techniques that another person would use if asked to judge your beliefs. According to this view, anyone who saw another person freely choose to behave in a certain manner would infer that his or her attitude corresponded with that behavior. Similarly, if you saw yourself giving a speech about an issue, you would infer that your attitude was consistent with the position that you took on the speech. In several experiments, Bem (e.g., 1965) showed that when the subjects' behavior in induced compliance experiments was described to observer-subjects, the observer-subjects' guesses about the attitudes of the original subjects were very close to the *real* attitudes of those subjects in the original experiments.

Impression management. Another alternative explanation to the dissonance findings has been offered under the term *impression management* (Tedeschi, Schlenker, & Bonoma, 1971). According to this view, people are motivated to appear consistent because they have been positively rewarded when it has looked as though they acted consistently, and negatively sanctioned when it has seemed that they acted inconsistently. Consequently, we learn to alter the impressions that we give others to produce the appearance of consistency and reliability. Tedeschi et al. believe that in laboratory situations, people attempt to rationalize or justify inconsistent behavior to the significant other in their immediate environment—that is, the high-status experimenter—just as they would in other situations. Thus, they change their attitude not out of some internal need for consistency, but *to appear* consistent.

Recently, Schlenker (1982) proposed a revision of the impression management view that he calls the identity-analytic model. According to this model, it is not a need to appear consistent that motivates the attitude change in dissonance experiments, but the desire to avoid appearing responsible for performing some reprehensible behavior.

A recent study by Baumeister and Tice (1984) addressed the debate between inconsistency and impression management as causes of dissonance. These authors found that dissonance can occur because of self-presentational (impression management) needs *or* because of consistency needs, and when the conditions are right for both of these factors to come into play, they will—producing even more attitude change than either cause would by itself.

Conclusions: Dissonance Theory   In general, dissonance theory has had a controversial but productive history. It has led to interesting and sometimes ingenious demonstrations in both laboratory and field settings. Dissonance theory phenomena have not been lacking in controversy, and numerous studies have attempted to provide alternative explanations for findings predicted by dissonance theory (Elms & Janis, 1965; Rosenberg, 1965). Since much of the knowledge gained in any discipline arises out of controversies like those that dissonance theory has engendered, the end product of dissonance theory research has been a useful accumulation of knowledge.

PSYCHOLOGICAL REACTANCE

We have considered the importance of allowing a person to feel at least an illusion of freedom to behave in attitude-discrepant ways if we wish to effect attitude change. From the point of view of dissonance theory, ordering someone to do something that is attitude discrepant will not evoke the motivational state that culminates in a change of attitude.

There are numerous illustrations of failures of plans that feature coercion as the mechanism for effecting changes of behavior. In a celebrated incident some years ago, a federal court ordered the busing of black and white children to achieve racial balance in the public schools in South Boston. This "do it" order met with extreme resistance and violence from many of the whites in South Boston, and as a result some parents withdrew their children from the public schools and set up their own private

Police clash with white parents after court-ordered busing integrated South Boston High School in 1974. *(Alex Webb/Magnum Photos, Inc.)*

"no busing" schools. This suggests that failing to induce feelings of free choice may not only be ineffective in producing the desired changes of opinion; it may also be counterproductive.

Brehm (1966, 1972; Brehm & Brehm, 1981) developed a theory to explain why the use of simple force can backfire in attempts to secure compliance and attitude change. Brehm based his theory on the assumption that each individual has a set of *free behaviors*. A free behavior is an act that the individual feels she can engage in at either the particular moment or at some time in the future, and that she knows she has the necessary physical or psychological ability to perform. For example, you may feel that going to the movie tonight is one of your free behaviors. The people in South Boston may have felt that choosing what school their child would attend was one of their free behaviors. Free behaviors can vary in importance, with the more important free behaviors being those that satisfy important needs.

According to Brehm, a threat to or elimination of the freedom to perform such behaviors will arouse the individual psychologically. This arousal, which will be aimed at restoring the threatened or eliminated freedom, is called *psychological reactance*. Reactance theory hypothesizes that the strength of psychological reactance will vary in a positive relationship to the importance of the free behavior and to the degree of threat to that behavior. For example, your freedom to eat is probably a more important freedom than your freedom to attend a movie tonight. Thus, if a friend told you that you could neither eat nor attend the movie tonight, greater reactance would be aroused by the first threat than by the second.

DENNIS the MENACE ®

"I DON'T *WANTA* GO OUTSIDE AN' PLAY...

UNLESS SHE SAYS I *CAN'T*."

Restricted behaviors can become more attractive due to psychological reactance. (*Courtesy of Hank Ketcham and © by Field Enterprises Inc.*)

Research has demonstrated three types of reactions to the arousal of reactance. First, the individual may attempt to reestablish freedom directly by performing the threatened free behavior. For example, Hammock and Brehm (1966) told children that they could choose to have one of a number of different candy bars. The experimenters then told the children that they should not choose candy bar X. The children reacted to this threat to freedom by choosing candy bar X and thus restoring their freedom to have that particular bar. In a study involving younger children, Brehm and Weintraub (1977) placed a barrier of different sizes between a two-year-old child and an attractive toy. The child could also play with an easily accessible toy in front of the barrier. Brehm and Weintraub varied the importance of the freedom to play with the toy behind the barrier by having it either different (high importance) or the same (low importance) as the toy in front of the barrier. The investigators found that male children went behind the barrier to play with the restricted toy if the freedom was important and if the barrier was large rather than small. Thus, two-year-old boys, but *not* two-year-old girls, restored their threatened freedom by direct performance of the threatened behavior.

A second reaction is that the threatened freedom increases in attractiveness as a result of the increased motivation to perform the threatened behavior. An event that occurred in the state of Florida will serve as an illustration. When social consciousness regarding the environment was being raised in the early 1970s, Dade County (Miami), Florida, enacted an ordinance banning the sale of laundry soaps containing phosphates. Mazis (1975) reasoned that delimiting the options of Dade County homemakers would make the restricted product seem more attractive than it had been before. Immediately following the enactment of the ordinance, Mazis asked consumers in Miami and consumers in a similar community (Tampa, Florida) in which phosphate detergents had not been banned to rate the effectiveness of phosphate detergents. Compared to the Tampa homemakers, Miami residents believed that the restricted product was better for whiteness, freshness, brightness, and virtually any other category that Mazis could generate. Apparently, the attractiveness of the product had increased as a function of the threat to the Miami homemakers' freedom to purchase it.

Finally, aggression aimed at the threatening agent has been found to follow the arousal of reactance. Worchel (1974) has suggested that aggressing against the threatening agent can reestablish freedom at the moment and ensure that that agent will not threaten freedom again in the future (see Chapter 8).

Reactance theory provides a basis for a better understanding of the reactions of whites in South Boston in 1974. We have said that before the court's ruling, the South Boston whites may have felt that they were free to decide where their children should attend school. The court order forcing busing eliminated this freedom. The response of many of the whites was to open their own schools so that they could choose to send their children to those schools (direct reestablishment of freedom) and to aggress against (through riots and acts of violence) the perceived source of the restriction of their freedom.

Thus, reactance theory suggests the need to pay attention to such details as "illusions of freedom" and the size of the incentives that people are given to adopt certain behaviors. If people feel that they are being forced to adopt a behavior, they are likely to experience reactance and to act against such force. As to the size of the incentive for adopting a behavior, it can be posited that the larger the incentive, the more pressure the individual will feel to perform a particular act. A large incentive may arouse reactance and result in the individual's refusing to adopt the

Reactance comes from eliminating people's choice to behave in particular ways. Ordering people to ride buses to integrate the public schools in South Boston may have produced reactance. Reactance, in turn, can lead to aggression. *(United Press International Photo)*

behavior. Brehm and Winer (reported in Brehm, 1966) demonstrated this in a grocery store study. When shoppers entered the store, they were met by an experimenter who asked them to buy brand X bread and then gave them either twenty-five cents or thirty-five cents. A loaf of brand X bread cost twenty-five cents, so the thirty-five cent payment was a very high incentive. The results showed that with female shoppers, over 60 percent who were given the low incentive (twenty-five cents) bought brand X bread, whereas only 40 percent of those who were given the high incentive (thirty-five cents) bought brand X bread. According to Brehm and Winer, the high incentive threatened the shoppers' freedom *not* to buy brand X bread, and the response to this was to resist the pressure and reestablish freedom.

In addition to affecting behavior, the arousal of reactance can affect attitudes. Brehm argues that the freedom to hold a particular attitude may be an important "free behavior" and that a threat to this freedom can arouse reactance. Worchel and Brehm (1970) demonstrated this by having subjects listen to a communication advocating equal treatment for the Communist party in the United States. Subjects in all conditions heard the same communication, except that in the high-threat condition the communication was liberally sprinkled with statements such as "You cannot believe otherwise" or "You have no choice but to believe this." These statements were included to threaten the subjects' freedom to hold the opposite position. The results showed that in the high-threat condition, only 50 percent of the subjects changed their attitudes in the direction of the communication whereas 67 percent of the subjects in the low-threat condition changed their attitudes in the direction advocated by the speech. Further, 40 percent of the subjects in the high-threat condition actually showed a "boomerang effect" (changed their attitudes in the direction opposite to that of the communication).

An Individual Difference Variable: Coronary-Prone Behavior   Loss of freedom is more important for some people than it is for others. The loss of freedom stems from a dread of having to give up personal control because of environmental constraints (Wortman & Brehm, 1975). Research over the past several years has shown that there is at least one personality type that cannot tolerate giving up control; these are people with so-called coronary-prone behavior patterns.

Hard-driving executives often experience coronary-prone behavior patterns. Research has shown that such people need a stronger sense of control over their environment. They are also more susceptible to heart attacks. *(Copyright Nancy J. Pierce/Photo Researchers, Inc.)*

As the name implies, coronary-prone behavior patterns are more likely to be associated with the incidence of heart attacks. Friedman and Rosenman (1959) identified a pattern of behaviors that seemed to be precursors of heart disease that included extreme competitiveness and achievement striving, a sense of time urgency, and hostility. People who demonstrate this behavior pattern are referred to as "Type A" personalities. By contrast, noncoronary-prone individuals (called "Type Bs") are characteristically laid-back, relaxed, and are less aggressive than Type As.

Rhodewalt and Comer (1982) reasoned that Type As would be more susceptible to reactance than Type Bs. A review of the coronary-prone behavior literature by Glass (1977) reports data showing that Type As feel that they have a high degree of personal control over their behaviors and outcomes. So it stands to reason that Type As will be extremely upset about anything that restricts their freedom and personal control. Rhodewalt and Comer (1982) subjected Type A and Type B students to pressures not unlike those in the Worchel and Brehm (1970) study reported above. The students' freedom to hold an opinion was threatened by a confederate who virtually told them that they had no choice but to hold a particular attitude. Type B subjects were not terribly upset by this restriction and continued to hold their opinion. Coronary-prone subjects (Type As), however, experienced reactance at this threat to their freedom and control. Unlike the Type B subjects, they sought to regain their control by altering their attitudes.

SUMMARY

Since La Pière (1934) showed that people's attitudes are not always consistent with their behavior, the question of attitude-behavior consistency has been a focus of study for social psychology. Research has evolved through three types of questions. The first is *Are* attitudes consistent with behaviors? The answer seems to be that sometimes they are and sometimes they are not. The second question is *When* are attitudes consistent with behaviors? Research has shown that attitudes formed through direct experience are more likely to be consistent with behavior. Attitude-behavior consistency is also greater when the attitude is made *relevant* and closely *matched* to the particular behavior. Finally, attitude-behavior consistency is greatest for certain personality types: low self-monitors are particularly apt to show attitude-behavior consistency. So too are people who define themselves as "doers," and people with high levels of self-consciousness and moral reasoning. Finally, research has turned to a third level of question: *How* do attitudes lead to behaviors? Ajzen and Fishbein proposed a *theory of reasoned action* in which people's attitudes and their judgments of subjective norms govern their behaviors. Fazio proposed an *automatic-processing model* in which the accessibility of the attitude is the critical factor in determining a behavior.

The *theory of cognitive dissonance* addresses the question of *when* behaviors lead to changes of attitudes. It holds that dissonance is experienced whenever one cognition that a person holds follows from the opposite of at least one other cognition that the person holds. Dissonance has a *magnitude* that is based on the number and importance of a person's discrepant and consonant cognitions.

According to the theory, dissonance is experienced as an uncomfortable *drivelike state*. People are motivated to reduce any dissonance that they experience. Dissonance can be reduced by (1) changing cognitions, (2) adding cognitions, or (3) altering the importance of the cognitions.

Much of the research in dissonance theory has been conducted on the paradigm of induced compliance. In the induced compliance paradigm, a person is persuaded to behave in ways contrary to his or her private beliefs. Research has shown that attitudes are likely to change to *restore consistency* between attitudes and behavior. Generally, the magnitude of attitude change is inversely proportional to the amount of *justification* that is provided to engage in the attitude-discrepant behavior. Induced compliance leads to dissonance arousal when (1) the behavior is engaged in *freely*, (2) the actor feels *committed* to his attitude-discrepant stance, (3) the behavior results in *unwanted consequences*, and (4) the actor feels *personally responsible* for bringing about the unwanted consequences.

Using variations of the induced compliance paradigm, several interesting phenomena have been identified. In the psychology of *effort justifications*, it has been shown that people come to love what they have suffered for (e.g., people who dislike snakes may be able to approach them after engaging in effortful behaviors). It has also been shown that *disconfirmed expectancies* can lead to dissonance arousal. In a case study of a cultlike group, it was shown that dissonance aroused by a disconfirmed expectancy could be reduced by gathering *social support* for the original belief.

In the *free-choice paradigm*, it is assumed that dissonance follows any freely exercised choice between cognitive alternatives. The positive features of the rejected alternative and the negative features of the chosen alternative are discrepant with the decision that was reached. Brehm has shown that attitudes change following decisions so that the alternatives will seem more *widely discrepant* in attractiveness after a decision than they seemed before it.

Some alternative models of dissonance have been proposed based on *self-concept, self-affirmation*, and *personal responsibility. Self-perception* and *impression management* have been offered as theories that compete with dissonance in explaining the experimental phenomena. These theories differ from dissonance in that they do not posit that any psychological arousal occurs due to inconsistency.

Following the discussion of dissonance, *reactance theory* was introduced. Reactance results when an individual feels that one or more of his or her *free behaviors* are being threatened. Three types of reactions have been found to follow reactance: (1) the individual may attempt to perform the threatened free behavior; (2) the threatened free behavior increases in attractiveness; and (3) the individual is instigated to aggress against the agent that created the reactance. Reactance theory can be used to explain negative attitude change, or the boomerang effect.

KEY WORDS

attitude-discrepant behavior	effort justification
automatic-processing model	foreseeability
aversive consequences	free-choice paradigm
boomerang effect	impression management
cognitions	insufficient deterrence
cognitive dissonance	personal responsibility
cognitive irrelevance	psychological reactance
commitment	reasoned action
consonance	reinforcement effect
direct experience	self-monitoring
disconfirmed expectancies	

SUGGESTED READINGS

Brehm, J. W. (1966). *A theory of psychological reactance.* New York: Academic Press.

Brehm, S. S., & Brehm, J. W. (1981). *Psychological reactance: A theory of freedom and control.* New York: Academic Press.

Cooper, J., & Fazio, R. H. (1984). A new look at dissonance theory. In L. Berkowitz (Ed.), *Advances in experimental social psychology* (Vol. 17, pp. 229–266). New York: Academic Press.

Fazio, R. H., & Cooper, J. (1983). Arousal in the dissonance process. In J. T. Cacioppo & R. E. Petty (Eds.), *Social psychophysiology.* New York: Guilford Press.

Festinger, L. (1957). *A theory of cognitive dissonance.* Stanford, CA: Stanford University Press.

Wicklund, R. A., & Brehm, J. W. (1976). *Perspectives on cognitive dissonance.* Hillsdale, NJ: Erlbaum.

Zanna, M. P., & Cooper, J. (1974). Dissonance and the attribution process. In J. Harvey, W. Ickes, & R. Kidd (Eds.), *New directions in attribution research* (Vol. 1, pp. 199–217). Hillsdale, NJ: Erlbaum.

SEVEN

INTERPERSONAL ATTRACTION

A young man of the House of Montague fell deeply in love with the beautiful daughter of the House of Capulet. It was a star-crossed romance, destined to end in the death of the lovers. Romeo, in Shakespeare's classic tragedy *Romeo and Juliet*, was by nature a lover. Impetuous and emotional, he had been deeply in love with another woman who failed to return his affections. With one glimpse at Juliet, his former love was forgotten and the consuming passionate romance was begun.

Juliet, by contrast, had been untouched by romantic love. Before meeting Romeo, she had been an obedient daughter, unfamiliar with the passions of love. When a marriage to Count Paris was arranged by her parents, she responded in a naive and intellectual fashion: "It is an honour that I dream not of. . . . I'll look to like, if looking move."

The action begins when Romeo, bemoaning his unrequited love, is cajoled by friends to attend a costume ball at the home of Capulet. Casting his eyes upon Juliet, he is enthralled by her beauty:

> Oh, she doth teach the torches to burn bright!
> It seems she hangs upon the cheek of night
> Like a rich jewel in an Ethiop's ear;
> Beauty too rich for use, for earth too dear!
> > (Act I, Scene 5)

Juliet, too, is instantly consumed by the passion of romance:

> My bounty is as boundless as the sea,
> My love as deep; the more I give to thee,
> The more I have, for both are infinite.
> > (Act II, Scene 2)

Both Romeo and Juliet are young and attractive, the offspring of established wealthy families. The impending tragedy has its roots in the long-standing feud between the Montagues and the Capulets. Shakespeare's Prologue states the insurmountable problem:

> Two households, both alike in dignity,
> In fair Verona, where we lay our scene,
> From ancient grudge break to new mutiny,
> Where civil blood makes civil hands unclean.
> From forth the fatal loins of these two foes
> A pair of star-crossed lovers take their life.

The balcony scene from Franco Zeffirelli's film version of William Shakespeare's play, *Romeo and Juliet*. (*Museum of Modern Art/Film Stills Archive*)

When the lovers find themselves attracted to each other, they maintain a sense of the supreme irony of the situation and of the likelihood of impending tragedy. Juliet says:

My only love sprung from my only hate!
Too early seen unknown, and known too late!
Prodigious birth of love it is to me,
That I must love a loathed enemy.

From the time of their initial meeting, events occur with extreme speed. This rapidity accentuates the passion of the romance and the inevitable tragedy of the outcome. On the following day, the two lovers are married secretly by Friar Laurence. While returning from the marriage vows, Romeo encounters Juliet's cousin, the fiery Tybalt of the House of Capulet. Although trying to avoid conflict, Romeo is forced into a fight, slays Tybalt, and is banished from Verona. The alternative is a sentence of death. Before leaving Verona, Romeo steals into his new wife's room. There they consummate their love. As fate will have it, they will never see each other alive again.

Angered by the murder of Tybalt, Lord Capulet announces the impending marriage of his daughter to Paris. Juliet devises a plan with Friar Laurence that will permit her to join Romeo and avoid the bigamous marriage to Paris. The friar prescribes a potion that will put Juliet to sleep, simulating the symptoms of death. After she takes the potion and is believed dead, she is brought to the Capulets' mausoleum.

Though the friar's plan was to let Romeo know of the trick by which Juliet would feign death, fate intervened. Romeo learned of Juliet's death, but not of the trick that was to return her to his side. Consumed by passion, Romeo raced to the mausoleum to join his love. Taking poison from an apothecary, he spoke his last words, "Thus with a kiss I die."

When Juliet awoke from her sleep, she saw her dead lover by her side. Ignoring the friar's exhortation to leave the tomb, Juliet thrust a knife into her breast and died.

ATTRACTION: A WORKING DEFINITION

Attraction takes many forms. Romeo's attraction to Juliet was passionate. A boy is attracted in different ways to his third-grade teacher, to his friend in the second row, and to the man who sells him ice-cream cones. In yet different ways, he is attracted to his mother and the other members of his family. *By attraction, we mean a positive attitude held by one person about another.* There are many kinds of attraction and many reasons for people to form attitudes of attraction or liking. Some people flatter us, and others earn our liking by being honest. Some people may be the source of sexual gratification whereas others are unattainable. We like some people because they are just like us, and others because they are different.

Some social psychologists have addressed the problem of why people are attracted to other people by adapting general theories of behavior to the area of interpersonal attraction. But more recently, social psychologists have started to develop both theories and methods that are designed more specifically for studying attraction in ongoing relationships, over longer periods of time, and in natural settings (Berscheid, 1983). This chapter will consider some of the theoretical positions regarding attraction and will look at what is known about the situations that cause people to like and to love each other.

A COGNITIVE VIEW: BETTER TO BE BALANCED

Balance theory has played an important role in many areas of social psychology. Chapter Five looked at Heider's balance theory as a model of attitude formation and Chapter Six discussed the related theory of cognitive dissonance. Each of those theories has spawned research on attraction (Darley & Berscheid, 1967; Davis & Jones, 1960; Tyler & Sears, 1977). In this chapter, however, we will consider a variant of balance theory that has been used extensively for understanding some of the issues involved in interpersonal attraction: Newcomb's symmetry model, often called the A–B–X model (Newcomb, 1956, 1961).

Newcomb's theory takes the perspective of person A who is in a network with another person, B, and an object, X. The system considers the positive and negative bonds that exist between the actor, the other person, and the attitudinal object. In this system, the attitudinal object, X, may be a "thing," such as a tree, a pineapple, or a brand of toothpaste; an issue, such as desegregation, population control, or television violence; or another person.

As in Heider's model, systems may be either balanced (symmetrical) or imbalanced (asymmetrical). An example of a balanced system can be seen in Figure 7–1(a). Romeo loves Juliet, and he is also favorable to (likes) marriage. Further, he knows that Juliet favors marriage. "If that thy bent be marriage," she says in the famous balcony scene, "send me word tomorrow. And all my fortunes at thy foot I'll lay." All of these harmoniously positive bonds are shown by the unbroken lines of Figure 7–1(a). As was pointed out in Chapter Five we can figure out whether a system is balanced by algebraically multiplying the signs of the relationships. In Figure 7–1(a), Romeo's relationship to Juliet and to marriage is positive, and he believes that her attitude toward marriage is positive. Since the product of three pluses is plus, the system is balanced.

Figure 7–1
Balance theory representation of relationships in Shakespeare's *Romeo and Juliet*

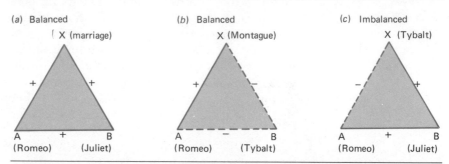

Note: Solid lines represent attraction; broken lines depict disliking.

Figure 7–1(*b*) shows that balance can also exist when all feelings are less than positive. In this example, Romeo loves his father (Lord Montague); Tybalt (Juliet's cousin) does not. But then again, Romeo does not care much for Juliet's cousin. The product of the three signs is again positive, and the system is balanced. Romeo loves Juliet, and Juliet loves her cousin Tybalt. But Romeo and Tybalt are enemies. As Tybalt says, "Romeo, the hate I bear thee can afford no better term than this—thou art a villain." The two positive relationships and the one negative relationship combine to form an imbalanced state. In Newcomb's terms, there is a "strain toward symmetry" such that the perception of asymmetry (or imbalance) will cause activity on the part of the actor (A) to restore symmetry.

How can a person restore symmetry if it does not exist? Your best friend disapproves of your fiancé; your wife or husband disagrees with you about the desirability of having a family; one of your very best friends thoroughly dislikes another of your close friends. Such situations are out of equilibrium and attempts must be made to restore symmetry. Consider Romeo's predicament in Figure 7–1(*c*). He loves Juliet; she loves him—but she also feels positively about Tybalt and Romeo does not. Romeo (A) could:

1. Try to persuade Juliet (B) to change her attitude about Tybalt (X).
2. Change his own attitude about Juliet (B).
3. Change his own attitude about Tybalt (X).

Changing any of the signs in the A–B–X system as proposed above would reduce the tension caused by the disequilibrium. In Shakespeare's play, Romeo did in fact try to alter his attitude about Tybalt. Although he was insulted and prodded by Tybalt, Romeo protested, "I never injured thee, but love thee better than thou canst devise."

There are other possibilities. The strain toward symmetry could be reduced if Romeo could:

4. Reduce the *importance* of the topic about which he and Juliet disagree.
5. Reduce the *common relevance* of the issue.

In the first of these alternatives, Romeo could come to feel that Tybalt is too trivial a person to worry about. In the second, he could feel strongly about both Tybalt and Juliet, but conclude that her opinion about a rivalry between gentlemen is irrelevant. Her opinion in this situation is not considered germane to areas that are common to him and his wife.

A REWARD MODEL OF ATTRACTION

A second model of interpersonal attraction is based on the simple notion that people associated with rewards are liked. Such models have been put forth by Albert and Bernice Lott (1968, 1974) and by Byrne and Clore (1970).

Consider a little girl sitting in a high chair who on this day, unlike every other day, picks up a spoon by herself and brings it to her mouth. Her mother responds with great delight; she smiles, kisses the baby, and gives her a cookie for her efforts. Picking up the spoon has now become a pleasurable response, since it has become associated with the pleasurable feeling generated by the mother's rewards of a kiss and a cookie. From then on, the little girl continues using the spoon to feed herself.

According to the reward model of attraction, the very same process is at the root of our interpersonal feelings: Those individuals who we associate with rewards that we experience become preferred and liked.

We should also note that attraction does not occur only when rewards have been received from someone in the past or are associated with them in the present. We also tend to be attracted to those who we believe will be associated with a reward in the *future* (Clore & Kerber, 1981; Tedeschi, 1974). The finding that people are sensitive to rewards that others can give them in the future may help to explain why we sometimes feel attraction to people we have known only briefly or know little about.

Loving That Pleasant Feeling   We are not surprised by the statement that we like people who give us rewards better than we like people who make us feel unpleasant. We can all think of occasions in which we left a situation fuming at a person who was obnoxious or unpleasant to us—the waiter who spilled soup on our sleeve, the cashier who insisted that the ten-dollar bill we gave her was actually a five—and we can think of as many instances of liking a person who was kind or rewarding to us.

However, the reward model of attraction goes further and indicates that a person who is associated with a pleasant feeling will be liked better than a person who is associated with an unpleasant feeling—regardless of whether that person was the cause of the feeling.

Griffitt and Guay (1969) conducted an experiment in which an innocent bystander was present when another person administered either a reward or a punishment to a subject. Although that bystander had absolutely nothing to do with the reward or punishment, he was liked better when the subject experienced a reward than when the subject experienced a punishment. In a subsequent study, Griffitt (1970) directly manipulated the pleasantness of an individual's experience by varying the temperature and the humidity of an experimental room. A hypothetical stranger was liked better when the room was comfortable than when the room was hot and humid. Similarly, Veitch and Griffitt (1976) found that after a subject had heard good news on a radio report, the subject liked a stranger more than he did after bad news was broadcast.

According to the reward model of attraction, a person's liking for another is influenced by the pleasantness or unpleasantness of the surroundings. (Left, © Susan Lapides/design conceptions; right, Nancy Durrell McKenna © 1985/Photo Researchers, Inc.)

Apparently, the stranger's association with the pleasantness or unpleasantness of the news report made the difference in his rated attractiveness —despite the undeniable fact that he had nothing to do with temperature or humidity in the first case, or with the nature of the news report in the last case.

The Exchange of Rewards: A Concern with Equity   Thus far, we have considered the effect of reward mainly from the perspective of its effect on a single individual. We have considered whether interaction with another person provides pleasure or displeasure to an actor. However, whether or not an interpersonal relationship leads to pleasure is often complex. Pleasure in a relationship depends not only on what a person receives, but also on what the cost is. Moreover, such pleasure is not just a function of a person's rewards and costs; it also is a function of the rewards and costs experienced by the other person in the relationship (Adams, 1965).

Equity may be said to exist when the ratio of a person's rewards to costs is equivalent to his or her perception of the partner's rewards-to-cost ratio. Relationships that are characterized by equity are more pleasurable and long lasting than those characterized by inequity. It is not just the person on the "short end" of an inequity who is uncomfortable in the relationship. Rather, inequity is expected to make the relationship less pleasant for both members (Kiesler & Baral, 1970; Walster et al., 1976).

Walster et al. (1978) studied the effect of equitable and inequitable relationships. They found that people who felt they were in equitable relationships reported that (1) they had been in the relationship longer than people who were in inequitable relationships, (2) they had greater expectations that the relationship would continue, and (3) they had greater intimacy in the relationship. It was also found that several months after the interview, the relationships that had been described as equitable were still ongoing.

Long-Term Relationships

Toward joint outcomes. Kelley and Thibaut (1978) are theorists who believe that attraction in a relationship is determined by the partners' joint rewards and costs.

But their observations on long-term interpersonal attraction are relevant here. Lasting intimate relationships are based on a transformation of the common concern with one's own outcomes (i.e., "What's in this situation for *me*?") to a concern with the joint outcomes of both partners in the relationship (i.e., "What's in this situation for *us*?").

In Kelley and Thibaut's view, then, a long-lasting interpersonal relationship is characterized not by both partners trying to maximize their individual payoffs, but rather by both trying to maximize their joint rewards. A couple may choose to attend a football game. One may truly enjoy it; the other may yawn from the first through the fourth quarter. Although one member of the partnership is temporarily pleased, the other is not. This, again, is inequitable. It is an example of the couple not paying attention to the best joint reward in the situation. Ultimately, it is not a pleasing situation for either partner. While one member of the dyad may truly enjoy football, the other may truly enjoy the ballet. They both may enjoy the theater. Longer lasting relationships are characterized by the kind of compromise that consists of finding that outcome that is equally pleasing to both partners, which may result in their agreeing to alternate their football and ballet attendance.

An interesting feature of the transformation from a concern with individual rewards to equitable joint rewards is that the partners in the relationship are usually aware of the transformation. Fleiner and Kelley (1978) interviewed ninety-six persons and had them rate their satisfaction in their personal relationships. They found that in successful partnerships, people did operate under the working rule of maximizing their joint rewards, and that each partner was aware that the other was attempting to do the same thing.

Keeping track of what you give and what you get. While Kelley and his colleagues have investigated the shift from individual to joint rewards, Clark and her colleagues at Carnegie-Mellon University (Clark, 1984; Mills & Clark, 1981) have examined the degree to which people feel a need to keep track of the rewards or benefits in different kinds of relationships. Clark has addressed the difference between what she refers to as "communal" and "exchange" relationships. People typically have exchange relationships with strangers, acquaintances, and those with whom they do business. But they enjoy a communal (i.e., deep, long term) relationship with family members, friends, and romantic partners.

In an *exchange* relationship, there is a concern for equity—or as Clark (1984) puts it, a concern for comparable benefit. Giving a benefit implies a debt for the partner. As one person gives in the relationship, he or she expects to be given something in return. Moreover, the partners keep track of the benefits they have given so that they can assess the benefits that they are entitled to receive. Such record keeping disappears in the *communal* relationship. Here people are responsive to each other's needs, implying a concern with joint outcomes.

Clark (1984) conducted a clever study to assess the degree to which

Is gift-giving always good for a relationship? Research suggests that failure to keep giving and receiving equitably can create problems for a long-term relationship. *(Joel Gordon 1979/1982)*

people in exchange and communal relationships engage in record keeping—that is, keep track of just how much they contribute to a joint venture with the presumed expectation of receiving a like amount from their partners in return. Students at Carnegie-Mellon entered into a relationship that they either hoped would become communal (in a romantic way) or that they knew would have to remain of the exchange type. In a game situation, the partners were given the task of locating and circling number sequences in a large matrix. As a function of the couple's performance, a reward could be won and divided between them. Clark predicted that subjects in an exchange relation would attempt to record-keep—to know just how much each had contributed to the joint product so that each would know exactly how much of the reward he or she would eventually be entitled to. On the other hand, Clark predicted that those subjects who thought they might share a communal relation would not record keep. Each would refrain from measuring his or her input into the relationship because the focus would be on the partnership's joint outcome.

The first person to begin the task was always the attractive female who served as the confederate of the experimenter; she circled numbers with a colored pen. The male subject's turn followed. He could use a pen of the same color as that used by his partner or he could use a pen of a different color. Which would he use? Obviously, if he wanted to keep track of just how many correct solutions he obtained compared to those of his partner, he would be motivated to use a different-colored pen. If he did not care about assessing the contributions made by each of them, he would not care very much which pen he used. The results showed that nearly 90 percent of all subjects in the exchange relationship chose to work with a different-colored pen, while only 12.5 percent of the people in the communal condition chose the pen of a different color. Apparently, Clark was correct in predicting that people are concerned with their individual equity when they are in an exchange relationship, and are concerned only with the joint rewards that the partnership can obtain when they are in a communal relationship.

Conflict due to misperceptions of joint reward. The notion that successful interpersonal relationships depend on the joint reward rule is also the source of some interpersonal conflict between partners. Fleiner and Kelley found in their interviews that respondents usually felt that they were following the joint payoff rule more than their partners. That is, they felt that they were more concerned with paying attention to the best common outcome than their partners were. Orvis, Kelley, and Butler (1976) also noted that when two partners in a relationship explain those instances in which joint rewards were not the outcome of a particular episode, the partners had very different explanations. The partner who was being interviewed usually blamed the inequity on a dispositional characteristic of the other partner ("He only thinks of himself when sports are on the television"; "He is never honest enough to tell me what he wants"; "She always ignores what I want"). On the other hand, when questioned about their own role in creating an inequity of outcomes, the partner who was interviewed rarely made a dispositional statement but almost always attributed the action to the environment or to circumstances. This, of course, is similar to the general differences between the attributions made by actors and observers when explaining behavior (recall the work of Jones & Nisbett, 1971).

In general, work on interpersonal attraction implicates not only the rewards that a person experiences when interacting with another person, but also the equity involved in the relationship. Longer lasting relationships characterized by greater intimacy are also characterized by a concern for equitable rewards and costs between the partners and a concern to maximize the pleasure that can be shared by both members of the relationship.

SIMILARITY AND ATTRACTION: I'LL LIKE YOU IF YOU'RE LIKE ME

The Basic Paradigm   Perhaps the greatest amount of research in interpersonal attraction has addressed the relationship between similarity and attraction. One reason for the popularity of the similarity and attraction connection is that most theories dealing with interpersonal attraction hypothesize that persons with similar attitudes should be more attracted to one another. Balance theories (for example, Newcomb, 1961) lead in a very straightforward manner to this prediction, as we have seen. If A feels positively toward X and B feels the same, then there is a strain toward balance such that A should feel positively toward B.

Reinforcement models make the same prediction, given the reasonable assumption that agreement is reinforcing.

Since both balance and reinforcement models have an interest in the similarity and attraction issue, a considerable amount of research on this question has been undertaken. Much of the research has been conducted by Donn Byrne and his colleagues. In a long series of investigations (Byrne, 1971), they have worked out a basic methodology for studying similarity and attraction. Subjects are first asked to fill out an attitude scale. Sometime later, they go to the laboratory and are asked to form judgments about a hypothetical person "on the basis of limited information." They are given a twelve-item attitude scale to read that has supposedly been filled out by another person. In fact, the attitude scale has been filled out by the experimenter on the basis of the subject's own attitude scale, which was completed earlier in the semester. The proportion of items on which the hypothetical other person agrees with the subject is varied. Then, the subject is given a scale to fill out regarding the stimulus person. Included in this scale are two items that measure interpersonal attraction.

The Importance of the Similarity If you were told that a stranger agreed with you on your favorite brand of paper towels, would you be inclined to date him or her? Probably not. It is not surprising to find that some issues are more important than others in producing the connection between similarity and attraction. Clore and Baldridge (1968) found much greater attraction when the hypothetical stimulus person agreed with the subject on important issues and disagreed on trivial issues than when the reverse was true. Of course, it is not always possible to know which items will be important to a person before considering the degree of attraction. For example, Touhey (1972) used the vehicle of a computer date to study attraction. Some of his couples were purposely matched according to religious attitudes, others according to sexual attitudes. Still others were *mis*matched on religious or sexual attitudes. After the couples had interacted, their attraction for each other was measured. First, pairs with similar attitudes were more attracted to each other than mismatched pairs. But the results also showed that males were most attracted to females who were most similar on sexual attitudes and least attracted to females with dissimilar sexual attitudes. Women, on the other hand, were most attracted to men with similar religious attitudes and least attracted to men with dissimilar religious attitudes. At least for this sample of subjects, males apparently found sexual attitudes more important whereas females found religious attitudes more important.

The Generality of Similarity and Attraction: Similar on What? What do you have to know about a person to be able to infer whether you like him or her? Most of the research that connects similarity and attraction deals with the matching of issue oriented attitudes, and uses college students as subjects. However, the similarity and attraction effect can be seen across a broad spectrum. Elementary school children (Byrne & Griffitt, 1966), as well as senior citizens (Griffitt, Nelson, & Littlepage, 1972), have shown the effect. Moreover, Byrne, Clore, and Worchel (1966) varied similarity of economic conditions, and Senn (1971) varied ability. In all cases, similarity led to attraction. The similarity-attraction hypothesis has been fairly robust across populations of subjects and has held up for various types of similarities. An exception to the general rule has been the difficulty of finding an effect for similarity of personality

Similarity leads to attraction.

characteristics (cf. Byrne, Griffitt, & Stefaniak, 1967), including sex-role orientation (Grush & Yehl, 1979).

Setting the Limits of Similarity and Attraction

1. Similarity: A laboratory phenomenon? In the neat world of the laboratory, the similarity-and-attraction effect has been fairly robust. When the hypothetical other person remains hypothetical, when the information about the person is severely limited by the experimenter, people are willing to make inferences about how much they like that person. But when Wright and Crawford (1971) tried to find evidence for similarity and attraction outside the laboratory, they were unable to do so. As a laboratory subject in the Byrne type of experiment, you know that the only information you will ever receive about a person are her responses to twelve attitudinal statements. As a human being in the real world, knowledge of twelve attitudes comprises a very small fraction of the important information that you hope to find out about someone.

However, in some nonlaboratory situations, similarity among people has been shown to have important influences on interpersonal attraction. For example, Kandel (1978) found that certain types of similarity were important in predicting friendship patterns among a large number of adolescents. Other investigators have found similarity relevant in predicting dating behavior (Byrne, Ervin, & Lamberth, 1970; Byrne & Rhamey, 1965). In a different context, Griffitt and Veitch (1974) studied the effect of similarity on people who had lived in a fallout shelter for ten days. Before entering the shelter, the participants filled out an attitude questionnaire. After several days, they were asked to name the two people whom they would most like to keep in the shelter with them and also to name the two whom they would most like to evict. The results indicated that the people selected to remain in the shelter were more similar in their attitudes to the subject than the people selected for eviction.

From a biosocial point of view, the effect of similarity on attraction is not at all surprising. Kenrick and Trost (1986) argue that bringing together people with similar but not identical genetic characteristics is the most adaptive strategy for the entire human species for purposes of mating. Obviously, the similarity and attraction effect that we have been examining is broader and pertains to more situations than heterosexual mating. Nonetheless, the biosocial point of view argues that the root of this effect—that is, the primary cause for us to prefer similar individuals—may derive from the adaptive evolution of the human species.

2. Similarity to whom? It is apparently true that being in agreement with people makes us feel pleasant and causes us to come to like the

Friendship patterns among young people can be predicted by the similarity of their backgrounds. *(David S. Strickler/The Picture Cube)*

people who agree with us. However, this statement may have broader implications than common sense and some data would acknowledge. Might there not be people whose agreement with us would make us feel uncomfortable rather than pleasant? A member of the House of Montague might be chagrined to learn that his attitudes are similar to those of Lord Capulet. Will he come to like Capulet as a result? Novak and Lerner (1968) conducted a study that bears on this question. They showed subjects that their attitudes and general background were similar or dissimilar to those of a mental patient. When compared to a group who received the same information about a "normal" stranger, people who found that they were similar to the mental patient liked him less than those who found that they were dissimilar to him (cf. Lerner & Agar, 1972). Similarly, Karuza and Brickman (1981) varied the status of a subject compared to the status of a confederate. Subjects liked similar confederates if the confederates were of high status. But subjects did not like being similar to a low-status confederate. In a like vein, Cooper and Jones (1969) showed that subjects took great pains to dissociate themselves from an obnoxious person whose attitudes were similar to their own.

The conclusions that can be drawn from these studies is that attitudinal similarity does not always lead to attraction. The characteristics of the target person also play an important role.

3. Similarity: Real or imagined? In an illustration presented in Figure 7–1(*c*), Romeo liked Juliet and disliked Tybalt. He must have been chagrined to learn that his wife liked Tybalt. In balance-theory terms, this asymmetry could lead to a lessening of the attraction between Romeo and Juliet. In the language of reward models, Juliet's disagreement with her husband might lead Romeo to associate a negative feeling with her, thereby decreasing her attractiveness. But there is an alternative. Romeo merely has to *imagine* that Juliet dislikes Tybalt. Then, as far as he is concerned, there is a state of balance. And if Juliet does not provide evidence to the contrary, Romeo might remain with this blissful distortion, using his *perceived* similarity to his wife as a further strengthening of his attraction to her.

Similarity, then, need not be real; it can be imagined. Good support exists for this possibility. Byrne and Blaylock (1963) found a moderate degree of similarity in the attitudes of married couples. But when they asked the husband or wife to predict the attitudes of his or her partner, the similarity scores increased markedly! The perception that each had of his or her similarity to the partner was much greater than the actual similarity. In a different investigation, Miller, Campbell, Twedt, and O'Connell (1966) asked students in dormitory suites at Northwestern University to describe their own personalities. They then asked other residents of the dormitories to describe the personalities of pairs of friends in the dorm. Friends were rated as having very similar personality traits, but when the self-descriptions of the pairs of friends were examined, there was much less actual similarity.

4. A time for complementarity. At the pole opposite to similarity is complementarity. In the Broadway show *Fiddler on the Roof,* Yenta the matchmaker says to the father of a homely prospective groom, "The way he looks and the way she sees, it's a perfect match!" We all know of instances in which two people are so dissimilar that they obviously fit well together. Examples from the media are manifold. Comedy teams such as the late Abbott and Costello have used the concept of complementarity. In the comic strip "Peanuts," the contrast between quiet naive Charlie Brown and his loud conniving friend Lucy makes them a perfect match. She may be domineering; he may be unassuming. He may be passive; she may be aggressive. It seems there is reason for the notion that attraction can result from complementary characteristics as well as from similar characteristics.

There is evidence to support this observation. Winch (1958) provided data to show that husbands who score high on standard measures of a particular need tend to marry wives who score low on that need or high on complementary needs. For example, a man who has a strong need to dominate is likely to marry a woman who has a need to be submissive and be dominated—though there is no evidence that complementarity leads to happier marriages (Meyer & Pepper, 1977; Katz, Glucksberg, & Krauss, 1960). Kerckhoff and Davis (1962) conducted a study with seriously attached couples, interviewing them at the beginning and end of a seven-month period. The couples were classified as having "stayed the same" in their relationship over seven months or as having moved "nearer to being a permanent couple." The investigators found that couples who had known each other only a short time showed progress toward permanence if they had similar needs and personalities. For couples who had been going together for a long time, however, complementarity was the best predictor of progress toward permanence. Thus, the evidence does support a role for complementarity—or a mixture of complementarity and similarity (Snyder & Fromkin, 1980)—leading to interpersonal attraction.

THE RECIPROCATION OF LIKING: I'LL LIKE YOU IF YOU LIKE ME

There is strong pressure to reciprocate liking (Gouldner, 1960). In the absence of other information, when someone likes you, you have every reason to like him. Tagiuri, Blake, and Bruner (1953) and others have found this to be so. This simple relationship suggests another interpretation of the similarity-attraction phenomenon.

After Walster and Walster (1963) provided evidence that people believe that similar others are attracted to them, Aronson and Worchel (1966) suggested that the entire similarity and attraction relationship could be accounted for by the pressure for reciprocal liking. The argument reasons that the similarity between the subject and the stimulus person causes an implicit assumption that the stimulus person would like the subject. Add to this the pressure to reciprocate liking, and we have another reason why similarities between two people should lead to attraction.

Aronson and Worchel put their explanation to the test by establishing a situation in which a similar or a dissimilar confederate was said to either like or dislike the subject. In other words, similarity information was manipulated independently of the stimulus person's evaluation of the subject. The investigators found that attraction to the stimulus person was affected only by the information that the stimulus person liked or disliked the subject, and not at all by information regarding similarity.

Research has shown that we are very sensitive to even small differences in how much we are liked. Berscheid, Walster, and Walster (1969)

PEANUTS ®   **By Schulz**

© 1953, United Feature Syndicate, Inc.

had subjects receive seven complimentary and one unflattering comment from a target. That target was liked significantly less than targets who made eight complimentary comments to the subject. The "I'll-like-you-if-you-like-me" effect may be short lived, as it may set the stage for the beginning of an attraction relationship but become less significant over time.

Backman and Secord (1959) had subjects meet as a group of strangers. They told each subject that personality tests they had taken indicated that specific members of the group were likely to like them. In fact, this information was bogus and not related to the personalities of the group members. The groups were to meet six times as informal discussion groups, but the members were told that there was a possibility that each group would be broken into two-member teams. They were asked to indicate with which members they would like to be paired. The data showed that after the first session, but not after later sessions, the subjects chose the group members who had been designated as likely to like them. After later sessions, this pattern broke down. For earlier sessions, subjects were attracted to those group members who they felt would be attracted to them. In time, apparently, feedback from group members superseded the information given by the experimenter.

Ingratiation: A Special Case   Although it is usually true that we enjoy being complimented and react to compliments with liking (Skolnick, 1971), this is not always the case. When we are complimented, we would like to believe that the compliments are attributable to our good nature, our fine qualities, and so on. We are less than happy if we must attribute the compliments to an ulterior motive on the part of the complimenter.

When a person acts in such a way as to illicitly enhance his image in the eyes of another, he may be said to be engaging in *ingratiation* (recall our discussion in Chapter Four). Jones (1964; Jones & Wortman, 1973) and his colleagues have considered the problem of ingratiation at some length. Flattery has been conceived as one tactic that an ingratiator might use to raise his or her esteem in the opinion of others. The question is: Is such a tactic successful?

The answer to this question depends on the perceived dependence of the flatterer on the object of his or her flattery. If you think that someone needs or wants something from you, you are much less likely to feel attracted to that individual as a result of compliments he may pay you than you are to someone who has nothing to gain by complimenting you. Evidence for this point of view can be found in studies by Dickoff (1961) and by Lowe and Goldstein (1970). In Dickoff's study, women students listened to an evaluation of themselves delivered by a graduate student who had been observing them through a one-way mirror. The graduate student (an accomplice of the experimenter) varied her proportion of compliments, depending on the experimental condition of the subject. The subject was (1) complimented excessively, (2) complimented within the bounds of her previously measured self-esteem, or (3) given neutral feedback.

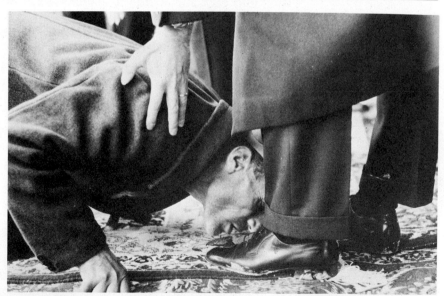

Praise, compliments, and favors may be genuine, but may also represent attempts to ingratiate. Ingratiation is a likely attribution when the recipient has greater power and status. *(Copyright Thomas Hopker 1981/Woodfin Camp & Associates)*

Dickoff manipulated whether the person giving the evaluation had anything to gain from the subject liking her. In the accuracy condition, the subjects were led to believe that the graduate student was trying to be as accurate and honest as possible. In the ulterior-motive condition, the subject was told that the graduate student was going to ask the subject to participate in one of her studies after the current experiment was concluded.

The feedback that the subject received strongly affected her evaluation of the graduate student. As Figure 7–2 shows, increasing the favorableness of the evaluation increases the liking—up to a point. When favorableness turns to flattery, the evaluation of the flatterer depends on the subject's perception of whether the flattery is in the service of ingratiation. When the possibility of an ulterior motive is present, attraction decreases as the favorableness of the compliments increases.

Note that these results present a double-edged dilemma. An ingratiator wishing to increase his esteem must conceal any possible ulterior motivation. If he cannot, it is best if he refrains from excessive flattery. On the other hand, a person who genuinely feels that another is worthy of considerable praise may be penalized for the expression of his feeling if the possibility of an ulterior motive is present.

Figure 7–2
Mean rating scale attraction scores in Dickoff study

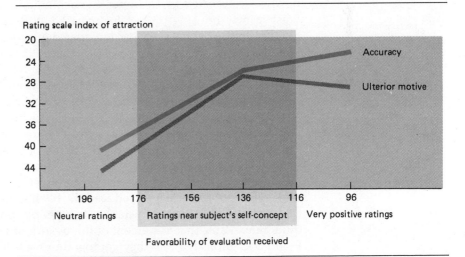

Source: Jones (1964).

Complimenting as a form of ingratiation is not the only technique that has been shown to lead to an ingratiator's dilemma. Continually agreeing with someone has been shown to lead to attraction except when the agreeing party has something to gain in a relationship (Jones, Jones, & Gergen, 1963). Similarly, the use of another's first name in the course of a conversation has been shown to be effective in producing attraction, with the same qualification. It led to less positive ratings when the name user was perceived to have something to gain by being viewed positively (Kleinke, Staneski, & Weaver, 1972).

PROPINQUITY BREEDS ATTRACTION—SOMETIMES

It is most probably true that throughout your life your closest acquaintances will live near you, that you will marry a person who lives close to you, and that the friends you make at work will occupy positions that are physically close to you. Bossard (1932) was one of the first to examine the importance of physical distance in mate selection for marriage. Examining five thousand marriage license applications in Philadelphia, he found an inverse relationship between the number of such applications and the physical distance of the addresses of the two engaged partners— as the distance increased, the number of applications sharply decreased.

Perhaps the most systematic investigation of propinquity and attraction was conducted by Festinger, Schachter, and Back in 1950. Westgate West, a new housing project for married students, was constructed in the form of small two-story garden apartment complexes. Each unit contained ten apartments. New residents did not have a choice about which apartment to live in; they were assigned on a nearly random basis—that is, they filled apartments as these became vacant. In addition, very few of the tenants knew one another before coming to Westgate West. After some time, all of the residents were asked which members of the complex they saw socially most often. The results are presented in Figure 7–3. The distance between people on the same floor and on different floors was closely related to friendship patterns—the closer two individuals lived to each other, the more likely they were to be friends. Living on different floors (bottom line) reduced the likelihood of friendship because this increased functional distance. For people on the same floor, it is quite remarkable that 41 percent of the next-door neighbors (marked *a* in Figure 7–3) indicated that they got together socially whereas only 10 percent of the people at opposite ends of the hall (marked *b*) mixed socially —especially since the maximum difference in distance between the closest and the farthest apartment was only sixty-nine feet.

Figure 7–3
Relationship between functional distance and liking

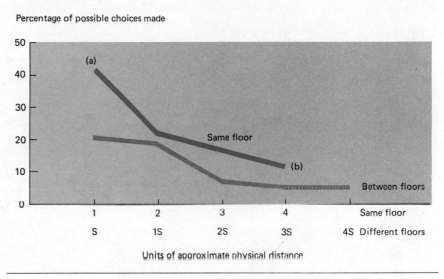

Source: Reprinted from *Social Pressures in Informal Groups*, by Leon Festinger, Stanley Schachter, and Kurt Back with the permission of the publishers, Stanford University Press. Copyright 1950 by Leon Festinger, Stanley Schachter, and Kurt Back (Copyright renewed).

Nahemow and Lawton (1975) examined friendship patterns in an inner-city housing project that serviced residents of various age groups and races. Consistent with the Festinger et al. (1950) finding, there was an overwhelming tendency for people of all ages and races to have their best friends within the same building (an average of 93 percent). But within the same building, an interesting pattern emerged. For people whose best friends were of a similar age or the same race, it was equally likely for the best friend to be on the respondent's floor or on a different floor. In other words, age and racial similarity were more important in predicting friendship than the floor on which the friends lived. However, if the best friend were of a different race or age, then it was overwhelmingly likely that the person resided on the respondent's floor. Apparently, attraction in a housing project can transcend the boundaries of propinquity to some degree if similarity on an important dimension exists. In the absence of such similarity, attraction seems very much a function of physical closeness.

Westgate West housing complex. This spatial design lent itself to a study of friendship patterns by Festinger, Schachter, and Back (1950). *(Used with permission of Stanford University Press.)*

Explaining the Effect of Propinquity: Rewards, Expectations, and Familiarity

Rewards. Why should propinquity lead to attraction? Why should people be more attracted to the people next to whom they live and work? One explanation is that we interact more with those who are near us and that such interactions are rewarding (Davis & Perkowitz, 1979; Werner & Latané, 1974). Newcomb has argued that "when persons interact, the reward-punishment ratio is more often . . . reinforcing" (1956, p. 576). That is, in normal everyday interaction, we are more likely to say nice things to others and to hear compliments in return than we are to say and hear negative things. So the more we interact with others, the more often we may be rewarded by them. Since it is thought that reward leads to greater liking, it would then follow that those who give us the greatest opportunity for frequent interaction would be rewarding to us and therefore would be liked by us.

Expectations. Those who are near us in our jobs, our houses, our dormitories, and so on are likely to be near us tomorrow and the next day as well. That is, we expect to interact with them again and again. As Newcomb's and Heider's balance theories would suggest, there is pressure to form a positive-sentiment relationship with those with whom we constantly interact. Darley and Berscheid (1967) conducted an experiment to demonstrate that a person's expectation of interacting with another person induces a tendency in that person to like the other. College women expected to participate in a study in which they were to discuss sexual standards for female college students. Before beginning the discussion, a subject was shown information about two other women students, one of whom was designated as the subject's partner for the discussion. Although the information about each of the two was of approximately equal attractiveness, the subjects answered the question "How probable is it that you would like this girl better socially?" by picking their prospective partner 70 percent of the time. In a subsequent study, Berscheid, Boye, and Darley (1968) found that a person with whom a subject was expecting to interact was liked better even when the future interaction was unforeseeably canceled and the person was objectively undesirable.

Familiarity or "mere exposure." A third explanation relates to what seems to be a general phenomenon of attraction. The more familiar we are with almost any object—that is, the more we have merely been exposed to that object—the more we seem to like it. Research has shown that the object may be a word, a picture, or another person. Merely being exposed to the person or object has the effect of our liking her or it more without there necessarily being a rational explanation.

Much of the work on "mere exposure" has been done by Zajonc and his colleagues (e.g., Moreland & Zajonc, 1979, 1982). In one study, Zajonc (1968) showed that words from a foreign language that subjects saw frequently were given greater positive value than words that were shown infrequently. In another study, Zajonc (1968) showed volunteer subjects a number of photographs. Some of the photographs were shown often; others were shown infrequently. Later, subjects were asked how much they like the people depicted in the photographs. People whose pictures were seen frequently were rated as more likable than people whose pictures were only seen once or twice.

Is liking affected by physical attractiveness? Some say people seek partners who are most attractive. Others say people seek partners who are as attractive as they are (the matching hypothesis). *(Top photos, Joel Gordon 1985/1979; bottom, copyright Ira Berger 1981/Woodfin Camp & Associates)*

Kunst-Wilson and Zajonc (1980) had subjects perform what is known as a dichotic listening task. Students were given earphones. In one ear, they heard a series of words. They had to match those words to words they were reading in a text that had been placed in front of them. In the other ear, they heard a series of melodies, although these were not referred to by the experimenter and seemed to have nothing to do with the task at hand. Later, subjects were asked to listen to a series of melodies, to indicate whether the melodies were familiar, and to indicate how much they liked each tune. Subjects could not remember hearing any of the tunes although, in truth, several had been played through the earphones during the earlier portion of the experiment. Despite the fact that the tunes were not consciously recognized, the students came to like them better. Thus, merely being exposed to the melodies—without the participants' remembering their previous exposure to the music—created greater liking.

The finding that repeated exposure to a stimulus object or person leads to liking is now well established (see Harrison, 1977, for a review). The effect appears to hold under many conditions, including instances in which the initial reaction to the stimulus is negative (Zajonc, Markus, & Wilson, 1974). And once attraction is induced by mere exposure, it is likely that increased opportunities will occur to increase further the degree of attraction.

In summary, propinquity appears to lead to attraction in a variety of situations. This may be attributable to (1) the phenomenon that mere exposure induces attraction, (2) the fact that those near to us have more opportunities to reward us, and/or (3) the expectation of future interaction with those who live and work near us. However, Berscheid and Walster (1978) have pointed out that attraction is not the only result of propinquity. They cite an FBI report that indicates that one-third of all murders occur within the family. In addition, the FBI report indicates that "most aggravated assaults occur within family units or between neighbors." Detroit police statistics for 1976 indicate that the majority of robberies occur between family members or neighbors, and a recent New York City statistic showed that muggings are more likely to be committed by people in the same neighborhood than by people from different neighborhoods. One reason that social psychological studies may demonstrate a liking-and-propinquity relationship is that the nature of the studies conducted leads to a high reward-punishment ratio. People in housing projects, for example, do not have to interact in an intimate fashion. Nodding one's head, giving compliments, or politely agreeing with a political comment made by a neighbor while picking up the newspaper may lead to a high number of rewarding situations and an avoidance of negative situations. Consequently, the nearness of superficial contacts may encourage attraction, but such attraction may be fragile and weak.

In general, propinquity may have the effect of magnifying the intensity of relationships. It may increase attractiveness *and* hatred, depending on other factors in the situation. Determining those "other factors" may be the future direction of research in the study of propinquity and interpersonal liking.

PHYSICAL ATTRACTIVENESS AND LIKING

Physically attractive people are liked better than homely people. Walster, Aronson, Abrahams, and Rottman (1966) arranged dates for subjects at a dance. The pairings were created randomly. Each participant was rated in terms of physical attractiveness by a group of judges. At a break in the dance, the participants were asked how much they liked their partners and how much they would like to have a future date with their partners. Walster et al. found that liking of the partner and desire for a future date were directly related to attractiveness—the more attractive the partner, the greater the liking.

Not all of the evidence indicates that people attempt to date the most attractive member of the opposite sex. The comment "She's out of your league" could be directed to an ordinary-looking person who seeks a date with the town's knockout. In fact, Walster et al. did not expect the desire for a future date to be a function of attractiveness. Instead, they had predicted a "matching" hypothesis: people would choose partners who were about as attractive as they themselves were. However, Walster et al. realized that arranging the date at the dance did not replicate a customary setting in which a person would find himself or herself. Usually, a fear of rejection or failure might accompany trying to win the most attractive member of the opposite sex. In a subsequent study by Walster and Walster (1969), subjects were led to believe that they would meet their prospective partners before the dance. They were then asked how attractive a partner they wished to have. With the fear of possible rejection reinstated, people chose potential dates who were about as attractive as they themselves were. Similar data have been collected by Berscheid, Dion, Walster, and Walster (1971) and by Huston (1973).

Dating an attractive person, then, is something that is desired but may be tempered by the fear of rejection. Kiesler and Baral (1970) conducted a study in which they temporarily lowered or raised men's self-esteem. With self-esteem lowered, we can predict that men will be more fearful of rejection; with self-esteem raised, they will have less fear of rejection. Kiesler and Baral found that men whose self-esteem had been lowered made more romantic advances toward a moderately attractive woman than toward a very attractive woman; men with raised self-esteem showed the opposite pattern.

The attractiveness data are probably a specific instance of Huston and Levinger's (1978) general position on the social choices that people make. They proposed that people usually consider two general issues when choosing a date or other social partner. First, how attractive do they find the potential partner's attributes (in the present case, physical attractiveness) and second, how likely is it that the potential partner will find their attributes attractive and therefore respond favorably?

Lest we believe that the greater liking of attractive dates is due purely or even primarily to sexual stimulation, some further data should be related. First, Dion, Berscheid, and Walster (1972) presented evidence that physically attractive people are seen as being happier and more successful than less attractive people. In addition, they are rated as having more socially desirable personality traits than less attractive people. Dion et al. also found that it did not matter whether a respondent was rating a member of the same or the opposite sex; sexual attraction did not seem to be involved.

The Jury Is Out   The gist of these studies is that we do not always act rationally when physical attractiveness is concerned. We tend to like attractive people more, regardless of their sex or age. Not only do we like them more, we may also evaluate their *behavior* differently. We may be inclined to like the behavior of attractive people more than that of unattractive people or to expect better behavior from them. For example, Clifford and Walster (1973) showed fifth-grade teachers a report card with information about a hypothetical student. Although all of the teachers saw the same information, the photograph of the student that was clipped to the card was varied so that either an attractive or an unattractive boy or girl was pictured. The teacher's assessment of the student's IQ and expected future level of attainment varied as a function of physical attractiveness. Although the test scores did not vary, an attractive child was seen as more intelligent and was expected to do better work than an unattractive child.

In another study, Landy and Sigall (1974) showed college students an essay that had been written by another student. The objective quality of the essay was made either good or bad, and a photograph attached to the essay revealed that the writer was either attractive or unattractive. (Control group subjects had no photo attached to the essay.) The subjects were asked to rate the quality of the essay. It is true that objectively good essays were rated better than poor essays, but it is also true that essays written by attractive writers were seen as being of better quality than essays written by unattractive writers. And, as the results presented

Table 7–1
Subjects' ratings of the general quality of the essay in each experimental condition

Essay quality	Writer's physical attractiveness			Total mean
	Attractive	Control	Unattractive	
Good	6.7	6.6	5.9	6.4
Poor	5.2	4.7	2.7	4.2
Total	6.0	5.5	4.3	

Note: The higher the rating number, the better the evaluation of the essay.
Source: Adapted from Landy and Sigall (1974).

in Table 7–1 indicate, the effect was somewhat stronger for the bad essay than for the good one. That is, a poor essay written by an attractive writer was given an extra benefit of the doubt by the judges.

It comes as no surprise that if opportunities in school can be influenced by attractiveness, then chances out in the job market can be similarly affected. Cash, Gillen, and Burns (1977) found that job recommendations were significantly influenced by whether the candidate was attractive or not, even when written by experienced personnel consultants and when looks could not possibly affect job performance.

Perhaps the most frightening situation in which physical attractiveness can affect judgments is in the courtroom, where physical attractiveness is supposed to be extraneous to the evidence of the case. But if beauty affects liking and our attributions of personality and behavior, then it may also affect courtroom judgments. As Clarence Darrow said, "Jurymen seldom convict a person they like or acquit one they dislike. . . . Facts regarding the crime are relatively unimportant." In a pioneering study, Landy and Aronson (1969) presented a case of negligent homicide to a simulated jury (student subjects pretending to serve as a jury). The defendant was accused of running over a pedestrian on Christmas Eve. The facts were identical in all cases. For half of the cases, however, the defendant was described positively (an insurance man who was going to spend Christmas Eve with his family), and for the other half he was described negatively (a janitor who was going to spend the evening with his girlfriend). Although the facts did not differ, the janitor was given significantly more years of imprisonment than the positively described defendant.

Landy and Aronson's study did not involve physical characteristics. However, a study by Efran (1974) took this additional step. He asked subjects to decide the fate of a defendant in a college cheating case.

Again, the facts were held constant, but a photograph of the defendant attached to the written information was varied according to the condition of the subject in the study. Each photograph had been rated by a separate group as either attractive or unattractive. Physically attractive defendants were liked better, judged less guilty, and received less punishment than defendants who were unattractive.

Why should attractiveness lead simulated juries to confer less guilt and punishment on a defendant? Sigall and Ostrove (1975) suggested that the reason may rest with the jurors' assumption that the attractive defendant is worthier, has greater potential, and is less likely to transgress in the future than an unattractive defendant. That people make this assumption was demonstrated in an earlier study by Dion (1972). In that study, judges attributed the transgressions of unattractive people to their stable dispositions whereas they attributed the transgressions of attractive people to momentary circumstances.

If these are the assumptions that jurors make, Sigall and Ostrove argued that the assumptions should apply only to crimes that are not directly related to appearance. That is, if a person uses his or her good looks to put over a "con game" or a swindle, then the notion that an attractive person will not get involved in such activities again loses its credibility. Sigall and Ostrove established a simulated jury to pass sentence on a defendant who was either attractive or, in another condition, unattractive. In a third condition, no information about attractiveness was provided. For half of the jurors, the crime was described as unrelated to the defendant's attractiveness. In this condition, the defendant burglarized a home of $2,200. For the other half, the defendant "ingratiated herself to a middle-aged bachelor and induced him to invest $2,200 in a nonexistent corporation." Presumably, the defendant's looks may have been a factor in this swindle.

The mean number of years of prison recommended by the jurors is depicted in Table 7–2. As can be seen, the results strongly support Sigall and Ostrove's reasoning. The attractive defendant who committed a burglary was given far less punishment than the unattractive defendant or the defendant about whom no attractiveness information was provided. However, the attractive defendant who had ingratiated herself to commit the swindle was sentenced to more years in prison than the defendants in all of the other conditions.

Why Does Physical Attractiveness Lead to Liking?   Although there are some limitations to the phenomenon, the effect of physical attractiveness on liking seems robust. People seem to like those who are more attractive; they praise their behaviors and characteristics and find them less culpable for transgressions. What reasons lead to this phenomenon?

The appearance and status of a defendant may influence a jury's estimation of guilt.

Why should rational human beings decide that people with more attractive physical characteristics are worthy of such praise?

First, it may be that people like attractive people for the status those people convey. We may have learned throughout our upbringing that people are impressed when we are with others who are attractive. Sigall and Landy (1973), for example, asked subjects to evaluate a man whom they saw seated either with an attractive or an unattractive woman. The man received far more positive ratings when seen with the attractive

Table 7–2
Mean sentence assigned, in years (n = 20 per cell)

| Offense | Defendant condition | | |
	Attractive	Unattractive	Control
Swindle	5.45	4.35	4.35
Burglary	2.80	5.20	5.10

Source: Sigall and Ostrove (1975).

rather than the unattractive woman. Kernis and Wheeler (1981) varied both the level of association that a target had with a confederate and the attractiveness of that confederate. When the target was portrayed as being a friend of, rather than someone merely seen with, the confederate, the target was rated as being more likable and more attractive. If we are seen as attractive when we associate with attractive people, then attractive people become very rewarding. It is reasonable to conclude, then, that we would come to evaluate attractive people highly.

A second principle that may govern the high regard given to attractive people comes from a study by Marks, Miller, and Maruyama (1981). These investigators asked people how similar several other people were to them on a variety of traits. Participants rated attractive people as being more similar to themselves. Could it be that there is a general tendency to view ourselves as being more similar to attractive than to unattractive people? Our positive regard for those who are attractive may not be due to their physical appeal, but rather to their assumed similarity to us.

A third explanation for the positive evaluations given to physically attractive people is that there may be a kernel of truth in that evaluation. Perhaps physically attractive people do have more pleasing personalities, more varied social contacts, and more interesting friends. Perhaps they do differ from the unattractive in their ability to achieve and to perform. Reis, Nezlek, and Wheeler (1980) collected extensive notes on the social interaction patterns of attractive and unattractive people. Important differences were indeed found between the two groups with regard to the number of friends, the initiation of social contacts, and the number and quality of conversations. The lives of attractive and unattractive people do appear to differ in significant ways. Further research may tell us whether these differences support the hypothesis that there is indeed a kernel of truth to the high ratings given to attractive people.

For Whom Is Physical Attractiveness Most Important? The Role of Self-Monitoring   People differ in the emphasis they put on physical attractiveness, personal attributes, religious affiliation, interpersonal styles, and so forth as they choose the people with whom they interact. Are there systematic differences among people that are related to the degree to which they take physical appearance into account in choosing a potentially romantic partner? Snyder, Berscheid, and Glick (1985) examined this question. They suggested that the concept of self-monitoring may provide that systematic difference.

As you may recall from our earlier discussions in Chapters Four and Six, people can be classified on a scale of high to low self-monitoring. Some people pay careful attention to presenting themselves according to what they believe is demanded by the situation. They are particularly responsive to situational cues for making decisions about appropriate behavior. And they tend to act more in accordance with what they believe is required by the situation than by what they truly believe or feel. Such people are considered high self-monitors. By contrast, low self-monitors are people who choose their behaviors in social situations based on their dispositions and attitudes, and not on what they think the situation demands. As we saw in Chapter Six, low self-monitors are more likely to demonstrate attitude-behavior consistency since they are usually more

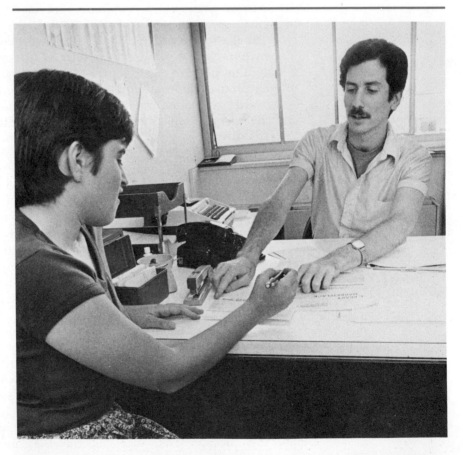

Is the man in this photograph a high self-monitor or a low self-monitor? Research has shown that high self-monitors are more influenced by the applicant's physical characteristics, whereas low self-monitors are more concerned with the applicant's qualifications on paper. (© *Tom Turner 1983/design conceptions*)

attuned to their own attitudes and less concerned with such distractions as making a good impression.

Since high self-monitors are more influenced by the appearance of a social situation, Snyder and his colleagues reasoned that they would be more inclined than low self-monitors to consider the physical attractiveness of a potential partner. Low self-monitors, on the other hand, would be more interested in discovering a potential partner's true attitudes and personal characteristics in deciding whom to choose as a potential partner.

In a first study, Snyder et al. gave male subjects at the University of Minnesota a choice of more than fifty files to examine. The files contained information on female students who could serve as potential partners for informal coffee dates at a nearby cafeteria. The subjects were known not to be involved with a steady romantic partner, so it was assumed that they would see the potential date as the possible start of a relationship.

Each file consisted of three pages. The first page consisted of information about the background, attitudes, and preferences of the particular woman; the second page contained some uninterpretable filler information; and the third page contained a photograph of the woman. The participants were able to spend as much time as they liked with as many of the files as they chose. Moreover, they could concentrate on any page of the file that they preferred—the physical information conveyed by page three's photograph, or the information about personal attributes on page one. Observers stationed behind a one-way mirror watched the subjects as they examined the files. One dependent measure was the degree to which participants looked at the first (personal information) page or the third (physical information) page. In addition, the subjects had to choose one of the women for a coffee date. Subjects were asked directly whether their choice was made more on the basis of the physical or the personal information.

The results were clear. High self-monitors were much more likely to pay attention to the photographs of the women than low self-monitors. On the other hand, low self-monitors were more likely to spend their time on page-one information (information on personal attributes). Table 7–3 adds further support to the hypotheses by showing the subjects' stated major reason for their choice of a dating partner. Clearly, high self-monitors stated that they were influenced by physical attractiveness; low self-monitors were affected by personal characteristics.

In a second experiment, Snyder, Berscheid, and Glick (1985) constrained the male subjects' choice of a dating partner to two potential choices. One was very attractive but had a series of unpleasant personal characteristics. The other was physically unattractive but had highly positive personal qualities. Subjects—selected so that they would be

Table 7–3
Reasons for choosing a dating partner: Investigation 1

	Individuals' self-monitoring category	
Stated reason	*Low*	*High*
Personal attributes	15	3
Photographs	5	10

Note: Entries in this table are number of participants in each self-monitoring category who offered each type of stated reason for choosing their dating partner.
Source: From Snyder, Berscheid, and Glick (1985). Copyright 1985 by the American Psychological Association. Adapted by permission of the authors.

either quite high or quite low in self-monitoring—were asked to choose one of the women for an evening date at a local restaurant. Which partner did the subjects select? Of the low self-monitors, 81 percent chose to date the partner with the desirable personality and the unattractive appearance. Only 31 percent of the high self-monitors made this choice. By contrast, 69 percent of the high self-monitors chose the physically attractive woman despite her undesirable personality, while only 19 percent of the low self-monitors made this choice.

It appears that while people may all be interested in the physical attractiveness of a potential partner in a dating situation, high self-monitors are particularly concerned with this dimension. Their preoccupation with presenting an appropriate image (or self-presentation) in the dating situation results in their focusing on the physical dimension. Low self-monitors are more concerned with personal qualities and attributes. Given a choice, they will trade physical beauty for inner qualities.

HOW TO WIN FRIENDS AND INFLUENCE PEOPLE BY BEING INSULTING AND CLUMSY

When Dale Carnegie sought to advise people on how to endear themselves to others in *How to Win Friends and Influence People,* he probably never dreamed of some of the less obvious and unusual facets of interpersonal attraction. Elliot Aronson and his colleagues have been active in exploring some of the more interesting situations that lead to attraction.

To Insult Is Divine   Earlier in this chapter, it was shown that people who compliment us are generally liked better than those who do not (see Skolnik, 1971; Sigall & Aronson, 1969; Tagiuri, Blake, & Bruner, 1953). However, this is not always true; after a while compliments can get boring. The doting husband who constantly compliments his wife on her clothing, makeup, and hairdo gets himself into a position where he is expected to be complimentary. His flattering statements, like the kneejerk reflex, begin to lose their meaning.

Aronson and Linder (1965) sought to investigate the *sequence* of flattering and insulting statements that a person received. The best way to understand their clever but complicated methodology is to imagine that you are the subject in their experiment. When you enter the laboratory, you are told that a second subject is expected. But since you arrived first, you will serve as the confederate in a study on "verbal conditioning." The experimenter tells you that the other subject will have a conversation with you and that she will then have a discussion with the experimenter, who will ask her what she thought of you. Actually, you are told, the entire purpose of the other subject's discussion with the experimenter is to allow the latter to "reinforce" with the response "mm hmm" or "good" all plural nouns that the subject utters. You, serving as the confederate, are to count the number of plural nouns that are used by the subject (which you can hear over a sound system).

You may ask what this has to do with interpersonal perception. The experimenter has not told you the full story. In fact, the other subject is the confederate; you are not. The hoax is designed to force you to "overhear" evaluative comments made about you. The four conditions of the experiment vary only the number and the sequence of the positive and negative evaluations the subject overhears; the positive and negative feedback are systematically varied over seven sessions. As depicted in Figure 7–4, in the positive-positive condition, the seven sessions are devoted to flattering statements that the "other subject" makes about you. In the negative-negative condition, the other subject's statements are all derogatory and insulting ("She seems to be a rather shallow and superficial person"). In the negative-positive (gain) condition, the confederate begins by describing you as dull, ordinary, and so on, but by the fourth session she begins to change her opinion, and at the end she is describing you in very flattering terms. The positive-negative (loss) condition is the mirror image of the negative-positive condition. Here you are described in glowing terms at first; the fourth session marks the change from flattery to insult, and by the end of the study you are described with purely insulting comments.

At the end, the experimenter asks you for your "gut feeling" about the "other subject." The results of this question are shown in Table 7–4. The most-liked person in the study is not the confederate in the positive-positive condition but the one in the negative-positive or gain condition. This is true even though over the course of the seven sessions the positive-positive confederate complimented you twenty-eight times

Figure 7–4
Four conditions of Aronson and Linder's study of the sequence of evaluative comments

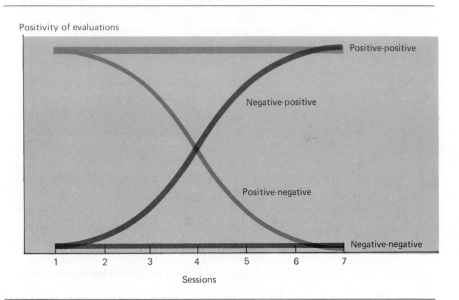

Note: Positive and negative feedback were systematically varied over seven sessions.
Source: Aronson and Linder (1965).

without an insult, and in the gain condition she complimented you only fourteen times after delivering eight insults. The reverse is also true. Subjects liked a person who consistently insulted them better than they liked someone who began by giving them fourteen compliments and ended with eight insults. It should be pointed out that the latter effect was not large enough to be statistically significant.

The Aronson and Linder study and a similar study by Mettee (1971) offer some potent advice about interpersonal attraction over time. The always complimentary husband may wonder why his wife flips for a guy who has always been insulting and belligerent and, just once, gives her an approving glance. Moreover, our doting husband should realize the bind that he has gotten himself into. On the one hand, he is at the mercy of the competitor with the one approving glance; but he dare not act disapprovingly himself, for if he does he could put himself in the loss condition. That is, he would be liked less than if he had always been insulting.

Table 7-4
Mean liking of the confederate in each condition

Experimental condition	Mean
1. Negative-positive (gain)	+7.67
2. Positive-positive	+6.42
3. Negative-negative	+2.52
4. Positive-negative (loss)	+0.87

Note: Higher numbers indicate greater liking.
Source: Adapted from Aronson and Linder (1965).

Why should such an effect occur? Aronson and Linder (1965) and Aronson (1969a) have suggested some possibilities, two of which should be mentioned. First, the person in the gain condition may be liked because she is seen as more discriminating. In effect, she establishes her credibility and proves that she is a discerning individual. To earn the praise of such a person who once insulted you indicates that you are really a good person. Second, the insulting person may upset you and cause some uncomfortable uncertainty about your self-esteem. But when she comes around to your side, she reduces that uncertainty. Aronson suggests that this produces a warm and pleasurable feeling—that is, it is rewarding—and therefore it leads to greater attraction.

Clumsiness Is Attractive: The Pratfall In the early days of his presidency, John F. Kennedy was riding a wave of very positive popular sentiment. But in 1961 there occurred the Bay of Pigs fiasco—a U.S.-supported invasion of Cuba. At the last possible moment, Kennedy withdrew support from the incursion. He advised the American public and shouldered full blame and responsibility for the event, though many analysts believed that he could have legitimately transferred a major proportion of the responsibility to former President Dwight D. Eisenhower. And a good many of his advisers, with their eye on the 1964 election, wished that he had. Kennedy's political opponents had their hearts set on the forthcoming opinion polls, which they believed would show a dramatic loss of popularity for the president. The results were indeed dramatic, for they provided Kennedy with the highest ratings he was ever to receive during his presidency.

What could account for this surprising turn of events? Aronson, Willerman, and Floyd (1966) argued that a blunder, mistake, or error of judgment can be an endearing quality in someone of extremely high competence. A man who seems to come from the land of Camelot—born

President John F. Kennedy with the Secretary of State, Dean Rusk, following the Bay of Pigs invasion. Kennedy's public acceptance of blame for the abortive invasion caused his popularity to soar. *(© Jacques Lowe/Woodfin Camp & Associates)*

to wealthy and influential parents; possessing superior intelligence, a likable personality, and good looks; and married to a beautiful woman—may be viewed with great admiration, but such a man does not always endear himself to us. He may seem too perfect, too unapproachable. A mistake, however, is something of which we are all capable. A man who commits one has human qualities. If he is otherwise highly competent, a mistake can humanize him in our eyes and serve to increase our liking for him.

Aronson, Willerman, and Floyd (1966) designed a situation in which they could test their hypotheses. Subjects listened to a tape-recorded session in which a stimulus person was being interviewed for a spot on a college team competing in a quiz competition (the old "College Bowl" television show). In one condition, the stimulus person was of extremely high ability. He was given a series of questions that he answered with a 92 percent score. During an interview, he said that he had been an honor student in high school, editor of the senior yearbook, and a member of the track team. The stimulus person on a second tape presented quite a different story. He answered only 30 percent of his questions correctly and said that he had received average grades in high school, that he had been a proofreader on the senior yearbook, and that he had tried out for the track team but failed to make it.

In half of the cases, both the competent and the incompetent stimulus person committed a clumsy pratfall. Near the end of the interview, a lot of shuffling was suddenly heard, and the stimulus person yelled, "Oh, my goodness, I've spilled coffee all over my new suit!" In the other half of the cases, the pratfall did not occur. At the end of the study, subjects were asked to give their impressions of the stimulus person by indicating how much they liked him. What results should be expected? In general, it is probably true that people who are clumsy are not liked as much as people who are not clumsy. It is also probably true that people who are as competent as the high-ability stimulus person are liked better than incompetent people. But putting the two together presents a more complicated prediction. In the Aronson et al. view, the highly competent stimulus person was expected to be liked better—*particularly* if he were the culprit in a clumsy accident. But the person of mediocre competence was not expected to benefit from his clumsiness. He had already demonstrated that he was far from perfect. Another example was hardly needed and could only work to his detriment.

The results of the study, presented in Table 7–5, supported the predictions. For the person of superior ability, attractiveness increased when he acted clumsily whereas, for the person of average ability, attractiveness was markedly reduced when he was clumsy. A later study by Helmreich, Aronson, and LeFan (1970) corroborated these results, with one qualification. It is important that the person making the judgment (the subject) consider himself to be of average, rather than of very high or very low self-esteem. As Helmreich et al. summarize it, "To err is humanizing—sometimes."

Table 7–5
Mean attraction scores of the interviewee

	Pratfall	*No pratfall*
Superior ability	30.2	20.8
Average ability	−2.5	17.8

Note: The higher the number, the greater the attraction.
Source: Aronson, Willerman, and Floyd (1966).

ON LOVE

When we speak about interpersonal attraction, we expect to encounter the consuming passion of lovers, the unbridled love of a Romeo for a Juliet. Social psychology has taught us little about such emotion, however. The rather extensive literature on attraction has focused on what we normally call "liking" or "respect" or "high regard." Love has been the Cinderella sister of like, being largely ignored by the discipline.

There are at least three major problems with studying love. First, the study of any topic (attitudes, aggression, leadership) requires good measurement techniques. Measuring love is difficult indeed. Second, most of us can describe what we mean by leadership, aggression, and so on, but many observers of human behavior including the playwrights and the poets have attempted to define love, and few have agreed. Kelley (1982) has cautioned that distinctions need to be made between altruistic love, attachment, friendship, and romantic love. And finally, many people have the attitude that love is a topic that should not be studied, that to study love is to ruin it. In 1975, a U.S. senator rose on the floor of Congress to denounce the appropriation of funds for the study of such an intimate topic, saying, "There are some things better left unstudied."

Nonetheless, recent inroads have been made in the study of romantic love, prompted largely by the question of whether loving is just more liking or whether the two differ in quality rather than quantity. Rubin (1973) boldly attempted to define love as the junction of three important components:

1. *Caring*—the feeling that another person's satisfactions are as important to you as your own. In Erich Fromm's words, "It is the active concern for the life and growth of that which we love."
2. *Attachment*—the need or desire to be with the other, to make physical contact, to be approved of and cared for.
3. *Intimacy*—the bond or the link between two people. It is manifested by close and confidential communication between people.

On the basis of his definition of love, Rubin set out to create a measurement device—a self-report scale—that could measure the emotion. He created items that were thought to measure each of the three elements of love. He also added items that would be responsive to the feelings of liking and respect, which form the cornerstones of interpersonal attraction in the more traditional studies. All of the items were administered to a large group of respondents and then submitted to a statistical technique known as factor analysis (this separates the items into clusters of similar items). The result of the factor analysis was the creation of two scales—one for love and one for liking (Figure 7–5).

Figure 7–5
Selected examples of love-scale and liking-scale items

Love scale

1. If ___ were feeling bad, my first duty would be to cheer him (her) up.
2. I feel that I can confide in ___ about virtually everything.
3. If I could never be with ___, I would feel miserable.

Liking scale

1. I think that ___ is unusually well adjusted.
2. I have great confidence in ___'s good judgment.
3. ___ is the sort of person whom I myself would like to be.

Source: Rubin (1973).

To see whether the scales really did discriminate between the two types of relationships, Rubin invited a large number of dating couples to participate in a study. Alone and confidentially, each member of a dating pair filled out the love and liking scales, with the other partner as the object of the questions. Later they were asked to complete the scales a second time with a same-sex friend as the object of the questions. The results are presented in Table 7–6. Friends and lovers were both well liked, but friends did not score highly on the love scale. This was as expected, and it offers some validation of Rubin's measurement technique.

In another aspect of his investigation, Rubin asked volunteer couples to come to the laboratory to participate in an experiment. The two partners were seated across a table from each other as they waited for the experiment to begin. Unknown to the partners, researchers were observing the room from behind a one-way mirror. They were keeping a close watch on the mutual glances that the partners gave to each other. Love,

Table 7–6
Average love and liking scores for dating partners and same-sex friends

	Women	Men
Love for partner	90.57	90.44
Liking for partner	89.10	85.30
Love for friend	64.79	54.47
Liking for friend	80.21	78.38

Source: Rubin (1973).

"What kind of marriage did you have in mind? Open marriage? Conventional marriage? Trial marriage?" *(From* The Wall Street Journal, *with permission of Cartoon Features Syndicate)*

we have learned to expect, is associated with mutual gazing, looking into each other's eyes. And, as Rubin predicted, partners who had scored high on the love scale looked at each other more than partners who had scored below the median of the scale.

Dermer and Pyszczynski (1978) obtained evidence for the usefulness of the liking and love scales in a study of sexual arousal and romantic love. Men were shown either sexually arousing material or neutral control material. They were then asked to fill out the liking and love scales with regard to the woman they were most attracted to. Scores on the love scale were significantly higher for men who had been exposed to the erotic material than they were for men who viewed the control material. As predicted, sexual arousal did not affect scores on the liking scale.

The Feeling of Love   What are the experiences of love? Do different social psychological factors affect the different types of love in different ways? Walster and Walster (1978) suggest a distinction between romantic love and companionate love. Romantic love is characterized by passionate emotional intensity. It is a state of complete absorption in the other, characterized by "a confusion of feelings: tenderness and sexuality, elation and pain, anxiety and relief, altruism and jealousy." Companionate love, on the other hand, is the long-term, deep affectionate attachment that people have for each other over time. Lovers, after the heat of romantic love has subsided, experience companionate love. So too may family members and best friends.

What makes romantic love so wonderful yet confusing? Walster and Walster have suggested a two-factor principle based on Schachter and Singer's theory of emotion. In that theory, we noted that emotion was created by physiological arousal and a cognitive label. That is, emotion involves both the body and the mind: general physiological arousal is combined with an interpretation to create any feeling. So too with romantic love: it is a combination of physiological arousal and an interpretation that tells us this is love.

If romantic love is, indeed, based on arousal and labels, then anything that alters that arousal should affect love. At this point, the research literature is only suggestive—it can only give some clues about the degree to which passionate love is affected by the two factors. White, Fishbein, and Rutstein (1981) had male subjects interact with an attractive or an unattractive female confederate. They altered the physiological arousal of the males in three unusual ways. Some men were asked to run in place, others were asked to watch portions of a Steve Martin comedy tape, while others were asked to watch portions of a grisly blood-and-gore film. In each of these conditions, physiological arousal was manipulated in ways that were quite independent of the attractiveness of the

Love comes in many forms. Romantic love and companionate love are two types of love relationships. *(Top left, © Susan Lapides 1982/design conceptions; top right, © Joel Gordon 1983; bottom, © Susan Lapides 1980/design conceptions)*

female confederate. The men were then asked to rate the attractiveness of that confederate. When the men were aroused in any of the ways that were just described, they found the attractive female more physically attractive than males who were not aroused. And what of the unattractive female confederate? She was perceived as uglier when rated by the aroused males than by the unaroused males. Apparently, the increased arousal led to increased feelings of attraction *and* revulsion.

Finally, Dutton and Aron (1974) conducted two fascinating experiments that lend further support to the two-factor theory. In one study conducted in the laboratory, male subjects met an attractive female confederate. Some of the males were anxious—they were anticipating being in an experiment in which they would have to undergo painful electric shocks. Other subjects anticipated no such shocks. The subjects were later asked how much they would like to date and to kiss the woman they had met. Subjects aroused through anxiety had more intense desires to kiss the woman than those who had not experienced the arousing anxiety.

In a second study, Dutton and Aron took their research to a 450-foot suspension walkway that hangs some 230 feet above the Capilano River in British Columbia. An attractive female approached male subjects as they traversed the 450-foot walkway. She asked them to help her fill out a questionnaire for her class. She also wrote down her name and phone number for the subject, inviting him to call. Did the physiological arousal that the subject was experiencing make the female seem like someone the male would like to be with? The comparison is to a similar request made by the same female to male subjects on a low solid bridge. Men approached on the high wobbly bridge were much more likely to call than men who were approached on the solid bridge. Men whose hearts were beating faster high above the Capilano were likely to interpret their arousal as romantic.

The Nature of Love and Long-Term Relationships   What are the feelings that go into the creation of long-term relationships—that deep companionate love shared by couples whose bond endures over time? This has been the subject of considerable interest by social psychologists in the last several years. Sternberg and Grajek (1984), for example, studied the components of love by carefully questioning eighty-five people in various stages of a love relationship. They found considerable agreement among the people questioned that love is comprised of several overlapping but important factors. No one factor was so crucial that if it did not exist love would not be experienced. But overall, love, for each of the people questioned, was comprised of most of these factors: (1) a deep understanding of the other, (2) sharing of ideas and information, (3) sharing of deeply personal ideas and feelings, (4) receiving and giving emotional support to the other, (5) personal growth through the relationship and helping of the other in his or her personal growth,

Love differs from friendship. According to Davis (1985), passion and caring characterize love. And love can happen at any age. (© *Joel Gordon 1983/1980*)

(6) giving help to the other, (7) making the other feel needed and needing the other, and (8) the giving and receiving of affection in the relationship.

Sternberg and Grajek (1984) also found that the Liking and Loving scales of Rubin that we discussed earlier were each related to the intensity and longevity of love. The Love scale was very important as a component between lovers, but the Liking scale was the single best predictor, for both sexes, of the long-term success of the relationship.

Keith Davis (1985) has reported the results of research identifying what he refers to as the tapestry of love. Love, like very close friendship, includes the partners' enjoyment of each other, their acceptance, trust, respect, mutual assistance, confiding, understanding, and spontaneity. But love has more. Davis's schematic drawing of love and friendship can be found in Figure 7–6. In addition to all of the factors involved in friendship, love contains two other clusters of factors: passion and caring. Passion includes the concept of fascination in which lovers tend to pay attention to each other even when they should be involved in some other activity. For example, a lover may not be able to concentrate on her or his homework because she or he is only able to think of the other. Passion also includes exclusiveness, that is, giving the romantic relationship priority over all other relationships in one's life. And passion includes sexual desire—wanting physical intimacy with the partner. Physical intimacy may not be acted on due to conflict with other values (e.g., moral, religious) or because of practical considerations (e.g., fear of pregnancy), but the desire is there nonetheless.

Figure 7–6
Love and friendship

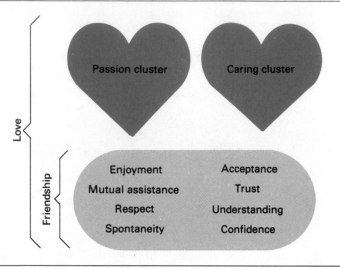

The initial model: Love is friendship plus the "passion cluster" and the "caring cluster."
Source: From Davis (1985).

Love, according to Davis's analysis, also includes a caring cluster that has two components. One is "giving the utmost." Davis reminds us to consider O'Henry's famous short story "The Gift of the Magi." In that story, a man pawns his favorite watch to have enough money to give his wife a set of combs for her beautiful, long hair. Unbeknownst to her husband, the wife has cut her hair and sold it to have enough money to buy her husband a gold chain for his watch. Each has given the utmost —and it is an expression of love. The caring cluster also contains the element of "being an advocate or champion" for the other, which is the notion that lovers will always take their partners' side in all disputes and see them as being able to do little wrong.

Davis reports the results of a questionnaire study of ninety-five women and fifty-five men concerning friendship and love relationships conducted to determine the factors that people consider essential. The results, some of which are shown in Figure 7–7, basically support the distinctions in Davis's model.

Romeo and Juliet: Alive, Well, and Temporary   One phenomenon that stands out in the literature on love is the poetic attachment of those who fight all odds to be together. In Shakespeare's play Romeo was from the family of Montague, Juliet from the House of Capulet. Although there had been an intense and long-lasting hatred between the two households, Romeo and Juliet cast eyes on each other and were in love. The intensity of the love affair was so great that it caused the lovers to abandon their families, marry in secret, feign death, and ultimately commit suicide.

Neither the balance theories that we have examined nor the research on similarity and attraction would have predicted that a Montague would love a Capulet. We might be tempted to say that their relationship existed despite balance pressures to the contrary. Driscoll, Davis, and Lipetz (1972), however, proposed that the intensity of a love relationship may increase *because* of interference from parents to stop it. Driscoll et al. employed a love scale much like Rubin's and found that couples scored higher on the scale as their perception of their parents' opposition to the relationship increased. In a similar vein, Rubin found that when lovers were of a different religious faith the intensity of the love relationship measured by the scale was greater than when they were of the same faith.

Apparently, the difficulties and turmoils that couples face—such as parental opposition and religious differences—can be associated with intense love relationships, and indeed those difficulties and turmoils may contribute to the intensity. But the "Romeo and Juliet effect" may not last forever. Rubin found that the strength of interfaith relationships was enhanced for couples who had been going together for less than eighteen months, but that among couples who had been together for a longer period, the pattern was reversed—couples of the same faith were higher on the love scale. One reason for the reversal may be that a relationship subjected to external pressures for a long time can begin to crumble.

Kelley and his colleagues (Kelley, 1979; Braiker & Kelley, 1979) have examined the consequences of nonreligious conflict among ongoing couples. They found that conflict, over the short term, was not disruptive to the growth and continuance of intimate relationships. However, unresolved conflict that endures over time does seem to have the effect of chipping away at the strength of the relationship (Rands, Levinger, & Mellinger, 1981). The precise explanation for the decline of the intensity of the love relationship is not clear, and the correlational nature of the study makes the attribution of a cause very difficult. The data that do

Figure 7-7
Close friends and lovers compared

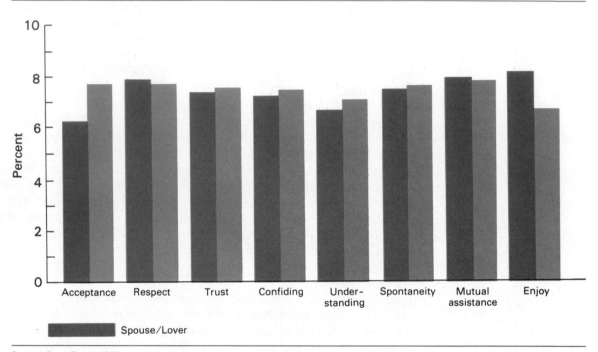

Source: From Davis (1985).

exist merely suggest that opposition to a relationship may at least temporarily magnify the intensity of the love.

The Rise and Fall of Love: Stages of a Love Relationship   Most social
psychologists agree that the concepts that determine interpersonal attraction are relevant for the beginning stage of long-term, intimate relationships. Present rewards, anticipation of future rewards, assessments of
the costs, and a concern for equity all play roles in initiating and maintaining relationships (Altman, 1974; Levinger, 1980). A number of theorists have gone on to suggest that relationships proceed through a series
of orderly stages as they become more and more intimate.

Backman (1981) and Secord and Backman (1974) have discussed their
view of the stages that a relationship goes through en route to becoming
intimate. First, there is an *exploration* stage in which the possible rewards

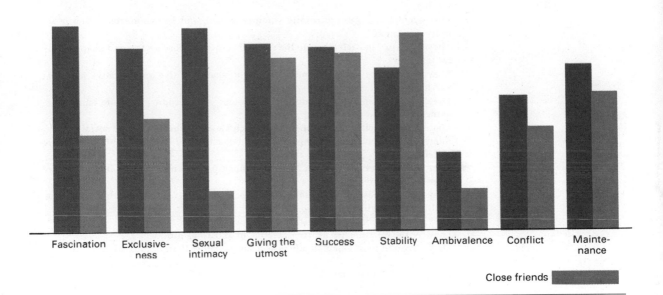

Fascination | Exclusive-ness | Sexual intimacy | Giving the utmost | Success | Stability | Ambivalence | Conflict | Mainte-nance

Close friends

and costs of a relationship are explored. Second, there is a *bargaining* stage in which the partners negotiate the terms of the relationship. This is not done in a formal bargaining session, of course, but there is a period of time during which partners must "feel out" the ground rules of the relationship. They learn which behaviors are rewarding, which are costly, and how to maximize the joint benefits. Third, there is a *commitment* stage characterized by increasing dependency on each other and on the relationship. Finally, Backman posits an *institutionalization* stage characterized by the emergence of shared expectations. It is also characterized by a recognition both by the partners and by observers that the relationship is exclusive.

Other theorists have discussed slightly different views of the stages through which intimate relationships develop (e.g., Levinger, 1980; Scanzoni, 1979). Research has not yet discriminated among the various

Table 7–7

The development of closeness in relationships

As partners grow increasingly closer, the following changes take place in their relationship:

1. They interact more often, for longer periods of time, and in a widening array of settings.
2. They attempt to restore proximity when separated, and feel comforted when proximity is regained.
3. They "open up" to each other, in the sense that they disclose secrets and share physical intimacies.
4. They become less inhibited, more willing to share positive and negative feelings, and to praise and criticize each other.
5. They develop their own communication system, and become ever more efficient in using it.
6. They increase their ability to map and anticipate each other's views of social reality.
7. They begin to synchronize their goals and behavior, and develop stable interaction patterns.
8. They increase their investment in the relationship, thus enhancing its importance in their life space.
9. They begin increasingly to feel that their separate interests are inextricably tied to the well-being of their relationship.
10. They increase their liking, trust, and love for each other.
11. They see the relationship as irreplaceable, or at least as unique.
12. They more and more relate to others as a couple rather than as individuals.

Source: Burgess and Huston (1979).

approaches. But while there may be disagreement about how to characterize the various stages, most theorists do agree on the changes that take place in the way partners act toward each other in deepening relationships (Berscheid, 1985). These changes have been summarized nicely by Burgess and Huston (1979) and are presented in Table 7–7.

LONELINESS

Intimacy in relationships has a flip side that has been receiving increasing attention from social psychologists (e.g., Wheeler, Reis, & Nezlek, 1983). People who do not have a reasonable number of relationships or whose relationships are less than intimate suffer the damaging unpleasant emotion of *loneliness*. The experience of loneliness is widespread. Weiss (1973) cites national survey data. When people were asked,

In the course of all relationships, there are sweet and bitter moments. Social psychologists have begun to trace the variety of stages that constitute a long-term relationship. *(Left, © Joel Gordon 1985; right, © 1981 Susan Rosenberg/Photo Researchers, Inc.)*

"During the past few weeks, did you ever feel very lonely or remote from other people?" 26 percent indicated that they did.

What is this experience? There is good evidence that it is actually two experiences that share a common core. Weiss (1973, 1974) has called our attention to the two kinds of loneliness. One is social loneliness. Here people feel lonely due to a lack of connectedness in a social network; they do not have a sufficient number of friends and companions with whom to share common interests and activities. The other loneliness is emotional loneliness, which derives from the lack of a close intimate attachment to another person. Emotional loneliness is related to the quality of a person's relationships, while social loneliness is related to the quantity of relationships.

Russell, Cutrona, Rose, and Yurko (1984) asked one thousand students at the University of Iowa about loneliness. They found evidence that, although there was a common core in the experience of loneliness, there were two distinct versions, as described by Weiss. They found that social loneliness was evoked when people felt a lack of satisfying friendship patterns, whereas emotional loneliness was evoked in the absence of a satisfying romantic relationship.

Loneliness is the flip side of intimacy. It is characterized by a lack of intimate social relationships. *(© Joel Gordon 1982)*

BREAKING UP: IS IT HARD TO DO?

Why do relationships end? Logically, it would seem that when two people no longer like each other, their relationship will end. Life and love, however, are not always so simple. Many factors other than attraction, or the lack of it, dictate whether a relationship will continue to develop or end.

Levinger (1976) has proposed that the continuance of a relationship depends on its "cohesiveness." This concept has three forces acting on it. The first is the attractiveness of the relationship itself. This is a multi-faceted concept but basically involves a consideration of whether the rewards in the relationship are worth the cost. Is the relationship satisfying; does it make each of the partners feel that their psychological investment is worthwhile? In this regard, we have already seen that an assessment of pleasure in a lasting relationship is not only a function of one's own personal rewards and costs but also a function of perceived equity (e.g., Walster, Berscheid, & Walster, 1978) and a concern for joint outcomes (e.g., Kelley & Thibaut, 1978). The second factor operating on cohesiveness is the potential alternatives to the relationship. Good relationships may be broken if better ones exist or are imagined. Poor relationships may be continued if they provide some minimal satisfaction and there are no alternatives on the horizon. Finally, cohesiveness is a function of the barriers that constrain the partners in the relationship. Barriers are factors that serve as costs to terminating the relationship. They may be institutional—as in the necessity to obtain a divorce to end a marriage; they may be social—as in ridicule or ostracism. These factors not only affect cohesiveness directly, but they may also interact. For example, Berscheid and Campbell (1981) point out that by decreasing the barriers to terminating a marriage (e.g., as divorce becomes simpler in most states), more eligible people become available as partners in a potentially new relationship. Having more potential partners available increases the likelihood that partners in an existing relationship may find an even more desirable partner outside of their relationship.

WHEN RELATIONSHIPS GO SOUR: REACTING TO DISSATISFACTION

Songwriter Paul Simon once wrote, "There must be fifty ways to leave your lover." Actually, recent research has identified two. Rusboldt and her colleagues (e.g., Rusboldt & Zembrot, 1983) have embarked on a systematic look at the way in which people respond to the potential dissolution of relationships. In one study, they asked twenty-five male and twenty-five female students at the University of Kentucky to describe a time when they became dissatisfied with a romantic relationship in which they were involved. In a second study, the same request was made of eighteen residents of Lexington, Kentucky, who ranged in age from twenty to sixty-seven. Their responses were analyzed and basically fit into four major categories.

One response to a dissatisfying relationship is to *exit*. Reactions of this type were actively destructive to the relationship. "I told him I couldn't

How do we respond to dissatisfaction with someone we have come to love? Rusboldt and her colleagues have identified several responses, including exit, neglect, voice, and loyalty. (© 1981 Susan Rosenberg/Photo Researchers, Inc.)

take it any more, and that it was over," and "I slapped her around a bit, I'm ashamed to say," were examples of the exit reaction.

Another way of responding to dissatisfaction was also destructive to the relationship's continuation. Unlike exit, this reaction is *passive.* Rusboldt and Zembrot call it *neglect.* "I guess I just kind of quit—I didn't try to salvage it—I just didn't know what to do," and "Mostly my response was silence to anything he might say, ignoring him," were examples of the neglect approach.

Alternatively, people who are dissatisfied with a relationship may act to salvage that relationship. Some of the Rusboldt and Zembrot respondents used the *voice* reaction. Here, people took active measures to try to make things better. "We talked it over and worked things out" was typical of this approach. And finally, some people answered with a variety of *loyalty* responses. In general, these were reactions that tried to keep the relationship going, but in a passive manner. "I loved her so much," said one student, "that I ignored her faults." "I prayed a lot," said another, "and left things in God's hands."

JEALOUSY: REACTING TO THREAT TO A RELATIONSHIP

Jealousy is a potential emotional consequence whenever a relationship is formed. Losing your partner, or the possibility of losing your partner, creates a complex of emotions, thoughts, and behaviors that can be devastating indeed. What makes jealousy different from similar emotions, such as anger? White (1981) has proposed that romantic jealousy is based on two losses: first, the loss of rewards that a partner enjoys in the relationship; second, the blow to self-esteem that occurs at the idea of rejection from the romantic partner.

Mathes, Adams, and Davies (1985) described five different situations to students at Western Illinois University. They were asked to imagine that they had just lost their boyfriend or girlfriend to a rival or to plain rejection (i.e., your partner decides he [she] does not love you anymore); or to destiny (i.e., your partner moves to a faraway city); or to fate (your partner is killed in an automobile crash); or to a no-loss control condition. Mathes and his colleagues reasoned that all of the loss conditions share one common element: they all deprived the person of the rewards that he or she enjoyed in the romantic partnership. But the rival and rejection conditions should be very damaging to the person's self-esteem. Losing a partner due to his or her having to take a position in another city is mildly self-esteem relevant whereas the fate condition does not involve self-esteem at all. Mathes et al. found that the emotion of jealousy was indeed greatest at the loss of a partner to a rival and least to the loss of a partner due to fate. Feeling jealousy does seem to depend not only on the loss of the rewards that the relationship held for the person, but also on the magnitude of the blow to self-esteem.

Hill, Rubin and Peplau (1976) examined the breakups of over one hundred student couples before marriage and couples whose breakups occurred after they began participation in Hill et al.'s two-year study. One fascinating factor discovered by Hill et al. was that the degree of involvement by the two partners in the relationship was considerably more uneven than for partners in relationships that lasted. In addition, those whose relationships dissolved tended to be less intimate when the study began. And finally, very few of the breakups occurred by the mutual agreement of both partners. It was far more prevalent for the relationship to be dissolved at the instigation of one of the partners. Reactions to the breakup were inversely related. The more one partner was pleased by the dissolution of the relationship, the more the other partner was upset.

In general, it may be said that interest by social psychologists in studying ongoing relationships is increasing (Berscheid, 1985). Much of the focus has been on describing the sequence through which casual relationships of liking turn to the more intimate relationship of loving (e.g., Backman, 1981; Levinger, 1980) and in describing the structure of the intimate relationship (e.g., Kelley, 1979). Research on the dissolution of intimate relationships is still in its infancy stage but it will undoubtedly grow and continue.

SUMMARY

Interpersonal attraction refers to the positive attitude held by one person about another. Attraction is based on many factors, one of which is our preference for balanced or symmetrical relationships. Newcomb's A–B–X model posits a "strain toward symmetry." For example, if A and B like each other, they will both tend to feel similarly toward X.

Reward models of attraction consider attraction to be based on associations with positive rewards. Pleasure in an interpersonal relationship depends on the rewards and costs experienced by both partners. Equity exists when the ratio of a person's rewards to costs is the same as his or her perception of the partner's rewards-to-cost ratio. Equitable relationships are more pleasurable and more long lasting than inequitable ones. Also, lasting relationships are characterized by a concern with maximizing the joint outcomes of both partners. Research has shown that people in short-term exchange relationships keep track of their contributions and rewards, whereas people in more meaningful, communal relationships do not care about keeping such records.

One of the most frequently researched relationships in liking is the relationship between similarity and attraction. In general, Byrne and his colleagues have shown that similarity leads to attraction, especially when the similarity is on important issues.

There is pressure to reciprocate attraction. We tend to like those whom we believe are attracted to us. In addition, physical closeness (propinquity) often produces attraction.

There is evidence that physical attractiveness leads to liking. This is true in heterosexual situations, but has other, more surprising effects as well. In simulated jury situations, attractive people are less often judged to be guilty of committing crimes than are unattractive people. In classroom situations, the work of attractive people is judged to be of greater value than that of unattractive people.

Some research in interpersonal attraction has examined the more unusual features that lead to attraction. Although we tend to like people who compliment us, it has been shown that insults can lead to greater attraction if a pattern of comments about us begins with insults and ends with compliments. Second, people of superior ability who have clumsy accidents can be seen as more attractive because of the accidents.

Recent attempts have been made to distinguish between liking and love. Rubin is among those who have validated scales that are specifically geared to the emotion of love. He has defined love as involving the components of (1) caring—the feeling that another's satisfactions are as important as your own, (2) attachment—the need to be with the other and to be cared for, and (3) intimacy—the bond between two people. Davis found that love, like friendship, includes the enjoyment of partners for each other, their acceptance, trust, respect, understanding, and spontaneity. In addition, love, as distinct from friendship, includes passion and caring.

Two factor theories contend that the experience of love is a function of physiological arousal and a cognitive label. If that cognitive label implies love, then the emotion will be experienced as love.

Recent research has also focused on emotions related to love: jealousy and loneliness. Research has also considered the ways in which relationships go sour. The stages of the breaking down of the love relationship have been attracting the attention of social psychologists.

KEY WORDS

A–B–X model
attraction
balance theory
behavioral communication
equity theory
gain-loss effect
immediacy

ingratiation
love
matching effect
similarity-complementarity
stages of a relationship
symmetrical relationships

SUGGESTED READINGS

Berscheid, E. (1985). Interpersonal attraction. In G. Lindsey and E. Aronson (Eds.), *Handbook of social psychology* (3rd ed.). Reading, MA: Addison-Wesley.

Berscheid, E., & Walster, E. (1978). *Interpersonal attraction*. Reading, MA: Addison-Wesley.

Byrne, D. (1971). *The attraction paradigm*. New York: Academic Press.

Davis, K. E. (1985, February). Near and dear: Friendship and love compared. *Psychology Today*, pp. 22–30.

Jones, E. E., & Wortman, C. B. (1973). *Ingratiation: An attributional approach.* Morristown, NJ: General Learning Press.

Kelley, H. H. (1979). *Personal relationships: Their structures and processes.* Hillsdale, NJ: Erlbaum.

Rubin, Z. (1973). *Liking and loving: An invitation to social psychology.* New York: Holt, Rinehart and Winston.

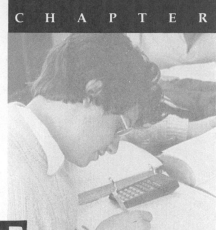

EIGHT

At 3:20 A.M. on March 13, 1964, thirty-eight residents of Austin Street, Queens, N.Y., peered from their apartment windows as a young woman was being attacked and beaten on the street below. Kitty Genovese was attacked three times by a man brandishing a knife. She struggled to free herself, and she managed to reach a street corner where she could be seen and heard by more of her neighbors. She was heard to yell, "He stabbed me! Please help me!"

Lights went on in several apartments overlooking the street. Ms. Genovese escaped, but she did not get far before she was again cornered by her attacker. Ms. Genovese screamed, "I'm dying! I'm dying!" This time, the attack was final. Ms. Genovese lay dead of stab wounds in an incident that was thought to have lasted nearly three quarters of an hour. Reporters from the *New York Times* sought to determine what the people whose windows faced that part of Austin Street did after they heard the screams. They discovered that although at least thirty-eight people had heard the screams, not one of the witnesses had attempted to come to the woman's aid (Rosenthal, 1964). Not one of them had so much as lifted the telephone to call the police. Had even one person done so, Ms. Genovese might have been saved. Why was Ms. Genovese attacked? And why did thirty-eight witnesses act so callously and indifferently to the human drama occurring below?

There are other examples of quite different responses to emergency situations—responses so selfless that we are awed and moved when we hear about them. On January 13, 1982, in the middle of a blinding snowstorm, Air Florida Flight 90 departed from National Airport in Washington, D.C., bound for Tampa and St. Petersburg, Florida. Shortly after the Boeing 737 took off, the plane lost altitude, slammed into the traffic-filled Fourteenth Street Bridge, and plunged into the icy waters of the Potomac River. In all, seventy-eight persons perished in the catastrophe, and the toll would surely have been higher if it were not for the heroic efforts of at least four individuals. Two of these persons were Donald W. Usher and M. E. Windsor, the pilot and copilot of the National Park Service helicopter that was the first rescue vehicle to arrive on the scene. Risking their own safety, the two men flew dangerously close to bridges, trees, and the wreck itself in a terrible winter storm to try to rescue the few survivors who had bobbed to the river's surface (Shribman, 1982a, b).

Two other individuals, however, acted in a particularly heroic manner. The first was an unnamed passenger, described as "a head bobbing in the water, slightly baldish, and in his mid-50s." As the two park rangers' helicopter hovered over the tail section of the downed aircraft dropping a life ring, this man gave the ring to those who needed it more than he—notably, another passenger with severe bleeding and head injuries. One

In life, Kitty Genovese drew little public notice. In death, she gained fame tragically when 38 witnesses did nothing as a killer stalked and stabbed her in a quiet Queens, New York, community more than twenty years ago. *(AP/Wide World Photos)*

by one, the survivors were shuttled to the shore; the man waited until all the others had been rescued. When the rangers finally returned for him, though, he was gone. He had given his life so that the others might survive (Gailey, 1982).

Then too, there is the story of M. L. Skutnik, a twenty-eight-year-old employee of the Congressional Budget Office, who had arrived on the scene and was pacing back and forth on the riverbank awaiting an opportunity to help with the rescue efforts if he could. As the Park Service helicopter attempted to drag Kelly Duncan, one of the Air Florida stewardesses who survived the crash, to the bank, she fell off the life ring and into the icy water. Without hesitating, Mr. Skutnik removed his boots and coat and plunged into the frigid waters to rescue Ms. Duncan (Clines, 1982). Even he was surprised by his selfless action and he remarked, "It's something I never thought I would do . . . but somebody had to go into the water." His actions surely saved the woman's life. Why did these individuals risk so much—even their own lives—to help others? What makes some people heroes and others simply spectators? What motivates individuals to help others?

This chapter concerns our capacities to help and to hurt others. It is about pro- and antisocial behavior. The lines that divide these two types of behavior are not clear-cut. There are times when our assistance is construed by those we try to help as a hindrance, and other times when our helping is genuinely appreciated. There are also times when we commit acts of violence for violence's sake, and other times when, to help someone in the long run, we must hurt them in the short run. Like the two faces of the Roman god Janus, pro- and antisocial behavior are intimately intertwined. Thus, in this chapter, we will examine the roots of human aggression as well as our capacity to help a person in need. We will consider the factors that move people to inflict injury on fellow human beings, and the factors that move them to help others. Like Messrs. Skutnik, Windsor, and Usher, we all know of people who have gone out of their way to help a person in need. And, like Ms. Genovese's killer, we know of people who inflict injury on others. We know of times when people have given unselfishly of themselves to help others and of times when people have refused to offer aid. What makes people act in prosocial ways sometimes but in antisocial ways at other times?

We often find it more comforting to think that instances such as the Genovese murder are isolated, that they stem from the deranged personality of the perpetrator, and that the bystanders' failure to help Ms. Genovese stems from the equally peculiar personalities of the people living in her Queens, N.Y., neighborhood. But the repetition of serious aggressive incidents through time and circumstance forces us to look for broader causes of aggression.

Divers search the wreckage of Air Florida Flight 90, in which 78 people died. A passerby, Mr. M. L. Skutnik, who is shown above (center), risked his life in the icy waters to save one of the victims. *(Top, Sygma; bottom, Charles Steiner/Sygma)*

And our failure to act in prosocial ways is also alarming. The failure of people to intervene and stop others like Ms. Genovese from becoming yet another crime statistic is also widespread. For example, eleven people watched a teenage boy bleed to death on a New York subway, and forty passersby did not intervene as they watched a telephone operator being raped and assaulted. In a 1974 incident in a crowded food shop, the victim of a sexual molester yelled, while imploring people to help her, "Is the Genovese case so old that you don't remember?" At least the lesson of the case was not remembered. No one did so much as call the police as the molester completed his attack, calmly strode from the store, hailed a taxi, and left.

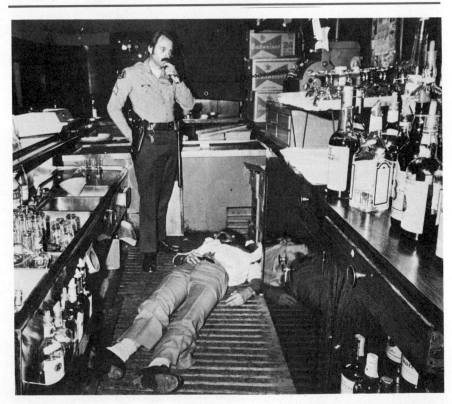

Violence is no stranger to today's society. In the United States alone, more than 20,000 murders are reported yearly. *(Patrice Chauvel)*

They Ignored Dying Old Man on Sidewalk

OKLAHOMA CITY (UPI)—For 20 minutes Clinton Collins, 77, lay dying on a downtown sidewalk. Pedestrians stepped across his body ignoring the pleas of a handful of persons who stopped to help.

Motorists hurrying home during rush hour honked their horns impatiently at other drivers who were about to stop. An ambulance with another patient happened by and took Collins to the hospital, but he was dead on arrival.

A hospital spokesman said he died of natural causes.

A psychologist said Thursday Collins was the victim of society's "full-gallop pace" and a city's depersonalization.

"Our society is set up for a kind of full-gallop pace, and since they are in a hurry to get places they just see the man, think somebody else will help him, or maybe they think he is drunk and go about their business," said Dr. Vernon Sisney.

"People are just not letting themselves get involved with other people. It seems like the closer we live, the less actual contact emotionally or involvement we have. It is unfortunate, but that is what happens."

Sisney said the timing of Wednesday's incident also worked against Collins.

"Had it not been at this particular rush hour, on the way home, and on the way to work, then it would not have been as likely to happen," he said.

He said some people who passed by the dying man now may "do something different" if they are confronted with a similar situation in the future.

"Even reading about it will cause some people to have an influx of feeling that perhaps they will help the next time, which is not to say they wouldn't have anyway," he said. "Maybe we should identify with these things a bit more closely."

Asked whether depersonalization must necessarily be a part of urbanization, Sisney said, "No, I think each individual needs to review his own standards or his own feelings and to see if we couldn't return a little bit more to being my brother's keeper instead of my keeper's brother."

Source: *Charlottesville Daily Progress.*

And ten years after the Genovese incident, New York's Austin Street was again the scene of a bizarre and chilling incident. At 3:20 A.M.—precisely the same time as the Genovese murder—on Christmas morning, 1974, the night's silence was broken by the chilling sounds of a woman's screams. Again and again, the screams rang out. Again neighbors heard the screams but failed to act. "Three screams, then no more. . . . I thought the superintendent would do something." Sandra Zahler lay dead. And again, no one had called the police. Why?

THE MEANING OF ALTRUISTIC BEHAVIOR

More than a thousand research papers have appeared trying to identify the how, what, when, and why of helping others (Dovidio, 1984). This research has ranged from the study of intervention in emergencies, to donations to charity, to doing a favor for a stranger. What is meant by altruism varies from study to study, and it is not possible to offer a definition that encompasses all of the research in the field. Typically, altruism means behavior that is motivated by a regard for another person; it is often accompanied by a disregard for the personal consequences to the helper. Krebs (1982), for example, described altruism as a "willingness to sacrifice one's own welfare for the sake of another" (p. 55). If we know that a person found a wallet and returned it anonymously, we are more likely to label the finder's behavior as altruistic than if the finder were to bring it personally to the $500,000 mansion of its owner. In other words, this view sees altruism as an internal attribution of a disposition to help another.

However, this type of definition eventually runs into difficulty. Suppose that a person does a favor for another person to receive a thank-you. Is the thank-you a sufficient reward to render the behavior non-altruistic, or is the reward so small that we would still call the favor altruistic? To compound this problem, we are not always aware of our own motivations. Did a man help a woman because he felt she was wealthy or sexy, or did he do it because he felt chivalrous? Often, in a real situation, neither the observer nor the actor is in a position to answer this question. Therefore, it would seem that altruism is better defined in terms of the behavior itself. We may say that *altruistic behavior is an act that renders help to another person.*

BYSTANDER INTERVENTION AND THE DECISION TREE

In an emergency situation, altruistic behavior would involve committing an action that would help the person in need. Latané and Darley (1970) pointed out that being altruistic involves not just one decision,

Purse Snatcher Nabbed by "Posse"

FORT WORTH, Texas (UPI) — Patricia Thomas was a witness Wednesday to an all too common occurrence lately in her neighborhood: a purse snatching.

"I figured if he got away with it this time, there's no telling what he might try next," she said.

The victim was crying and clutching her baby when Miss Thomas arrived at the corner. She calmed the woman and then said, "Let's get him."

"We began pursuing the thief, and as we were driving (after him), another young man came out of a church and also began chasing him."

The newest addition to the pursuing posse was John Lahue, who lumbered along on crutches. Lahue, 31, had recently broken both legs.

After pursuing the purse snatcher several blocks, Miss Thomas, the victim, and Lahue cornered him. But the man screamed, "Leave me alone or I'll shoot you."

Lahue threw both crutches down and staggered at the man, who turned and again fled.

As they drove down the street, Miss Thomas began screaming, "Thief, thief," and asked for help.

Residents — including one elderly man with a claw hammer — poured into the streets in pursuit of the assailant, who had by now thrown away the purse and was running for his life.

The group again cornered the suspect and forced him to return to the place where he had thrown away the purse. "Now leave me alone," he told Miss Thomas.

"Nothing doing," she said. "You're going to jail."

The thief escaped for a third time, but was soon cornered, this time in an apartment complex. He was threatened with a brick, a hammer, and a pair of crutches if he ran again.

He didn't. He surrendered peacefully to police.

"I just got tired of all the crime in this area," Miss Thomas told police.

"I decided I wasn't going to just sit back and do nothing. If people would try to help their neighborhood and be better citizens, I think the police would have a lot better job of cutting down on crime."

Source: *Charlottesville Daily Progress,* September 17, 1976.

but a series of separate decisions. Only if a person makes an appropriate decision at each decision point will he or she intervene in the emergency. Figure 8–1 outlines these decision points in what has been called the *decision tree.* At each point, branches are available that may cause the bystander to go about his or her business without altruistic intervention.

The first crucial decision is whether to *notice* the incident at all. If a person staggers from the side of the road and waves his arms in front of your car, and your headlights shine directly on him, you have very little alternative but to notice him. A scream at a crowded snack bar at Grand Central Station, however, could go completely unnoticed, and any intervention by passersby would thus be forestalled. Somewhere in the

Figure 8–1
Decision tree analysis of intervention in an emergency

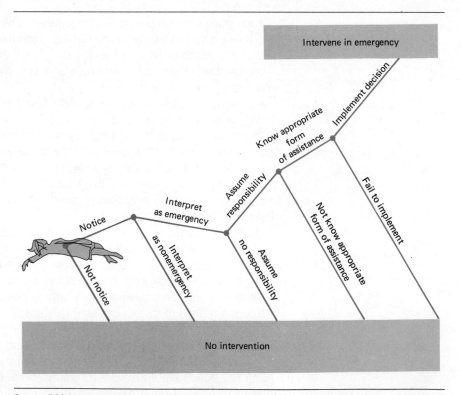

Source: Bibb Latané and John M. Darley, *The Unresponsive Bystander: Why Doesn't He Help?*, © 1970, p. 23. Adapted by permission of Prentice-Hall, Inc., Englewood Cliffs, New Jersey.

middle of these extremes lie most of the situations that would call for our intervention.

Second, we have to *interpret* an event as an emergency. Evidence will be presented shortly on just how crucial this decision is. However, we might imagine that the neighbors on Austin Street who heard screams interpreted them as something other than calls for help. "I thought I heard hammering noises," explained one of the neighbors. We can see two factors operating here. One is at the level of *perception*. If the screams really sounded like the crash of a hammer, then it might be difficult to make the interpretation necessary for intervention. The second factor is at the level of *motivation*. It may well be that people are far from passive in making their interpretations of situations. They may actively want to make a nonemergency interpretation whenever possible so that they will not have to intervene.

The third decision point is whether we, as bystanders, are *responsible* for helping. If we see two brothers fighting and notice that one of them is getting hurt, we may not view it as our responsibility to intervene if their father is standing there. The factors that may play a role in this decision include whether an appropriate authority who can intervene is present and, as Darley and Latané's study demonstrated, the number of people who witness the emergency.

Fourth, we must decide on the *appropriate form of assistance*. We may believe that a situation requires direct or indirect intervention. People seeing the Genovese murder may have been loath to intervene directly, yet may have decided that they should contact someone. But who? In the anxiety of the moment, they may not have been able to provide the answer. In short, intervention may not take place because the bystanders cannot decide on the appropriate form of assistance, so they continue to tend to their own business.

Finally, people who notice an event that they interpret as an emergency and have decided on the appropriate form of intervention must still decide to *implement the decision*. People who observe a mugging in process may know what to do but, out of fear, may decide not to implement their decisions. Those who heard the Genovese attack may have felt embarrassed about describing the event to the police or may have been fearful about the consequences of reporting the event if the assailant were not apprehended.

It is clear from the decision tree analysis that intervening in an emergency is a complex act. A series of interlocking decisions must be made, yet the final outcome may have to be achieved in a matter of seconds. Dissecting this speedy decision process is difficult, but research is now accumulating that sheds light on the components that culminate in the final decision regarding intervention.

Noticing a request for help is the first stage in Latané and Darley's (1970) decision tree analysis. A scream for help in New York's crowded Grand Central Station may well go unnoticed. *(Ewing Galloway)*

WHY DOESN'T THE BYSTANDER INTERVENE? DIFFUSING RESPONSIBILITY

Many factors can account for bystanders' failure to intervene: their personalities, the large city in which they live, the "dehumanization" of today's technological society, and so on. To shed more light on this social phenomenon, Darley and Latané (1968) set out to isolate the variable that they thought accounted for the witnesses' behavior in the Genovese incident. They reasoned that the *number of persons* watching the crime was primarily responsible for the inaction of the group.

> When only one bystander is present in an emergency, if help is to come, it must come from him. Although he may choose to ignore it . . . any pressure to intervene focuses uniquely on him. When there are several observers present, however, the pressures to intervene do not focus on any one of the observers; instead the responsibility for intervention is shared among all the onlookers and is not unique to anyone. As a result, no one helps. (pp. 377–378)

To test this hypothesis, Darley and Latané asked New York University students to participate in an honest discussion about problems they were having in adjusting to college life. Each student was to talk from a separate booth to prevent any possible embarrassment about face-to-face communication; the booths were connected by a sound system. The experimenter also explained that he would not listen to the discussion so that students could have more freedom in their comments.

Actually, only one subject participated in the experiment at a time. Each of the other voices he was to hear was a tape-recorded simulation; no other "discussants" were present. The ruse enabled the experimenters to standardize their procedure for each subject and to set the stage for the emergency.

In the "discussion," the future victim always spoke first. He talked about his difficulties in adjusting to college and then, very hesitantly, mentioned that he was prone to seizures during times of stress. The other prerecorded discussants then took their turns. The actual subject spoke last. When it was the victim's turn to talk again, the emergency took place. The victim began by making a few calm comments and then appeared to be gripped by a seizure. Over the subject's loudspeaker came the following: "I-er-um-I think I-I need-er-if-if- could-er somebody er-er-er-er-er-er- give me a little-er give me a little-er give me a little help here because I-er-I'm . . ." (chokes, then quiet) (p. 379).

The experimenter sat outside the subject's room and recorded the amount of time it took him to seek assistance for the victim. Recall that Darley and Latané were interested in the effect of the number of witnesses to the emergency. Consequently, they systematically varied the alleged size of the discussion group. In some cases, the subject was led to believe that the group consisted of six persons: himself, the victim, and four other witnesses. In another set of cases, the subject believed that the group consisted of three persons. In the remaining cases, the subject believed that he and the victim were the only people in the discussion.

The percentage of subjects who responded to the staged emergency and the speed of their responses are shown in Table 8–1. It took subjects who believed that they were the only witness to the emergency an average of 52 seconds from the beginning of the seizure to swing the door open and attempt to find help. However, as the group became larger, the average amount of time that elapsed before the subject sought help increased to 166 seconds. Moreover, only 31 percent of the subjects who thought that they were only one of a large group of witnesses ever came out to help, but an overwhelming percentage of the subjects (85 percent) eventually tried to help the victim if the responsibility for helping rested squarely on their shoulders—that is, if they believed that they were the only person to hear the attack. Thus, by systematically varying one of the factors in the actual emergency, Darley and Latané could conclude that the number of witnesses to an emergency is a critical determinant of whether any witnesses will take action to intervene.

Table 8–1
Effect of group sizes on the likelihood and the speed of response

Group size	Number of subjects	Percent response by end of seizure	Mean time (seconds)
2 (subject and victim)	13	85	52
3 (subject, victim, and 1 other)	26	62	93
6 (subject, victim, and 4 others)	13	31	166

Source: Adapted from Darley and Latané (1968).

It is now a well-established finding in quite a variety of situations both inside and outside of the laboratory that the number of witnesses present reduces the likelihood that anyone will intervene. For example, Latané and Darley (1970) arranged to have a series of thefts occur in a New York discount store. Cases of beer were stolen in front of either one or two customers. Customers who had been lone witnesses were more likely to report the crime to the store clerk than customers who had been one of a pair of witnesses.

Schwartz and Gottlieb (1980) provided the first direct evidence that the number of bystanders had an effect on helping by affecting a witness's feeling of personal responsibility. Subjects observed an emergency situation while they were either alone or in the presence of another bystander. The presence of the bystander inhibited the subject from offering help. Subjects were then asked about their decision to help. Eighty percent of the people who were alone specifically mentioned that they felt it was their responsibility to help; only 17 percent of the people who were with another bystander felt it was their responsibility to help.

INTERPRETING THE SITUATION: A NEED FOR HELP OR A FAMILY QUARREL?

Before we offer help to a person in need, we have to define that person as being in need. Observers may have viewed the Genovese assault as a family quarrel or as a quarrel between two lovers. Given such an interpretation, the scene takes on a different meaning and the appropriate form of action changes. People may feel that it is appropriate to come to the aid of a woman in distress, but not to become involved in an encounter between lovers. In an experimental study, Shotland and Strau (1976) had observers witness a fight in which a woman was attacked by a man. If the woman yelled "I don't know you" in the course of the fight, 65 percent of the male bystanders intervened to help. But if she indicated that they knew each other, the same fight was rated as less intense, as less of an emergency, and the rate of intervention dropped to 19 percent.

The point here is a general one: the context in which an emergency takes place may also affect the way in which we interpret the event. People may be inclined to interpret situations in a way that does not call for their intervention or help.

De Jong, Marber, and Shaver (1980) examined the effect of a victim's reaction to an emergency in another way. They carried out their study in the engineering and business library at Dartmouth College. Users of the library saw an experimenter drop a ten-dollar bill that was then snatched up by another person. The experimenter then acted as if he were unaware of the loss, or began to search his pockets and look around. Subjects were more likely to notify the victim of the theft when he appeared to know he was missing the ten dollars. De Jong et al. argue that the reaction of the victim when he knew he had lost the ten dollars helped witnesses *define the situation* as one that was not ambiguous, but rather as one that called for help.

An intriguing study by Rodin (in Latané & Darley, 1970, pp. 81–85) demonstrates in a different way the motivation of bystanders in an emergency to redefine the situation to which they are witnesses. Subjects came to the laboratory individually, ostensibly for a market research study. Each subject was placed in a room and asked to fill out some questionnaires. While alone, he overheard two children playing in an adjacent room. Soon the play turned into a fight, and an older bully was heard mercilessly beating a younger child. In one condition of the experiment, the subject believed that only he was aware of what was happening in the next room. Therefore, breaking up the fight was the subject's responsibility. In the no-responsibility condition, the subject believed that an adult supervisor was present at the time of the fight.

Only one subject out of eight tried to help in the no-responsibility condition; this is not surprising because an adult was with the children. But could the adult subjects possibly resist going in to break up the fight in the responsibility condition? Yes. Only one of the twelve subjects tried to help. Why was this the case, considering that there was no opportunity for responsibility diffusion? Apparently, the answer lay in the subjects' *altered perception* of what was going on. As Table 8–2 points out, three-fourths of the subjects in this condition did not believe that the fight was real. "Children don't really fight like that," said some of the subjects. Of course, they were correct; it was not a real fight. Perhaps the experimenter did a poor job of staging the fight. However, the startling finding in Rodin's study was that in the no-responsibility condition, only

Table 8–2
The frequency of believing that the fight was real in study

Condition	N	Believe	Do not believe
Responsibility (children are alone)	12	25%	75%
No responsibility (children are supervised)	8	88	12

Source: Rodin (1970).

one of the eight subjects questioned the authenticity of the fight. The only conclusion that can be reached is that the subjects who felt that they were responsible for taking some helping action were *motivated* to perceive the situation as unreal.

WHY DON'T PEOPLE HELP? AN ANALYSIS OF THE COSTS

In considering people's motivation to avoid helping, we have seen that if people can avoid responsibility, they will do so (Darley & Latané, 1968) and that if they can redefine the situation, they will do so (Rodin, 1970). Why shouldn't people want to help? Why don't people want to get involved? There are no entirely satisfactory answers to these questions, but a model proposed by Piliavin, Piliavin, and Rodin (1975) provides some insight. According to Piliavin et al., witnessing an emergency situation is arousing. Generally, this arousal is experienced as uncomfortable tension that a person is motivated to reduce. In most cases, the bystander will choose the response to an emergency that most rapidly and completely reduces the arousal.

Intervention in the emergency is not the only behavior that can reduce arousal: interpreting the situation as one that does not call for help, leaving the scene, and failing to notice the situation are other possible reactions. Which behavior will be chosen is a function of the analysis of the net costs of helping. *In general, as the costs of helping go up, direct intervention becomes less likely.* These costs are of two types. The first is the *cost of intervention to the bystander.* If the attacker on Austin Street was a truly vicious person, then attempting to help could result in a direct physical cost to the bystander (that is, the bystander could be stabbed).

The second type of cost is the *cost to the victim* if the bystander fails to help. How much trouble is the victim in? How much potential benefit can the bystander provide? A person attacked by a mob of people may be in genuine jeopardy, but little extra cost may be involved if the bystander fails to intervene directly since the bystander simply may not be able to accomplish very much. Table 8–3 provides the Piliavin et al. schema. Direct intervention is expected to occur when the bystander does not accrue high costs for trying to help and the victim will suffer great harm if the bystander fails to act. When the cost to the bystander is high, then the bystander is motivated to reduce arousal by choosing an alternative method. The right-hand column of Table 8–3 suggests some of the alternatives. The most common alternative may be a redefinition of the situation so that it is viewed as a nonemergency or as a situation that does not call for a response by the bystander. The last redefinition is akin to Darley and Latané's concept of diffusion of responsibility. If the situation can be responded to by people other than a particular bystander, that bystander is especially likely to diffuse responsibility when the costs of intervention are high.

Testing the Costs Model   The potential cost of intervention to a bystander can come from a variety of sources. As a bystander, you may incur costs because of the amount of effort you expend to help, because of the danger you incur by helping, or because of the lack of internal reward that you derive by being of help. As we pointed out earlier, helping in a situation of physical danger like that of the Genovese case bears

---

Table 8–3
Predicted modal responses of moderately aroused observer as a joint function of costs of direct help and costs of no help to victim

Cost of no help to victim	Cost of direct help	
	Low	*High**
High	*(a)* **Direct intervention**	*(c)* **Indirect intervention** **or** **Redefinition of situation, disparagement of victim, etc.**[†]
Low	*(b)* **Variable (largely a function of perceived norms in situation)**	*(d)* **Leaving scene, ignoring, denial, etc.**

*There are some situations, generally those in which victims themselves are very likely to perish, such as severe fires, explosions, cave-ins, and ship accidents, in which the costs for helping become so high that they will be perceived as total, incalculable, or infinite. Under these limiting conditions, the actions and reactions of bystanders will deviate somewhat from those predicted in Table 8–3.
[†]This lowers the cost of not helping, leading to (d).
Source: Piliavin, Piliavin, and Rodin (1975).

a rather salient cost. According to the model of Piliavin et al., this fact should reduce the degree of direct helping.

Consider the situation devised by Allen (in Latané and Darley, 1970, pp. 21–24). In a New York City subway train, a wide-eyed, lost-looking person asks a subway rider whether a particular location is uptown or downtown. In the presence of a second subway rider, the person who has been asked gives the questioner the wrong information. The second subway rider is the real subject in this study. Both the questioner and the respondent are experimental confederates.

What this study varied were events that occurred prior to the asking of directions. In one condition, the person who gave the misinformation had been sitting with his feet propped up on another seat. When an innocent bystander (another confederate) tripped over the outstretched feet, the seated passenger looked up from his *Muscle* magazine and threatened the bystander with physical violence before letting the incident pass. In a second condition, he looked up and shouted some verbal abuse at the bystander. In a third condition, the bystander was neither threatened nor insulted.

The subject who witnessed these events was aware that the muscle-bound respondent had given the stranger misinformation. It would be easy to help the stranger by correcting the respondent, but what would it cost? As Figure 8–2 indicates, when the costs were small because the stranger had been neither threatened nor insulted, 50 percent of the subjects corrected the respondent. When the respondent had verbally abused a bystander, only 28 percent of the subjects corrected him, and when he had physically threatened a bystander, only 16 percent of the subjects dared to correct him.

Sterling and Gaertner (1984) tested an important assumption of the costs model. Recall that helping is based on the experience of arousal. It is arousal that motivates people to come to the aid of a victim. Sterling and Gaertner argued that if arousal is the basis of the helping response, then increasing arousal in an unambiguous emergency situation should increase the helping rate. They had male subjects perform push-ups as a part of a study that supposedly was investigating physical distraction (see photo, p. 406). Some subjects performed a large number of push-ups (ten) and therefore experienced a heightened degree of physiological arousal; others performed a moderate number (five); and others performed none. The subjects then witnessed an unambiguous emergency. They believed that they heard a female student fall and become pinned under a heavy metal ladder in a room next to theirs. As in Darley and Latané's (1968) experiment, the question was the length of time it took subjects to leave their room to see if they could be of assistance to the female student. The results were clear: when the accident was unambiguous, subjects who

Figure 8–2
Correcting a stranger as a function of threat

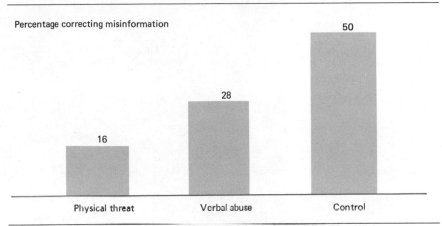

Percentage correcting misinformation

Source: Adaptation of Table 7, p. 23, Latané and Darley. *The Unresponsive Bystander: Why Doesn't He Help?* © 1970, Englewood Cliffs, New Jersey: Prentice-Hall. Reprinted by permission.

had performed ten push-ups and therefore experienced the greatest physiological arousal helped the female confederate more than subjects in either the moderate or no-exercise conditions. Apparently, then, helping *does* seem to be based on a witness's degree of arousal.

The analysis of helping in terms of costs to the helper and the victim has provoked a considerable amount of research and has provided a guide for understanding the motivations of people who chose not to help in an emergency. But any single analysis should not be thought of as sufficient to explain the complex reasons that come together to prevent someone from helping another. For example, a study by Gruder, Romer, and Korth (1978) suggests one limitation. Gruder et al. proposed that the social rules and norms that exist in a situation may alter the effect of the costs-to-the-victim variable in a dramatic way.

Gruder et al. had a female confederate call potential helpers in their homes. Using the "wrong number" technique that had been developed in several previous studies (Gaertner, 1970; Kriss, Indenbaum, & Tesch, 1974), the confederate asked for Ralph's Garage. Of course, the confederate had not reached Ralph's Garage and the subject typically informed the caller that she had the wrong number. The caller then pleaded, "Oh, I'm sorry. Please don't hang up. I'm calling from a pay phone out here on the expressway. . . ."

Sterling and Gaertner (1984) had subjects experience physiological arousal by performing push-ups. The more aroused they were, the more likely they were to intervene in a potential emergency. (© *Jim Anderson 1978/Woodfin Camp & Associates*)

For half of the phone calls, the confederate indicated her extreme reliance on the subjects' help. She continued by saying, "and I don't have any more change for the phone. Do you think you could do me a favor and call Ralph's Garage for me?" For these subjects, it appeared that not being helped would have high costs for the victim. Without a dime and stranded on the highway, it is not clear what she could have done. The other half of the subjects received their call from someone for whom the costs of not being helped were low. No mention about the lack of money was made, and the subject could presume that the caller would be able to dial Ralph's Garage again.

According to the Piliavin et al. (1975) costs analysis, the subjects should have been considerably more likely to help the caller when their failure to help entailed high costs to the victim. This did not always happen, however. In addition to manipulating the costs, Gruder et al. manipulated the requester's negligence for bringing about the emergency. For half of her phone calls, the requester added, "I was supposed to take the car into the shop last week to be repaired, but I forgot to. Now it's broken down." For the other half of her phone calls, the requester substituted, "The car was just repaired last week, and it just broke down."

Gruder et al. believed that at least one principle other than the costs to the victim would bear on the decision of the potential helpers. They reasoned that it is embedded in the fabric of our social rules that people are supposed to take care of themselves, to take reasonable precautions, and to avoid negligence. They termed this concept the "norm of self-sufficiency." Clearly, the people who forgot to take their car into the shop violated this norm. Gruder et al. reasoned that the norm would be invoked to withdraw assistance from its violators if they were not greatly in need of help. Subjects who received the low-dependency call were expected to be more helpful to the caller when the emergency was not the result of the caller's negligence. On the other hand, when the potential costs of a failure to help the caller were high, the caller's negligence was expected to be viewed as just one more illustration of the caller's incompetence and need for help. In this condition, the caller's negligence was expected to strengthen the subject's decision to help.

The results are presented in Figure 8–3. When the costs of not helping the caller were high (high dependency), the subjects made more phone calls for the negligent caller than for the nonnegligent caller. However, when the dependency of the victim was low, the norm of self-sufficiency was apparently invoked and the subjects made significantly more calls to aid the nonnegligent victim than the negligent victim. An analysis purely in terms of the net costs to the victim of the subjects' refusal to help would not have predicted the findings of this study. People's motivations for not getting involved remain complex. Costs are undoubtedly a major component, but future research will most likely uncover further qualifications and components of this process.

Expanding the Costs Model   The analysis of helping, in terms of its costs to the victim and the bystander, has, as we have seen, attracted a

Figure 8-3
Percentages of subjects helping in the experimental conditions

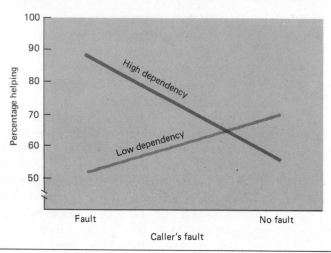

Source: Gruder, Romer, and Korth (1978).

considerable amount of attention. There have also been efforts to expand the model to make it more comprehensive (e.g., Lynch & Cohen, 1978). Perhaps the most ambitious of the models was proposed by Piliavin, Dovidio, Gaertner, and Clark (1982). They suggest that three general factors affect the likelihood that a bystander will intervene in a situation. Costs, they argue, are just one of those factors. First, factors that affect the degree of *empathy* between the bystander and the victim have to be considered. How much does the potential helper feel identified with the victim? Factors that affect feelings of empathy include (1) situational characteristics such as the ambiguity of the event and the number of bystanders that are present; (2) bystander characteristics such as age, sex, and competence to help; and (3) victim characteristics, such as sex, race, and attractiveness.

The bystander's empathy for the victim determines the second factor in the helping process: psychological arousal. The arousal must not only be experienced, it must also be interpreted as having been caused by the victim's distress. Finally, once arousal has occurred and has been interpreted as being due to the victim's plight, the actual decision to offer direct help, indirect help, or no help at all will be a function of the perceived costs, as specified in the earlier model.

WHY DO PEOPLE HELP?

As we have seen, the model of bystander helping proposed by Piliavin, Dovidio, Gaertner, and Clark (1982) posits that people help when they experience physiological arousal. In reviewing the literature, Dovidio (1984) confirms that there is now sufficient empirical evidence that people *are* aroused by the distress of others. What form does that arousal take?

Batson and his colleagues (e.g., Batson & Coke, 1981) have presented a theoretical model of helping that is based on two different forms of arousal. They posit that people react to the distress of others by experiencing *(a)* empathic feelings and *(b)* personal distress. Empathic feelings lead a person to take truly altruistic actions. These are actions that are directed only at alleviating the distress of another person. Personal distress, on the other hand, leads to egoistic behaviors. These are actions that may offer relief to another but are motivated by one's need to avoid personal discomfort.

When people see another person in trouble, then, they may feel aroused. Some people may describe that arousal as alarmed, upset, worried, disturbed, or distressed. They are suffering personal distress since they describe their feelings in terms of their own discomfort. Others, observing the same person in difficulty, may describe themselves as empathic, concerned, warm, and compassionate. These adjectives suggest an empathy for the person in distress and thus suggest empathic arousal. Batson and Coke (1981), as well as Archer, Diaz-Loving, Gollwitzer, Davis, and Fonshee (1981), asked people to describe their feelings after witnessing a person in distress. They found that the empathic and personal distress adjectives were independent clusters—that is, they described two very different types of reactions.

It makes sense that these two forms of arousal will sometimes lead to similar behaviors and sometimes lead to different behaviors. Consider the following: people who see another person in distress will contemplate helping that person. Why? Because they need to lower *their own* arousal state, which derived from witnessing the event. If that arousal is of the personal distress type, then the helping behavior is predicted to be "egoistic." That is, the helping behavior will occur if it helps the *witness* alleviate his or her own arousal in the most efficient manner. Therefore, if the witness can reduce arousal by merely escaping from the situation, he or she may very likely do so. Personal distress may also lead someone to intervene in a potential helping situation if there is no convenient way to avoid the victim. On the other hand, people who experience empathic arousal will act on the basis of pure altruism. They will come to the aid of a victim because they are truly moved by the victim's plight.

To test this idea, Batson and Coke (1981) introduced subjects to Elaine. Female students served as observers in an experimental study in which Elaine was considered the worker. Elaine's job was to perform a sequence of recall tasks for two minutes. At random intervals, Elaine was to receive a series of electric shocks. Subjects watched the proceedings on video-tape but believed they were watching live action on closed-circuit TV. From the tape, it was clear that Elaine was very disturbed by the electric shock. Naturally, the subjects were also disturbed. The experimenters manipulated the attribution that the subjects made about their feelings: half were made to attribute their arousal to empathic feelings; the other half to personal distress. In addition, half of the subjects thought they could leave very soon whereas the other half thought they would have to stay for a full block of ten two-minute trials. While watching the TV, sub-jects found out that Elaine had had an earlier experience with shocks that made them extremely difficult for her to bear. Presumably, the sub-jects realized that they would not find the shocks quite as intolerable as Elaine did.

Subjects were then given an opportunity to help Elaine by trading places with her and receiving the shock instead. Batson and Coke pre-dicted that all subjects would want to relieve their arousal by helping Elaine—except those who were experiencing personal distress and who believed they could leave at any moment. The results confirmed the predictions. Empathic subjects helped Elaine regardless of whether they had to stay for all ten trials or could leave at any time. Personal distress subjects volunteered to help Elaine only if they thought they would have to stay to witness her dilemma for the full ten trials.

Batson, O'Quinn, Fultz, Vanderplas, and Isen (1983) replicated this experiment and obtained further support for the importance of the dis-tinction between empathic and personal distress arousal. Instead of manipulating what subjects thought they were experiencing after watch-ing Elaine, Batson et al. (1983) asked subjects to describe their emotions after watching Elaine suffer. Based on their responses, the subjects were categorized as either personally distressed or empathic. Once again, subjects who were categorized as empathic chose to help regardless of whether escape (leaving the situation) was easy or difficult. Distress subjects helped primarily if leaving was difficult. The data are shown graphically in Figure 8–4. It should be added that in a subsequent study in this series, Batson et al. (1983) raised the cost of helping—that is, in this version of the study, the shocks were described as *very* painful. With the cost of helping thus raised, even empathic subjects stopped behaving altruistically. Consistent with Piliavin et al.'s (1981, 1978) model, the cost of helping caused even empathic subjects to refrain from giv-ing assistance.

Figure 8–4
Results of Batson et al.'s (1983) study comparing empathic versus distressed feelings and ease of victim's escape on the probability of giving help

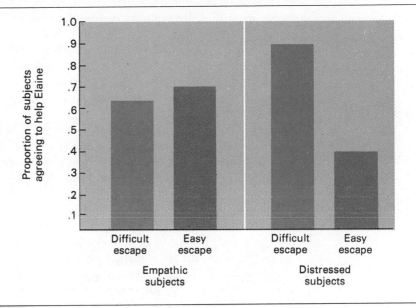

Source: From Batson, O'Quinn, Fultz, Vanderplas, and Isen (1983). Copyright 1983 by the American Psychological Association. Adapted by permission of the author.

WHOM DO PEOPLE HELP?

Those We Like   Some people are more likely than other people to get our help if they need it. It is quite obvious that a member of the family who might be in trouble will receive our quick assistance. In most cases, friends will be helped more readily than strangers, although Tesser and Smith (1980) did show that if helping means the helper might be embarrassed, he or she is less likely to help a friend than a stranger.

However, as we have seen, strangers may or may not be helped even if their need seems urgent. It is not surprising then that some research efforts have shown that greater help is given to those who are liked than to those who are disliked (Goodstadt, 1971). Benson, Karabenick, and Lerner (1976) conducted a field experiment in an airline terminal to test the effect of physical attractiveness on the likelihood of receiving help. The subjects were persons who used a particular telephone booth in which a completed graduate school application, a photograph, and a stamped envelope had been placed. It was apparent that the application was to be mailed but that the applicant had left it in the booth. Would the subject offer help by placing the application in the envelope and mailing it? Observations of the responses of the subjects showed that this depended on the attractiveness of the applicant as shown in the photograph. The subjects were much more likely to mail the application if the photograph was of an attractive rather than an unattractive person.

IN WHAT SITUATIONS DO PEOPLE HELP?

When We Are Rewarded Much of our behavior, our values, and our goals are molded and shaped by the pattern of rewards and punishments that we receive. It would be surprising if a tendency toward altruistic behavior were not shaped during childhood by myriad events involving parents, siblings, and peers. More specifically, a tendency to help may depend on the way in which similar helping was very recently rewarded. If I try to help a senior citizen cross the street and get kicked in the shins for my efforts, I probably will not try it again soon. On the other hand, if that person responds with great warmth and pleasure and even offers me a tea biscuit in return, I will probably be more inclined to help on the next similar occasion.

Using a situation not unlike this one, Moss and Page (1972) set out on the streets of Dayton, Ohio, to find a relationship between rewarded helping and subsequent helping. A passerby was first approached by a stranger and asked directions for getting to a particular part of town. Almost always, the passerby willingly gave the stranger the directions. The stranger, actually an experimental confederate, responded by saying something positive such as "Thank you"; or by grumbling, "I can't understand what you're saying. Never mind, I'll ask someone else"; or by saying something neutral, such as "OK." After being reinforced positively or negatively (or not at all in the control condition), the passerby next saw a woman drop a small bag on the ground and apparently fail to notice it. Who stopped to help the lady in this staged accident? Figure 8–5 shows that people who had been positively reinforced in their earlier encounter with a stranger were much more likely to try to help the lady retrieve her package than people who had been negatively reinforced the last time they offered help to someone. Rushton and Teachinan (1978) found support for a similar proposition using children as subjects.

When We Feel Good Strange things happen when we are in a good mood: we may sing on the street, offer our seat to someone on the bus,

Figure 8–5
The frequency and type of helping after being positively or negatively reinforced

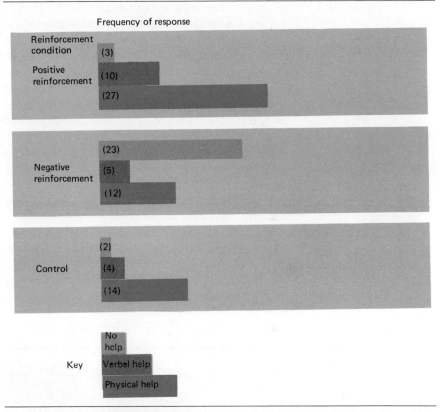

Note: Physical help = helping to pick up a dropped bag; verbal help = calling attention to dropped bag.
Source: Moss and Page (1972).

maybe even offer help to people who need it. Isen (1970) had teachers in a suburban school system believe that they had done either well or poorly at a task. Afterward, a confederate entered the room and asked for a contribution to a fund to purchase air conditioning for the school. Teachers who had done well, and presumably felt happy and successful, contributed more money than teachers who had done poorly. Similarly, Isen and Levin (1972) varied the subjects' happiness by sneaking into a telephone booth and planting dimes in the coin-return slot for subjects to find serendipitously. When such a subject came out of the phone booth, a female confederate dropped a pile of manila folders directly in his path.

Buoyed by their lucky feeling, the subjects who had found a coin in the phone booth were much more likely to offer help than the subjects who had not been so fortunate (cf. Isen, Clark, & Schwartz, 1976).

In a more recent field experiment, people emerging from a local movie theater were asked to donate money to the Muscular Dystrophy Foundation. Fewer donations were made to the charity if the moviegoers had seen a sad movie than if they had seen a happy movie (Underwood, Berenson, Berenson, Cheng, Wilson, Kulik, & Wenzel, 1977).

Finally, we should note that there are some special occasions in which good moods do not lead to greater helping, or bad moods to less helping. Isen and Simmonds (1978) found that people in good moods do not wish to interrupt their happiness by taking on helping behavior that is itself unpleasant. And Rosenhan, Salovey, and Hargis (1981) showed that the happiness that does lead to helping is happiness that pertains to oneself. They found that if people were made happy because of someone else's good fortune, the happy mood did not lead to greater helping. On the other side of the coin, people who are in a bad mood because of something that happened to them are indeed less likely to be altruistic. But if they are in a bad mood because of something that happened to someone else (e.g., a friend), they seem to develop greater empathy for the victim and thus increase their helping (Thompson, Cowan, & Rosenhan, 1980).

Who will stop to help this woman stranded at the roadside? *(Joel Gordon)*

Drawing by Alan Dunn; © 1962 The New Yorker Magazine, Inc.

When Someone Else Does The concept of modeling has wide use in psychology. Many of the things we do are learned from observing the behavior of a model such as a parent, a teacher, or a friend (Bandura & Walters, 1963). If we observe the model acting in a certain way, we are likely to try that behavior ourselves. Bryan and Test (1967) wanted to see whether male motorists would stop on a highway to assist a woman who was trying to fix a flat tire. They found that motorists were much more likely to stop if they had recently passed a scene in which a male driver had stopped to help another woman change a tire. That is, in the presence of a helping model, people were much more likely to help. Macaulay (1970) has given additional support to Bryan and Test's modeling hypothesis; she found that contributions to a Salvation Army collection box increased markedly when a model was observed making a contribution. The modeling of charitable behavior is perhaps best used in TV telethons. There we are asked to contribute both based on the need of the charity and because our neighbor from Teaneck, Seattle, Columbus, or Wichita just contributed too.

When Time Permits You are probably familiar with the parable of the Good Samaritan.

A man was going down from Jerusalem to Jericho and he fell among robbers, who stripped him and beat him, and departed, leaving him half dead. Now by chance a priest was going down the road, and when he saw him he passed by on the other side. So likewise a Levite. . . . But a Samaritan, as he journeyed, came to where he was; and when he saw him, he had compassion on him and bound his wounds . . . then set him on his own beast and brought him to an inn. (Luke 10:29-37)

According to the parable, the religious outcast—the Samaritan—had more goodwill in his heart than the priest and the Levite who were hurrying off to Jericho to conduct their business. Darley and Batson (1973) used Jesus's story in considering some of the factors that might affect intervention to help those in need. They set up a situation to show (1) that people who are thinking ethical or moral thoughts are no more likely to help a person in need than people who are thinking other thoughts, and (2) that people who are in a hurry to attend to their business will be less likely to help someone in need than people who are not in a hurry.

Students from a theological seminary volunteered to make short speeches. Half of them were asked to speak on the ethical, moral, and social implications of the parable of the Good Samaritan. The other half were asked to make a speech on interesting employment opportunities open to seminarians. The speeches were to be tape recorded, and the room with the recording equipment was in another building. Half of the subjects were sent on their way with the knowledge that they were quite late for their appointments; the other half believed that they had ample time.

On the route between the two buildings, each of the subjects encountered a man who was sitting in a doorway, head down, eyes closed, not moving. As the subject walked by, the man coughed and groaned. The following illustration shows the scene as it looked to the subject making his way between the buildings.

Did the subject stop to find out what was wrong or to offer assistance? Did it matter whether the subject was thinking about the parable of the Good Samaritan as he passed by the stranger in need? Did it matter whether he, like the Levite and the priest in the original parable, was in a hurry to get to his destination? The victim in need of help carefully rated the reaction of each subject on a six-point scale, ranging from failing to notice the victim at all to insisting on taking him somewhere for help.

The results supported Darley and Batson's predictions. In their words,

A person not in a hurry may stop and offer help to a person in distress. A person in a hurry is likely to keep going—even if he is hurrying to give a

A stranger in need of help in Darley and Batson's study. Rushing to get to an appointment increased the likelihood that people would pass by his slumped and moaning body. *(Courtesy of John M. Darley)*

talk on the parable of the Good Samaritan, thus inadvertently confirming the point of the parable. Indeed, on several occasions a seminary student going to give his talk on the parable of the Good Samaritan literally stepped over the victim as he hurried on his way! (p. 107)

Could it be argued that another interpretation of the parable of the Good Samaritan is possible? Batson, Cochran, Biederman, Blosser, Ryan, and Vogt (1978) suggested that it is conceivable that the priest and the Levite in the original parable may have made the decision to bypass the needy person because their business in Jericho was so important that it would result in greater good. In sum, the costs of not helping the needy person may have been less than the costs of failing to arrive in Jericho. Batson et al. repeated the basic procedure of the Darley and Batson study. Half of the subjects were in a hurry; half were not. In addition, some of the subjects were made to believe that their mission was extremely important; the rest thought their mission less urgent. This time, the parable of the Good Samaritan was replicated only when the subject's hurry was combined with his perception that his mission was extremely important.

A note should be added to Good Samaritan studies. In our discussion of the decision tree model of helping behavior, it was suggested that the first important decision point is to notice that the event is occurring. Darley and Batson report that many subjects who were rushing to combat the time pressure placed on them failed to even look in the direction of the groaning victim and denied ever having heard his coughs and groans. The time pressures of our daily lives may cause us to fail to notice events that, from a more dispassionate perspective, would appear to call out for our attention.

When Making the Attribution of Altruism   People who believe that they are altruistic may be more likely to act in an altruistic manner. Earlier we noted that people use instances of behavior and the cues that exist in situations to make attributions about themselves and others. Therefore, people who act altruistically may be more apt to act that way in the future if they attribute the cause of their initial behavior to an altruistic disposition.

Paulhus, Shaffer, and Downing (1977) showed that blood donors who were sensitized to the altruistic nature of donating blood (i.e., the humanitarianism and selflessness) indicated a greater willingness to donate again in the future compared to donors sensitized to the personal benefits of the donation (e.g., the donor's free use of blood-bank supplies). This was particularly true for first-time donors, who were probably less certain of what attribution to make for their own behavior.

In a related context, Batson, Coke, Jasnoski, and Hanson (1978) showed that people who behaved altruistically might attribute a low degree of altruism to themselves if possible external causes existed for their behavior. Students who entered the University of Kansas administration building were met by an experimental accomplice who requested help in filling out a questionnaire. Some of the subjects received no payment for their help. Others received payment, but were only told about it after they finished providing assistance. Still other subjects were promised payment before agreeing to help. This situation closely resembles the "overjustification" studies of Lepper and his colleagues (Lepper, Greene, & Nisbett, 1973) in which intrinsic motivation was undermined because of the promise of an attractive reward. As in those studies, the University of Kansas students rated themselves as less altruistic if they helped while knowing of a reward. Even though the reward was a mere twenty-five cents, the subjects who behaved altruistically and knew about the reward were less able to convince themselves that they helped because of the kind of persons they were. The subjects who only learned of the reward afterward and the subjects who received no reward saw themselves as altruistic. As the Paulhus et al. (1977) study suggests, such people are likely to behave more altruistically in the future.

When Norms Direct Us to   We have already looked at several norms that prescribe altruistic behavior. The general idea that we should help those who need it can be termed a *social responsibility norm.* We saw too that helping was part of normative behavior to those we consider our friends. However, it is clear that we do not always behave altruistically and that we can, in fact, tolerate considerable inconsistency between the norms we say we hold and our actual behavior.

The *reciprocity norm* provides a promising approach for understanding conditions under which altruism occurs. People tend to match a partner's intimate self-disclosure with an equally intimate one of their own. Gouldner (1960) believed that the reciprocity norm is more general in its statement that we should help those who help us and not harm those who have helped us. He has argued that the only people exempt from the norm of reciprocity are the old, the very young, or the weak and sick —just those people targeted for aid by the social responsibility norm.

If you ever want someone you know to do you a favor, you may be inclined to remind him of the great number of favors you have done for him: "Remember the time you asked me for a. . . ." This folk wisdom is usually effective, as an experiment by Goranson and Berkowitz (1966) demonstrated. The subjects were done a favor by an experimenter who was either acting voluntarily or was compelled to do so. Later, the subjects had a chance to help the experimenter. Even when the subjects did not expect to see the experimenter again, they were inclined to do a favor for him if he had previously done them a favor. This effect was much more pronounced when the experimenter had performed his favor voluntarily (see also Kahn & Tice, 1973).

REACTIONS OF THE RECIPIENTS: DO THEY ALWAYS LOVE THE HELPER?

During the first decade of intensive research on helping behavior, almost all attention was focused on the helpers. Their costs, their rewards, their arousal, and their responsibility were the focus of research. The reaction of the recipients of aid was assumed to be positive, as might be predicted by simple reinforcement theories. After all, seeking and receiving help usually results in increased material benefit for the recipient (Gross, Wallston, & Piliavin, 1975). More recently, though, attention has been paid to the psychology of receiving help. Several social psychological theories predict negative reactions by the recipients of help under some conditions. Let us turn to the application of some of these theories (some encountered in previous chapters and others that will be discussed in full in ensuing chapters) to helping situations.

She's Alive Thanks to Passer-by

STOCKTON—When Victoria White tried to avoid running over a dog yesterday morning, she almost lost her life.

If it weren't for a heroic passing motorist with keen eyesight and quick reflexes, she would have lost her battle with the grim reaper.

The day began as usual for the 21-year-old sales manager at Square Nickel Jewelers at Turntable Junction, Flemington. But minutes after she left her Stockton home for work, she found herself upside down and trapped in her car in Lockatong Creek, Kingwood Township.

"I was on my way to work and I had just dropped my daughter off at my brother's house (on Route 519). I was heading north on 519 doing about 35 or 40 miles an hour and I saw a dog in the road. I think it was only about 200 yards from my brother's house," she recalled.

"I tried to stop. But the road was really wet and slippery and I skidded through a guard rail, which was old and rotted, flipped over, and landed upside down in the creek," she said.

The roof of the car was crushed, the back windshield broke on impact, and "the car began filling up with water fast," she said.

She wasn't going to give up without a fight.

"I was holding my foot on the horn and trying to get the door open on the passenger side of the car. But it was stuck in the mud and wouldn't open.

"I finally went away from the horn and managed to wedge the door open about a quarter of an inch. Then I started screaming at the top of my lungs. That's why I'm so hoarse now," she said.

That was when Steve Trstensky, Jr., of Kingwood-Locktown Road, Stockton, drove up to the scene and went into action.

"He drove up and saw the guard rail was out and stopped. Then he heard me screaming, He came down the bank into the creek, forced open the car door, and got me out. If he hadn't stopped, I wouldn't be alive."

When the Kingwood First Aid and Rescue Squad arrived on the scene a few minutes later, Trstensky simply got back into his truck and left, said State Police Sgt. John DiLorenzo of the Flemington station.

"There couldn't have been more than three or four inches of air left in that car when he got her out," DiLorenzo said. "She had some bruises, but she was fine. But if he hadn't stopped, that young woman would have died."

"The man was working and he had to be somewhere by noon," Ms. White said. "He just waited until help came and he left."

Ms. White said she is bruised and badly shaken up and her car, a 1977 Chevy Malibu, was destroyed.

"I just thank God I'm alive," she said. "And I thank God he stopped."

Source: Story by Rita Yost, photograph by Herman Laesker. Reprinted by permission of *The Trenton Times*.

Equity Theory: Is It as Equal to Give as to Receive?   The heart of equity theory is the proposal that individuals will not only attempt to maximize their rewards in a relationship, but they will also try to achieve an equitable relationship. For equity to exist, the ratio of one person's rewards to costs should be equal to his or her partner's rewards-to-costs ratio. People who find themselves in an inequitable relationship will feel distressed. A helping situation is often inequitable, with the recipient of help feeling that he or she is indebted to the helper. Several investigations have demonstrated that the recipient of help may feel negatively toward the helper when the recipient has no opportunity to reciprocate (Castro, 1974; Gross & Latané, 1974; Clark, Gotay, & Mills, 1974).

Equity theory proposes that, in an inequitable relationship, both the individual who has contributed more *and* the individual who has contributed less will be distressed. However, research on helping situations has demonstrated only that the recipient of help is distressed. Helpers often feel good about their actions.

Social Exchange Theories: Helping Is Power   According to social exchange theories, any time individuals interact, certain *costs* must be paid and certain *rewards* result. According to Worchel (1984), an increased sense of power is one of the rewards the helper receives from the interaction. This is due to the fact that he or she demonstrated useful abilities and resources and was able to influence other people. This increased sense of power is independent of anything the recipient does to repay the helper, and Worchel (1984) maintains that often the increased sense of power offsets the cost of helping. From the helper's point of view, this makes the interaction worthwhile. In contrast, an increased sense of powerlessness is a cost that the recipient experiences from the interaction, for the recipient has been forced to acknowledge dependence.

Recipients' Reactions: A Postscript   The foregoing discussion should not be taken to mean that help is never appreciated. To the contrary, people who are truly in need of help respond favorably to a person who comes to their aid. But research in the area of helping has identified what might be called the helper's dilemma. The more the helping goes beyond what is absolutely required (Schwartz, 1977), or the more the favor is unsolicited, or the less the opportunity for reciprocation, the more likely that the recipient will react negatively to the help. This may be as true of nations that relate to each other as it is of individuals. So, while partners in a relationship may offer aid as a way of both being of assistance and getting the other partner to like them, the reaction to the assistance may be the opposite of what was desired. Rather than seeming to bring benefit, the assistance may be viewed as a restriction of freedom, the creation of inequity, and the usurping of power.

ANTISOCIAL BEHAVIOR: AGGRESSION

Up to this point, we have focused on when and why people help or fail to help others. But consider the person who killed Kitty Genovese. Why did his aggression manifest itself as it did? Why did it surface on that lonely Queens street? And why was Ms. Genovese the target of the savage attack? It is to the general issues raised by these questions that we shall now turn.

Violence in today's society is, unfortunately, not difficult to document. Fears and concerns about aggression have come to dictate many important parts of our lives. Almost every large city has its no-man's land, an area that people are afraid to enter for fear of being the victim of an attack. Women at many of our colleges and universities are warned not to venture out alone at night because of the danger of assault. In response to increased violence against students and teachers in public schools, many schools have requested police protection and instituted periodic searches of students to find weapons. Incidents of fan violence at sports contests have necessitated the placing of police and other guards at these events. While many nations spend billions of dollars to defend themselves against attack by other countries, these same nations are suffering deep wounds from the violence within their borders.

We have already discussed the conditions that make people come to—or refrain from coming to—the aid of a person in need. We now turn our attention to understanding why people commit aggression against others and how aggression can be controlled. Such an understanding could help us all make our world a safer and happier place in which to live. As we will see in this section, psychologists have made some major steps in explaining why people behave violently.

What Is Aggression? Before examining the research and theories on aggression, we must take a careful look at what is meant by the term *aggression*. At first glance, defining the term may seem like an absurdly simple task. Of course, we all know what aggression is! But do we really? For example, imagine a situation in which you see Mary hit John on the back. Most of us would quickly agree that this is an act of aggression. Our position would be supported if we found out that Mary was angry with John and wanted to hurt him. However, would we also consider this an act of aggression if we found out that Mary was trying to knock a wasp off John's back? Or would we consider Mary an aggressor if

Spontaneous acts of aggression and violence at sporting events have cost numerous lives. One of the most brutal incidents occurred in Brussels, Belgium, on May 29, 1985. Shortly before the European Cup final game, English fans of the Liverpool team savagely attacked the Italian fans in the stadium. A supporting wall collapsed, killing forty-one people and injuring three hundred. *(Stuart Franklin/Sygma)*

we found that she accidentally hit John while swatting a mosquito from her own face? In all three cases, the result was the same: John was hit in the back. However, in each case, the goal of Mary's act was different.

This example raises the question of whether we define aggression by the nature of a behavior or by the intentions behind the behavior. There has been considerable disagreement about this point. Most investigators (Dollard, Doob, Miller, Mowrer, & Sears, 1939; Baron, 1977) define aggression as *an act that is intended to injure the person or persons toward whom it is directed.* Other investigators (Buss, 1961) point out that it is often difficult to measure intent. They suggest that aggression be defined solely by the nature of the act: aggression is any act that delivers noxious stimuli to another organism. Overall, most investigators (Kane, Joseph, & Tedeschi, 1976) use both the nature of the act and the intentions of the actor to define aggression. Our legal system also follows this pattern. For example, first-degree murder, which is punishable by life imprisonment or death, involves a premeditated act in which the person clearly intended to kill the victim. On the other end of the continuum are acts such as involuntary manslaughter where death results without intent or foresight.

Another issue related to intent involves the ultimate goal of the act. A person who intentionally hurts another person may do so with the belief that the victim may ultimately be benefited. Parents who spank their children believe that they are doing so for the child's welfare. Similarly, Baron and Eggleston (1972) found that some subjects who delivered shocks to a victim in an experiment believed the shocks would help the victim learn the necessary material.

INSTINCT THEORIES: AGGRESSION FROM WITHIN

When we begin to study human aggression, one point quickly becomes evident: aggression is an extremely popular behavior. Although most aggressive acts do not involve the extreme violence committed by Kitty Genovese's attacker, it is nearly impossible to find an individual who can honestly say that he or she has not acted aggressively. Aggression is a behavior that is practiced by everyone, regardless of age, sex, race, religion, or personal creed.

Among the oldest and most controversial theories of aggression are those that state that aggression is an *instinct*. This concept implies that a behavior is inherited rather than learned, and that the behavior pattern is common to all members of the species. After witnessing the death and destruction in World War I, Sigmund Freud stated that humans are born with the instinct to aggress. He argued that the drive for violence arises from within people and that human aggression cannot be eliminated. It is, therefore, important to give people the opportunity to channel their aggression in nondestructive ways.

Another theory of instincts has been proposed by *ethologists*, those who study animal behavior. The Nobel-Prize winner Konrad Lorenz (1968) points out that the instinct to aggress is common to many animal species. Lorenz, however, differs from Freud, because he states that aggressive behavior will not occur unless it is triggered by external cues. Unlike Freud, who saw aggression as destructive and disruptive, Lorenz viewed intraspecies aggression as adaptive and essential for the survival of animal species. An animal protects its territory and, hence, its food supply by attacking other animals that invade the territory. Aggression serves to spread out animal populations and to prevent overcrowding. In

There is little evidence of an instinct for interspecies aggression. *(Malcolm Perkins/Stock, Boston)*

addition, as a result of the fights that animals wage over mates, the strongest animals win the mates and reproduce the species. Thus, only the fittest members of a species reproduce and the defective members are weeded out.

There have been a number of attacks on instinct theories. One focuses on the issue of natural releasing mechanisms. Many instinct theories argue that certain animals have built-in releasing mechanisms. However, such mechanisms have not been identified for many animal species and for humans. Zing Yang Kuo (1930) raised some kittens with rat-killing mothers, other kittens in isolation, and a third group of kittens with rats as constant companions. After a period of time, the grown kittens were placed in the presence of rats. Of those that had been raised with the rat-killing mothers, 85 percent killed the rats whereas only 17 percent of those that had been raised with rats attacked the rats.

A second criticism of instinct theories is most directly concerned with human aggression. If humans are instinctively aggressive, we would expect to find a great deal of similarity in the style and amount of aggression displayed by people. However, one of the main characteristics of human aggression is its diversity. Some people are often violent while others are seldom violent. For example, in 1970, there were 213 homicides in Tokyo, a city of eleven million people. During that same year, there were 1,117 homicides in New York City, a city of eight million. Looking at the kind of aggression, we find some people who use weapons while others use words. Some people aggress directly and openly while others engage in passive aggression.

Therefore, even if we were to argue that people have a natural tendency toward violence, we still have not explained human aggression. To make progress in this direction, we need to understand social-psychological conditions that must at least interact with instinct to provoke aggression and determine how people aggress (Kenrick, Dantchik, & MacFarlane, 1983).

Biological Theories of Aggression   Biological theories also locate the seat of aggression inside the individual. These theories, however, differ from the earlier instinct theories because they attempt to identify specific *biological* mechanisms that excite people to aggression.

Proponents of one biological approach have attempted to locate specific parts of the brain that might trigger aggression. Work in this area often involves either stimulating or severing various parts of an animal's brain and observing the effect of these procedures on aggression. This research has made some headway in identifying certain neural centers that give rise to violent behavior when stimulated (Moyer, 1971). However, this approach does not identify the conditions that cause stimulation of these aggression "seats."

A second line of research has focused on the relationship between aggression and hormones. More specifically, this research has suggested that male sex hormones may be responsible for aggressive behavior. Along these lines, numerous investigators (Maccoby & Jacklin, 1980) have argued that there are definite sex differences in aggressive behavior. These investigators argue that males are more aggressive than females because of hormonal differences. According to this position, the difference is innate. This argument has been vigorously attacked by other researchers (Eron, 1980; Tieger, 1980) who state that the sex differences in aggressiveness are due to learning and socialization rather than differences in hormones. One of the major battlegrounds for proponents and opponents of the biological predisposition theory centers on whether sex differences in aggression can be found in young children. Presumably, if these sex differences are found only at a later age, learning rather than biological predisposition must play a role in aggressive behavior. At this time, there are no conclusive answers on this issue.

We are left in a position similar to that of the instinct theories. Even if we accept the view that biological mechanisms play a role in instigating violence, we must explain what triggers these mechanisms. To understand aggression fully, we must also look outside the person. We must investigate the ways in which these external conditions affect when and how people aggress.

FRUSTRATION-AGGRESSION THEORY

One of the earliest theories to focus on the role of external conditions was the frustration-aggression theory (Dollard et al., 1939), which postulates that "aggression is always a consequence of frustration" and that "frustration always leads to some form of aggression" (p. 1). According to this theory, the instigation to aggress should increase as the strength of frustration increases. Based on these seemingly simple premises, Dollard and his associates attempted to make precise predictions about when people aggress and against whom they direct their aggression. However, the statement that frustration always results in aggression is not as uncomplicated as it appears to be.

Frustration   Dollard et al. included some very formal definitions of the terms used in their theory. *Frustration* was defined as an "interference with the behavior sequence" (p. 7). This statement may be translated to say that frustration will occur when someone cannot have what he wants when he wants it. A study by Davitz (1952) provides an example of frustration. He gave children candy bars and showed them a very interesting movie. Just before the climax of the movie, he took the candy bars away from the children and escorted them out of the film room. Needless to say, the children were frustrated.

The theory also postulates that the greater the frustration, the greater the resulting aggression. This hypothesis was supported by Harris (1974), who had confederates cut into lines of people waiting in theaters, grocery stores, and movies. The confederates either cut into line in front of the second person or in front of the twelfth person in line. Observations showed that the second person reacted more aggressively (verbal abuse) to the line breaker than the twelfth person. Supposedly, the frustration was greater for the second person because he or she was closer to reaching the goal than the twelfth person.

Although the definition of frustration seems straightforward, there are still questions about what constitutes a frustration. One such question is whether frustration is an external state or an internal feeling. For example, in the Davitz illustration given above, is the frustration the experimenter's action of taking the children's candy bars and removing the children from the film room, or is the frustration the feelings that these actions aroused in the children? Dollard et al. (1939) viewed frustration as an operation.

Aggression   According to Dollard et al.'s theory, *aggression* is a behavior whose goal is the "injury of the person toward whom it is directed." Supposedly, this includes physical and verbal aggression.

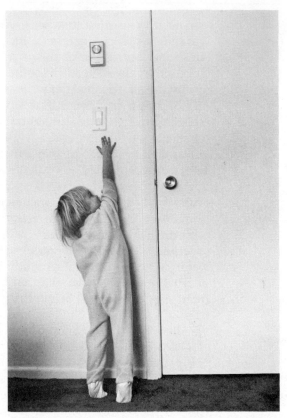

Frustration is a situation in which people cannot get what they want when they want it. Frustration often motivates people to aggress. *(Gabor Demjen/Stock, Boston)*

Displaced aggression. The investigators recognized that one cannot always aggress without reprisal from either the target of the aggression or some other person. Older children are aware of this possibility; parents often mete out punishment when an older child aggresses against a younger one. Dollard et al. stated that although frustration instigates aggression, the actual act of aggression may be inhibited if punishment for aggression is expected. According to frustration-aggression theory, "the strongest instigation, aroused by a frustration, is to acts of aggression directed against the agent perceived to be the source of frustration and progressively weaker instigations are aroused to progressively less direct acts of 'aggression.'" Consequently, those who are frustrated should aggress directly against the frustrating agent. However, if the frustrating agent is unavailable or if the aggressor fears punishment for aggressing against the frustrating agent, an aggressor may "displace" aggression to some other target.

Identifying the targets of displaced aggression has led to some controversy. Miller (1948) hypothesized that the target of displaced aggression will have some similarities with the original frustrating agent. Thus, if the frustrating agent is the father, aggression may be displaced to the mother, since both the mother and the father are parents. However, Miller's hypothesis does not include a clear method for determining the similarity dimension. Berkowitz and Knurek (1967) found that aggression may be displaced to a target with a name similar to that of the frustrator. In this study, subjects who were prevented from winning money attributed more unfavorable characteristics to a bystander with the same name as that of the frustrator than to a bystander with a different name.

Frustration-aggression theory also deals with the types of aggression that can be expected to follow frustration. Dollard et al. suggest that direct physical and verbal aggression will be the most preferred types. However, if the use of direct aggression is inhibited or blocked, an alternative type of aggression, such as spreading rumors about the frustrator or making him or her the butt of jokes, may be employed. Such displacements of aggression can occur in both the target and the type of aggression.

Reducing aggression. Knowing what causes aggression is only partly satisfying. It is also important to understand how to diminish aggression. Dollard and his colleagues believed that if aggression does not follow frustration, the frustrated person retains a residue of frustration and a readiness to aggress. Each frustration that is not followed by an aggressive response adds to the residue. Finally, the residue builds up to a point at which any further addition sets off a very violent aggressive reaction. A person who is constantly frustrated at work may go home and blow up at a minor offense committed by his or her child. Normally, this offense would not upset the person. The situation is analogous to blowing air into a balloon—one breath is not enough to cause the balloon to explode but one breath can indeed cause an explosion if the balloon is already filled to capacity with air.

Frustration-aggression theory describes two ways of reducing the instigation to aggression after an individual has been frustrated. First, the frustration can be removed, thus removing the motivation to aggress. Second, the individual may be allowed to aggress. *Catharsis* is the term that is applied to the case in which aggression reduces future instigation to aggression. Frustration-aggression theory holds that the act of aggression should remove some of the built-up residual instigation, just as

Aggression in sports may be a way of releasing tension and thereby reducing future aggression. *(Joel Gordon 1975)*

opening a balloon valve removes some of the air inside so that the balloon is less likely to explode.

According to the catharsis hypothesis, two effects should follow aggression. First, the act of aggression should reduce the individual's arousal, and second, the individual should be less likely to aggress in the near future *because* of the reduced arousal. It is important to note that the reduction of future aggression should occur because of the reduced arousal and not because of some other process, such as guilt or the fear of retaliation. The catharsis hypothesis is extremely important because frustration-aggression theory considers catharsis one of the main methods by which future instigations to aggression can be reduced. However, the evidence for the catharsis effect has been far less than compelling.

For example, Hokanson and his colleagues (Hokanson, Burgess, & Cohen, 1963; Hokanson & Shelter, 1961) demonstrated that under certain conditions, aggression reduces physiological arousal (systolic blood pressure and heart rate).

However, Geen and Quanty (1977) have emphasized that these effects occur only under *certain conditions*. In their review of the catharsis literature, they point out that aggression does not lead to a reduction of arousal when the target of aggression is of high power or status, when the aggressor feels that his or her aggression is foolish or inappropriately intense, and when there exists a strong possibility of counteraggression. Thus, while there are some situations in which a little aggression can feel good, there are also many situations in which it can result in discomfort and guilt.

Let us turn to the question of whether the expression of aggression reduces the instigation to future aggression. We find the picture even more clouded. Some studies have found that allowing people to participate in controlled real or fantasy aggression does reduce further aggression (Nosanchuk, 1981; Doob & Wood, 1972; Tedeschi, 1979). While these studies suggest that aggression reduces future aggression, other studies have failed to find this catharsis effect. For example, Ryan (1971) allowed some angry subjects to pound on a box with a hammer. Some of the subjects were competing with a person who had previously angered them whereas others were not. A group of control subjects were not allowed to pound on the box. All of the subjects were then given the opportunity to shock the individual who had angered them. The results showed that the subjects who had pounded on the box were as aggressive as the control subjects. This result would not have been predicted by the catharsis hypothesis.

Further, in our discussion of social learning theory and media violence, we will examine a number of other studies that suggest that aggression leads to more aggression. Taken together, the research shows that the conditions under which a true catharsis of hostility will occur are rather limited. The minimum conditions for catharsis are that the aggressor be angry and that the aggressor be allowed to attack the antagonist directly. Even given these conditions, catharsis may not result; and we shall see later in this chapter that aggression often leads to more aggression—not less.

THEORY OF AGGRESSION CUES

The presence of items or events that people have learned to associate with aggression has also been proposed as influencing the violence of the expression. For example, we might ask whether the easy availability of weapons not only made it easier for the murderer of Kitty Genovese to carry out his act of destruction, but also played a role in bringing out his aggressiveness. According to Berkowitz (1965), the presence of weapons may well elicit aggression. In fact, he has suggested that it may be the "trigger that pulls the finger." Berkowitz argued that frustration leads to a readiness to aggress, an emotional state that can be labeled *anger.* Actual aggression occurs only when there are appropriate aggression-eliciting cues in the environment. *Aggression cues,* which are defined as stimuli associated with the source of frustration and with aggressive behavior in general, may be anything from a weapon to a disliked person to a name associated with the frustrator. A cue assumes its aggression-eliciting quality when an individual associates certain instruments, situations, or persons with aggression. Further, since learning plays an important role, an object that serves as an aggression cue for one person may not be an aggression cue for another person. To predict the occurrence of aggression, one needs to know whether the individual has been frustrated and whether the immediate environment contains aggression cues.

To demonstrate the role of aggression cues in eliciting aggression, Berkowitz and his colleagues devised a number of "weapon effect" studies. They reasoned that weapons such as knives and guns would be aggression-eliciting cues and that the presence of a weapon should therefore elicit aggression from an angry individual. In one study, Berkowitz and LePage (1967) had a confederate either anger or not anger subjects. The subjects were then given the opportunity to administer electric shock to the confederate. In some conditions, a twelve-gauge shotgun and a thirty-eight-caliber revolver were lying on the table next to the shock apparatus (weapons condition), and in other conditions, two badminton rackets were placed next to the shock apparatus. The results indicated that when the subjects were angry they gave more shocks to the confederate (aggressed more) in the weapons condition than in the badminton condition. Berkowitz interpreted these results as supporting his hypothesis that the weapons elicited aggression from the angry subjects.

The conclusion derived from the Berkowitz and LePage study has important implications, but the study has not escaped criticism. Some investigators (Page & Scheidt, 1971; Buss, Booker, & Buss, 1972) believed that subjects may have been thinking about and reacting to demand characteristics in the situation. The subjects in the weapons condition may have used the presence of weapons not as a cue eliciting aggression in the sense suggested by Berkowitz, but as a cue from the experimenter that it was alright to aggress or that he wanted them to aggress in this situation. A number of attempts have been made to replicate this study (some successful and others not), and there is still some controversy about exactly what role the weapons do play (aggression cue or demand characteristic).

Berkowitz's cue theory has also been criticized because of its stand that cues are necessary before aggression will occur (Rule & Nesdale, 1976). In an extensive review of the literature, Rule and Nesdale cite many examples in which anger alone resulted in aggression. Berkowitz

(1969, 1974) incorporated these criticisms into an amended version of his theory by stating that in some cases anger may have aggression-eliciting properties of its own.

In the final analysis, it seems that the presence of aggression cues will increase the likelihood of aggression following anger. However, violence may well occur in the absence of these cues.

EROTICA, VIOLENT PORNOGRAPHY, AND GENERAL AROUSAL

Does pornography engender aggressive acts? Certainly, watching a pornographic movie or reading a pornographic novel are arousing stimuli and their effects may follow from those of general arousal on aggression.

In an earlier chapter we discussed Schachter's (1964; Schachter & Singer, 1962) work on emotions. It will be recalled that Schachter postulated that once individuals become aroused, they search the environment to determine the cause of their arousal and to label the arousal. Schachter believed that arousal is nonspecific and that environmental cues determine in large part the type of emotion that aroused individuals manifest.

Zillman and his associates (Zillman, 1971, 1978; Tannenbaum & Zillman, 1975) transported the labeling theory of emotions to the aggression paradigm. They reasoned that an angry individual who is further aroused by some other source may attribute the additional arousal as anger. As a consequence of this misattribution, the individual will *feel* even more angry and will therefore be more likely to aggress. According to this *excitation-transfer theory*, what is important is not the real source but the perceptions that people have about the arousal.

Sexually explicit stimuli should fit the excitation-transfer model proposed by Zillman. And indeed several studies have tested this hypothesis. Zillman (1971) investigated the effects of sexual arousal on aggression. The subjects watched a violent film about a prizefight (*Body and Soul*), a sexually arousing film (*The Couch*), or an interesting but nonarousing documentary (*Marco Polo's Travels*). The subjects were then either angered or not angered by a confederate. Finally, the subjects were allowed to act as teachers and to shock the confederate. The results showed that the subjects who had watched the sexually arousing film were the most aggressive (delivered the strongest shocks) whereas the subjects who watched the nonarousing documentary were the least aggressive. Supposedly, the sexual arousal created by the erotic film was interpreted as anger by the subjects, and the result was heightened aggression.

Yet a second group of studies suggests that we need to be even more comprehensive in answering the pornography and aggression question. Baron and his colleagues (e.g., Baron, 1974; Baron & Bell, 1973; Frodi, 1977) showed that exposure to erotic stimuli can actually reduce subsequent aggression. Further, the studies that have shown that people will aggress against a victim after exposure to erotic movies require that the viewers were angered before their opportunity to aggress. The somewhat ambiguous state of the early research led the Presidential Commission on Obscenity and Pornography to conclude that "there is no reliable evidence to date that exposure to explicitly sexual material plays a significant role in the causation of delinquent or criminal sexual behavior among youth or adults."

Donnerstein, Donnerstein, and Evans (1975), argued that pornographic material could either enhance or reduce eventual aggressive behavior. They argued that pornography's arousal properties led to increased aggression. But erotic stimuli can also be distracting; and if a person is distracted, he or she is not likely to aggress. Donnerstein et al. found that mildly arousing sexual stimuli significantly reduced the amount of aggression whereas the highly arousing sexual stimuli did not. Baron (1979) found similar effects for females viewing sexually arousing pictures of males.

Over the past several years, investigators have been increasingly concerned with aggressive erotica—films that combine sexual arousal with violence. Scenes of forcible rape, sex at gunpoint, and so forth are commonplace in films bearing the "X" rating. Malamuth and his colleagues have shown that such films have disturbing attitudinal effects on male viewers. They have demonstrated that people who see such films have (1) more fantasies about rape (Malamuth, 1984), (2) a reduced sensitivity to rape (Malamuth & Check, 1981), and (3) harbor greater feelings that they too could commit rape (Malamuth, Haber, & Feshbach, 1980).

Donnerstein (1980, 1983) argued that aggressive pornography could result in greater aggression, particularly by males against females. He posited that watching a female become the victim of sexual aggression caused arousal in males, and caused the female to become associated with aggression. Recall our discussion of aggression cue theory (Berkowitz, 1965). As this theory is applied to aggressive erotica, the female could become an aggressive cue that, in a future incident, might trigger aggression by the viewer.

Donnerstein (1980) had male subjects angered or treated in a neutral manner by a confederate. They were then given the opportunity to view one of three films. One was a control film that showed neither sex nor violence. The other two films were highly erotic. One of the erotic films was entirely nonaggressive but the other depicted the rape of a woman by a man who broke into her house and forced her into sexual activity at gunpoint. After the film, the subjects had the opportunity to deliver electric shocks to the confederate during what the subject thought was a learning task. The amount of electric shock that the subject wished to administer served as the dependent measure of aggression.

The results are depicted in Figure 8-6. While the erotic film had a mild effect on increasing the amount of electric shock, the aggressive-erotic film had a major effect. The aggressive-erotic film caused a major increase in the amount of aggression shown by the subject, especially when the subject had been angered and when the confederate was a female. In summarizing much of the recent literature, Donnerstein (1983) concludes that a direct causal link has been demonstrated between exposure to aggressive erotica and violence against women.

Reducing Violence by Misattribution   Until now, we have been looking at research in the excitation-transfer tradition that showed that arousal

Figure 8-6
Mean shock intensity as a function of sex of victim, film, and anger

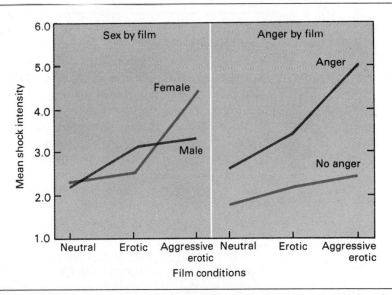

Source: From "Aggressive Erotica and Violence against Women" by E. Donnerstein, 1980, *Journal of Personality and Social Psychology, 39,* pp. 269–277. Copyright 1980 by the American Psychological Association. Reprinted by permission of the author.

Figure 8–7
Mean shock intensity as a function of noise and anger

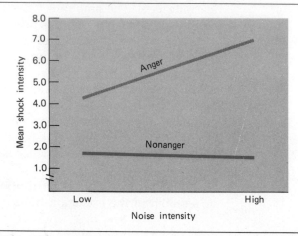

Source: From "Effects of Noise and Perceived Control on Ongoing and Subsequent Aggressive Behavior" by E. Donnerstein & D. W. Wilson, 1976, *Journal of Personality and Social Psychology, 34*, pp. 774–781. Copyright 1980 by the American Psychological Association. Reprinted by permission of the author.

from another source (e.g., sexual arousal) could be transferred, or misattributed, to aggression. Arousal from nonsexual sources ought to be misattributed as well. Subjects in a study by Donnerstein and Wilson (1976) were either angered by an insulting confederate or were not angered. The subjects were then given the opportunity to shock the confederate. Half of the subjects were placed in a situation in which high-intensity noise was played into the room, and the other half heard low-intensity noise. The results, presented in Figure 8–7, indicated that high-intensity noise increased the amount of aggression from angry subjects but had no effect on nonangry subjects. It should be pointed out that in the majority of the excitation-transfer studies, the arousing stimuli increase aggression only in angry subjects and have no effect on nonangry subjects.

The above research is interesting because it demonstrates that arousing stimuli can be misattributed as anger and thus increase aggression. Although the focus has been on how arousing stimuli can increase aggression, the reverse effect is also possible. That is, misattribution may result in decreased aggression. For example, if an individual were angered and then watched a sexually arousing movie, the instigation to aggression should be reduced if he misattributed his anger as sexual arousal rather than anger. Geen, Rakosky, and Pigg (1972) demonstrated this reverse effect. The subjects received electric shocks while reading sexually arousing material. They were then led to believe that their arousal was caused by the shock, the sexually arousing reading material, or a drug. The subjects who were told that their arousal was due to the reading material or the drug were less aggressive and reported feeling less anger than the subjects who felt that their emotional arousal was a result of the electric shock.

The important question that is left unanswered by the research is what factors determine whether the additional arousal will lead to heightened or to reduced aggression. In a recent study (McCarty, Diamond, & Kaye, 1982), investigators examined the effects of alcohol on ratings of sexually arousing pictures. The results indicated that alcohol led to increased ratings of arousal only when subjects did not know they were drinking an alcoholic beverage (told they were only drinking tonic). This suggests that the direction of the excitation transfer will be influenced by the salience of the stimuli and/or the individual's knowledge about the arousal-inducing qualities of the stimuli.

Drugs and Aggression   A familiar movie theme concerns the man who is angered by a business partner or his wife, goes to the bar and downs a half dozen strong drinks, and then returns and kills the person who had previously angered him. Unfortunately, such incidents are not confined to the movies. Consequently, a number of people have linked alcohol, and more recently such drugs as marijuana, with violence. Taylor and his associates (Taylor & Gammon, 1975; Taylor, Gammon, & Capasso, 1976; Taylor, Vardaris, Rawitch, Gammon, & Cranston, 1976) studied the effects of alcohol and marijuana on aggression. Subjects in the studies were given either alcohol or marijuana, in large or small doses. They were then either angered or not angered by a confederate and given the opportunity to attack the confederate. The results indicated that even in rather large doses, alcohol by itself does not instigate aggression. However, large doses of alcohol do lead to increased aggression if the subject is angered or threatened.

Marijuana, on the other hand, has a different effect. Subjects who have consumed a large dose of marijuana and are later threatened react significantly less aggressively than either subjects who have consumed small doses of the drug or subjects who have not consumed the drug. Further, subjects who have consumed large doses of marijuana are significantly less aggressive than subjects who have consumed large doses of alcohol.

Recently, research has uncovered another interesting effect of alcohol. Schmutte and Taylor (1980) placed intoxicated and nonintoxicated subjects in a reaction-time task in which they could shock and be shocked by their opponent. In some conditions, the subjects received little pain feedback from the opponent and in other cases, they heard the opponent express a great deal of pain and discomfort when shocked. The results showed that intoxicated subjects were more aggressive than nonintoxicated subjects *and* that the aggression of the intoxicated individuals was not influenced by the pain cues. On the other hand, the nonintoxicated subjects decreased their aggression in the pain feedback condition. Along a similar line, Zeichner and Pihl (1979) found that feedback about the effects of aggression did not affect the aggressiveness of intoxicated subjects. It did, however, influence the aggression of nonintoxicated subjects. Overall, these results suggest that high quantities of alcohol reduce people's awareness or concern with situational conditions and the effects of their aggression.

Thus, drugs can significantly affect aggressive behavior, but the direction of the effect is dependent on the type of drug, the size of the dose, and whether or not the subject is threatened.

UNDERSTANDING ACTUAL AGGRESSION

Summing up the work on the frustration-aggression theory, we can raise the question: Can frustration-aggression theory and derivative themes be used to enhance our understanding of "real" cases of aggression?

Recall Ms. Genovese's attacker. In reality, we know very little, if anything, about him. Suppose, though, we had found out that he was a person who had been experiencing considerable frustration. Suppose we learned that he had lost his job, that his wife had left him, and that he had come within one number of winning the New York State lottery.

We would know that the perpetrator of the Genovese murder was experiencing considerable frustration. If we added to this hypothetical example the idea that he carefully restrained himself from venting aggression toward people he knew well, we would get a picture of a man experiencing a buildup of frustration, a man holding in any expression of that frustration until it exploded into full-scale aggression on Austin Street on March 13, 1964. Frustration-aggression theory certainly would have predicted an act of aggression. But frustration-aggression theory does not explain why this aggression manifested itself in the unprovoked attack on someone he did not even know. The killing may certainly have been an instance of displaced aggression, but frustration-aggression theory does not explain why the slayer singled out Ms.

Genovese. Perhaps the murderer was aggressing against someone who reminded him of his mother—or some other agent of frustration.

Frustration-aggression theory is one of the principal theories dealing with aggression, and researchers generally agree that frustration does lead to aggression. However, although the theory can suggest some causes for the Genovese attack, it is imprecise in predicting when frustration will lead to aggression, how the aggression will be expressed, and against whom it will be aimed.

SOCIAL LEARNING THEORY

To obtain a foundation on which to base more specific predictions about the situations under which aggression will be exhibited and the forms that aggression will take, we can turn to a theory that relates aggressive behavior to learning. The major proponents of *social learning theory* (Bandura & Walters, 1963; Bandura, 1973) suggest that children learn when to aggress, how to aggress, and against whom to aggress. Although the bulk of this learning comes from observing parents, additional learning of aggression comes from peer groups and from mass-media portrayals of aggression and violence. In extreme forms, children may actually be schooled in the techniques of aggression by parents or teachers.

Learning to Aggress: Reinforcement   There are two main mechanisms by which such learning occurs. The first is *reinforcement*. Children are often rewarded for acting aggressively; the reward may take the form of praise from a father when his son beats up a larger boy or makes a particularly vicious tackle in a football game. The child is also reinforced through the added attention that he or she receives for aggressing. Even when parents and teachers disapprove of a child's aggressive behavior, they make the child the center of attention by scolding him or her or by trying to change the behavior. The child who desires attention from adults may be very willing to suffer such negative sanctions in return for the attention that the aggression brings. Positive reinforcement is also gained directly when the aggressor reaps the fruits of the aggressive acts—when Johnny beats up Jim to get Jim's football and is rewarded by taking possession of the ball. The child can learn from instances such as these that aggression pays.

There is a great deal of evidence to support the position that individuals learn aggression through reinforcement. Geen and Stoner (1973) found that subjects increased the intensity of aggression when they received verbal reinforcement for violence. Cowan and Walters (1963)

demonstrated that the schedule of reinforcement is important in determining future aggression. Small children were rewarded for hitting a
doll. Some of the children were rewarded for every aggressive act (continuous reinforcement) whereas others were rewarded only periodically
(partial reinforcement). The hitting behavior of the children increased
while they were being rewarded. After a time, the experimenter stopped
rewarding the aggressive behavior and studied the children's behavior.
Interestingly enough, the children who had been on a partial reinforcement schedule continued to hit the doll longer than the children who had
been continuously rewarded. The Cowan and Walters study is important
because people are not always rewarded when they act aggressively—
their aggression is successful only some of the time. The results of the
study show that such partial reinforcement may be enough to sustain
continued aggression even without rewards.

Modeling   Bandura and Walters also suggest that aggression is learned
through *imitation*. People are prone to imitate the behaviors of other
persons—especially persons whom they admire or like. A son who sees
his father aggress or a boy who sees his favorite television cowboy wipe
out twenty-five Indians may come to believe that violence must be a
good thing because "good" people act violently. Wolfgang and Fenacuti
(1967) pointed out that children are surrounded by lessons that violence
is good. They are taught that the security of our nation is based on our
ability to use violent weapons if we are attacked. Violence permeates
our advertising—it is the hero who overcomes obstacles and brings the
beer home.

   In addition to learning that aggression may be "good" behavior because "good" people aggress, children can learn how to aggress from
models. The television cowboy teaches them how to use their fists or
tongues to aggress; Agent 007 gives lessons in karate and teaches how to
fabricate ingenious weapons. The child will be motivated to try out these
new behaviors so he can act like father, or Roy Rogers, or James Bond.

   The research on imitative learning has shown that not all models are
imitated to the same degree. Bandura, Ross, and Ross (1961, 1963a,
1963b) conducted a number of studies in which nursery school children
first observed a model aggressively playing with an inflated plastic clown
(a "Bobo doll"). The model hit the doll, beat it with a hammer, kicked it,
and sat on it. After watching the model, the children were put in a room
with some toys—one of the toys being the Bobo doll. Their behavior was
carefully observed. By varying the characteristics of the model, Bandura
and his associates could study the influence of different types of models.
In one study (Bandura et al., 1961), they demonstrated that children are
more likely to imitate same-sex models—the boys imitated the male

model more than they imitated the female model, and the reverse was true for the girls. Further, imitation is more likely if the model is of high status than of low status (Turner & Berkowitz, 1972).

In another study, Bandura et al. (1963a) found that children imitated a real-life adult, an adult on film, or a cartoon figure that aggressed against a Bobo doll. Thus, even cartoons can teach aggression. Myer (1972) found that adults too will imitate the behavior of a model displaying real or staged aggression. In still another example of adult imitation, Arms, Russell, and Sandilands (1979) found that spectators of sporting events involving aggression (wrestling and ice hockey) were more likely to feel hostile and express aggression than people who had watched a competitive but nonaggressive sporting event (swimming). This suggests that it is not competition that teaches aggression; it is aggressive acts themselves that teach aggression.

Other studies have focused on the act that the model performs. These studies have shown that subjects are more likely to imitate aggression when the model is rewarded, rather than punished, for acting violently (Bandura et al., 1963b; Bandura, 1965; Walters & Willows, 1968) and when the model's aggression is justified rather than unjustified (Geen & Stoner, 1973). Bandura (1965) allowed children to observe a model beating the Bobo doll. In one condition, the children observed no consequences to the model for the aggressive action. In a second condition, the children saw the model rewarded and praised by another adult. In a third condition, the children saw the model being punished and being called a bully for acting aggressively. The children were then allowed to play with the Bobo doll. The children who observed the punished model played less aggressively than either the children who observed the rewarded model or the children who saw no model at all.

Performing Aggression Social learning theory makes an important distinction between learning to aggress and actually performing aggression. People can learn to aggress by being rewarded for this activity or by observing models. However, they will generally only express this aggression when there are rewards for doing so in the particular situation. For example, in the Bandura (1965) study, we saw that children did not act aggressively after watching a model being punished for aggressive behavior.

Although these results seem to suggest that watching an aggressive model will not increase aggression if the model is punished, Bandura questioned whether the effect of punishment was on the acquisition of the aggressive behavior or on its performance. That is, did the children who saw the punished model fail to learn aggressive behavior, or did they learn how to aggress but simply inhibit the behavior? To find the answer, Bandura offered all of the children a reward if they could imitate the behavior of the model that they had observed previously. All of the subjects, including those who had seen the punished model, were able to reproduce the aggressive behavior with the same degree of accuracy. This suggests that the children who observed the punished model had learned how to behave aggressively but had simply inhibited such behavior. When the circumstances were right, they too acted aggressively. This finding is important because it shows that punishing aggressive models will not keep observers from learning aggression. To accurately predict when people will aggress, we need to examine their past learning opportunities *and* conditions in the present situation.

Reducing Aggression   The social learning theory of aggression is important for a number of reasons. First, it supplies answers to questions that cannot be handled by the frustration-aggression theory. For example, frustration-aggression theory cannot explain why in the same frustrating situation one individual will lash out with fists, another will use a gun, and a third will not aggress at all. According to social learning theory, early experiences and learning determine how an individual will express aggression. We might expect, therefore, that the first individual grew up in an environment where he or she witnessed or was rewarded for fist fighting. The second individual may have been reared in a family in which guns were constantly present and "shoot em up" movies were popular. The third individual may have grown up in an environment in which aggression was discouraged and not rewarded.

In addition to explaining why people aggress as they do, social learning theory provides a foundation on which a program to reduce aggression can be based. Bandura and Walters (1963) point out that the parents' use of physical punishment for their children's misdeeds may actually lead to increased future aggression. In this case the parents serve as a model for the children. The children observe the parents' use of aggression (punishment) to obtain what they want (a reduction in the children's aggression). Although the children may not aggress at home because of fear of retaliation, they are likely to use the aggressive responses learned at home in other situations. Sears, Whiting, Nowlis, and Sears (1953) found that children who had been severely punished for aggression at home were more likely to act aggressively outside the home than children whose parents had punished them less severely for aggressive acts.

According to social learning theory, aggression can be decreased by using withdrawal of love or withholding some other desired object as punishment for aggression. In this way, the child receives no reinforcement or attention for aggression and does not witness an aggressive model to imitate in a later situation. Thus, social learning theory suggests that, in teaching the child not to aggress, aggression must not be employed as the deterrent. Brown and Elliot (1965) demonstrated this principle by having nursery school teachers reward children's cooperative and nonviolent behavior and ignore their aggressive behavior. After two weeks of this treatment, there was a significant reduction in the aggressive behavior displayed by the children. The children's aggressive behavior was reduced further when the teachers repeated this program of rewards three weeks later.

VIOLENT TELEVISION AND AGGRESSION

Turn on your television set most any evening and odds are you will be confronted with violence. In 1979, for instance, it was estimated that 70 percent of all prime-time programs contained physical violence; on the average, 5.7 violent encounters occurred per hour. Weekend daytime shows (mostly for children) were even more violent; 92 percent of these programs had at least one violent scene and, on the average, seventeen violent encounters occurred per hour (Gerbner, Gross, Morgan, & Signorielli, 1980). Because children watch up to three to four hours of television per day (Lyle & Hoffman, 1972), they almost inevitably are exposed to a heavy dose of violence. Waters and Malamud (1975) estimated that the average sixteen-year-old has seen 13,000 murders on television.

Because television viewing is one of the most common American pastimes, and violence is one of the most common acts portrayed on television, it should not be surprising that both laypersons and social psychologists have been interested in the effects of violent television on aggressive behavior. Such groups as Citizens Action for Better Television have called for a decrease in media violence. They assume that such programming leads to increased aggressive behavior in viewers. As we shall see, research has generally supported this contention (Huesmann, 1982). The picture, however, may not be as clear as it is sometimes painted to be.

The two major theories about human aggression (frustration-aggression and social learning) make different predictions about the effects of television violence. On the one hand, the catharsis hypothesis of frustration-aggression theory states that participation in an aggressive act will lessen the instigation to future aggression. This would suggest that if people are allowed to play aggressively or if they vicariously experience aggression by watching violence on television, they will be less likely to aggress. From this point of view, it could be argued that violence on television (and in other media) should be allowed, if not encouraged. By witnessing violence, viewers can reduce their own needs to act aggressively, since the vicarious experience of violence can lead to catharsis. On the other hand, social learning theory and Berkowitz's cue theory suggest that witnessed aggression should lead to more aggression rather than to catharsis. Portrayed aggression serves as a model for the viewer to imitate, and it can provide aggression cues that are sufficient to release the viewer's aggressiveness. Moreover, in many cases, the viewer also sees the aggressor on the screen rewarded for his or her actions. This makes the aggressor an even more attractive model to follow.

Research attempting to resolve this dispute has fallen into two categories. One approach has been correlational. In these studies (cf., Huesmann, 1982), measures are taken of aggression and of television viewing as they occur naturally. The two measures are then correlated to see if any relationship emerges. What has been consistently found is that violent television viewing and aggressive behavior are mildly but positively related to one another. In other words, the more a person shows a preference for violent television, the more aggressive that person is. This has held true not only in the United States but in Finland, Poland, and Australia as well. This finding poses problems for a catharsis explanation of the effects of violent television; it seems more consistent with social learning theory. However, correlation does not necessarily imply causation. It could be, for instance, that people who are more aggressive to begin with prefer violent television. They may find it more exciting, or a means of justifying their own aggression. If this were true, a positive correlation would be seen between the viewing of violence and aggressive behavior, but *not* because television *caused* the aggressive behavior.

To answer more clearly this question of cause, researchers have turned to experiments as a second avenue of inquiry. Some of the earliest and most influential studies were conducted by Bandura and his colleagues (Bandura, Ross, & Ross, 1961, 1963a), and have been described earlier in this chapter. However, as Stein and Friedrich (1975) have observed, it is unclear how far we can generalize from these studies to violence as it occurs on commercial television. Bandura used films constructed specifically for his experiments. These films were brief and simple; the model's aggressive behavior dominated the action that occurred. But violence on commercial television may be harder to understand; the shows are longer and more complex. As such, the person's attention may be less focused and the violence may be less salient. Also, we do not know from Bandura's studies whether the aggression observed in subjects was lasting or more general. Typically, aggression was assessed immediately after viewing the model's behavior; the subject was given an opportunity to aggress in a similar situation using similar behaviors as the model. Would the aggression also be observed in a different situation? And more importantly, would different, even *more* aggressive behaviors be observed in a different context?

Further research has been somewhat contradictory. Some studies report an actual decline in aggressive behavior after witnessing violence. Feshbach (1961) demonstrated that witnessing an aggressive film can lower the viewer's subsequent aggression. He had angry and nonangry subjects watch either an aggressive film (a prizefight scene) or a non-aggressive film. Feshbach found that when given the opportunity to aggress, the angry subjects who had witnessed the aggressive film were less aggressive than the angry subjects who had seen the nonaggressive film. However, the nonangry subjects who saw the aggressive film reported feeling more hostile than the nonangry subjects who saw the nonaggressive film. This suggests that witnessing aggression can reduce the instigation to aggression of a viewer who is angry when he sees the film.

In a field study involving 625 boys between the ages of ten and seventeen, Feshbach and Singer (1971) found that watching violent movies reduced aggressive behavior. The subjects were upper-class boys at private boarding schools and boys in state institutions for the homeless. They were assigned to watch six weeks (one hour each night) of either aggressive programs or nonaggressive programs. Their behavior was rated for aggressiveness by staff members of the institutions. The results showed that the boys in the state institutions who watched the aggressive movies engaged in only half as many fights as, and were rated as less aggressive than, the boys who watched the nonviolent programs. There was no effect for the type of program on the behavior of the boys in the private schools. The Feshbach and Singer study has been cited as supporting the catharsis hypothesis. However, the study has been severely criticized on methodological grounds. For example, boys at the state institution preferred aggressive programs. Thus, those boys assigned to view *nonaggressive* programs may have felt deprived and resentful over losing their favorite programs. This in turn may have led them to behave more aggressively.

A second body of research has suggested that violent television increases aggressive behavior. Friedrich and Stein (1973) allowed nursery-school children to watch aggressive, neutral, or prosocial programs for a four-week period (see Figure 8–8). The behavior of the children was observed before, during, and after the television period. Interestingly enough, the behavior of the children who had been rated as below-average aggressive before viewing the programs was not affected by them. For children who were initially high in aggressiveness, the results were more complex. Highly aggressive children who saw neutral and prosocial programs *decreased* their aggressiveness over time; those who

Figure 8–8
Mean change scores for interpersonal aggression[1,2]

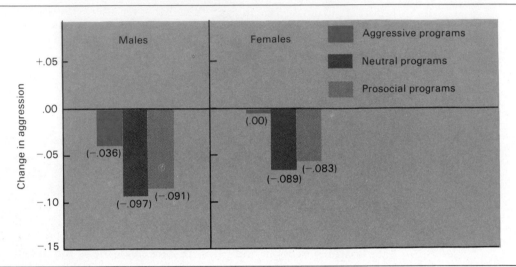

[1]The lower the score, the greater the reduction in aggression after viewing the programs.
[2]Scores are for subjects high in initial aggression.
Source: From "Aggressive and Prosocial Television Programs and the Natural Behavior of Preschool Children," by L. K. Friedrich & A. H. Stein, 1973. © Monographs of the Society for Research in Child Development, *38*, Whole No. 151. Chicago: University of Chicago Press. Reprinted by permission.

saw aggressive programs also decreased their aggressiveness, but less so. Friedrich and Stein interpreted this to mean that aggressive programs maintained what otherwise would have been a pattern of decreasing aggression, and that such shows thus encouraged aggression. It is important to keep in mind, however, that the aggressive programs did not *increase* subjects' aggressiveness. It is possible that the aggressive shows had little or no impact, and that the neutral and prosocial programs served to decrease aggression. This has been found in several studies with adult subjects (Zillman & Johnson, 1973; Donnerstein, Donnerstein, & Barrett, 1976), and is an interesting finding in its own right.

An experiment that did show an increase in aggression after viewing violent films was reported by Parke, Berkowitz, Leyens, West, and Sebastian (1977). They conducted three extensive studies (two in the United States and one in Belgium) with juvenile delinquents in minimum-custody institutions. The subjects' behaviors were observed for a three-week period to get a baseline measure of general aggressiveness. The subjects were then randomly divided into two groups, and for the next

Evidence suggests that children may learn violent behavior by watching aggressive models on television.

week, half of the subjects watched aggressive movies each night and the other half watched nonaggressive movies. During the final three-week phase, the subjects were observed in their day-to-day routines and their behavior was evaluated on an aggressiveness dimension. Figure 8–9 presents results from the first study. In each case, the subjects who watched the aggressive movies behaved more aggressively than the subjects who saw the neutral movies. This is consistent with social learning theory. However, the implications of this study for understanding the impact of *television* violence on *typical* individuals is unclear. The films used were unedited, feature-length selections that were much more violent than television fare. Also, the subjects were from institutions for juvenile delinquents. As such, at least one of the problems that Feshbach and

Figure 8-9
General aggression index

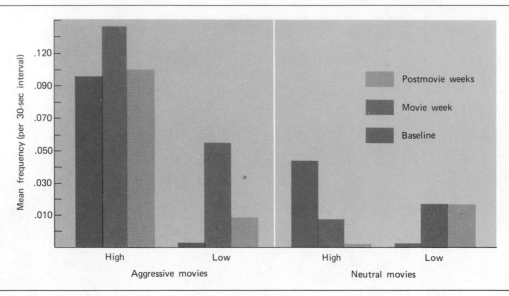

Note: High and low refer to initial tendencies to aggress.
Source: Parke, Berkowitz, Leyens, West, and Sebastian (1977), p. 146.

Singer were criticized for—the use of an overly aggressive, atypical subject population—was also true of this study. Subjects from this population may have reacted differently than most other people.

WHAT CAN WE CONCLUDE?

We have examined research that has supported the notion that viewing televised aggression causes the viewer to increase his or her aggressive behavior. We have also seen research that supports the opposite position. Other research, too numerous to detail in this text, offers ambiguous and inconclusive evidence. Are there any clear and definitive answers that can be given to the question of whether there is a causal relationship between TV viewing and aggressive behavior? Probably not. A report prepared by the National Institute of Mental Health (NIMH) conceded that the television-aggression link has not been established conclusively in any single study (Pearl & Bouthilet, 1982). However, the report did conclude that the weight of the evidence suggested that violent television programs increased subsequent viewer aggression.

Jonathan Freedman (1984) reviewed not only the one hundred studies that comprised the NIMH report, but also what he described as "every available published study." He reviewed all studies that used correlational methods as well as all field experiments. He concluded that the weight of the available evidence leads to no conclusion at all. It is not that the evidence tells us that televised aggression does not lead to increased aggression. It is not that the social learning theory is unreasonable. It is just that the evidence at hand is not sufficient to prove the theory's hypothesis.

Freedman offers some reasons for the inconclusive findings. Suppose that there is an effect, as has been shown in the laboratory, for televised aggression to lead to aggressive behavior. In the nonlaboratory world, television watching has to be placed in the context of many other behaviors and many other influences. Television viewing itself, even for a person who watches a great deal of televised violence, has to be seen in relation to other programs in which aggression does not take place. Consequently, the "real-world" context provides so many other influences that the effect of television viewing may be mitigated by those influences.

We have placed considerable emphasis on the television-aggression question for several reasons: (1) it is a phenomenon of obvious social importance; (2) it is a phenomenon that brings together several theories of social psychology, each of which has received considerable support in the laboratory; and (3) it is an area that demonstrates the rewards and frustrations of bringing basic research to bear on a problem of immense societal significance. At the present time, we concur with Freedman's (1984) analysis that the causal link between television and aggression has not yet been proved.

PREJUDICE AND DISCRIMINATION: WHAT AND WHY?

One of the most destructive and widespread human behaviors is discrimination based on prejudice. In examining this area, we must begin by identifying three terms that are often confused. The first is *stereotype*. Stereotypes are oversimplified mental images of some category of person or event that are shared by a large number of people (Tajfel, 1981). In other words, they are generalizations that people assign to other groups of people. A stereotype can be negative (dirty, cheap), or it can be positive (intelligent, strong, moral). *Prejudice* refers to an unjustified negative attitude toward an individual based solely on that individual's membership in a group. In a sense, prejudice involves negative stereotypes.

Finally, *discrimination* refers to negative, often aggressive behaviors aimed at a person and based on that person's membership in a group.

Prejudice and discrimination are perplexing for a number of reasons. First, prejudice is often baseless—that is, prejudiced attitudes are generally not based on factual data or personal experience. Second, discrimination may be exhibited even when it has negative consequences for the discriminator; thus, an individual who is prejudiced against blacks may hire a less qualified white to fill a job rather than employ the black. Third, prejudice is extremely resistant to change.

There are other points about prejudice and discrimination that lend added urgency to studying them. First, they are found in all, or nearly all, cultures in the world (Milner, 1981). Second, almost any imaginable group can be the object of prejudice. Prejudice can be aimed at people because of their race (racism), sex (sexism), religion, sexual preference, culture, and even regional location. Finally, the study of prejudice and discrimination involves almost every area and topic of research in social psychology. We will now focus our attention on the theories of aggression that can help us understand this concept.

Displaced Aggression   During the 1940s and 1950s, one of the more popular explanations of prejudice was based on frustration-aggression theory. This explanation, which became known as the "scapegoat theory" (Hovland & Sears, 1940; Allport, 1954), suggests that prejudice and discrimination against minorities are the result of displaced aggression. Supposedly, members of the majority group are frustrated in their day-to-day lives and are forced to inhibit this aggression. A woman on the job is frustrated by her boss but cannot aggress against the boss or she will lose her job. A man may be frustrated by his wife and children at home, but there are laws that prohibit his aggressing directly against them. The frustration builds up, and the woman and the man look for a target onto which they can displace their aggression. A minority group may be a good scapegoat because it is generally weak and cannot retaliate. Further, a number of other people are expressing hostile attitudes toward this group, and it seems acceptable to do so. If there are laws that prohibit aggressing against the minority group, they may not be enforced.

Numerous studies have supported the scapegoat theory. Hovland and Sears (1940) found a negative correlation between cotton prices in the South for the years 1882 and 1930 and the number of lynchings of blacks. That is, the lower the price of cotton, the greater the likelihood that there would be a larger number of lynchings. The authors believed that because the Southerners depended on cotton for their livelihood, low cotton prices would be frustrating to them. The aggression resulting

"Ms. Ryan, send me in a scapegoat." *(From* The Wall Street Journal, *with permission of Cartoon Features Syndicate)*

from this frustration would be displaced onto a minority group, and thus the lynchings were a sign of displaced aggression. Campbell (see Allport, 1954, p. 224) found that the more dissatisfied people were with their jobs, the more anti-Semitism they expressed. Supposedly, they were displacing onto Jews the aggression caused by job frustration. Miller and Bugelski (1948) found that when they frustrated men in a CCC camp by not letting them go to see an attractive movie, these men became more hostile toward Mexicans and Japanese. Again, this was supposedly an example of displaced aggression.

Although the scapegoat theory of prejudice has been criticized as being too simple, there does seem to be some relationship between frustration and prejudice. A question can be raised about why certain groups are chosen as the scapegoats. Why is there prejudice against blacks in the South rather than against Scots? Why were the Jews singled out as the target of discrimination by the Germans during World War II? According to frustration-aggression theory, the target of the displaced aggression must bear some resemblance to the frustrating agent. It is, however, difficult to see the similarity between the boss who frustrates a woman and the blacks onto whom she may displace her aggression. What is the similarity between a frustrating experimenter in the Miller and Bugelski study and Mexicans and Japanese? Thus, similarity to the frustrator cannot be the only factor that makes certain groups the focus of prejudice and displaced aggression.

Berkowitz (1962) identified four other factors that may play a role in determining which group will be chosen as the target for displaced aggression:

1. *Safeness:* The target group is so weak that it can be attacked without fear of strong retaliation. Although this may be the case for some prejudices, Berkowitz points out that it cannot be the only factor, as many times the target of prejudice is not the weakest group that could have been chosen.
2. *Visibility:* The group must have qualities that make it visible and make it stand out from other groups. Color, physical characteristics, or different customs can make a group visible.
3. *Strangeness:* There is a certain fear of strangeness, and Berkowitz believes that humans have an instinct to hate what is strange to them. He points out that children become emotionally upset and tend to draw away when a stranger approaches.
4. *Prior dislike for the group:* Berkowitz believes that aggression may be displaced from one disliked person or group to a previously disliked group.

Perceived Threat   Some investigators (LeVine & Campbell, 1972) have suggested that there may be a more direct link between frustration and prejudice. In many cases, the object of prejudice and discrimination may be perceived as being a direct threat. For example, Hovland and Sears (1940) explained their negative correlation between the price of cotton and the lynching of blacks as an example of displaced aggression. However, it is possible that as economic conditions became depressed, southern whites began to see blacks as competing for scarce goods and resources. More recently, Kinder and Sears (1981) pointed out that today, some people feel direct threats from blacks whom they perceive as wishing to move into their neighborhoods, take their jobs, and displace their children from their schools. Perceived threat may also underlie some prejudice against women. In this case, some males see the women's liberation movement with alarm because they fear that women will be competing directly for jobs once reserved for men.

While this point of view may explain some prejudice and discrimination, it is clearly limited. For example, it is difficult to apply the perceived-threat hypothesis to explain children's prejudices. Further, Brewer (1979) pointed out that people often harbor prejudices against groups with whom they have had no contact and do not expect to have contact.

Personality   Personality may also play a role in selecting the target of and general orientation to displaced aggression. Following World War II, a great deal of attention was focused on the conditions that could give rise to prejudiced and stereotyped attitudes toward groups of people. Of central concern to a project funded by the American Jewish Committee was the wholesale genocide that resulted from anti-Semitism in Germany. Was anti-Semitism an isolated attitude held by individuals who had had unpleasant personal experiences with Jews, or was it related to a network of attitudes, personality, and family background? Adorno, Frenkel-Brunswick, Levinson, and Sanford's *The Authoritarian Personality* (1950) went some distance in providing answers to these questions.

The investigators approached a large number of people who belonged to groups ranging from college fraternities to San Quentin prison inmates. The respondents, most of whom were white, middle-class Americans, were given a battery of questionnaires, and many of them were interviewed in depth about their feelings toward themselves, their families, and their childhood. The data from the questionnaires and the extensive clinical interviews provided the material for the investigation.

Respondents filled out an anti-Semitism scale, an ethnocentrism scale, and a political and economic conservatism scale. The anti-Semitism scale tapped respondents' attitudes toward Jews in a variety of situations and circumstances. The ethnocentrism scale measured the degree to which negative, stereotyped attitudes were held for a variety of other groups. In general, ethnocentrism refers to the tendency to reject those who are culturally dissimilar while blindly accepting those who are culturally alike (Sumner, 1906). Adorno et al. found that the correlation between the specific attitude of anti-Semitism and the general quality of ethnocentrism was extremely high: those who were anti-Semitic endorsed similar attitudes toward other ethnic, religious, and cultural groups. There was a slight tendency for ethnocentric anti-Semites to express right-wing attitudes on the political and economic conservatism scale, but the data were not conclusive in this regard.

Finally, assessments of the respondents' personalities were made by means of a test constructed especially for the occasion (potential for fascism scale, or F scale) and by the clinical interviews. The major findings were extremely interesting from the standpoint of viewing childhood development, personality, and attitudes as inextricably inter-related. Adorno et al. found that people with anti-Semitic and ethnocentric attitudes tended to come from homes in which discipline was severe and threatening. The parents of highly prejudiced subjects tended to have very high aspirations for their children and to measure them in terms of their own needs rather than the children's needs. The products of this upbringing idealized their parents in questionnaire and interview responses; they were more likely to see their fathers as the most influential, likable, and successful person, and their mothers as the most giving and helpful person. Prejudiced subjects saw no weakness in either themselves or their parents, whereas unprejudiced respondents were more apt to admit to some human shortcomings. The irony in the prejudiced subjects' parental adoration is that hostility was found seething beneath the surface. Although it was difficult to find prejudiced subjects who would introspect and examine their feelings, the investigators detected a great deal of hostility directed against authority figures and parents.

A study of the size and scope of Adorno et al. is bound to draw criticism, and *The Authoritarian Personality* has drawn its share. Problems have been raised regarding the selection of the respondents (Hyman & Sheatsley, 1954), the construction of the scales (Couch & Keniston, 1960), and the analysis of the interview material (Brown, 1965). The study also suggested other problems. Spurred by a concern with fascism and anti-Semitism, it focused on the authoritarian with Rightist political views. But is there also an authoritarianism of the Left? Can communists, national socialists, or even middle-of-the-roaders exhibit the kinds of ethnocentric attitudes and feelings about authority that qualify them as "authoritarian personalities"? There has been debate about this (for example, Christie, 1956; Eysenck, 1956), and the questions are as yet unanswered. Finally, Milner (1981) argues that while personality may influence the development of prejudice, the theories are simply too limited to explain a phenomenon as broad and pervasive as prejudice.

Group Categorization   The three theories that we have discussed focus on prejudice as the result of individual experiences or characteristics. Tajfel (1981) and Milner (1981) argue that prejudice is too widespread to explain solely on the basis of "individual" theories. These investigators point out that prejudice and discrimination are group phenomena and that we must look at group dynamics if we hope to develop broad explanations. Tajfel (1978) has suggested that prejudice and discrimination may be one of the byproducts of belonging to a group. He argued that groups have a need to create and maintain a positive social identity. Just as individuals develop their self-concept by comparing themselves with others, so groups also develop an identity by comparing with other groups. Because of this, members of one group are motivated to perceive their own group in a positive light while evaluating outgroups in negative terms. According to this position, the roots of prejudice are sown as soon as an ingroup and outgroup is created.

While this may seem too simple a process to explain prejudice, numerous studies demonstrate that people evaluate members of their own group positively and assign positive outcomes to these members, while they evaluate outgroup members negatively and discriminate against them. These effects occur even in cases where people have been randomly assigned to groups and they have never met members of their own group or the outgroup (Billig & Tajfel, 1973; Brewer, 1979; Brown & Turner, 1979, 1981). Further, research by Jones and his colleagues (Jones, Wood, & Quattrone, 1981; Quattrone & Jones, 1980; Quattrone, 1985) has found that people tend to see outgroup members as being relatively similar while they perceive greater variability in their own group.

While such research adds a great deal to understanding the dynamics of prejudice and discrimination, Hamilton (1979) raises an important issue. He points out that, at any one time, a single individual belongs to many groups. Given this, why do strong prejudices develop toward some outgroups but not others? Unfortunately, there has not been a great deal of research on this issue. Hamilton points out, however, that the salience of group characteristics may be one of the features that determines the strength of a prejudice. People tend to be most attentive to salient or distinctive stimuli (Taylor & Fiske, 1978) and such stimuli serve as easily recognizable boundaries between groups. Salience, in this case, may include Berkowitz's dimensions of strangeness and visibility. For example, one can quickly distinguish groups on the basis of race, sex, age, or dress. Therefore, group categorization research suggests

Tajfel argues that prejudice may be a consequence of people being categorized into groups. Almost any characteristic, such as the clothing of the monks pictured above, can create group boundaries. *(Joel Gordon 1979)*

that the simple act of differentiating people into groups may sow the seeds of prejudice and that the more salient the boundaries between the groups, the more likely these seeds are to be manifested into prejudice and discrimination. This position is supported by research (Worchel, Axsom, Ferris, Samaha, & Schweitzer, 1978; Worchel & Norvell, 1980) showing that discrimination can be reduced by reducing the salience of group boundaries.

Sociocultural Learning   Approaches based on learning theories attempt to explain why certain groups are the object of prejudice and why people, including young children, may harbor prejudices against groups with which they have little or no contact. Numerous investigators (e.g., Kelly, Ferson, & Holtzman, 1958) have suggested that prejudice, like most other behaviors, is a learned response. A child may see its parents discriminate against blacks, hear their disparaging remarks about blacks, and find that they will quickly whisk him or her away when black children come out to play. Bird, Monachesi, and Burdick (1952) found that almost half of the white families that they interviewed had rules against playing with black children. As the children grow older, they are told by peers that blacks are bad, and they are excluded from peer groups if seen playing with blacks. Their parents may point out newspaper stories telling how a gang of blacks raped an innocent white girl. Each of these incidents teaches a child to be prejudiced against blacks. This model of prejudice closely parallels social learning theory. The children have models in their parents who teach them to dislike blacks. They are positively reinforced by parents and peers for discriminating against blacks, and punished by these parents and peers for associating with blacks. Thus, children are neatly taught to hate.

The learning approach can explain why there are such wide variations in the object of prejudice. Children in different countries, or in different regions of the same country, can be taught to hate different ethnic groups. Interestingly enough, the learning approach allows for the formation of prejudice in children even if they have never seen a member of the group against which they become prejudiced. Parents can instill in their children the idea that they should hate blacks (or some other group) and can tell the children frightening stories about what will happen to them if they interact with blacks. The result of this schooling will be a child who hates and is afraid of blacks, even though he or she may never have interacted with a black person.

The learning of prejudice can be further facilitated by the media. Stories in the newspaper and television programs often support stereotypes about groups. For example, blacks are often cast as being lazy, superstitious, or dangerous, and they are shown holding inferior occupations. Until recently, television commercials were a "whites only club";

commercials aimed at portraying glamor and beauty used only white models. The traditional stereotype of women also dominated the media; women were shown as being rather dull, submissive, and inferior to men. These stereotypes were also found in books written for very young children.

There have indeed been many attempts to "clean up" the media and eliminate the portrayal of blatant prejudices. Further, societal values today stress equality; and discrimination, especially racial discrimination, receives almost universal disapproval. However, Sears and his colleagues (Sears & McConahay, 1973; Kinder & Sears, 1981) argue that blatant racism has been replaced by *symbolic racism*. Symbolic racism "represents a form of resistance to change in racial status, based on moral feelings that blacks violate such traditional American values as individualism and self-reliance, the work ethic, obedience, and discipline." According to this position, people do not learn the traditional racial stereotypes that blacks are lazy or intellectually inferior. Rather, they learn that blacks are a threat to the symbols and values that Americans hold dear. Kinder and Sears conducted a survey of white voters in the Los Angeles area to determine the factors that influenced their decision to vote for a white or black mayoral candidate. They found that symbolic racism rather than direct racial threats to whites' private lives (jobs, neighborhoods, schools) was a major determinant of voting behavior. Because of its roots in moral principles and values, symbolic racism may be more difficult to combat than prejudice based on the perception of direct personal threats.

Although learning can implant the seeds of prejudice, Pettigrew (1958, 1959) suggests that discrimination is most likely to surface when the individual is in a group of other prejudiced people. Pettigrew believes that conformity plays an important role in determining prejudice; that is, the individual sees what attitudes his peers hold, and will shape his own attitudes to conform. In support of this notion, Pettigrew (1959) found that women, churchgoers, and the individuals who were most concerned about upward social mobility were the most prejudiced people in the South. It is exactly such people who were the most conforming. Other supporting data come from studies such as that of Newcomb (1943), who found that individuals' racial attitudes change when they go to college; the new attitudes come to more closely resemble the attitudes of other college students. Thus, individuals do conform to the prevailing racial attitudes of their reference groups, and when a person changes group membership or moves to another part of the country, his racial attitudes are likely to change.

THE CONSEQUENCES OF PREJUDICE

As we have seen, there are many possible channels through which prejudice develops. Regardless of how it develops, investigators have found that prejudice exerts some interesting and disturbing influences on both the holder of prejudice and the victim. These effects of prejudice offer an explanation for why it is so difficult to change prejudiced attitudes and discriminatory behavior. Because we have examined many of these effects in earlier chapters, we will only briefly review them here.

Prejudice affects the *attributions* made about the victim's behavior. For example, Deaux (1976) suggested that when a victim's behaviors are consistent with an observer's prejudices, they will be attributed to stable

People who belong to groups whose stereotype is that they are not supposed to succeed are rarely given credit for their own success. Did this woman become a pilot because she is good or because she is lucky? Work by Deaux suggests that observers will make the latter attribution. (© Niépce-Rapho/Photo Researchers, Inc.)

characteristics of the victim (e.g., ability). However, when the behavior is not consistent with the observer's stereotype, he or she will attribute the victim's behavior to an unstable attribute such as luck or task difficulty. Deaux and Emswiller (1974) found data supporting this prediction. As you can see, this type of biased attribution serves to maintain the prejudice. For example, a male who believes that women are not athletic may attribute his loss to a female tennis opponent as due to his not feeling well. However, if he had lost to a male, he may have congratulated his opponent (seen him) as a good tennis player.

Prejudice affects the *processing of information* (Hamilton, 1979) about the target of prejudice. For example, recall the study of the football game played between Princeton and Dartmouth in 1951 (Hastorf & Cantril, 1954). In the reports of that game, Princeton students saw the Dartmouth team's behavior as aggressive and provocative while the Dartmouth students viewed the Princeton team's behavior in this light. Sagar and Schofield (1980) showed both white and black school children pictures of either white or black models engaged in aggressive behaviors. As can be seen from the results in Table 8–4, both white and black children viewed the black model's behavior as more threatening and mean than the same behavior exhibited by a white model. Along a different line, Howard and Rothbart (1980) found that subjects were more likely to remember the negative features of the outgroup and positive traits of the ingroup members. Further, Park and Rothbart (1982) found that subjects recalled

Table 8–4
Mean ratings of both white and black actors' behaviors by both white and black subjects

Subject group*	Actor race†	Rating scale	
		Mean/threatening	Playful/friendly
White	**White**	8.28	6.43
	Black	8.99	6.24
Black	**White**	7.38	7.19
	Black	8.40	6.74

Note: Means are based on sums of paired 7-point scales indicating how well the given adjective described the behaviors, from 1 (not at all) to 7 (exactly).
*$n=40$ for each group.
†Each subject rated two white and two black actors and two white and two black targets. Means are not broken down by target race, since no statistically significant main effects or interactions were found for this variable.
Source: Adapted from Sagar and Schofield (1980). Copyright 1980 by the American Psychological Association. Adapted by permission of the authors.

more stereotyped information about an outgroup member than an in-group member.

Finally, prejudice may initiate *self-fulfilling prophecy behaviors.* Earlier, we examined experiments by Rosenthal and his colleagues (Rosenthal, 1964; Rosenthal & Fode, 1963; Rosenthal & Jacobson, 1968) that demonstrated that people's expectations can unwittingly influence their behavior to create situations that support their expectations. Similarly, research (Word, Zanna, & Cooper, 1974) found that interviewers' nonverbal behaviors were influenced by the race of the interviewee. The interviewers gave more negative cues to, and spent less time with, blacks than they did with whites. Behaviors such as these will increase the psychological distance between members of the two racial groups and can intensify hostile and prejudiced feelings.

There is clearly a wide range of effects of prejudice. These effects involve attitudes, attributions, and behaviors. In looking at these effects, we can also see why prejudice is so resistant to change. Each of these effects helps cement and perpetuate prejudiced attitudes and justify discrimination. Thus, a vicious cycle is created where prejudice tends to support and feed off itself.

SUMMARY

This chapter has been about altruistic and aggressive behavior. Altruistic behavior refers to an act that renders help to another person. Aggressive behavior defines an act that is intended to injure another person. In an emergency situation, altruistic behavior frequently occurs. In the rescue of victims of the Air Florida crash, altruism was manifested despite great danger to the rescuers. In the failure of witnesses to intervene in the Kitty Genovese slaying, it was not. Latané and Darley studied the factors leading either to the action or inaction of bystanders during emergencies. The bystander must (1) notice the event, (2) interpret it as an emergency, (3) assume the responsibility to act, (4) know the appropriate form of assistance, and (5) implement the decision to help.

Much of the research on bystander intervention has revolved about the question of responsibility. Darley and Latané showed that the number of witnesses to an emergency is related to the likelihood of acting: the more witnesses, the less action. The presence of a number of bystanders makes any single bystander feel less responsible for intervening, and therefore less likely to act altruistically.

A cost model of helping has been developed to account for situations that do and do not lead to helping. According to the expanded version of the model, helping increases when empathy and psychological arousal are high. If those conditions are met, the likelihood of intervention increases as the cost to the bystander decreases. Intervention also increases as the cost to the victim for the bystander's not helping increases.

Batson and his colleagues have stressed the distinction between empathic feelings and personal distress. Both may result in help giving. The first emotion leads to altruistic behavior based solely on the desire to alleviate the stress of another. The latter, however, results in offering relief to another based on the desire to alleviate one's own personal discomfort.

Research on the situations that are more likely to produce helping behavior has shown that helping increases when (1) we have been positively rewarded for previous helping, (2) we are in a positive mood, (3) we observe someone else helping, (4) the rules or norms permit behavior that can lead to helping, (5) we are not otherwise preoccupied or hurried, and (6) we are reciprocating a favor done by another.

The recipient's response to helping may not always be positive. Favorable responses depend on the use of the attribution process in determining the meaning of the helpful action.

Aggressive behavior may have an instinctual or a biological basis. Nonetheless, we have argued that social-psychological theories are necessary to understand when and why aggressive behavior takes place.

One of the most popular theories of human aggression posits that frustration always leads to aggression and that aggression always presupposes the existence of frustration. Dollard, Doob, Miller, Mowrer, and Sears predicted that the expression of aggression (either directly or vicariously) would result in a decrease in the drive to aggress (catharsis). The frustration-aggression theory also states that aggression might be displaced if it cannot safely be directed against the thwarter. Critics of the theory argue that frustration does not always lead to aggression, and aggression does not always presuppose the existence of frustration. Further, evidence for catharsis has not been found consistently in research.

Another theoretical approach suggests that frustration only produces the readiness to aggress; the presence or absence of aggression cues will determine whether people will actually express aggression. The excitation-transfer theory argues that the attributions people make for arousal affect aggressive behavior. According to this position, arousal—regardless of its real source—will increase the likelihood of aggression if people attribute it as anger. These theoretical approaches have been applied to the question of the effect of violent, pornographic erotica in the media and suggest that such pornography can provoke violence against women.

Social learning theory suggests that aggression is learned like any other behavior. The learning occurs through reinforcement and modeling. However, even if an individual knows how to aggress, he or she will not express aggression unless rewarded for doing so. Research has shown that people will imitate aggressive models. Social learning theory suggests that aggression can be reduced by not supplying aggressive models and not rewarding aggressive behavior.

Research on television violence has generally found that watching violent programs is associated with increased aggression. Whether watching aggression on TV actually causes aggressive behavior is still a matter for debate. The sex and age of the viewer are two variables that influence the relationship between television and violence. Still other research has shown that watching many violent programs may reduce the viewer's sensitivity to aggression and empathy with the victim of aggression.

Prejudice is an unjustified negative attitude toward an individual, based solely on that individual's membership in a group. Discrimination includes negative, often aggressive, behaviors aimed at a person and motivated by prejudice. Some types of personalities, such as the authoritarian personality, may be more prone to prejudice. Displaced aggression may also be at the root of prejudice and discrimination. Research has shown that simply becoming a member of a group can lead to discrimination against outgroup members. Prejudiced attitudes tend to influence the holder's attributions and processing of information about outgroup members.

KEY WORDS

aggression	ethnocentrism
aggression cue	ethologist
altruistic behavior	excitation-transfer theory
arbitrary frustration	frustration
authoritarian personality	imitative learning
catharsis	instinct
cost model of helping	norm of reciprocity
decision tree	prejudice
diffusion of responsibility	reciprocation
discrimination	social exchange
displaced aggression	social learning theory
empathy	stereotype

SUGGESTED READINGS

Austin, W., & Worchel, S. (Eds.). (1979). *The social psychology of intergroup relations.* Monterey, CA: Brooks/Cole Publishing.

Dollard, J., Doob, L., Miller, N. E., Mowrer, O. H., & Sears, R. R. (1939). *Frustration and aggression*. New Haven, CT: Yale University Press.

Freedman, J. L. (1984). Effect of television violence on aggressiveness. *Psychological Bulletin, 96*(2), 227–246.

Geen, R. G., & Donnerstein, E. I. (Eds.). (1983). *Aggression: Theoretical and empirical reviews*. Volume 1. New York: Academic Press.

Krebs, D., & Miller, D. T. (1985). Altruism and aggression. In G. Lindzey & E. Aronson (Eds.), *Handbook of social psychology* (3rd ed.). New York: Random House.

Latané, B., & Darley, J. M. (1970). *The unresponsive bystander: Why doesn't he help?* Englewood Cliffs, NJ: Prentice-Hall.

Lorenz, K. (1968). *On aggression*. New York: Bantam Books.

Piliavin, J. A., Dovidio, J., Gaertner, S., & Clark, R. D., III. (1981). *Emergency interventions*. New York: Academic Press.

Staub, E., Bar-Tal, D., Karylowski, J., & Reykowski, J. (Eds.). (1984). *Development and maintenance of prosocial behavior*. New York: Plenum Press.

Turner, J., & Giles, H. (1981). *Intergroup behavior*. Chicago: University of Chicago Press.

NINE

INTERPERSONAL AND INTERGROUP CONFLICT

A haggard-looking pilot leaned out of the window of the lonely jet to speak to reporters standing on the tarmac. "We are continuously surrounded by many, many guards. The gunmen are constantly changing" (*Time*, July 1, 1985, p. 19). TWA Flight 847 began as a routine trip from Athens to Rome, but it had now become the focus of international attention and a symbol of the conflict that exists between people of different nations, different religions, and different cultures.

Soon after Flight 847 took off from Athens, two Arab gunmen armed with pistols and grenades seized control of the plane. In a wild frenzy, the terrorists brutally beat and then shot a young U.S. Navy diver who had been a passenger on the plane. For two days, the plane crisscrossed the skies between Beirut and Algiers before coming to a final resting spot at the Beirut airport. About one hundred passengers, mostly women, children, and non-United States citizens, were allowed to leave the plane at earlier stops. Now, the remaining thirty-seven American male passengers were secreted off the plane, but they were not allowed to go free, as the other passengers had been. Instead, these thirty-seven were taken in small groups to hiding places in Beirut. The three American crewmen remained on board the plane along with numerous terrorist gunmen.

These forty men became the bargaining chips of the terrorists, who demanded that Israel release 776 Shi'ites who had been detained during Israel's withdrawal from Lebanon some months before. Some of the concern for the hostages was reduced when the brutal terrorists who had hijacked the plane were replaced by members of the Amal organization controlled by Nabih Berri. But the resolve of this new group was soon apparent when one of the members told the Beirut flight control tower that if no progress was made on the demands by the next morning, the plane would be loaded with explosives and blown up over Tel Aviv.

The stage was set: the Amal gunmen would hold the American passengers hostage until the United States put pressure on Israel to release the Lebanese detainees. What was to be the response of the United States? The irony of the situation was not lost on the world. The president of the United States, Ronald Reagan, had ridden into office criticizing his predecessor's (Jimmy Carter) handling of the Iranian hostage crisis in which American embassy personnel were held for 444 days; Reagan had publicly blasted Carter for not having been tough enough with the kidnappers. Thus, for President Reagan and his advisers, the task was not only to gain the release of the hostages, but also to preserve their image as being tough on terrorism. To add another ironic twist to the situation, President Reagan felt that the Israelis had acted unlawfully in taking the Shi'ite prisoners. However, he believed that he could not openly express these feelings given the hijackers' demands.

Officials from the United States and the Amal group negotiated for days over the fate of the forty hostages. Anger and distrust increased as the conflict wore on. Each side voiced strong demands and each made threats before a compromise was reached. (R. Bossu/Sygma)

Israel too was caught in an ironic bind. The Israelis had been planning to release the Shi'ites. The Shi'ites, who had been taken to protect Israel's earlier withdrawal from Lebanon, now served no purpose; thus, their continued imprisonment was a headache for Israel. But the Israelis now felt that they could not release the prisoners because to do so might damage Israel's image of not capitulating to terrorism.

Even Nabih Berri found himself in an uncomfortable position. As leader of the Amal militia, he faced the difficult task of maintaining control over his followers. Some of the more radical militia members wanted to kill the hostages and wage a suicidal struggle against the United States and Israel. The more moderate members, on the other hand, were concerned that such action would result in a serious setback to the group's power in Lebanon. Thus, Berri wanted to have his demands met and release the hostages without losing his leadership position; he was like "a man riding a tiger" (*Time,* July 1, 1985, p. 22).

While each of the parties in the conflict may have had some common goals, these were forgotten during the early days of the crisis. President Reagan made the tough public statement that "Americans will never make concessions to terrorists," but he resisted suggestions that he escalate the conflict by threatening military action. The Israelis also avoided making direct threats against the Amal, but they proclaimed that they would not release the Shi'ites in the face of terrorist demands.

The stalemate continued. After a week had passed, the captors set up a press conference in which they paraded five of the hostages before an army of media people. The purpose of this media event was not clear, but it did reassure the world that the hostages were alive. In fact, the hostages reported that they were getting along, but urged an end to the conflict. Israel attempted to lessen the tension by releasing thirty-one Shi'ites. The Israelis insisted that the release had nothing to do with the hostage crisis, but negotiators suggested that Berri could respond in good faith by releasing some of the hostages. Berri's initial response was "What should we do now? Should we release half a hostage?" (*Time,* July 8, 1985, p. 11). But one hostage who had a heart ailment was later set free.

The negotiation process, however, began to bog down as each side waited for the other to make further concessions. Distrust increased and rumors began to crop up. One rumor was that six hostages with Jewish-sounding names had been turned over to a radical group of terrorists. A group of several hundred Shi'ites chanting anti-American slogans marched at the Beirut airport in support of the hijackers.

While publicly it seemed that negotiations were at a standstill, a great deal of behind-the-scenes work was taking place. Convinced that direct negotiations would not work, U.S. officials attempted to find a third

Through negotiations and the intervention of Syrian President Assad, the deadlock was finally broken and the hostages were released. A motorcade carried the hostages safely into Syria. *(Alain Nogues/Sygma)*

party to seek a resolution. This third party had to be someone the terrorists trusted: President Assad of Syria emerged as a candidate. Syria had a history of supporting terrorism, but Assad wanted the hostage crisis ended so he could increase his control over Lebanon. Thus, he offered to accept the hostages from the Amal. He also obtained promises that Israel would release the Shi'ite prisoners—but not as a condition of the release of the hostages.

This solution seemed acceptable to everyone: Berri could release the hostages to a trusted party with the understanding that the prisoners would be released; and neither Israel nor the United States would be seen as making direct concessions to the terrorists. Just when it seemed that the hostages would be released, Berri halted progress and demanded that President Reagan give assurances that he would not retaliate against Lebanon after the release. These assurances were probably unnecessary since six other Americans were still being held hostage somewhere in Lebanon.

With the details worked out, the hostages were finally taken to Syria and then sent home. Some days later, Israel released the Shi'ite prisoners. The immediate crisis was over, but mixed with sighs of relief and tears of happiness was the realization that a similar conflict could happen again. And ironically, in January 1987, the shadow of Flight 847 again visited the international scene. One of the terrorists involved in the TWA highjacking was caught in West Germany. Soon afterwards, four hostages were taken from the American University in Beirut. The kidnappers were not only concerned with the fate of the terrorist in West Germany, but they also demanded that Israel release 400 Arab prisoners.

DEFINING CONFLICT

Our discussion of the plight of TWA Flight 847, as well as the broader context of events in the Middle East over the last forty years, can be used to illustrate a number of social psychological phenomena. One of the most poignant is *conflict*. In the hostage case, we can identify conflict at many levels. For example, there was the *intrapersonal conflict* experienced by President Reagan as he tried to decide how to respond to the hijacking: Should he negotiate or use massive force and retaliate? Showing the effects of this internal struggle, Reagan stated, "I'm as frustrated as anyone. I've pounded a few walls myself, when I'm alone, about this" (*Time,* July 1, 1985, p. 8). There was the *interpersonal conflict* between Reagan and Berri, between Berri and members of his Amal militia, and between President Reagan and his advisers. And there was *intergroup* and *international conflict* involving the United States, Israel, and the Amal faction.

Conflict plays a central role in almost all social psychological theories. As a result, there are many different views of the concept. For example, we can look within the individual and define conflict as "a state that obtains for an individual when he is motivated to make two or more mutually incompatible responses" (Jones & Gerard, 1967, p. 709). We can also focus on the relationship between individuals or groups and describe conflict as "tension between two or more social entities (individuals, groups, or larger organizations) which arise from incompatibility of actual or desired responses" (Raven & Kruglanski, 1970, p. 70). A common element in these definitions is the existence of opposing forces that create tension and demand a response. Earlier chapters have dealt with the intrapersonal conflict that occurs in decision making (Chapter Six), attributions (Chapter Three), and helping behavior (Chapter Eight). Therefore, this chapter will focus on those conflicts that occur between people (interpersonal) and between groups (intergroup).

TYPES OF INTERPERSONAL CONFLICT

Although we can supply a single definition of conflict, there are actually a number of different types of conflict. One type is called *zero-sum conflict* (Table 9–1), indicating that one party's gain is the other party's loss. The zero-sum conflict exemplifies true *competition*; parlor games such as checkers or chess are examples of true competition because one player's gain is the other's loss.

However, most conflict situations do not fit the definition of competition; rather, they fall under the heading of *nonzero-sum conflict* or *mixed-motive conflict*. As the name implies, mixed-motive conflicts do not present the parties with a situation in which one must win while the other must lose. Rather, these conflicts can be resolved to benefit both sides. But there is a unique twist in mixed-motive conflicts that makes it difficult to choose the best solution. The twist is that the solution that offers the best payoff to both sides is not best from the individual's standpoint. Hence, each side must decide whether to work for the best *joint* or the best *individual* payoff, which means that concerns about trust, greed, and being doublecrossed weigh heavily in mixed-motive conflicts. In a broad sense, the conflict between individual and group interests has been referred to as a *social dilemma*, and global problems such as pollution and overpopulation have been cast in this framework (Samuelson & Messick, 1986). Because this type of conflict is so common, let us examine two specific examples that illustrate its intriguing characteristics.

Prisoner's Dilemma   President Reagan wanted desperately to catch and punish the terrorists who murdered the navy diver. But he pointed out, "You can't just start shooting without having someone in your sights." In other words, he had to be sure who was responsible for the murder before he could punish anyone. Let us go on with our scenario and assume that the U.S. officials were able to capture two men whom they

Table 9–1
A zero-sum, or pure conflict situation

Person B \ Person A	Response 1	Response 2
Response 1	+4, −4	+1, −1
Response 2	+7, −7	−6, +6

Board games such as checkers represent true zero-sum conflicts because one person's gain is another's loss. However, most of the conflict situations we face in our lives are of the mixed-motive or nonzero-sum type. (© Michael Weisbrot and Family/Stock, Boston)

believed were responsible. These men (we'll call them Abdul and Achmed) are turned over to the attorney general who must develop the case against them. As it turns out, eyewitness accounts are vague, contradictory, and will not stand up in court. The attorney general needs a confession, but how can he get these men to confess to a crime that will bring them long jail sentences or even the death penalty?

Fortunately, our attorney general is a good student of human behavior. He begins by placing Abdul and Achmed in separate cells where they cannot communicate with each other. He then visits both men and tells them their choices: each can confess to killing the navy diver or each can remain silent and not confess. The attorney general points out that he does not yet have enough evidence to convict either man of murder, but he does have evidence that will convict both of lesser crimes. He now offers each suspect a deal (Table 9–2). If neither man confesses, he will charge each with the lesser crime, such as possession of stolen property and trespassing, and will fight to get the longest prison sentence possible (four years) for both. On the other hand, if one of the men confesses and testifies against the other, the attorney general will let the

Table 9–2

Matrix representation of the prisoner's dilemma

Achmed \ Abdul	Not confess	Confess
Not confess	4 years, 4 years	99 years, Freedom
Confess	Freedom, 99 years	20 years, 20 years

Note: Cooperative responses (not confess) from both parties would lead to relatively light sentences for each, but each party must trust the other before he will make a cooperative response.

confessor go free, but will prosecute the one who did not confess (ninety-nine years in prison). However, if both confess, the attorney general will recommend reduced terms for each (twenty years) since he could not possibly let them both go free. As you can see, our crafty attorney general has set up a conflict between Abdul and Achmed.

This conflict, known as the *prisoner's dilemma*, has the characteristics of the mixed-motive situation. First, one person's gain is not necessarily the other's loss; both men could receive rather short sentences (four years). Second, motives of both cooperation and competition are involved. For example, looking at Table 9–2, a competitive response would be a confession since a confession by either man hurts the other by increasing the other's sentence. Clearly, the competitive response is the "safe" response if the person does not *trust* his partner; it would be disastrous not to confess when the other person confesses. A cooperative response would be not to confess. This is, however, a difficult course to follow for two reasons. First, the individual can achieve the highest outcome for himself if he acts competitively (confesses) and the partner does not. Hence, the person is tempted away from cooperation by greed. In addition, we pointed out the risk of cooperation if there is any uncertainty about the partner acting cooperatively.

Looking at the situation from both players' points of view, their joint payoff will be best if they both cooperate and neither confesses. In this way, both will get a light sentence. Thus, on the one hand, the player is motivated to cooperate and obtain a good joint payoff; on the other hand, he is motivated to compete and obtain the best possible payoff for himself.

Social Traps Social traps are another situation in which individuals are faced with the dilemma of furthering their own immediate self-interest

In the Prisoner's Dilemma, each party must be concerned with how the other will behave. If distrust is high, it is likely that both parties will attempt to protect their self-interest by making a competitive response. *(© David Powers, 1986/Stock, Boston)*

or acting for the long-term good of the group. The classic social trap is represented by the "Tragedy of the Commons" (Hardin, 1968). Old New England towns were often built next to or around a pasture; this pasture was called the commons because it was used by all the farmers to graze their cattle. The commons served everyone's needs as long as it was not overgrazed. Overgrazing would destroy the grass and ruin the area for everyone. This situation posed a dilemma for each farmer; adding an extra cow or two to the commons would increase a farmer's personal profit, but if everyone did this the commons would be ruined. If you are a farmer, what do you do in this situation? All too often, the farmers chose to add the extra cattle, resulting in the tragedy of the commons (the destruction of the pasture).

In examining the situation, we can see why this occurred. If you were a farmer, two points might come to your mind. First, you might think that adding only one or two cows to the commons would not hurt or be noticed. The problem here is that if all the farmers think this way, the result will be disaster. Second, even if you foresee this ultimate disaster, you may suspect that your neighbors will not. Hence, you fear that they will sneak their cattle into the commons; this will result in increased

A social trap results when an individual faces the conflict of acting only for self-interest or acting for the good of the group. Removing the pollution device from your car may give you a peppier and more economical vehicle, but if everyone did this action, the air becomes poisoned. *(Ellis Herwig/Stock, Boston)*

profits for them while you suffer because you tried to help the group. There is no way you will let them profit by their selfish actions, so you decide to add cattle and increase your profits too.

This social trap is not, of course, confined to grazing cattle on the commons. It occurs in any situation where there is a renewable resource that can be depleted by overuse. The dilemma here is the trap of immediate self-interest versus long-term group welfare. Many situations have these characteristics. For example, your automobile probably has pollution controls that require that you use unleaded gasoline, cut down on your mileage, and reduce the power of your engine. It would be to your personal advantage to remove these controls; you could use cheaper fuel and have a peppier automobile. The extra pollution from your car alone would make no difference. But if many automobile owners removed their pollution controls, the air would be poisoned for everyone.

Investigators (Allison & Messick, 1983; Samualson & Messick, 1986) have developed a social trap situation for use in the laboratory. Groups are given a resource pool of points or money and told that the pool will increase at a given rate such as 10 percent after each round of the experiment. Each subject is then given the opportunity to withdraw any amount from this common pool. After everyone has taken their amount, the pool is increased by the agreed-upon amount. The individual's goal is to get as much as he or she can, but if each person withdraws too much, the pool will be depleted and everyone will be poor in the end. This situation can be compared to a family that has a joint savings account. The account earns interest (replenishes itself) so that if each member withdraws a reasonable amount, the account will always be there. However, if one or more members becomes greedy and withdraws too much, the account diminishes so that in the end, the family will have no savings at all.

These dilemmas have proved notoriously difficult to resolve. We could argue that a reward/punishment system could be developed to encourage concern for the group good. However, this would require a complex organization to police individual behavior and in most common social dilemmas, people know that their behavior cannot be identified. Recently it has been suggested (Lynn & Oldenquist, 1986) that solutions to these dilemmas cannot rely on individual rewards and punishments. Rather, they must be aimed at developing concerns for the group by increasing altruistic motives, moral motives, and a deeper sense of identification with the group. Unfortunately, developing these motives may prove as difficult as policing individual behaviors.

THE ESCALATING PATH OF CONFLICT

If we examine a situation such as the social trap, we might be tempted to argue that it is an easy one to resolve. It is in everyone's long-term interest to cooperate, and this should be clear. But conflicts do not always follow the most logical path. In the case of the hijacking, for example, Nabih Berri wanted to release the American hostages; not only did their presence intensify conflicts within his Amal group, but Berri had a former wife and six children living in Dearborn, Michigan, who might have been harmed if the hostages had not been released safely. President Reagan wanted to get the hostages home *and* he wanted Israel to free the Shi'ite prisoners. The Israelis wanted to release the Shi'ites; these prisoners served no function for Israel and their continued detention was creating friction with Israel's allies. But with all these forces pointing toward a speedy resolution of the crisis, the conflict among the parties escalated, as threats and counterthreats were hurled with increasing frequency. Ultimately, intervention by Assad of Syria was necessary to help resolve the tension.

Conflict often resembles a snowball rolling downhill; it increases in size and intensity rather than taking a course toward diminution and resolve. This circumstance is referred to as the *conflict spiral* (Deutsch, 1973). As we will see, conflict often leads to increased distrust between the parties, which in turn heightens the conflict. Attitudes become more extreme and polarized (Cooper & Fazio, 1986) and the parties resist compromise. "Each group (or individual) believes that its beliefs are 'true' and 'objective,' and the beliefs of the other group (or individual) are either 'false,' 'incorrect,' or 'distorted' " (Bar-Tal & Geva, 1986, p. 123).

Conflict reaches out and embraces the parties. And people become entrapped in escalating conflict even when there are reasonable and rational means to reduce it (Brockner & Rubin, 1985). The entrapment results as people find that both reducing and remaining in the conflict situation are costly. For an elegant example of this dilemma, consider yourself in the following situation. You and three other students arrive at an experiment and are told that the experimenter will auction off a dollar bill. The rules of the auction are a bit unusual: although the winning bidder will get to keep the dollar, the next highest bidder must pay the amount that he or she bid, even though he or she gets nothing in return. At first this wrinkle seems unimportant to you. The bidding begins; you bid five cents, another student bids ten cents, and so on. After a while, the bidding boils down to you and one other student: you bid seventy-five cents and he bids eighty cents. Now that insignificant rule applying to the losing bidder takes on new importance. You realize that if you stop here, you will have to pay seventy-five cents and get nothing in return; therefore, you up the bid to eighty-five cents. Your opponent has also become aware of the plight that awaits the losing bidder and he bids ninety cents. Now the two of you are trapped in the escalating conflict. How high do you go?

In an experiment (Teger, 1980) using these rules, it was found that the bidding almost always went past the one-dollar level, and sometimes went as high as twenty dollars! As the bids increased in size, all joking and friendly conversation ceased. Anxiety and tension rose and participants showed increasing signs of stress, such as elevated heart rate. The bidders reported that they were forced to remain in the conflict (keep bidding) because of their opponents' bids. And they could not understand why their opponents kept bidding! As the bidding level increased, the participants no longer thought of winning cheap money; now they wanted to beat their opponents and avoid appearing weak or foolish. Was this what prolonged the conflict over the hostages on TWA Flight 847?

This conflict scenario is not an appealing one. What begins as a mild disagreement can quickly escalate into a major confrontation. Let us

examine in more detail how people's reactions to conflict can increase
that conflict.

THE USE OF THREAT

Almost as soon as Flight 847 landed in Beirut, threats and counterthreats began to surface. The terrorists threatened to kill the hostages
and blow up the plane over Israel. At one point in the negotiations,
President Reagan threatened to retaliate against the terrorists; this threat
led Berri to delay releasing the hostages until he was given assurances
that there would be no reprisals. In one of the more bizarre incidents
of the hijacking, five of the hostages were allowed to hold an interview with the media. Their spokesman, Allyn Conwell, pleaded for the
parties to stop threatening each other and to work constructively for
their release.

The use of threats by parties to conflict is very common. In fact, it has
been found that threat is the most common method used by classroom
teachers to change their students' behaviors. The present nuclear arms
race between the Eastern and Western powers is based on the belief that
the party that has the greatest threat potential will fare best in the conflict (Markey, 1985). The use of threat is widespread because it demonstrates power and strength. The parties believe that they can frighten
their opponent into making concessions and seeking a quick solution to
the conflict if they can demonstrate their superior strength.

Does this tactic work or was the advice of many of President Reagan's
advisers to avoid any hint of threat wise? There is considerable evidence
that rather than resolve conflicts, threats increase and prolong them.
Jamison and Thomas found that the use of threat caused students to
become distrustful of their teachers. Examining threat at another level,
Smith (1980) and Wallace (1980) found that a majority of international
wars have been preceded by arms races in which each side increased its
threat potential.

In one of the earliest experiments on the effects of threat (Deutsch &
Krauss, 1960), two subjects were asked to imagine that they were heads
of opposing trucking companies (Acme and Bolt). The players' task was
to move their truck from the start to the finish as quickly as possible; the
quicker the trip, the more money the player earned. The subjects were
then shown a road map (Figure 9–1) that indicated that each player
could take two routes to the finish. The longest route was filled with
curves so that a player taking this route was sure to lose money on the
trip. The second route was the most direct but had a stretch of one-lane
road. If the players' trucks met on this road, neither could proceed

"It's not a war toy, madam.
It's a cease fire toy." (*From*
The Wall Street Journal,
*with permission of Cartoon
Features Syndicate*)

Figure 9–1
Road map in the trucking game

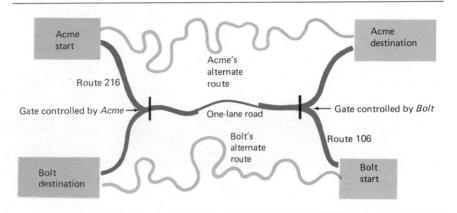

unless one of the trucks backed up. Here was the point of conflict: Which player would back up and let the other pass?

To make matters more interesting, Deutsch and Krauss also built in a manipulation of "threat." At each end of the one-lane section, there was a gate that was under the control of the player whose starting point was closest to that end. By closing the gate, one player could prevent the other player's truck from passing through the one-lane section. Each player's gate was a threat because the player could close it (thus preventing the other from passing) and then take the alternate route. Deutsch and Krauss ran three conditions by varying the availability of the gates: no threat (no gates), unilateral threat (only one player has a gate), and bilateral threat (both players have gates). After each trial, the experimenter announced how much each player had won or lost. The game was played over twenty trials.

There are two ways to view the results of this study. The first is to look at the joint payoff or the sum of the profits (or losses) earned by both players (Table 9–3). The better the joint payoff, the less time it took for the players to arrive at a procedure for sharing the one-lane road and the faster the conflict was resolved. The results indicate quite dramatically that the quickest resolution (and the best payoff) occurred when neither player had access to threats and that the slowest resolution

Table 9–3

Payoffs in the Deutsch and Krauss trucking game

| | | Means | |
| | | | |
Variable	No threat	Unilateral threat (Acme has threat)	Bilateral threat
Summed payoffs (Acme and Bolt)	203.31	−405.88	−875.12
Acme's payoff	122.44	−118.56	−406.56
Bolt's payoff	80.88	−287.31	−468.56

Note: The highest payoff for each party occurred under the no-threat condition, and the lowest payoff resulted in the bilateral-threat condition.

Source: Deutsch and Krauss (1960). Copyright 1960 by the American Psychological Association. Reprinted by permission of the authors.

occurred when both could threaten. In fact, profit was realized only in the no-threat condition.

A second way to view the results is to look at each player's payoff separately. These results indicated that both players received the highest payoffs when neither player had access to threats. The second highest payoffs for each player occurred in the unilateral-threat condition. This was true for the player having the threat (Acme in Table 9–3) and for the player (Bolt) not having the threat. The worst payoff for both players occurred in the bilateral-threat condition. It is interesting to note that the payoff for Bolt was higher when she did not possess the threat capacity that her opponent had than when she did have the capacity to counterthreaten her opponent (bilateral threat). These results suggest that the greater the threat potential in a conflict situation, the more difficult it is to resolve the conflict.

This study set off a flurry of research aimed at taking a close look at the effects of threats (Deutsch, Canavan, and Rubin, 1971; Gallo, 1966; Shomer, Davis, & Kelley, 1966). On the whole, the results confirmed that threat retards the resolution of conflict. The greater the threat used by the parties, the more likely it was that the conflict would escalate and the parties would become entrapped in the situation. Threat begets threat on two levels: People tend to match the threat they receive both in kind and in strength (Youngs, 1986). This would suggest that a threat by Berri to kill the hostages would be met by a threat from the United States to kill the terrorists. Interestingly, this same research suggests that parties to a conflict are most likely to overmatch (escalate) conflict in response to low levels of threat as opposed to more intense threat or punishment.

Participants disliked the distrusted people who used threats, and they often changed their orientation from trying to resolve the conflict to trying to beat the opposing party. The threats increase concerns about power and lead both sides to "arm" themselves. This is an unfortunate consequence because the greater the availability of threats, the greater the likelihood that they will be used.

The last point has been particularly disturbing to psychologists who have been studying the nuclear arms race (Wagner, 1985; Nelson, 1985). They caution that the increase of nuclear weapons as threats against war is likely to have the opposite effect. That is, instead of reducing the likelihood of war, these weapons actually increase that likelihood because having the ability to threaten the opponent increases the chance that the weapons will actually be used. They are concerned that people attempt to deny this possibility, which paves the way for the continued buildup of weapons.

Our discussion has cast doubt on the role of threat and power in the resolution of conflict. Before leaving this important issue, one point

President Reagan was forced to take a tough stand against the terrorists in order to protect his public image. He had criticized President Carter for being soft on terrorists. (© *Barbara Alper/Stock, Boston*)

should be made. While having the availability to threaten an opponent may escalate conflict and result in poor payoffs, not having the power to threaten a powerful opponent may be distressing and damaging to one's self-esteem (Apfelbaum, 1974, 1979). Apfelbaum suggested that, although the actual payoffs may be higher in unequal power relationships, the low-power party may not be happy or satisfied with such a relationship. The points raised by Apfelbaum have also been at the center of discussions about slavery in the Old South, apartheid in South Africa, and maintaining traditional family patterns in which the wife remains at home, dependent on her husband to fulfill her basic needs. In each case, the argument in support of the imbalance in power and freedom is that the system works well to take care of the low-power person. The slave in the Old South (blacks in South Africa, women in the traditional family) receives food, clothing, housing, protection, and other desirable commodities without having power or needing to compete. If these people gain power and begin competing with the high-power people in the system, their lot may be worse because no one will guarantee that these basic needs will be met. This argument, however, fails to consider the psychological effects of being the low-power person in the relationship. Clearly, there are some advantages to being taken care of by high-power persons, but what are the effects on self-esteem and self-concept?

Obviously, there are many unanswered questions about the effect of threat on conflict. However, continued research in this area is of great importance since threat is so commonly used by people who find themselves in conflict.

THE CONCERN WITH APPEARANCE: SAVING FACE

One of the unusual characteristics of the conflict over Flight 847 was the amount of media coverage. The terrorists allowed reporters to talk with the crew. News conferences were held in which the hostages were paraded before cameras and allowed to speak and answer questions. During the weeks of the conflict, the world was able to watch events unfold much like a soap opera. The terrorists felt that this media coverage would put greater pressure on the United States and Israel to capitulate to their demands. Yet the results were not as expected. The conflict escalated and dragged on. People were angered by the use of the hostages in this way. One hostage commented, "It's a bloody circus, all this television stuff. We are just serving their ends, and we wonder sometimes what it is all about" (*Time*, July 8, 1985, p. 15).

If we take a careful look at the feelings of people in conflict, we can understand why this tactic of public display was not successful.

Individuals in conflict situations generally have two aims: one is to obtain as much as possible from the conflict; the other is to appear strong and tough. The second goal is often more important than the first for a number of reasons. First, if the opponent perceives weakness or lack of determination on the part of the other party, he or she may seek out other opportunities for confrontation. Numerous interviews with experts on terrorism conducted during and after the Flight 847 conflict suggested that one of the reasons for continued terrorism was the weak response from the United States and its allies to the terrorists. These experts argued that if terrorists believe that they can "get away" with these acts, they will continue to use terrorism. One expert stated, "The U.S. is paying the price for years of refusing to respond to the terrorists" (*Time*, July 1, 1985, p. 14). A second reason for the concern with appearances is the desire to impress supporters who observe the conflict. Both Nabih Berri and President Reagan wanted to show their supporters that they were strong and in control. Reagan had, in fact, implied during the 1980 election campaign that Jimmy Carter had been "too soft" on the terrorists who took Americans hostage in Iran. This "weakness" severely damaged Carter's bid for reelection.

The concern with appearances in dealing with conflict is referred to as *face saving*. A number of investigators (Brockner & Rubin, 1985; Streufert & Streufert, 1986) have suggested that the desire to save face often motivates people to resort to threats and escalates conflict. People feel that yielding is an admission that the other person in a conflict is stronger. Such an admission is not only a blow to one's self-esteem, but it can lead to embarrassment and distress if other people witness this weakness. Therefore, to avoid embarrassment, the individual will not want to show any sign of weakness. This desire may well lead him or her to respond with a threat when conflicts arise. Brown (1968) reasoned that subjects who had been publicly embarrassed would resort to the use of threat as a means of restoring face even if doing so resulted in costs to themselves. He had subjects play against a confederate in a trucking game experiment. The subjects were told that they were being observed by other subjects through a one-way mirror. During the first half of the experiment, the confederate had the greatest power and exploited the subjects. At one point in the experiment, the subjects were given notes that had supposedly been written by the observers. Half of the subjects received insulting notes saying that they looked like suckers, and the other half received more flattering notes. After receiving the notes, the subjects were given control of the gates and could charge the confederate a high toll to allow them to pass through. The one catch was that using the gates and charging a high toll would also reduce the subject's ability to win. The results showed that subjects who felt that they had lost face

Prime Minister Margaret Thatcher admitted that Great Britain had to go to war with Argentina over the Falkland Islands to preserve the reputation of her country and save face. The Falkland Islands had no economic or strategic value for Great Britain, but war was waged to maintain the country's image. (© *Bob Nickelsberg 1983/Woodfin Camp & Associates*)

during the first part of the study (that is, received insulting notes from the observer) were more likely to use threats than subjects who had not lost face.

In addition to public observation, there are other conditions that are influential when people attempt to save face in conflicts. Teger (1980) suggested that the more a person has invested in a conflict, the more he or she will attempt to save face and resist yielding to demands. This investment can take the form of time, effort, personal commitment, or material. Realization of this point led U.S. Congressman Edward Markey (1985) to suggest that the incredible cost of military preparedness may actually be prolonging conflict between the United States and the Soviet Union. He pointed out that every four hours, the world's militaries spend the equivalent of the year's United Nations Children's Fund (UNICEF) budget. While it can be argued that this money is spent for defense and national safety, it also serves the purpose of increasing nations' commitments to conflict. A second factor affecting face-saving responses is the possibility of future conflict; the greater the likelihood of future conflict, the greater the efforts to save face in the present conflict (Hiltrop & Rubin, 1981).

CONFLICT IN THE EYE OF THE BEHOLDER: PERCEPTIONS OF THE OTHER

President Reagan referred to the hijackers as "criminals" whose main purpose was to spread terror. He felt that these acts of terrorism were forcing him to take an aggressive stand against those who supported terrorism. His view was expressed again as the United States increased naval and air power off the coast of Libya after terrorists killed sixteen civilians in the Rome and Vienna airports during the 1985 Christmas holidays. Nabih Berri, on the other hand, expressed a very different view. He perceived the United States and Israel as aggressors who had forced the Arabs to take action. He argued that the hijackings would not have occurred if Israel had not taken the Shi'ites prisoners. Thus, each side saw itself as reasonable and as acting only in response to the aggressive responses of the other. These perceptions became more entrenched as the conflict increased, and in turn, they helped to escalate the conflict.

One point that must be remembered is that conflict is shaped by the parties' perceptions of the situation rather than what the situation may actually be. In other words, perceptions become reality (Cooper & Fazio, 1986).

Kelley and Stahelski (1970a, 1970b) clearly demonstrated the role of perceptions in the escalation of conflict. They proposed that there are basically two types of individuals: competitive and cooperative. These two types have different views of the way in which other people intend to respond. The competitive type of person sees other people as being homogeneously competitive, and the cooperative person sees other people in a more heterogeneous light—some as cooperative and some as competitive. Kelley and Stahelski (1970b) further assumed that the manner in which individuals interact with others is partly determined by the intentions that they attribute to others. If these two assumptions are correct, competitive people should always interact competitively because they attribute competitive intentions to others. Cooperative people, however, should act cooperatively with a cooperative other and competitively with a competitive other. According to this view, competitive individuals are responsible for setting the tone of a relationship since they do not adapt to their partner's behavior whereas cooperative individuals do adapt.

To test their hypotheses, Kelley and Stahelski (1970b) devised a number of experiments using the same paradigm. Generally, the experiments began by showing the subject a modified prisoner's dilemma

How real is the threat from the Sandinistas in Nicaragua? Many politicians have argued that there is a real danger that the Nicaraguan government will incite a communist revolution in Central America. Research cautions us to carefully examine such statements because conflict leads parties to view the opponent as a threat. (© *Bob Nickelsberg 1983/ Woodfin Camp & Associates*)

Table 9–4
The prisoner's dilemma game used in the study of competitive and cooperative individuals

Person B \ Person A	Y	W
Y	5 \ 5	10 \ −10
W	−10 \ 10	−5 \ −5

Source: Kelley and Stahelski (1970b).

situation (Table 9–4) and asking him how he expected to interact— cooperatively or competitively. In this manner, competitive and cooperative players could be identified. Then, players were paired so that in some dyads both players were cooperative, in other dyads both players were competitive, and in still other dyads one player was cooperative and one competitive. The subjects were then asked what type of play they felt that other players might exhibit. It can be seen in Table 9–5 that the cooperative subjects expected more equal amounts of cooperative and competitive play from others than the competitive subjects, who expected others to act overwhelmingly competitive.

Table 9–5
Expectations of the players

	Expected typical play of others	
Self	*Cooperative*	*Competitive*
Cooperative ($n = 52$)	39%	61%
Competitive ($n = 49$)	24	76
	$TI = 30$	

Note: Competitive players expected more competition from their partners than did cooperative players.
Source: Kelley and Stahelski (1970a).

Table 9–6
Percentage of cooperative responses

| | Partner | | | | | |
| | First ten trials | | Second ten trials | | Third ten trials | |
Actor	Cooperative	Competitive	Cooperative	Competitive	Cooperative	Competitive
Cooperative	85%	64%	90%	67%	92%	69%
Competitive	34	32	31	18	25	27

Note: Competitive individuals gave very few cooperative responses, regardless of the behavior of their partners. The behavior of cooperative players was more affected by the behavior of their partners.
Source: Kelley and Stahelski (1970b).

Next, the subjects participated in a number of trials of the game, and the percentages of cooperative and competitive moves were recorded. Given the matrix presented in Table 9–4, a cooperative play would be Y, both for A and for B. As can be seen by the results in Table 9–6, the competitive players made about the same percentage of cooperative moves, regardless of whether the partner was competitive or cooperative. The cooperative players, on the other hand, made significantly more cooperative moves when the partner was cooperative than when he or she was competitive. Thus, the results supported the hypothesis that the cooperative players would adapt their behavior to match that of their partners more than the competitive players would.

The bottom line in this discussion and in that of the previous section is that the process of conflict both affects and is affected by the perceptions people have of themselves and their opponent. Perceiving the other as competitive and as concerned with one's own appearance adds fuel to conflict and feeds the conflict spiral.

TRUST AND DISTRUST

One of the most significant features that characterized the hostage crisis was the distrust that existed among the parties involved. Berri did not trust the United States, so he moved the hostages to hiding places so that the United States could not attack and free the hostages. The radical element of the Amal group did not trust Berri so they took a group of hostages, supposedly with "Jewish-sounding" names, to another hiding place so that Berri could not easily give in to demands by the United States and Israel. And it was distrust that delayed the release of the hostages into Syrian custody, as Berri feared that Reagan would order military retaliation once the hostages were freed.

"The perceptions of the other group as untrustworthy is probably a major source of tensions leading to conflict. The history of labor/management strife, interracial violence, war, and revolution demonstrates the significance of distrust" (Webb & Worchel, 1986, p. 213). Trust is especially critical to the conflict spiral; the lack of trust helps create conflict, and conflict leads to increased distrust between the parties. Thus, we have a vicious circle of distrust-conflict-increased distrust-increased conflict.

Although *trust* has emerged as a widely used and important concept in interpersonal relations, there is some question about how to define it. A number of investigators (Rotter, 1971) refer to trust as the expectancy that the word, promise, or verbal or written statement of another can be relied on. Put simply, this means that others will do what they say they will do. Pruitt (1965) adds another dimension to the definition, viewing trust as the expectancy that others will act in a helpful rather than hurtful manner.

Research (Pelton, 1974; Schlenker, Helm, & Tedeschi, 1973; Swinth, 1976; Zand, 1972) using the prisoner's dilemma and other similar situations suggests that for trust to develop, one person has to let down his or her guard and become vulnerable to see whether the other person abuses that vulnerability. Many such tests are necessary before a trusting relationship can be established.

There are three factors that influence the development of trust. One is the individuals' *personalities*. Ainsworth (1979) suggests that people develop the tendency to trust or distrust others during infancy and early childhood; infants who were brought up in a secure environment in which they could rely on consistent and appropriate behavior from their parents (especially the mother), were most likely to develop a readiness to trust. Scales such as the Philosophies of Human Nature Scale (Wrightsman, 1964) and the Interpersonal Trust Scale (Rotter, 1971) have been developed to distinguish between people who have a tendency to trust others and those who tend to distrust. A second influence on trust is the presence of *environmental cues* indicating the probabilities of harmful consequences. These cues include the perception that the opponent has much to gain by betrayal, and knowledge that the other has acted in a self-serving way in the past. A study illustrates this effect (McGillicuddy, Pruitt, & Syna, 1984). Subjects observed a negotiation in which one person was conciliatory (made many concessions), cooperative (matched the opponent's concessions), or self-serving (made few concessions). They saw the self-serving negotiator as strong and unfair and when they later negotiated with that person, they made few concessions and rarely

Infants raised in a secure environment in which they can rely on consistent and appropriate care from their parents are most likely to develop a trusting approach to their world. An unstable or unpredictable environment may inhibit the development of trust in infants. (© *MCMLXXX Peter Menzel*)

reached an agreement. The final characteristic influencing the development of trust is the *individual's motivation for positive outcomes.* If one person has little at stake and does not care about the outcomes, it is relatively easy for him or her to risk trusting the other person. However, if the stakes are high, as they were in the hostage crisis, trust is more difficult to develop.

Although trust is difficult to develop and a series of positive encounters are often required to develop a trusting relationship, Webb and Worchel (1986) report that it "may take only one betrayal to establish distrust." Further, "once aroused, distrust is extremely resistive to change." Distrust is difficult to change because it leads to the perception that the other person is a threat, and that perception leads to greater distrust. Once an individual has committed one betrayal, it is difficult for him or her to "make up" with another person, because the wronged individual may believe that the betrayal will recur in the future.

We have presented distrust as a rather terminal state; that is, once it occurs it will remain. This is certainly true in many cases. However, the tide of distrust can be reversed. For this to happen, the wrongdoer must confess the betrayal and convince the wronged person that he or she is remorseful. Further, if the wrongdoer has gained from the betrayal, he or she must attempt to make restitution. There has been little experimental research to test these hypotheses. However, it is interesting that some of the most popular presidents (George Washington, Abraham Lincoln, Harry Truman) in U.S. history were involved in situations in which they made public apologies for events and accepted personal blame. Truman, in fact, had a plaque on his desk that read "The buck stops here." On the other hand, a number of presidents who lost popularity while in office were involved in questionable situations where they failed to take responsibility or show remorse. For example, Lyndon Johnson failed to admit that his judgment on the Vietnam War may have been in error. Richard Nixon steadfastly refused to admit wrongdoing in the Watergate affair.

COMMUNICATION

As the hijacking unfolded, comments from the White House suggested that the United States would not negotiate or make concessions to the terrorists. The message was that "we will not talk to you until you release the hostages." This stand soon gave way to the desire to talk with the terrorists and determine who they were and what they wanted. The terrorists worked feverishly to keep the lines of communication open; they invited reporters to the airplane, they held news conferences, and they got their allies to communicate with the United States. Toward the end of the crisis, the level of communication increased among all parties as they tried to work out the complicated details for the hostage release.

Whether we talk about couples in conflict or countries in conflict, we constantly hear that it is important to keep the lines of communication open. Communication is an important key to resolving conflict. Yet, if we study the progress of conflict, we often find that it follows the course of the hostage crisis. The first response of parties in conflict is "I'm not going to talk to you." This response has been referred to as *autistic hostility*; people in conflict tend to withdraw and avoid interaction (Newcomb, 1947).

To communicate or not to communicate creates an interesting dilemma for the parties (McClintock, Stech, & Keil, 1983). On the one hand, neither side wants to give the other information about its strengths, weaknesses, and desires that may be used against it. On the other hand,

A dilemma that often faces people in conflict is that while communication is often necessary to resolve conflict, one does not want to give an opponent an advantage by disclosing too much information. *(Philippot/Sygma)*

communication is vital to ascertain the issues and develop solutions to the problem. In addition to this dilemma, there is concern about the type of information to communicate. A party could gain an advantage by misrepresenting its position or concealing information. However, this advantage could be disastrous if the other side believed it was being manipulated or acted on false information. For example, Berri could have gained an advantage if he could have made Reagan believe that the hostages would be killed unless rapid progress was made. On the other hand, if President Reagan believed this, he might have ordered an all-out attack, figuring that he was unlikely to get the hostages back alive. In fact, one U.S. official suggested military action because he felt that "we probably are not going to get all these people back in any event" (*Time,* July 8, 1985, p. 17).

These points should help us to better understand the effect of communication on conflict. Overall, the results of many studies show that communication increases the chances for a positive resolution of conflict. But people in conflict often choose not to communicate, and they,

Table 9–7
Mean joint payoffs (Acme plus Bolt) per trial in modified trucking game

	No threat	Unilateral threat	Bilateral threat
Compulsory communication	6.09	− 5.14	−41.73
Permissive communication	8.54	−34.58	−41.32
No communication	10.41	−22.13	−47.44

Note: Deutsch and Krauss (1962) replayed the trucking game with three types of communication conditions: a no-communication condition in which the subjects were not given the opportunity to communicate; a permissive-communication condition in which the subjects could communicate if they wished; and a compulsory-communication condition in which the subjects were told that they must communicate. Forced communication had the most dramatic effect in the unilateral condition.
Source: From "Studies of Interpersonal Bargaining," by M. Deutsch and R. M. Krauss, in *Journal of Conflict Resolution, 6,* 1962, pp. 52–76. Reprinted by permission.

therefore, must be encouraged or forced to engage in communication (Deutsch & Krauss, 1962, see Table 9-7). Finally, the content and timing of communication are important. For example, Caldwell (1976) found that communications between groups of subjects in a prisoner's dilemma situation increased cooperation when the communications contained information about sanctions that would be applied to subjects who did not cooperate. In addition, it has been found (Stech & McClintock, 1981) that communication later in the conflict is more likely to have a positive effect than communication early in the conflict. Late communication may focus attention on cooperative aspects of the relationship and ways to reduce conflict while early communication often focuses on the conflict and on threats.

Taken together, the results suggest that communication is not a natural event in conflict; it must be encouraged and nurtured. Further, people must be taught constructive ways to communicate. Communicating in the "wrong" ways can increase distrust and conflict.

RESOLVING CONFLICT

By this time, we may have thoroughly depressed the reader; you may be thinking that conflict is an affliction for which there is no cure. A glance at the daily newspaper will reinforce this gloomy picture, as it seems that the world abounds in conflict. It is, indeed, true that we are confronted by a great deal of competition and conflict in our lives. But we do learn to resolve our disagreements, and often these resolutions lead to progress and deeper understanding. The crisis over Flight 847 was resolved and Shi'ite prisoners were released by Israel (although our relief is only partial given the brutal murder of the innocent navy diver).

While the many incidents of conflict weigh heavily on us, their existence poses a very real challenge for social scientists: to identify constructive ways to resolve conflict. It is important that conflict be resolved in just and fair ways; resolutions that are viewed as unjust by either side do not result in lasting or stable settlements. In a sense, unjust resolutions perpetuate conflict. Let us now examine some of the factors that influence the resolution of conflict. This discussion should serve to demonstrate how far we have come in developing ways to resolve conflict *and* how far we have yet to go to find constructive ways to settle crises such as the hostage situation.

Correctly Perceiving the Conflict   The immediate reaction by both the terrorists and the United States and Israel was for each to perceive the other as a threat and a competitor. The initial view was that the sides had nothing in common and that one side's gains would be the other's losses. However, when the situation was examined more closely, common ground was found.

It is not unusual for people to perceive their conflicts as pure competition (zero-sum), when in fact the parties share common goals but disagree about the means of achieving these goals. Filley (1975) suggests that attempts to resolve conflict should begin by the parties listing their specific goals; they should refrain from taking positions on how these goals will be met. After specifying their goals, the parties should then discuss methods by which the goals can be achieved. This approach turns the conflict into an *integrative problem-solving* situation rather than a competition. Filley reports that this method leads to a quicker, more lasting resolution to interpersonal conflict than methods that rely on negotiation or compromise.

Knudson, Sommers, and Golding (1980) also found that conflict resolution is enhanced when parties share their perceptions about the situation. These investigators videotaped married couples while they discussed a conflict. Later, each member of the couple was shown the tape and asked to give his or her perceptions of the conflict at different stages. The results indicated that those couples who shared similar perceptions of the conflict tended to engage in constructive problem solving to resolve the conflict. However, when the couple did not share the same perception of the conflict, they tended to resort to avoidance and other tactics that inhibited conflict resolution.

The bottom line here is that conflict resolution can be enhanced if people carefully examine the conflict and clearly identify the nature of the conflict. This step not only helps them develop a plan for reducing their disagreements, but it also encourages communication.

Reducing Conflict by Reducing Threat   Earlier in this chapter, we examined the destructive effects of threat on conflict resolution; we added a depressing note to this discussion by pointing out that threat is often resorted to because it is easy to use. Further, threat not only escalates conflict, but conflict often motivates the use of threat. Osgood (1962) recognized this and pointed out that negotiations in the cold war between the United States and Russia were proceeding on a path directly contrary to conflict resolution. Each side was amassing threat potential, and the huge increase in weapons was making the possibility of accidental war more likely. Osgood suggested a way out of this spiraling increase in conflict. He called his plan the *graduated reciprocation in tension reduction* (GRIT) policy. The first phase, which is aimed at enlisting public support, involves having one party publicly announce that it intends to reduce tension and having that side clearly state the unilateral initiatives that it plans to take to do so. That party should also invite the other party to reciprocate with its own initiatives. The second phase is aimed at establishing the initiator's credibility and authenticity. During this phase, the initiator must carry out the announced tension-reducing moves in a way that is unambiguous and open to verification. These steps must be taken even in the absence of reciprocation. The final points of the GRIT strategy relate to the need to have the initiator retain enough power to avoid being exploited by the other party. These steps specify that the initiatives should be risky and create a vulnerability in the initiator; yet they should not be so drastic that the initiator loses the ability to protect itself or to retaliate if the opponent responds aggressively.

The idea behind GRIT is that moves by one nation or person to reduce threat capabilities would be met with similar reductions by others (Lindskold, 1986). The aim of the GRIT strategy is to reduce the threat potential in conflict situations, so that the parties will communicate and work toward resolution of their differences.

Overall, the research suggests that GRIT does work; that is, unilateral reductions of threat are often responded to with cooperative efforts on the part of an opponent. Research has found this effect even when the competition is very keen and has lasted for some time (Walters & Lindskold, 1982). Other research has found that GRIT is most likely to be successful when the opponent has equal or less power than the initiator (Lindskold & Aronoff, 1980). High-power people are often slow to give up their advantage. This effect was seen in the hijacking crisis. After almost a week of the standoff, Israel released thirty-one Shi'ite prisoners.

There was hope that the hijackers would respond by releasing a number of the hostages. But this attempt at reducing the level of conflict did not have the immediate results that many had hoped for since after a time, only the hostage with the serious heart condition was freed. Looking at the GRIT formula, we can see two possible reasons why this effort was not successful. First, the hijackers felt that they had the greatest power in the conflict; with the hostages hidden, neither the United States nor Israel could do much except negotiate. Second, Israel went to great lengths to convince the world that the release of the Shi'ites had nothing to do with the present conflict, that it had been planned well in advance. A clear statement of Israel's intentions and an invitation to the hijackers to reciprocate were not made. Hence, reducing threat can initiate conflict reduction, but the way in which threat reduction is carried out is important to consider.

Negotiation and Bargaining   The hostage crisis on TWA Flight 847 offers an opportunity to watch the process of conflict resolution. Each side began by stating its demands, and then each negotiated to get as many demands met as possible. The process involved *overt bargaining* in which (1) the parties in conflict have divergent interests, (2) some form of communication is possible, and (3) the parties can make provisional offers or concessions (Chertkoff & Esser, 1976). In our everyday lives, we often bargain to resolve conflicts. Anyone who has bought an automobile or a home knows that lengthy bargaining is often necessary to settle on a price. Further, anyone who has been in these situations quickly learns that some strategies are more successful than others for achieving a favorable resolution. Let us examine some of the strategies that affect the outcome of bargaining.

Initial position. The hijackers quickly made their demands known after the plane finally settled on the runway in Beirut; they wanted Israel to release all of the Shi'ite prisoners before a single hostage was freed. Their position seems rather extreme; a more reasonable position would have been the swap of one hostage for a set number of Shi'ites. But their extreme demands seem to have worked in that all prisoners were released without jeopardizing the hijackers' safety. Research supports the wisdom of taking an extreme initial position in obtaining a favorable outcome.

In one study (Chertkoff & Conley, 1967), subjects believed that they were either buying or selling an automobile. The subjects could send messages back and forth and were to signal when they had agreed on a price. Actually, the experimenter intercepted the messages that were sent and supplied messages of his own. The first message that the subjects

If you are interested in purchasing an automobile, research suggests that it is to your advantage to begin with a rather extreme position and make only moderate concessions in a tit-for-tat manner. Taking a very extreme initial position may lead the other party to break off negotiations. And making unmatched or too-large concessions will invite the other party to take advantage of you. (© *Burk Uzzle 1984/Woodfin Camp & Associates*)

received was either moderately or highly discrepant from the price they wished to get (or pay) for the automobile. When the final price that the subject agreed to receive (or pay) for the automobile was examined, it was found that the subjects were willing to accept less or to pay more for the automobile when the experimenter's initial bid was highly discrepant (Table 9–8). This suggests that from the individual bargainer's point of view, it is better to begin by making highly discrepant offers or very strong demands.

Taking an extreme initial position works because it causes the opponent to lower his or her expectations about the interaction. Seeing the extreme position, the opponent begins to think, "I'll be lucky if I can get anything out of this situation." The effect of the hijackers' initial position on U.S. officials could be seen when those officials stated that they would be fortunate to get any of the hostages out alive. However, before you decide to guide your life by this strategy of a tough initial stand, we must add one word of caution; if the initial stand is *too* extreme, the other person may either break off negotiations or take extreme actions. Again,

Table 9–8
Mean final price for automobile

	Subject's role	
Experimenter's initial offer	*Buyer*	*Seller*
Extreme	**$1,302.60**	**$1,221.01**
Moderate	**$1,189.13**	**$1,368.78**

Note: When the subject was the buyer, he ended up paying the highest price when the experimenter's initial offer was extreme. When the subject was the seller, he received the lowest price when the experimenter's offer was extremely low.

in the hijacking situation, some officials felt the crisis was hopeless and they urged immediate military action. Hence, the hijackers' demands almost destroyed the bargaining process before it began.

The Pattern of Concessions   As we have seen, bargaining is a give-and-take process; each side states its demands and then the process of compromise begins. However, within the bargaining framework, each side can structure its responses in many ways. At the extremes, a person can decide to be competitive all the time and never make concessions or to be cooperative regardless of the opponent's actions and consistently make large concessions. A middle ground might be to match the opponent's responses in a *tit-for-tat* manner; cooperation begets cooperation and competition begets competition.

Placing yourself in the position of a bargainer, your interests should include (1) reaching an agreement, and (2) having that agreement be most beneficial to you. In other words, you want to get as much as possible out of the resolution. Given these desires, the research indicates that you should make small rather than large concessions (Komorita & Brenner, 1968). Second, you are best advised to use a tit-for-tat strategy rather than being unconditionally cooperative or unconditionally competitive (Shure et al., 1965). This tit-for-tat strategy not only develops a reward/punishment contingency, but also affects the attributions your opponent may make about you. Subjects who observed a bargaining session rated an opponent who followed a matching strategy as stronger than one who adopted a soft cooperation strategy and fairer than one who took a tough competitive stance (McGillicuddy et al., 1984). Hence, if you always cooperate, your opponent may perceive you as weak (Swingle, 1970) or think you are attempting to manipulate him or her. In bargaining "nice guys (women, groups) do finish last" and get exploited.

On the other hand, if you make no concessions and are always competitive, your opponent may break off negotiations or become consistently competitive to save face. One additional piece of advice is necessary here. Research examining people's responses in social traps found that cooperation was more likely when cooperative behavior was rewarded than when competitive behavior was punished (Komorita & Barth, 1985). This finding suggests that it is especially important for you to match (i.e., reward) the cooperative behavior of your opponent.

Using Time as an Ally   Almost as soon as the plane landed for the final time in Beirut, the terrorists attempted to put time pressures on the United States and Israel; they threatened to blow up the plane with the hostages if the Shi'ite prisoners were not released immediately. When Nabih Berri took over, he threatened to "wash his hands" of the situation and turn the hostages back to the original hijackers if progress on the demands was not quickly forthcoming. Throughout the crisis, President Reagan felt the pressures of time. These events lead us to investigate the effects of time on the bargaining process.

Kelley (1966) stated that bargaining tends to fill up the available time. Procrastination has utility, as each party waits for the other party to make additional concessions. Looking at another side of this issue, numerous studies (Hamner, 1974; Pruitt & Johnson, 1970; Yukl, 1974) have found that time pressures lead to faster concessions from negotiating parties. Taken together, these positions suggest that it is to the advantage of one party to convince the other party that it can "wait forever" for the other party to make concessions.

Attempts to use time pressures, however, can backfire; time pressures may give rise to the use of threat and coercion. Thus, the party that feels that time is about to run out may resort to force. In fact, some of Reagan's advisers urged him to use force to end the crisis because they feared that time *was* running out. In addition, while time pressures may facilitate a quick resolution to conflict, these pressures inhibit communication, increase feelings of competitiveness, and often result in poor joint outcomes (Carnevale, Sherer, & Pruitt, 1979; Yukl, Malone, Hayslip, & Pamin, 1978). Thus, time can be a valuable weapon, but it can also work against cooperation and problem-solving approaches to conflict resolution.

DEPERSONALIZING CONFLICT: THE USE OF NORMS

As the crisis continued, focus shifted away from the issues and toward the men involved in the conflict. The conflict began to be viewed as a

Concern that "time was running out" led police to storm the Howard Johnson Motor Lodge in New Orleans in order to free hostages. Time pressures may be used to gain concessions, but this strategy may also backfire. *(Mitchel L. Osborne/Gamma)*

test of who (Berri or Reagan) was the strongest bargainer, and interest focused on how the crisis' outcome would affect these men's standings in the eyes of their supporters. In other words, the conflict quickly became personalized, which added additional roadblocks to a resolution of the situation.

One way to remove this type of impediment in conflict resolution is to resort to norms to resolve differences. *Norms* (see Chapter Eleven) are rules that determine how behavior should legitimately progress. They are impersonal in that they are concerned with the situation rather than the personalities of people in conflict. Norms center on what is a just and fair solution rather than who is stronger or more capable. Because this is the case, norms are often used to resolve conflict—especially when both parties can use threats to the same degree and when concern with face saving is high (Thibaut, 1968).

Some norms focus on the procedure of conflict resolution. For example, the *norm of reciprocity* suggests that behavior should be reciprocated in kind. In addition, *norms of distribution* are of vital importance in conflict resolution. These norms dictate a solution by identifying how resources should be divided between the parties.

One such norm focuses on the *needs* of the two parties. Simply put, this norm states that the more need a person has, the more he or she should receive. This norm would suggest that if two people work on the same job, the person who has the greatest need should receive the most payment.

A second norm is based on *equality*. According to this norm, resources should be divided equally among the people involved in a social relationship. This is a relatively simple norm to apply because it involves looking only at the available resources and the number of people involved. If two people receive $1,000 for completing a job, each should receive $500 regardless of how much work each person did. This type of division tends to reduce resource and power differences between people.

The third and most studied norm is *equity*. According to this position, the amount people receive from a relationship should be determined by how much they put into it. Equity theorists (Adams, 1963, 1965; Walster, Berscheid, & Walster, 1978) argue that people are motivated both to maximize their gains *and* achieve equity in their relationships. A relationship is equitable when a person scrutinizing that relationship can conclude:

$$\frac{(\text{Outcomes}_A - \text{Inputs}_A)}{\text{Inputs}_A} = \frac{(\text{Outcomes}_B - \text{Inputs}_B)}{\text{Inputs}_B}$$

For example, suppose that you work eight hours painting a fence and your friend works two hours. Together you receive one hundred dollars for the job. The relationship will be equitable if you receive eighty dollars (80 percent of the pay for 80 percent of the work) and your friend receives twenty dollars (20 percent of the pay for 20 percent of the work). As can be seen, resolving conflict on the basis of equity can perpetuate differences in power and resources between people.

Norms do have strong influences on people's behavior. For example, it has been shown that people who feel they are receiving more for a job than is equitable experience uneasiness and will often increase the amount of work to establish equity (Austin & Walster, 1974; Adams, 1965). Even more strongly, people become uncomfortable and angry when they receive less than they deserve from a relationship. When people cannot restore actual equity by changing their work or payoffs, they attempt to restore *psychological equity* by changing their perceptions of the relationship (Austin & Hatfield, 1980).

However, the availability of norms does not ensure a smooth resolution of conflict. Disagreement can arise over which norm is most appropriate to use in the situation (Austin, 1986). For example, in some employment settings, males have argued that they should receive more pay than females because they must support families (norm of need). Females have countered by pointing out that they must also support families and that fairness dictates equal pay for equal work (equity). Another disagreement can arise over the value of inputs or outputs even if there is agreement about the norm to be used in distributing rewards. For example, assume that you are an inventor who needs money to develop your invention. Your friend gives you $10,000 so that you can continue your work. Your invention is a tremendous success and you make $1 million. How do you compare your time, effort, and skills with your friend's money to arrive at an equitable distribution of the profits? Evaluations of input may be considered in light of the alternatives the parties had to the present relationship. In other words, your friend might argue that the $10,000 represented a greater input if he or she had passed up another attractive investment to give you that money, as opposed to the situation in which your friend had no other opportunity for investment. Another way to evaluate inputs and outcomes is to compare with relevant others. Research (Major, McFarlin, & Gagnon, 1984) has found that men and women compare their outcomes from work with others of the same sex to determine what is fair pay.

Equity and equality norms are used to resolve conflicts. Equality norms are most likely to be used in cohesive groups where a positive socioemotional climate exists, while equity norms will be most salient in noncohesive groups. Deutsch (1975) argues that equity norms will be used in groups whose greatest concern is productivity, while equality norms will be used when the main concern is developing positive social relations.

As you can see, there are many advantages to using norms to resolve conflict; the norms depersonalize the conflict and make it easier for the parties to make concessions without losing face. However, there are numerous conditions that determine which norm will be used and how the parties will perceive inputs and outcomes. Norms, therefore, cannot always offer a "yellow brick road" to conflict resolution.

THE IMPORTANCE OF PROCEDURE

In the last section, we focused on norms dictating the outcome from conflict. Yet outcome is not the only point to consider in conflict; the

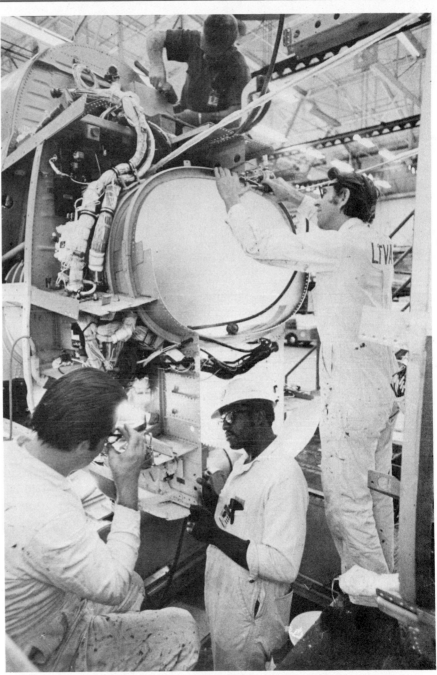

It has been suggested that groups whose greatest concern is productivity tend to use equity norms to resolve conflict. Equality norms, on the other hand, are used in groups whose major concern is social relationships. *(Cary Wolinsky/Stock, Boston)*

procedure used to arrive at the outcome is also very important. For example, Israel had planned to release the Shi'ite prisoners before the hijacking. Yet, when the hijackers demanded the prisoner release Israel refused, saying that the prisoners would not be released under the conditions established by the hijacking.

Research in the area of *procedural justice* has examined how the procedure used to resolve conflict affects the parties' perceptions of fairness of the outcomes. Much of the research focuses on procedures used in courts of law (Thibaut & Walker, 1975, 1978). In the *adversary system,* each party has its own lawyers that present its side in front of a judge. This is the system that is most frequently practiced in U.S. courts. On the other hand, there is the *nonadversary system,* where a single representative appointed by the court gathers information from both sides and presents findings to the court. This system is often used in British and French courts of law.

In general, the studies suggest that people prefer the adversary procedure and that decisions reached using this procedure are perceived as more fair, satisfying, and unbiased than decisions arrived at using the nonadversary system (Lind, Kutz, Musante, Walker, & Thibaut, 1980). However, there is evidence that preference for the adversary procedure occurs only in Western cultures where autonomy and competitiveness are stressed; Chinese students in Hong Kong (a culture stressing harmony and group solidarity) did not prefer the adversary procedure (Leung & Lind, 1986). Careful examinations of the procedures indicate that the important aspect of the adversarial system is that it allows participants to have *voice* (Folger & Greenberg, 1985); that is, people feel that their opinions are heard. Active participation generally makes people feel that both the procedure and the outcome are fair. More recently, it has been found that the addition of an appeals process further enhances the perceptions of fairness and satisfaction (Sheppard, 1985). Whether or not the appeals procedure is used, its existence is comforting to the participants.

Before concluding this discussion, we must add an important exception. Because participation may raise people's hopes that a certain decision will be reached, they will be especially disappointed when this does not occur. This negative effect of participation is most likely to occur when the individual receives a negative decision and learns that others also view it as unfair.

As you can see, both the outcome and the procedure used to reach the outcome are important in determining people's satisfaction and the ultimate success of conflict resolution.

WITH A LITTLE HELP FROM FRIENDS: COALITION FORMATION

When it became clear that he had a real crisis on his hands, President Reagan began to recruit support from others to help him settle the conflict. Although the hostages were all United States citizens, Reagan attempted to show leaders from other countries how their interests were involved in this crisis. Israel was quickly involved, but Reagan also tried to get help from France, Great Britain, Egypt, and Switzerland. The development of coalitions to deal with conflict has become a common response to international crises; when the Rome and Vienna airports were bombed by terrorists in December 1985, Reagan again sought the support of allies to put sanctions on Libya. The balance of world power rests on an entangled configuration of coalitions including the North Atlantic Treaty Organization countries (NATO), the Soviet Bloc countries, and nonaligned countries. At a more individual level, people successfully use coalitions to help them deal with stress and personal conflict (Shinn, Rosario, Morch, & Chestnut, 1984).

A *coalition* has been defined as "two or more individuals who formally agree to cooperate in order to obtain some mutually desired outcome" (Urruti & Miller, 1984, p. 825). Coalitions seem like such an obvious way to resolve conflicts that we are tempted to question why they are not always used. The answer is that the formation of coalitions is a complex process that can lead to additional conflict and negotiation.

People enter coalitions to beat their adversary. However, once a coalition is formed, the parties are quickly faced with the additional problem of how to divide payoffs should they win. For example, a coalition can divide payoffs based on how much each party contributes to the coalition (*equity*); the party who controls the most receives the most. On the other hand, it can be argued that the payoffs should be divided equally because the coalition would not be successful if *any* of the participants backed out. This is what makes it difficult to predict what coalitions will form and how these coalitions will function. To understand this process, let us examine one popular theory of coalition formation. The *bargaining theory of coalitions* emphasizes the negotiation process that occurs within coalitions (Komorita & Esser, 1977; Komorita & Kravitz, 1983). The theory proposes that each member of a coalition has a maximum expected outcome, a minimum expected outcome, and a *most probable expected outcome*. For the high-power person in a coalition, the maximum expected outcome is equity (payoffs based on contribution) and the minimum expected outcome is equality (a fifty-fifty split of the rewards). For the low-power person, the maximum expected outcome is equality and the

minimum expected outcome is equity. The most probable expected outcome for both parties is the average of equity and equality. Individuals
enter into coalitions because of their desire to establish relationships that
will yield the highest possible outcome. Continuing this reasoning, the
bargaining theory of coalitions makes the additional prediction that coalitions will often be unstable because those who are excluded from a
coalition will entice defectors by offering them higher outcomes than
they are getting from the present coalition.

Because of these difficulties with negotiation, coalitions generally
form with the smallest number of parties needed to beat the adversary
(Gamson, 1961, 1964). People join coalitions that they feel will give them
maximum payoff. The power of any party in a coalition is based on the
resources that party controls, the value (or expected profit) of alternative
coalitions, *and* the number of available alternative coalitions that party
could enter (Komorita & Miller, 1986). In other words, you can be successful in extracting promises of reward from a coalition if you have
many resources to add to that coalition *and* if there are a number of other
coalitions you could enter into. Finally, coalitions are often unstable
because there is the constant temptation to defect to other coalitions that
may promise greater rewards.

Thus, rather than offering simple solutions to conflict resolution, coalitions may create new dilemmas. In addition, the inclusion of outside
parties that may not be directly involved in the initial conflict often
widens the conflict. Coalitions may, therefore, resolve conflict, or they
may encourage the conflict spiral.

SOME SPECIAL CONSIDERATIONS OF INTERGROUP CONFLICT

Thus far we have been examining conflict in a rather general way. Our
discussion could apply to conflict between individuals, between an individual and a group, or between groups. In many situations, however,
conflict results because we belong to groups. The resolution of this form
of conflict has some distinct characteristics (Worchel & Austin, 1986). For
example, the hostages were taken because they belonged to a group
(United States citizens) and not because the hijackers had anything
against the individuals. President Reagan and Nabih Berri were drawn
into negotiating a resolution because of the groups to which they belonged, and *not* because they had any personal relationship. Hence,
much of our behavior and much of what we observe is based on group
membership. Tajfel (1979) makes this point when he states, "Whenever
individuals belonging to one group interact collectively or individually

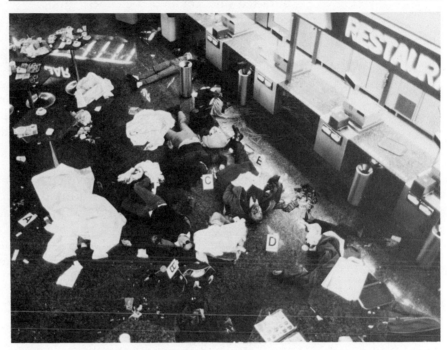

People are often drawn into conflicts because of the groups to which they belong. Arab terrorists killed a number of people in the Rome airport on December 27, 1985, because they believed the passengers were waiting to board an Israeli airliner. *(Gianni Giansanti/Sygma)*

with another group or its members, *in terms of their group identification,* we have an instance of intergroup behavior."

A great deal of research has focused on intergroup conflict and conflict resolution.

The Basis for Intergroup Conflict

Competition. One of the earliest studies in this area examined the hypothesis that competition leads to intergroup hostility. Carolyn and Muzafer Sherif and their colleagues (Sherif, Harvey, White, Hood, & Sherif, 1961) conducted a number of studies at boys' summer camps in Connecticut, New York, and Oklahoma. The same basic design was employed in all of the studies. The subjects at each camp were randomly divided into two groups. The subjects were given a week to become attracted and committed to their group. They lived in bunkhouses, cooked their own meals, cleaned up their own campsites, and organized so that group members could play games with each other. The groups developed their own leadership structures, and some groups coined such names as Pythons, Eagles, or Red Devils for themselves.

Following this period of group formation, the experimenters brought the two groups together. Each time the groups met it was to compete for some prize—for example, they met on the sports field to play touch football, tug-of-war, and baseball against each other for attractive prizes. And they competed to see who could put on the best skit, have the cleanest cabin, or pitch a tent faster.

The effects of introducing competition between the groups were striking. The serene camp setting was turned into a miniature battleground as the two groups began to hurl insults and names at each other. Such terms as *pigs, dirty bums, jerks,* and several other objectionable words were used to describe the rival team; and posters were made showing the other team being bombed or trampled. Guerrilla tactics were employed; one group raided and vandalized the other group's bunkhouse. There were also incidents of open warfare as food fights erupted between the two groups; open scuffles occurred between rival groups on the camp field; and there were full-blown artillery attacks in which apples were used as ammunition.

The Sherif studies were followed by the work of Blake and Mouton (1961, 1962, 1986). These investigators examined intergroup relations in business settings (e.g., labor-management) and found that competition resulted in intergroup hostility. They reported that "a 'win' orientation between two groups has a spontaneous, mobilizing effect with a number of predictable consequences."

Minimal intergroup situation. While we know that intergroup competition leads to a dislike of the out-group and a preference for the in-group, we can ask whether or not competition is necessary for the development of intergroup hostility. That is, must competition exist before intergroup hostility will result? The answer to this question is that competition is not necessary. Research shows that simply placing people in groups leads to in-group favoritism and out-group discrimination.

This point has been clearly demonstrated by Tajfel and his colleagues (Tajfel, 1970, 1972; Tajfel, Flament, Billig, & Bundy, 1971). In these experiments, the investigators assigned schoolboys to groups based on the performance on trivial tasks. For example, in one study, subjects believed that they had been assigned to a particular group based on their judgment of two abstract paintings. Following their assignment to the groups, the subjects were asked to divide up a sum of money between the two groups. The results indicated that more money was given to the in-group than to the out-group. In addition to this bias in favor of the in-group, the results indicated that when subjects had the choice of giving money either to increase in-group profit or to maximize the difference in payoff between in-group and out-group, they chose the last division. They made this choice even when it lowered the in-group's payoff. Thus, the boys seemed to be competing rather than following the strategy of maximum gain for the in-group. The in-group bias that results from simply being assigned to groups has been referred to as the *minimal intergroup situation* (Brewer, 1979; Tajfel & Turner, 1986).

Why does this effect occur? An explanation that has received support focuses on the social comparison process (see Chapter Three). According to this theory, people define themselves and develop self-esteem by comparing themselves to others in their own group (Lemyre & Smith, 1985; Turner, 1981). Because of this phenomenon, people want to enhance the status of their own group in comparison to other groups. The effect here is to increase the differences between in-group and out-group and to perceive the in-group in a favorable light. This explanation for the minimal intergroup situation effect has received support in studies (Turner & Brown, 1978) showing greater out-group discrimination when group assignment is based on important or personally relevant dimensions than when the assignment is based on irrelevant dimensions.

In addition to initiating discrimination, the formation of groups affects perceptions of both the in- and out-group (see Chapter Eleven). In general, the in-group is perceived as being good and the members are seen as possessing diverse qualities. On the other hand, the out-group is viewed in a negative light and its members are seen as all being similar. These data help us to better understand why the hijacking developed into such a long and difficult conflict. The seeds of conflict were evident with the clear distinctions drawn between the Arabs and United States citizens; boundaries existed along national, political, cultural, and religious lines. Thus, the hijacking became one more fuse to ignite a wide-scale conflict that still burns today.

THE RESOLUTION OF INTERGROUP CONFLICT

Our world is filled with examples of intergroup conflict. American warships are cruising the coast of Libya following a series of terrorist activities. Fighting rages in the Middle East, in Afghanistan, and in Central America. Racial conflict in South Africa threatens to erupt into revolution. Bickering between Canadians of British and French backgrounds surfaces periodically. The United States is faced with issues of racial

Examples of intergroup conflict and violence can be found in almost every part of the world. In Afghanistan, Moslems are fighting government and Russian troops, while in Northern Ireland, fighting continues between the Catholics and Protestants with British troops often caught in the middle. *(Left, © Jacques Charles/Stock, Boston; right, Cary Wolinsky/ Stock, Boston)*

conflict and sexism. Indeed, it has been found that conflict between individuals is easier to resolve than conflict between groups; one study (Allison & Messick, 1985) found that individuals do better at resolving social traps than groups. Despite these examples and problems, however, there are numerous other examples of the reduction or resolution of intergroup conflict. Moreover, the social science literature has been able to identify constructive ways of dealing with this type of conflict.

Contact   Some of the earliest attempts to reduce intergroup and interracial conflict focused on contact (Cook, 1985; Stephan, 1985). It was argued that contact between the groups would lessen conflict and tension.

The early results of this approach, however, were not consistently positive. Contact sometimes reduced conflict but in other situations, it actually increased conflict. In fact, there is some evidence (Brewer, 1986) that conflict is most likely to erupt between groups that are close together and therefore likely to have frequent contact.

A closer examination of these results identified the conditions under which contact was most likely to have positive effects. First, it was found that *equal status contact* was a key (Amir, 1969); that is, the situation under which the group members have contact must ensure that they have equal status or power. For example, in many attempts to integrate schools, whites who had superior previous schooling were placed in schools with blacks who had previously been forced into inferior schools. The students were then given tasks that the whites were better prepared to handle because of their past history. This contact emphasized the differences between blacks and whites and often increased the conflict. Second, the contact situation must *allow group members to interact on a personal basis* (Wilder, 1986). One of the tendencies in intergroup conflict is to deindividuate (see Chapter Eleven) or depersonalize out-group members; they are seen as different and as having different concerns. Thus, the contact situation must promote perceiving out-group members as individuals. Third, the contact situation must *encourage people to see the relationship between the group members with whom they have contact and their group* (Wilder, 1986). There is a tendency to perceive out-group members with whom we have positive interactions as "exceptions," people who are not like the others in their group. Here contact may facilitate the personal relationship but it will not reduce the intergroup conflict. Fourth, the contact must *encourage cooperation and interdependence.* We will examine this point in a later section.

Contact then can help to reduce intergroup conflict. However, attention must be given to the conditions under which the contact occurs so that it does not increase the conflict.

Helping   In Chapter Eight we discussed the research on helping and altruism. As you will recall, helping often promotes attraction and may be used to bring parties closer together. This might lead us to believe that conflict could be resolved if one group were to offer aid or help to the other. We can find examples of this approach in the international arena where foreign aid is used to enlist the support of other nations.

Yet we must be cautious in suggesting this approach as a means for reducing intergroup conflict. Since the conflict relationship is characterized by distrust, the offer to help by one group may be seen by the other group as manipulative and self-centered (Rosen, 1984). In addition, it has been argued that helping tends to emphasize differences between helper and recipient and the power differences between the two (Worchel, 1984). The result here may be to make boundaries more salient and enhance the tendency to categorize or stereotype people according to their group. Research has shown that helping enhances relations between groups that have already established positive inter-actions. However, the offer to help has a negative effect on the relation-ship between groups with a history of conflict and distrust.

Cooperation and Interdependence   One of the most productive means for reducing intergroup conflict involves cooperation. In the Sherif et al. (1961) camp studies discussed earlier in this chapter, a number of meas-ures were taken to reduce intergroup hostility. Adults at the camp lec-tured the groups on the necessity of coming together and being friends. This method did not succeed. Then the two groups were united to com-bat a common enemy—a group from another camp that had been invited to compete against the two warring groups. The two groups did com-bine and hostility was diminished while they competed against the new group, but after the "common enemy" withdrew, the intergroup hostility recurred. Further, this method merely serves to redirect and widen inter-group conflict and aggression.

The method that proved most effective in reducing intergroup hos-tility involved having the two warring groups work together toward a superordinate goal. A *superordinate goal* is one that is attractive to the members of two groups but cannot be achieved without cooperation between the groups. To test the hypothesis, a number of tasks were designed that required intergroup cooperation for success. For example, while the boys were on a camping trip, a truck that was to go for their food stalled. The only way to get it started was to push it some distance, and neither group could do this by itself. Thus, the two groups were forced to cooperate to get the food. After the two groups had cooperated on a number of tasks, there was a significant decrease in the hostility between them.

Aronson and his colleagues (Aronson, Bridgeman, & Geffner, 1978; Aronson, Stephan, Sikes, Blaney, & Snapp, 1978) developed a unique method to encourage cooperation between interracial groups in the classroom. The *jigsaw method* involves six-person groups of students who must learn a body of material. Each member of the group is given a part of the lesson that he or she must present to the other group members. Successful group performance is therefore dependent on each member mastering his or her part of the lesson. Under these circumstances, all the group members become motivated to help each other learn their parts of the lesson. When the groups were composed of people from dif-ferent racial or ethnic groups, Aronson found that the jigsaw method reduced ethnic stereotyping and increased attraction between members of the various ethnic groups.

Follow-up studies on cooperation (Worchel, Andreoli, & Folger, 1977) suggested that cooperation is effective if the groups succeed in their effort. However, failure in the cooperative effort may result in scapegoating (blaming the other group) and increased intergroup hostility.

Cooperation is a good method for reducing hostility for a number of reasons. First, it focuses the group members' attention away from their conflict and onto trying to solve the problem that confronts them. Earlier, we pointed out the value of transforming conflict into problem-solving efforts. Second, cooperation reduces the salience of the in-group/out-group distinction (Worchel, 1986). Groups that work together become more concerned with the task at hand and are less likely to categorize into in-group/out-group. In a sense, all the members are now one group with increased motivation to see others in a positive light because each person is dependent on all the others.

As you can see, reducing conflict between groups is no small task, which may explain why we are surrounded by examples of intergroup conflict. It also helps explain why the conflict over the hostage crisis was so difficult to resolve; the conditions that existed did not promote contact or cooperation between the parties. The hopeful sign, however, is that intergroup conflict *can* be resolved and we *can* identify the steps that are most likely to lead to this resolution.

THE OTHER SIDE OF THE COIN: THE VALUE OF CONFLICT

Throughout this chapter, and indeed throughout much of our lives, we view conflict as negative; we try to avoid conflict and when it occurs, we work to quickly reduce it. Clearly, conflict such as that leading to the hostage crisis is negative and can lead to negative consequences. Yet, there is another side: conflict can have positive influences on people, groups, and relationships.

Conflict often identifies problems and motivates people to work on these problems. The hostage crisis focused attention on the destructiveness of the Middle East situation and emphasized the need to find a solution for the problems there. It also identified problems in airport security around the world and resulted in cooperative efforts to improve that security. Conflict may bring people together who are otherwise separated and offer them a chance to exchange information. The intervention of Syria in helping to gain the release of the hostages was seen as a positive step. Tension between the United States and Syria had been high before the crisis, and President Assad's actions offered fleeting hope that cooperative efforts would be forthcoming in other areas of tension between the two nations. From a group's standpoint, conflict may be useful in identifying its boundaries and establishing an identification (Worchel, 1984). There are numerous cases in which groups use and even invite conflict as a way of solidifying membership and establishing an identity. In the hostage crisis, the Amal group became very prominent; the crisis resulted in a clear definition of its boundaries and its membership.

Sociologist George Simmel (1955) suggested two additional positive roles of conflict. First, conflict gives rise to social change. Open conflict between blacks and whites in the United States, for example, has led to numerous social changes that have afforded opportunities for more equality in our society. Simmel also pointed out that conflict between groups may result in a new unity and solidarity within each group: "One unites in order to fight." In the United States, the black power movement that has resulted in new solidarity among blacks was a direct result of racial conflict.

Deutsch (1973) sums up the positive roles of conflict.

> It [conflict] prevents stagnation; it stimulates interest and curiosity; it is the medium through which problems can be aired and solutions arrived at; it is the root of personal and social change. Conflict is often part of the process of testing and assessing oneself and, as such, may be highly enjoyable as one experiences the pleasure of the full and active use of one's capacities. In addition, conflict demarcates groups from one another and thus helps establish group and personal identities; external conflict often fosters internal cohesiveness. (p. 9)

SUMMARY

Interpersonal conflict can be described as tension between two or more social entities that arises from an incompatibility of actual or desired responses. Two major types of interpersonal conflict have been defined: *zero-sum* and *mixed-motive*. The zero-sum conflict is a pure competition situation in which one party's loss is exactly equal to the other party's gain. In the mixed-motive situation, the individual player is tempted to compete with the opponent to maximize personal gain and to cooperate with the opponent to maximize the joint payoff. The *prisoner's dilemma* and *social trap* are examples of the mixed-motive conflict. Once conflict begins, it has a tendency to spiral as people become entrapped; entrapment results because people realize that there are costs associated with reducing conflict as well as staying in it.

Threat is a common response to conflict. On the whole, research suggests that threat escalates rather than reduces conflict. People often remain in conflict because of their concern with saving face and appearing strong. Concern with *face saving* is especially prevalent when people's responses to conflict are public. The perception of others as competitive also feeds the *conflict spiral*; research suggests that some people tend to view most others as competitive while others may see more heterogeneity in the responses of others.

Distrust widens a conflict. It has been found that *trust* is difficult to develop and requires one party taking risks to see how the other party will respond. It only takes one betrayal for distrust to occur, and once people distrust each other, it is difficult to reestablish trust. While communication may help reduce conflict, people in conflict often do not want to communicate with each other. Communication must contain accurate information to facilitate conflict resolution, but information may be used by an opponent to gain an advantage in negotiations.

Conflict can be resolved more easily if people will clarify their perceptions of the situation. Further, work on the *GRIT* has shown that reducing threat potential will help reduce conflict.

Bargaining involves situations where individuals can communicate and exchange *concessions.* The research suggests that one party in a conflict will achieve the highest payoff if that party takes a very extreme first position and makes only small concessions during the bargaining process. Further, a party that continually responds in a cooperative manner will be taken advantage of by the opponent. Thus, unwavering cooperation does not necessarily beget cooperation. The best strategy is the *tit-for-tat* program that matches the behavior of the opponent. Placing time pressures on an opponent may force concessions, but it may also reduce communication and lead the opponent to resort to threats.

Norms can be used to resolve conflicts because they tend to depersonalize the situation and reduce the need to save face. Norms of *reciprocity* and *equity* have received the most attention in conflict-resolution research. In addition to *outcomes*, the *procedure* used to mediate conflict influences how people feel. Research has shown that procedures that allow for a great deal of individual participation are most effective in resolving conflict.

Coalitions that involve two or more parties getting together against an opponent may be used to influence conflict resolution. In general, coalitions are formed between parties that have barely enough resources to overcome the opponent. This grouping reduces the problems of deciding how the outcomes should be divided between the members of the coalition.

Intergroup conflict can result when people are assigned to groups; it is found even when the group assignment is done on a random basis and group members do not interact. Competition heightens the degree of conflict. Groups in conflict tend to view the out-group as bad and see themselves in a positive light. There is also a tendency to see more diversity in the in-group than in the out-group.

Contact between groups will reduce conflict if it places the groups on equal status, allows the group members to interact at a personal level, promotes the perception of a relationship between the individual and group, and encourages cooperation and interdependence. While helping may reduce conflict between groups that have a history of positive interaction, it may increase conflict between groups that lack trust and have previously competed. Intergroup cooperation that results in a successful outcome reduces intergroup conflict. Cooperation focuses attention on solutions rather than on the conflict and it reduces the salience of in-group/out-group boundaries.

While conflict can produce negative outcomes, it can also have positive effects. Conflict initiates social change, motivates creative solutions to problems, promotes individual and group identity, and initiates self-evaluation.

KEY WORDS

autistic hostility	minimal intergroup situation
coalition	mixed-motive conflict
competition	norm of reciprocity
conflict spiral	norms
distributive justice	overt bargaining
equality norm	prisoner's dilemma
equity theory	procedural justice
face saving	social trap
GRIT	threat
integrative problem solving	tit-for-tat
intergroup conflict	trust
interpersonal conflict	voice
jigsaw method	zero-sum conflict

SUGGESTED READINGS

Bacharach, S., & Lawler, E. (1981). *Bargaining*. San Francisco, Jossey-Bass.

Brockner, J., & Rubin, J. Z. (1985). *Entrapment in escalating conflicts*. New York: Springer-Verlag.

Caplow, T. (1968). *Two against one: Coalition in triads.* Englewood Cliffs, NJ: Prentice-Hall.

Deutsch, M. (1973). *The resolution of conflict.* New Haven, CT: Yale University Press.

Druckman, D. (Ed.), (1977). *Negotiations: Social perspectives.* Beverly Hills, CA: Sage Publications.

Kelly, H., & Thibaut, J. (1978). *Interpersonal relations: A theory of interdependence.* New York: John Wiley & Sons.

Rubin, J., & Brown, B. (1975). *The social psychology of bargaining and negotiations.* New York: Academic Press.

Turner, J., & Giles, H. (1981). *Intergroup behavior.* Chicago: University of Chicago Press.

Walster, E., Walster, G. W., & Berscheid, E. (1978). *Equity theory and research.* Boston: Allyn & Bacon.

Worchel, S., & Austin, W. (Eds.), (1986). *The psychology of intergroup relations.* Chicago: Nelson-Hall Publishers.

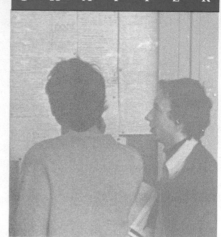

TEN

SOCIAL INFLUENCE

On July 1, 1975, nationally syndicated advice columnist Ann Landers published her "most difficult column." She told her readers, "The sad fact is that after thirty-six years of marriage Jules and I are being divorced." She went on to say that even though her marriage to Jules Lederer had been a wonderful one, "it didn't make it to the finish line." Most poignantly she wrote, "How did it happen that something so good for so long didn't last forever? The lady with all the answers does not know the answer to this one" (Howard, 1982).

Writing this column was personally difficult and professionally risky for Eppie Lederer, the woman behind the name Ann Landers. Eppie's column gave advice to people all over North America about personal problems. It had made her one of America's most influential leaders of opinion and arbiters of social behavior. She also had a wealth of information about free services available to people in need in every community in which her column appeared. Sometimes, even U.S. government officials came to her for information about human services. How would people react to the fact that the author of an advice column couldn't make her own marriage last? Eppie had complete faith that her readers would rally around and remain loyal—and she was right. Eppie Lederer —known to millions of people as Ann Landers—had had a strong following for twenty years and today, after more than thirty years, she is still going strong. She continues to serve as long-distance counselor to countless numbers of people. Who is Eppie Lederer and how has she become so influential?

Eppie was born Esther Pauline Friedman on July 4, 1918, in Sioux City, Iowa. A twin sister, Pauline Esther Friedman, was born seventeen minutes later; the identical twin sister was nicknamed Popo. Six months after Eppie became Ann Landers in 1955, Popo became Abigail Van Buren, author of the "Dear Abby" advice column. It was not unusual for the twins to do things together. They were brought up together in a well-to-do family in Sioux City, the daughters of Russian Jewish immigrants, and they graduated from Central High School together in 1936. They were married in a double wedding just before their twenty-first birthdays in 1939. Despite some very rough spots in their relationship—imagine the competition that must accompany being the two most widely known and syndicated newspaper advice columnists in the country—they are still doing things together. Abby announced in her column in early 1986 that both she and Ann would attend their fiftieth high school reunion in Sioux City, and they were there together in June.

Although they are remarkably similar, each woman has had her own life history and interests. Eppie's early interests were politics and public affairs, interests she has maintained to this day. Living in Wisconsin after World War II, she was elected a county chair for the Democratic party.

Ann Landers has become one of America's most influential leaders. Her advice column affects people's thinking about a variety of important issues, from proper decorum at weddings to premarital sex. *(UPI/ Bettmann Newsphotos)*

She became a close and lifelong friend of the late Hubert Humphrey, former senator from Minnesota and vice-president of the United States. Her energy and commitment were intense, but when she moved to Chicago in 1954 she found herself displaced from politics. The Chicago Democratic machine, under the control of Mayor Richard Daley and others, had little interest in a reformist woman newcomer: she was given the message that it would be dangerous to get involved.

Eppie needed to find something else. She took an interest in the Ann Landers advice column in the *Chicago Sun-Times* and contacted a friend at the paper asking if she could assist in answering the mail. When her friend told her that the woman who wrote the column had recently died, Eppie boldly suggested that she could become the next Ann Landers. Her friend said that that was impossible since she had no experience, but he agreed to let Eppie apply for the job. The job was to be given to the applicant who wrote the best answers—judged anonymously—to typical letters. The surprise winner turned out to be Eppie. She began writing the column immediately.

Ann Landers has had a great deal of influence for a number of reasons. First, simply by dealing with certain topics, she acknowledges that they are problems that deserve attention. In 1955, venereal disease and homosexuality were not discussed in newspapers (Howard, 1982). Now they are. Second, her advice about a range of personal matters such as premarital sex, handling troublesome neighbors, and who to invite to weddings helps set standards for social behavior. Further, because of her interest in politics, Ann Landers has given her fifty million or more readers advice about public affairs. For example, she once asked her readers to write their congressmen suggesting that they support funding for cancer research; that advice generated stacks of mail in Washington. As a result of her enormous clout, Ann Landers has frequently been listed by UPI as one of America's ten most influential women. When she visited Vietnam during the war, the commanding general William Westmoreland gave her the best VIP treatment; he fully understood that anything she said about the war in her column could have a staggering impact. Most of her advice about public affairs is given privately, however. A few years ago at a Washington dinner, she told her old friend Caspar Weinberger, currently secretary of defense, that the MX missile was "a dog." The Ann Landers column remains an advice and not a political column, but it does include a concern with public affairs that distinguishes it. Eppie Lederer is going strong and will continue to be an influential voice as Ann Landers. Because she is so well known as the woman who authors the column, when Eppie stops writing, the name Ann Landers will be retired too. Until that time, however, Eppie's more than thirty-year perspective will continue to inform and influence her readers.

THE SCOPE OF SOCIAL INFLUENCE

In its broadest sense, social influence includes almost all of social psychology. It can be thought of as any change, whether physiological, attitudinal, emotional, or behavioral, that occurs in one person as the result of the real, implied, or imagined presence of others (Latané, 1981). For our purposes, however, we will define social influence more narrowly as the exercise of power by a person or group to change the opinions and/or behavior of others. Ann Landers is a physically small woman who might not seem like a powerful person. However, as we will soon see, she has a great deal of power that she uses to influence the opinions and behavior of letter writers who seek her guidance.

Social influence is pervasive in our everyday lives. Some of its forms are direct and obvious while others are indirect and subtle. In this chapter, we will consider several different aspects of social influence. First, we will focus on the influence exerted by individuals. In that connection, we will consider different kinds of power and discuss both leaders and leadership. Then we will consider obedience to authority. Later, we will turn to the influence exerted by groups and consider conformity. Finally, we will discuss resistance to social influence.

RESPONSES TO SOCIAL INFLUENCE

It will be helpful if, at the outset, we identify three different types of responses to the pressures of social influence (Kelman, 1961). As you will see, different kinds of individual power and group pressure result in different kinds of opinion and behavior change. The first kind of response to social influence is *compliance*. When people comply, they simply go along overtly with certain kinds of social influence; there is no genuine internal or private opinion change in the case of compliance. For example, as a result of peer pressure, a person might participate in a rally demanding that her college fight apartheid by divesting itself of stock in companies that do business in South Africa. This person is demonstrating compliance because she does not really *believe* that divestiture is effective or helpful.

Compliance is public; that is, it does not involve private opinion change. There are, however, two kinds of responses to social influence that are marked by genuine opinion change. The first is called *identification*. Identification occurs when an individual adopts the standards of a person or group that he or she likes, admires, and wants to establish a relationship with. The individual privately accepts the new standards, but maintains them only as long as he or she continues to admire the other person or group. For instance, a student may willingly participate in divestiture rallies as long as she likes one of the antiapartheid group leaders. When that admiration ends, however, the student may find herself surprisingly disinterested in divestiture.

The third response to social influence involves genuine, long-lasting, private opinion change based on congruence between a new opinion and the individual's overall value system. This kind of response to social influence is called *internalization*. The student who not only participated in the divestiture rally, but also believes in that policy because of his or her values provides an example of internalization.

The distinction between compliance and internalization is important, as it enables us to predict how an individual will act when influence pressures have been removed. If the individual is simply complying with individual or group pressures, but retains private attitudes that are inconsistent with those pressures, we would not expect his or her behavior to be the same once the social influence pressure has been removed. Thus, the person whose attendance at the divestiture rally only reflects public compliance will not follow through with other antiapartheid actions.

The distinction between compliance and internalization alerts us to the other side of the coin; that is, the fact that influence can result in private acceptance without producing public compliance. Sometimes, for example, people respond to societal minorities by accepting their ideas privately while publicly ignoring them (Nemeth, 1986).

SOCIAL POWER

As our definitions imply, power forms the basis of an individual's or group's ability to influence others. In fact, power is generally defined as the capacity or the potential to influence other people's outcomes (see Chapter Four). The critical difference between power and influence is that power is the ability to affect other people and therefore to change their behavior, while influence involves the actual exercise of that power to produce personal or social change. That is, sometimes a person with power may not use that power to influence someone else. A parent, for example, may have a great deal of power over a child but may not always use it to influence the child. In this section, we will consider several different kinds of power and the ways in which people use them.

Types of Power and Their Use   People gain the potential to influence others through many routes. For example, both a policeman and a doctor may be able to influence you to refrain from using certain drugs;

however, the basis of influence is very different for these two sources. French and Raven (1959) identified five bases from which individuals gain power. They and others (Aries, 1976; Michener & Burt, 1974; Bonoma, 1976) point out that in most cases people derive power from more than one base and that they must decide which type of power to use in a particular situation. Further, the base of power often determines the situations in which it can be used.

Coercive power. *Coercive power* involves the potential to deliver threats and punishment to force another person to change his or her behavior. A parent uses coercive power when he or she threatens to spank a child if a certain behavior is not carried out.

Coercive power is based on access to weapons or other resources that increase strength and the credibility of threat. Two important drawbacks deter the use of coercive power. First, the low-power individual in a coercive relationship is going to be motivated to end the relationship if the opportunity presents itself. Dictatorial governments that rely on coercive power must go to great lengths to keep citizens from leaving the country. Second, the coercive power base requires surveillance of the low-power person (Shaw & Condelli, 1986). The power of coercion is only as effective as the surveillance system. Rarely does a child rush in and announce to its mother, "I just sneaked three cookies from the cookie jar."

The necessity of surveillance is a problem for a number of reasons. First, it is very difficult, if not impossible, to maintain close surveillance. Hijackings continue to occur despite the millions of dollars that have been spent on the surveillance of passengers at airports. Second, surveillance leads to distrust and fosters conflict (Strickland, 1968). Distrust on the part of the high-power individual may occur through a dissonance-reduction process (for example, "I'm spending all this effort on surveillance; therefore that individual I'm having watched must be untrustworthy"). Finally, surveillance does not lead to internalization; it influences individuals only while they are under surveillance. One reason for this is that the individual does not experience dissonance following behavior performed while under surveillance because he can justify such behavior by saying, "I was only doing that to avoid punishment" (see Chapter Six).

Given these negative aspects of coercive power, one may ask why coercion is ever used. One reason is that it is relatively easy to use; it takes little effort to make a threat. Another reason is that coercion may enhance the self-esteem of its user (Raven & Kruglanski, 1970; Kipnis, 1974). Being able to force another person to act in a prescribed manner leads to a feeling of mastery and superiority. Hence, Kipnis reports that supervisors who lack confidence and self-esteem often resort to coercive power. However, coercive power is the type of power that is least likely to sustain change and it is the most difficult to maintain. It is generally used as a last resort.

Reward power. *Reward power* involves giving positive reinforcement to produce change. The reinforcement may take the form of material commodities such as money, or it may take a more intangible form such as praise. Reward power is based on access to commodities that others value. Hence, an individual may have reward power over one person but not over another, depending on the value that these people place on the commodities.

Reward power, unlike coercive power, motivates the low-power individual to stay in the relationship. Although surveillance is required for the effective use of reward power, the degree of such surveillance need not be as high as that required by coercive power. It is not uncommon for

When people use coercive power they must maintain constant surveillance to make sure others are behaving in a desired way. Coercive power does not produce internalization. *(Andrew Brilliant/The Picture Cube)*

a child to announce, "Come, look, I've just cleaned up my room." When the desired behavior is performed, the actor is likely to call the attention of the high-power individual to that performance. Canavan-Gumpert (1977) found that reward power (praise) is more effective than coercive power (criticism) in increasing performance in children. Hence, reward power should be preferred to coercive power.

However, reward power may be costly to the user, especially when the reward is based on material assets, such as money. In addition, because the reward may justify behavior, the exercise of reward power may not result in internalization, or attitude change. Remembering dissonance theory again (see Chapter Six), the actor may say, "I am doing this because of the reward and not because I believe in what I am doing." Thus, reward power will be effective only so long as rewards are dispensed.

Legitimate power. The power that one derives from being in a particular role or position is *legitimate power*. Legitimate power is authority, and it is generally limited to a particular domain. For example, your boss may have the legitimate power to influence how you behave at work, but he or she does not have legitimate power to determine how you behave toward your spouse or what you do on your days off. Pruitt (1976) notes that legitimate power is based on the norm of "oughtness"; we are socialized to believe that we should follow the orders of persons in legitimate positions. For example, the child is taught that he should "do what his parents say because they are his parents."

Possessors of legitimate power do not have to explain why they want individuals to act in a certain way. People with legitimate power are influential not because they say the right things, but because they have the right to influence. Laws may be used to assign legitimate power to certain people. And often, people who have others power types may pass laws to ensure legitimate power for themselves. For example, a dictator who overthrows a government by the use of coercive power may then "pass laws" that give him or her legitimate power.

Expert power. Often people gain power because others see them as knowledgeable in a particular area. Ann Landers gains much of her influence through expert power. People regard her as having a great deal of expertise on a wide range of personal problems, as well as the judgment and knowledge necessary to make recommendations about where they can find special kinds of help. Expert power, like legitimate power, is usually limited to a specific area. Thus, Ann Landers may be able to influence you on personal and social matters, but you would not seek her advice about what new car to buy. People often attempt to increase their expert power by using diplomas and citations that testify to their knowledge in a certain area. It is not uncommon to walk into a doctor's office and see a whole wall of diplomas. Even garage mechanics may bolster their expert power by displaying diplomas and citations from courses they have taken.

Expert power has some of the advantages and disadvantages of legitimate power. It does not require surveillance; it is clearly vested in the individual; it often covers only a limited domain. It does, however, have the added advantage that internalization of attitudes may follow its use. That is, people not only follow an expert because they are awed by the credentials that he or she possesses, but they also believe that he or she has the correct information.

Referent power. People gain the ability to influence us because we admire and like them. We want to be similar to the people we admire, and hence we often imitate them and try to act as we think they would. Referent power was useful for Ann Landers when she announced her divorce. Not only did people respect her expertise, but many of them had come to know and like her through the occasional glimpses she offered of her personal life (e.g., proudly announcing her thirtieth wedding anniversary and talking about her career and marriage in a 1969 column). Such referent power added to the acknowledged expert power that forms the basis of Ms. Landers's influence.

Given the available evidence, it seems that referent power is the most *usable.* It does not require surveillance, and it tends to bring the user and the target closer together; that is, it does not create the "power distance" that other forms of power engender—especially expert power (Mulder, 1981). Referent power is also likely to lead to the internalization of attitudes, rather than simply a change in behavior. The belief in the effectiveness of referent power was one of the motivating factors in the formation of group psychotherapy and such behavior-change groups as Weight Watchers and Alcoholics Anonymous. In these cases, peers with similar backgrounds, and not experts, are relied on as the agents of influence.

Informational power. Raven and Kruglanksi (1970) added a sixth basis of power to those suggested by French and Raven (1959). The five types of power that we discussed above are all dependent on the source; the basis of power lies within the particular person. That person's power may be limited to particular situations, but it is independent of the information that the person actually possesses. On the other hand, eyewitnesses to crimes have the power to influence juries solely because of the information they have and not because of their characteristics. This type of independent power has been labeled *informational power.* As Pruitt

People with information have a special kind of power. It can be very influential but it may lose value once it is used. (Lionel J-M Delvoigne/Stock, Boston)

(1976) points out, "Knowledge is power." It should be noted, however, that once the person who possesses informational power dispenses the information, power is reduced. For example, once the eyewitness has testified, he or she no longer has the power to influence the behavior of the jury.

Sex Differences in the Use of Power   Although the type of power influences when and how power will be used, there are also many characteristics of the target that influence how power will be used. One factor is sex.

In an interesting study on the use of power by married couples, Raven, Centers, and Rodrigues (1969) interviewed 776 husbands and wives in the Los Angeles area. They gave examples of behaviors and asked the respondents to tell what type of power would be used by their spouses to influence those behaviors. They found that referent and expert power were used most frequently, and coercive power least frequently. Wives were most likely to attribute expert power ("knew what was best in the case") to their husbands, and husbands saw their wives as using referent power ("both part of the same family") most often.

Table 10-1

Percentage attributing each basis of power to the spouse as a function of the domain of power

Domain of power	N	Predominant basis of the power attributed to spouse				
		Reward	Coercion	Expert	Legitimate	Referent
"Visit some friend or relative"	768	7%	8%	15%	43%	27%
"Change some personal habit"	758	6	9	35	30	20
"Repair or clean something around house"	766	5	13	28	35	19
"Change station on TV or radio"	766	14	13	8	30	35
"Go somewhere for outing or vacation"	760	10	3	10	37	40
"Go see a doctor"	768	1	2	55	22	20

Source: Raven (1974), p. 186.

Further, expert power was used more by younger couples than by older ones, and the use of referent power increased with age. Finally, as can be seen in Table 10-1, the use of power was also dependent on the type of behavior being influenced.

Following up on this gender difference, Falbo and Peplau (1980) had subjects write an essay describing "how I get (their intimate partner) to do what I want." These essays were then analyzed to see what power strategy was used. The results indicated that heterosexual males tended to prefer direct and interactive strategies (bargaining, talking, reasoning, and persistence), while heterosexual females tended to use indirect and solitary strategies (withdrawal, negative affect). They also found that the strategies (direct-interactive) used by males were more likely to promote a satisfying relationship. Rather than indicating that males are more socially sensitive than females, Falbo and Peplau argue that because males expect compliance in their relationship, they have the "luxury" of being able to rely on these methods. Females, on the other hand, often see their position as the weaker one in the relationship. As a result, they must resort to the solitary strategies that are used when the goal is important but compliance is not expected.

LEADERSHIP

In any group, large or small, some individuals have more power and influence than others. The person with the most influence often assumes a position of prominence in the group and comes to be regarded as the leader. In fact, we can define a leader as *the person who exerts the most influence in a group* (Hollander, 1985; Shaw, 1981). There are many different kinds of leaders and leadership. Ann Landers is a leader in our society because of the influence she exerts. Her advice about matters such as what to tell a spouse about past sexual affairs has considerable impact on the way many people in America behave. Another more obvious kind of leader in our society is the president of the United States. Recently, psychologists and political scientists discussed different kinds of presidential leadership and identified the "transformational leader," one who senses the unexpressed "wants" of the populace and tries to bring those desires to expression for the purpose of changing the political system (Burns, 1984). Franklin Roosevelt fit the definition of a transformational leader, as does Ronald Reagan. Despite the many different kinds of leaders in this and other countries, all leaders have the common characteristic of exerting the most influence. A person may be a leader for only a short time and in a limited situation, but in that time or place he or she has the greatest influence.

Leadership Behavior   Just as there are numerous types of power, so too are there numerous types of leadership behavior and functions. There have been literally hundreds of studies aimed at finding out exactly what a leader does in and for a group.

One of the most widely cited studies on leadership was conducted at Ohio State University in the late 1940s. In one phase of that investigation, Halpin and Winer (1952) asked subjects to record what characteristics of a leader they felt were most important. The two most widely mentioned characteristics fell under the headings of *consideration* and *initiating structure*. The consideration category included such characteristics as (1) initiates communication, (2) explains actions, and (3) promotes trust. The initiating structure dimension included the behaviors of directing the actions of the group and group planning. Two minor factors were also found: *production emphasis* (stresses "getting the job done") and *social sensitivity* (flexibility in adjusting plans and scapegoating others). Lieberman, Yalom, and Miles (1973) point out that these duties of a leader are often contradictory. For example, it is difficult for an individual who is concerned with getting the job done or initiating new tasks to

All kinds of people have been great leaders. Factors other than personal qualities determine who becomes a leader and how a person leads effectively. *(Top left to right [FDR], Topham/The Image Works; [G. Meir], Richard Sobol/Stock, Boston; [I. Ghandi], Lehtikuva/Woodfin Camp & Associates; bottom left to right [R. Reagan], Peter Southwick/Stock, Boston; [M. Luther King, Jr.], © Dan Budnick 1980/Woodfin Camp & Associates)*

be involved in fraternization or in being "just a member" of the group. Similarly, it is difficult to be an evaluator of a member's performance and also to be concerned about that member's feelings.

The duality of leadership and the contradictory pressures that accompany having to be concerned about both the task and the feelings of the people working on the task would seem to ensure that one could not be an effective leader: it should be almost impossible to perform both functions at the same time. However, Bales and Slater (1955) found that one person does not generally perform both functions; usually, one person leads on task related issues, and another assumes the person oriented functions. These investigators studied groups of three to six members working on a discussion task. They found an increasing tendency over time for the best-liked individual not to be rated as the person who came up with the best ideas. The tendency was to see the individual with the best ideas as the leader because he or she provided suggestions about how the group should solve its problems. Bales and Slater named that leader the *task specialist*—mainly concerned with getting the job done. The best-liked person was called the *socioemotional leader* by Bales and Slater and the *maintenance specialist* by Thibaut and Kelley (1959). His or her chief concern was to create a good social climate in the group. Zelditch (1955) studied families in fifty-six societies and found that in most families there was a task specialist and a maintenance specialist. Generally, the male was the task specialist and the female the socioemotional leader.

Thus, it is very likely that there are two leaders in many groups: one leader pushes the group members to get the job done and the other works to keep the group members happy. It is probably also true that the two types of leaders use different types of power in their roles. Task leaders use legitimate, expert, and coercive power to get group members to work. On the other hand, socioemotional leaders should be most effective if they use referent and reward power.

What Makes a Leader?   Thus far, we have seen that a leader is an individual who exercises power to influence the direction of group activity. We have seen that there are many leadership behaviors and many ways to measure leadership. We can now ask, Why do some individuals arise as leaders while others do not? Did Ann Landers become an opinion leader because of her personal characteristics, her honest, clear, and direct style? Or did she become a leader because of the situation that existed when she started her column, a situation in which more and more people were seeking advice about social values in a rapidly changing world? Perhaps she became a leader due to the combination of what the times demanded and the way in which she responded to that demand. Hollander (1985) pointed out that the study of leadership has historically progressed by considering the following three factors in the following order: the person, the situation, and the combination of the two. As a result, we have *trait theories, situational theories,* and *interactionist theories* of leadership.

The "Great Person" Theory of Leadership When we look at great leaders such as Martin Luther King, Jr., Franklin Roosevelt, Abraham Lincoln, and Golda Meir, we get the impression that these were not ordinary people; there must have been something special about them that enabled them to be great leaders. The earliest studies on leadership were based on the premise that there is something that sets leaders apart from followers—that leaders are born, not made. If this assumption is correct, it should be possible to identify certain unique traits that characterize leaders. The theory that encompasses these ideas has been labeled the "great person theory of leadership" or the "trait theory." In its simplest form, the theory states that history, or the direction of a group's behavior, is shaped by the particular person in the leadership position and that the course of events would be completely different if another person were in that position (Jacobs, 1971). In the case of Martin Luther King, Jr., for example, the theory would emphasize the fact that King shaped and determined the direction of the civil rights movement in our country, and that the movement would have had a different look if someone else had been its leader.

Key assumptions of the trait theory have not been supported by empirical studies. First, the same people tend not to be the leaders in all situations and at all times. Second, leaders are not a breed apart. Sometimes they are not so different from followers. That is, many different kinds of people can be both leaders and followers at different times in different places. Still, there have been hundreds of studies of the characteristics of leaders that show that leaders do tend to have distinctive traits (Stogdill, 1948). To reduce the data to manageable proportions, we will briefly review the literature on traits and leadership under three categories: physical traits, personality traits, and acquired traits.

Physical traits. Terman (1904) points out that primitive tribes chose their leaders based on size, strength, or age. In certain tribes the leader was the individual who could lift the largest beam and carry it longest. In one Colombian Indian tribe, an individual was allowed to lead only after he had passed a test in which he was covered by stinging ants or whipped by other tribe members. Stogdill's data indicate that even in our own culture, leaders tend to be slightly older, taller, heavier, healthier, and more energetic than the average group member. The data on physical traits make sense if one is considering such groups as football teams, exploring expeditions, or hunting parties, where physical prowess is important. However, it is difficult to see why the strongest individual would be the leader of a debate team, where physical strength is irrelevant to the task. Since Stogdill did not differentiate his data according to the task that the group performed, generalizing from these data is somewhat risky. It is interesting to note that such great leaders as Gandhi, King, Napoleon, and Hitler were no stronger, taller, or heavier than most of their followers.

Sex or gender has also been found to be related to leadership, though the picture is rapidly changing. Both men and women expect men to be leaders, and in early studies women were less likely to view themselves as potential leaders (Megargee, 1969). This stereotype of men as more natural leaders than women means that women leaders face an extra handicap in trying to be effective and in being perceived as such. They must "be like gold to be seen as silver" (Hollander, 1985).

Two recent studies of male and female leaders at the U.S. Military Academy at West Point suggest how fast matters may be changing. A

People are getting accustomed to having women leaders. While some people still believe that leaders should be men, women are proving that they can lead successfully too. (© Jim Anderson 1983/Woodfin Camp & Associates)

1980 study showed that while women performed as well as men and had equally good morale in their groups, their successes were attributed to luck while men's were attributed to ability. These negative attributions were not present in a 1984 study, although female subordinates still rated female leaders quite negatively (Rice, Bender, & Vitters, 1980; Rice, Instone, & Adams, 1984).

Studies of men and women in natural leadership positions are beginning to show increasingly fewer differences between the sexes in both their behaviors and their effectiveness. Laboratory studies in which men and women are assigned leadership positions still show lower ratings for women, probably because of continuing stereotypes suggesting that leaders should be men (Hollander, 1985). As more and more women actually fill leadership positions, we can anticipate that their effectiveness will be the same as men's and that discrimination against them will lessen. Increasing numbers of people may realize that women like Ann Landers have been leaders all along and will expect to see more women in more leadership positions in the near future. Geraldine Ferraro was candidate for vice-president of the United States in 1984. The time is not too distant when women will routinely be on national presidential tickets, including the top spot.

Personality traits. Two personality related traits have most often been associated with leadership. The first is intelligence. The leader in most groups is somewhat more intelligent than the followers (Gibb, 1969; Mann, 1959; Stogdill, 1948). The correlation between intelligence and leadership, however, is not high; Mann reports the median correlation to be around .25, and some studies (for example, Loretto & Williams, 1974) found no relationship between intelligence and leadership. One possible reason for this low correlation is that a leader who is much more intelligent than the other group members will not be able to relate to them.

A second trait that paves the road for an individual's rise to leadership is verbosity, or talkativeness. A number of investigators (Riecken, 1958; Bass, 1949; and McGrath & Julian, 1963) have consistently found evidence supporting the "big mouth" theory of leadership; that is, the most talkative member of the group is seen as the leader.

The relationship between talkativeness and leadership was demonstrated in a study (Bavelas, Hastorf, Gross, & Kite, 1965) in which the subjects first met in four-person discussion groups and the observers recorded the amount of time that each member spent talking. After the first discussion, the subjects rated each other on the leadership dimension. In the next session, each subject had a box in front of him with a red and green light. The subjects were told that they would receive feedback about how well they performed; a green light would signify good performance, and a red light, poor performance. One subject who had been near the bottom in verbosity in the first session was chosen to receive positive feedback for talking. During the second session, he received more green lights than anyone else in the group. This positive reinforcement for talking caused him to more than double his verbal output, and the group then came to view him as the leader. A third session was run without lights. The previously reinforced subject's verbal output remained high, and so did his ratings on leadership. This study strikingly demonstrated the importance of verbosity as a determinant of leadership. In support of these findings, Sorrentino and Boutillier (1975) manipulated both the quantity and quality of a confederate's remarks during a group discussion. While quality had little effect on the confederate's leadership ratings, the more he talked, the higher he was rated on leadership ability by the other group members.

While it seems that talking is a sure road to leadership, there have been some important qualifications of this rule. First, Ginter and Lindskold (1975) found that the amount of talking did not affect leadership ratings of persons introduced to the group as experts on their topic of conversation. Amount of talking, however, was positively related to leadership ratings of nonexperts. Second, talking may be negatively related to leadership if the comments involve negative statements about the group's effectiveness; in other words, if the person rejects the group, the group will reject the person (Morris & Hackman, 1969).

Motives are also important in leadership. Recent research shows that being oriented toward achieving success and being oriented toward affiliating with others are both important in emerging as a leader in a long lasting group (Sorrentino & Field, 1986).

One other "trait" that is often associated with leadership has received little empirical study: *charisma,* a term used to describe the magnetic pull that certain leaders appear to have. It has been applied to such leaders as Martin Luther King, Jr., John F. Kennedy, Adolf Hitler, and Ho Chi Minh. While some leaders seem to have charisma, others do not. Max Weber (1946) used the term to mean the "gift of grace." Charisma has almost supernatural qualities that are difficult to describe and may be impossible to study. Weber felt that a leader's charisma is especially evident in times of crisis and that situational events seem to "draw it out." A leader's charisma is also, in part, determined by the followers' needs and emotional states. Because of this, not everyone is affected by the leader in the same way; as a result a charismatic leader often has a group of strongly devoted followers and a number of strong opponents. This was the case with Martin Luther King, Jr., who had both close followers and vocal antagonists among blacks.

Although there are leaders who appear to have charisma, a better understanding of the trait awaits future research and a better operational definition. It is, however, interesting to note that many political figures have attempted to "build" charisma. For example, campaign leaders attempted to build charisma in Richard Nixon; they trained him to say the right things, wear the proper clothes, sit in the proper way, and even joke and laugh to show the country that he had a sense of humor. Although few would agree that Nixon emerged from the campaign as a charismatic leader, these efforts to change Nixon's image did help him to win the 1968 and 1972 elections.

The Zeitgeist Theory: A Situational Approach to Leadership   Psychologists found the trait approach to leadership unsatisfactory because it cannot, by itself, predict who will become a leader or explain why an individual becomes a leader. The emphasis in the study of leadership therefore shifted from investigating traits of individuals to investigating characteristics of particular group situations that might determine who emerges as the leader. This situational or time approach shuns the hypotheses that certain people are born to lead. Situational theorists espouse the position that the particular time or situation determines who will become the leader:

> At a particular time, a group of people has certain needs and requires the services of an individual to assist it in meeting its needs. Which individual comes to play the role of leader in meeting these needs is essentially determined by chance; that is, a given person happens to be at the critical place at the critical time (Cooper & McGaugh, 1969, p. 247).

The point has been made that had Hitler espoused his doctrine in the United States rather than in Germany, he would probably have been thrown in jail or committed to a mental institution. In Germany, however, the time and the situation were right for the people to follow the lead of such an individual.

The situational approach may also explain Ann Landers's great impact when she started her column in 1955. The United States was right in the middle of the baby boom and changes in American society were taking place quickly. When the 1960s began, change started to occur even more rapidly. Ann Landers was well positioned to be influential during these years of change. She responded to situations that were real, such as the increase in premarital sexual experimentation, and she helped people to realize that birth control and premarital sex were realities that they needed to think about and deal with.

Several situational factors affect leadership, and some that are unsuspected can be highly influential. For example, Howells and Becker (1962)

John F. Kennedy was a very charismatic leader. The concept of charisma is difficult to research because of disagreement about how it should be defined. (© *Jacques Lowe/Woodfin Camp & Associates*)

suggested that *seating arrangement* would influence leadership. They suggested that communication would naturally tend to flow across a table. They used five-man groups in which two individuals sat across the table from three. They hypothesized that if communication is important in determining the leader and if communication flows across the table, then people seated on the two-person side of the table would tend to be seen as leaders, since they would be communicating to three other persons. The groups were instructed to work on a number of simple tasks, and the group members were then asked to identify the leader of their group. The results indicated that persons seated on the two-person side of the table were chosen as leader more than twice as often as persons seated on the three-man side. It has also been found that leaders naturally choose seats at the head of rectangular tables rather than seats along the sides (Lécuyer, 1976).

Seniority is also an important factor in determining who will emerge as leader. Insko, Thibaut, Moehle, Wilson, Diamond, Gilmore, Soloman, and Lipsitz (1980) studied experimental groups over a period of time. During the experiment, subjects were removed, one by one, from a group and replaced with new members. The results indicated that groups at the hub of communication had the greatest influence and, within groups, members with the most seniority were accorded leadership roles. While the seniority-leadership norm emerged in all groups, this norm was particularly strong in powerful groups. As you can imagine, having this type of norm allows for orderly change in leadership and reduces the chances of intragroup conflict.

The situation facing the group will also affect leadership. Numerous investigators (Hamblin, 1958; Klein, 1976; Worchel, Andreoli, & Folger, 1977) have found that groups facing threat or competition are more likely to accept an authoritative leader than groups not facing such difficulties. Crisis seems to cause people to rally around their leader. In an interesting series of studies on Dutch subjects, Rabbie and Bekkers (1976) found that leaders who were threatened with losing their positions of leadership tried to engage their groups in competitive and threatening situations. Apparently, they felt that they would be less likely to lose their positions if they caused the groups to perceive an external threat than if no such threat existed.

Finally, the situational theorists of leadership state that the particular *needs of the group* determine who will emerge as leader. As these needs change, the leader of the group is also likely to change. Barnlund (1962) found that when task requirements changed, leadership tended to shift to an individual with more appropriate qualifications. Identification of the leader at a particular time depends on the task on which the group is working. Thus, the situational theory argues that there are no general leadership traits and that the traits that make an individual a leader in one situation may not qualify him or her to lead in another. In this regard, it is interesting that Ann Landers has managed to retain her position of influence during a period when the concerns of the nation have changed dramatically. For example, only in the past few years have people become concerned about AIDS and faced issues such as whether to allow young children afflicted by the illness into the public schools. Ann Landers has been willing to deal with any issue that comes along.

Her style and personality have not changed, but she has responded to changing needs to maintain her position of leadership and influence.

Interactionist Theories While both the trait and situational theories give us some answers about the emergence of leaders, both are incomplete. More recent theories have suggested that the emergence of a leader is the result of characteristics of the leader, the followers, and the situation (Katz & Kahn, 1978; Hollander, 1978). Certain traits may make an individual the center of attention. However, if his or her abilities do not satisfy the needs of the members, leadership will not result. The situation influences the needs of the followers and the need of the group for a leader. Thus, the leader is influenced by the followers, and the followers are influenced by the leader (see Figure 10–1). As the situation and needs of the followers change, the person who is accepted as leader will change. But the leader must possess certain abilities before he or she will be elevated to a position of leadership. As we will see later in the chapter, the interactionist approach has also been used to predict who will be an effective leader.

The Effective Leader Having examined research on the emergence of a leader in a group, we can consider the kind of leader who is likely to be effective, and the factors that influence that effectiveness. The question of leader effectiveness is distinct from the question of leader emergence, although the two questions are related.

Democratic versus Autocratic Styles of Leadership One early study on leadership asked the question, What type of leader will be most effective? Lewin, Lippitt, and White (1939) closely observed four comparable groups of 10-year-old boys under autocratic, democratic, and laissez-faire adult leaders. The leaders were trained to respond in one of these styles and were rotated every six weeks so that each group had each type of leader. The autocratic leader determined the policy of the group, dictated all the steps and techniques for attaining the group goals, assigned tasks and task partners, and remained aloof from the group. The democratic leader allowed the group to determine policy, offered suggestions about procedures and tasks, allowed members to choose their own tasks and task partners, was objective in his praise and criticism, and participated in the group tasks. The laissez-faire leader allowed his group complete freedom and did not participate in the group tasks. The group engaged in such hobbies as making masks and building objects.

The results showed that under the authoritarian leader, the boys were thirty times as hostile and eight times as aggressive as they were under the democratic leader. Subjects under the authoritarian leader tended to

Figure 10–1
The elements of leadership

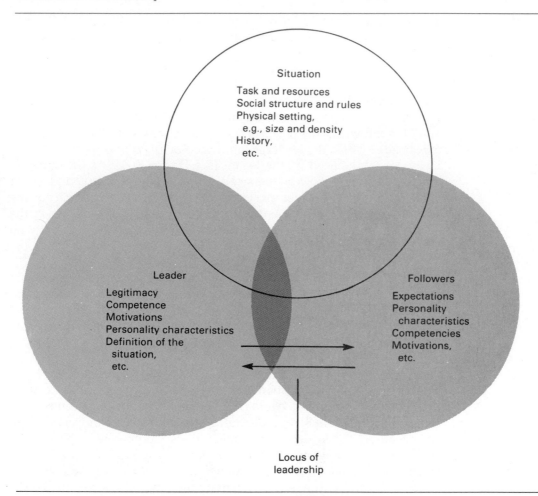

Note: Three elements involved in leadership—the situation, the leader, and the followers—with some of their relevant attributes. The crosshatched area represents their intersection, which is the locus of leadership. The arrows indicate the social exchange that occurs there between the leader and the followers.
Source: Reprinted with permission of The Free Press, a division of Macmillan, Inc., from *Leadership Dynamics: A Practical Guide to Effective Relationships*, p. 8, by Edwin P. Hollander. Copyright © 1978 by The Free Press.

pick out scapegoats as the target of their aggression (two such scape-goats actually left the groups). This behavior did not occur under the democratic leader. Group unity was higher under the democratic leader than under the authoritarian leader. Although the constructiveness of work sharply decreased when the authoritarian leader temporarily left the room, it remained constant in the democratic group. Experimentally induced frustrations were very disruptive to the authoritarian-led group, but the democratic-led group tended to meet these difficulties with organized attacks.

Interesting sequential events occurred when the groups changed leaders. Figure 10–2 shows the effect of leader change in two groups. The most noticeable effect is the sharp increase in aggression when the group shifted from an autocratic leader to a laissez-faire leader. This is

Figure 10–2
The effect of different leadership styles on aggressiveness in a group

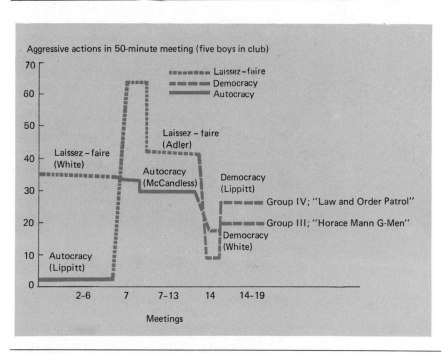

Note: Aggressiveness greatly increases in the group when an autocratic leader is replaced by a laissez-faire leader.
Source: "Patterns of Aggressive Behavior in Experimentally Created Social Climates," by K. Lewin, R. Lippitt & R. White, 1939. In *Journal of Social Psychology,* Vol. 10. Reprinted with permission of the Helen Dwight Reid Educational Foundation. Published by Heldref Publications, 4000 Albemarle St., N.W., Washington, D.C., 20016. Copyright © 1939.

supposedly the result of repressed aggression under autocratic supervision. The boys may have become angry under the autocratic leader, but they feared the leader and were afraid to disrupt the group by expressing their anger. The laissez-faire leader gave the group a freer atmosphere which allowed the release of pent-up aggression. It is interesting to note that this type of effect often occurs after the overthrow of an autocratic ruler. In the history of nations, we have often seen a people, liberated after years of an autocratic reign, release pent-up hostility and frustration in a bloodbath like the one that followed Louis XV's demise in France.

Turning from the psychological atmosphere of the group to the question of productivity, Lewin et al. found that the boys worked longer and turned out more products under the autocratic leader than under the democratic leader. They did, however, tend to turn out products of somewhat better quality under the democratic leader.

Again, however, we find that the effectiveness of the leader is influenced by the situation. Research (Rosenbaum & Rosenbaum, 1971) has found that groups are more productive with an autocratic leader under stressful conditions. But, when conditions are nonstressful, groups are more productive with a democratic leader. Thus, the most effective style is partly a function of the situation.

The Contingency Theory of Leadership   It is clear from the early work that leadership effectiveness is not simply a function of the leader's style. As the interactionist theories imply, the demands of the situation and the interaction between leaders and followers need to be considered as well. For example, in trying to understand Ann Landers's influence in our society, one would need to consider her style, the situations facing the people who seek her advice, and the relationship between Ann and the public. Her effectiveness would best be understood in light of all these factors. A significant step forward in understanding leadership effectiveness was made by Fiedler (1964, 1978), who developed a theory of leadership effectiveness that considers both personal and situational factors. Fiedler's *contingency model* has been important in combining insights of the trait and situational approaches and in paving the way for other contingency models (Hollander, 1985).

Fiedler identifies two different leadership styles. One is the task oriented leader who is primarily concerned with getting the job done. The other is the relationship oriented leader who is more concerned with feelings and relationships in the group. These two styles are similar to Bales and Slater's (1955) task versus maintenance specialists. They also remind us of the two broad categories of leadership behavior, initiating structure (getting the task done) and showing consideration (thinking

Fiedler's contingency theory suggests that different kinds of people are effective in different situations. In some situations a directive leader is needed, in others a person-oriented, egalitarian leader is better suited. (© *John Maher/Stock, Boston*)

about relationships). The key idea in Fiedler's contingency model is that whether the task oriented or the relationship oriented leadership style is most effective will depend on the situation the leader faces.

Situations can be classified according to how favorable they are for the leader. Favorability of the situation depends on three factors. The first is the quality of *leader-group relations*. The situation is favorable to the leader if these relations are good, if he or she is trusted, admired, and respected. The second factor is the *task structure*. Here the situation is favorable to the leader if the task is clear and everyone knows who needs to do what. The third factor is the *leader's position power*. If the leader has a position with a great deal of power (for example, a head of state with no legislature), the situation is more favorable to that leader.

Fiedler hypothesized that the task oriented leader would be most effective under conditions that were either highly favorable or highly unfavorable to the leader. In the first condition, where leader-group relations are good, the task is clear, and the leader's position is powerful, it is easy for the leader to be directive and task oriented without worrying too much about feelings, for here is a group where everything is going well and people's feelings do not require much attention. In the second condition, where the situation is chaotic, unpleasant, and ambiguous, a take-charge, task oriented style will also be more effective; here, the relationship oriented leader is likely to be swamped by the chaos. On the other hand, in situations where favorability to the leader is in the middle ranges, where people need to be shown consideration, where there is some tension and relations between group members need to be coordinated and clarified, a relationship oriented leader will do better than a task oriented leader who tends to overlook interpersonal relations.

Fiedler's theory is a complex and ambitious one. It has been tested in numerous laboratory and field studies with a wide variety of groups, such as Belgian naval officers, postmasters, basketball players, store managers, workers on open-hearth furnaces, B-29 bomber crews, and research chemists. In general, the relationship oriented leaders were most effective in the moderately favorable situations whereas the task oriented leaders were most effective in either very poor or highly favorable situations (Fiedler, 1978; Chemers & Skrzypek, 1972; Hardy, 1976).

The contingency model of leadership effectiveness has generated a great deal of research and, as you might imagine with so complex a theory, a great deal of controversy (Fiedler, 1977; Schreisheim and Kerr, 1977a, 1977b). Recent reviews of studies of this model suggest that while it has been supported in many ways, a complete understanding of leadership effectiveness will require consideration of factors beyond leadership style and the favorability of the situation to the leader (Rice & Kastenbaum, 1983).

In addition to generating a large body of research and focusing attention on the interaction of personal and situational variables, the contingency theory has had practical impact in the leadership area. The usual approach to finding leaders for businesses and organizations was to rely on personality tests to identify the individual with general potential for leadership. If an individual happened to be in a position of leadership, attempts would be made to train him or her to be a better leader. Millions of dollars were spent on sending people to leadership conferences or training sessions. Essentially, the idea was to reshape the person to fit the situation. According to Fiedler, this approach will not succeed. He believes that it is extremely difficult to change a person's leadership style. We should instead change a person's rank, job, or power to fit his personality or leadership style (Fiedler, 1964); that is, we should make the environment fit the person instead of trying to make the person fit the environment. Along these lines, Fiedler, Chemers, and Mahar (1976) have developed the LEADERMATCH program, which is aimed at helping leaders to identify and create situations that are most suited to their style of leadership. Here again, the position is that it is easier to change the situation than a person's style of leadership. The LEADERMATCH program has proved successful in preliminary studies (Fiedler, 1978). However, as with the theory, there is some controversy about this program (Kabanoff, 1981; Shiflett, 1981).

OBEDIENCE

An individual like Ann Landers leads in an indirect and gentle way. She can only offer advice to those who ask for it. Her printed answers often mold public opinion about what is appropriate, but she cannot direct interpersonal behavior, unlike an authoritarian leader. She has neither the legitimate nor coercive power that is needed to do so. By contrast, if we consider the power of an authority figure to command obedience, we find chilling examples of the extent to which people will do what their leaders or authorities direct. Perhaps the most vivid example of people's willingness to follow those with authority is seen in the atrocities committed against the Jews by the Nazis during World War II; six million men, women, and children were tortured and executed. At the Nuremberg War Trials, the Germans who served as executioners in the concentration camps maintained that they were not responsible for the deaths because they were merely following orders. This seemed a poor excuse indeed for their actions, and the executioners who were tried were themselves executed or imprisoned. The general feeling was that no human being could intentionally torture or kill another human being simply because he or she was following orders; anyone with feelings would certainly have resisted or disobeyed such orders.

Although the most common examples of blind faith in following orders occur in emergency or wartime situations, there is nowhere a more striking and, we think, more terrifying example of how blindly people follow orders than in the demonstrations of Stanley Milgram (1963, 1965). Imagine yourself in the following situation:

You arrive at an experimental room, sit down, and begin talking to another subject who has signed up for the same experiment. The experimenter enters and tells you both that the experiment concerns the effects of punishment on learning. You draw straws to see which of you will be the "learner" and which the "teacher," and you draw the teacher straw. The experimenter tells you both that the teacher will ask the learner questions and that the learner will be shocked each time he answers incorrectly. The learner is led away and is supposedly hooked up to a shock apparatus in a small enclosed booth.

You are shown the "teaching machine," which supposedly generates shock. There is a lever and a row of numbers starting at 15 volts and running to 450 volts, with each 15-volt interval labeled. The lower range of numbers is marked "Slight Shock," and the upper end is labeled "Danger: Severe Shock"; 450 volts is marked "XXX." The experimenter tells you that you are to read a prepared list of questions to the learner and that, if he answers a question incorrectly, you are to shock him. You are to increase the shock by one level after each incorrect answer so that the first shock will be 15 volts, the next 30 volts, and so on.

You begin reading the questions. The learner misses one, then another, and another. After each incorrect answer you increase the voltage by 15 volts, shock the learner, and read the next question. At 90 volts, the learner cries out in pain. At 150 volts, he screams and asks to be let out of the experiment. You look to the experimenter, and he simply says: "Proceed with the next question." At 180 volts, the learner cries out that he can no longer stand the pain and bangs on the wall of the booth. You look at the experimenter and ask to stop the experiment. However, the experimenter calmly tells you: "You have no other choice; you must go on." At 300 volts, the learner refuses to answer any more questions and begs to be let out of the experiment. The experimenter tells you to continue. From this point on, however, there is no further response from the learner.

What would you do in this situation? Would you continue to administer shock to the 450-volt maximum? What percentage of the people in this experiment do you think would continue to the maximum shock? These were the questions that Milgram wanted to answer. He described the situation to fourteen Yale University seniors in psychology and to a group of psychiatrists, and asked them to predict what percentage of subjects would continue to the 450-volt level. They predicted that less than 2 percent of the subjects would "go all the way."

Milgram ran the actual study at Yale University. His subjects were twenty to fifty years old; 40 percent of them had unskilled jobs, 40 percent had white-collar sales jobs, and 20 percent were professionals. He found that twenty-six of forty subjects, or 65 percent, continued to shock until they reached the 450-volt level! Almost two-thirds of the subjects followed orders to directly inflict intense pain on an innocent victim. In actuality, the "victim" was an experimental accomplice who had been trained to make mistakes on the questions and really did not receive any shock. However, the subjects genuinely believed that he was in pain.

The amount of obedience displayed in his studies surprised even Milgram. This was not wartime Nazi Germany; it was New Haven,

Connecticut, in 1960. The subjects were not people who had been trained to injure and kill; they were everyday businesspeople. Some critics (Baumrind, 1964; Orne, 1962; Orne & Holland, 1968) argued that the high obedience rate was obtained because the experiment was run at Yale University and because the subjects believed that the experimenter would not let anything bad happen to the victim. Therefore, Milgram moved the experiment to a run-down office building in Bridgeport, Connecticut. The subjects were told nothing of an affiliation with Yale,

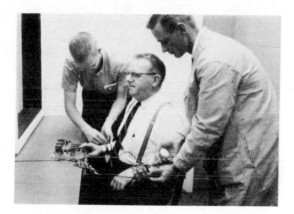

Stanley Milgram used a shock generator to study obedience to authority. The shock generator is shown in the photo in the upper left. In the upper right photo, the learner is strapped into a chair and electrodes are attached to his wrists. The photo in the lower left shows the teacher, the real subject, receiving a sample shock from the generator. The lower right photo shows the subject refusing to continue the experiment. *(Copyright 1965 by Stanley Milgram. From the film* Obedience, *distributed by the New York University Film Library)*

and the experimenter did not wear a white laboratory coat, as he did in the first study. Although obedience dropped somewhat, the drop was not significant; 48 percent of the subjects administered maximum shock.

Milgram felt that he had dramatically demonstrated obedience, and he ran a series of additional experiments to determine what variables would affect obedience. In one study, he varied the closeness of the authority figure. Three conditions were run. In one condition, the experimenter sat a few feet away from the subject as the subject was punishing the learner. In a second condition, the experimenter gave his instructions and left the room while the subject shocked. And in the third condition, the subject received his instructions on a tape recorder and never saw the experimenter. Obedience dropped sharply when the authority figure was removed. The number of subjects who obeyed when the experimenter was present was three times as large as the number who obeyed when he was absent. In a follow-up study, Rada and Rogers (1973) found a high degree of obedience if the experimenter gave the orders in person and then left the room.

In another study, Milgram varied the closeness of the learner. In the remote-feedback condition, the learner was placed in an isolation booth and the teacher could neither see nor hear him, except for an occasional pounding on the booth's walls. In a second condition (voice feedback), the teacher could hear the learner but could not see him. In the proximity condition, the learner was in the same room with the teacher so that he would be seen *and* heard. Finally, Milgram introduced a touch-proximity condition in which the learner was seated right next to the teacher and the teacher had to force the learner's hand onto the shock-plate when he delivered the shock. Figure 10–3 shows the results of this experiment: the closer the learner, the lower the obedience level.

Although these studies demonstrated an amazing degree of obedience, Milgram reported that his subjects suffered even though they obeyed. Many of the subjects became tense; some broke into nervous fits of laughter; and some sweated profusely and begged the experimenter to stop the study.

Although Milgram's experiments are the most often cited studies of obedience, researchers have also found high degrees of obedience in other situations. For example, Hofling, Brotzman, Dalrymple, Graves, and Pierce (1966) ordered nurses in a hospital to administer unusual doses of drugs to patients. In the study, the nurses were telephoned by a doctor who was unfamiliar to them. The doctor ordered the nurses to administer to a patient a drug that was not in common use in the hospital. The doctor also told the nurses to administer the drug in double the amount of the maximum dose stated on the drug box. Of the twenty-two nurses, twenty-one followed the doctor's order even though it was

Figure 10–3
The effect of the proximity of the "victim" on the average shock delivered

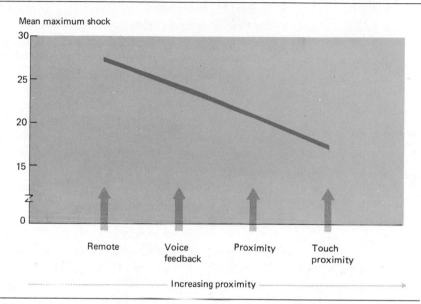

Note: The more feedback the subject received from the victim, the less shock he administered to him.
Source: Milgram (1965).

in violation of hospital policy and could have had very harmful effects on the patient. Orne and Evans (1965) found that subjects would follow an experimenter's orders to conduct such dangerous tasks as grasping a venomous snake, taking a coin from a jar containing acid, and throwing acid onto another person.

The Milgram studies and similar studies raise a number of questions about obedience. One such question is: Why did the subjects obey? Orne (1962) suggested that one reason for the high degree of obedience was the experimental procedure itself. The subjects were placed in a situation that was totally unfamiliar to them; they had had little experience with electric shock; and they had no power in the study. Further, they were faced with an experimenter who seemed very aware of the procedure and showed no signs of concern when the victim was shocked. The experimenter's behavior may have convinced the subjects that there was little need for concern. A second reason for the high degree of obedience may have been that the subjects did not feel responsible for their behavior (Milgram, 1974). The experimenter explicitly told them that the experimenter was the person responsible. A number of studies have shown that when subjects are made to feel responsible for their behavior in the Milgram paradigm, obedience drops drastically (e.g., Tilker, 1970). Further, Milgram (1965) found that obedience decreased when the subjects saw others disobey. It is possible that seeing others disobey caused subjects to feel that if they continued to shock the victim, they would be responsible for their actions.

Ethical questions are also raised by the Milgram studies. Milgram ran his studies in the early 1960s and spent many years responding to criticisms concerning the ethics of his research (see Chapter One). A number of ethical questions can be leveled at his obedience studies. First, the studies put the unsuspecting subjects through a great deal of psychological pain—they were forced to behave in a way that made them extremely uncomfortable. Second, the subjects learned something about themselves that they may have had no desire to know—that they could be made to follow orders that might lead to the injury, and possibly even the death, of innocent individuals. This is certainly a painful thing to learn about oneself. Critics also chastised Milgram for not stopping the research when he observed the extreme discomfort that the subjects experienced. Milgram was surprised by the degree of criticism he received. He argued: "I'm convinced that much of the criticism, whether people know it or not, stems from the results of the experiment. If everyone had broken off at slight shock or moderate shock, this would be a very reassuring finding and who would protest?" (Milgram, 1977, p. 98). Milgram sent the subjects a follow-up questionnaire after they had been in the study. One question asked them how glad they were to have participated. Almost 84 percent of the subjects reported that they were glad they had participated.

The question of ethics is a difficult one, especially in regard to the Milgram studies. On the one hand, the results of the studies were valuable, as the studies dramatically demonstrated that an individual would typically obey orders to hurt another individual. The impact of the results would have been lessened had Milgram used a more mundane task, such as asking subjects to write random numbers on paper. On the other hand, the subjects in the study clearly suffered psychological pain and were forced to learn a disturbing fact about themselves (that they would follow orders to hurt another individual). This is a difficult dilemma to resolve, but it should be pointed out that today it would be very difficult to get a departmental ethics committee to approve a study embodying Milgram's methodology.

CONFORMITY

Many of the letters that Ann Landers receives ask about conformity. People wonder whether they should do something that most of their peers do and want them to do too. For example, many letters come from teenage girls, and some boys as well, who feel peer pressure to have sex. They wonder how many teenagers really are having sex, whether they should resist the conformity pressure, and how they actually can resist. Ann Landers's answers generally recognize the power of the conformity pressures that people feel. She offers the best support she can for their efforts to be independent. There are occasions, however, when her answers suggest that people *should* go along with certain social conventions, at which times her voice is added to the pressure to conform.

Conformity is a change in behavior or belief toward a group's standards as a result of the group's power. In some cases, conformity results from conflict between the way the individual thinks or acts and the way the group pressures him or her to think or act (Moscovici, 1985). For example, conformity may result when a group pressures a teenage girl into having sex before she feels ready for it. In other cases, conformity results from imagined group pressure (Kiesler & Kiesler, 1969). That is, the teenage girl thinking about whether to have sex may imagine that others want her to conform when that is not really true. In still other cases, conformity results when the individual is uncertain about what is correct or appropriate and adopts the group's standards, believing that they are a reliable guide. In this instance, the teenage girl may not know whether it is good for her to have sex but she goes ahead because the group's standards suggest that doing so is the correct and satisfying way to behave.

The kind of group power that produces conformity varies considerably from case to case. For example, the group may use coercive or reward power to pressure someone into a certain action. In this case, the conformity would be an instance of compliance as we defined it at the beginning of the chapter. The compliance may lead to internalization through cognitive dissonance or self-perception (see Chapter Six), but it is compliance at the outset. In other instances, particularly where the person is uncertain about what is correct, the group's referent or expert power may produce conformity. Referent power is likely to produce identification while expert power may produce internalization.

Why Conform?   Some early theories (Crutchfield, 1955) suggested that certain personality traits made individuals prone to conformity. However,

There are many instances of conformity in human behavior. One common example is conformity in dress. We also conform in matters of opinion and judgment. *(Jean-Claude Lejeune/Stock, Boston)*

this approach is of limited value because few people conform all the time, and everyone conforms sometimes. Therefore, we cannot develop a satisfying explanation simply by focusing on individual traits.

For this reason, most investigators began to examine groups to determine how they influenced their members. This research identified the types of power that groups can use to "keep members in line." One of the powers that groups have is *information* (Asch, 1952; Kelley, 1952; Deutsch & Gerard, 1955). If you don't know the answer to a question, or don't know the correct way to behave or believe, you turn to other people for the answer. This is especially true if you doubt your own judgment (Campbell, Tesser, & Fairey). You may accept an answer supplied by one person, but you are more likely to accept an answer if many people supply it.

Festinger (1950) and Kelley (1952) pointed out that when we rely on others for social information, they acquire the capacity to produce what is called *informational social influence*. We conform to them because of the information that they provide. In other words, information is power. Ann Landers's use of expert and informational power illustrates this point. Her experience with people's problems and her investigation of human resources have given her a tremendous amount of varied information. She knows a great deal about social services in communities across the country, the impact of having an affair on the quality of a marriage, and what happens when parents refuse to listen to their children. This information gives her considerable influence over people's behavior.

While information is power, we also know that groups influence people's behavior even when people are not looking for information. A teenager may know that smoking is bad for his health and he may hate the taste of cigarettes. Yet, he is quick to light up when he sees his friends smoking. From where does this type of group power come? Anyone who has been in a group and has wanted to remain part of that group knows the anxiety that is aroused by the thought that he or she might be rejected by the group. This is not an unfounded fear; such rejection is painful. Further, anyone who has been part of a group knows that groups often reject members who act differently from the other group members, who fail to follow the rules of the group, or who consistently hold and express beliefs that are different from those expressed by the group. The group may remove the nonconformist's power by denying him or her the right to vote; it may inflict physical or psychological abuse by beatings or calling out unflattering names; it may see that the nonconformist does not share in any of the rewards that the group obtains.

The individual, believing that deviancy from the group may lead to rejection, feels pressure to conform to the group model. This pressure, which is referred to as normative pressure, produces *normative social influence*. We conform because of the group's capacity to reward and punish us. In particular, the group acquires its capacity to exert normative pressure from the individual's fear of the group's response to deviating from its expectations. It should be pointed out that the group may never make it explicit that deviants will receive negative sanctions, and the individual may or may not have seen the group carry out such sanctions. In reality, sanctions for deviation may not even exist. However, the group's normative power results from the fact that the individual believes that deviants will be rejected.

Given these two types of group pressures, it is interesting to examine how they lead to different types of conforming behavior. The consensus among psychologists (cf. Allen, 1965) is that normative pressure is likely to result in public compliance without an accompanying private acceptance. An individual who reacts to normative pressure is reacting out of fear or anxiety and will often conform overtly without doing so covertly.

One example of this phenomenon is the prisoners of war during the Korean and Vietnamese wars who openly expressed anti-American views while in the hands of their captors, but held on to their private pro-American beliefs and chose to return to the United States when the opportunity was presented to them. They were responding to normative pressures from their captors, but no private acceptance accompanied their public compliance.

On the other hand, an individual who conforms to informational pressures is more likely to evidence private acceptance. This compliance to the group norm is based, not on fear, but on the desire to do the correct thing. Because the group is used to decide the correct course of action or belief, public compliance is often accompanied by private acceptance. Despite these differences, investigators (Shaw, 1981) point out that in most cases, groups influence individuals by using both types of pressure.

Studying Conformity: The Conformity Paradigm   It is interesting to find that one of the earliest studies of conformity was not really aimed at studying conformity at all. Rather, Sherif (1935) wanted to examine how groups develop norms (see Chapter Eleven). Using a phenomenon known as the *autokinetic effect*, he demonstrated that groups will establish norms that individuals in the groups will follow. He showed individual subjects a single pinpoint of light in a dark room and asked them to judge how far the light moved. In fact, the light was stationary, but to an individual focusing on the small spot of light in a dark room, the light appears to move. The amount of movement seen differs from one person to another, but it is relatively constant for each individual.

After the individual reported his estimation of the light movement, he was brought together with one or two other naive subjects. The subjects were then asked to continue estimating the light movement and to announce their estimates so that the other group members could hear. Interestingly enough, the estimates of the group members converged so that after a time each person reported that he saw about the same amount of movement as the other group members (see Figure 10–4). Sherif also found that when the individual was later asked to estimate the movement of the light in a situation in which he was alone, his estimates were very similar to those that he had given by the end of the group estimates.

Figure 10–4
The convergence of judgments of the autokinetic movement in two groups

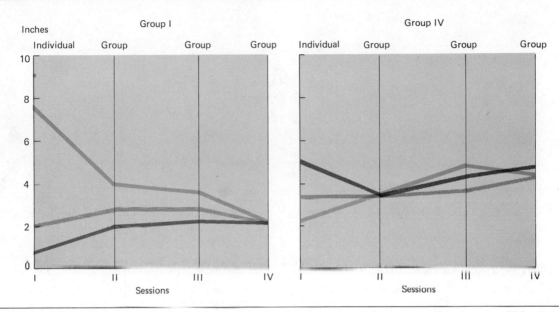

In session I the subjects judged alone. In sessions II and III they heard the judgments of other group members. In session IV they judged alone. The results show that the subjects' judgments conformed to the group norm and that this conformity continued even when the subjects were alone again in the last session.
Source: First and Fourth Group graphs from "Medians in Groups of Three Subjects" (p. 209), in *Social Psychology* by Muzafer Sherif and Carolyn W. Sherif. Copyright © 1969 by Muzafer Sherif and Carolyn W. Sherif. Reprinted by permission of Harper & Row, Publishers, Inc.

The Asch Paradigm   Although Sherif's study was not aimed at demonstrating conformity, many interpreted the results as showing that humans are a conforming breed. Solomon Asch did not believe this. He felt that one reason why subjects conformed in Sherif's study was that the stimulus they were judging was so ambiguous. Asch (1951) devised a unique method for studying conformity. Imagine that you are a subject who has volunteered for an experiment. You enter the experimental room at the appointed time, and you see that six other subjects are already there. You take an empty seat at the table around which everyone is seated. The experimenter enters and tells the subjects that the experiment is concerned with accuracy and visual perception. He shows the group two cards (Figure 10–5). On one card is a single line, and on the other card are three lines labeled A, B, and C. The lone line is actually 10 inches long. Line A is 8¾ inches long, line B is 10 inches long,

Solomon Asch used a group of confederates in a "line judgment" experiment to study conformity to group opinion. In the photo above, only subject number six, seated second from the right, is naive. The first five "subjects" have just given an incorrect response and subject number six must decide whether to give the correct response or the conforming one. *(William Vandivert and* Scientific American*)*

and line C is 8 inches long. The experimenter tells the subjects that their task is to match the lone line with the line of equal length from the three-line card. You are to respond next to last.

The experimenter asks each subject in turn to call out the letter of the matching line. The first subject calls out B. This is the line that you also feel is correct. The next four subjects also call out B. When it's your turn, you call out B. The next trial goes the same as the first. The experimenter shows a two-inch standard line, and everyone before you matches it to another two-inch line. You do the same, and you wait for the next trial.

On the next trial, the experimenter shows a three-inch standard line, and the three lines A = 3¾ inches, B = 4¼ inches, and C = 3 inches. You see that line C is the correct answer, and you wait for the first subject to report line C. You may also be thinking that this is really a simple-minded experiment. Suddenly, your whole world begins to collapse! The first subject reports line A. You wonder what's wrong with him; line C is obviously the correct answer. You might even laugh at the obviously

Figure 10-5
Stimulus material used by Asch in early conformity research

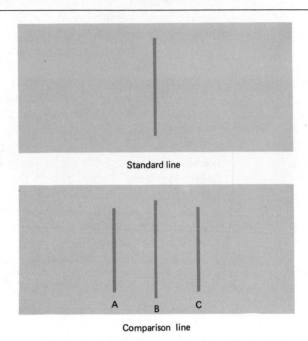

Standard line

Comparison line

incorrect response. You wait for subject two to report line C. Subject two looks the line over carefully and calls out, "Line A is correct." You sit back in disbelief, and you listen while the other subjects who precede you confidently report line A. It's your turn now. What do you do?

This was the question that Asch asked when he devised this procedure for studying conformity. Actually, the first five subjects were experimental confederates who had been told how to respond. On twelve of the eighteen trials, they were to respond unanimously with an incorrect answer. The second-to-the-last subject—you in this case—was really the only naive subject, and the experimenter was interested in finding out whether he or she would conform to the group's opinion or stick to the correct answer.

Asch set out to show that people do not conform to group opinion when they know that their own behavior is correct and that the behavior of the group is incorrect. He developed the line-judging task because he found that when people were asked to judge the lines alone, without group influence, they performed almost without error. However, Asch found that his subjects conformed to the group's incorrect opinion over a third of the time, even when they knew that the group was wrong. When faced with the group's unanimous incorrect opinion, most of the subjects conformed at least once, and only about one-fourth of the subjects were able to turn in a completely error-free performance.

Ross, Bierbrauer, and Hoffman (1976) enumerated the pressures on the subject in the Asch situation. First, it is probably clear to everyone that the subject must wonder about his own ability to judge lines. The subject must think, "How can everyone but me see it that way? Is there something wrong with me?" There is, however, an additional pressure on the subjects. If they report the situation as they see it (differently from the group response), are they not challenging the "competence, wisdom, and sanity of the other group members"? By deviating from the group opinion after the other members have stated their judgment, the subject will be telling the other members that they don't have the ability to do a simple task, such as judging line lengths. This is a tough position to be in.

Despite these pressures, the results obtained by Asch surprised a number of psychologists and created a great deal of interest in studying conformity. In an effort to add more flexibility and eliminate the need for confederates, a modification of the Asch design was developed (Crutchfield, 1955; Deutsch & Gerard, 1955). Instead of having subjects in a face-to-face situation, this technique places subjects in individual booths and allows them to communicate using switches and lights (see photo). Subjects believe that they are seeing the responses of other subjects. However, the experimenter determines the information received by each subject and monitors the subjects' responses.

Factors Affecting Conformity   Conformity often involves conflict between a person's beliefs or inclinations and the group's norms. The way this conflict is resolved varies a great deal from person to person, time to time, and situation to situation. The determinants of conforming versus resisting group pressure are complex. In this section, we will consider how both situational factors and personal concerns affect the degree of conformity.

Situational factors.   There are a variety of factors in the conformity situation that affect the degree to which people yield to the majority. These include the difficulty of the judgments people have to make, the size of the group, and the group's unanimity. Let us first consider the way the difficulty of the judgment affects conformity. Asch predicted that there would be more conformity on ambiguous or difficult judgments than on easy ones. Although Asch found far more conformity than he expected on relatively easy judgments, it is nonetheless true that conformity drops when the judgments become easier (Blake, Helson, & Mouton, 1956). For example, Asch (1952) found that conformity was greater when the differences between the lengths of the comparison lines were small than when they were large. In Figure 10-6, it is very difficult to determine the correct comparison line for judgment (*a*), but easy for judgment (*b*). Asch found greater conformity for the hard judgment than the easy one. From this finding, we can infer that people use the group as a source of information when the task is difficult or ambiguous.

The size and unanimity of the group are also important. Asch (1951) varied the size of the group that the naive subject confronted, using one, two, three, four, eight, or fifteen confederates. He found that conformity increased with group size until the group consisted of three confederates.

Figure 10-6
Examples of difficult (*a*) and easy (*b*) line-judging tasks

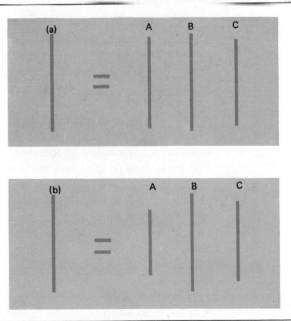

Source: Asch (1952). Reprinted by permission.

Figure 10-7
Errors made by critical subjects to conform with unanimous majorities of different size

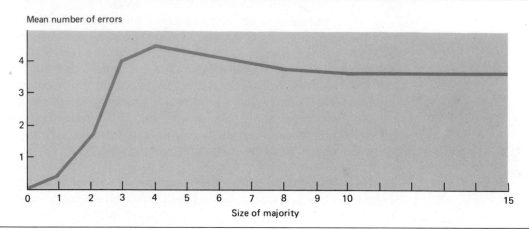

Source: Asch (1951). Reprinted by permission

Then the amount of conformity leveled off so that there was no more conformity to a majority of fifteen members than to a group of three (see Figure 10-7). More recent research shows that increasing the majority beyond the number three does produce more conformity, but the increases are slight (Gerard, Wilhelmy, & Conolley, 1968). Three or four people are generally enough to produce very strong conformity effects.

However, other research has shown that the group size under which maximum conformity is achieved is dependent on a number of factors. The type of task may be one factor. For example, Mann (1977) studied queuing behavior (waiting in line). He had groups of two, four, six, or eight people line up at bus stops in Jerusalem, and then observed how many first arrivers would conform and get into line. He found that conformity increased as group size increased, with the greatest amount of conformity given to the eight-person group. Thus, the relationship between group size and conformity depends on the setting and task (Shaw, 1981).

A second issue relating to group size involves the association that may exist between majority members. Wilder (1977) suggests that when people are categorized as belonging to a group, others respond to them as a group rather than as individuals. That is, if three people from the American Red Cross ask you for a donation, you will not respond to the request as if it came from three separate individuals; rather, you will view it as a request coming from "a group from the Red Cross." Wilder argues that, as a result of this categorization process, a group may lose some of its ability to influence others. He therefore suggests that instead of counting the number of people in a majority, we should be concerned with examining the number of subgroups to determine the pressures toward conformity. To illustrate this point, Wilder found more conformity to a majority of four unrelated persons than to a majority of two groups of two persons each (still four people); and more conformity to a majority of six unrelated persons than to two groups of three people. Thus, both number and group categorization are important variables influencing conformity.

Asch's (1956) original research also looked at the issue of group unanimity. He studied the effect of having just one person deviate from the unanimous majority and found that deviation by that one group member reduced the amount of conformity to the group. In one set of conditions, Asch instructed one confederate to give correct judgments on all trials, even when the remainder of the confederates did not. In other conditions, all of the confederates were instructed to agree on their responses. When the group gave a unanimously incorrect answer, conformity occurred about 35 percent of the time. However, when there was one deviant who gave correct answers, conformity dropped to about one-fourth of that level. Further, it did not seem to matter whether the group size was three or fifteen—one deviant drastically reduced the

Asch's studies of conformity show that a group of three can exert strong pressure on a single individual to conform. There are a variety of factors that determine whether we give in to conformity pressure. (© *Hazel Hankin/Stock, Boston*)

Table 10–2
Mean conformity

	Total
Unanimous	1.87
Deviant 4	1.13
Deviant 1	.94

Source: Adapted from Morris and Miller (1975a), p. 219.

---

amount of conformity. Interestingly enough, conformity by naive subjects decreased even when the deviant gave an incorrect answer.

Numerous other investigators have examined the effect of a single deviant on conformity (see Allen, 1965). Shaw, Rothschild, and Strickland (1957) found that the deviant does not even have to give an answer to reduce conformity. In their study, one of the confederates was instructed to respond by saying that he could not make up his mind about an answer. This ambiguous response also reduced the amount of conformity from naive subjects. In another study, Morris and Miller (1975) found that a group member who deviated early (the first to respond) reduced conformity more than a deviant who responded later (fourth) in the group (see Table 10–2). This effect may be due to the fact that the early deviant created more uncertainty about the correct answer than the deviant who responded fourth. On the other hand, the subject may have received more information (about how the group would react to deviants) with the first deviant as opposed to the fourth; in other words, when the deviant responded first, the subject was able to see whether or not any of the other group members rejected or ridiculed that person.

Why does a single deviant have such a drastic impact on conformity? Allen and Wilder (1980) suggest that a unanimous majority may force the individual to reinterpret the situation; the presence of a deviant, even one, shows the individual that there may be many ways to view the situation and that a reinterpretation is not necessary. While this explanation may apply to situations where there is some doubt about the meaning of events, a broader interpretation focuses on the deviant's effect on normative pressure. If an individual feared group rejection for not conforming, a deviant who was not rejected could alleviate this fear and significantly reduce the amount of normative pressure. The effects of the deviation would quite likely have been very different had the remainder of the group laughed at or threatened the deviant. Then the group's response to the deviant might have actually increased conformity. The group must ensure that the deviant does not "get away with it" lest additional group members decide to act against the desires of the group. One function of brutal public executions is to demonstrate how badly a deviant will be treated by the group. Supposedly, such penalties will cause others to think twice before they try to break away from the group's norms.

Other research on group characteristics has investigated how the position taken by the majority of group members affects conformity. Olmstead and Blake (1955) used a task in which the subjects had to guess the number of clicks they heard. The naive subjects heard the majority report a number that was close to the correct answer, moderately discrepant from the correct answer, or highly discrepant from it. The greatest conformity occurred in the slightly and highly discrepant conditions. Kiesler (1969) suggested that the subjects in the highly discrepant conditions were responding to normative pressures, as they knew that the group answer was incorrect but were afraid to deviate from it. According to Kiesler, this should bring about public compliance without private acceptance. However, the subjects in the slightly discrepant condition did not know the correct answer and were using the group responses to gain information on it. Private acceptance should be most evident in this condition.

Personal factors. A variety of personal factors affect conformity. One such factor may be cultural values favoring conformity over independence. A study of British subjects showed much lower rates of conformity than those found in American studies (Perrin & Spencer, 1980). This result was taken to indicate that conformity in American studies is essentially a cultural phenomenon. However, a study in response to this conclusion was conducted in Belgium and showed conformity rates comparable to those found in American studies (Doms & Van Avermaet, 1980). Thus, the degree of cross-cultural differences in conformity is an unresolved issue that warrants further research (Moscovici, 1985).

Another personal factor that affects conformity is the individual's concern about his or her position or status in the group, especially when the individual is attracted to the group. Overall, the research indicates that people who feel insecure about their position are most likely to conform. For example, Hancock and Sorrentino (1980) found a high degree of conformity in subjects who had received no support from the group in previous meetings and who expected future interaction with the group. The lack of prior support reduced the subjects' self-confidence and the expectation of future interaction made acceptance as group members an important issue. Related research has found that conformity is greater when people are attracted to the group (Back, 1951; Brehm & Festinger,

1957), and when the individual has somewhat lower status than other group members (Raven & French, 1958; Stang, 1972).

In these cases, it seems that individuals are responding to normative group pressures and trying to "buy" themselves a secure position in the group by conforming. Hollander (1958), in fact, suggested that people earn *idiosyncrasy credits* when they conform to group expectations. These credits give individuals status in the group, and they also allow him or her the opportunity to deviate without being rejected by the group. Each time members deviate, they must pay for this action by giving up some of their credits. Therefore, conformity may well help an individual buy a more secure place in the group.

While some research has focused on personal characteristics in isolation, most research has studied how person and situational variables interact to influence conformity. Let us examine two lines of research that show the value of this approach. The first area is sex differences in conformity. A number of early studies (Gerard, Wilhelmy, & Conolley, 1968; Julian, Regula & Hollander, 1968) found that women were more likely to conform than men. These results were often explained by focusing on sex roles: men were expected to be independent while women were expected to be "reasonable" and sensitive to others. While this explanation fit many of the earlier results, it did not explain subsequent findings. For example, Sistrunk and McDavid (1971) found that females conformed more than males when the task was one at which males should have been expert. However, when the task involved female related items, males conformed more than females. Eagly, Wood, and Fishbaugh (1981) found that females conformed more than males when their behavior was being observed, but that there was no sex difference when there was no surveillance. While surveillance did not affect the amount of conformity shown by females, males conformed less under surveillance than under no surveillance conditions. The investigators suggest that surveillance increased concerns with self-presentation: males conformed less than females under these conditions because they were more interested than females in presenting themselves as being independent. Thus, sex and sex roles do not necessarily breed conformity; rather, they breed concern with presenting a certain image to others. While there is still some debate about why sex differences in conformity occur (Eagly & Carli, 1981), these studies show that sex alone does not determine conformity; sex interacts with the situation to determine conformity.

Santee and Maslach (1982) also adopt a self-presentation approach to explain conformity. They argue that people vary in the degree to which they want to be seen as distinct and separate from others (this desire can be measured by a number of scales). However, the situation determines when this personality variable will influence conformity. For example, individuals can more readily present themselves as distinct by deviating from a unanimous group as opposed to a nonunanimous group. If other people are already dissenting, an individual who also dissents will not look particularly unique. Santee and Maslach found, in fact, that desire for distinctiveness had a greater influence on conformity in the face of a unanimous group, compared with a nonunanimous group. Once again, the role of individual characteristics can best be understood in relation to situational variables.

SOCIAL IMPACT THEORY

Obedience and conformity are two important consequences of social influence pressures. They can lead to behaviors that few people would have predicted had they not actually been demonstrated in laboratory research. The research on these phenomena help us to understand a variety of dramatic instances of social influence, including the murder of six million Jews under the direction of Adolf Hitler and the mass suicide that took place in Jonestown in 1978 under the direction of the fanatical preacher Jim Jones.

A recent general theory of social influence helps us to understand and relate some of the factors that affect obedience, conformity, and other kinds of social influence. It is called social impact theory (Jackson, 1986, 1987; Latané, 1981). Social impact theory states that the social impact or force felt by a person, or target, is a function of the strength, immediacy, and number of sources of social influence that are present. That is, a person will be more affected when there are stronger sources of influence, when the sources are physically closer or more immediate, and when there are more of them. Social impact works just like physical impact. For example, the amount of light falling on a table is a function of the strength of the lights overhead, their distance from the table, and their number. Let us consider how these basic principles of strength, immediacy, and number might apply to obedience and conformity.

Social impact theory predicts more impact and thus more influence when the source of influence is strong. Thus, in Milgram's procedure, we would predict more obedience when the authority is strong (e.g., highly credible or distinguished) and more conformity when the group is composed of high-status or physically strong peers. This prediction regarding source strength is supported by research on attitude change showing that more persuasion was produced by credible communicators (Hass, 1981). The theory also predicts more impact and influence when the source is closer. This prediction is directly applicable to Milgram's

Social impact theory suggests that a strong teacher who is close to her students will have more impact than a weak teacher or one who stands further away. (© *Susan Lapides 1986*)

experiments on obedience that showed more obedience when the experimenter—one source of social impact—was closer to the subject, but less obedience when the learner—another source of social impact—was closer to the subject (Milgram, 1974). Ann Landers operates at a long distance from her targets of influence. She contacts them through the newspapers or through the mail. Her impact would be even stronger, according to the theory, if she were closer. For example, if she delivered her message by telephone or in person, that message would have more impact. It is a testimony to Ms. Landers's strength as a source of social impact that she can have so much influence from such a great distance.

Third, social impact theory predicts more influence when there are more sources. Consistent with this prediction are the findings showing more conformity with more group members. You may recall that while there was greater conformity when there were more group members, the effect of adding additional members beyond three or four was relatively small. This finding is consistent with another principle of social impact theory that says that the mathematical relationship governing all three variables—strength, immediacy, and number—is a power function. This means that initial increases in strength, immediacy, and number have large effects but that additional increases have less and less impact. Not surprisingly then, adding a few group members at the beginning increases conformity dramatically, but each additional member after that affects conformity relatively little.

Another principle of social impact theory states that the impact of any source of social influence is diffused as the strength, immediacy, and number of the targets of social influence increase. For example, there should be less impact on a strong target than a weak one. We just saw that people with less status in a group conform more. As their strength (measured by status) increases, the group's impact is diffused and they conform less. This finding is exactly what social impact theory predicts. The number of targets was explored in one of the variations of Milgram's (1977) research. When there were two other confederates posing as real subjects, the experimenter's orders to the actual subject had less impact. These confederates also modeled defiance of the experimenter's orders, so it is unclear if the number of targets *alone* reduces social impact; their behavior also has an effect. However, it is plausible to conclude that their number alone reduces the experimenter's impact (Brown, 1986). The immediacy variable in the case of cotargets of influence suggests that as other people who are also targets of the source are closer to you, the impact of the source will be diffused away from you and onto those cotargets.

While the principles of social impact theory are applicable to obedience and conformity studies, they have also been supported in a number of other contexts. For example, research on stagefright by Jackson and Latané (1981) shows that people singing in front of an audience experience more impact as the size of the audience, which constitutes the source of impact, increases. This study also shows less impact as the number of singers, that is, cotargets, increases. In the last case, the audience's impact is diffused. Research on bystander intervention by Latané and Darley (1970) discussed in Chapter Eight also shows that the impact of a source, for example, a person in distress, is diffused if there are a large number of bystanders.

The research supporting social impact theory is impressive, as is its wide applicability. In recent years, similar theories that consider strength, immediacy, and number have also been proposed (Knowles, 1983; Tanford & Penrod, 1984). Their fundamental ideas are compatible with those of social impact theory.

DEVIATION AND RESISTANCE TO SOCIAL INFLUENCE

Our discussion thus far has shown many of the factors that lead people to respond to social influence. There are many pressures that act on us as targets of social influence, pressures that can be very difficult to resist. There are, indeed, many risks run by a person who deviates and refuses to go along with the crowd. In one demonstration of such risks, Schachter (1951) set up groups of naive subjects and planted three experimental confederates who acted as subjects in each of the groups. The task of the groups was to discuss how to handle a juvenile delinquent named Johnny Rocco. One of the confederates (the deviant) consistently disagreed with the group's opinion about how to handle Johnny. A second confederate (the slider) began by disagreeing with the majority opinion, but soon switched positions to conform to that of the majority. The final confederate (the mode) agreed with the majority opinion throughout the discussion. Schachter manipulated cohesiveness by making half of the groups believe that they would be working on very attractive tasks (high cohesive) and by making the other half believe that they would be working on relatively unattractive tasks (low cohesive). After the groups had discussed the Johnny Rocco case, the subjects were asked to rate how much they liked the other members of the group and to nominate group members to serve in various functional positions in the group.

With regard to the deviant, the group first reacted by directing a great deal of its communication and attention to him, apparently in an attempt to persuade him to conform to group opinion. Finally, the group members seemed to give up and to cease talking to him; in essence, they rejected him. When the jobs in the group were divided up, the deviant was consistently given the worst job. Thus, he was not only rejected; he was also punished for not conforming to group opinion. Interestingly enough, the rejection of the deviant was greatest in the highly cohesive groups. Schachter also found that the slider, who began by deviating but later switched to a conforming posture, was liked as much as the mode, who consistently agreed with the group. The slider was often assigned popular and attractive jobs, and he received a great deal of the group's attention. Apparently, the slider's switching to conformity was seen by the group as admitting that he had seen the light and was "mature enough" to admit it. Thus, consistent deviation from a group is met with rejection whereas conformity is rewarded.

However, despite all the pressures to comply, noncompliance is often as common as, if not more common than, compliance. In every study of conformity there were incidences of nonconformity by subjects—in fact, nonconformity to the majority was more common than conformity in the Asch studies. Many of the great men of history have been nonconformists. Galileo was tortured because he argued that the earth revolved around the sun when the prevailing view was that the earth was the focal point of the universe. Columbus was ridiculed because he believed that the world was round at a time when most people believed that it was flat. Freud was not allowed to publish many of his writings because his theories offended his contemporaries. Why do such men deviate from the majority and risk ridicule and punishment?

Before examining the reasons for noncompliance, one point should be made. A number of researchers (for example, Hollander & Willis, 1964; Willis, 1965, 1972) have suggested that there may be many different types of nonconformity. As far back as 1903, the French sociologist Tarde suggested that there are at least two types of nonconformity. The first is "counterimitation," which involves doing the exact opposite of what the individual observes being done by others. The second is "invention," or simple "nonimitation," which involves making up one's own mind about how to act and not simply responding to group pressures. Tarde's counterimitating behavior has been relabeled *anticonformity,* and his inventive behavior has been relabeled *independence.*

It is interesting to note that the anticonformist, like the conformist, is influenced by group pressures. However, instead of conforming to group pressures, he or she opposes them. This type of person "zigs" when the group "zags." The independent, on the other hand, is our hero. This is the individual who "makes up his own mind, being able to 'take the group or . . . leave it,' as his own good sense would dictate" (Krech, Crutchfield, & Ballachey, 1962). The independent looks at the group's behavior, decides whether that behavior is right or wrong, and then on the basis of this decision either conforms to the group or does not.

The majority of the social psychological work on conformity has studied the conformist, not the deviant or the nonconformist. However, there are some theories that apply to the question of why a person does not conform. One of these is *reactance theory* (Brehm, 1966; West & Wicklund, 1980). As Chapter Six noted, Brehm hypothesized that if an individual's freedom to perform certain behaviors is threatened or eliminated, he or she will experience a motivational arousal that is aimed at regaining the freedom. This motivational arousal is labeled "reactance." When individuals feel pressure from the group to conform, whether that pressure be normative or informational, they should experience reactance because the pressure threatens their freedom not to conform. Nonconformity should then become a more attractive behavioral option, and individuals should attempt to demonstrate that they are free not to conform. In the reactance view of nonconformity, therefore, pressures from the group to conform cause individuals to experience reactance, and result in their nonconformity. Such nonconformity is a direct result of felt pressures toward conformity, and thus it is an example of anticonformity rather than independence.

The desire to be unique is another reason why people resist influence (Maslach, 1974; Snyder & Fromkin, 1980). Most of us believe that we

People do not always conform to social norms for appropriate behavior. This is especially true if they feel deindividuated. For example, aggressive behavior is more likely when people feel deindividuated. (© *Trefonides/The Picture Cube*)

have certain traits or abilities that are different from those possessed by others. Further, in most societies value is placed on being different and standing apart from the crowd. One way of demonstrating this uniqueness is by not conforming to the group. Santee and Maslach (1982) found that people who place a high value on uniqueness resist conformity, especially when the rest of the group adopts a unanimous position. Further, being different attracts the attention of others. As we saw in the Schachter (1951) study, early in the group's life the majority of communication was aimed at those people who held a deviant attitude. Thus, people may adopt anticonformity as a way of showing their *uniqueness* and *attracting attention.*

Another area of research that sheds some light on nonconformity is the study of *deindividuation* (see Chapter Eleven). Individuals in groups often exhibit behaviors that they would normally not exhibit if they were alone. For example, some people who might act violently if they were submerged in a mob, would not behave aggressively if they were acting alone. Festinger, Pepitone, and Newcomb (1952) suggested that people in groups do not feel responsible for their behaviors because they cannot readily be identified as individuals. This lack of personal identifiability, which results from the individual's submergence in the group, leads to a decrease in the individual's inhibitions about performing certain behaviors. The more submerged individuals feel, the more deindividuated they are, and the more restraint reduction should occur. Based on this reasoning, Singer, Brush, and Lublin (1965) suggested that there should be more independence in deindividuated groups than in more individuated groups. In one condition of their study, the subjects wore white laboratory coats and were not readily identifiable (deindividuated group). In a second condition, the subjects were asked to wear "a dress or suit and heels and hose" and were given name tags to wear; thus, they were readily identifiable. An Asch-type task was used, with one naive subject and three confederates in each session. The results indicated that more nonconforming responses were given by the deindividuated group than by the more individuated group. Thus, conditions that increase an individual's feeling of being deindividuated may lead to more nonconformity. It would seem that the nonconformity found in deindividuated groups fits into the category of "independent" behavior. Such individuals are not simply acting in a manner opposite to that of the group, as do the anticonformists. They know how they want to act, irrespective of the group, and deindividuation allows them to remain independent and to follow their own desires.

As this discussion illustrates, there are many factors that influence nonconformity. Some of these factors involve the group and the situation while others involve personal characteristics of the deviant. It is important to identify the reasons for deviation if we wish to determine whether the action is anticonformity or independence.

SUMMARY

Social influence involves the exercise of power by a person or group to influence the behavior of others. *Power* is viewed as the potential to influence others. There are many bases of power including coercive, legitimate, expert, referent, and informational.

A *leader* is the individual who exerts the most influence in a group. Leaders tend to be either *task oriented* or *relationship oriented*. Often groups have two leaders, each taking a different orientation. One of the earliest theories suggested that leaders have certain *traits* that make them leaders. This position, however, has received little support. The *Zeitgeist* theories argue that the situation determines who will become the group's leader. While some situational factors such as seniority and physical position do influence leadership, this approach has proved too limited in scope. The most accepted view is that the situation, personal characteristics of the individual, and the followers interact to determine who will be leader. Research on leadership style shows that, while *autocratic leaders* may have productive groups, members are most happy with a *democratic leader*. The *contingency theory* of leadership suggests that the situation determines what will be the most effective style of leadership.

Obedience involves following the direct orders of a person in a position of authority. Milgram's research found that people are surprisingly obedient. One reason is that they feel that the leader will assume responsibility for their behavior.

Conformity involves yielding to the real or imagined pressures of the group. Groups use *informational* and *normative pressure* to get members to conform. Conformity is affected by both situational and personal factors.

Social impact theory states that the impact of a source or sources on a target of influence increases with the strength, immediacy, and number of the sources. Social impact is diffused across targets as the strength, immediacy, and number of the targets of influence increase.

Deviation from group opinion can lead to rejection from the group. There are at least two types of nonconformity behaviors. *Anticonformity* involves doing the opposite of what is dictated by the group. *Independence* occurs when the individual resists group influence to act as he or she deems appropriate. *Reactance,* the desire to appear *unique,* and the desire to *attract attention* may underlie anticonformity. *Deindividuation* facilitates independent behavior.

KEY WORDS

anticonformity	informational pressure
autocratic style of leadership	internalization
charisma	leader
coercive power	legitimate power
compliance	obedience
conformity	power
democratic style of leadership	private acceptance
diffusion of impact	referent power
expert power	reward power
identification	social impact theory
independence	social influence
informational power	

SUGGESTED READINGS

Cialdini, R. B. (1985). *Influence: Science and practice.* Glenview, IL: Scott, Foresman.

Fiedler, F. E., & Chemers, M. M. (1974). *Leadership and effective management.* Glenview, IL: Scott, Foresman.

Freeman, J. L., & Doob, A. N. (1968). *Deviancy.* New York: Academic Press.

Hollander, E. P. (1985). Leadership and power. In G. Lindzey and E. Aronson (Eds.), *The handbook of social psychology* (Vol. 2, pp. 485–537). New York: Random House.

Milgram, S. (1977). *The individual in a social world.* Reading, MA: Addison-Wesley Publishing.

Moscovici, S. (1985). Social influence and conformity. In G. Lindzey and E. Aronson (Eds.), *The handbook of social psychology* (Vol. 2, pp. 347–412). New York: Random House.

Schopler, J., & Layton, B. D. (1972). *Attributions of interpersonal power and influence.* New York: General Learning Corporation.

Tedeschi, J. (Ed.), (1974). *Perspectives on social power.* Chicago: Aldine Publishing.

Wheeler, L., Deci, E., Reis, H., & Zuckerman, M. (1978). *Interpersonal influence* (2nd ed.). Boston: Allyn & Bacon.

ELEVEN

GROUP DYNAMICS

The museum director smiled at the young man. "That's an interesting theory but it has one major flaw. It would have been impossible for anyone to sail a balsa raft from Peru to the Polynesian Islands. Do you realize that the journey is over 4,300 miles?"

Thor Heyerdahl pressed his point. "Look at the similarity between these artifacts found in Peru and on the Polynesian Islands. And how do you explain the fact that both the ancient Incas of Peru and the Polynesians have a god named Kon Tiki? The Polynesian Islands must have first been settled by peoples from Peru."

"You will never be able to make a strong case by showing similarities in artifacts and gods," responded the director. "These coincidences mean nothing if it is impossible to get from Peru to Polynesia by raft. You have to show that this feat could be done before your theory will be taken seriously."

Thor left this meeting more determined than ever to prove his theory. He would show that it was possible to sail a raft from Peru to Polynesia. He spent weeks in the library studying the type of raft that was used by the Incas during the period between A.D. 500 and 1100. Thor found that they built large rafts out of balsa trees and lashed these logs together with hemp rope. They erected cloth sails and used long rudders to steer the rafts. Could such a raft make a 4,300-mile trip over some of the roughest ocean in the world?

Clearly, Thor could not make the trip by himself. Someone had to man the helm at all times and there were many chores to do on board. With little effort, Thor talked five other men into accompanying him on the trip. Herman would keep the instruments and measure the currents and winds. Erik was an expert at patching sails, splicing ropes, and navigating. Knut and Torstein had experience with wireless radios during World War II, and they would be responsible for communication. Bengt would make scientific notes and act as quartermaster. And Thor would captain the expedition and keep the logbook.

With the crew assembled and financial backing secured, the group set off to Peru to build their raft. They had to go deep into jungles to find large balsa trees, and with great effort they moved nine gigantic logs to Callao harbor. There they worked on lashing the logs together, building a small cabin on the deck, and making their sails. They followed drawings of the ancient Inca rafts, and they accepted no help from the curious audience that gathered each day to watch them build their raft. The native Peruvians watched the strange raft take shape, and each day the size of the crowd grew.

Finally the raft was ready. The logs ranged from thirty to forty-five feet long. On the large sail, they painted a picture of the *Tiki* and they christened their raft the *Kon Tiki*. Each man had worked with the knowledge

The *Kon Tiki* crew built and piloted their unusual craft from Peru to Polynesia. The crew became a close-knit group during the 101-day journey. (Science Illustrated, *UPI/Bettmann Newsphotos*)

that the raft would be only as good as the worst piece of work. Finally, on April 27, 1947, food and water were brought on board and the *Kon Tiki* was ready.

Early the next morning, the raft was slowly towed out to sea. As they waved farewell to the tugboat, each man knew that these were the last people he would see for at least three months—if all went well.

Three days into their voyage, the men held a meeting to discuss rules. Although each man had been assigned certain duties, all the difficult jobs like steering, watch, and cooking were divided equally. Every man had two hours each day and two hours each night at the steering oar. All meals were to be eaten outside the cabin, and "the 'right place' was only at the farthest end of the logs astern" (Heyerdahl, 1950). Each position also had its rules. For example, the night watch had to wear a rope around his waist at all times.

Days wore into weeks, weeks into months. The sturdy raft was battered by high waves and fierce storms, but it always emerged the victor. Each morning, the men would anxiously check the ropes to make sure that their raft was holding together.

Coordination of effort was essential if the voyage was to succeed. Each man had to do his part, and they all had to work together during crises such as storms. Living in such close quarters offered little room for bickering, so when trouble arose, the group held a powwow.

Finally, ninety-three days into their journey, the watch shouted, "Land ahead!" All the men scrambled to the deck and saw the island of Puka Puka in the distance. However, the winds were not in their favor, and they sailed past this island. During the next several days, they passed a number of islands; the inhabitants would often row out toward the raft. At these times, the men busied themselves cleaning up the *Kon Tiki* so that they could show off their proud craft.

On the 101st day, a strong wind blew them onto a reef off a small Polynesian island. They had made it! They had shown that it was indeed possible that ancient inhabitants of Peru could have been the first settlers of Polynesia. These six men had overcome storms, navigational problems, and interpersonal squabbles. Using only the most primitive means, they had duplicated a trip that may have been made over one thousand years earlier. They were hailed as heroes throughout the world. President Truman received members of the expedition.

The voyage of the *Kon Tiki* is notable in many respects. One of the most interesting stories of the trip involves how six individuals from very different backgrounds could be formed into a closely knit group capable of undertaking such a trip. This group of men was able to work together and make the complex decisions that ensured success.

Each man had a role in the *Kon Tiki* crew. Thor Heyerdahl, shown here, was the captain who was responsible for the voyage. (Science Illustrated, *UPI/Bettmann Newsphotos*)

WHAT IS A GROUP?

A number of years ago, Allport (1924) stated that groups were only an illusory phenomenon—not something real. He made the seemingly profound statement that nobody ever stumbled over a group. Although this may be true, more recent research has demonstrated that groups do have definite boundaries. People know where their group stops and other groups begin, and there is an identifiable transition through which people go to become full members in a group (Moreland & Levine, 1984). An even more cogent defense of groups was presented by Lewin (1948), who argued that groups are real because they have real effects on people.

A group is defined as two or more people who are interacting with one another in such a manner that each person influences and is influenced by each other person. Group members generally feel that they belong together and can identify the boundary of their group. (*Top left, Chris Maynard/Stock, Boston; top right, David S. Strickler/The Picture Cube; bottom left, © John Maher 1980/EKM-Nepenthe; bottom right, Joel Gordon 1983*)

As we will see, groups have dramatic effects on almost every aspect of our lives; they influence our attitudes, perceptions, performance, interpersonal relations, and decisions. In fact, it might be argued that we never escape the influence of the groups to which we belong!

Determining the nature of this entity that we call a group is an important step. The conclusion we reach has a profound effect in guiding our research and theories on groups. If we agree with Allport, we will focus our study solely on individuals, with little reference to groups or categories. However, if we adopt the position that groups are real and have describable qualities, we then must concern ourselves with studying the development of groups and the effect of the group on the individual and on interpersonal behavior.

Today, social psychologists view the group as a dynamic whole that is different from the sum of its parts; it is neither greater nor less than these parts, but it is clearly different than the collection of individual members. Although investigators have offered somewhat different definitions of the group, most would be comfortable with the position that a group involves "two or more persons who are interacting with one another in such a manner that each person influences and is influenced by each other person" (Shaw, 1981, p. 8). Group members generally feel that they belong together; they see themselves as forming a single unit. This feeling of self-awareness usually results because the group members share common beliefs and attitudes and accept certain norms of the group. Group members also share at least one common goal.

As we can see, the crew of the *Kon Tiki* fit the definition of a group. They were involved in constant face-to-face interaction during their voyage. They saw themselves as forming a group, and felt that they belonged together. In talking with others, they often referred to themselves as "the *Kon Tiki* crew." In other words, the awareness of being a group became part of their own identity. Finally, they shared the common goal of completing the journey from Peru to Polynesia. We can contrast this group with the collection of people who gathered to watch them build their raft. These people did not interact with each other and had no feeling of belonging together. They simply happened to be in the same place at the same time, and thus engaged in a similar activity. The term *collective* has been used to define a gathering of individuals who do not have face-to-face interactions but are engaged in a common activity (Milgram & Toch, 1968).

THE STRUCTURE OF GROUPS

If we consider the crew of the *Kon Tiki* a group, we begin to see some of the features that characterize groups. First, groups have boundaries;

Laws are written norms that specify what must or must not be done. They often describe the punishment that will follow the breaking of the norm. *(© Joel Gordon 1982)*

we can determine who is a crew member and who is not. Further, within these boundaries, groups have structure. As we will see, this structure is made up of rules and positions to guide behavior.

Norms   As the men developed into the crew, they spent a lot of time discussing their structure and the rules by which they would live. Some of the rules they formed applied to everyone. For example, each person was to spend four hours a day at the helm and no one was allowed to eat inside the cabin. Each crew member was allowed only one quart of water a day. *Norms* are rules that govern specific behaviors and apply to everyone in the group. In other words, "Norms specify what must or must not be done when" (Steiner, 1972).

In some cases, the norms may be explicit and developed through group discussions. However, in other cases, the norms may develop through practice and they are unwritten and unspecified. In either case, group members are expected to follow norms. For example, Milgram and his colleagues (Milgram et al., 1986) found that people waiting in line objected when someone broke the unwritten norm about "cutting" into the line. Interestingly, the highest rate of objection came from the person immediately behind the "cutter." In another example, Roethlisberger and Dickson (1939) showed the effect of norms in their study of workers at the Western Electric Company in Hawthorne, Illinois. Work teams in this plant were responsible for wiring switchboard panels. Although each worker's pay was determined by the number of boards he wired, the workers developed informal norms about the number of panels a worker "should" wire each day. If everyone followed these norms, no individual could be singled out as being better or worse than any other.

Early research in industrial settings found that workers often develop norms about how much each worker should produce. Rate-busters or chiselers are harassed until they conform to the norm. (© *MCMLXXXVI Peter Menzel*)

If a worker exceeded ("rate buster") or failed to meet ("chiseler") these standards, he was harassed by his fellow workers. This harassment took the form of good-natured but pointed kidding and "binging." A bing involved one of the workers punching the norm breaker in the upper arm; the bing was hard enough to get the point across, but not so hard that it could injure the individual.

In Chapter Ten, we discussed another interesting characteristic of norms. Jacobs and Campbell (1961) conducted a study showing that groups developed norms about the amount of movement seen in the autokinetic effect. After the norm was developed, individual group members were replaced one at a time with new people. Even when all the old members had been replaced, the norm regarding the amount of movement remained intact. This study demonstrated that norms often outlive the group members who form them. This point can be seen by examining the laws in many states. Such an examination will show that there are still laws about where people may tie their horses, what position may be used during sexual intercourse, and the number of spittoons that must be placed in public places. It seems that old norms die slowly! Fortunately, reasonable norms tend to last longer than unreasonable and arbitrary norms (MacNeil & Sherif, 1976).

Roles   In addition to rules that governed everyone's behavior, the crew of the *Kon Tiki* also had rules that applied only to certain positions. For example, at night the helmsman was required to wear a safety rope around his waist. *Roles* define the obligations of and expectations for people in particular positions. Roles specify *who* should do what, when, and how. We may view roles as positions in groups, along with the rules that govern the behavior of people who occupy these positions. For example, Thor Heyderdahl was in the role of leader. Being in this position, he had certain responsibilities, such as acting as spokesman for the group and seeing that his men performed the necessary duties. He also had certain privileges, such as dining with dignitaries and accepting honors for the crew.

In an ideal world, roles and norms should ensure that the group functions smoothly; members should not only know how to act, but they should also know what to expect from others. But groups are rarely perfect systems, and conflicts often arise to some degree. One of the more common conflicts concerns roles; there are actually two types of *role conflict* that can occur. One type of conflict may reside within the role itself. A role may require a person to perform conflicting behaviors. For example, many parents struggle with the duties of providing warmth and love to their children while also having to punish and discipline them. A second type of conflict arises because we belong to many groups at the same time; the

Role conflict often exists for married people who find that the demands of their job often conflict with the demands of their family role. Closer to home, students may find that the role of student conflicts with their social roles on campus. *(Eric A. Roth/The Picture Cube)*

role requirements of one group may conflict with those of another. A common example of this conflict involves the work and family roles. The work role may demand that the person spend large amounts of time at the office or traveling, while the role of spouse or parent dictates that the person should spend time with the family.

There are many ways to deal with these role conflicts. One involves simply ignoring competing roles or demands within a role (Stryker & Statham, 1985). While doing this may make life easier for the individual faced with the conflict, it makes his or her behavior more difficult to predict by other group members. A second approach is to choose groups that do not present conflicting roles. For example, a woman may choose a less fulfilling job because it gives her greater freedom to spend time with her family. While this approach reduces the conflict between the roles of work and family, the woman may experience resentment because her job does not meet her needs. As these examples point out, roles are generally developed to solve the needs of the group rather than those of the individual. As such, role conflict is often difficult to resolve and may be the source of considerable tension.

In addition to role conflict, we can identify some other trouble spots with roles and norms. For example, both norms and roles may be ambiguous: people may not know what is expected of them in specific situations or positions. There is also the problem of role overload in which too much is expected of a person by the roles that he or she occupies.

In summary, norms and roles give structure to the group. They are important for the group members because they allow them to predict how others will behave. They also relieve individuals from having to make a conscious decision for every action they make in the group, thereby playing a vital role in helping the group function smoothly. Finally, they may help avoid or resolve conflict. For example, the crew of the *Kon Tiki* decided that everyone would have equal night duty. If a crew member attempted to avoid this duty, the other crew members would simply have had to remind him of their agreement. In this case, the norm becomes a third party that mediates an agreement and eliminates the need for the use of personal power or coercion. However, norms and roles that are too rigid can hinder individual creativity and make it impossible for the group to respond to new situations (see Chapter Four). Likewise, norms and roles that are ambiguous or demand too much can be troublesome for the individual and group.

Now that we have discussed the structure of groups, let us turn our attention to the research and theory on group behavior. We will approach this examination in two ways. First, we will consider the group as a unit and examine how that unit functions. For example, we will discuss conditions that influence how productive the *group* will be and we will investigate how groups arrive at decisions. Second, we will change our focus to the individual group member and ask how being a member of a group affects that person's behavior, perceptions, and attitudes. Here, we will discuss, for example, how being a member of a group affects an *individual's* performance. In several of the earlier chapters, we discussed many of the social processes that occur in groups; for example, in Chapter Ten we examined conformity, leadership, and obedience. In this chapter, therefore, we will focus mainly on how groups influence perceptions, performance, and decisions. Let us begin by considering the group as a unit.

GROUP PRODUCTIVITY

Some of the earliest studies on groups were concerned with the problem of comparing group and individual productivity. Assuming that there is a problem to be solved or a task to be completed, is it better to have a single individual work on the problem/task or to assemble a group that will work together? For example, Thor Heyerdahl had numerous drawings of ancient Incan rafts. He was faced with the problem of designing his own raft based on these old drawings. How was he to solve this problem? On the one hand, he could study the drawings on his own and arrive at a solution; or he could assemble his crew, show them the drawings, and have the group arrive at a plan for the raft.

To advise Heyerdahl on the best strategy to use, we would need to know whether groups are more efficient than individuals at solving problems. This seems like a simple question to answer. One need merely give a group of people a problem to work on and then compare the group's performance to that of an individual. However, the procedure raises some difficult questions. Is it fair to compare a group of six people to an individual working alone? Certainly six people working on a problem, whether individually or together, should have a better chance of arriving at the correct solution than one person working alone. A finding that the group does better than the individual may simply mean that six people working individually on a problem are better than one person, or it may mean that something is added because the six people work together as a group.

One possibility would be to average the work of six people working alone. This arrangement would constitute a *nominal group* (a number of persons working on a problem independently). Comparing the real group's solution to the nominal group's solution would indicate whether working in a group did aid in problem solving. This is the usual manner in which research in the area of group productivity has proceeded. Looking at a different issue, we could compare the group's product to that of the best of the six individuals working alone. Or the group's product could be compared to the product of the weakest member of the nominal group to see whether a group is more effective than its weakest member. All of these questions are important in determining whether a group is more productive than an individual, and research has been devoted to each of them.

The early research on group versus individual efficiency proceeded in a haphazard fashion without theory or structure to guide it. In one early experiment, Marjorie Shaw (1932) asked individuals and groups to arrive at a solution to the following problem:

> On one side of a river are three wives and three husbands. All of the men but none of the women can row. Get them all across the river by means of a boat carrying only three at one time. No man will allow his wife to be in the presence of another man unless he is also there. (p. 492)

Shaw found that 60 percent of the groups, and only 14 percent of the individuals who worked alone, arrived at correct solutions to the problem.

Groups are more likely to accept solutions to problems when those solutions are proposed by a high status rather than a low status member. *(Rick Smolan/Stock, Boston)*

While these early studies suggested that groups were generally more effective than individuals, more recent efforts have focused on explaining the group advantage and identifying when this advantage is most likely to occur.

For example, careful examination of working groups has found that groups are more effective at problem solving than individuals only when one of the group members has known the correct solution (Laughlin & Futoran, 1985). This may seem like a rather insignificant statement, but it adds an important piece to the puzzle of understanding group productivity. Solving a problem involves at least two steps: one is developing the correct solution and the other is recognizing that solution as correct and adopting it. The above finding suggests that groups are not necessarily better at generating solutions than individuals working alone, but they are superior at recognizing the correct solution once it has been proposed.

Although we might be tempted to adopt the position that groups are superior at recognizing the correct solution, we must add one caveat to complete this statement: *Groups are superior at recognizing correct solutions, especially when these solutions are presented by members who have high status in the group.* In a study that examined the problem-solving behavior of B-26 bomber crews, it was found that the crew recognized and adopted the correct solution 94 percent of the time when it was proposed by the high-status pilots (Torrance, 1954). However, when the correct solution was proposed by gunners who held the lowest status in the crew, it was adopted only 62 percent of the time in permanent crews.

In attempting to identify when groups would be most effective, Steiner (1972, 1976) suggested that the efficiency of a group is dependent on the *process loss*—the difference between the group's potential and its actual productivity. There are two types of process losses that can occur in groups. First, there is *coordination* loss, which is determined by how well the group can combine and use the individual member's contributions. For example, when rowing the *Kon Tiki* out to sea, coordination loss would be high if the members all rowed at different times. Second, there is also *motivation loss* in groups; this loss occurs when members do not put their maximum effort into the task.

Recognizing the importance of group process on performance, Hackman and Morris (1975) have identified three variables that impact on process. They argue that group performance will be strongly influenced by the *task performance strategies* that groups adopt; these strategies are the decisions that groups make about how they will approach their tasks. Unfortunately, Hackman and Morris point out that most groups don't want to "waste time" talking about strategies and instead jump directly into working on the task. There is evidence (Hackman, Brousseau, & Wiess, 1976) that groups perform better when they do take the time to determine strategies before working on tasks. Clearly, the type of task facing the group will influence the need to develop a strategy and the type of strategy that will be best suited for the task. A second variable is *member effort*; that is, how hard the group members work on the task. This variable will be strongly influenced by the members' motivation to contribute to the group and their attraction to the group. Finally, group members' *knowledge and skills* will influence the final outcome.

As we can see, both of these approaches to group productivity suggest that having resources and adequate membership are not enough to ensure a successful group. The group must blend these talents together and motivate its members to contribute. There are, in fact, many factors that will influence how well the group will be able to do this. Two of these factors fall under the heading of task type and group characteristics.

TASK TYPE AND PERFORMANCE

Looking first at the type of task, Steiner offered a classification system for tasks. He pointed out that not all tasks have the same requirements, and that performance potential is affected by the requirements of the task. Given this situation, it is important for groups to recognize the type of task and develop an appropriate strategy for working on the task.

Disjunctive Tasks   This type of task requires an "either-or" decision. The problem of the three wives and husbands presented earlier is an example of a disjunctive task. In this problem, the group must decide among a number of alternative answers. It is unlikely that the group will arrive at the correct answer unless at least one of its members has the correct answer. On disjunctive tasks, the group's maximum potential is dependent on the capacities of its most capable members. There may be motivation losses because the less capable members perceive that their efforts are unimportant.

Conjunctive Tasks   In a conjunctive task, all of the group members perform essentially the same subtask, and the overall performance of the

In conjunctive tasks, the group's performance is often only as good as the least capable group member. In the above example, the dragon can move only as fast as the slowest person. *(Laimute E. Druskis/Stock, Boston)*

group is dependent on the combination of these subtasks. An example is a team of mountain climbers. Here, as with all conjunctive tasks, the group's maximum performance is dependent on the capacities of its least capable member; the group of climbers can reach the mountaintop no faster than the slowest climber. On such conjunctive tasks, it is likely that the average performance of the individuals in the group will be better than the group's performance since a group will be severely penalized by even one bad member. On this problem, unlike the disjunctive task, motivation loss is likely to result because the most capable members reduce their effort.

Additive Tasks   Additive tasks are those in which the final group product is the sum of the group members. A tug-of-war is an example of an additive task. In additive tasks, the group product will almost always be better than the product of the single individual, even if the average individual in the group does not perform as well as the single individual performing alone. Such a case occurred in the Ringelmann rope-pulling study. The individual performing alone exerted an average pull of 63 kilograms on a rope whereas the average group of eight individuals exerted a pull of 248 kilograms. Hence, the group was better than the individual even though each member in the group exerted an average of only 31 kilograms of the pull.

Both coordination loss and motivation loss may occur with additive tasks. It is important that the members' efforts be coordinated to get the maximum effort. For example, it does little good for every member to put maximum effort into the rope-pulling task if those efforts are not made simultaneously. As we will see in our discussion of social loafing, motivation loss may occur if members do not feel responsible for the final group product.

Discretionary Tasks   Discretionary tasks require the group to arrive at a group decision. For example, deciding which route the *Kon Tiki* would follow was a discretionary task. As Steiner points out, this decision does not involve an either-or-answer, as does the disjunctive task. Further, the final group decision can be arrived at in a number of ways. In the above example, the crew could have given a total weight to the estimates of their leader, Thor. Or the group decision could have been reached by taking the average of each member's course. Thus, discretionary tasks allow the use of a number of alternative means by which the group can arrive at a decision, and the decision of the group will be strongly affected by the means chosen. Because of this, coordination loss is the major problem faced in this type of task.

On additive tasks, the product is the sum of the group members' efforts. As in the picture above, every little bit of effort will help. *(Dan Chidester/The Image Works)*

GROUP CHARACTERISTICS AND PRODUCTIVITY

Just as the type of task can influence how productive a group will be, so too can group characteristics affect productivity. If we look at the *Kon Tiki* crew, we can ask a number of questions relating to the makeup of the group. One question focuses on size. Would the voyage have been accomplished more easily with a larger crew? We can also examine the members' feelings for each other. Heyerdahl chose men who knew and liked each other. Was this factor important for the success of the voyage, or would he have been equally successful choosing people based solely on their expertise? There are many other characteristics to consider, such as the personality of group members and the particular structure of the group. However, we will examine group size, cohesiveness, and communication structure.

Group Size   Heyerdahl's decision to use a six-man crew was based on space considerations and the amount of provisions that could be taken on the voyage. Assuming that he had adequate space and rations, would he have been wiser to take a larger group?

There are many reasons to expect a large group to perform better than a smaller group. If the task is a disjunctive one, the larger the group the greater the likelihood that someone will have the solution. If the task is additive, each additional member will add something to the group and, therefore, the large group should perform better than the small group.

However, increasing the size of a group also creates problems. One involves coordination loss. On the *Kon Tiki*, it was relatively easy to coordinate the work of the six crew members. If there had been sixty crew members, the problem of seeing that each member performed the correct task at the correct time would have been much more difficult. Time and effort would have been wasted on trying to coordinate members' efforts.

An even more serious problem in large groups is the motivation and dissatisfaction of group members. Numerous studies have found that as group size increases, there is a decrease in group members' motivation to work and in their satisfaction with the group. For example, Wicker, Kirmeyer, Hanson, and Alexander (1976) found greater variability of involvement in large groups as opposed to small groups. In the larger groups, some members seemed to feel very involved whereas others felt almost no involvement. In larger groups, individuals tend to get "lost in the shuffle," and this reduces their desire to contribute to the group. On the *Kon Tiki*, each member felt that he played a vital part in the voyage. Had the crew been much larger, it is less likely that the members would have felt this importance. As a result, they may not have tried as hard to make the trip a success.

Another problem is that large group size may cause members to feel inhibited. No one wants to be made a fool of in front of a large group of people. Hence, in large groups, members may withhold suggestions. You have probably experienced such inhibitions when you have considered asking a question in a large class. You raise your hand to ask a question, and the professor calls on you. Suddenly you feel six hundred eyes focusing on you. The pressure is on; you'd better ask a "good" question! You may have struggled through such an experience, vowing never to get yourself in that position again.

Overall, there are advantages and disadvantages to increasing the size of the group. Larger groups have more resources to focus on the task, but the increase in size also increases the likelihood of significant process loss. Later in this chapter, we will examine juries; here, we will see that group size also affects the way in which groups work on tasks.

Cohesiveness   One of the most studied variables in group behavior is cohesiveness. We can best view *cohesiveness* as the desire of members to stay in the group; it is often measured by examining how attracted group members are to each other. One important question that can be asked is, Do highly cohesive groups perform better than less cohesive groups? Our first response to this question might be to answer "Certainly." Imagine how difficult it would have been for the crew of the *Kon Tiki* to work together for over one hundred days if they had disliked each other.

There have been a number of studies suggesting that our initial response is correct. In general, group members are happier and more satisfied in cohesive groups (Zander, 1982). Looking at performance, Van Zelt (1952) examined work groups composed of carpenters and bricklayers. In some of the groups, the men all liked one another (high cohesive); in other groups, fewer men liked one another. Workers in the high-cohesive groups expressed greater job satisfaction and had lower turnover and less absenteeism. The high-cohesive groups also performed at a higher level. Research on volleyball and baseball teams found that cohesive teams are generally winning teams (Bird, 1977; Long, 1972).

Continuing with this line of reasoning, Japanese business firms have gone to great lengths to build cohesive work groups (Vogel, 1979). They have hired friends from the same school and tried to put friends on the same work teams. They sponsor parties and clubs for their employees. To increase commitment to the company, they have promised workers jobs for life, given large bonuses, and even provided economical housing for the workers. One result of these efforts is that Japanese workers seldom change companies.

While this research argues for an exalted position for cohesiveness, there is another side to the issue. First, a number of organizational psychologists have questioned the nature of the relationship between cohesiveness and performance. While a happy group may be a productive group, these investigators suggest that the mirror relationship may also be true. That is, a productive group may be a happy one. Research (Porter & Lawler, 1968) has found that success increases group cohesiveness.

Japanese businesses often go to great lengths to build cohesive work groups. Workers may be given lifetime jobs, housing, and uniforms. It is not unusual for a Japanese worker to stay with the same company throughout his or her lifetime. (© *MCMLXXXV Peter Menzel*)

A second approach that somewhat tarnishes the image of cohesiveness is research that has found no relationship between cohesiveness and productivity (Terborg, Castore, & DeNinno, 1976).

There are a number of reasons for this last effect. One of the most important is that *members of cohesive groups are generally more influenced by their groups than members of less cohesive groups* (McGrath, 1984). In other words, people who are highly attracted to a group conform to the norms set up by that group. In some cases, such as in the Western Electric plant studied by Roethlisberger and Dickson (1939), these norms may set work levels below an individual's capability. When this happens, members of cohesive groups will reduce their productivity to meet the group norm. Another possible effect of cohesiveness is that members will be reluctant to question the direction of the group. In their desire to maintain the positive atmosphere that exists in the group, members may remain quiet even when they feel the group is incorrect (Forsyth, 1983). We will see the disastrous consequences that can result from this situation in our examination of groupthink later in this chapter.

In the final analysis, we can conclude that cohesiveness usually leads to higher group productivity. However, there are exceptions to this rule which must also be considered. Thus, it is likely, but not a certainty, that the camaraderie among the *Kon Tiki* crew contributed to the success of their voyage.

Success breeds cohesiveness, just as cohesiveness can enhance a group's performance.
(© *Rick Mansfield/The Image Works*)

Communication and Communication Networks   To the casual observer, the crew of the *Kon Tiki* may have appeared without structure. Closer observation, however, would show that each of the men had a job for which he was responsible and tasks he had to complete. This arrangement was decided upon before the crew left on their voyage. There was, however, no explicit decision made about how communication would flow or who would talk to whom. However, a pattern soon developed on the raft. Thor and Eric, "a painter and a big hefty chap who can play the guitar and is full of fun," were the most talkative members of the crew. Although Thor wanted to have a rather informal organization, his account showed that much of the communication was directed to him, even when the crew members were relaxing after a long day.

It is, in fact, not unusual to find that communication patterns develop in groups. As was the case on the *Kon Tiki*, research (Stephan & Mishler, 1952) shows that, regardless of group size, over 50 percent of the talking is usually done by only two members. In groups of eight, they found that two members usually accounted for over 60 percent of the talking. Further, leaders generally talk more than other group members (Ruback, Dabbs, & Hopper, 1984) and their communication generally is directed at the group as a whole rather than at individual members. Other research (Hurwitz, Zander, & Hymoritch, 1960) found that low-status persons direct their communication toward high-status persons and that high-status persons also communicate with high-status persons. Thus, communication is directed upward in the status hierarchy so that low-status persons are often ignored. Much communication may be aimed upward by individuals who wish to improve their standing in the group.

Studying communication patterns in groups is more than just an interesting exercise; communication patterns can have direct influence on member's satisfaction and group productivity. Therefore, it is important that groups focus on this factor when they are planning their strategy for working on tasks. In the late 1940s and early 1950s, a number of investigators (Bavelas; 1948, 1950; Leavitt, 1951; Shaw, 1954) were concerned with the effects of structured channels of communication (*communication networks*) on group processes and group productivity. Leavitt varied the communication networks within groups of five people, using four types of networks (see Figure 11–1) The networks allow direct communication only between persons one link away from each other. In the circle, for example, person A can communicate with only two persons, person B and person E. Each member of a group was given a card with symbols on it. The group task was to identify which of the symbols was the common symbol. After the experiment, the subjects were asked how happy they had been in their group and were requested to identify the leader of the group. The results showed that the more freedom individuals had to communicate with others—that is, the more central they were in the communication network—the happier they were and the more likely they were to be identified as leaders. Leavitt also found that the groups with a more centralized structure (the wheel and the Y) made fewer errors and required less time to solve the problem than the less centralized groups (the chain and the circle).

Leavitt's results present an interesting paradox to the student of small group behavior: the more centralized group performs well, but it is likely to have a number of unhappy members. On the other hand, the decentralized network does not perform well, but it will have satisfied members. Shaw (1954), however, offered a resolution to this paradox. He studied the efficiency of the different networks in solving more difficult and complex problems. His results indicated that the less centralized networks found solutions to such problems more quickly and corrected mistakes more efficiently than the more centralized networks. Presumably, the individual in the central position became saturated with messages and could not

Figure 11–1
Four types of communication networks

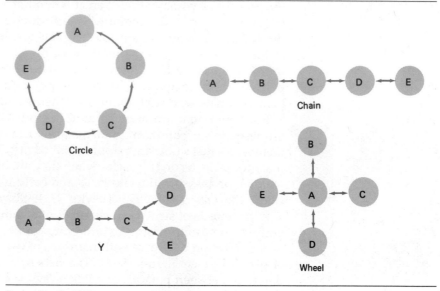

Source: Leavitt (1951).

coordinate group activities when the group was faced with a complicated task. This was not a problem when the task was simple.

GROUP DECISION MAKING

Up to this point, our examination of groups has focused mainly on
how well or how quickly groups can complete a specific job or make a
product. In this light, we could view the voyage of the *Kon Tiki* as a job or
product, and ask how well the group performed. However, if we examine the voyage more carefully, we find that the group was called on to
perform many tasks. Some involved producing a specific product, such
as building the raft or sailing it through a storm. Many others involved
making decisions, such as what course to follow and how much food to
carry aboard. To produce products, groups must often make decisions
about how to work and what the final product should be. In addition, the
sole task of other groups such as juries is making decisions. Therefore, let
us now turn our attention away from questions of material products and
focus on a specific type of product: group decisions.

Groupthink   There are many reasons for believing that groups should make better decisions than individuals; groups have members with different experiences, expertise, and points of view. Based on our earlier discussion of cohesiveness, we might further expect that highly cohesive groups would be best able to use the diverse talents of the members and arrive at the best decisions. Indeed, there is evidence that groups often make better decisions than isolated individuals (Shaw, 1981). However, there are so many examples to the contrary that we cannot conclude that groups are always superior decision makers. One of the clearest examples of a situation in which a group made a poor decision occurred on April 17, 1961. On that day, a group of 1,400 Cuban exiles landed at the Bay of Pigs in Cuba. Their mission was to establish a beachhead and to unite with Cuban rebels in the Escambray Mountains. Together, these forces were expected to unite the Cuban people in a rebellion to overthrow Premier Fidel Castro. The exiles were armed by the United States. Their mission had been planned by one of the best intelligence organizations in the world, the Central Intelligence Agency (CIA), and approved by one of the most popular leaders of the time, President John F. Kennedy. Despite all of these advantages, the whole plan fell flat on its face. Castro's army was well prepared for the invasion; there was little discontent among the Cuban people; and eighty miles of dense swamp separated the Bay of Pigs from the Escambray Mountains. Within two days of the invasion, the exiles had been surrounded by Castro's army and the entire force either killed or captured. The United States suffered a severe political setback, and it was beseiged with cries of outrage and indignation from countries throughout the world.

It is easy to see why the invasion failed. It is, however, not so easy to see how such a misconceived plan could have been devised and set into motion. Janis (1972, 1982) carefully analyzed the decision-making process that produced the Bay of Pigs fiasco and similar blunders (lack of preparedness for the Pearl Harbor attack and increasing U.S. involvement in Vietnam). From these analyses, he concluded that a situation of *groupthink* may result in cohesive decision-making groups. Groupthink results because the group members become so concerned with keeping a high degree of consensus and cohesiveness that they suspend their reality-testing powers and fail to exercise their ability to critically evaluate ideas. A major aim of groupthink is to avoid or reduce stress in the group. Janis outlined a number of symptoms that characterize groupthink:

1. The group develops the illusion of *invulnerability*. As Schlesinger (1965) reports, the Kennedy group felt that they had the Midas touch; they had done everything right and won the election against all odds.

They were euphoric, and the possibility of failure hardly crossed their minds.

2. The group members view themselves as having a high degree of *morality*. Kennedy's advisers saw themselves as fighting the evil forces of communism.

3. The group members share *common stereotypes*. In the Bay of Pigs case, Kennedy's cabinet members reinforced one another's view that the Cubans were a bunch of unorganized bandits who could not fight.

4. One of the most disastrous symptoms is that the group develops an *illusion of agreement and unanimity*. Each person simply assumes that the other group members hold the same opinions and that there is no need to encourage discussion on issues on which everyone agrees.

5. As a result of this illusion, there are strong group *pressures toward conformity* and the group members become *reluctant to express disagreement*. A member or members of the group assume the role of "mindguards" and work to protect the agreement and cohesive feeling of the group.

6. A *strong and respected leader* reinforces the tendency toward agreement and docility. Kennedy played an active role in the discussions, and the other discussants saw him as a good person who could hardly be wrong.

7. Another possible reason concerns *discussion patterns* that develop in groups. In a careful analysis of group communication, investigators (Stasser & Titus, 1985) found that information is more likely to enter group discussion if it is shared by all or most group members. Groups tend to avoid considering unique information that is not already known by most group members. Further, group discussion is generally biased in favor of preferences that already exist in the group. This suggests that if only one member of Kennedy's cabinet knew of the conditions that existed at the Bay of Pigs site, it is unlikely that the other group members would have given that information much consideration, even if the initial member proposed that they do so. Referring back to our earlier discussion of group communication, this effect is especially likely if the member has low status in the group.

Having painted a rather dismal picture, we must ask whether groupthink is the inevitable result when cohesive groups with strong leaders are charged with making important decisions. Fortunately, it is not. First, it has been pointed out that groupthink may not necessarily be a phenomenon solely related to groups; an individual who rationalized decisions and failed to carefully examine the risks involved would also make poor decisions (Abelson & Levi, 1985). Group pressures may increase the likelihood of this faulty process, but they are not solely responsible for it. Second, cohesive groups do not always fall prey to groupthink; in fact, such groups can make excellent decisions if they take steps to avoid groupthink. To demonstrate this point, Janis cited another decision made by Kennedy's cabinet. Just over a year after the Bay of Pigs invasion, Kennedy learned that the Russians were deploying missiles with nuclear warheads in Cuba. Kennedy called a series of meetings of his advisers; many of the advisers were the same men who had planned the Bay of Pigs invasion. However, this time Kennedy pushed to ensure that numerous proposals for action were discussed and carefully weighed; recommendations were considered and reconsidered. Persons outside the group of advisers were called on to supply information and opinions. Kennedy intentionally excluded himself from many of the meetings so that the discussants would not be unduly influenced by him. In this case, groupthink was avoided and a "good" plan was adopted by the group. A shipping blockade was used to prevent the Russians from delivering additional men and supplies to Cuba. Ensuing events led to the eventual removal of the missiles already in Cuba.

The Russian attempt to deploy nuclear warheads in Cuba presented the Kennedy administration with another opportunity to make an important decision. Groupthink was avoided by considering numerous alternative proposals, seeking recommendations from people outside the administration, and allowing the group to work in discussions without Kennedy being present. (*United Press International Photo*)

As this example illustrates, groupthink is most likely to be avoided if the following steps are taken: (1) the leader should avoid stating a preference and should encourage group members to consider all alternatives; (2) group members should be encouraged to play the role of devil's advocate and force group discussion to focus on unique information; (3) when possible, persons outside the group should be brought in to express opinions and offer suggestions; (4) there should also be a continual reassessment of new information; (5) recent research (Callaway, Marriott, & Esser, 1985) has shown that groups composed of highly dominant members who were not prone to anxiety about disagreement were less likely to show symptoms of groupthink than groups composed of low-dominant members. Thus, groupthink can be reduced by paying attention to the characteristics of group members, group structure, and group process.

Decisions of Juries   Juries are a rather unique group because they are composed of strangers whose sole purpose is to make a decision: an individual's guilt or innocence and length of sentence.

The jury concept has its roots deep within the justice system. There is evidence that juries were used during the Trojan period in 1200 B.C. (Nemeth, 1981). Over the last three hundred years in which it has been used in U.S. courts, the jury system has undergone many changes. For example, before 1670, a judge could punish a jury by imprisonment if he felt that the jury's verdict was in error. Through changes in law and practice, the most common jury used in the United States today involves twelve people who must reach a unanimous verdict before sentence can be passed.

Recently, a growing interest in applying social psychological techniques to understand juries has developed; this interest is theoretical, practical, and historical. As we pointed out earlier in the chapter, the jury offers a unique arena to examine theories of group decision making and group dynamics. On the practical side, the last few years have seen the use of social psychologists in the legal process (Saks, 1976; Saks & Hastie, 1978). Specifically, social psychologists have assisted attorneys in the jury selection process; they have used their knowledge of theory and methodology to help attorneys identify and exclude prospective jurors who might harbor prejudice toward their clients (Tapp, 1981). The historical interest derives from the fact that the court system has come under a great deal of recent attack. Critics have argued that the legal process is too slow and cumbersome. Thus, many of the suggestions aimed at streamlining the court system have focused on the jury. We will briefly focus on some of the research that has identified how certain factors influence (or do not influence) the jury's decision.

Looking first at jury size, the Supreme Court ruled in 1970 (*Williams* v. *Florida*) that juries of six members were permissible. In 1978, the Court ruled that six was the minimum allowable size for state criminal juries (*Ballew* v. *Georgia*). At the heart of these rulings were questions about how jury size affects (or does not affect) decisions. To a large degree, research has suggested that the verdicts of six- and twelve-member juries do not differ significantly. For example, Padawer-Singer, Singer, and Singer (1977) had six-member and twelve-member juries watch a three-hour, videotaped reenactment of a real trial. Following that trial, the juries discussed the information until they reached a verdict. There was little difference in the verdicts reached by the two types of juries. One exception is the finding that smaller juries (three or six members) are more likely than larger juries (twelve members) to hang (fail to reach a verdict) if they have a prescribed amount of time in which to make their decision and guilt or innocence is not clear from the start (Kerr & MacCoun, 1985).

Overall, we may assume that six- and twelve-member juries will reach similar verdicts. However, investigators argue that this finding does not necessarily eliminate jury size as an issue. It has been demonstrated that six-member juries are less likely to be representative of the community than twelve-member juries (Saks, 1976). For example, if a community were 10 percent black and 90 percent white, only 41 percent of randomly constituted six-member juries would have a black member while 80 percent of the twelve-member juries would contain at least one black member. A second issue concerns the different pressures on dissenting members in the two juries. A dissenter in a five to one split would feel a great deal more pressure to go along with the majority than dissenters in a ten to two split. (Recall our discussion of conformity in Chapter Ten in which we showed that having an ally reduces the pressure to conform.) Thus, while the verdicts (decisions) of the two juries may be similar, the process used to arrive at these decisions and the degree to which the jury represents the community may be very different.

Turning next to the unanimity issue, the Supreme Court ruled (*Johnson* v. *Louisiana*, 1972) that nonunanimous verdicts by juries were permissible; in fact, the Court suggested that in many areas, 75 percent agreement was acceptable. This decision is consistent with a 1966 British court system ruling holding that agreement by ten out of twelve jury members is sufficient for a verdict. Thus, when comparing unanimous and nonunanimous jury decision rules, we are again faced with the differences in decision and process.

A series of studies (Davis, Kerr, Atkin, Holt, & Meek, 1975; Davis, Bray, & Holt, 1977) found that the majority generally wins; that is, the view held by the majority before beginning discussion usually determines the verdict. Thus, if we find that ten out of twelve jurors believe the defendant is guilty, it is likely that a guilty verdict will be returned if the jury is forced to deliberate to unanimity. On the other hand, there are some important process differences to consider. For example, Foss (1981) formed twelve-member mock juries and had them listen to a trial proceeding. Some of the juries were told that they had to reach a unanimous decision before a verdict could be accepted while others were told that a verdict supported by a majority of members could be accepted (quorum). The results indicated that the verdicts reached by the two types of juries were roughly the same. However, the quorum juries reached a decision twice as fast and were less likely to be "hung" than the unanimous juries. Further, members of the quorum juries were more cooperative and willing to compromise than the members of the unanimous juries. The individual has much less power in the quorum juries than in the unanimous juries; in the second type of jury, one member can hang the jury. These findings are important because they may mean that juries required to reach a unanimous verdict are more likely to consider all the evidence carefully than juries using the majority rule. (If you were on trial, it would not be very comforting to know that the members of your jury were willing to compromise so that they could reach a quick verdict!)

Minority Influence on Decisions   Our discussion of group decision making and juries suggests that if you find yourself with a minority opinion, you should give up; you will never get the group to see things your way. This advice may be sound in many situations, but there are times when the minority *can* influence the group. An example of *minority influence* can be seen in the movie *Twelve Angry Men*. Henry Fonda portrayed one of twelve jurors responsible for arriving at a verdict in a murder trial. After hearing the evidence, the jury retired to the jury room to reach a verdict. Many of the jurors wanted to decide quickly because they had other things planned after the trial. On their first ballot, eleven jurors found the defendant guilty. The one not-guilty vote was cast by Henry Fonda, who believed strongly that there was not enough evidence to prove beyond a reasonable doubt that the defendant was guilty. The remainder of the movie shows how the other eleven jurors tried to get Fonda to change his vote. When he held to his convictions, one-by-one, the other jurors began agreeing with him; at the end, the jury voted unanimously for acquittal.

How could Fonda or any other minority change the opinion of the majority? According to investigators (Moscovici & Mugny, 1983), minorities become influential to the extent that they can *become visible* to other group members and *create conflict* and tension within the group. Often the group attempts to silence the minority, but the tension may lead others to consider the minority position. Others may be willing to examine other positions because the minority has broken the *norm of conformity* by deviating from the group's position. As we saw in Chapter Ten, the presence of one deviate reduces conformity in the group because others see that the group's position may be wrong or questionable.

Moscovici and Personnaz (1980) suggest that the majority and minority influence people in different ways. According to these investigators, individuals faced with disagreement by a majority focus their attention on the majority: not wishing to face rejection, they overtly conform to the majority. However, the disagreeing minority causes the individual to focus on the task. Since the person agrees with the majority and is not concerned with rejection, he or she attempts to determine why the minority adopted the discrepant position. The focus on the task may not lead to immediate overt compliance, but it may result in real attitude or perceptual change. (For a discussion of private acceptance, see Chapter Ten). Another interesting possibility is that the majority and minority influence group members thinking in different ways. Nemeth (1986) suggests that majorities induce people to focus on the one position they propose while minorities motivate people to consider the aspects of the situation and search for novel solutions. Further, disagreeing with the

Small groups of people who take clear, consistent positions and remain firm and uncompromising may influence the opinion of members of the larger group. The possibility that radical views may actually persuade others often leads to demands from the majority to silence radical groups. (© Jean-Claude Lejeune/Stock, Boston)

majority is highly stressful and the result is to seek a quick solution to reduce the stress. Disagreeing with the minority is not as stressful and therefore, attention does not become so narrowly focused.

This being the case, we may question why some minorities succeed while others fail in swaying the group. The answer seems to be in the way that the minority presents itself to the group (Papastamov & Mugny, 1985). A minority is most likely to be successful if it takes two steps. First, the minority must take a *consistent* position; consistency is the most important attribute in minority influence, as it clearly defines the minority view. Nemeth (1979) points out that it is often difficult for the minority to remain consistent because it is disliked and subjected to attacks from the majority. Second, the minority must *remain firm, uncompromising, and resolute in adhering to this position.* By taking a different stand from that of the majority, the minority casts doubt on the correctness of the majority's position and thereby offers an alternative. The one caution here is that the minority must be consistent and firm without appearing rigid and unthinking.

To summarize, we can conclude that groups often make better decisions than isolated individuals. However, when groups become too concerned with maintaining a good emotional climate, they can experience groupthink and make poor decisions. It is generally the majority that determines the group's decision. At times, however, the minority can influence the group. The minority is most likely to be successful if it adopts a clear consistent position and remains uncompromising.

THE GROUP'S EFFECT ON THE INDIVIDUAL

Thus far, we have focused primarily on group behavior; we have studied how groups perform and make decisions. We will now change our focus and examine how groups influence the individual. With this new focus, we become interested in whether being in a group influences the way individual members perceive, behave, and work. We will therefore be asking whether membership in the *Kon Tiki* crew had an effect on each crew member.

The Influence of Groups on Self-Identity   The crew of the *Kon Tiki* returned to a large parade in the United States. They met with President Truman. A crew member could walk into any sailing club in the world and be greeted with respect. Being a member of the *Kon Tiki* crew became part of each member's self-concept; it gave that person an identity. The groups to which we belong also help form our own self-concepts. If someone asks us to describe who we are, we will include information

The groups to which we belong give us a social identity and help shape our self-concept. We are motivated to join groups that will enhance our image. *(Top, Michael Hayman/Stock, Boston; bottom, Ellis Herwig/Stock, Boston)*

about the groups to which we belong (Tajfel, 1982); we might describe ourselves as a student at The Ohio State University, a member of the band, a Delta Delta Iota, and a Lutheran.

The role of groups in determining our identity sets into motion a number of processes. Most of us want to have a positive view of ourselves. Hence, we attempt to join groups that enhance this image. Along these lines, people tend to disassociate themselves from groups that fail, while associating themselves with groups that are successful (Snyder, Lassegard, & Ford, 1980). At another level, we want to see the groups to which we belong as good, and the groups to which we do not belong as bad. This desire leads us to perceive and emphasize the positive aspects of our own group and the negative characteristics of the relevant out-groups (Mackie & Goethals, 1987; Tajfel & Turner, 1986). Further, our desire to be in good groups and to have no part of bad groups causes us to discriminate against the out-groups; we make our own group appear more positive in comparison to the out-group.

Discrimination often results in self-defeating behavior. For example, in one study (Tajfel, 1970), people were randomly divided into two groups. They were then given the opportunity to choose how to divide rewards between the two groups. One option gave both groups a high reward level; the other option gave both groups less absolute reward but emphasized the difference between the two groups. Subjects overwhelmingly chose the last option, even though it penalized their own group by giving it less absolute reward. It did, however, place the in-group in a more favorable position compared to that of the out-group. Therefore, discrimination (see Chapter Eight) occurs even when it hurts the individual and his or her own group.

As a final note on this issue, we should be reminded of the work discussed in Chapter Nine, which demonstrated the ease with which people form in-groups and out-groups. People distinguish between their own groups and other groups even when they are assigned to groups randomly or based on trivial matters such as a preference for a painting or a political attitude (Hymas, 1986). Even within groups, members may make in-group, out-group distinctions based on the most scant criteria. For example, a distinction between "newcomers" and "oldtimers" may develop and influence the way these members treat and perceive each other (Moreland, 1985). This potentially disruptive distinction, however, diminishes over time.

The Influence of Groups on Perceptions and Evaluations   Belonging to a group not only colors how we see ourselves, but it also has pervasive effects on the way in which we view others and their products.

In-group = good; out-group = bad.   One of the more consistent findings in research is that people tend to perceive their own group and its efforts as good and the out-group and its efforts as bad. This effect is

Conflict often leads to distorted perceptions in which each side sees itself as being defensive while the other side is offensive and hostile. Israel viewed its invasion of Lebanon in 1982 as defensive and self-protective, while the Palestine Liberation Organization (PLO) and other Arabs saw the invasion as an offensive act of aggression. *(Moshe Milner/Sygma)*

clearly seen in performance ratings. At one point in the Sherif et al. (1961, see Chapter Nine) study, campers were told to gather as many beans as possible. Following this, the campers were asked to estimate the number of beans that each of the boys had collected. The results indicated that the in-group estimated its total as being larger than that of the out-group. Hinkle and Schopler (1986) report a series of studies that also found an overevaluation of in-group performance and an underevaluation of out-group performance.

This tendency to see the in-group as better than the out-group is not confined to evaluations of performance; it also occurs in the judgment of traits. White (1966) illustrated this point clearly by examining conditions that have historically led to wars. For example, he points out that as conflict increases, nations form a "diabolical-enemy image" whereby they view their antagonist as evil and warlike. Hitler saw the Jews as evil and as plotting to take control of Germany. The view of the evil enemy is generally accompanied by a moral and virile self-image. Hitler described Germany and Germans as strong and courageous (virile) and he argued on numerous occasions that his intentions were peaceful. "I wish to point out first that I have not conducted any war; second, that for years past I have expressed my abhorrence of war" (Hitler's speech, April 28, 1939, in White, 1966). This pattern of perceptions repeated itself as the United States and the Soviet Union prepared for a summit meeting in November 1985. President Reagan painted a picture of the United States as peace loving and saw his proposals for arms reduction as positive and constructive. He characterized the Russians as expansionists who desire world conquest. He saw their arms proposals as hollow and as a trick to

Because we see members of our in-group in a variety of situations, we are generally aware of the diversity that exists within the group. On the other hand, we generally see out-group members in a limited number of situations and tend to perceive homogeneity in that group. *(Left, Elizabeth Crews/Stock, Boston; right, © Ellis Herwig/Stock, Boston)*

gain a propaganda edge. Soviet Prime Minister Gorbachev presented almost identical views, with the major exception that the names were switched; the Russians were the good guys while the United States was the threat to world peace.

Taking research a step further, one study (Howard & Rothbart, 1980) found that people were also more likely to remember the unfavorable behaviors of out-group members than the unfavorable behaviors of in-group members. Therefore, being assigned to a group not only leads us to see our own group more favorably than the out-group, but also structures our memories so that we will be most likely to remember the unfavorable behaviors of the out-group.

In-group members = dissimilar; out-group members = similar. When the *Kon Tiki* arrived in Polynesia, it was met be a number of excited islanders. Heyerdahl discussed the different reactions of each of his crew members to this historic landing. However, he refers to the welcoming party of Polynesians as the collective "they"; they looked this way, or they acted in this manner.

There is a tendency to notice variability within our own groups and to perceive similarities within the out-group. For example, Jones, Wood, and Quattrone (1981) asked members of various "eating clubs" at Princeton

University to indicate how members of their own and other clubs could be described on a number of trait dimensions. There was a significant tendency to indicate greater variability in one's own club compared to the other clubs.

If people do see the out-group as being composed of homogeneous members, we might expect them to attribute the *same* traits to all out-group members. Quattrone and Jones (1980) had subjects watch a target person make decisions regarding a number of activities. The target person was presented as a member of their own group (from the same college) or as a member of an out-group (from a neighboring college). After watching the target make the decisions, subjects rated the person and indicated how the "average" person from the target person's college would have acted in a similar situation. The results indicated that there was a greater tendency to generalize from the target person's behavior to that of his group if he came from a different college (out-group) than the subject. This effect did not occur if subjects had strong prior expectations about how people would act in the particular setting.

A number of explanations for this effect have been offered (Quattrone, 1986; and see Chapter Two on stereotypes). One explanation concerns the frequency of exposure; we have more contact with members of our own groups than with members of out-groups. Therefore, we will see more variability in the behavior and attitudes of in-group members than in those of out-group members. A second explanation is that we interact with in-group members over a wider range of situations; our interaction with out-group members is often confined to a narrow range of settings. Therefore, we have information about how the behavior of in-group members varies across situations, but we do not have this information about out-group members. For example, Heyerdahl observed his crew members as they readied for the voyage, as they faced the difficulties at sea, and as they experienced success. He worked, played, and attended formal functions with his crew. On the other hand, he interacted with the Polynesians in only one situation—when they were surprised by the arrival of the strange craft. Finally, due to this limited range of experience with out-group members, Quattrone suggests that we often explain away disconforming information about members of the out-group—that is, we see members of the out-group who do not conform to our expectations as "exceptions." It is relatively easy to ignore these "exceptions" because we have little opportunity to determine the correctness of this assumption.

Before leaving this discussion, one point should be raised. There is evidence (Worchel, 1984) that this effect is most likely to occur in groups that have been well established. Worchel, in fact, found the *opposite* relationship between group and perceptions during the early stages of group formation. That is, people perceived more similarity among in-group members than among out-group members. This perception may reflect people's lack of information about other in-group members early in the group's life. Or it may reflect the individual's desire to see himself or herself as similar to other in-group members. The concern with similarity will be high during this early stage because (1) the person wants to clearly define the in-group and (2) ensure that he or she will be accepted by that group.

THE INFLUENCE OF THE GROUP ON PRODUCT EVALUATION

The *Kon Tiki* crew felt that their voyage was a major contribution to history since it showed that people from South America could have been the first settlers in Polynesia. There were, however, many critics of the voyage who argued that it proved very little. Verbal battles raged for years over the contribution of the *Kon Tiki* voyage; those who made the voyage proclaimed its merits while outsiders expressed doubts. The ensuing discussion touches on an interesting area in group dynamics: how group members judge their performance and products.

A number of studies have investigated group product evaluation by establishing situations in which groups believed that they were in competition on a series of tasks. Two competing groups performed tasks; then each group was asked to rate the quality of its own product and that of the competing group. The results consistently showed that group members overestimated the quality of their group's product, whereas they underestimated the quality of the other group's product (Blake & Mouton, 1961; Ferguson & Kelley, 1964; Sherif et al., 1961). While several explanations for these results have been suggested, the one that is most widely accepted involves balance theory (Hinkle & Schopler, 1986). These researchers reason that group members are associated with their own group in a positive unit relationship (+). The group's product is also related to the group in a positive unit relationship since it belongs to the group (+). Therefore, to balance this relationship, group members should like the product (+). The opposite reasoning is applied to a group's evaluations of the product of the competing group. The subject is not a member of that group (−), and the product of that group is positively associated with it (+). Therefore, balance theory (see Chapter One) would predict that the subject would dislike (−) the competing group's product to achieve a state of balance.

While balance theory suggests that people will overvalue their group's product, there are other forces that may moderate this effect. It was found that group members did not significantly overvalue their group's product when their group won a competition and expected to be competing again in the future (Worchel, Lind, & Kaufman, 1975). Further, group members tended to de-emphasize the evaluation of a poor performance by their group when they expected to be competing again in the future. It was argued that people use group product evaluations to influence the motivations of other group members. In the first situation (win and expect future competition), group members refrained from giving high ratings to their group's product in an effort to avoid complacency and overconfidence. If group members felt that their group was too good, they may have lessened their efforts in the next round of competition. We often see this effect when coaches discuss a winning effort by their team. In a serious tone of voice, the coach will say, "The win was nice, but [the team] still needs a lot of work to get ready for [to win] the next one." On the other hand, when a group loses a competition and must get ready for another competitive event, members will be motivated to put the best light on their performance to boost group morale. We rarely hear a losing coach proclaim that his team was terrible; rather, these coaches often say that the loss was a tough one, but there were many bright spots in the team's performance.

GROUP INFLUENCE ON INDIVIDUAL PERFORMANCE

We will now address the question of whether people work harder and better when in a group than when alone. This is a particularly important question for businesses that are concerned with productivity. Clearly, some jobs require that people work together, but others do not. For example, assume you are manager in a plant that makes Cabbage Patch dolls. You could have your employees work in small groups sewing and painting the dolls or you could isolate them in small cubicles so that they work alone. What would be your choice?

Social Facilitation   Social scientists have been interested in questions like this since the turn of the century. In 1897, Triplett made the observation that cyclists rode more rapidly when they raced in head-to-head competition than when they tried to "beat the clock" while racing alone. To investigate whether the group really had an effect on individual performance, Triplett devised one of the first social psychology experiments. Children were given the task of winding string on a fishing reel as fast as possible. In half of the trials, each child performed alone; in the other half, two competing children worked side by side. Triplett found that the children worked faster in competition than when alone.

Triplett found that cyclists raced more rapidly when they competed in a head-to-head manner than when they simply rode against the clock. (*Susan Lapides/Design Conceptions*)

Much of the research that followed Triplett's studies also found that people performed better in groups or in front of audiences than alone (Travis, 1925; Allport, 1924). This effect of others has even been found with animals and insects. For example, Chen (1937) counted the balls of dirt that the ants excavated when building their tunnels. In some cases he had an ant work alone, and in other cases the ant worked with one or two other ants. Chen found that the individual ant worked harder (removed more balls of dirt) when it worked with other ants than when it worked alone. These results suggest that the presence of others facilitates performance. Since the subjects performed in front of a passive audience in a number of the studies, it seems that the *social facilitation* effects are due to the mere presence of others rather than to direct competition between individuals.

Given these results, we might conclude that groups are good for people (and other animals). Unfortunately, the picture is not quite so clear. At about the same time that the social facilitation results were reported, a number of investigators reported *social inhibition* effects. For example, Pessin and Husband (1933) found that the presence of an audience slowed the learning of a maze task and a nonsense-syllable task. Interestingly, *after* the subjects had learned the maze and nonsense-syllable tasks, they performed better in front of spectators. These contradictory results caution us against indiscriminately using groups to upgrade an individual's performance.

It was not until Zajonc (1965) proposed his theory of social facilitation that some theoretical sense was made of the contradictory results. Zajonc drew a distinction between the learning or acquisition phase of task performance and the performance or emission phase. Zajonc (1965, 1972) proposed that the mere presence of others increases an individual's arousal and drive. He argued that the presence of others in the environment increases the alertness of the individual. The alertness (or arousal) results because the presence of others may require that the individual act quickly or in novel or unique ways. The arousal is important because it has been shown that increased drive increases the likelihood that an individual will perform the dominant response. The dominant response is the one that the individual is most likely to make in a particular situation. Hence, Zajonc proposed that the mere presence of others facilitates the performance of the dominant response due to the increased drive and arousal. He further pointed out that in situations in which an individual is learning a new behavior, the dominant response would be the correct behavior. Thus, according to Zajonc, the mere presence of others should inhibit the learning of new or complicated responses but facilitate the performance of well-learned behaviors.

Overall, there has been agreement about the effect groups have on individual performance, but there has been considerable disagreement about why these effects occur (Berger, Carli, Garcier, & James, 1982; Guerin & Innes, 1982). One alternative position is that audience effects are due to the performer's concern about being evaluated (Cottrell, Wack, Sekerak, & Rittle, 1968). According to this position, people learn that others are potential sources of evaluation, and the presence of these others creates an anticipation of positive or negative outcomes. Therefore, social facilitation should occur only when the audience is in a position to evaluate the individual's performance. In support of this position, Henchy and Glass (1968) found greater social facilitation when the audience was perceived as being experts on the task than when the audience knew little about the task. Supposedly, the experts were in a better position to evaluate performance than the nonexperts.

Other research, however, suggested that concern about evaluation is not necessary to achieve social facilitation. For example, one study (Haas & Roberts, 1975) found that a blindfolded audience that could not evaluate performance did improve the worker's performance, but not as much as an audience that was not blindfolded. More recently, research by

In an interesting study, Markus (1978) found that the presence of another person in the room facilitated the speed with which subjects put on familiar clothes. But the presence of this other person inhibited the speed with which subjects put on unfamiliar clothes. (© Donald Dietz/Stock, Boston)

Baumeister, Hamilton, & Tice (1985) has found that too much concern with evaluation may lower performance. Results from this study showed that people performed less well in front of an audience that expected success than in front of an audience that did not hold such high expectations.

Another alternative explanation (Sanders, 1981) suggests that the audience serves as a distraction for the performer. In such a situation, the performer is placed in the conflictual position of having to decide whether to pay attention to the audience or to the task. This conflict leads to increased drive and facilitates the performance of simple tasks. In support of this position, a number of studies (Sanders & Baron, 1975) found that low levels of distraction enhanced the performance of simple tasks. Although the distraction/conflict hypothesis has been criticized as being imprecise (Geen, 1981; Markus, 1981) and not accounting for much of the social facilitation data, it does offer an interesting alternative approach to the area.

In conclusion, it seems that many factors including arousal, concern for evaluation, and distraction may enhance social facilitation effects. In fact, all of these processes may occur simultaneously in some situations.

Social Loafing   The results on social facilitation *seem* quite straightforward and clear. However, as is often the case, human behavior manages to create some interesting wrinkles and challenges for social psychologists. The first hint of such a wrinkle was reported by Ringelmann (Dashiell, 1935) who had male subjects pull as hard as they could on a rope. They pulled either alone or in groups of two, three, or eight persons. Ringelmann found that two-man groups pulled 1.9 times as hard as a single individual, that three-man groups pulled 2.5 times as hard, and that eight-man groups pulled 4 times as hard. Hence, the larger the group, the greater the force that was exerted on the rope. However, as the size of the group increased, the output from each individual decreased. In other words, people worked less hard or "loafed" when they worked in the group.

Appropriately, this effect has been called *social loafing* (Latané, Williams, & Harkins, 1979), and research has replicated it many times. For example, it has been found that people clap less loudly when in a group than when alone. And a result that will interest waiters and waitresses is that individuals leave smaller tips when they are part of a group than when they are tipping alone (Latané, 1981).

Before we scrap everything that we learned about social facilitation, let us examine some of the explanations for the loafing effect. As you will remember, in the studies on social facilitation, subjects performed alone or in front of a group: in each case, the person knew that his or her performance could be observed and identified by others. In the social loafing research, on the other hand, the person is a member of the group and believes that only the group product can be measured. Further, the group product has little personal implication for the individual. In this case, the individual believes that his or her output cannot be specifically identified. In an effort to demonstrate the importance of identifiability, Williams, Harkins, & Latané (1981) had subjects perform the shouting task either alone or in groups. However, in some conditions, subjects believed that their individual performance was always being monitored (always identifiable); in others, they believed it was only identifiable when alone; and in other conditions, they believed their output was never identifiable. As can be seen in Figure 11–2, performance was lower whenever subjects felt that their efforts were not being identified.

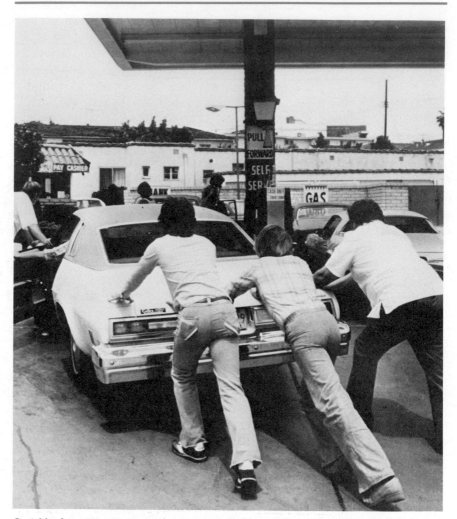

Social loafing occurs in groups because people do not believe that their output can be identified. The effect may also be the result of people feeling that the group can function without their efforts and/or a desire not to "carry the load" for other group members. *(Tony Korody/Sygma)*

Further support for this position comes from research showing that social loafing does not occur if the result of the group performance has clear personal relevance for the individual members (Brickner, Harkins, & Ostrom, 1986). Hence, one explanation for loafing suggests the effect results when the individual cannot be identified with a specific output and the output has little implication for the individual.

A second explanation has been termed the *free rider* explanation (Kerr & Brunn, 1983). To understand this effect, assume that you are a crew member on the *Kon Tiki*. The job is to pull up the sail. Everyone is pitching in and you see the sail going up nicely. Because all is going well, you may feel that great effort is not needed from you in this situation; you therefore reduce your efforts and become a "free rider." Loafing in this case results because the group members believe that their contributions are dispensable and that the group will succeed without them. From

Figure 11–2
Sound pressure as a function of size of pseudogroup and identifiability: Experiment 2

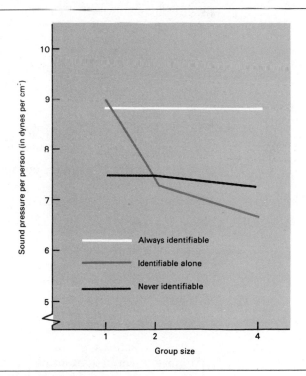

Source: After Williams et al. (1981), pp. 303–11.

the group's point of view, this is a dangerous situation because if all the members become free riders, the task performance will suffer.

Another interesting explanation for social loafing has been called the *sucker effect* (Kerr, 1983). Again, assume that you are working to pull up the sails on the *Kon Tiki*. This time you are working your hardest and turn to see another crew member doing very little. You realize that it is the crew as a whole and not you as an individual who will get credit for getting the job done. This lazy member is, therefore, playing you for a sucker; you are doing all the work and he will receive much of the credit. As a result, you may reduce your efforts and not work as hard as when you were working alone. In a study demonstrating this effect, subjects worked on a task with another group member who did poorly (Kerr, 1983). The subjects believed that the other member either had or did not have the ability to do better. They reduced their efforts (loafed) to the greatest extent when they felt the other person could do better but simply was not trying. It seems that we especially want to avoid being a sucker for others who can do well but are intentionally acting lazy.

In conclusion, being in a group enhances individual performance when a person's output is clearly identifiable and the task is easy. However, when the output cannot be matched to the individual, social loafing may occur. Loafing may result from this lack of identifiability, or it may result from free rider or sucker effects.

THE INFLUENCE OF GROUPS ON INDIVIDUAL DECISIONS

One of the critical activities engaged in by the *Kon Tiki* crew was decision making. From the beginning, they were faced with a number of tough issues. First, they had to decide how to build the raft. They had to decide on the kinds and quantities of provisions to take with them. They had to decide who performed which tasks, and they had to make numerous rules to govern their behavior during the voyage. The decisions they made determined the success or failure of the voyage; and some of these decisions would affect their very lives. Often the group would discuss the issues, but the final decisions and actions would rest with the individual crew members. This situation leads to a number of interesting questions concerning how being a member of a group affects individual decisions and actions.

We have previously examined how groups make decisions; now our focus is on the individual. One of the earliest questions to be researched in this area was how making a decision in a group affects the individual's behavior (Lewin, 1943). Kurt Lewin's interest arose out of a practical problem that existed in this country during World War II. The price of foods, especially meats, increased rapidly and there was some shortage of supply. There was no shortage of beef entrails such as kidneys, brains, and sweetbreads; however, the American homemaker was not accustomed to serving these to her family. The government, interested in getting the homemaker to serve these entrails, launched an extensive media campaign to persuade her to do so. Lewin reasoned that this method would not be effective. He believed that, since groups to which the homemakers might belong were responsible for the norm of not serving these products, propaganda attempts should be aimed at the groups, not at the individual.

Lewin felt that it was important to change the group norms regarding these products, and he set up an experiment to demonstrate how this could be done. He brought Red Cross volunteers together in groups of thirteen to seventeen. Half of the groups heard a lecture on the positive values of using the entrails and on how their use would help the war effort (lecture condition). The lecturer told how the entrails could be cooked, and even passed out recipes. The other half of the groups were in the group-decision condition, in which a trained group leader summarized the problem briefly and then let the women discuss their feelings about using the entrails. The discussion leader succeeded in getting a 100 percent vote in favor of the proposal that at least one meal a week be served using these meats. One week later, the women from all of the groups were interviewed to see who had actually served entrails. Ten percent of the women in the lecture condition, compared to 52 percent of the women in the group-decision condition, had done so. Later research (Pennington, Harary, & Bass, 1958) found that the group discussion is also very important in determining group members' conformity to group norms.

The Lewin study clearly demonstrates that group discussion and decision can be used to change the norms and the behavior of group members. It is sometimes difficult, however, to have every member of a group involved in the discussion and decision-making process. Hence, it would be nice to find that the same change can be achieved by using group representatives instead of the whole group. Coch and French (1948) had a chance to investigate this question when they were asked to look at productivity at the Harwood Manufacturing Corporation, a pajama factory. The plant often had to make minor adjustments in the work procedure. Although management expected temporary decreases in productivity following such changes, it found that there were often drastic, long-lasting declines in productivity. Supervisors explained the reasons for the work adjustments to the employees, but these explanations failed to increase productivity. Coch and French designed a study in which some groups of workers (no involvement) were simply told the reasons for the changes and exhorted to work harder. Other groups (total involvement) were given the opportunity to discuss with management the reasons for the changes and how they could improve work conditions. A third condition (representatives) involved bringing group representatives together to discuss the changes with management. The results indicated that workers in the total-involvement condition adjusted more quickly to the changes than the no-involvement workers, and that the productivity of the total-involvement workers rose to a much higher level than that of the no-involvement workers. The performance of the workers in the representative condition was higher than that of the no-involvement groups but did not reach the level of the total-involvement groups. Hence, direct involvement in discussions by all group members is the most effective way to bring about group change.

GROUP POLARIZATION

When Heyerdahl began thinking about the voyage, he proposed his idea to a number of people in the scientific community. He met with disbelief and discouragement that began to shake his commitment to the trip. With somewhat dampened spirits, he had a chance meeting with other sailors and explorers at the New York Explorers Club. After a long discussion of the pros and cons of the trip, Thor emerged completely committed to taking the risky voyage. What could have magically transformed Thor's growing caution into absolute certainty?

If we were to look at the early literature on group decision making, we would be surprised at this turn of events; we would expect Thor to have emerged from the group in a more cautious frame of mind. William Whyte, in his insightful analysis of business bureaucracies *The Organization Man* (1956), speculates that the group lowers the creativity and risk of its members to the least common denominator. Rarely do people risk being creative and innovative out of fear that they will be ridiculed by the more conservative power structure.

The view of group effects on individuals was challenged in a dissertation study. Stoner (1961) found that people chose riskier courses of action when in groups than when alone. Following up on this result, a group of investigators (Wallach, Kogan, & Bem, 1962) asked a large group of college students to fill out a Choice Dilemma questionnaire (see Table 11–1). The form consisted of twelve potential choices that a person might face in life, with each choice presenting a risky and a conservative alternative. The risky alternative had a very high payoff if successful, but if unsuccessful it had dire consequences. For example, the subjects were shown the following dilemma:

Table 11–1
Other choice dilemmas

---

1. A captain of a college football team, in the final seconds of a game with the college's traditional rival, may choose a play that is almost certain to produce a tie score, or a more risky play that would lead to sure victory if successful, sure defeat if not.

2. The president of an American corporation that is about to expand may build a new plant in the United States where returns on the investment would be moderate, or may decide to build in a foreign country with an unstable political history where, however, returns on the investment would be very high.

3. A college senior planning graduate work in chemistry may enter university X where, because of rigorous standards, only a fraction of the graduate students manage to receive the Ph.D., or may enter university Y which has a poorer reputation but where almost every graduate student receives the Ph.D.

4. A low-ranked participant in a national chess tournament, playing an early match with the top-favored man, has the choice of attempting or not trying a deceptive but risky maneuver that might lead to quick victory if successful or almost certain defeat if it fails.

Source: Wallach et al. (1962), p. 77.

A man with a severe heart ailment must seriously curtail his customary way of life if he does not undergo a delicate medical operation that might cure him completely or might prove fatal.

The students were asked what probability of success they would require before they recommended the risky alternative. When the subjects had completed the questionnaire, they were asked to get together in groups of five to discuss the various dilemmas and arrive at a group consensus—a recommendation that could be agreed to by all members of the group. On ten of the twelve items of the questionnaire, the groups arrived at decisions that were riskier (required less of a prior probability of success) than the average risk that had been acceptable only moments earlier to the individuals who made up the groups.

In a final step in the Wallach et al. study, the subjects were retested individually. The group shift to a risky position may have been one that the individual group members publicly agreed to but did not actually accept; perhaps they had acceded to the will of a few strong individuals. The results showed that the group discussion and decision had caused a change of attitude. The subjects' opinions in the second individual testing remained at the risky position that they had adopted in the group

Research on betting at the racetrack showed that groups were more conservative and bet on the "favorite" more often than an individual acting alone. *(Mark Antman/The Image Works)*

discussion. Some subjects who were tested as much as six weeks after the group session continued to show the shift toward risk.

This and a number of studies with similar results (Muhelman, Bruker, & Ingram, 1976; Cartwright, 1973) led investigators to conclude that being in groups led individuals to adopt riskier positions; the term *risky shift* was coined to refer to this effect. But the picture became cloudy when other studies discovered that people in groups adopted more conservative positions than they had had on entering the group. For example, Fraser, Gouge, and Billig (1971) were able to write several items on which the subjects shifted toward caution. McCauley, Stitt, Woods, and Lipton (1973), and Knox and Safford (1976) examined bets on horses at the racetrack. In their field studies, the subjects either bet alone or after group discussion. In both of these cases, groups were more cautious than individuals, as groups bet on the "favorite" more often than individuals.

The general picture that emerged was that groups do not necessarily produce a risky shift. Rather, they seem to produce a polarization effect in the direction that was initially preferred. That is, the average post-group response was more extreme in the same direction as the average pregroup response. If there was an initial tendency toward risk, the group response was more risky; if there was an initial tendency toward conservatism, the group response was even more conservative. This area of study became known as *group polarization*. Given that groups do lead to polarization in decisions, the next question centered on why this effect occurred. A number of different hypotheses were suggested.

One explanation that focuses on *social comparison* (see Chapter Three) suggests that people do not want to be seen as taking wishy-washy or neutral positions; they want to appear at least as certain and extreme as others (Myers, 1982). According to this explanation, people use group discussion to compare their position to that of others. As a result of this comparison, they move their own position to be at least as extreme as that of other group members.

Social comparison may be responsible for some of the polarization effects, but not all. Studies of the impact of simply exchanging information about preferred positions without group discussion typically show some degree of polarization, but not as much as is found with full discussion. If people simply want to compare their position with that of others, this information exchange should produce complete polarization effects. This suggests that social comparison by itself is one factor affecting polarization, but that other factors are important as well.

A second hypothesis (Burnstein & Vinokur, 1977; Burnstein, 1982) suggests that it is not the position of the other people, but the arguments they use to support their positions that create group polarization. According to this hypothesis, members listen to the arguments presented by people during the group discussion, and they shift their opinion in the direction of the position that has the *most persuasive arguments*. Laughlin and Earley (1982) found that the direction of polarization was related to the number of persuasive arguments supporting a position: risky shift occurred when the risky extreme had the most arguments, and conservative shift occurred when the conservative side had the most arguments.

Although the persuasive arguments theory does have support, Sanders and Baron (1977) argue that the theory does not explain why the most compelling arguments favor a particular and relatively extreme position. That is, would it not be just as likely that strong arguments might favor a more neutral and middle-of-the-road stand?

In an effort to reconcile the various positions several social psychologists (Isenberg, 1986; Brown, 1986) suggested that both social comparison and persuasive arguments work together to produce group polarization. According to these investigators, group members first compare their position to that of other group members. This comparison motivates them to present arguments supporting their position. These arguments not only influence the presenter, but other members are influenced as well. Recent evidence suggests that this polarization process is enhanced when people clearly identify with the group (Mackie, 1986). The identification leads members to perceive their group's position as even more extreme than it is and these biased perceptions augment social comparison and the effectiveness of the presented information.

DEINDIVIDUATION: GETTING LOST IN THE GROUP

Before leaving our discussion of group dynamics, we will examine one of the more dramatic effects of groups on individuals. Herman Watzinger, one of the crew members on the *Kon Tiki*, anticipated our discussion when he stated that as the voyage wore on, he lost his concern about himself and focused on "the crew." He felt that his own identity became that of the group. For Watzinger, the effect was enjoyable and enhanced his performance on the voyage. In other cases, the effect has not been positive. In the now infamous "snowball" game between the Denver and San Francisco football teams during the 1985 season, a snowball was hurled from the crowd as San Francisco was preparing to kick a short field goal. The snowball distracted the players and San Francisco missed the goal; Denver won the game by two points. The young man who threw the snowball said he was ashamed of his actions; he had become carried away in the excitement of the crowd, and had acted without thinking of the consequences.

As far back as 1895, French sociologist Le Bon observed that individuals often become "lost" in crowds and perform acts in crowds that they would not perform if they were alone. He observed:

> Whoever be the individuals that compose it, however like or unlike be their mode of life, their occupations, their character, or their intelligence, the fact that they have been transformed into a crowd puts them in possession of a sort of collective mind. (p. 20)

In addition to having a collective mind, a crowd is irrational, and its intellectual level is always below that of the isolated individual. Le Bon also described crowds as emotional and said that when in them, the individual begins to feel and express the emotions of a "primitive being." According to Le Bon, three mechanisms are responsible for creating the monster known as a crowd. First, because the individual is anonymous, he or she loses the sense of individual responsibility and thus participates in acts that he or she would not normally engage in. Second, contagion (see Chapter Ten) causes the individual in the crowd to act as he or she likes but would not under other circumstances. Contagion reduces the individual's inhibitions and allows him or her to behave as the model behaves. Third, people become more suggestible in crowds; the crowd

Table 11–2
Representation of the deindividuation process

Input variables →	Inferred subjective changes →	Output behaviors
A. Anonymity B. Responsibility: shared, diffused, given up C. Group size, activity D. Altered temporal perspective: present expanded, future and past distanced E. Arousal F. Sensory input overload G. Physical involvement in the act H. Reliance upon noncognitive interactions and feedback I. Novel or unstructured situation J. Altered states of consciousness, drugs, alcohol, sleep, etc.	Minimization of: 1. Self-observation-evaluation 2. Concern for social evaluation Weakening of controls based on guilt, shame, fear, and commitment Lowered threshold for expressing inhibited behaviors	a. Behavior emitted is emotional, impulsive, irrational, regressive, with high intensity. b. Not under the controlling influence of usual external discriminative stimuli. c. Behavior is self-reinforcing and is intensified, amplified with repeated expressions of it. d. Difficult to terminate. e. Possible memory impairments; some amnesia for act. f. Perceptual distortion—insensitive to incidental stimuli and to relating actions to other actors. g. Hyperresponsiveness—"contagious plasticity" to behavior of proximal, active others. h. Unresponsiveness to distal reference groups. i. Greater liking for group or situation associated with "released" behavior. j. At extreme levels, the group dissolves as its members become autistic in their impulse gratification. k. Destruction of traditional forms and structures.

Source: Reprinted from the 1969 *Nebraska Symposium on Motivation*, P. Zimbardo, by permission of University of Nebraska Press. Copyright © 1970 by the University of Nebraska Press.

hypnotizes the individual, who then follows the suggestions of other members or the crowd's leader.

Other investigators have expanded the view of the *deindividuation* process. They have suggested that conditions such as large groups, anonymity, and a heightened state of arousal (see Table 11–2) are the precursors of deindividuation. These conditions lead individuals to become submerged in the group, losing their own sense of identity (Zimbardo, 1970). When this identity loss occurs, people no longer feel responsible for their behavior; their attention is drawn to the group and behavior

Research found that trick-or-treaters were more likely to steal when they wore masks and were anonymous than when they were clearly identifiable. (© William McBride/Southern Light)

becomes regulated by fleeting cues in the immediate situation (Diener, Fraser, Beaman, & Kelem, 1980). As can be seen from the model presented in Table 11–2, when people lose a sense of personal responsibility for their actions, they are no longer governed by the norms and inhibitions that are present in most situations. Their behavior becomes impulsive, emotional, and difficult to terminate.

At the extreme, this view suggests that becoming deindividuated releases the beast inside each of us. For example, Watson (1973) studied the warfare patterns of over two hundred cultures. He found that in cultures whose warriors deindividuated themselves by wearing masks and paint, there was a greater tendency to torture captives than in cultures whose warriors were not deindividuated. Taking a somewhat different approach, Worchel and Andreoli (1978) found that aggressors deindividuated their victims before harming them. This deindividuation of the victim occurred when the aggressor selectively recalled information, thereby removing the victim's identity and uniqueness. Hence, it was easier to attack a deindividuated victim than a more individuated one. Finally, Diener et al. (1976) found that trick-or-treaters were more likely to steal when they wore masks and remained anonymous than when they were clearly identifiable.

While this model of deindividuation has received wide acceptance, there is another position of interest. Many of us may find losing our identity to the group disturbing or uncomfortable. At many large universities, students complain of being lost in the crowd; they are treated like numbers and no one knows or cares about them. Feeling lost in the crowd may motivate people to do something that makes them stand out from the group, to gain identity, and to be recognized. Hence, the animated, exaggerated, and sometimes antisocial behavior may be people's attempt to gain recognition (Maslach, Stapp, & Santee, 1985). We might therefore explain the snowball hurler at the football game by focusing on loss of responsibility; being in the group freed him from inhibitions against throwing the snowball. On the other hand, we might argue that being submerged in the crowd motivated him to do something to gain recognition; throwing the snowball separated him from the rest of the crowd.

Clearly, deindividuation is a complex process that may be partially explained by both explanations. Before leaving our discussion of this process, let us point out another side of deindividuation. We have shown that deindividuation can lead to negative antisocial behaviors; but there are also positive consequences from deindividuation. As we pointed out in Chapter Ten, deindividuation often leads to a reduction in conformity

It has been suggested that the unrestrained behavior of some people in deindividuating situations may be efforts to gain individual recognition. *(Peter Southwick/Stock, Boston)*

to group norms. In some cases, freeing the individual from the shackles of group norms can give rise to creativity that would otherwise be inhibited. For example, some authors adopt pseudonyms because they feel fewer restraints when writing anonymously. Finally, we find deindividuation in some professions in which individuals must violate social norms to carry out their jobs. For example, surgeons must handle and cut into their patients' bodies. For many years, it was believed that surgeons should not become well acquainted with their patients; and when the operation took place, the surgeon was covered from head to foot and the patient was draped with a cloth so that only the affected area was visible. We might speculate that deindividuation here freed the surgeon from concerns and fears that might have interfered with his or her job. However, many patients and doctors complained that they felt uncomfortable with this impersonal transaction; today many doctors spend time getting to know their patients before operations. Thus, while deindividuation has its darker side, it can also have positive effects.

SUMMARY

A group may be defined as two or more people who are interacting with one another in such a manner that each person influences and is influenced by each other person. People in groups experience themselves as belonging together and sharing common goals. Group structure includes boundaries, norms, and roles. Although the structure is designed to help groups function smoothly, conflict can occur within and between roles.

Groups generally perform better than individuals working alone. Groups are superior at recognizing correct solutions, especially when these solutions are presented by members with high status. The efficiency of groups is diminished by process loss, which includes coordination and motivation loss. Performance is also influenced by the type of task on which the group is working. For example, large groups may perform better than small groups on *additive* tasks, but may be hindered by motivation loss on *disjunctive* and *conjunctive tasks*. In general, cohesive groups perform better than noncohesive groups unless the cohesive groups develop norms that limit production. *Cohesiveness* is promoted by similarity of group members, outside group threat, member sacrifice to the group, and group success.

Communication in groups is usually directed toward higher status members. Some groups have definite *communication networks*. Group members tend to be happiest in decentralized networks. Groups with decentralized networks perform difficult tasks better than groups with centralized networks; the reverse is true for simple tasks.

Groupthink occurs when group members make a quick and ill-conceived decision in an effort to maintain group harmony. Groupthink is most likely to occur in highly cohesive groups that have a strong and respected leader. The chances of groupthink occurring can be reduced by encouraging a careful consideration of proposals, by having the leader avoid stating a clear preference, and by soliciting opinions from persons who are not members of the group.

Research on juries has shown that six-person and twelve-person juries generally arrive at the same decision. However, the process used by each is often different; twelve-person juries are more likely to be representative of the community. Although the majority usually determines the group's decision, the minority can be effective if it adopts a consistent and unyielding stand. Minorities are effective because they create conflict and challenge the group norm of conformity.

Groups influence members' self-concept. As a result, people attempt to join "good" groups and perceive their own group as positive. Discrimination results when members attempt to enhance the difference between the in-group and out-group. In most cases, people perceive in-group members as dissimilar and out-group members as similar. This effect is particularly pronounced in more established groups.

Research has shown that group members usually overvalue their own group's performance and undervalue the performance of a competing group. However, the magnitude of the *over-* and *underevaluation* is dependent on the group members' expectations about future interactions and on whether they believe that their group won or lost the competition.

Groups may influence the performance of individual members. Research on *social facilitation* shows that people perform simple and well-learned tasks better in groups than alone, but that learning new material will be inhibited by the presence of others. The last effect seems to occur because others arouse the individual and increase the drive to exhibit the dominant response. There have been many explanations for the social facilitation effect including *evaluation apprehension, distraction,* and *social comparison. Social loafing* involves the individual working less hard in groups than when alone. This effect may be the result of not feeling responsible for the final product and the lack of identifiability of individual performance in a group. The *free rider* effect and *sucker* effect have also been used to explain social loafing.

Decisions made in groups following group discussion are most likely to influence an individual's behavior. Being in groups often leads individuals to adopt more extreme positions than they held before they became part of the group. This effect may result from the reduction of responsibility that people feel in group-based decisions. Group polarization has also been explained by social comparison and persuasive argument processes.

Deindividuation occurs when people lose their personal identity and adopt that of the group. It generally results in large groups where anonymity and heightened arousal are present. People in deindividuated conditions focus on immediate cues and do not feel responsible for their actions. Doing so often lowers inhibitions against performing socially disapproved actions. An alternative explanation for deindividuation effects is that people are attempting to gain recognition and stand out from the crowd.

KEY WORDS

additive task
collective
conjunctive task
coordination loss
deindividuation
discretionary task
disjunctive task

free-rider effect
group
group cohesiveness
group polarization
groupthink
juries
minority influence

motivation loss
nominal group
norms
process loss
roles
role conflict

rumor
sharpening
social facilitation
social inhibition
social loafing
sucker effect

SUGGESTED READINGS

Forsyth, D. (1983). *An introduction to group dynamics.* Monterey, CA: Brooks/Cole Publishing.

Hare, A. P. (1976). *Handbook of small group research.* New York: Free Press.

Janis, I. (1982). *Victims of groupthink.* Boston: Houghton Mifflin.

McGrath, J. (1984). *Groups: Interaction and performance.* Englewood Cliffs, NJ: Prentice-Hall.

Moscovici, S., Mugny, G. & van Avermaet, E. (1985). *Perspectives on minority influence.* Cambridge, Eng.: Cambridge University Press.

Mullen, B., & Goethals, G. R. (1987). *Theories of group behavior.* New York: Springer-Verlag.

Saks, M., & Hastie, R. (1978). *Social psychology in court.* New York: Litton.

Shaw, M. (1981). *Group dynamics: The psychology of small group behavior.* (3rd ed.). New York: McGraw-Hill.

Steiner, I. (1972). *Group process and productivity.* New York: Academic Press.

Zander, A. (1982). *Making groups effective.* San Francisco: Jossey-Bass.

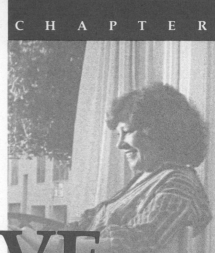

TWELVE

CHAPTER

THE ENVIRONMENT

One of the more popular movies in 1985 was entitled *The Gods Must Be Crazy.* Its plot was rather simple but very prophetic. A Coke bottle, thrown from a passing airplane, was found by a tribe of primitive Bushmen in the Kalahari Desert. The Bushmen had been isolated from contact with the modern world. This simple change in their environment drastically altered the tribe's daily routine and social relationships. Outside the theater, the year 1985 offered many real reminders that the environment in which we live strongly influences our lives. In Bhopal, India, a cloud of methyl isocyanate leaked from a Union Carbide chemical plant and killed over two thousand people who lived in the crowded neighborhoods around the plant. A drought that had toyed with Eastern Africa for five years tightened its grip. Daily television programs aired heart-rendering pictures of starving people in Ethiopia that touched the world; food poured into the country and a worldwide rock concert raised millions of dollars. But despite these efforts, thousands starved to death and hundreds of thousands were forced to move from their homes. Two earthquakes hit the coast of Mexico and buildings in Mexico City toppled like dominoes. *Rainbow Warrior,* the flagship of the environmentalist group Greenpeace, was sunk in its harbor in New Zealand. As the incredible story unfolded, it was clear that the ship had been sunk by the French secret service to prevent it from protesting the destruction of the environment by nuclear testing in the Pacific (Jones, 1985).

These events serve as dramatic reminders of the delicate relationship that exists between people and their environment. They stand out because of their scope and international importance, but they do not stand alone in bringing us this message. Ten years earlier, an energetic sailor, Tristan Jones, dazzled an audience in the Explorers Club in New York City when he pulled open a curtain to the stage on the Waldorf Astoria to reveal a nineteen-foot sailboat. Jones was the last of a distinguished panel of speakers that had included astronaut James Lovell and industrialist William Rockwell. While these other speakers talked about the wondrous conquests that had been made, Jones spoke of the cost of these conquests, calling for reason and caution. He had just completed a ten-year, sixty-thousand mile voyage in his small craft, the *Sea Dart*, and had viewed the world from a perspective that few of us have either the patience or opportunity to use.

He had flown into New York some months earlier marveling that it took seven hours to complete a trip that would have taken him eleven weeks on the *Sea Dart*. But he also noted that the speed of the trip gave him no opportunity to enjoy the seas or land below, or to pause to talk with the people along the way. Still obsessed with transportation, he noted that in America, unlike Europe, a car is not a luxury; it is an absolute necessity. He found that the public transportation system in the

From the cabin of his tiny craft, Tristan Jones had a unique perspective of the relationship between people and their physical environment. Jones, a Fellow in the Royal Geographical Society, London, and the Explorer's Club, New York, holder of nine world sailing records, and author of numerous books and articles, was very concerned with making people more aware of their environment. *(Photo: Carl Paler)*

United States was hopelessly inadequate and that the sheer size of the United States made it necessary to own an automobile. Being penniless and friendless in a new environment, Jones made two interesting observations. First, travel by car is isolating; unlike traveling on public transportation, people in a car do not have the opportunity to interact with others or to closely observe their environment. He also found that "it is much more frustrating to be poor in America than it is in Britain. . . . The country is so huge compared to tiny Britain, that for someone to pull up stakes and move to another part of the land by public transport is a major undertaking" (Jones, 1980, p. 107).

Jones had hoped to find a boat that he could transport to the Caribbean so that he could earn money. While searching for work, he spent a great deal of time walking through New York. He was struck by the enormous diversity of the environment he found and by its effect on the people. One such walking tour particularly stuck in his mind.

> Walking through Pelham Park, on the mainland side of the City Island causeway, I was closely surveyed three times by different police cars that slowed down and cruised by me slowly, the cops inside eyeing me suspiciously. I just kept plodding along until I was at Westchester, an urban center. From then on I was seemingly in more criminal surroundings, for I was ignored by passing police.
>
> At first the south side of The Bronx wasn't too bad. Long, long avenues surrounded by boxlike factories and apartment buildings. But further on, closer to Manhattan, there were more and more burned-out buildings, more and more potholes in the road, and more and more an air of sleazy hopelessness. By now just about everyone in the area was black. In the street there was a continual procession of gleaming steel behemoths, Fords, Chevys, Cadillacs, green, blue, red, black, streaming along. The sun reflected hostility from their chrome, their riders were hidden behind tinted windows. On the sidewalks, sitting on broken door stoops, ambling around and lounging, was group after group of people, most of them staring sullenly at the passing parade. There was a lot of noise, both from the traffic and the locals. Unlike the poor I had seen in many parts of the world, these people did not seem to be hungry or very ill-clad or sick, especially the younger ones. (Jones, 1980, p. 105)

In addition to these sights, the variety of bars in New York also delighted Jones.

> There's an extravagant variety of bars in New York. Irish bars and Polish bars, journalists' bars, singles' bars, doubles' bars, theatrical bars, "gay" bars, topless dancing bars, literary bars, painters' bars, sculptors' bars—I suppose there must be an undertakers' bar somewhere. (Jones, 1980, p. 119)

Each bar catered to one type of patron and those who did not fit the acceptable category were quickly made to feel unwelcome with unkind stares and cold shoulders.

Jones observed that there were great differences in the way seafarers and land dwellers approached their environment. He felt that the world of the sailor was unstable and naturally confusing. It did not have the predictability and opportunities for control available to people who live on the land. As a result, the life of a seafarer was aimed at learning skills to aid his survival by cooperating with his environment. The land dweller, on the other hand, viewed the land and the sea as "an empty wilderness or a promising prairie. They seem to think that if something could not be controlled, it ought to be exploited" (Jones, 1980, p. 281).

In his talk at the Explorer's Club, Jones argued that people who live on the land were losing touch with their environment; they were largely unaware of it and the role it played in their lives. He made the observation that "the landsman, at base, is a farmer. He improves the land. He tries to make things grow where they never grew before. . . . Successful agriculture creates comfort for many and it allows capital—in the form of grain, for example—to be accumulated in good years and set aside against setbacks in poor years" (Jones, 1980, p. 231). As a result of this security, Jones argued, people often fail to pay attention to their environment until disaster or catastrophe strikes.

Jones left the Explorer's Club and in his wake, he left a questioning audience. Was this unusual man simply a preacher of doom or was he a prophet? Jones seemed to care little what people thought of him. After sailing in all the oceans and seas of the world, he had planned a new trip, one that would allow him to carefully observe the relationship between land dwellers and their environment. But it was also a trip that would allow him to stay tucked away in the *Sea Dart* on the fringes of this relationship that intrigued and frightened him. He planned to sail through the heart of the United States, down the Mississippi River from Minneapolis to New Orleans. As president of the Atlantis Society, he would also devote his efforts to investigating and providing the means for young disabled people to earn their livelihood at sea.

ENVIRONMENTAL PSYCHOLOGY: WHAT IS IT AND WHY STUDY IT?

Looking at the world through Tristan Jones's eyes offers a unique picture of our lifestyle. Because he spent so much time isolated from the modern world while sailing on his small boat, Jones's observations give us a chance to explore a question that many have asked at one time or another: "What would someone from another place or time think about our world if he or she suddenly arrived on the scene?" It is interesting to note that while Jones commented on the politics and social relationships that he found in the countries he visited, much of his attention was captured by the relationship between people and their physical environment. He was interested not only in how people affected their environment, but in how the environment affected the way people behaved, believed, and interacted.

It is precisely because of this last observation that an examination of the environment is an appropriate topic for social psychology. Our physical environment, as we will see, has a strong influence on our attitudes, perceptions, and social interactions. In studying the relationship between people and their environment, we will draw on almost all the theories we have covered earlier in this text. We'll see the role of attitudes (Chapter Five) in influencing our approach to our environment; we'll see how our self-concept (Chapter Three) is affected by and reflected in our use of the environment; we'll find that attributions (Chapter Two) and social cognition (Chapter Two) play a major part in determining how we respond to our physical environment; and we'll see how our environment influences our social behavior such as attraction (Chapter Seven), helping (Chapter Eight), frustration and violence (Chapter Eight), conflict (Chapter Nine), and group behavior (Chapter Eleven). In a sense, studying the relationship between people and their environment allows us to put many of the theories of social psychology to the test; we have the opportunity to determine whether these theories enable us to better understand this relationship and to apply these theories to the creation of a better relationship between people and their surroundings.

With this background in mind, we can begin to examine the area that has become known as *environmental psychology*. This area of study is relatively new, tracing its history back only a few decades. Environmental psychology is the scientific study of the relationship between people and their environment (Stokols, 1978). The field has a unique character because it has attracted researchers from such diverse areas as social psychology, architecture, urban planning, engineering, anthropology, and sociology.

PEOPLE AND THEIR ENVIRONMENT: A HISTORICAL PERSPECTIVE

Tristan Jones's description of the difference in the seafarer's and land-dweller's view of the environment presents an interesting contrast—interesting in that it not only shows the difference in these two groups,

In our modern-day world, we change our environment by traveling to another location. As the temperature in the north drops, the number of people on southern beaches increases dramatically. *(Tim Carlson/Stock, Boston)*

but it also parallels historical differences in the way people have felt about their environment.

Jones suggested that the mariner sees his or her surroundings as uncontrollable and unpredictable; the environment is the master and the sailor must learn to survive in it. Altman and Chemers (1980) suggest that this view was characteristic of people early in history; they too saw the environment as master. In early times, people's lives were controlled by nature. It determined the types of homes they built: the Eskimo lived in a home made of ice because the environment supplied only this type of building material. The environment determined where people lived: villages were built close to the rivers because people needed water and used the river for travel. When it was hot, people were forced to seek shade for protection; and when it was cold, they shivered together around fires.

In contrast to the mariner's approach was that which Jones felt that land dwellers held, the view that they were the masters of nature: their aim was to gain complete control of their environment. Jones (1980) protested this approach because he saw it as threatening his domain. "Now

Native Americans viewed the environment as a master with whom they must live in harmony. Their dances and ceremonies often portrayed this partnership. *(John Running/ Stock, Boston)*

he [land dweller] was about to invade the ocean using the same phi-losophy and methods that had done so much harm ashore" (p. 233). According to Altman and Chemers (1980), the view that people were *above* nature became common during the Industrial Revolution when people developed many devices to control nature. In time, people could control their climate with air conditioners and heaters. The environment no longer determined where people could build homes; they could dig deep wells for water and move mountains to make room for houses. Improvements in transportation allowed people to seek out environ-ments that catered to their immediate needs. Their attitude was that the environment was something to be controlled and conquered.

In recent years, this view has changed, and a new understanding and respect for the environment has begun to emerge. Pollution and the scar-city of environmental resources have become topics of major concern. We are slowly realizing that our relationship with the environment is a reciprocal one; we both influence it and are influenced by it. We are now beginning to see ourselves as part of nature. Research has shown that our environment has a broad effect on a variety of behaviors. Recently, for example, Nadler (1986) found differences in helping behavior between city and kibbutz dwellers.

STUDYING THE ENVIRONMENT: SOME UNIFYING CONCEPTS

If you examine your own environment, you will begin to appreciate the enormous task facing environmental psychologists who wish to study the relationship between people and their surroundings. The environment is composed of many variables. These include the physical space around you, the shape of the room you are in, the temperature of the air, the amount of noise, and the size of the city in which you live. These and more variables are part of our environment and, as we will see, research has shown that each variable can influence our behavior.

A concept that consistently crops up in the literature on environmental studies is the *person-environment fit* (Altman, Lawton, & Wohlwill, 1984; Holahan, 1982). The heart of this concept is that the relationship between people and their environment is a dynamic one. We cannot simply sug-gest that a particular environment will have the same effect on all people; the effect of the environment on an individual will be influenced by the individual's characteristics, attitudes, expectations, and personal history. Hence, we must draw on a wide variety of theories and research to better understand and predict this relationship. As we suggested earlier, many if not most of the theories of social psychology are used to help further our understanding of the person-environment relationship. However, some stand out as more central than others.

One concept that is frequently relied on is *attribution*, often referred to as *interpretation* or *appraisal* (see Chapter Three). Attribution theories argue that the way people feel and react to others (and their environment) is a function of the interpretation they give to situations and events. For example, Jones got a job to sail a boat, the *Star Rider*, from New York to the West Indies. He took a crew of four men who had little sailing experience. After several days of sailing in light breezes, the wind changed direction and picked up velocity. The crew felt that this was a welcome change, for it offered them a new challenge and increased the speed at which they sailed. Tristan Jones, however, interpreted the change as a sign that a menacing storm was approaching and he became worried and concerned. The same environment, therefore, led to different interpretations and reactions. Lazarus (1982) argued that the degree to which people will view an event or situation as stressful is determined by their appraisal of that event. Thus, it is not only the environment that affects people; their interpretation of the environment plays a major role.

A second important concept is *control*. Jones felt that people strive to control their surroundings and that their lack of control was very disquieting. Similarly, environmental psychologists have found that control is a central issue in predicting how people will respond to the environment (Baum, Singer, & Baum, 1981). People can endure very extreme conditions when they feel that they have control over their environment. On the other hand, seemingly benign environments can become very stressful when people feel that they have no control over their surroundings.

A third unifying concept that runs through many environmental studies is *cognitive overload*. According to this theory, people are able to deal with a limited amount of stimulation at any one time. If the environment becomes too complex so that the individual is "overloaded" with stimulation, he or she will experience stress, performance will deteriorate, and effort will be directed at reducing the amount of stimulation. This concept is most applicable to explaining the effects of urban environments, but it has also been used to explain the circumstances in which people will suffer crowding and ill effects from noise. Along these lines, investigators (Costanzo, Archer, Aronson, & Pettigrew, 1986) found that people are often overloaded with information about energy conservation programs, but that they do not have an accurate understanding of these programs.

More than in most areas of social psychology, research on environment and behavior has focused on *arousal*. Investigators are not only interested in how the environment affects an individual's state of arousal,

An approaching storm may elicit different reactions from farmers and city dwellers. One may view the storm with relief while the other may see it as fearful or as a nuisance. *(Top, Mark Antman/The Image Works; bottom, Jack Prelutsky/Stock, Boston)*

but they are also concerned with how this arousal then affects the individual's health and performance in that environment (Gatchel & Baum, 1983). Arousal has become a key concept because it may explain behavior in a given situation. As we will see, investigators (Worchel & Brown, 1984) have also been interested in how the environment affects the way people interpret their arousal. It has been argued that two people may experience similar arousal (heart rate, blood pressure, galvanic skin responses [GSR], and so on) but each will interpret that arousal differently depending on characteristics of the environment. The interpretation subsequently influences their behavior and their "fit" with their environment.

With this background in mind, let us examine some of the specific areas that have been studied by environmental psychologists.

SPATIAL FEATURES OF THE ENVIRONMENT

When we think about our environment, one of the first features that comes to mind is space. Do we have too little or too much of it? Are there too many people in it or too few? Can we control what is in that space? While these questions may come to mind when we examine our surroundings, there are some other intriguing questions that should also be asked. Why do we need or want space? What happens when we do not have sufficient space? What qualities make some space more desirable than other space? Because of its prominence, there has been a great deal of research on how people use and are affected by the space around them. As we will see, this research not only examines areas such as the places in which we live and work, but it also focuses on the space that immediately surrounds our bodies.

Personal Space   It was an odd crew that signed on to deliver the forty-foot ketch *Star Rider* to the West Indies. There was the British captain Tristan Jones. Jerry, the cook, was black and in his early twenties. Johnny, the first mate, was Korean-American and had just turned twenty. The two white American crew members could hardly have been more different. Al, the mechanic, was in his early twenties and had been a pipe fitter before the voyage. Hank, the navigator, was a middle-aged man who owned a restaurant and "was the image of a suburban American." At the beginning of the voyage, Jones noted that the crew members generally kept to themselves, trying to be very careful not to bump into one another, and apologizing when a sudden lurch brought on an unavoidable collision. In a sense, regardless of where on the ship a man happened to be, he tried to protect the space around him from uninvited

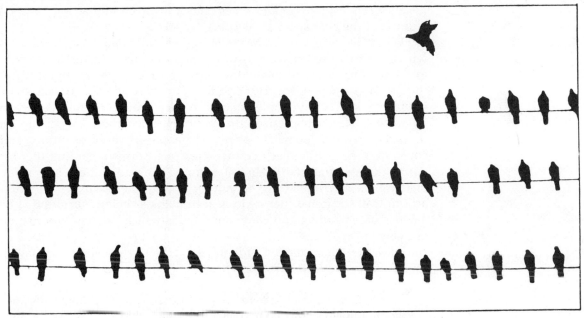

One need merely observe animal behavior to see evidence of personal distances. (*Charlottesville Daily Progress, September 15, 1977, p. E5*).

intrusion. However, as the voyage progressed, the concern about close contact abated and the crew often chose to eat together in close quarters; no apologies were uttered or discomfort displayed as they crawled over one another while carrying out their daily duties. Still, each man viewed the space around him as personal, but the size of that personal space was smaller than at the outset of the voyage.

The behavior of the *Star Rider's* crew was not accidental or haphazard. For decades, social scientists have observed that animals and people use the space around them in rather predictable ways. This is especially true of the space that directly surrounds the body; we can consider this space "mobile territory" because it is always present and goes wherever the animal or person goes. Thus, each crew member had a zone of personal space whether he was on shore, on the ship's deck, or in the ship's galley. This zone of personal space, then, went wherever the crewman went.

The existence of personal space was first observed in animals. Hediger (1950) noticed that animals tend to space themselves when around other animals of the same species. These spacing distances remain constant within species and across situations. Animals will move and attempt to position themselves to keep this normal spacing. Hediger called this distance *personal distance* and noted that it involved interaction between animals of the *same* species.

Hall (1959, 1966), an anthropologist, was fascinated by the way in which animals used space and wondered whether humans used space in a similar manner. He coined the term *proxemics* to denote the study of the human's use of space. He used the term *personal space* to denote the bubbles of space that people attempt to keep around themselves when interacting. Hall hypothesized that people feel a certain "ownership" of the space around them. He observed people in various cultures and concluded that within each culture there are norms regarding the distances that persons hold when interacting. The size of these interaction distances is determined by the culture and by the nature of the interaction. Hall suggested that we look at humans as being "surrounded by a series of expanding and contrasting fields which provide information of many kinds."

Hall (1966) characterized individuals in Western societies as having four definite interaction distances, each with a close and far phase:

1. The first is *intimate distance*. The close phase of intimate distance involves having the two parties touch each other. This is the distance at which we make love, wrestle, protect, and comfort. In the far phase, six to eighteen inches separate the two parties. This phase is used when touching is not permitted and conversation is conducted in very low tones, as in telling secrets.
2. *Personal distance* involves a close phase of eighteen to thirty inches and a far phase of thirty to forty-eight inches. Close personal distance is used by close friends or by a man and his wife when conversing. Hall says that "keeping someone at arm's length" is one way to characterize the far phase of personal distance. This is the distance for ordinary social interactions between friends and acquaintances who wish to discuss matters of personal interest but do not want to engage in physical contact.
3. In *social distance*, the close phase (four to seven feet) is used for personal business and for conversations at casual social gatherings. The far phase (seven to twelve feet) is used for more formal business and social discourse. Desks in the offices of important people are usually large enough to hold people at the far phase.
4. Formal interactions occur in the close phase (twelve to twenty-five feet) of *public distance*. This is usually one way in nature. The far phase (twenty-five feet or more) is the distance that is automatically set around important public figures.

The distance at which we interact with others is affected by personal variables, the nature of the relationship, and the topic of conversation. We keep greater distances when we argue with a stranger than when we talk of intimate subjects with a friend. *(Left, © Greg Platka/Southern Light; right, Deborah Kahn 1985/Stock, Boston)*

Reviews of hundreds of studies have found that people keep predictable distances between themselves and others (Altman & Vinsel, 1977; Hayduk, 1978, 1983). However, as we will see, the exact distances that are used are more complex than the picture presented by Hall.

One fascinating aspect of spatial behavior is that, despite the regularity involved, people seem unaware of it. Love and Aiello (1980) had pairs of unacquainted females discuss a prearranged topic. After the discussion, the investigators asked the subjects to replicate the spatial behavior they had used during the discussion. Subjects were given dolls to use in indicating their behavior. It turned out that the subjects were unaware of the interaction distances they had kept during their conversation.

Before we become too complacent and accept the image of a world populated by people navigating through their environment encapsulated in perfect bubbles of space, we must caution that the size and shape of personal space are affected by a wide range of factors. Our view of this orderly world must first take into account that the shape of personal space is not necessarily the circle suggested by Hall. Research suggests that frontal distances are often slightly larger than rear distances (Strube & Werner, 1982). However, one caveat here is the finding that violent or delinquent individuals protect larger areas behind them than in front of them (Lothstein, 1972). Other investigators (see Figure 12–1) have developed even more complex representations of personal space.

These observations open the door for us to ask what other factors affect the shape and size of personal space. A complete answer to this question would fill at least one volume the size of this text, so let us take a selective look at some of the more interesting variables.

Factors Affecting Personal Space

Sex and age. In general, research has found that the distance kept between males when interacting with other males is larger than that kept in female-female interactions and mixed-sex interactions (Brady & Walker, 1978). There is also some support for the hypothesis that greater distance is maintained in mixed-sex interactions than in interactions between females. Overall, these patterns argue that males have larger personal spaces than females. We can speculate about the reasons for these differences. In Western cultures, there are strong taboos against homosexuality—especially male homosexuality. Children are often punished by their parents for touching or caressing another child of the same sex. However, direct teaching and models inform children that heterosexual touching is acceptable. Hence, children's spatial behavior may, in part, be a response to norms about permissible sexual behavior.

In light of this speculation, it is interesting to note that stable personal space norms do develop around the time that the child reaches puberty. Investigations reveal that children do not begin to exhibit consistent spatial behavior before the age of four or five. After that age, the size of personal space increases until the age of twelve or thirteen when it stabilizes (Aiello & Aiello, 1974; see Figure 12–2).

Byrne and his colleagues (Byrne, Baskett, & Hodges, 1971; Fisher & Byrne, 1975) found another difference between the spatial behavior of males and females. Males responded most negatively to frontal invasions of their space whereas females reacted most negatively to invasions from the side. This finding led Fisher and Byrne to predict that males would be more likely to protect their frontal space than their lateral space, whereas females would be most concerned about protecting their lateral space. To test this hypothesis, observers watched the behavior of males and females in the library. They found that males were most likely to place their books and possessions in front of them on a table, thereby keeping others from taking a seat across the table. Females, on the other hand, placed their possessions at their side and thus reduced the likelihood of invasion from that direction.

Culture. Culture also affects personal space distances. Latin Americans, French, and Arabs interact at closer distances than individuals

Figure 12–1
A three-dimensional view of the shape of personal space

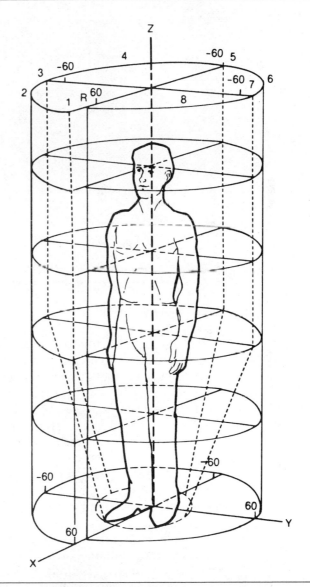

Source: After Hayduk, L. The vertical profile of personal space, Edmonton, Alberta, Canada T6G 2H4: University of Alberta, unpublished.

Figure 12–2
Mean interaction distances of male and female dyads at six grade levels

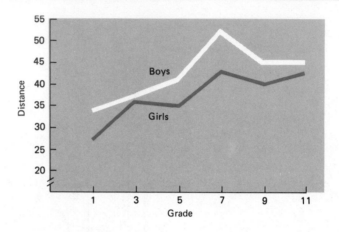

Source: Aiello and Aiello (1974).

from the United States, England, or Sweden (Hall, 1966). Little (1968) asked subjects from five countries to place dolls in a "comfortable interaction" position. He found that people from Italy and Greece placed the dolls closer than subjects from the United States, Sweden, and Scotland.

Cultural differences in personal space have been the subject of many humorous stories. One such story involves a Latin American and a North American who were conversing at a party. The Latin American continually moved closer and closer to the North American because he was comfortable interacting at a close distance. The North American, on the other hand, felt comfortable with more space and countered the other's approach with movements backward. The result was a "Latin Waltz" in which the Latin American moved in and the North American moved back, and the two crossed the room during the course of their conversation.

The existence of cultural variations in personal space norms has some important implications. Inner-city populations represent a mixture of racial and ethnic backgrounds, which may be a source of constant stress. This stress arises not only from differences in language or customs but also from cultural differences in the norms regarding personal space. For example, given that Puerto Ricans like to interact at close distance, whereas Germans like to maintain rather large spacing, interactions between members of the two nationalities are likely to be marked by stress. When an interaction occurs between members of two nationalities, each of the two persons involved will attempt to locate himself at a comfortable spacing for the interaction. This type of spacing conflict is more acute in North American cities such as New York and Toronto than in such cities as Hong Kong because there is much greater cultural mixing in North America.

It is also interesting to find that the crew of the *Star Rider* was composed of adult males from different cultural and racial backgrounds. According to our discussion, the men may have had different requirements for personal space zones, and these differences may have accounted for some of the awkwardness and apologies for unplanned contact that occurred during the early stages of the voyage.

Contextual factors. There are many factors that are characteristic of the situation in which an interaction takes place that are not directly related to the participants (age, sex, race) or the nature of their interaction (friendly, unfriendly, strangers). We might consider these characteristics *contextual factors* (Worchel, 1986). A wide variety of such factors have been shown to influence the size of personal-space zones. For example, people maintain greater distances in small rooms than in large rooms (White, 1975) and in rectangular rooms than in square rooms (Worchel, 1986). People interacting in inside locations keep greater distance than people interacting outdoors (Cochran, Hale, & Hissam, 1984). When people are in settings that are likely to arouse a great deal of tension (student infirmary, dean's office waiting area), they maintain greater distances than in less anxiety-provoking settings (television lounge, commuter lounge) (Long, 1984). Even ceiling height has an effect; males maintain greater distances when room ceiling heights are low than when they are high (Savinar, 1975). Two other contextual findings are also of interest. First, strangers who are discussing an intimate or potentially embarrassing topic (sexual behavior) keep greater distances than when the topic is less intimate (university classes) (Baker & Shaw, 1980). Finally, people who expect to be interacting over a long period set greater distances than people who expect only a short interaction (Worchel, 1986).

Reactions to Invasions of Personal Space

We have presented a great deal of evidence that shows that humans do have clearly defined personal-space zones, although the size of these zones is dependent on a number of variables. It is also clear from the evidence that, when possible, individuals avoid intruding into the personal space of others. However, there are numerous times in our daily lives when such intrusions are impossible to avoid, when we violate the personal space of others and they violate ours. What are the effects of such violations?

Some thirty inches from my nose
The frontier of my Person goes
And all the untilled air between
Is private pagus or demesne.
Stranger, unless with bedroom eyes
I beckon you to fraternize,
Beware of rudely crossing it:
I have no gun but I can spit.

Source: W. H. Auden, "Prologue: The birth of architecture," *About the house.* New York: Random House; London: Faber and Faber, Ltd., 1965. Copyright © 1965 by W. H. Auden. Reprinted from W. H. Auden: *Collected Poems,* edited by Edward Mendelson, by permission of Random House, Inc.

The answer to this question is that two general types of reactions can occur. On one hand, people may respond negatively, experience stress, and attempt to move away from the intruder. One of the most common reactions to violations of personal space is arousal and stress. Numerous investigators (e.g., Worchel & Teddlie, 1976) found that subjects reported feeling uncomfortable and ill at ease when their personal space was violated. Such feelings of discomfort are accompanied by physiological arousal. McBride, King, and James (1965) found elevated galvanic skin responses (GSR) when the personal space of subjects was violated. Their GSR was also higher when the violations occurred from the frontal position than when they occurred from the side.

In addition to experiencing arousal, individuals often react by moving to reestablish the proper spacing or by fleeing the situation. Sommer (1969) examined reactions to spatial invasion, using normal female subjects who happened to be sitting alone at a table in the library. When a subject was located, Sommer's female colleague went to the same table and either violated the subject's personal space or did not. The results showed that when the experimenter chose the adjacent chair and moved closer to the subject (violated personal space) 70 percent of the subjects had left the table after thirty minutes, as compared with 10 percent when personal space was not violated. Many subjects attempted to stand their ground before fleeing by moving their chairs, changing their posture, and trying to erect barriers between themselves and the intruder. Interestingly, out of 149 subjects who were run in the manner just described, only 3 verbally expressed their discomfort or asked the invader to allow more space.

While these findings suggest that people become stressed and move away from intruders, other investigators have found the opposite effect. Some studies (Schnieder & Harsuick, 1979) found that people responded to violations of personal space by moving still closer, and that they did not feel stressed by these violations.

How can we explain such conflicting results? Patterson (1976) suggested that the answer lies in the interpretation given to the violations. If the violations are seen as unfriendly or there is uncertainty about why they occurred, people will experience stress and move away from the intruder. However, if the violations are seen as a sign of friendship, people may reciprocate and actually enjoy the violation. This theory may explain the reactions of the *Star Rider* crew. Early in the voyage, they did not know each other and were uncertain about the intentions behind violations of their personal space. However, as they got to know each other, they saw the violations as accidents caused by sudden motion of the boat or as overtures of friendship. Because of these attributions, they were not stressed by the violations.

WHY PERSONAL SPACE?

Given that spatial behavior is so predictable, and violations engender such strong responses, we are led to ask why personal space occurs. What is the function of the sack of behavior that we keep around our bodies? There have been a number of answers to this question and all probably have merit.

1. One of the functions of personal space may be to give the person a sense of identity. By claiming the space around themselves, people can signal that they are indeed unique individuals who are independent from others. Thus, the act of claiming personal space may be a symbolic means of declaring independence.
2. Personal space may be an important mechanism for achieving privacy. According to this position, people can use the space around them as a buffer to protect their privacy. In fact, Altman states that the desire for privacy may be one of the factors that determines the amount of space individuals claim as personal.
3. Hall (1966) points out that the distances used in most social interactions are those that keep others at arm's length. Individuals who have a history of violence or who are angry keep even greater distances. These arm's length distances allow the individual to see the hands and feet of others and *protect* against surprise physical assaults.

4. Distance plays an important role in interpersonal communication. The distance at which we interact with others determines the channels of communication that can be used. For example, if we communicate with others at the public distance (twelve to twenty-five feet), we may hear their voices, but it is difficult to determine whether they are maintaining eye contact, frowning, smiling, or expressing anger. As we move closer to such individuals, we can begin to observe more of these nonverbal behaviors; we can distinguish eye contact, smiling, slight changes in the angle of the head, and even sweating. Thus, interpersonal distance determines the channels through which communication can take place.

5. Probably the most widely quoted function is the regulation of intimacy. Many studies (Gifford and O'Connor, 1986) have found that people interact at closer distances with others whom they like than with people they dislike. The closer people are to one another, the more intimate their relationship. But distance is not the only way we communicate intimacy. We can also signal attraction for others by looking into their eyes, smiling, and leaning toward them. We can communicate dislike by moving away from people, reducing eye contact, frowning, turning our shoulder toward them ("giving them the cold shoulder"), and leaning away. Hence, Argyle and Dean (1965) suggested that nonverbal behaviors are used to form an equilibrium system through which intimacy is communicated. Individuals form a comfortable level of intimacy, and if that level is upset, the individuals will attempt to compensate and reestablish equilibrium by using any or all of the behaviors associated with intimacy.

Interpersonal distance determines which channels of communications are available. As can be seen in the pictures, when we get closer to another person, facial features become more evident and other nonverbal modes of communication (e.g., posture and hand gestures) are not visible.

Argyle and Dean tested equilibrium theory by having subjects converse with a confederate at distances of two, six, or ten feet. An observer behind a one-way mirror recorded the amount of eye contact maintained by the subject. As the distance between the subject and confederate decreased, so did the amount of eye contact (see Figure 12–3). Patterson (1977) found that as interaction distance decreased, not only did subjects

Figure 12–3
The relation between eye contact and distances for different combinations of confederates and subjects

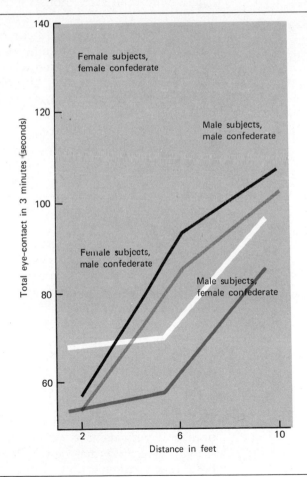

Source: Argyle and Dean (1965).

reduce eye contact, but they positioned their bodies to be less open to the confederate (placed their shoulders between themselves and the other person).

TERRITORIALITY

Thus far, we have been discussing the small bit of mobile territory that immediately surrounds our bodies. There is, however, another type of territory that has a strong influence on our behavior. Tristan Jones sailed more than sixty thousand miles on a nineteen-foot boat named the *Sea Dart*. He sailed her in every ocean in the world and ferried her across continents. He worked at jobs such as janitor to buy rigging and paint for his tiny craft. When he was on the *Sea Dart*, he was king in his own small realm. He decided who could come aboard and who could not. He knew every inch of his boat and he took pride in her appearance. The *Sea Dart* was Jones's territory and he would risk his life to save her.

The desire to possess territory has been observed in both animals and humans. *Territoriality* involves the mutually exclusive use of areas and objects by persons or groups. In humans, territoriality involves a sense of ownership in that people can dispose of their territory as they wish. Further, most descriptions of territoriality state that territory will be defended even to the point of using aggression.

Types of Territory   An interesting feature of human territorial behavior is that people have many types of territory. Altman (1975) identifies three types of human territories: primary, secondary, and public. *Primary territories* are exclusively owned and controlled by individuals or groups; they are relatively central to the lives of those individuals and are generally owned on a permanent basis. One's home or apartment or even one's bedroom within a home is a primary territory, as was the *Sea Dart* for Tristan Jones. He often lived on the boat and his life revolved around this craft.

Secondary territories are less central, and it is not usually clear who owns them. They serve as a bridge between the primary territories and the more public areas that can be used by everyone. Often a limited number of persons have access to a secondary territory. An example of a secondary territory may be your "regular seat" in a classroom. You may become accustomed to sitting in a particular seat every time you attend a certain class. If another person sits in "your" seat, you may not throw that person out but you are likely to feel somewhat stressed — the chances are that you will arrive early at the next meeting of the class to regain

The *Sea Dart* was Tristan Jones's primary territory. The boat was central to his life and he controlled who could board her and what they could do on her rolling deck.

control over "your territory." Cavan (1963, 1966) reported that neighborhood bars are examples of secondary territories. Patrons who use these bars frequently feel a sense of control over them. Outsiders who wander into these bars often receive cold stares or insulting questions. The message that they do not belong there is made very clear. As we reported in the opening pages of this book, Jones observed those behaviors clearly in New York bars; if one wasn't the 'type" to fit into the bar, he or she did not belong in that territory and the patrons gave this message clearly. Thus, while secondary territories are not owned, people usually exercise control over them. Interestingly enough, because secondary territories involve feelings of control but not clear ownership, the potential for conflict and misunderstanding in these areas is very high.

Public territory is "open to the public," and individuals or groups do not feel that they have a claim on such territory unless they are occupying it. For example, you may feel that you have exclusive access to a particular spot on the beach while you are occupying that spot; no one should trespass on your spot while you are there. However, you do not feel that you should be entitled to that particular spot if you come back to the beach the next day.

Notice how often you sit in the same seat in the classroom. "Your" classroom seat is an example of secondary territory; while you don't own it, you do feel a sense of control over the chair. *(Elizabeth Crews/Stock, Boston)*

People are most protective of their primary territories and least defensive of public territories. These behaviors were clearly shown in a recent cross-cultural study by Worchel and Lollis (1982). These investigators pointed out that Greeks draw a clear distinction between private and public territory; there is very little secondary territory surrounding their residences. Most Greek homes have a fence or hedge separating private property from public property; in fact, in many cases the fence is erected before the home is built. The private-public distinction is not as clear in the United States and Canada. In these countries, people often view the areas in front of their homes as secondary territories. These secondary areas include the sidewalk and street curb in front of the home; while other people may pass through these areas, the residents feel that they control this territory. Fences around homes in the United States and Canada are not generally found.

To demonstrate how these different perceptions of territory affect behavior, Worchel and Lollis placed plastic bags of litter in three locations in residences in the United States and Greece. Early in the morning, the litter was put either (1) in the front yard, (2) on the sidewalk in

Table 12–1
Mean speed for the removal of litter

Culture	Yard	Walkway	Street	Across street
		Location of drop		
Greece	1.53*	5.00	5.25	—
	(17)	(15)	(16)	
United States	2.27	2.00	2.25	5.57
	(15)	(15)	(16)	(7)

*Scores range from 1 to 6 with lower scores indicating quicker removal. Numbers in parentheses indicate number of houses in the condition.
Source: Worchel and Lollis (1982), pp. 370–375.

front of the house, or (3) on the curb in front of the house. The investigators returned every four hours to see if the litter had been removed. (If the litter had not been removed by the following morning, the experimenters collected it.) As can be seen from Table 12–1, litter in the front yard (private territory) was removed with equal speed in Greece and the United States. However, litter on the sidewalk and street curb was removed significantly quicker in the United States than in Greece. To determine whether all areas around the home are considered secondary territory in the United States, Worchel and Lollis located homes wih a vacant lot across the street. They placed bags of litter on the curbs in front of these lots and across the street from selected homes. As can be seen from the results, the litter was rarely removed in these cases. It therefore seems that secondary territory in the United States does not extend across the street.

The Functions of Territory The owning and control of territory play many important roles in our lives.

1. Territoriality helps provide a stable social organization. Rosenblatt and Budd (1977) found that married couples exhibited more territorial behavior than cohabiting couples. Married couples were likely to have a clear understanding about who slept on what side of the bed, to have separate closets or closet areas, and to have specific seating positions at the dinner table. Supposedly, married couples were in a longer term relationship than cohabiting couples and social organization was more important to them. You might imagine what your own living situation would be if there were no territorial rules;

you would not know what bed you would be sleeping in or what desk you could study at or even which room you would have for the night.

2. Territoriality aids in the regulation of privacy (Ittelson, Proshansky, Rivlin, & Winkel, 1974). Privacy is "an individual's freedom to choose what he will communicate about himself and to whom he will communicate it in a given circumstance." Thus, privacy is a chosen isolation. Usually, periods of privacy are intermingled with periods of social interaction.

Privacy is an important and necessary condition for humans. Four needs that are fulfilled by privacy have been identified (Westin, 1967).

a. It allows the individual some personal autonomy or self-identity in that it provides a means by which he can control his environment.

b. It provides opportunities for emotional release from the tensions caused by everyday life.

c. It gives the individual an opportunity for self-evaluation by allowing him to withdraw and take stock of himself.

Elderly Lady Lives with Horde of Rats

MIAMI (AP)—A petite, gray-haired widow is living in apparent harmony with a house full of scurrying rats. "You can see dozens of them from the windows," says a neighbor. "Tails hanging out all over. Rat heads sticking out."

But police say she turned away an offer of assistance with a shout of, "I don't need your help," and is doing nothing wrong. She will be left alone as long as the rats stay home and create no public health hazard.

"You can do whatever you want in your own house," said Dr. Richard Morgan, Dade County health director.

"She refused the aid," said Dade County's assistant environmental health director, Luis Benavides, who had sent the county rodent control director to offer help in removing the rats.

"We have no jurisdiction. A man's home is his castle. Nobody's got jurisdiction inside a house. Maybe she keeps them as pets."

As this report shows, we tend to view people's primary territory as an area where they have strict privacy and can do almost whatever they like. *(Source: Charlottesville Daily Progress, March 8, 1978. Courtesy of The Associated Press.)*

Richard's side   Judy's side

Territorial behavior helps promote social order. Couples in long-term relationships tend to
have clear territorial understanding such as what side of the closet belongs to whom.
(*Judy S. Gelles 1981/Stock, Boston*)

  d. It allows the individual limited and protected communication by
    permitting him to decide when and with whom he will share his
    thoughts and feelings.

  By controlling territory, a person can achieve privacy whenever
desired. Tristan Jones was a prime example of this. When he wanted
privacy he retreated into the *Sea Dart*; when he really wanted to
ensure his privacy, he set sail.

3. A third function of territoriality for humans is analogous to the protection function for animals. Humans seem to have a "home-court
  advantage"; they perform better on their own territory. Worchel and
  Sigall (1976) found that Atlantic Coast Conference basketball teams
  win 88 percent of their home games and less than 65 percent of their
  games on the road. Familiarity with the home territory seems to play
  some role in these statistics; the basketball player knows how the ball
  will bounce on the home court and knows "the action" of the familiar home-court backboards. More recently, however, investigators
  (Baumeister & Steinhilber, 1984) found that there is actually a slight

tendency for home teams to lose decisive championship games. According to the researchers, the pressure to perform well in these decisive games is much greater on the home-court players than the visitors; the players do not want to make mistakes in front of their own fans. This added pressure may make them self-conscious, cautious, and inhibit their performance.

Moving out of the sports arena, we again find a home-court advantage. Results of a number of studies (Edney, 1975; Taylor & Lanni, 1981) have found that people on their home territory tend to dominate social interactions and play leadership roles. One investigator (Lee, 1973) found that students who were bused to schools outside their neighborhoods performed less well than students who were not bused. After ruling out alternative explanations, such as effect of the bus ride and school quality, Lee concluded that students felt more uncomfortable outside their familiar area, and this discomfort influenced their performance.

4. A final important function of territory involves personal identity; people use territory to establish their independence and self-identity. Having territory allows people to define who they are and draw

A homecourt advantage exists in a variety of sporting contests. The home team wins a majority of the games. One important exception may be in important championship games. *(Frank Siteman MCMLXXX/The Picture Cube)*

Individuals or groups often use clear markers to delineate and protect their territory. *(United Press International Photo)*

boundaries between themselves and others. Territory also lets people "advertise" their self-identity to others. If you walk through a dormitory or office, you will see that people have decorated their areas to reflect their identity. The skier has pictures of snow-covered mountains; the political activist has pictures of favorite candidates and political slogans.

Establishing and Protecting Territory Both animals and humans use markers to define and clearly distinguish their territory so that others will observe that a certain plot is "owned." Some animals, such as deer, mark their territory by scraping the bark off trees around the boundary. Other animals, such as domestic dogs will urinate or defecate around the boundaries of their territory. Humans may erect high fences or hedges to protect their territory. Often these markers are accentuated with "No Trespassing" signs or even armed guards. Territorial markings are often very effective in defending against intrusion. One study (Brown, 1978)

Figure 12-4
The appearance of a home can influence its chances of being burglarized (left, nonburglarized; right, burglarized)

Source: Brown, 1979, reprinted by permission.

found that a home was less likely to burglarized if it had clear territorial markings such as a fence or name plate than a home that was not clearly marked (see Figure 12-4). At another level, investigators (Sommer & Becker, 1969) examined the effectiveness of various markers in protecting secondary territory. In a crowded study hall, the experimenters placed different markers in a chair and observed how often someone would invade the territory and sit in that chair. The results, presented in Table 12-2, indicate that the greater the number of markers and the more personal the markers, the more effective they were in protecting the territory.

Table 12-2
Effectiveness of markers in protecting territory

Markers	*Percentage of trials in which chair was taken*
Sportcoat, textbook, and notebook	0
Sportcoat	20
Textbook and notebook	20
Stacked journals	60
Scattered journals	100
Unmarked chair	100

Source: Sommer and Becker (1969).

We use our territory to establish and advertise our self-identity. What do the two pictures indicate about the identity of the people involved? *(Top, P. Davidson © 1983/The Image Works; bottom, Ellis Herwig/The Picture Cube)*

It seems, therefore, that people have very clear norms about how to claim territory. However, people do not have clear norms about how to react when territory is invaded. What do you do if you have left your coat to claim a library chair and return to find someone has moved your coat and taken your chair? Some of us might march up and loudly demand our territorial rights. However, Becker and Mayo (1971) found that confrontation is seldom used by humans to protect secondary or public territory. Often the individual will retreat and find a new territory. On the other hand, the situation is probably very different when primary territory is involved. Although there have been no studies of the protection of primary territory, the newspapers often carry stories of individuals who barricade themselves in homes and threaten to shoot anyone who attempts to take possession of their territory.

DENSITY AND CROWDING

Jones came to New York in an effort to find work; his trusty craft, *Sea Dart*, had been impounded in London, and Jones had no money to pay the port tax on her. He had to get her out of bondage and he felt he could find work in New York. When he arrived, he was penniless and hence searched through New York for a flophouse where he could find a bed for a few dollars a night. He finally happened on the Uncle Sam that in "its hey-day, had been a medium class full-blown hotel." It was anything but a hotel when Jones found it. "Now it had the air of being—not just condemned—damned. . . . Upstairs, many of the walls that had once separated rooms had been removed; now there were several big dormitories, each crowded with single beds so that there was only eighteen inches of walkway between them" (p. 188). Jones vividly remembered trying to sleep in these cramped quarters.

> All night there was muttering in different quarters, coughing, sputtering, wheezing, moaning, a continual going to and from the men's room, the rustle of brown paper bags, the gurgle of "Irish Rose," and the cries of those who even asleep found no peace, no comfort of spirit. There were a half-dozen night-ramblers, mostly very old men who found it impossible to sleep. They spent the night creeping around and around the dormitory. . . . The first night I was exhausted, but I slept only in snatches. (p. 194)

Jones found it terribly stressful being in the center of the room surrounded by people, and he bribed the night attendant with a precious dollar to give him a bed on the side of the room. At least here he did not have a sea of humanity completely around him.

Up to this point, we have been examining space that was personal and did not contain other people. Now we turn our attention to space in which other people exist. We will focus on *density* and *crowding*; the two terms are often used interchangeably, but as we will see, the distinction between them is an important one.

Density and Behavior   Much of the concern with density resulted from two sources. First, there are the startling statistics concerning the growth rate of the world's population. In 1650, the world's population was five hundred million. It had reached one billion by 1850, taking two hundred years to double (Ehrlich, 1968). There were two billion people in the world by 1930, a doubling in eighty years. Ehrlich estimated that it would take only thirty-five years for the world's population to double again. Clearly, these figures indicate that our planet is growing dramatically in human density.

The second source of concern was a number of animal studies that indicated negative effects of high density. For example, Calhoun (1962) conducted careful observations on a colony of rats that were confined to a limited amount of space. As the rat population and density increased, a number of alarming events resulted. Social order broke down; aggression, homosexuality, cannibalism, and abnormal sexual behavior increased. Female rats failed to build suitable nests or take care of their young. In addition, health problems dramatically increased; many females developed cancer of their sexual organs and mammary glands, and miscarriages were more frequent. These problems occurred despite the fact that there was sufficient food, water, and nesting material for the animals to maintain a high standard of living. Thus, the cause of these problems was attributed to the increasing density.

Armed with this evidence, researchers expected to find similar villainous effects of density in humans. In support of this position, Cox, Paulus, and McCain (1984; McCain, Cox, Paulus, Luke, & Abadzi, 1985) found that as the number of inmates in a prison unit increased, so too did the number of behavioral and medical problems. For example, suicide rates at large institutions (population greater than 1,400) were ten times as high as in small units (population less than 1,100), and the number of disciplinary infractions increased as density increased.

However, despite these and a smattering of findings on the negative effects of high density, most other carefully controlled research failed to show that high density, by itself, created behavioral, performance, or health problems (Sundstrom, 1978). The conclusion presented by this research was that with the possible exception of highly stressful environments such as the prison, high density was not the ogre it had been feared to be.

While the density may be lower in the library than at the sporting event, people in the library may feel more crowded when faced with someone seated next to them. Crowding is a motivational state rather than a physical measure of the environment. *(Top, Ellis Herwig/The Picture Cube; bottom, © Richard Wood 1980/The Picture Cube)*

Crowding   The conclusion from the density research seems to contradict the personal experience that many people have. Most of us would argue that being packed together with other people does affect our mood and performance in some situations. Many investigators were also unsatisfied with the conclusion that people are not affected by spatial restrictions in their environment. These investigators began to search for the factors that determine when people are affected by spatial restrictions.

As a first step, researchers (Stokols, 1972) distinguished crowding from density. In most of the earlier research, the two terms had been used interchangeably. However, Stokols pointed out that density is a purely spatial concept. Crowding, on the other hand, is a "motivational state aroused through the interaction of spatial, social, and personal factors" (1972, p. 275). Further, Stokols observed that crowding is stressful and can result in a number of negative effects on performance, social interaction, and personal behavior.

To understand the distinction between density and crowding, think of a rock concert and a library. At the rock concert, tens of thousands of people may be jammed together on a hillside. This situation obviously involves high density, yet the music lovers in attendance may not report feeling crowded. On the other hand, an individual in the library may feel crowded when three other people sit at the table where he or she is studying. The density in the library may be far lower than the density at the rock concert, yet greater crowding may be experienced in the library than at the rock concert. This distinction is important because it may be that humans are more affected by the experience of crowding than by variations in density.

Such reasoning dictates that we turn our attention away from density and focus on crowding. Many researchers have taken this direction and have developed theories to explain when individuals will feel crowded and how they will respond to crowding.

Privacy and crowding. Altman (1975) suggested that crowding results when "privacy mechanisms" do not function effectively and the individual is subjected to an undesired amount of social contact. Essentially, crowding results when the achieved privacy is less than the desired privacy. As we pointed out earlier, space is an important feature in regulating privacy.

Greenberg and Firestone (1977) tested Altman's hypothesis by asking subjects to participate in an interview session. In half of the conditions (surveillance), two confederates were present in the room during the interview whereas in the other conditions (no surveillance), the subject was alone with the interviewer for the session. During half of the interviews, the experimenter intruded on the subject's personal space by maintaining steady eye contact and touching the subject's knee (intrusion); there was no intrusion in the other half. Greenberg and Firestone reasoned that surveillance and intrusion would reduce the subject's privacy and lead to heightened perceptions of crowding. These predictions were confirmed. The highest level of crowding was found in the surveillance-intrusion condition, and the lowest level of crowding was found in the no surveillance-no intrusion condition. Another interesting finding was that the subjects revealed the least information about themselves during the interview in the surveillance-intrusion condition. Apparently, if they could not regain their privacy through spatial behaviors, they would protect it by withholding personal information and refusing to open up during the interview.

Crowding and control. There is an ironic inconsistency in Tristan Jones's view of landdwellers and mariners. He complains that "the landsman's society tends toward centralized control" and that people on land are oriented toward controlling their surroundings. Jones, the mariner, however, had supposedly learned to accept and live with unpredictability and lack of control. But Jones's experience in the Uncle Sam hotel showed that he was not immune from the need for control. He found it very disturbing that he could not control the noise and the intrusions from the night stalkers, and he went so far as to bribe the attendant to give him a space over which he could exercise more control.

For more than a decade, psychologists have examined the effects of loss of control (Wortman & Brehm, 1975; Seligman, 1975). Seligman postulated that an individual who perceives that he or she has no control over the environment will experience a state of *learned helplessness*. Because of the feeling that they have no control over the environment, such individuals stop trying to affect their surroundings.

Rodin and others (Rodin & Baum, 1978; Baron & Rodin, 1978; Cohen & Sherrod, 1978) applied the concept of loss of control to crowding. They suggested that some high-density situations cause individuals to lose control over social interaction. In these conditions, individuals are forced to interact with one another and have no means for regulating that interaction. According to Rodin, this loss of control leads both to the experience of crowding and to feelings of learned helplessness. High density that does not involve a loss of control will not result in crowding.

There have been a number of demonstrations that control does play a central role in the experience of crowding. One study (Rodin, 1976) found that children from high-density homes did show symptoms of learned helplessness. Children who came from homes where a large number of people lived in a small amount of space attempted to exercise less control in a laboratory task than children from less densely populated homes.

The children from high-density homes were more willing to let the experimenter or a machine determine what happened to them, even when they had the opportunity to make their own choices.

In another manipulation of control, Rodin, Solomon, and Metcalf (1978) studied crowding in elevators. A team of four confederates waited until they spotted a single person waiting for the elevator in the Yale University library. When the elevator arrived, the four confederates and the subject entered it. In half of the conditions, the confederates positioned themselves so that the subject did not have access to the control panel of the elevator (no control). In the other half of the conditions, the confederates manipulated the subject so that he or she was standing in front of the controls. When the elevator reached the subject's destination, he or she was asked by a confederate posing as an architecture student to complete a questionnaire dealing with the elevator. The results obtained on the questionnaire indicated that the subjects in the control condition felt less crowded and gave a larger estimate of the size of the elevator than the subjects in the no-control condition. Hence, the perception of control does affect the experience of crowding.

Attribution, stimulus salience, and crowding. There were many events that competed for Jones's attention on his first night in the Uncle Sam. The architecture of the building was a fascinating combination of Victorian and Gothic. Jones met some interesting people who became steadfast friends. Yet the feature that stood out in Jones's mind was how crowded he felt in the setting. Given the wide variety of experiences and possible emotions that Jones could have had, why was crowding so prominent?

In an effort to answer this question, a number of investigators (Schmidt & Keating, 1979; Worchel & Teddlie, 1976) developed a model of crowding based on attribution theory and social cognition (see Chapters Two, Three). The investigators suggested that crowding results when people become aroused by events such as violations of personal space and then attribute that arousal to a lack of space or to other people being too close. Crowding will not occur if people are not aroused or if they do not view their arousal as resulting from spatial violations. As you can see, this model suggests that spatial restrictions or violations of personal space will not always lead to the experience of crowding. Strangers intrude into one another's personal spaces at basketball games, football games, theaters, and rock concerts. Yet people do not report feeling crowded at these events. In fact, Tuan (1977) reports that in some cases, individuals find that crowds are exhilarating and add to the enjoyment of an experience.

An important feature in determining whether people will feel crowded is the salience of others in their environment. When other people are salient (see Chapter Two), individuals will be likely to attribute their arousal to these others and crowding will result. However, if other people are not salient, people may not attribute their arousal to crowding, even though spatial violations have occurred. This model would explain Tristan Jones's experience in the Uncle Sam; when he lay down to sleep the salient features in his environment were the other people in the room, especially the silent monklike figures who often passed quietly by his bed.

In support of this model, one study (Worchel & Teddlie, 1976) found that crowding could be reduced if people were distracted from paying attention to others in their environment. Subjects in a densely populated room reported less crowding if there were attention-grabbing pictures on the walls than if there were no pictures. Along similar lines, investigators (Webb, Worchel, Reichers, & Wayne, 1986) found that crowding could be reduced if people in the environment were categorized in groups rather than identified as individuals. Categorization reduced the attention given to individuals in the environment.

Demonstrating the importance of the attribution process, subjects in one study (Worchel & Brown, 1984) were seated either very close together or at comfortable distances. The subjects watched a movie that was either arousing and attention gathering (fight film, sexually arousing film, or humorous film) or was not arousing and not as likely to capture their attention (documentary). Two results from this study are of special interest. First, subjects who watched the films under close spatial conditions reported being more crowded when they watched the documentary as opposed to the arousing films (see Table 12–3). Second, subjects enjoyed the arousing films more when they watched them under close spatial

Table 12–3
Mean ratings of crowding

Interpersonal distance	Televised program			
	Humorous	Sexual	Violent	Nonarousing
Close	6.34*	7.17	6.80	5.43
	(12)†	(10)	(9)	(8)
Far	7.31*	8.16	7.89	8.39
	(8)	(8)	(9)	(10)

*Subjects asked to rate, "How crowded did you feel during the experiment? (1 = very crowded, 10 = not crowded).
†Number of groups in parentheses.
Source: Worchel and Brown (1984). Copyright 1984 by the American Psychological Association. Reprinted by permission of the author.

People may not feel crowded while watching an exciting movie because they attribute their arousal as being caused by the movie rather than the other people around them. *(© MCMLXXXV Peter Menzel)*

conditions than under comfortable conditions; the close spatial conditions actually enhanced their enjoyment of the films. The investigators argued that subjects watching the arousing films attributed their arousal to the films; this attribution reduced crowding and thus enhanced their enjoyment of the films. While the arousing films were the salient features in these subjects' environments, the documentary was not salient. Therefore, people watching the documentary attributed their arousal to spatial restrictions present in the room; as a result, they felt crowded.

This study not only showed the importance of attribution and stimulus salience, but it also demonstrated that high density can actually have positive effects. A similar process may explain why fans enjoy athletic events so much when they are seated in a packed stadium. In this case, the contest on the field is the salient event in their environment, and consequently, they may view their arousal as resulting from this action.

Summing It Up   Taken as a whole, the research and theories suggest that high density, by itself, is not always unhealthy or even unpleasant. However, when high density is associated with such factors as overstimulation, loss of personal control, and violations of personal space, the experience of crowding is likely to result. Crowding is an uncomfortable state; task performance, interpersonal relationships, and possibly health are negatively affected by it.

If we are interested in improving the quality of human life, this focus on crowding rather than density offers some room for optimism. The world's population is growing rapidly, but the amount of space available is fixed. Hence, density will necessarily increase. However, the experience of crowding does not necessarily have to grow at the same rate. If we can structure the environment so that individuals have havens of privacy or feel control over their daily lives, we can reduce crowding and the negative effects associated with it.

NONSPATIAL ENVIRONMENTAL VARIABLES

Noise   In addition to complaining about the lack of space in the Uncle Sam, Jones was also uncomfortable with the noise. People's talking, snoring, and moaning kept him from sleeping at night. The noise inside the hotel, along with the constant rumble of traffic and blaring horns outside, distracted Jones so that he had difficulty writing. In desperation, he set up a small closet in which to do his writing. Jones was constantly aware of the changing sounds in New York. One event particularly demonstrated his awareness. "The first fall of snow in New York is pure magic. I went to bed wrung out after another twelve-hour stint of writing. Next morning I was awakened by silence. It was as if the world slept. . . . But the city government seemed to be affronted by this cold charity that like a quiet forgiveness, hid its sins. Soon its henchmen in incredibly rowdy, fume-spouting snow-plough-rigged garbage trucks had restored 'normality' " (p. 230). As Jones was well aware, in addition to becoming more crowded, our world is becoming more noisy.

Is this dangerous? Are we being unwittingly affected by the sounds we have created in our environment? In answering this question, environmental psychologists begin by making a distinction between sound and noise. *Sound* includes changes in air pressure that are detected by the ear. It is measured in decibels (dB) with 0 dB being the weakest sound that can be heard by people with good ears. *Noise*, on the other hand, is sound that is unwanted by the listener because it is unpleasant and bothersome.

As a general rule, three qualities determine when sound will be perceived as noise: volume, predictability, and controllability. The most bothersome sounds are those that are loud, unpredictable, and uncontrollable (Fisher, Bell, & Baum, 1984).

Noise has a wide variety of effects on us. At the most basic level, loud noise can damage hearing. As a startling example, it has been found that seventy year old Sudanese tribesmen who live in a quiet area have the

We are often unaware of the noise of the city until an event such as a snowstorm causes a drastic reduction of that noise. (© *MCMLXXXV Peter Menzel*)

Figure 12–5
Systolic and diastolic blood pressure as a function of school noise level and duration of exposure for cross-sectional third grade replication study

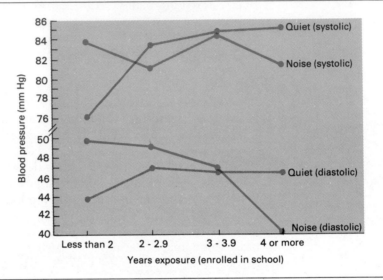

Note: Each period on the years exposure coordinate represents one quarter of the sample.

hearing ability of a twenty year old in America (Rosen et al, 1972). We have all probably complained that noise gives us a headache, but recent research suggests that we better not take an aspirin to alleviate that headache if we are staying in a noisy environment. This research (Raloff, 1982; Miller, 1982) suggests that certain drugs such as antibiotics and aspirin might interact with noise to increase the damage caused by that noise. Finally, a study in Los Angeles found that students who attended schools in the noisy flight corridor of the airport had higher blood pressure than students in quiet schools; as can be seen in Figure 12–5, these effects were most likely in students who had attended the schools for a relatively short time (Cohen, Krantz, Evans, & Stokols, 1982).

Noise can also affect our performance; it was not only Jones's imagination that he could not concentrate on his work in the noisy hotel. Turning back to the studies of the children in Los Angeles, the investigators found that children in noisy schools made more errors on a puzzle task and were more likely to give up on the task than children in quiet schools (Cohen, Evans, Krantz, & Stokols, 1980). Further, the effects of noise were found even after steps were taken to reduce the noise in the classrooms (Cohen et al., 1981). Even over the short term, noise can produce negative aftereffects on performance. In a series of studies, Glass and Singer (1972) found that subjects who had been exposed to uncontrollable and unpredictable noise for period of less than an hour, performed less well on tasks in a quiet room than subjects who had never been exposed to the noise.

Noise can also have negative effects on our social interactions. This has been shown in a number of behaviors. For example, we are less attracted to others in a noisy environment. Mathews, Cannon, and Alexander (1974) found that subjects chose greater interpersonal distances when a background noise was played into the experimental room. We are also less likely to help someone when a loud noise is present (Mathews & Cannon, 1975). As can be seen from Figure 12–6, this effect is strongest when the victim of an accident has a high need for help.

Figure 12–6
Percentages of subjects offering help as a function of noise level and need of victim

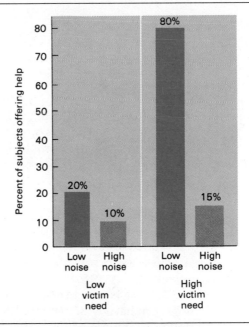

Source: Adapted from Mathews and Canon (1975). Copyright 1975 by the American Psychological Association. Reprinted by permission of the publisher.

Figure 12-7

Mean intensity of shock delivered by subjects as a function of noise condition and anger arousal

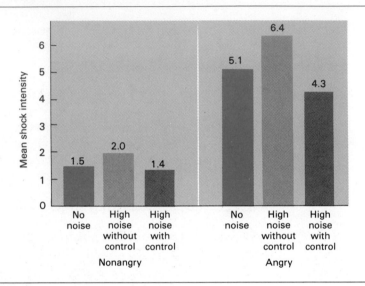

Source: Adapted from Donnerstein and Wilson (1976).

Finally, a number of studies have found that noise can increase human aggression. In one of the more complex studies on this topic (Donnerstein & Wilson, 1976), subjects worked on a task in the presence of either no noise, loud noise they could control, or loud noise over which they had no control. The noise was then terminated and subjects were given the opportunity to shock another person under the guise of a learning experience. Some of the subjects were angered during this task while others were not. As can be seen from Figure 12-7, having experienced high noise that was uncontrollable resulted in higher aggression than either no noise or controllable noise. It was also found that these differences were strongest for angry subjects.

All noise is not created equal. The studies presented above show that noise can have wide-ranging effects on human behavior. Two additional findings from the research stand out as interesting and important. First, not all noise has the same effects. Noise that is composed of conversation seems to have the most negative effects on performance (Olszewski, Rotton, & Soler, 1976) and is reported to be the most disturbing (Topf,

Research has shown that children who attend schools in the flight path of airports have higher blood pressure and perform less well on some tasks than children in quiet schools. (*Courtesy U.S. Environmental Protection Agency*)

1985). Second, not all people are affected by the same noise. In studies of hospital patients, Topf (1983, 1985) found that patients who scored high on a scale of social desirability were less bothered by routine hospital noise than people who scored low on this scale. Further, the research showed that some people were generally more sensitive to noise than others, and people who reported this general sensitivity were indeed particularly disturbed by the noises in the hospital. Hence, there are individual differences in sensitivity and reactions to noise.

Why does noise affect us? The general picture that emerges from the research on noise is that it can have negative effects, especially when we are working on complex tasks or must use environmental cues such as a victim's need to determine our responses. How do we explain these curious sets of circumstances that influence the effect of noise? Broadbent (1978) argued that the exposure to noise causes people to become aroused. This heightened arousal, in turn, causes them to narrow their attention; they focus on important environmental stimuli and neglect ones that they consider unimportant. As a result of this narrowing of attention, performance on some tasks (simple problems or ones requiring visual performance) may actually improve because the individual pays close attention to the task. However, performance becomes impaired on more complex tasks requiring coordination or reasoning. Social interactions may also suffer because people pay less attention to each other and do not discriminate others' needs and desires.

Weather: Focus on Heat   One of our favorite topics of conversation when we meet a stranger seems to be the weather. When we don't know where to begin a conversation, we can safely talk about the weather. On his flight from England to the United States, Jones found himself in the awkward situation of wanting to talk with a stewardess, but not knowing what to say. Their conversation settled on the weather and sailing.

The stewardess asked Jones whether he preferred to sail alone or with a companion. Jones responded, "If the weather is rough then I'm thankful I have no one else to worry about but myself." The stewardess then questioned, "But when it is fine weather and the sun is shining on the sea?" Jones responded with a smile, "Ah, then . . . then I want to *share*" (p. 42).

This conversation shows that the weather is more than something to talk about; it can well influence our moods and social interactions. Investigators have studied almost every aspect of weather including wind, sunlight, heat, cold, barometric pressure, and moon phases. Because of limited space, let us examine only one component of climate: heat.

In 1969, the United States Riot Commission stated that a large proportion of civil riots have occurred during the hot summer months. This

There is evidence that heat may be related to violent acts and aggressive crimes. *(Michele Bogre/Sygma)*

Figure 12–8

Aggressive crime ratio as a function of maximum ambient temperatures

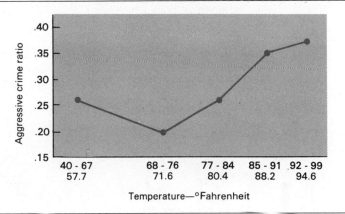

Note: The aggressive crime ratio is the number of murders and rapes divided by the number of robberies and arsons. (Note that along the abscissa points are plotted at the category-weighted average temperature, as indicated by the small-sized digits. The larger digits indicate the range of temperatures included in each category. The categories were constructed to represent approximately equal numbers of days.) Source: From "Ambient Temperature and Violent Crime" by C. A. Anderson and D. C. Anderson, 1984, *Journal of Personality and Social Psychology, 46,* p. 96. Copyright 1984 by the American Psychological Association. Reprinted by permission of the author.

announcement gave rise to a flurry of studies attempting to relate temperature to aggression. The studies have taken two forms: archival research and laboratory experimentation. The archival research involved choosing a time period, charting temperature and violent acts, and examining how these two measures related. Although there has been some disagreement as to the exact relationship, the majority of the findings suggest that violence increases as temperature increases. For example, Anderson and Anderson (1984) found that aggressive crimes (murder and rape) in Houston, Texas, tended to increase as the temperature increased (see Figure 12–8).

The relationship between heat and aggression becomes a bit more murky when we examine laboratory studies. In a number of studies in which temperature was manipulated, Baron and his colleagues (Baron & Bell, 1976; Bell & Baron, 1977) found that angry subjects aggressed less in very hot rooms (92° to 95°F) than in rooms with more comfortable temperature. On the other hand, nonangry subjects were more aggressive in hot than in comfortable rooms. One explanation for these results is that heat, like other environmental variables, acts as a stressor that arouses

Figure 12-9
Theoretical relationship between negative affect and aggression (up to a point, uncomfortable conditions facilitate aggression; past that point, more severe conditions decrease aggression)

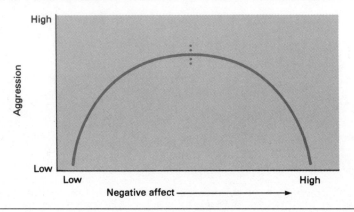

Source: From Baron, R. A., & Bell, P. A., 1976, "Aggression and heat: The influence of ambient temperature, negative affect, and a cooling drink on physical aggression." *Journal of Personality and Social Psychology, 33*, 245–255. Copyright 1976 by the American Psychological Association. Reprinted by permission of the author.

people. At moderate levels of arousal, the heat leads to anger and aggression. However, at excessively high levels of arousal, people seek to withdraw from social interaction, and aggression is reduced. This high level of arousal is reached when people are angered in a very hot room. This reasoning would lead us to expect a curvilinear relationship between heat and aggression (see Figure 12–9).

How do we reconcile the differences in the results of the laboratory and field research? In attempting to develop an explanation for this discrepancy, we can demonstrate the application of social psychological theory. One possibility is simply that the enclosed laboratory rooms were hotter and more uncomfortable than conditions found in the outside world. In other words, the curvilinear relationship is correct, but the field studies have not examined the very hot end of the scale. However, anyone who has spent time in Houston in August will argue that only the baker's oven can exceed the heat found there! Another explanation draws on attribution and social cognition theories (see Chapter Two). It is possible that the excessive heat is the salient feature in the laboratory; it is certainly unusual to be in a room with ninety-five degree temperatures. However, the heat is only one of the outstanding features on a sunny day in Houston; there is the traffic, the actions of many other people, and the performance of the Houston Astros. Hence, in the laboratory, arousal will be attributed to the salient feature of heat and will not be interpreted as anger. However, in the field setting, arousal is less likely to be attributed to the heat and more likely to be interpreted as anger (Anderson & Anderson, 1984). There is not as yet a clear resolution of the issue, but we can conclude that with the possible exception of very high temperatures, there is a relationship between heat and aggression.

The research on heat and performance also presents conflicting results. On July 16, 1979, the Emergency Building Temperature Restriction Plan was put into effect in the United States. The plan required public buildings not to be heated above 65°F in the winter and not to be cooled below 78°F in the summer. A number of reports indicated that the summer temperature restriction caused decreases in performance. For example, a company in Norfolk, Virginia, reported a drop of 15 percent to 20 percent in clerical work output (King, 1980). A number of more carefully controlled studies (Mackworth, 1961; Link & Pepler, 1970) also found that performance decreased with high temperatures. However, other studies (Provins & Bell, 1970) found that heat led to short-term improvements in performance that often dissipated over time.

Clearly, more research is needed to understand the effects of heat on human behavior. The research on heat is complicated by the fact that many variables influence human comfort level. Rohles (1981) listed seven variables: (1) air temperature, (2) relative humidity, (3) radiant temperature (temperature from surfaces such as windows), (4) air velocity, (5) clothing, (6) physical activity, and (7) length of exposure. For example, Table 12–4 on page 688 shows how humidity affects people's experiences with temperature.

ARCHITECTURE AND DESIGN

In the previous sections, we have seen that we cannot make a blanket statement that a certain environmental condition is always bad or always good; much depends on the purpose to which that environment will be put. For example, we saw that crowding can have negative effects in some cases, but positive effects in other cases. An important feature in determining the person-environment fit is the activity that will take place in the environment (Darley & Gilbert, 1985). Nowhere will this principle become more clear than in our discussion of architecture and design.

To begin, we can consider Tristan Jones's reactions when he first saw the *Star Rider*. The forty-four footer was a Nova Scotia-built wooden vessel

Table 12–4
Effective temperature (°F) at 0 percent humidity as a function of actual temperature and humidity

Relative humidity (percent)	Thermometer reading (°F)					
	41°	50°	59°	68°	77°	86°
			Effective temperature			
0	41	50	59	68	77	86
20	41	50	60	70	81	91
40	40	51	61	72	83	96
60	40	51	62	73	86	102
80	39	52	63	75	90	111
100	39	52	64	79	96	120

Source: From *Environmental Psychology*, 2nd ed., by Jeffrey D. Fisher, Paul A. Bell and Andrew Baum. Copyright © 1984 by CBS College Publishing. Copyright © 1978 by W. B. Saunders Company. Reprinted by permission of Holt, Rinehart & Winston, Inc.

fitted with the best sailing gear for a boat her size. But Jones (1980) was not delighted. "I can see she's a fine sea boat, but for charter in the West Indies? Forget it. Look, Tom [her owner], her ventilation hatches are tiny—she's built for the cold North Atlantic—there'll never be any air down here [the berths], and in the island heat . . . she's not built for finicky charterers; they'll mutiny!" (p. 113). As if this were not enough, Jones delivered the final blow when he proclaimed, "The only people who will be happy chartering this vessel are coal miners or circus acrobats. She was built for eight-foot giants and four-foot dwarfs" (p. 113).

With this in mind, let us consider the research on our built environment.

Rooms   Investigators found that variables such as color, the number of windows and doors, and the arrangement of furniture dramatically affect the behaviors of the people who use a room. For example, people associate moods with certain colors (Hesselgren, 1975; Wexner, 1954). In the Wexner study, the subjects were asked to ascribe moods to various colors. With a high degree of agreement the following match was reported:

Blue: secure, comfortable, tender, soothing, calm, serene.
Red: exciting, protective, defending, defiant.
Orange: distressed, upset.
Black: despondent, powerful.
Purple: dignified.
Yellow: cheerful.

Further, Wilson (1966) found that subjects were more physiologically aroused (as measured by GSR) when viewing red slides as opposed to green slides. The research suggests that if subdued activities such as reading, sleeping, and studying are to take place in a room, less arousing colors such as blue and green should used.

The arrangement of furniture is another important design feature that should be taken into account when planning a room. The layout of a room regulates communication and also communicates the purpose of the environment. Osmond (1957) conducted an intensive study of a newly completed geriatric ward. He noted that the design of the environment had marked effects on the patients' behavior. He classified design arrangements into two types. *Sociopetal spaces* involve arrangements that "encourage, foster, and even enforce the development of stable interpersonal relationships." *Sociofugal spaces,* on the other hand, are arrangements that tend to separate people and reduce social interaction. The arrangement of furniture in a room can create either a sociopetal or sociofugal atmosphere.

A study by Sommer and Ross (1958) in a newly remodeled geriatric ward in a Canadian hospital clearly demonstrates the effects of furniture arrangement. The designers of the ward carpeted and painted a dayroom and installed new furniture. They hoped that these improvements would foster social interaction among the women patients and increase their involvement in the hospital routine. However, the patients continued to exhibit apathetic behavior and social interaction was minimal. Sommer observed that the patients were "like strangers in a train station waiting for a train that never came." Sommer and Ross noted that the new furniture had been lined up in long straight rows so that the patients sat shoulder to shoulder and back to back. This arrangement was clearly sociofugal, as it did not foster social interaction. The investigators rearranged the furniture so that four chairs were grouped around small square tables. At first, the patients and the staff grumbled about this arrangement; it was unfamiliar to the patients, and it was harder for the staff to keep the room clean. After a few weeks, however, interactions among the patients had nearly doubled. Thus, the organization of the furniture in a room can have important effects on the behaviors of the individuals who use the room. The arrangement of room furniture should fit the room's use. Sociopetal arrangements should be used in rooms where interaction will take place (living rooms, dayrooms, dormitory lounges), and sociofugal arrangements should be used in low-interaction rooms (bus stations, airports, libraries).

Offices   Recently, social scientists have looked at the designs of offices. Wells (1972) studied an insurance company in Manchester, England, that

Many waiting rooms are designed to reduce social interaction. The arrangement of furniture can have a important influence on social interactions. (© *Gabor Demien/Stock, Boston*)

had two types of office arrangements: small offices and large open office space. He found that people in the small offices tended to form small but cohesive groups whereas those working in the open offices interacted with a larger number of people but did not form close relationships. There have been several studies (McCarrey, Peterson, Edwards, & von Kuniz, 1974; Howard, 1972) of "open-office" design, which separates workers by the use of low, movable partitions, furniture, or plants, thereby eliminating ceiling-to-floor separating walls. The results from these studies have been rather mixed. Although workers report that the open office fosters interpersonal contact, they also feel that it offers less privacy and is noisier than the room-type office design.

Once again, we are reminded of our person-environment fit relationship. Certain jobs will be facilitated by the open-office design while others will be hindered by it (Sundstrom, Town, Brown, Forman, & McGee, 1982). Hence, the office must be designed with the job in mind.

BUILDINGS AND INSTITUTIONS

When we walk into a large building such as a bank, department store, or hospital, we often marvel at its imposing exterior design and fancy interior. In our awe, however, we may forget that its design and layout play a major role in determining our behavior while in that building. A review of the research on hospital design (Reizenstein, 1982) produced a rather impressive list of the behaviors influenced by the hospital design (Table 12–5). In addition to this list, other investigators have found that design can influence social conflict and friendship patterns.

One of the best examples of the pervasive influence of building design on human behavior is the Pruitt-Igoe complex in St. Louis. In 1954, forty-three eleven-story high-rise apartment buildings were erected on a fifty-seven-acre tract in St. Louis. Nearly twelve thousand people were relocated in these apartments, and the project was hailed as a great advance in low-income housing. Each apartment had all the most modern facilities, and each family was assured ample living space. Very soon, however, bragging about the Pruitt-Igoe project stopped. Windows were smashed; the elevators became repositories for human waste; gangs roamed the project; and rape and robbery were commonplace. By the early 1970s only sixteen of the forty-three buildings were occupied, and in April 1972 demolition of the entire project began.

Why was the project such a failure? Could anything be done in the future to ensure against such failures? Several studies indicated that

---

Table 12–5
Factors affected by hospital design

Confidentiality
Control over social interaction
Cross-infection
Disclosure
Image
Organizational climate
Perception
Post-operative delirium
Post-operative medication
Travel time

Source: Baum and Singer (1982).

Looks are not everything. Despite winning architectural awards for design, the Pruitt-Igoe complex did not fit the needs of the residents. The residents moved out of the complex and it was eventually demolished. The story of the project stands as a testimony to the importance of person-environment fit. *(UPI/Bettmann Newsphotos)*

the housing complex, though architecturally well designed, did not fit the needs of the tenants. Yancey (1971) interviewed numerous residents and found that, although they were satisfied with the space and the facilities of the apartments, they were upset because the building design did not foster interactions among neighbors and because they could not supervise their children once the children were out of the apartment. Further, Newman (1972) points out that there was too much indefensible territory in the project. According to Newman, when there is no clear way to mark ownership or to patrol territory, vandalism is likely to occur. The stairwells, elevators, and alleyways were indefensible space in the Pruitt-Igoe complex. They could not be adequately patrolled, and they were not open to visual inspection. It was impossible to see who lurked in the stairwells or elevators, and as a result the residents were afraid to use these necessary areas. The sheer size of the complex was also a problem. Individuals feel insignificant in the presence of such large structures and feel little control over their environment.

Newman (1973, 1975) put his views on defensible space to use in renovating two public townhouse developments in New York City. Among other things, he added fences to create individual front yards and private areas and provided more attractive lighting. These changes were directed at giving people more control over their areas. These changes did increase residents' use of outside areas and made them feel safer. But these changes did not reduce vandalism in the developments (Kohn, Frank & Fox, 1975).

Designing Space for the Mentally Retarded   One of the most ambitious studies on the effects of design took place at the Belchertown State School of the mentally retarded in Western Massachusetts (Zimring, Weitzer, & Knight, 1982). As a result of a court settlement, $2.6 million was designated for renovation of the old institution. The residents had previously lived in large open-ward rooms where fifteen to twenty residents slept in one room.

In the renovation, three different designs were used. The *module design* retained the ward quality but drew on the open-office plan. Beds were set up in the ward with low (four and one-half foot) privacy partitions; twelve residents were assigned to a ward that had a small lounge. The *suite design* followed that of many apartments; partitions divided the wards into three separate bedrooms and a bathroom with a lounge area serving this area. The bedrooms housed two to four residents and privacy could be obtained by closing the bedroom door. The third *corridor design* followed that used in many college dormitories. Small one- or two-person bedrooms lined long corridors; each corridor had a common bathroom and lounge area.

Interviews and careful observations of resident and staff behavior were performed over a thirty-month period. A wide range of behaviors was examined. A summary of the results is presented in Figure 12–10. As can be seen, the module design had little effect on the behavior of the residents or the staff. On the other hand, the greatest improvement in adjustment and resident interactions was found in the corridor design. Residents became more verbal and alert and interactions between the residents increased dramatically. There were fewer undesired intrusions by staff into the residents' private space and residents made more use of their bedroom areas.

The investigators explained the effects by focusing on personal control. They argued that the corridor design gave individuals the greatest control over their space. For example, each person or pair had access to the light switch and could close the door. People could obtain privacy by going into their room and closing the door. This is especially important for mentally retarded individuals who do not have the verbal or social skills to request privacy in other ways. The renovation also gave the staff private areas where they could work and get their needed "time out."

Figure 12–10
Overview of major quantitative results from the institutional design study

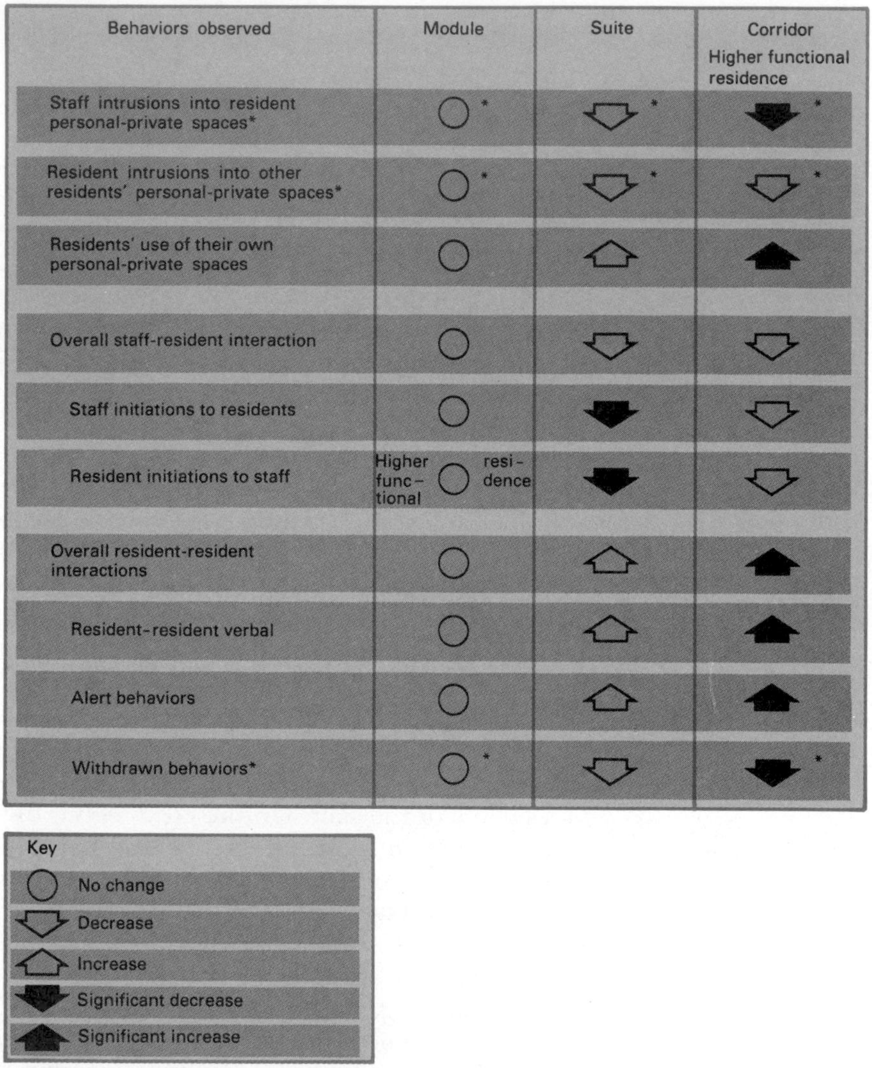

Behaviors observed	Module	Suite	Corridor Higher functional residence
Staff intrusions into resident personal-private spaces*	◯ *	⬇ *	⬇ *
Resident intrusions into other residents' personal-private spaces*	◯ *	⬇ *	⬇ *
Residents' use of their own personal-private spaces	◯	⬆	⬆
Overall staff-resident interaction	◯	⬇	⬇
Staff initiations to residents	◯	⬇	⬇
Resident initiations to staff	Higher func-tional ◯ resi-dence	⬇	⬇
Overall resident-resident interactions	◯	⬆	⬆
Resident-resident verbal	◯	⬆	⬆
Alert behaviors	◯	⬆	⬆
Withdrawn behaviors*	◯ *	⬇	⬇ *

Key	
◯	No change
⬇	Decrease
⬆	Increase
⬇	Significant decrease
⬆	Significant increase

Source: Zimring et al., 1982. Published with permission of L. Erlbaum, Publisher.

Designing the Dormitory   We might be tempted to conclude from the Zimring et al. study that all institutions should be based on the corridor model. In doing so, however, we would not be paying attention to our cautions about person-environment fit; we must design buildings to fit the needs of the people who will use them. Jones's experience with the *Star Rider* made this point very clearly. This position can also be seen in research on college dormitories that also compared the effect of the corridor design and suite design.

In a series of studies, Baum and Valins (1977) examined the behavior of students living in two-person rooms in a corridor-style dormitory with those of students living in suite-type dormitories (see Figure 12–11). The density (space per person) was roughly the same in the two types of dormitories. Baum and Valins, however, predicted that the design would have a marked effect on students' behaviors. Unlike the mentally retarded residents in the Belchertown State School, college students are generally skilled in social interaction, very mobile, and have need for space to study and carry on a wide variety of social interaction. With these features in mind, Baum and Valins argued that residents in the corridor dormitories have less meaningful control over their environment than do residents in the suite dorms. The former group is often faced with unpredictable and unwanted social interaction in the long corridors, bathrooms, and lounges that are shared by many residents. This lack of control should lead the corridor residents to feel more crowded and less comfortable with social interaction than the suite residents.

These predictions were indeed supported. First, questioning the residents indicated that corridor residents did feel more crowded than suite residents. The effects of dormitory-type social interaction were revealed in a more subtle way. Residents in the two types of dormitories were invited to participate in a laboratory experiment. When each resident arrived at the experiment, he or she was asked to wait with a confederate before the experiment began. Corridor residents tried to withdraw from social contact with the confederate by sitting further away, maintaining less eye contact, and carrying on less conversation than suite residents. Apparently, the tendency for corridor residents to withdraw from social interactions generalized beyond their dormitory into other settings. Further, corridor residents attempted to exert less control in the experimental setting than did suite residents.

When we compare the Zimring et al. research on the school for mentally retarded and the Baum and Valins studies on the dormitory, we can see why we cannot conclude that one type of building design is always better than another. The design that best fits the needs of one group did

Figure 12–11
Floor plan of (*a*) a corridor-style dormitory and (*b*) a suite-style dormitory

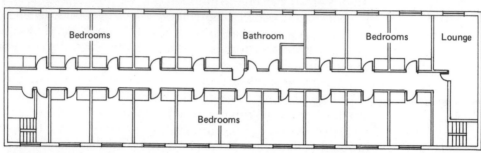

(a) Floor design of corridor dormitory

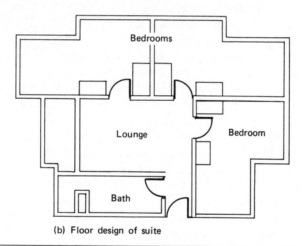

(b) Floor design of suite

Source: Baum and Valins (1977). Published with permission of L. Erlbaum, Publisher.

not work best for the other group. On the other hand, the underlying principle of control over the environment was important for both groups.

THE CITY

Tristan Jones had a love-hate relationship with large cities. He was consistently attracted to cities such as New York, London, and Buenos Aires to make professional contacts, work, and enjoy the cultural activities. On the other hand, he found himself easily disoriented in cities and felt that they were an affront to natural beauty. Despite Jones's feelings, cities seem to be attracting and holding an increasing number of the world's population.

In 1850, only 2 percent of the world's population lived in cities. Today about 25 percent of the people live in cities and, by the year 2000, 40 percent of the people will live in urban areas (Fischer, 1976). This fact makes it important to learn how the cities we have built affect our lives. Large cities present the individual with an enormously complex environment. There is huge variety in the types of housing, the types of buildings, the types of people, and the types of noise. In addition, large cities have more of these variables—more buildings, more people, and more noise—

The city environment presents people with an incredible array of stimuli. People must develop ways to process these stimuli in order to avoid cognitive overload. (© *Joel Gordon* *1980*)

than suburbs or rural areas. For example, Milgram (1970) reports that, whereas an individual working in a New York suburb might meet 11,000 people within a ten-minute radius of his or her office, an individual working in midtown Manhattan might meet 220,000 people within the same radius of the office.

What are the effects of such an intense and compact environment? On the one hand, people report that the city environment offers fascinating and exciting opportunities. The city offers a wide variety of cultural opportunities, more restaurants than one could try in a lifetime, and almost unlimited shopping possibilities. The city itself presents a unique cinema in which one can simply spend time looking at the varied actions of its very large cast of people.

Although the city has numerous advantages over the less populated rural or suburban areas, the price that its inhabitants pay for these advantages is high. Physical disease is higher in the inner city than in any other area. McHarg (1969) mapped the incidence of eight diseases (heart disease, tuberculosis, diabetes, syphilis, cirrhosis of the liver, salmonellosis, and two types of dysentery) in the Philadelphia area. The highest incidence of all these diseases occurred in the inner city, with a reduction in incidence toward the suburbs. In addition, many people view the city as a hostile unfriendly environment. In the city, people push and shove and fail to observe the usual social courtesies; they are abrupt and cold; no one seems willing to offer help to persons in need.

There are a number of possible causes for the higher disease and crime rates of cities. Living conditions in the inner city are often woefully inadequate. Harris and Lindsay (1972) surveyed urban welfare families in the United States and found that 24 percent had no hot and cold running water, that 22.4 percent had no private use of a bathroom with a shower, and that 30.1 percent did not have enough space for each member of the family. Also, the inner city is often populated with individuals from widely different cultural backgrounds, who tend to be poorly educated and of low socioeconomic status.

Although such conditions may explain the higher urban disease and crime rates, they do not adequately explain why the psychology of the city is often characterized as cold and unfriendly. Milgram (1970) suggested that the seeming aloofness and unfriendliness of the city dweller may be a defensive response to a highly overloaded environment. The city is characterized by hustle and bustle — people constantly moving into and out of view. There are bright lights, something to see in every store window, and different types of vehicles passing by. Since individuals can only comprehend and respond to a limited number of events, they have difficulty in accommodating to such an overloaded environment.

Milgram hypothesized that individuals give less time to each event or input as the total number of events increases. They either do not respond to or they disregard unimportant events, and they attempt to devise formal channels through which their interaction with others takes place. Above all, Milgram suggests that individuals depersonalize or deindividuate the other people in the environment. Because of the complexity and the huge number of social interactions that take place in the city, it is impossible to respond to each person on an individual basis. Thus, in order to reduce the incoming stimuli to manageable amounts, individuals remove the uniqueness from events and people and respond to them only as classes. They also pay less attention to other people.

This depersonalization results in the "unfriendliness" that the newcomer often perceives in the city. This depersonalization is often blamed for the lack of altruism that is reported in the city. In Chapter Eight, we discussed the case in which onlookers failed to respond in the Kitty Genovese incident. The depersonalization of other people eliminates empathy, and empathizing with persons in distress is one of the motivating forces behind helping behavior.

This description paints a rather dismal picture of the city dweller. It must be pointed out, however, that no one could function in this overloaded complex environment unless it were possible to organize the incoming stimuli. The depersonalization of other people and the screening out of less important inputs are simply means of coping with such an environment.

PERCEIVING OUR ENVIRONMENT

One point that should stand out from much of our discussion of social psychology is that we do not necessarily respond to events or people as they are; rather, we respond as we see or interpret them. The same is true of the environment: our reactions are dictated by our perception of the environment. And our perceptions of the environment are often selective. For example, one study (Rowles, 1984) found that the elderly make clear distinctions in their perceptions of their environment; they see their environment as a set of zones encircling their home (Figure 12–12).

In examining how we perceive our environment, much attention has been focused on *cognitive maps.* These maps are the mental images that we hold of our environments (Holahan, 1982). For example, we tend to use five features in developing cognitive maps of the cities in which we live (Lynch, 1960).

Figure 12–12
A hierarchy of environmental spaces

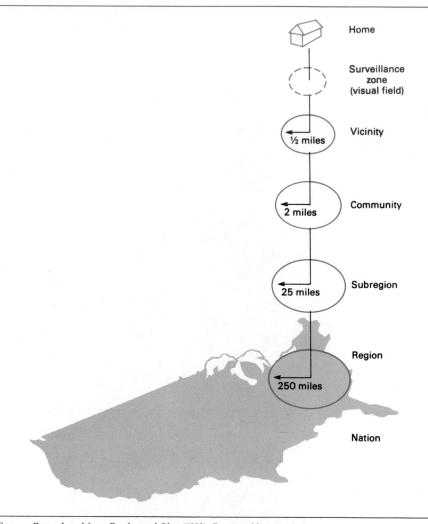

Source: Reproduced from Rowles and Ohta (1983). Reprinted by permission.

1. Paths: streets, sidewalks, railroads, and other movement channels.
2. Edges: rivers or barriers, such as walls.
3. Nodes: intersections or junctions of paths where activity often occurs.

4. Districts: regions that are characterized by some common element, such as Chinatown in San Francisco.
5. Landmarks: reference points that "stand out" in the environment, such as the Empire State Building in New York City and the Washington Monument in Washington, D.C.

According to Lynch, some environments are more *legible* than others; the more legible the environment, the easier it is to form a cognitive map of the area. However, regardless of how legible an area is, our cognitive maps are often inaccurate representations of the environment. Three types of errors are most often found in our maps (Fisher et al., 1984). First, the maps are generally *incomplete*; details are left out. Second, we *often add features* to our maps that are not present in the environment; we may include a house in a lot that is actually vacant, or a sidewalk where none exists. Finally, our map is often distorted; we place objects closer together or farther apart than they actually are. As might be expected, maps of familiar areas tend to be more accurate than maps of unfamiliar areas.

Cognitive maps play a number of important roles in our lives. First, we use these maps to navigate through our environment; the more accurate

The increasing complexity of our environments makes it more important that we develop clear cognitive maps to help us become oriented and move from place to place. *(Ellis Herwig/The Picture Cube)*

our map, the easier it is for us to deal with our environment. We all have experienced the stress and feelings of helplessness of being lost in a strange area or being unable to find our automobile in a crowded parking lot. Zimring cited a newspaper story about a college professor who started "gibbering mathematical equations and tearing off his clothes" when he became lost in the huge Dallas-Fort Worth Airport. Cognitive maps are also used when we communicate about our environment. When Jones wrote about New York, he did not present a road map for his readers to follow; rather, he gave descriptions of certain buildings, major roads, neighborhoods, and waterways. Finally, our maps are used to present our self-identity; they describe our memories, fantasies, beliefs, and feelings about our surroundings.

Because cognitive maps play such a central role in our lives, it is important that planners develop legible environments. This is important for everyone, but it is especially important for people such as the elderly who may become disoriented in unfamiliar surroundings. Having clear cognitive maps is also becoming increasingly important as we travel at greater speeds through our environment; most of us have experienced the sense of panic when approaching a complicated highway interchange while driving at a fast speed in our automobile. Environments that are clear, relatively simple, and have prominent features help us to gain a sense of control and facilitate our adjustment to new surroundings (Lynch, 1960).

SUMMARY

Environmental psychology is the scientific study of the relationship between people and their environment. The way in which people view the environment has changed throughout history. The earliest view was that the environment was the master; during the Industrial Revolution, people felt that *they* could be the masters. Today, the prevailing attitude is that people are partners with the environment. In examining environmental effects, the concept of *person-environmental fit* guides the research and theory. The effects of the environment on people are best understood by examining attributions, feelings of control, cognitive overload, and arousal.

Personal space is the "private space" that surrounds an individual. Personal space is often conceptualized as a series of concentric circles—although this picture may be misleading. The size of personal space is affected by numerous variables such as sex, culture, age, and the nature of the given interaction, as well as contextual variables such as room size and shape. Invasions of personal space may lead to people's arousal and subsequent attempts to restore appropriate spacing. Depending on how they interpret the invasion, people may enjoy and reciprocate the invasions. Interpersonal distance determines the channels of communication that can be used during an interaction; it can also be used to regulate intimacy. One of the major messages that people communicate through their spatial behavior is attraction. Equilibrium theory deals with the relationship between spatial communication and other nonverbal modes of communication. Territoriality involves the exclusive use of a fixed area by an individual or a group; both humans and animals exhibit territoriality. The three types of human territory are primary, secondary, and public. Territory serves many functions—including defining social organization, regulating privacy, and defining personal identity. People establish territory by using personal markers to demonstrate their control.

Density is a spatial measure of the number of square feet per person in a situation. Although demographic and animal research has suggested that high density has negative consequences, laboratory research has failed to confirm this hypothesis.

Crowding is a psychological state rather than a simple spatial measure. Although crowding is related to density, it is a distinct concept. The major theories of crowding hypothesize that lack of privacy, loss of control, and attribution affect people's experience of feeling crowded. In general, research has shown that crowding often leads to impaired task performance, discomfort, and stress. The theories in this area imply that the crowding experience can be lessened without necessarily increasing the amount of space.

Noise is sound that is unwanted by the listener because it is unpleasant or bothersome. Loud noises can damage hearing. The most bothersome types of noise are loud, unpredictable, and uncontrollable; research suggests that background conversation is one of the more disruptive types of noise. Noise has both immediate and aftereffects on performance and social interactions. One reason for these effects is that noise increases arousal and thus makes people focus their attention on a few stimuli.

Research on *heat* suggests that within commonly experienced temperature ranges, increasing heat is associated with increasing aggression. There is some disagreement between field and laboratory studies about the effect of heat on aggression in very hot temperatures.

Recent studies have found that rooms may be designed to either facilitate (sociopetal space) or inhibit (sociofugal space) social interaction. Other room variables, such as the presence of windows and doors, not only affect people's perceptions of a room, but also influence behavior inside the room. Buildings that are not designed to "fit" human behavioral needs may be either misused or not used at all. No single design will be best in all cases; rather, designs must take into account the people who will use the area and the types of activities that will take place. This effect was clearly evident in studies on institutions for the mentally retarded and college dormitories.

Complex urban environments often lead to cognitive overload. As a result, individuals may depersonalize the environment and exercise selectivity over the stimuli to which they pay attention. Because of the complexity of the urban environment, individuals form *cognitive maps* that aid them in locomoting through that environment. Variables such as paths, edges, nodes, districts, and landmarks are the principal features of these cognitive maps.

KEY WORDS

arousal	personal distance
cognitive maps	personal space
cognitive overload	primary territory
crowding	privacy
density	proxemics
environmental psychology	public distance
heat	public territory
intimate distance	secondary territory
learned helplessness	social distance
legibility of an environment	sound
noise	territoriality
person-environment fit	

SUGGESTED READINGS

Altman, I. (1975). *The environment and social behavior.* Monterey, CA: Brooks/Cole Publishing.

Altman, I., & Chemers, M. (1980). *Culture and environmental.* Monterey, CA: Brooks/Cole.

Baum, A., & Epstein, Y. M. (1978). *Human response to crowding.* Hillsdale, NJ: Lawrence Erlbaum.

Baum, A. & Singer, J. E. (1982). *Advances in environmental psychology.* Vol. 4. Hillsdale, NJ: Erlbaum.

Fisher, C. S. (1984). *The urban experience* (2nd ed.). New York: Harcourt Brace Jovanovich.

Fisher, J., Bell, P., & Baum, A. (1984). *Environmental psychology* (2nd ed.). New York: Holt, Rinehart and Winston.

Geller, E., Winett, R., & Everett, P. (1982). *Preserving the environment: New strategies for behavior changes.* New York: Pergamon Press.

Glass, D. C., & Singer, J. E. (1972). *Urban stress.* New York: Academic Press.

Sundstrom, E. & Sundstrom, M. G. (1983). *Work places: Psychology of the physical environment in offices and factories.* Monterey, CA: Brooks/Cole.

Zube, E. (1980). *Environmental evolution: Perception and public policy.* Monterey, CA: Brooks/Cole.

GLOSSARY

A–B–X model A system that involves the relationship of two persons and an attitude object. The model holds that the relationship between the persons and the attitude object will strain to become symmetrical.

Additive task Task where final group product is the sum of members' performances.

Aggression Behavior aimed at injuring a specific target.

Aggression cue Stimuli associated with the source of frustration and with aggressive behavior, in general. When paired with frustration, aggression cues may elicit aggression.

Altruistic behavior An act that renders help to another person.

Anticonformity Behaving opposite to what the individual observes being done or said by others.

Arbitrary frustration Thwarting that is viewed as unreasonable or unwarranted.

Attitude-discrepant behavior Actions that are contrary to a person's private attitude.

Attraction A positive attitude held by one person toward another.

Audience pleasing Self-presentational behavior designed to make an audience happy.

Authoritarian personality A set of attitudes and personality characteristics first studied by Adorno et al. following World War II. Authoritarian personalities are characterized by a high degree of prejudice and ethnocentrism. Development of the authoritarian personality is characterized by severe discipline and deference to authority.

Autistic conspiracy Tendency for ingratiator and target person to pretend or believe that ingratiation is not occurring, because neither one wants to acknowledge it.

Autistic hostility The tendency of people in conflict to withdraw and avoid interaction.

Autocratic style of leadership Directive leadership style emphasizing the completion of tasks with little concern for other people's feelings.

Availability bias The increased likelihood that a stimulus will be seen as the cause of an event, as a function of the ease with which that stimulus can be brought to awareness.

Aversive consequences In the research on cognitive dissonance, aversive consequences are events resulting from a behavior that an individual would rather not have occur.

Balance theory The notion that people prefer orderly, consistent, and harmonious relationships among their cognitions.

Baserate information Data or information about the frequency of specific events or behaviors in particular groups.

Beneffectance The tendency to see oneself as responsible for good, rather than bad, outcomes. Also known as the self-serving bias.

Boomerang effect Attitude change in a direction opposite to that professed in a communication.

Case history method Method of inquiry that examines the responses of a few individuals and analyzes their reactions in depth.

Category-based expectancy An expectancy about a person based on knowledge of the categories or groups the person belongs to.

Catharsis The reduction in the instigation to aggress following some instances of aggression.

Charisma Personal attribute possessed by certain leaders that tends to "draw" others' support and admiration.

Circumplex Leary's classification scheme for interpersonal behavior which arrays behaviors in a circle created by crossing dominant-submissive dimension and friendly-hostile dimension.

Coalition A coalition occurs when two or more parties cooperate and combine their resources to beat an opponent.

Coercive power Capacity to deliver threats and punishments to force compliance from another individual.

Cognition An element of knowledge. Any thought that an individual has about him- or herself or the environment.

Cognitive conservatism The resistance to change of self-conceptions.

Cognitive dissonance A relationship among cognitions such that one cognition follows from the opposite of another. Also, a theory proposed by Leon Festinger that unpleasant psychological tension arises when an individual possesses cognitions that are dissonant.

Cognitive irrelevance A relationship among cognitions such that one cognition has no psychological implication for the other cognitions.

Cognitive map Individual's mental image of a particular area of space.

Cognitive overload Overload results when the individual is confronted with more stimuli than he or she can process.

Cohesiveness The result of all forces that impel individuals to remain in or leave a group. Often measured by how attractive individuals find their group.

Collectives Gatherings of persons who do not have a face-to-face interaction but are engaged in a common activity.

Commitment The degree to which a behavior or decision cannot be undone, rescinded, or taken back.

Communication network Group situation where communication can only flow through prescribed channels.

Competition Interpersonal conflict involving an incompatibility of goals.

Compliance Overt behavioral conformity while maintaining one's own attitude.

Conflict spiral Situation where individuals in a conflict invoke threats thereby increasing the degree of conflict.

Conformity A change in behavior or belief toward a group as a result of real or imagined group pressure.

Conjunctive task Task where all group members perform essentially the same subtask, and the overall performance is dependent on the combination of these subtasks.

Consonance A relationship among cognitions such that each fits with or psychologically follows from the others.

Coordination loss Reduced group productivity due to the group's inability to combine and use the individual members' contributions.

Correlation Statistical measure of an association or relationship between two variables.

Correspondence bias (also known as **fundamental attribution error**) Tendency of perceivers to infer that behavior reflects internal dispositions and to ignore external factors tha might explain it.

Correspondent inference An inference that a behavior was caused by and corresponds to a personal disposition in the actor.

Cost model of helping A model of altruistic behavior that considers the observer's cost of helping and the cost to the victim of not helping.

Crowding Motivational state aroused through the interaction of spatial, social and personal factors.

Deception (in an experiment) Deception is used to keep the subject from knowing the purpose of the manipulations. It involves the experimenter giving subjects false information about the reasons for the study or the manipulations.

Decision tree A model of intervening in emergencies that considers decisions about noticing, interpreting, assessing responsibility; knowing an appropriate form of assistance and implementing the decision.

Defensive attribution An attribution of causality that is made to reduce the perceiver's anxiety.

Deindividuation A condition whereby the individual becomes "submerged into the group" and feels relatively anonymous.

Demand characteristics Cues in the experimental setting that communicate what behavior is expected of subjects.

Democratic style of leadership Egalitarian style of leadership emphasizing broad participation and concern with other people's ideas and feelings.

Density Simple physical measure of the amount of space available for each individual in a defined area.

Dependent variable Represents subject's response in the study.

Diffusion of responsibility The sharing of responsibility among several individuals. The concept is used to explain why bystanders may not intervene in emergencies.

Dilution effect The weakening of an inference about a person due to the presence of other irrelevant information about the person.

Disconfirmed expectancies A paradigm of research relevant to cognitive dissonance theory in which inconsistency is created by the occurrence of an event that is at variance with an expected event.

Discounting principle In Kelley's attribution theory the tendency to attribute a behavior to a given cause less when there are other plausible explanations for the behavior.

Discretionary task Task that requires group members to agree on a decision.

Discrimination Negative, often aggressive, behaviors aimed at the target of prejudice.

Disjunctive task Problem requiring an "either-or" decision.

Displaced aggression Aggression that varies either in type or target from that most preferred by the attacker.

Display rules Norms about the emotions that are appropriate to display in particular situations.

Distributive justice View of justice and fairness that focuses on people's satisfaction with the resources they receive from social relationships.

Effort justification A paradigm of research relevant to cognitive dissonance theory in which inconsistency is created by inducing a person to expend a large amount of effort in order to achieve a specific goal state.

Egocentricity   Bias toward perceiving oneself as the central actor and causal agent in events.

Emblems   Gestures used in particular cultures to express certain ideas or feelings.

Empathy   The ability to share in another's emotions or feelings. In helping behavior, empathy leads to actions that are directed solely at alleviating the distress of another person.

Environmental psychology   Study of relationship between the environment and behavior.

Equal status contact   Means for reducing intergroup hostility in which members of groups in conflict have equal status or power when they interact.

Equity theory   Theory stating that individuals compare their inputs and outcomes with those of the other party to determine the fairness of a relationship.

Ethnocentrism   The tendency to reject those who are culturally dissimilar while accepting without question those who are culturally alike. Ethnocentrism is characteristic of the *authoritarian personality*.

Ethologist   Scientist who studies animal behavior in natural settings. The ethologist often attempts to draw comparisons between animal behavior and human behavior.

Excitation transfer   The transfer of arousal produced by one source to the energization of an unrelated response.

Excitation-transfer theory   A theory, usually applied to aggression, that holds that arousal from one source can be misperceived and therefore transferred to another source.

Exemplification   Behavior designed to get others to believe that one is moral and self-sacrificing.

Experiment   Method of study aimed at determining the cause-and-effect relationship between events. Experimenter exercises control over independent variable.

Experimental realism   Degree to which experimental manipulations have impact and are involving to subjects.

Experimenter bias   Influence on subjects' behavior as a function of the investigators' expectations.

Expert power   Power an individual derives by being seen as possessing special insight or knowledge about a particular area.

External locus of control   Perception that one's outcomes are due to factors outside of one's control, such as luck, chance, or fate.

External validity   Describes the degree to which research findings may be generalized to situations outside the laboratory.

Face   The positive social value we claim for ourselves in social interaction.

Face-saving   Behaviors designed to create a positive public image.

Facework   In Goffman's theory of self-presentation, behavior designed to maintain other people's faces.

False consensus effect   Tendency to believe that other people think and act like you do more than they actually do or more than others believe it.

False uniqueness effect   Tendency to believe that others behave like you do less than they actually do.

Field experiment   Experiment that is run in a natural setting, and subjects often do not know they are in an experiment. The added realism should allow greater opportunity for generalization and more mundane realism.

Flight distance Distance one animal will let another approach before it retreats.

Foreseeability In the research on cognitive dissonance, it is knowledge of the consequences that will accrue to a decision before the decision is made.

Free-choice paradigm A strategy for research in cognitive dissonance in which an individual is asked to choose a gift from among two or more consumer items. Dissonance is said to be aroused by the choice, due to rejection of desirable aspects in the rejected item and acceptance of undesirable aspects in the chosen alternative.

Free rider Explanation for social loafing that suggests that people may reduce their effort when they observe that their contributions to the group are dispensable and the group will succeed without them.

Frustration Interference or thwarting of an ongoing behavior.

Fundamental attribution error *see* **Correspondence bias**.

Gain-loss effect The finding that people are most attracted to those who initially dislike them but eventually like them and are least attracted to those who initially like them but eventually dislike them.

Gender schema General knowledge and expectations about the behavior of males or females.

GRIT Graduated reciprocation in tension reduction. Policy developed by Osgood to reduce international tension through the unilateral reduction of threat capability.

Group Two or more persons who are interacting with one another in such a manner that each person influences and is influenced by each other person.

Group polarization Process where group discussion causes an individual to make a more extreme decision than he or she would make alone.

Groupthink Decision-making situation where group suspends objectivity and careful analysis in an effort to preserve group cohesiveness.

Hypothesis Statement that expresses the nature of the relationship between events. Expresses *what* (not *why*) relationship exists between the events.

Idealized performance Behavior suggesting we live up to ideal standards of social behavior more than in fact we do.

Illusory correlation The erroneous perception of a correlation between two characteristics based on specific instances when the two characteristics do occur together.

Imitative learning Learning that occurs through the observation of models. This is one of the major ways in which people learn aggressive behavior.

Immediacy The degree of directness and intensity of interaction between two persons or entities. It is measured behaviorally by the direction of the head, arm position, the lean of the torso, shoulder orientation, physical proximity, and eye contact.

Immediacy behaviors Nonverbal behaviors regulating intimacy.

Impression management Behavior designed to control what others think, especially so as to maintain power in relation to them.

Independence Self-determination about how to act or believe rather than simply responding to group pressure.

Independent variable Variable manipulated by the experimenter. Experiment designed to study the effect of the independent variable on the dependent variable.

Induced compliance A paradigm of research in cognitive dissonance theory in which individuals are persuaded to behave in ways that are discrepant from their private attitudes.

Informational power Power derived by the possession of a specific piece of information.

Informational pressure Power the group has over the individual because of its possession of information.

Informed consent An attempt to safeguard subjects by giving them a choice of participating or not participating in an experiment after they have been told of the procedures that will be used.

Ingratiation A term that describes a variety of strategies whereby a person acts in ways that illicitly enhance his or her image in the eyes of others.

Ingratiator's dilemma Problem posed by the fact that low power position makes a person want to ingratiate but alerts target person to possibility of ingratiation and thus makes it more difficult. Also, problem posed by person wanting to ingratiate but not wanting to see himself as ingratiating.

Instincts Innate and unlearned behavior tendencies common to all members of a species.

Insufficient deterrence A paradigm for research in cognitive dissonance theory in which an individual is induced to refrain from an activity for a minimally effective reason.

Integrative problem solving Attempt to solve conflict by identifying common goals rather than focusing on means.

Internal locus of control Perception that one's outcomes are due to one's own efforts and actions.

Internal validity Describes experimental design free from contamination by extraneous variable. Allows investigator to state that manipulations of the independent variable are responsible for changes in dependent variable.

Internalization Process of opinion change where one genuinely accepts and internalizes an opinion as a result of its good fit with one's other values and opinions.

Interpersonal style Person's characteristic style of behaving in a group categorized by degree of dominance, positivity, and task-orientation.

Intimate distance The distance people use for intimate activities such as making love, protection, comfort, or whispering.

Intimidation Behavior designed to get others to believe that one is dangerous.

Jig-saw method Technique for reducing intergroup conflict that has been used with school children in the classroom. It involves giving a racially mixed group of students a problem to solve such that each member holds a part of the solution. In order for the group to succeed, each member must master his or her part.

Leader Individual who influences the activities of a group.

Learned helplessness State resulting when the individual perceives no control over his or her environment.

Legitimate power Power an individual derives from occupying a particular role or position.

Love In the research on attraction, love has been identified as including the notions of caring, attachment, and intimacy.

Matching effect The notion that in heterosexual situations people prefer partners who are about equally attractive to themselves.

Matching to standards Attempts to meet ideal standards of behavior in a situation; caused or increased by self-awareness.

Mediator Neutral third party whose task is to help bargainers achieve a fair solution.

Minimal intergroup situation Research showing that in-group bias results from the simple assignment of individuals to groups. This bias occurs even when the assignment is made on a random basis.

Misattribution The incorrect attribution of causality, generally attributing internal arousal to incorrect internal or external causes.

Mixed-motive conflict Conflict where both parties may gain by responding in a cooperative manner.

Motivation loss Loss of group productivity that occurs when members do not put their maximum effort into the task.

Mundane realism Degree to which the experimental setting approximates "real-life" settings.

Noise Sound that is unwanted by the listener because it is unpleasant and bothersome.

Nominal group A number of persons working independently on a problem.

Norm Rule that governs a specific behavior and applies to everyone in the group.

Norm of equality Norm that attempts to resolve conflict by dividing resources equally between the parties.

Norm of reciprocity The generally shared expectation that we should treat others as they treat us.

Normative social pressure Group's power to influence based on individual's fear of being rejected by the group.

Norms of distribution Norms for resolving conflict that determine how resources should be divided.

Obedience Conforming to direct orders from a high-status individual.

Outcome In social exchange theory, the outcome of a relationship is equal to rewards – costs.

Overjustification effect The tendency not to like activities for which too much reward is given, thereby overjustifying engaging in the activity.

Overt bargaining Situation where parties have divergent interests, some form of communication, and can make provisional offers and concessions.

Pay-off matrix Schematic used to illustrate behavioral alternatives available to individuals in a relationship and the outcome of each alternative.

Person-environment fit This concept concerns the relationship between people and their environment and indicates that this relationship is a dynamic one.

Personal distance Space kept between organisms when interacting with member of the same species.

Personal responsibility The concept that the cause of individual behavior is internal. In the research on cognitive dissonance, personal responsibility is the blending of choice and foreseeability.

Personal space That area around an individual which he or she feels ownership and control of.

Prejudice Unjustified negative attitude toward an individual based solely on that individual's membership in a group.

Primacy effects Impressions that are based on the first information a perceiver has about an actor rather than later information.

Primary territory Area or object that is exclusively owned or controlled on a permanent basis by an individual or group and is viewed as a central part of the individual's life.

Prisoner's dilemma A mixed-motive conflict where the best individual choice leads to the worst joint pay-off. Paradigm used to study trust.

Privacy An individual's freedom to choose what he or she will communicate about self and to whom the information will be communicated. Privacy may be viewed as chosen isolation.

Private acceptance Changing both attitudes and behavior to be more congruent with group norms.

Private self-consciousness Awareness of one's own feelings and internal states.

Procedural justice Study of justice and fairness that focuses on the procedure by which resources are allocated.

Process loss The difference between a group's potential and its actual productivity.

Prototypes The organization of impressions around various central tendencies.

Proxemics The study of interpersonal space.

Psychological reactance A state of arousal generated by blocking or the threat of blocking a person's free behaviors.

Public distance The distance used in formal interactions and that placed around public figures.

Public self-consciousness Awareness of how others react to or evaluate oneself.

Public territory Area or object that is temporarily controlled by an individual but over which no feeling of ownership exists.

Random assignment In a study situation, assigning conditions to subjects so that each subject has an equal opportunity to be in each experimental condition.

Recency effects Impressions that are based on the last or most recent information perceiver has about an actor rather than early information.

Reciprocity Norm specifying that people should reciprocate another's degree of self-disclosure and altruism.

Reference group A group toward which one orients oneself. It forms the basis of comparison for attitudes, values, and behaviors.

Referent power Power an individual derives from being admired and liked.

Reflected appraisal A view of self based on other people's appraisal of oneself.

Reinforcement effect In attitude change research, the greater the incentive for stating a position on an attitude issue, the most positive the private belief toward that issue becomes.

Related attributes hypothesis In social comparison theory the hypothesis that we evaluate our opinions or abilities by comparing with people who should have similar opinions or performance levels based on their standing on characteristics related to the opinion or performance level.

Representativeness heuristic Judging whether a person belongs to a specific group on the basis of how similar he or she is to typical members of the group.

Reward power Capacity to give positive reinforcements to achieve compliance from another person.

Role Set of norms that defines how a particular person in a given position must act.

Role conflict Situation that results either when the various requirements of a role demand incompatible behaviors, or when the different roles occupied by a single person demand incompatible behaviors.

Schema General knowledge and expectations about a person, group, or event.

Science Set of rules guiding the inquiry and study of events.

Script Knowledge about the sequence of events that usually takes place in a situation.

Secondary territory Area or object that is temporarily controlled by an individual or group.

Self-awareness (also called **self-focused attention**) State of paying attention to and being aware of oneself.

Self-construction Self-presentational behavior designed to confirm a desired view of self.

Self-disclosure The act of revealing personal information to others.

Self-handicapping Putting obstacles in the way of one's own attempts to perform successfully. Done in order to provide an excuse for poor performances.

Self-monitoring Modifying one's behavior to meet the expectations of others.

Self-perception theory Theory arguing that people make inferences about their attitudes and feelings based on their behaviors and the situations in which they were performed.

Self-promotion Behavior designed to get others to believe that one is competent and talented.

Self-schemata General knowledge about oneself and the traits one possesses.

Similarity-complementarity The degree to which a person is like or unlike a target person.

Similarity hypothesis In social comparison theory the hypothesis that we evaluate ourselves by comparing our opinions or abilities to those of other people who are similar.

Situated identity Conception one has of oneself in a specific situation.

Social cognition An approach to understanding social behavior as a function of the way in which information is processed, organized, and retrieved.

Social comparison process The process whereby individuals reduce the uncertainty about their opinions, abilities, and emotions by observing the opinions, etc., of similar others.

Social distance The distance used for personal business and at social gatherings.

Social-exchange theory Theory that views human interaction as a cost-reward transaction.

Social facilitation Condition where presence of audience or co-actors improves the quality of an individual's performance.

Social influence The exercise of power by a person or group to change the opinions or behavior of others.

Social inhibition Situation where presence of audience or co-actors hinders individual's performance.

Social isolation Removing the individual from all social contact.

Social-learning theory Hypothesis that individuals learn behavior through imitating others and receiving rewards.

Social loafing Occurs when individuals work less hard in a group setting than alone. The effect may be due to the lack of individual identifiability or reduced feelings of personal responsibility.

Social psychology Discipline that employs scientific methods to understand and explain how the thought, feeling, and behavior of individuals is influenced by the actual, imagined, or implied presence of others.

Social trap Conflict that exists when behaviors bring short-term pleasures but have negative long-term effects. This conflict also involves choosing between one's self-interest and that of the group.

Sociofugal space Arrangements that tend to separate people and reduce social interaction.

Sociopetal space Arrangements that foster and encourage social interaction.

Sound Changes in air pressure that are detected by the ear.

Stages of a relationship The notion that relationships go through a series of orderly stages as they progress toward intimacy.

Statistically significant In psychology, a finding is taken as reliable (statistically significant), if a statistical test indicates that the event could have occurred by chance less than 5 times out of 100 ($p < .05$).

Stereotype A set of beliefs about the characteristics of people in a group that is generalized to nearly all group members.

Sucker effect Explanation for social loafing that argues that people will reduce their efforts if they think other group members are not putting in maximum effort.

Superordinate goal Goal that is attractive to members of two groups but cannot be achieved without cooperation between the two groups.

Supplication Behavior designed to make others feel sorry for you and want to help.

Survey method Involves asking questions of a large sample of subjects.

Symmetrical relationships In the perception of individuals, a set of relationships that are harmonious and consistent.

Target-based expectancy An expectancy about a person based on knowledge of the person's other characteristics or behavior.

Territoriality Involves the mutually exclusive use of areas and objects by individuals or groups.

Theory A systematic statement of relationships that seek to explain *why* two or more events are related.

Tit-for-tat response A response to conflict where an opponent's cooperative actions receive a cooperative response and his or her competitive responses beget competitive reactions.

Totalitarian ego The biased organization of information about the self that functions to preserve a favorable self-impression.

Trucking game Experimental paradigm developed by Deutsch and Krauss. Involves two players attempting to move trucks toward opposite destinations. Cooperation is required for both players to receive positive pay-offs.

Trust Defined by Pruitt as a general expectancy that another individual will respond in a helpful rather than a harmful manner.

Two-factor theory of emotions Schachter's theory that emotional experience is based on the combination of physiological arousal and cognitive labeling or interpretation of the causes of arousal.

Visual dominance behavior Staring or other assertive, dominating nonverbal behavior.

Zero-sum conflict Pure competition conflict where one party's gain is the other party's loss.

REFERENCES

Abelson, R. P. (1981). The psychological status of the script concept. *American Psychologist, 36,* 715–729.

Abelson, R. P. (1982). Three modes of attitude behavior consistency. In M. P. Zanna, E. T. Higgins, & C. P. Herman, (Eds.), *Consistency in social behavior: The Ontario symposium* (Vol. 2). Hillsdale, NJ: Erlbaum.

Abelson, R., & Levi, A. (1985). Decision making and decision theory. In G. Lindsey & E. Aronson (Eds.), *The handbook of social psychology (3rd ed.).* New York: Random House.

Abramson, L. Y., Seligman, M. E. P., & Teasdale, J. D. (1978). Learned helplessness in humans: Critique and reformulation. *Journal of Abnormal Psychology, 87,* 49–74.

Adair, J. G., & Epstein, J. S. (1968). Verbal cues in the mediation of experimenter bias. *Psychological Reports, 22,* 1045–1053.

Adams, G. R., & Huston, T. L. (1975). Social perception of middle-aged persons varying in physical attractiveness. *Developmental Psychology, 11,* 657–658.

Adams, J. S. (1963). Toward an understanding of inequity. *Journal of Abnormal and Social Psychology, 67,* 422–436.

Adams, J. S. (1965). Inequity in social exchange. In L. Berkowitz (Ed.), *Advances in experimental social psychology* (Vol. 2). New York: Academic Press.

Adorno, T. W., Frenkel-Brunswick, E., Levinson, D. J., & Sanford, R. N. (1950). *The authoritarian personality.* New York: Harper.

Aiello, J. R., & Aiello, T. (1974). The development of personal space: Proxemic behavior of children 6 through 16. *Human Ecology, 2(3),* 177–189.

Ainsworth, M. (1979). Infant-mother attachment. *American Psychologist, 34,* 932–937.

Ajzen, I. (1982). On behaving in accordance with one's attitudes. In M. P. Zanna, E. T. Higgins, & C. P. Herman (Eds.), *Consistency in social behavior: The Ontario symposium* (Vol. 2). Hillsdale, NJ: Erlbaum.

Ajzen, I., & Fishbein, M. (1980). *Understanding attitudes and predicting social behavior.* Englewood Cliffs, NJ: Prentice Hall.

Alexander, C. N., Jr., & Rudd, J. (1981). Situated identities and response variables. In J. T. Tedeschi (Ed.), *Impression management theory and social psychological research.* New York: Academic Press.

Allen, H. (1970). Lost in the subway. In B. Latané & J. M. Darley (Eds.), *The unresponsive bystander: Why doesn't he help?* (Pp. 21–24). Englewood Cliffs, NJ: Prentice-Hall.

Allen, V. L. (1965). Situational factors in conformity. In L. Berkowitz (Ed.), *Advances in experimental social psychology* (Vol. 2). New York: Academic Press.

Allen, V. L., & Wilder, D. A. (1980). Impact of group concensus and social support on stimulus meaning: Mediation of conformity by cognitive restructuring. *Journal of Personality and Social Psychology, 39,* 1116–1125.

Allington, R. (1980). Teacher interruption behaviors during primary grade oral reading. *Journal of Educational Psychology, 72,* 371–377.

Allison, S. T., & Messick, D. M. (1983). Effects of experience on performance in replenishable resource trap. *Journal of Personality and Social Psychology, 49,* 943–948.

Allport, F. H. (1924). *Social psychology.* Cambridge, MA: Riverside Press.

Allport, G. W. (1954). *The nature of prejudice.* Reading, MA: Addison-Wesley.

Allport, G. W. (1985). The historical background of social psychology. In G. Lindzey & E. Aronson (Eds.), *Handbook of social psychology* (3rd ed., Vol. 1, pp. 1–46). New York: Random House.

Altman, I. (1974). The communication of interpersonal attitudes: An ecological approach. In T. L. Huston (Ed.), *Foundations of interpersonal attraction.* New York: Academic Press.

Altman, I. (1975). *The environment and social behavior.* Copyright © 1975 by Wadsworth Publishing, Inc. Reprinted by permission of the publisher, Brooks/Cole Publishing Company, Monterey, California 93940.

Altman, I., & Chemers, M. (1980). *Culture and environment.* Belmont, CA: Wadsworth.

Altman, I., Lawton, M. P., & Wohlwill, J. (1984). *Elderly people and the environment.* New York: Plenum Press.

Altman, I., & Vinsel, A. M. (1977). Personal space: An analysis of E. T. Hall's proxemics framework. In I. Altman & J. F. Wohlwill (Eds.), *Human behavior and environment: Advances in theory and research* (Vol. 1). New York: Plenum Press.

Amir, Y. (1969). Contact hypothesis in ethnic relations. *Psychological Bulletin, 71,* 319–341.

Anderson, C., & Anderson, D. (1984). Ambient temperature and violent crime: Tests of the linear and curvilinear hypotheses. *Journal of Personality and Social Psychology, 46,* 91–97.

Anderson, D., & Rosenthal, R. (1968). Some effects of interpersonal expectancy on institutionalized retarded children. *Proceedings of the 76th annual convention of the American Psychological Association,* 49–480.

Anderson, J. R. (1982). *The architecture of cognition.* Cambridge, MA: Harvard University Press.

Anderson, N. H. (1965). Averaging versus adding as a stimulus-combination rule in impression formation. *Journal of Experimental Psychology, 70,* 394–400.

Anderson, N. H. (1968). Likeableness ratings of 555 personality trait words. *Journal of Personality and Social Psychology, 9,* 272–279.

Anderson, N. H., & Hubert, S. (1963). Effects of concomitant recall on order effects of personality impression formation. *Journal of Verbal Learning and Verbal Behavior, 2,* 379–391.

Anderson, N. H., & Jacobson, A. (1965). Effect of stimulus inconsistency and discounting instructions in personality impression formation. *Journal of Personality and Social Psychology, 2,* 531-539.

Andreoli, V., & Worchel, S. (1978). Effects of media, communication, and message position on attitude change. *Public Opinion Quarterly, 42,* 59–70.

Apfelbaum, E. (1974). On conflicts and bargaining. In L. Berkowitz (Ed.), *Advances in experimental social psychology* (Vol. 7). New York: Academic Press.

Apfelbaum, E. (1979). Relations of domination and movements for liberation: An analysis of power between groups. In W. G. Austin & S. Worchel (Eds.), *The social psychology of intergroup relations.* Monterey, CA: Brooks/Cole.

Archer, D., & Akert, R. M. (1977). Words and everything else: Verbal and nonverbal cues to social interpretation. *Journal of Personality and Social Psychology, 35,* 443–449.

Archer, R. L. (1980). Self-disclosure. In D. M. Wegner & R. R. Vallacher (Eds.), *The self in social psychology.* New York: Oxford University Press.

Archer, R. L., & Burleson, J. A. (1980). The effect of timing of self-disclosure on attraction and reciprocity. *Journal of Personality and Social Psychology, 38,* 120–130.

Archer, R. L., Diaz-Loving, R., Gollwitzer, P. M., Davis, M. H., & Fonshee, H. C. (1981). The role of dispositional empathy and social evaluation in the empathic mediation of helping. *Journal of Personality and Social Psychology, 40,* 786–796.

Argyle, M., & Dean, J. (1965). Eye-contact, distance and affiliation. *Sociometry, 18,* 289–304.

Aries, D. (1976). Interaction patterns and themes of male, female and mixed groups. *Small Group Behavior, 7,* 7–18.

Arkin, R. M. (1980). Self-presentation. In D. M. Wegner & R. R. Vallacher (Eds.), *The self in social psychology.* New York: Oxford University Press.

Arkkelin, D., Oakley, T., & Mynatt, C. (1979). Effects of controllable versus uncontrollable factors on responsibility attributions: A single subject approach. *Journal of Personality and Social Psychology, 37,* 110–115.

Arms, R. L., Russell, G. W., & Sandilands, M. L. (1979). Effects on the hostility of spectators of viewing aggressive sports. *Social Psychology Quarterly, 42,* 275–279.

Aronson, E. (1969a). Some antecedents of interpersonal attraction. In W. J. Arnold & D. Levine (Eds.), *Nebraska symposium on motivation* (Vol. 17). Lincoln: University of Nebraska Press.

Aronson, E. (1969b). The theory of cognitive dissonance: A current perspective. In L. Berkowitz (Ed.), *Advances in experimental social psychology* (Vol. 4). New York: Academic Press.

Aronson, E., Brewer, M., & Carlsmith, J. M. (1985). Experimentation in social psychology. In G. Lindzey & E. Aronson (Eds.), *Handbook of social psychology* (3rd ed., Vol. 1, pp. 1–46). New York: Random House.

Aronson, E., Bridgeman, L., & Geffner, R. (1978). The effects of cooperative classroom structure on student behavior and attitudes. In D. Bar-Tal & L. Saxe (Eds.), *Social psychology of education.* New York: Halsted Press.

Aronson, E., & Linder, D. E. (1965). Gain and loss of esteem as determinants of interpersonal attractiveness. *Journal of Experimental Social Psychology, 1,* 156–171. © 1965 by the American Psychological Association. Adapted by permission of the authors.

Aronson, E. & Mills, J. (1959). The effect of severity of initiation on liking for a group. *Journal of Abnormal and Social Psychology, 59,* 177–181. © 1959 by the American Psychological Association. Adapted by permission of the authors.

Aronson, E., Stephan, C., Sikes, J., Blancy, N., & Snapp, M. (1978).

The jigsaw classroom. Beverly Hills, CA: Sage Publications.

Aronson, E., Turner, J., & Carlsmith, J. M. (1963). Communicator credibility and communicator discrepancy as determinants of opinion change. *Journal of Abnormal and Social Psychology, 67,* 31–36. © 1963 by the American Psychological Association. Adapted by permission of the authors.

Aronson, E., Willerman, B., & Floyd, J. (1966). The effect of a pratfall on increasing interpersonal attractiveness. *Psychonomic Science, 4,* 227–228. © 1966 by the American Psychological Association. Adapted by permission of the authors.

Aronson, E., & Worchel, P. (1966). Similarity versus liking as determinants of interpersonal attractiveness. *Psychonomic Science, 5,* 157–158.

Asch, S. (1946). Forming impressions on personality. *Journal of Abnormal and Social Psychology, 41,* 258–290.

Asch, S. (1951). Effects of group pressure upon the modification and distortion of judgment. In H. Guetzkow (Ed.), *Groups, leadership and men.* Pittsburgh: Carnegie Press.

Asch, S. (1952). *Social psychology.* New York: Prentice-Hall, 1952. Material reprinted by permission of Prentice-Hall, Inc., Englewood Cliffs, New Jersey.

Asch, S. (1956). Studies of independence and conformity: I. A minority of one against a unanimous majority. *Psychological Monographs, 70*(9).

Ashmore, R., Ramchandra, V., & Jones, R. (1971, April). *Censorship as an attitude change induction.* Paper presented at Eastern Psychological Association Convention, New York.

Auden, W. H. (1965). Postscript, "Pro-

logue: The birth of architecture." *About the house.* New York: Random House.

Austin, W. G. (1986). Justice in intergroup conflict. In Worchel, S. & Austin, W. G. (Eds.), *The psychology of intergroup relations* (pp. 153–176). Chicago: Nelson-Hall.

Austin, W. G., & Hatfield, E. (1980). Equity theory, power, and social justice. In G. M. Kula (Ed.), *Justice and social interaction.* Bern, Switzerland: Hans Huber.

Austin, W. G., & Walster, E. (1974). Participants' reactions to "equity with the world." *Journal of Experimental Social Psychology, 10,* 528–548.

Ayllon, T., & Azrin, N. (1968). *The token economy: A motivational system for therapy and rehabilitation.* New York: Appleton-Century-Crofts.

Back, K. W. (1951). Influence through social communication. *Journal of Abnormal and Social Psychology, 46,* 9–23.

Backman, C. W. (1981). Attraction in interpersonal relationships. In M. Rosenberg & R. Turner (Eds.), *Social psychology: Sociological perspectives.* New York: Basic Books.

Backman, C. W., & Secord, P. F. (1959). The effect of perceived liking on interpersonal attraction. *Human Relations, 12,* 379–384.

Bales, R. F. (1958). Task roles and social roles in problem-solving groups. In E. E. Maccoby, T. M. Newcomb, & E. L. Hartly (Eds.), *Readings in social psychology* (3rd ed.). New York: Holt, Rinehart & Winston.

Bales, R. F. (1970). *Personality and interpersonal behavior.* New York: Holt, Rinehart & Winston.

Bales, R. F., & Slater, P. (1955). Role differentiation in small decision-making groups. In T. Parsons & R. F. Bales (Eds.), *Family, socializa-*

tion and interaction processes. Glencoe, IL: Free Press.

Bandura, A. (1973). *Aggression: A social learning analysis.* New York: Holt, Rinehart & Winston.

Bandura, A., Ross, D., & Ross, S. A. (1961). Transmission of aggression through imitation of aggressive models. *Journal of Abnormal and Social Psychology, 63,* 575–582.

Bandura, A., Ross, D., & Ross, S. A. (1963a). Imitation of film-mediated aggressive models. *Journal of Abnormal and Social Psychology, 66,* 3–11.

Bandura, A., Ross, D., & Ross, S. A. (1963b). A comparative test of the status envy, social power and secondary reinforcement theories of identificatory learning. *Journal of Abnormal and Social Psychology, 66,* 527–534.

Bandura, A., & Walters, R. H. (1963). *Social learning and personality development.* New York: Holt, Rinehart & Winston.

Barnlund, D. C. (1962). Consistency of emergent leadership in groups with changing tasks and members. *Speech Monographs, 29,* 45–52.

Baron, R. A. (1974). The aggression-inhibiting influence of heightened sexual arousal. *Journal of Personality and Social Psychology, 30,* 318–322.

Baron, R. A. (1979). Heightened sexual arousal and physical aggression: An extension to females. *Journal of Research in Personality, 13,* 91–102.

Baron, R. A., & Bell, P. A. (1973). Effects of heightened sexual arousal on physical aggression. *Proceedings of the 81st Annual Convention of the American Psychological Association, 8,* 171–172.

Baron, R. A., & Bell, P. A. (1976). Physical distance and helping: Some unexpected benefits of "crowding in" on others. *Journal of Applied Social Psychology, 6,* 95–104.

Baron, R. A., & Eggleston, R. J. (1972). Performance on the "aggression machine:" Motivation to help or harm? *Psychonomic Science, 26,* 321–322.

Baron, R. A., & Rodin, J. (1978). Perceived control and crowding stress. *Advances in Environmental Psychology, 1.*

Bar-Tal, D., & Geva, N. (1986). A cognitive basis of international conflict. In Worchel, S., & Austin, W. G. (Eds.), *The psychology of intergroup relations.* Chicago: Nelson-Hall.

Bass, B. M. (1949). An analysis of the leaderless group discussion. *Journal of Applied Psychology, 33,* 527–533.

Batson, C. D., Cochran, P. J., Biederman, M. F., Blosser, J. L., Ryan, M. J., & Vogt, B. (1978). Failure to help when in a hurry. Callousness or conflict? *Personality and Social Psychology Bulletin, 4,* 97–101.

Batson, C. D., & Coke, J. S. (1981). Empathy: A source of altruistic motivation for helping? In J. P. Rushton & R. M. Sorrentino (Eds.), *Altruism and helping behavior: Social, personality, and developmental perspectives.* Hillsdale, NJ: Erlbaum.

Batson, C. D., Coke, J. S., Jasnoski, M. L., & Hanson, M. (1978). Buying kindness: Effect of an extrinsic incentive for helping on perceived altruism. *Personality and Social Psychology Bulletin, 4(1),* 86–91.

Batson, C. D., O'Quinn, K., Fultz, J., Vanderplas, M., & Isen, A. M. (1983). Influence of self-reported distress and empathy on egoistic versus altruistic motivation to help. *Journal of Personality and Social Psychology, 45,* 706–718.

Baum, A., & Singer, J. E. (1982). *Advances in environmental psychology*

(Vol. 4). Hillsdale, NJ: Erlbaum. Material reprinted with permission.

Baum, A., Singer, J., & Baum, C. (1981). Energy: Psychological perspectives. *Advances in Environmental Psychology, 3.*

Baum, A., & Valins, S. (1977). *Architecture and social behavior: Psychological studies in social density.* Hillsdale, NJ: Erlbaum. Material reprinted with the permission of the authors and Lawrence Erlbaum Associates, Inc., Publishers from Baum and Valins (1977).

Baumeister, R. F. (1982). A self-presentational view of social phenomena. *Psychological Bulletin, 91,* 3–26.

Baumeister, R. F. (1985, April). The championship choke. *Psychology Today,* pp. 48–52.

Baumeister, R. F. (1986). *Public self and private self.* New York: Springer-Verlag.

Baumeister, R. F., Hamilton, J., & Tice, D. (1985). Public versus private expectancy of success: Confidence booster or performance pressure? *Journal of Personality and Social Psychology, 48,* 1447–1457.

Baumeister, R. F., & Hutton, D. G. (1986). A self presentational perspective on group processes. In B. Mullen & G. R. Goethals (Eds.), *Theories of group behavior.* New York: Springer-Verlag.

Baumeister, R. F., & Jones, E. E. (1978). When self-presentation is constrained by the target's knowledge: Consistency and compensation. *Journal of Personality and Social Psychology, 36,* 608–618.

Baumeister, R. F., & Steinhilber, A. (1984). Paradoxical effects of supportive audiences on performance under pressure: The home field disadvantage in sports championships. *Journal of Personality and Social Psychology, 47,* 85–93.

Baumeister, R. F., & Tice, D. M. (1984). Role of self-presentation and choice in cognitive dissonance under forced compliance: Necessary or sufficient causes. *Journal of Personality and Social Psychology, 46,* 5–13.

Baumeister, R. F., & Tice, D. M. (1985). Toward a theory of situational structure. *Environment and Behavior, 17,* 147–172.

Baumrind, D. (1964). Some thoughts on ethics of research: After reading Milgram's "Behavioral Study of Obedience." *American Psychologist, 19,* 421–423.

Bavelas, A. (1948). Some problems of organizational change. *Journal of Social Issues, 3,* 48–52.

Bavelas, A. (1950). Communication patterns in task-oriented groups. *Journal of the Acoustical Society of America, 22,* 735–742.

Bavelas, A., Hastorf, A. H., Gross, A. E., & Kite, W. R. (1975). Experiments on the alteration of group structure. *Journal of Experimental Social Psychology, 1,* 55–71.

Beaman, A. L., Klentz, B., Diener, E., & Svanum, S. (1979). Objective self-awareness and transgression in children: A field study. *Journal of Personality and Social Psychology, 37,* 1835–1846.

Becker, F. D., & Mayo, C. (1971). Delineating personal distance and territoriality. *Environment and Behavior, 3,* 375–381.

Beckman, L. (1970). Effects of students' performance on teachers' and observers' attributions of causality. *Journal of Educational Psychology, 61,* 76–82.

Bell, P. A., & Baron, R. A. (1977). Aggression and ambient temperature: The facilitating and inhibiting effects of hot and cold environments. *Bulletin of the Psychonomic Society, 9,* 443–445.

Bem, D. (1965). An experimental analysis of self-persuasion. *Journal of Experimental Social Psychology, 1,* 199–218. © 1965 by the American Psychological Association. Adapted by permission of the author.

Bem, D. (1972). Self-perception theory. In L. Berkowitz (Ed.), *Advances in experimental social psychology* (Vol. 6). New York: Academic Press.

Bem, S. L. (1981). Gender scheme theory: A cognitive account of sex typing. *Psychological Review, 88,* 354–364.

Benson, P. L., Karabenick, S. A., & Lerner, R. M. (1976). Pretty pleases: The effect of physical attraction, race and sex on receiving help. *Journal of Experimental Social Psychology, 12,* 409–415.

Bentler, P. M. & Speckart, G. (1981). Attitudes "cause" behaviors: A structural equation analysis. *Journal of Personality and Social Psychology, 40,* 226–238.

Berg, J. H., & Archer, R. L. (1978, August). Disclosure or concern: A look at liking for norm-breakers. In *Self-disclosure and responsivity: An attributional analysis.* Symposium presented at the meeting of the American Psychological Association, Toronto.

Berger, S. M., Carli, L. C., Garcier, R., & James, J. B. (1982). Audience effects in anticipatory learning: A comparison of drive and practice inhibition analysis. *Journal of Personality and Social Psychology, 42,* 478–486.

Berglas, S., & Jones, E. E. (1978). Drug choice as a self-handicapping strategy in response to noncontingent success. *Journal of Personality and Social Psychology, 36,* 405–417.

Berkowitz, L. (1962). *Aggression: A social psychological analysis.* New York: McGraw-Hill.

Berkowitz, L. (1965). The concept of aggressive drive: Some additional considerations. In L. Berkowitz (Ed.), *Advances in experimental social psychology* (Vol. 2). New York: Academic Press.

Berkowitz, L. (Ed.). (1969). *Roots of aggression: A reexamination of the frustration-aggression hypothesis.* New York: Atherton.

Berkowitz, L. (1974). Some determinants of impulsive aggression: Role of mediated associations with reinforcements for aggression. *Psychological Review, 81,* 165–176.

Berkowitz, L., & Knurek, D. (1967). Label-mediated hostility generalization. *Journal of Personality and Social Psychology, 5,* 364–368.

Berkowitz, L., & Le Page, A. (1967). Weapons as aggression-eliciting stimuli. *Journal of Personality and Social Psychology, 7,* 202–207.

Berscheid, E. (1983). Emotion. In H. H. Kelley, E. Berscheid, A. Christensen, J. Harvey, T. L. Huston, G. Levinger, E. McClintock, A. Peplau, & D. R. Peterson (Eds.), *Close relationships.* San Francisco: Freeman.

Berscheid, E. (1985). Interpersonal attraction. In G. Lindzey & E. Aronson (Eds.), *The handbook of social psychology* (3rd ed., Vol. 2). New York: Erlbaum.

Berscheid, E., Boye, D., & Darley, J. M. (1968). Effects of forced association upon voluntary choice to associate. *Journal of Personality and Social Psychology, 8,* 13–19.

Berscheid, E., & Campbell, B. (1981). The changing longevity of heterosexual close relationships: A commentary and forecast. In M. Lerner (Ed.), *The justice motive in times of scarcity and change.* New York: Plenum Press.

Berscheid, E., Dion, K., Walster, E., & Walster, G. W. (1971). Physical attractiveness and dating choice: A test of the matching hypothesis. *Journal of Experimental Social Psychology, 7,* 173–189.

Berscheid, E., Graziano, W., Monson, T., & Dermer, M. (1976). Outcome dependency: Attention, attribution, and attraction. *Journal of Personality and Social Psychology, 34,* 978–989.

Berscheid, E., & Walster, E. (1978). *Interpersonal attraction.* Reading, MA: Addison-Wesley.

Berscheid, E., Walster, G. W., & Walster, E. (1969). Effects of accuracy and positivity of an evaluation on liking for the evaluator. In E. Berscheid and E. Walster, *Interpersonal attraction.* Reading, MA: Addison-Wesley.

Biggers, T., & Pryor, B. (1982). Attitude change: A function of emotion-eliciting qualities of environment. *Personality and Social Psychology Bulletin, 8,* 94–99.

Billig, M., & Tajfel, H. (1973). Social categorization and similarity in intergroup behavior. *European Journal of Social Psychology, 3,* 27–52.

Bird, A. (1977). Team structure and success as related to cohesiveness and leadership. *Journal of Social Psychology, 103,* 217–223.

Bird, C., Monachesi, E. D., & Burdick, M. (1952). Studies of group tensions: III. The effect of parental discouragement of play activities upon the attitudes of white children toward Negroes. *Child Development, 23,* 295–306.

Birdwhistell, R. L. (1952). *Introduction to kinesics.* Louisville, KY: University of Louisville Press.

Blake, R. R., Helson, H., & Mouton, J. S. (1956). The generality of conformity behavior as a function of factual anchorage, difficulty of task

and amount of social pressure. *Journal of Personality, 25,* 294–305.

Blake, R. R., & Mouton, J. S. (1961). Loyalty of representatives to ingroup positions during intergroup competition. *Sociometry, 24,* 177–183.

Blake, R. R., & Mouton, J. S. (1962). The intergroup dynamics of win-lose conflict and problem-solving collaboration in union-management relations. In M. Sherif (Ed.), *Intergroup relations and leadership* (pp. 94–140). New York: Wiley.

Blake, R. R., & Mouton, J. S. (1986). From theory to practice in interface problem-solving. In Worchel, S., & Austin, W. G. (Eds.), *The psychology of intergroup relations.* Chicago: Nelson-Hall.

Blanck, P. D., & Rosenthal, R. (1982). Developing strategies for decoding "leaky" messages: On learning how and when to decode discrepant and consistent social communications. In R. S. Feldman (Ed.), *Development of nonverbal behavior in children* (pp. 203–229). New York: Springer-Verlag.

Bogart, K., Loeb, A., & Rittman, J. D. (1969). *Behavioral consequences of cognitive dissonance.* Paper presented at Eastern Psychological Association.

Bogart, L. (1981). *The press and the public: Who reads what, where, and why in American newspapers.* Hillsdale, NJ: Erlbaum.

Bonoma, T. V. (1976). Social psychology and social evaluation. *Representative Research in Social Psychology, 7,* 147–156.

Bootzin, R. R., Herman, C. P., & Nicassio, P. (1976). The power of suggestion: Another examination of misattribution and insomnia. *Journal of Personality and Social Psychology, 34,* 673–679.

Borgida, E., & Nisbett, R. E. (1977).

The differential impact of abstract vs. concrete information on decisions. *Journal of Applied Social Psychology, 7,* 258–271.

Bossard, J. (1932). Residential propinquity as a factor in marriage selection. *American Journal of Sociology, 38,* 219–224.

Bradley, G. W. (1978). Self-serving biases in the attribution process: A re-examination of the fact or fiction question. *Journal of Personality and Social Psychology, 35,* 56–71.

Brady, A., & Walker, M. (1978). Interpersonal distance as a function of situationally induced anxiety. *British Journal of Social and Clinical Psychology, 17,* 127–133.

Braiker, H. B., & Kelley, H. H. (1979). Conflict in the development of close relationships. In R. L. Burgess & T. L. Huston (Eds.), *Social exchange in developing relationships.* New York: Academic Press.

Brehm, J. W. (1956). Post-decision changes in desirability of alternatives. *Journal of Abnormal and Social Psychology, 52,* 384–389. © 1956 by the American Psychological Association. Adapted by permission of the author.

Brehm, J. W. (1966). *A theory of psychological reactance.* New York: Academic Press.

Brehm, J. W. (1972). *Responses to loss of freedom: A theory of psychological reactance.* Morristown, NJ: General Learning Press.

Brehm, J. W., & Festinger, L. (1957). Pressures toward uniformity of performance in groups. *Human Relations, 10,* 85–89.

Brehm, S. S., & Brehm, J. W. (1981). *Psychological reactance: A theory of freedom and control.* New York: Academic Press.

Brehm, S. S., & Weinraub, M. (1977).

Physical barriers and psychological reactance: 2-year-olds' responses to threats to freedom. *Journal of Personality and Social Psychology, 35,* 830–836.

Brewer, M. B. (1979). In-group bias in the minimal intergroup situation: A cognitive-motivational analysis. *Psychological Bulletin, 86,* 307–324.

Brewer, M. B. (1986). The role of ethnocentrism in intergroup conflict. In Worchel, S., & Austin, W. G. (Eds.), *The psychology of intergroup relations.* Chicago: Nelson Hall.

Brickner, M., Harkins, S., & Ostrom, T. (1986). Effects of personal involvement: Thought-provoking implications for social loafing. *Journal of Personality and Social Psychology, 51,* 763–769.

Broadbent, D. E. (1978). The current state of noise research: reply to Poulton. *Psychological Bulletin, 85*(s), 1052–1067.

Brock, T. C. (1965). Communicator-recipient similarity and decision change. *Journal of Personality and Social Psychology, 1,* 650–654.

Brock, T. C., & Buss, A. H. (1962). Dissonance, aggression and evaluation of pain. *Journal of Abnormal and Social Psychology, 65,* 192–202.

Brockner, J., Mahan, T., Thomas, B., Weiss, W., Winters, L., & Mitchell, A. (1983). The roles of self-esteem and self-consciousness in the Wortman-Brehm model of reactance and learned helplessness. *Journal of Personality and Social Psychology, 45,* 199–209.

Brockner, J., & Rubin, J. Z. (1985). *Entrapment in escalating conflicts.* New York: Springer-Verlag.

Brockner, J., & Swap, W. C. (1976). Effects of repeated exposure and attitudinal similarity on self-disclosure and interpersonal attraction. *Journal* *of Personality and Social Psychology, 33,* 531–540.

Brophy, J. E. (1982). *Research on the self-fulfilling prophecy and teacher expectations.* Paper delivered at annual meeting of the American Educational Research Association, New York City.

Brown, B. R. (1968). The effects of need to maintain face on interpersonal bargaining. *Journal of Experimental Social Psychology, 4,* 107–122.

Brown, B. (1979). Territoriality and residential burglary. Paper presented at the American Psychological Association meeting, New York.

Brown, P., & Eliot, R. (1965). Control of aggression in a nursery school class. *Journal of Experimental Child Psychology, 2,* 103–107.

Brown, R. (1965). *Social psychology.* New York: Free Press.

Brown, R. (1986). *Social psychology: the second edition.* New York: Free Press.

Brown, R. J., & Turner, J. C. (1979). The criss-cross categorization effect in intergroup discrimination. *British Journal of Social and Clinical Psychology, 18,* 371–383.

Brown, R. J., & Turner, J. C. (1981). Interpersonal and intergroup behavior. In J. C. Turner & H. Giles (Eds.), *Intergroup behavior.* Chicago: University of Chicago Press.

Bruner, J. S., Busiek, R. D., & Minturn, A. (1952). Assimilation in the immediate reproduction of visually perceived figures. *Journal of Experimental Psychology, 44,* 151–155. © 1952 by the American Psychological Association.

Bryan, J., & Test, M. (1967). Models and helping: Naturalistic studies in aiding behavior. *Journal of Personality and Social Psychology, 6,* 400–407.

Burger, J. M., & Petty, R. E. (1981). The low-ball compliance technique:

Task or person commitment? *Journal of Personality and Social Psychology, 40,* 492–500.

Burgess, R. L., & Huston, T. L. (Eds.). (1979). *Social exchange in developing relationships.* New York: Academic Press.

Burns, J. R. (1984). *The power to God: the crisis of the American presidency.* New York: Simon & Schuster.

Burnstein, E. (1982). Persuasion as argument processing. In M. Brandstatter, J. M. Davis, & G. Stocker-Kreichgauer (Eds.), *Group decision processes.* London: Academic Press.

Burnstein, E., & Vinokur, A. (1977). Persuasive argumentation and social comparison as determinants of attitude polarization. *Journal of Experimental Social Psychology, 9,* 123–137.

Buss, A. H. (1961). *The psychology of aggression.* New York: Wiley.

Buss, A. H., Booker, A., & Buss, E. (1972). Firing a weapon and aggression. *Journal of Personality and Social Psychology, 27,* 296–302.

Byrne, D. (1971). *The attraction paradigm.* New York: Academic Press.

Byrne, D., Baskett, C. D., & Hodges, L. (1971). Behavioral indicators of interpersonal attraction. *Journal of Abnormal and Social Psychology, 1,* 137–149.

Byrne, D., & Blaylock, B. (1963). Similarity and assumed similarity of attitudes between husbands and wives. *Journal of Abnormal and Social Psychology, 67,* 636–640.

Byrne, D., & Clore, G. L. (1970). A reinforcement model of evaluative responses. *Personality: An International Journal, 1,* 103–128.

Byrne, D., Clore, G., & Worchel, P. (1966). The effect of economic similarity-dissimilarity on interpersonal attraction. *Journal of Personality and Social Psychology, 4,* 220–224.

Byrne, D., Ervin, C., & Lamberth, J. (1970). Continuity between the experimental study of attraction and real-life computer dating. *Journal of Personality and Social Psychology, 16,* 157–165.

Byrne, D., & Griffitt, W. (1966). Developmental investigation of the law of attraction. *Journal of Personality and Social Psychology, 4,* 699–702.

Byrne, D., Griffitt, W., & Stefaniak, D. (1967). Attraction and similarity of personality characteristics. *Journal of Personality and Social Psychology, 5,* 82–90.

Byrne, D., London, O., & Reeves, K. (1968). The effects of physical attractiveness, sex, and attitude similarity on interpersonal attraction *Journal of Personality, 36,* 259–271.

Byrne, D., & Rhamey, R. (1965). Magnitude of positive and negative reinforcements as determinants of attraction. *Journal of Personality and Social Psychology, 2,* 884–889.

Cacioppo, J. T., & Petty, R. E. (1979a). Attitudes and cognitive response: An electrophysiological approach. *Journal of Personality and Social Psychology, 37,* 2181–2199.

Cacioppo, J. T., & Petty, R. E. (1979b). Effects of message repetition and position on cognitive responses, recall, and persuasion. *Journal of Personality and Social Psychology, 37,* 97–109.

Cacioppo, J. T., & Petty, R. E. (1981a). Effects of extent of thought on the pleasantness ratings of P-O-X triads: Evidence for 3 judgmental tendencies in evaluating social situations. *Journal of Personality and Social Psychology, 40,* 1000–1009.

Cacioppo, J. T., & Petty, R. E. (1981b). Electromyograms as measures of extent and affectivity of information processing. *American Psychologist, 36*(5), 441–456.

Cacioppo, J. T., & Petty, R. E. (1981c). Electromyographic specificity during covert information processing. *Psychophysiology, 18,* 518–523.

Cacioppo, J. T., & Petty, R. E. (1986). Stalking rudimentary processes of social influence: A psychophysiological approach. In M. P. Zanna, J. M. Olson, & C. P. Herman (Eds.), *Social influence: The Ontario symposium* (Vol. 5). Hillsdale, NJ: Erlbaum.

Cacioppo, J. T., Petty, R. E., Losch, M. C., & Kim, H. S. (1986). Electromyographic activity over facial muscle regions can differentiate the valence and intensity of affective reactions. *Journal of Personality and Social Psychology, 50,* 260–268.

Callahan, T. (1982, October 11). Some people build the roads. *Time Magazine,* p. 80.

Caldwell, M. D. (1976). Communication and sex effects in a five-person Prisoner's Dilemma game. *Journal of Personality and Social Psychology, 33,* 273–280.

Calhoun, J. B. (1962). Population density and social pathology. *Scientific American, 206*(3), 139–148.

Callaway, M., Marriott, R., & Esser, J. (1985). Effects of dominance or group decision making: Toward a stress-reduction explanation of group think. *Journal of Personality and Social Psychology, 49,* 949–952.

Campbell, D. T., & LeVine, R. A. (1970). Field manual anthropology. In R. Naroll & R. Cohen (Eds.), *A handbook of method in cultural anthropology.* Garden City, NY: Natural History Press.

Campbell, D. T., & Stanley, J. C. (1963). *Experimental and quasi-experimental designs for research.* Chicago: Rand McNally.

Campbell, J. D. (1986). Similarity and uniqueness: The effects of attribute type, relevance, and individual differences in self-esteem and depression. *Journal of Personality and Social Psychology, 50,* 281–293.

Campbell, J. D., Tesser, A., & Fairey, P. J. (1986). Conformity and attention to the stimulus: Some temporal and contextual dynamics. *Journal of Personality and Social Psychology, 51,* 315–324.

Canavan-Gumpert, D. (1977). Generating reward and cost orientations through praise and criticism. *Journal of Personality and Social Psychology, 35,* 501–514.

Cann, A., Sherman, S. J., & Elkes, R. (1975). Effects of initial request size and timing of a second request on compliance: The foot in the door and the door in the face. *Journal of Personality and Social Psychology, 32,* 774–782. © 1975 by the American Psychological Association. Adapted by permission of the authors.

Cantor, N., & Mischel, W. (1977). Traits as prototypes: Effects on recognition memory. *Journal of Personality and Social Psychology, 35,* 38–48.

Cantril, H. (1940). *The invasion from Mars: A study in the psychology of panic.* Princeton, NJ: Princeton University Press. Copyright 1940, © renewed 1968 by Princeton University Press. Excerpt, p. 52, reprinted by permission of Princeton University Press.

Carlsmith, J. M., Collins, B. E., & Helmreich, R. L. (1966). Studies in forced compliance: 1. The effect of pressure for compliance on attitude change produced by face-to-face role playing and anonymous essay writing. *Journal of Personality and Social Psychology, 4,* 1–13.

Carlsmith, J. M., Ellsworth, P. C., & Aronson, E. (1976). *Methods of research in social psychology.* Reading, MA: Addison-Wesley.

Carnegie, D. (1936). *How to win friends and influence people.* New York: Simon & Schuster.

Carnevale, P., Sherer, P., & Pruitt, D. G. (1979). *Some determinants of concessions rate and distributive tactics in negotiation.* Paper presented at American Psychological Association, New York.

Carson, R. C. (1969). *Interaction concepts of personality.* Chicago: Aldine.

Cartwright, D. (1973). Determinants of scientific progress: The case of research on the risky shift. *American Psychologist, 28,* 222–231.

Cartwright, D., & Harary, F. (1956). Structural balance: A generalization of Heider's theory. *Psychological Review, 63,* 277–293.

Carver, C. S., & Scheier, M. F. (1981). *Attention and self-regulation: A control-theory approach to human behavior.* New York: Springer-Verlag.

Cash, T. F., Gillen, B., & Burns, D. S. (1977). Sexism and "beautyism" in personnel consultant decision making. *Journal of Applied Psychology, 62*(3), 301–310.

Castro, M. A. C. (1974). Reactions to receiving aid as a function of cost to donor and opportunity to aid. *Journal of Applied Social Psychology, 4,* 194–209.

Cavalli-Sforza, L. L., & Feldman, M. W. (1981). *Cultural transmission and evolution: A quantitative approach.* Princeton, NJ: Princeton University Press.

Cavalli-Sforza, L. L., Feldman, M. W., Chen, K. H., & Dornbush, S. M. (1982). Theory and observation in cultural transmission. *Science, 218,* 19–27.

Cavan, S. (1963). Interaction in home territories. *Berkeley Journal of Sociology, 8,* 17–32.

Cavan, S. (1966). *Liquor license.* Chicago: Aldine.

Cavior, N., & Dorecki, P. R. (1969, April). *Physical attractiveness and popularity among fifth grade boys.* Paper presented at the meeting of the Southwestern Psychological Association, Austin, Texas.

Chaiken, S. (1980). Heuristic versus systematic information processing and the use of source versus message cues in persuasion. *Journal of Personality and Social Psychology, 39,* 752–756.

Chaiken, S., & Baldwin, M. W. (1981). Affective-cognitive consistency and the effect of salient behavioral information on the self perception of attitudes. *Journal of Personality and Social Psychology, 34,* 605–614.

Chaiken, S., & Eagly, A. H. (1976). Communication modality as a determinant of message persuasiveness and message comprehensibility. *Journal of Personality and Social Psychology, 34,* 605–614. © 1976 by the American Psychological Association. Adapted by permission of the authors.

Chaiken, S., & Eagly, A. H. (1983). Communication modality as a determinant of persuasion: The role of communicator salience. *Journal of Personality and Social Psychology, 45,* 241–256.

Chaiken, A., Sigler, E., & Derlega, V. A. (1974). Nonverbal mediators of teacher expectation effects. *Journal of Personality and Social Psychology, 30,* 144–149.

Chemers, M. M., & Skrzypek, G. J. (1972). Experimental test of the contingency model of leadership effectiveness. *Journal of Personality and Social Psychology, 24,* 172–177.

Chen, S. C. (1937). Social modification of the activity of ants in nest-building. *Physiological Zoology, 10,* 420–436.

Chertkoff, J. M., & Conley, M. (1967). Opening offer and frequency of concession as bargaining strategies. *Journal of Personality and Social Psychology, 7,* 181–185. Copyright © 1967 by the American Psychological Association. Adapted by permission of the authors.

Chertkoff, J. M., & Esser, J. K. (1976). A review of experiments in explicit bargaining. *Journal of Experimental Social Psychology, 12,* 464–486.

Christie, R. (1956). Eysenck's treatment of the personality of Communists. *Psychological Bulletin, 53,* 411–430.

Cialdini, R. B. (1985). *Influence: Science and practice* (pp. 183–188). Glenview, IL: Scott, Foresman.

Cialdini, R. B., Borden, R. J., Thorne, A., Walker, M. R., Freman, S., & Sloan, L. R. (1976). Basking in reflected glory: Three (football) field studies. *Journal of Personality and Social Psychology, 34,* 366–375.

Cialdini, R. B., Cacioppo, J. T., Bassett, R., & Miller, J. A. (1978). The low-ball procedure for producing compliance: Commitment then cost. *Journal of Personality and Social Psychology, 36,* 463–476.

Cialdini, R. B., Vincent, J. E., Lewis, S. K., Catalan, J., Wheeler, D., & Darby, B. L. (1975). Reciprocal concessions procedure for inducing compliance: The door-in-the-face technique. *Journal of Personality and Social Psychology, 31,* 206–215.

Clark, M. S. (1984). Record keeping in two types of relationships. *Journal of Personality and Social Psychology, 47,* 549–557.

Clark, M. S., Gotay, C. C., & Mills, J. (1974). Acceptance of help as a function of the potential helper and opportunity to repay. *Journal of Applied Social Psychology, 4,* 224–229.

Clifford, M., & Walster, E. (1973). The effect of physical attractiveness on teacher expectation. *Sociology of Education, 46,* 248.

Clines, F. X. (1982, January 14). Plane hits bridge over the Potomac: 12 dead, 50 missing. *The New York Times,* pp. A1, B6.

Clore, G. L., & Baldridge, B. (1968). Interpersonal attraction: The role of agreement and topic interest. *Journal of Personality and Social Psychology, 9,* 340–346.

Clore, G. L., & Kerber, K. W. (1981). *Toward an affective theory of attraction and trait attribution.* Unpublished manuscript.

Coch, L., & French, J. R. P. (1948). Overcoming resistance to change. *Human Relations, 1,* 512–532.

Cochran, C., Hale, W., & Hissam, C. (1984). Personal space requirements in indoor versus outdoor locations. *Journal of Psychology, 117,* 121–123.

Cohen, A. R. (1958). Upward communication in experimentally created hierarchies. *Human Relations, 11,* 41–53.

Cohen, A. R. (1962). An experiment on small rewards for discrepant compliance and attitude change. In J. W. Brehm & A. R. Cohen (Eds.), *Explorations in cognitive dissonance.* New York: Wiley.

Cohen, S., Evans, G. W., Krantz, D. S., & Stokols, D. (1980). Physiological, motivational, and cognitive effects of aircraft noise on children. *American Psychologist, 35,* 231–244.

Cohen, S., Evans, G. W., Krantz, D. S., Stokols, D., & Kelly, S. (1981). Aircraft noise and children: Longitudinal and cross-sectional evidence on adaptation to noise and the effectiveness of noise abatement. *Journal of Personality and Social Psychology, 40*(2), 331–345.

Cohen, S., Glass, D., & Singer, J. (1973). Apartment noise, auditory discrimination, and reading ability in children. *Journal of Experimental Social Psychology, 4,* 407–422.

Cohen, S., Krantz, D., Evans, G., & Stokols, D. (1982). Community noise, behavior, and health: The Los Angeles Noise Project. In A. Baum & T. Singer (Eds.), *Advances in Environmental Psychology* (Vol. 4). Hillsdale, NJ: Erlbaum.

Cohen, S., & Sherrod, D. (1978). When density matters: Environmental control as a determinant of crowding effects in laboratory and residential settings. *Journal of Population, 1,* 189–202.

Cohen, S., & Weinstein, N. (1981). Nonauditory effects of noise on behavior and health. *Journal of Social Issues, 37*(1), 36–40.

Cohn, N. B., & Strassberg, D. S. (1983). Self-disclosure reciprocity among preadolescents. *Personality and Social Psychology Bulletin, 9,* 97–102.

Coke tampers with success. (1985, May 6). *Newsweek,* pp. 50–52.

Collins, B. E., & Hoyt, M. G. (1972). Personal responsibility for consequences: An integration and extension of the "forced compliance" literature. *Journal of Experimental Social Psychology, 8,* 558–593.

Collins, B. E., & Raven, B. (1969). Psychological aspects of structure in the small group: Interpersonal attraction, coalitions, communication and power. In G. Lindzey & E. Aronson (Eds.), *The handbook of social psychology (Vol. 4), Group psychology and phenomena of interaction* (2nd ed.). Reading, MA: Addison-Wesley.

Comer, R., & Rhodewalt, F. (1979). Cue utilization in the self-attribution of emotions and attitudes. *Personality and Social Psychology Bulletin, 5,* 320–324.

Cone, J. D., & Hayes, S. C. (1980). *Environmental problems behavioral solutions.* Belmont, CA: Wadsworth.

Conn, L. K., Edwards, C. N., Rosenthal, R., & Crowne, D. (1968). Perception of emotion and response to teachers' expectancy by elementary school children. *Psychological Reports, 22,* 27–34.

Cook, S. W. (1985). Experimenting on social issues: The case of school desegregation. *American Psychologist, 40,* 452–460.

Cook, T. D., Gruder, C. L., Hennigan, K. M., & Flay, B. R. (1979). History of the sleeper effect: Some logical pitfalls in accepting the null hypothesis. *Psychological Bulletin, 37,* 131–146.

Cooley, C. H. (1902). *Human order and the social order.* New York: Scribner's.

Cooper, H., & Baron, R. (1977). Academic expectations and attributed responsibility as predictors of professional teacher's reinforcement behavior. *Journal of Educational Psychology, 69,* 409–418.

Cooper, J. (1971). Personal responsibility and dissonance: The role of foreseen consequences. *Journal of Personality and Social Psychology, 18,* 354–363.

Cooper, J., & Axsom, D. (1982). Effort justification in psychotherapy. In G. Weary & H. Mirels (Eds.), *Integrations of clinical and social psychology.* London: Oxford University Press. Copyright © 1982 by Oxford University Press, Inc. Reprinted by permission.

Cooper, J., & Croyle, R. T. (1982). *From experimental bias to social interaction: The self-fulfilling prophecy in social psychology.* Paper presented at the annual meeting of the American Educational Research Association, New York.

Cooper, J., & Croyle, R. T. (1984). Attitudes and attitude change. *Annual Review of Psychology, 35,* 395–426.

Cooper, J., & Fazio, R. H. (1984). A new look at dissonance theory. In L. Berkowitz (Ed.), *Advances in experimental social psychology* (Vol. 17). New York: Academic Press.

Cooper, J., & Fazio, R. H. (1986). The formation and persistence of attributes that support intergroup conflict. In Worchel, S., & Austin, W. G. (Eds.), *The psychology of intergroup relations.* Chicago: Nelson-Hall.

Cooper, J., & Jones, E. E. (1969). Opinion divergence as a strategy to avoid being miscast. *Journal of Personality and Social Psychology, 13,* 23–30.

Cooper, J., & Worchel, S. (1970). Role of undesired consequences in arousing cognitive dissonance. *Journal of Personality and Social Psychology, 16,* 199–206. © 1970 by the American Psychological Association.

Cooper, J., Zanna, M. P., & Taves, P. A. (1978). Arousal as a necessary condition for attitude change following induced compliance. *Journal of Personality and Social Psychology, 36,* 1101–1106.

Cooper, J. E., & McGaugh, J. L. (1969). Leadership: Integrating principles of social psychology. In C. A. Gibb (Ed.), *Leadership.* Baltimore: Penguin Books.

Costanzo, M., Archer, D., Aronson, E., & Pettigrew, T. (1986). Energy conservation behavior: The difficult path from information to action. *American Psychologist, 41,* 521–528.

Cotton, J. L. (1981). A review of research on Schachter's theory of emotion and the misattribution of arousal. *European Journal of Social Psychology, 11,* 365–397.

Cottrell, N., & Wack, D. (1967). The energizing effect of cognitive dissonance on dominant and subordinate responses. *Journal of Personality and Social Psychology, 6,* 132–138.

Cottrell, N., Wack, D., Sekerak, G., & Rittle, R. (1968). Social facilitation of dominant responses by the presence of an audience and the mere presence of others. *Journal of Personality and Social Psychology, 9,* 245–250.

Couch, A., & Keniston, K. (1960). Yeasayers and naysayers. Agreeing response set as a personality variable. *Journal of Abnormal and Social Psychology, 60,* 151–174.

Cowan, P. A., & Walters, R. H. (1963). Studies of reinforcement of aggression: 1. Effects of scheduling. *Child Development, 34,* 543, 551.

Cox, V., Paulus, P., & McCain, G. (1984). Prison crowding research: The relevance for prison housing standards and a general approach regarding crowding phenomena. *American Psychologist, 39,* 1148–1160.

Cozby, P. C. (1972). Self-disclosure, reciprocity and liking. *Sociometry, 35,* 151–160.

Crider, A. B., Goethals, G. R., Kavanaugh, R. D., & Soloman, P. R. (1986). *Psychology* (2nd ed.). Glenview, IL: Scott, Foresman.

Crocker, J., Hannah, D. B., & Weber, R. (1983). Person memory and causal attributions. *Journal of Personality and Social Psychology, 44,* 55–66.

Crowne, D. P., & Marlow, D. (1964). *The approval motive: Studies in evaluative dependence.* New York: Wiley.

Croyle, R., & Cooper, J. (1983). Dissonance arousal: Physiological evidence. *Journal of Personality and Social Psychology, 45,* 782–791.

Crutchfield, R. A. (1955). Conformity and character. *American Psychologist, 10,* 191–198.

Cunningham, J. D. (1981). Self-disclosure intimacy: Sex, sex-of-target, cross-national, and "generational" differences. *Personality and Social Psychology Bulletin, 7,* 314–319.

Danheiser, P. R., & Graziano, W. G. (1982). Self-monitoring and cooperation as a self-presentational strategy. *Journal of Personality and Social Psychology, 42,* 497–505.

Darley, J. M., & Aronson, E. (1966). Self-evaluation vs. direct anxiety reduction as determinants of the fear-affiliation relationship. *Journal of Experimental Social Psychology, 2,* 66–79.

Darley, J. M., & Batson, C. D. (1973). "From Jerusalem to Jericho": A study of situational and dispositional variables in helping behavior. *Journal of Personality and Social Psychology, 27,* 100–108. © 1973 by the American Psychological Association. Reprinted by permission of the authors.

Darley, J. M., & Berscheid, E. (1967). Increased liking caused by the anticipation of personal contact. *Human Relations, 10,* 29–40.

Darley, J. M., & Fazio, R. H. (1980). Expectancy and confirmation processes arising in the social interaction sequence. *American Psychologist, 35,* 867–881.

Darley, J. M., & Gilbert, D. (1985). *Social psychological aspects of environmental psychology* (3rd ed.). New York: Random House.

Darley, J. M., & Gross, P. H. (1983). A hypothesis-confirming bias in labeling effects. *Journal of Personality and Social Psychology, 44,* 20–33.

Darley, J. M., & Latané, B. (1968). Bystander intervention in emergencies: Diffusion of responsibility.

Journal of Personality and Social Psychology, 8, 377–383. © 1968 by the American Psychological Association. Reprinted by permission of the authors.

Darley, S. A. (1976). Big-time careers for the "little woman": A dual-role dilemma. *Journal of Social Issues, 32,* 85–98.

Darwin, C. (1872). *The expression of the emotions in man and animals.* London: John Murray.

Dashiell, J. F. (1935). Experimental studies of the influence of social situations on the behavior of individual human adults. In *A handbook of social psychology,* Worcester, MA: Clark University Press.

Davidson, A. R., & Jaccard, J. (1979). Variables that moderate the attitude-behavior relation: Results of a longitudinal survey. *Journal of Personality and Social Psychology, 37,* 1364–1376. © 1979 by the American Psychological Association. Adapted by permission of the authors.

Davidson, L. R., & Duberman, L. (1982). Friendship: Communication and interactional patterns in same sex dyads. *Sex Roles, 8,* 809–822.

Davis, D., & Perkowitz, W. T. (1979). Consequences of responsiveness in dyadic interaction: Effects of probability of response and proportion of content-related responses on interpersonal attraction. *Journal of Personality and Social Psychology, 37,* 534–550.

Davis, J., Bray, R., & Holt, R. (1977). The empirical study of decision processes in juries. In J. Tapp & F. Levine (Eds.), *Law, justice, and the individual in society: Psychological and legal issues.* New York: Holt, Rinehart & Winston.

Davis, J., Kerr, N. L., Atkin, R. S., Holt, R., & Meek, D. (1975). The decision processes of 6- and 12-person mock juries assigned unanimous and two-thirds majority rules. *Journal of Personality and Social Psychology, 32,* 1–14. © 1975 by the American Psychological Association.

Davis, K. E. (1985, February). Near and dear: Friendship and love. *Psychology Today,* pp. 22–30.

Davis, K. E., & Jones, E. E. (1960). Changes in interpersonal perception as a means of reducing cognitive dissonance. *Journal of Abnormal and Social Psychology, 61,* 402–410. © 1960 by the American Psychological Association. Adapted by permission of the authors.

Davis, K. E., & Florquist, C. C. (1965). Perceived threat and dependence as determinants of the tactical usage of opinion conformity. *Journal of Experimental Social Psychology, 1,* 219–236.

Davis, O. K. (1983). *Grambling's gridiron glory: Eddie Robinson and the Tigers' success story.* Ruston, LA: M&M Printing.

Davis, O. K. (1985). About coach Eddie Robinson. Louisiana Sports Writers Association, p. 3–4.

Davitz, J. R. (1952). The effects of previous training on post-frustrative behavior. *Journal of Abnormal and Social Psychology, 47,* 309–315.

Dawes, R. M., & Smith, T. L. (1985). Attitude and opinion measurement. In G. Lindzey & E. Aronson (Eds.), *The handbook of social psychology* (3rd ed., Vol. 1, pp. 509–566). New York: Random House.

Deaux, K. (1976). Sex: A perspective on the attribution process. In H. Harvey, W. J. Ickes, & R. F. Kidd (Eds.), *New directions in attribution research.* Hillsdale, NJ: Erlbaum.

Deaux, K., & Emswiller, T. (1974). Explanations of successful performance on sex-linked tasks: What is skill for the male is luck for the female. *Journal of Personality and Social Psychology, 29,* 80–85.

Deaux, K., & Farris, E. (1977). Attributing causes for one's own behavior: The effects of sex, norms and outcome. *Journal of Research in Personality, 11,* 59–72.

DeJong, W. (1979). An examination of self-perception mediation of the foot-in-the-door effect. *Journal of Personality and Social Psychology, 37,* 2221–2239.

DeJong, W. (1981). Consensus information and the foot-in-the-door effect. *Personality and Social Psychology Bulletin, 7,* 423–430.

DeJong, W., Marber, S., & Shaver, R. (1980). Crime intervention: The role of a victim's behavior in reducing situational ambiguity. *Personality and Social Psychology Bulletin, 6,* 113–118.

Dermer, M., & Pyszczynski, T. A. (1978). Effects of erotica upon men's loving and liking responses for women they love. *Journal of Personality and Social Psychology, 36,* 1302–1309.

Desor, J. A. (1972). Toward a psychological theory of crowding. *Journal of Personality and Social Psychology, 21,* 79–83.

Deutsch, M. (1973). *The resolution of conflict.* New Haven: Yale University Press.

Deutsch, M. (1975). Introduction. In M. Deutsch & H. A. Hornstein (Eds.), *Applying social psychology: Implications for research, practice, training* (pp. 1–12). Hillsdale, NJ: Erlbaum.

Deutsch, M. (1980). Fifty years of conflict. In L. Festinger (Ed.), *Retrospectives on social psychology.* New York. Oxford Press.

Deutsch, M., Canavan, D., & Rubin, J. (1971). The effects of size of conflict and sex of experimenter upon interpersonal bargaining. *Journal of Experimental Social Psychology, 7,* 258–267.

Deutsch, M., & Gerard, H. (1955). A study of normative and informational social influences upon individual judgment. *Journal of Abnormal and Social Psychology, 51,* 629–636.

Deutsch, M., & Krauss, R. M. (1960). The effect of threat upon interpersonal bargaining. *Journal of Abnormal and Social Psychology, 61,* 181–189. Copyright © 1960 by the American Psychological Association. Adapted by permission of the authors.

Deutsch, M., & Krauss, R. M. (1962). Studies of interpersonal bargaining. *Journal of Conflict Resolution, 6,* 52–76.

Dickoff, H. (1961). *Reactions to evaluations by another person as a function of self-evaluation and the interaction context.* Unpublished doctoral dissertation, Duke University, Durham, NC.

Diener, E., Fraser, S., Beaman, A., & Kelem, Z. (1976). Effects of deindividuation variables on stealing among Halloween trick-or-treaters. *Journal of Personality and Social Psychology, 33,* 178–183.

Diener, E., Lusk, R., Defour, D., & Flax, R. (1980). Deindividuation: Effects of group size, density, number of observers, and group member similarity on self-consciousness and disinhibited behavior. *Journal of Personality and Social Psychology, 39,* 449–459.

Dion, K. K. (1972). Physical attractiveness and evaluation on children's transgressions. *Journal of Personality and Social Psychology, 24,* 207–213.

Dion, K. K., Berscheid, E., & Walster, E. (1972). What is beautiful is good. *Journal of Personality and Social Psychology, 24,* 285–290.

Dodson, J. A., Tybout, A. M., & Sternthal, B. (1978). Impact of deals and deal retraction on brand switching. *Journal of Marketing Research, 15*(1), 72–81.

Dollard, J., Doob, L., Miller, N., Mowrer, O., & Sears, R. (1939). *Frustration and aggression.* New Haven, CT: Yale University Press.

Doms, M., & Van Avermaet, E. (1980). Majority influence, minority influence and conversion behavior: A replication. *Journal of Experimental Social Psychology, 16,* 283–293.

Donnerstein, E. (1980). Aggressive erotica and violence against women. *Journal of Personality and Social Psychology, 39,* 269–277.

Donnerstein, E. (1983). Erotica and human aggression. In R. G. Geen & E. Donnerstein (Eds.), *Aggression: Theoretical and empirical reviews* (Vol. 1). New York: Academic Press.

Donnerstein, E., Donnerstein, M., & Barrett, G. (1976). Where is the facilitation of media violence: The effects of nonexposure and placement of anger arousal. *Journal of Research in Personality, 10,* 386–398.

Donnerstein, E., Donnerstein, M., & Evans, R. (1975). Erotic stimuli and aggression: Facilitation or inhibition. *Journal of Personality and Social Psychology, 32,* 237–244.

Donnerstein, E., & Wilson, D. W. (1976). Effects of noise and perceived control on ongoing and subsequent aggressive behavior. *Journal of Personality and Social Psychology, 34,* 774–781. © 1976 by the American Psychological Association. Adapted by permission of the authors.

Doob, A. N. (1972). Catharsis and aggression: The effect of annoyance and retaliation on aggressive behavior. *Journal of Personality and Social Psychology, 22,* 387–392.

Dovidio, J. R. (1984). Helping behavior and altruism: An empirical and conceptual overview. In L. Berkowitz (Ed.), *Advances in experimental social psychology,* (Vol. 17), New York: Academic Press.

Driscoll, R., Davis, L., & Lipetz, M. (1972). Parental interference and romantic love: The Romeo and Juliet effect. *Journal of Personality and Social Psychology, 24,* 1–10.

Dutton, D. G., & Aron, A. P. (1974). Some evidence for heightened sexual attraction under conditions of high anxiety. *Journal of Personality and Social Psychology, 30,* 510–517.

Dutton, D. G., & Lake, R. A. (1973). Threat of own prejudice and reverse discrimination in interracial situations. *Journal of Personality and Social Psychology, 28,* 94–100.

Duval, S., Duval, V. H., & Neely, R. (1979). Self-focus, felt responsibility, and helping behavior. *Journal of Personality and Social Psychology, 37,* 1769–1778.

Duval, S., & Wicklund, R. A. (1972). *A theory of objective self-awareness.* New York: Academic Press.

Dweck, C. S. (1975). The role of expectations and attributions in the alleviation of learned helplessness. *Journal of Personality and Social Psychology, 31,* 674–685.

Eagly, A. H. (1983). Gender and social influence: A social psychological analysis. *American Psychologist, 38,* 971–981.

Eagly, A. H., & Carli, L. (1981). Sex of researchers and sex-typed communications as determinants of sex differences in influenceability: A meta-analysis of social influence studies. *Psychological Bulletin, 90,* 1–20.

Eagly, A. H., & Chaiken, S. (1984). Cognitive theories of persuasion. In L. Berkowitz (Ed.), *Advances in experimental social psychology* (Vol. 17). New York: Academic Press.

Eagly, A. H., Chaiken, S., & Wood, W. (1981). An attribution analysis of persuasion. In J. H. Harvey, W. Ickes, & R. F. Kidd (Eds.), *New directions in attribution research* (Vol. 3). Hillsdale, NJ: Erlbaum.

Eagly, A. H., Wood, W., & Fishbaugh, L. (1981). Sex differences in conformity: Surveillance by the group as a determinant of male nonconformity. *Journal of Personality and Social Psychology, 40*, 384–394.

Ebbinghaus, H. (1913). *Memory* (H. A. Ruger & C. E. Bussenius, Trans.). New York: Teachers College. (Originally published as *Uber das Gedachtnis*, Leipzig, Germany: Duncker, 1885).

Edney, J. J. (1975). Territoriality and control: A field experiment. *Journal of Personality and Social Psychology, 31*, 1108–1115.

Edney, J. J. (1980). The commons problem: Alternative perspectives. *American Psychologist, 35*, 131–150.

Efran, M. G. (1974). The effect of physical appearance on the judgment of guilt, interpersonal attraction, and severity of recommended punishment in a simulated jury task. *Journal of Experimental Research and Personality, 8*, 45–54.

Ehrlich, P. (1968). *The population bomb.* New York: Ballantine Books.

Eiser, J. R. (Ed.). (1984). *Attitudinal judgment.* New York: Springer.

Ekman, P., & Friesen, W. V. (1969). Nonverbal leakage and clues to deception. *Psychiatry, 32*, 88–106.

Ekman, P., Friesen, W. V., & Ellsworth, P. C. (1982). What are the similarities and differences in facial behavior across cultures? In P. Ekman (Ed.), *Emotion in the human race* (Vol. 2, pp. 56–97). Cambridge, Eng.: Cambridge University Press.

Elashoff, J. R., & Snow, R. E. (1971). *Pygmalion reconsidered.* Worthington, OH: Charles A. Jones.

Ellsworth, P. C., & Carlsmith, J. M. (1968). Effect of eye contact and verbal consent on affective response to a dyadic interaction. *Journal of Personality and Social Psychology, 10*, 15–20.

Elms, A. (1975). The crisis of confidence in social psychology. *American Psychologist, 30*, 967–976.

Elms, A. C., & Janis, I. L. (1965). Counter-norm attitudes induced by consonant versus dissonant conditions of role-playing. *Journal of Experimental Research in Personality, 1*, 50–60.

Eron, L. D. (1980). Prescription for reduction of aggression. *American Psychologist, 35*, 244–252.

Eysenck, H. J. (1956). The psychology of politics and the personality similarities between fascists and communists. *Psychological Bulletin, 53*, 431–438.

Exline, R. V., Ellyson, S. L., & Long, B. (1975). Visual behavior as an aspect of power role relationships. In P. Pliner, L. Krames, & T. Galloway (Eds.), *Nonverbal communication of aggression* (Vol. 2). New York: Plenum Press.

Falbo, T., & Peplau, L. S. (1980). Power strategies in intimate relationships. *Journal of Personality and Social Psychology, 38*, 618–628.

Fazio, R. H. (1981). On the self-perception explanation of the overjustification effect: The role of the salience of initial attitude. *Journal of Experimental Social Psychology, 17*, 417–426.

Fazio, R. H. (1986). How do attitudes

guide behaviors? In R. M. Sorrentino & E. T. Higgins (Eds.), *The handbook of motivation and cognition: Foundations of social behavior.* New York: Guilford.

Fazio, R. H., & Williams, C. J. (1985). *Attitude accessibility as a moderator of the attitude-perception and attitude-behavior relations: An investigation of the 1984 presidential election.* Unpublished manuscript, Indiana University, Bloomington.

Fazio, R. H., & Zanna, M. P. (1981). Direct experience and attitude-consistency. In L. Berkowitz (Ed.), *Advances in experimental social psychology,* Vol. 19. New York: Academic Press.

Feather, N. T., & Simon, J. G. (1975). Reactions to male and female success and failure in sex-linked occupations: Impressions of personality, causal attributions, and perceived likelihood of different consequences. *Journal of Personality and Social Psychology, 31,* 20–31.

Feldman, N. S., Higgins, E. T., Karlovac, M., & Ruble, D. N. (1976). Use of consensus information in causal attributions as a function of temporal presentation and availability of direct information. *Journal of Personality and Social Psychology, 34,* 694–698.

Fenigstein, A. (1979). Self-consciousness, self-attention, and social interaction. *Journal of Personality and Social Psychology, 37,* 75–86.

Fenigstein, A., Scheier, M. F., & Buss, A. H. (1975). Public and private self-consciousness: Assessment and theory. *Journal of Consulting and Clinical Psychology, 43,* 522–527.

Ferguson, C. K., & Kelley, H. H. (1964). Significant factors in overevaluation of own group's product. *Journal of Abnormal and Social Psychology, 69,* 223–228.

Feshbach, S. (1961). The stimulating versus cathartic effects of a vicarious aggressive activity. *Journal of Abnormal and Social Psychology, 63,* 381–385.

Feshbach, S. & Singer, R. D. (1971). *Television and aggression: An experimental field study.* San Francisco: Jossey-Bass.

Festinger, L. (1950). Informal social communication. *Psychological Review, 57,* 271–282.

Festinger, L. (1954). A theory of social comparison processes. *Human Relations, 7,* 117–140.

Festinger, L. (1957). *A theory of cognitive dissonance.* Stanford, CA: Stanford University Press.

Festinger, L. (1964). *Conflict, decision and dissonance.* Stanford, CA: Stanford University Press.

Festinger, L. (1980). *Retrospections on social psychology.* New York: Oxford University Press.

Festinger, L. & Carlsmith, J. M. (1959). Cognitive consequences of forced compliance. *Journal of Abnormal and Social Psychology, 58,* 203–210. © 1959 by the American Psychological Association. Adapted by permission of the authors.

Festinger, L., Pepitone, A., & Newcomb, T. (1952). Some consequences of deindividuation in a group. *Journal of Abnormal and Social Psychology, 47,* 382–389.

Festinger, L., Riecken, H. W., & Schachter, S. (1956). *When prophecy fails.* Minneapolis: University of Minnesota Press.

Festinger, L., Schachter, S., & Back, K. (1950). *Social pressures in informal groups: A study of a housing community.* Material reprinted with the permission of the publishers, Stanford University Press. Copyright © 1950 by Leon Festinger, Stanley Schachter, and Kurt Back.

Fiedler, F. E. (1964). A contingency model of leadership effectiveness. In L. Berkowitz (Ed.), *Advances in experimental social psychology* (Vol. 1). New York: Academic Press.

Fiedler, F. E. (1977). A rejoinder to Schriesheim and Kerr's premature obituary of the contingency model. In J. G. Hunt and L. L. Larson (Eds.), *Leadership: The cutting edge.* Carbondale: Southern Illinois University Press.

Fiedler, F. E. (1978). Recent developments in research on the contingency model. In L. Berkowitz (Ed.), *Group process* (pp. 209–225). New York: Academic Press.

Fiedler, F. E., Chemers, M. M., & Mahar, L. (1976). *Improving leadership effectiveness: The leader match concept.* New York: Wiley.

Filley, A. (1975). *Interpersonal conflict resolution.* Glenview, IL: Scott, Foresman.

Fincham, F. D., & Jaspers, J. M. (1980). Attribution of responsibility: From man the scientist to man as lawyer. In L. Berkowitz (Ed.), *Advances in experimental social psychology* (Vol. 13, pp. 82–139). New York: Academic Press.

Fischer, C. S. (1976). *The urban experience.* New York: Harcourt Brace Jovanovich.

Fischoff, B. (1975). Hindsight = foresight: the effects of outcome knowledge on judgment under uncertainty. *Journal of Experimental Psychology: Human Perception and Performance, 1,* 288–299.

Fishbein, M., & Ajzen, I. (1975). *Belief, attitude, intention and behavior: An introduction to theory and research.* Reading, MA: Addison-Wesley.

Fisher, J., Bell, P., & Baum, A. (1984).

Environmental psychology (Vol. 2). New York: Holt, Rinehart & Winston.

Fisher, J., & Byrne, D. (1975). Too close for comfort: Sex differences in response to invasions of personal space. *Journal of Personality and Social Psychology, 32,* 15–21.

Fiske, S. T., & Taylor, S. E. (1984). *Social cognition.* Reading, MA: Addison-Wesley. Copyright © 1985 by Newbery Award Records, Inc. and Random House.

Fleiner, S., & Kelley, H. H. (1978). Study cited (but not referenced) in H. H. Kelley, *Personal relationships: Their structures and processes* (p. 5). Hillsdale, NJ: Erlbaum.

Fleming, E. S., & Anttonen, R. G. (1971). Teacher expectancy as related to the academic and personal growth of primary-age children. *Monographs of the Society for Research in Child Development, 36* (Serial no. 145).

Folger, R., & Greenberg, J. (1985). Procedural justice: An interpretive analysis of personnel systems. In K. Rowland & G. Ferris (Eds.), *Research in personnel and human resource management.* Greenwich, CT: JAI Press.

Forsyth, D. (1983). *An introduction to group dynamics.* Monterey, CA: Brooks/Cole.

Foss, R. D. (1981). Structural effects in simulated jury decision making. *Journal of Personality and Social Psychology, 40,* 1053–1062.

Frank, R. E., & Greenberg, M. G. (1980). *The public's use of television: Who watches and why.* Beverly Hills, CA: Sage.

Fraser, S., Gouge, C., & Billig, M. (1971). Risky shifts, cautious shifts and group polarization. *European Journal of Social Psychology, 1,* 7–29.

Freedman, J. L. (1984). Effect of television violence on aggressiveness. *Psychological Bulletin, 96*(2), 227–246.

Freedman, J. L., & Fraser, S. (1966). Compliance without pressure: The foot-in-the-door technique. *Journal of Personality and Social Psychology, 4,* 195–202.

French, J. R. P., Jr., & Raven, B. H. (1959). The bases of social power. In D. Cartwright (Ed.), *Studies in social power* (pp. 150–167). Ann Arbor: University of Michigan.

Friedman, M., & Rosenman, R. H. (1959). Association of specific overt behavior patterns with blood and cardiovascular findings: Blood cholesterol level, blood clotting time, incidence of arcus senilus, and clinical artery disease. *Journal of the American Medical Association, 169,* 1286.

Friedrich, L. K., & Stein, A. H. (1973). Aggressive and prosocial television programs and the natural behavior of preschool children. *Monographs of the Society for Research in Child Development, 38*(4), Whole No. 151.

Frieze, I., Parsons, J. E., Johnson, P. B., Ruble, D. N., & Zellman, G. L. (1978). *Women and sex roles: A social psychological perspective.* New York: W. W. Norton.

Frieze, I., & Weiner, B. (1971). Cue utilization and attributional judgments for success and failure. *Journal of Personality, 39,* 591–606.

Frodi, A. (1977). Sexual arousal, situational restrictiveness, and aggressive behavior. *Journal of Research in Personality, 11,* 48–58.

Froming, W. J., & Carver, C. S. (1981). Divergent influence of private and public self-consciousness in a compliance paradigm. *Journal of Research in Personality, 15,* 159–171.

Fromm, E. (1956). *The art of loving.* New York: Harper & Row.

Gabrenya, W. K., & Arkin, R. M.

(1980). Self-monitoring scale: Factor structure and correlates. *Personality and Social Psychology Bulletin, 6,* 12–22.

Gaertner, S. L. (1970). A "call" for help: Helping behavior extended to black and white victims by New York City Liberal and Conservative Party members. *Proceedings of the 78th Annual Convention of the American Psychological Association* (Vol. 5), pp. 441–442.

Gailey, P. (1982, January 15). Four rescuers praised: Courage of fourth is known, but not the name. *The New York Times,* p. D14.

Gallo, P. S. (1966). Effects of increased incentives upon the use of threat in bargaining. *Journal of Personality and Social Psychology, 4,* 14–20.

Gamson, W. A. A. (1961). A theory of coalition formation. *American Sociological Review, 26,* 373–382.

Gamson, W. A. A. (1964). Experimental studies of coalition formation. In L. Berkowitz (Ed.), *Advances in experimental social psychology* (Vol. 1). New York: Academic Press.

Gatchel, R. J., & Baum, A. (1983). *An introduction to health psychology.* Reading, MA: Addison-Wesley.

Geen, R. G., & Stoner, D. (1973). Context effects in observed violence. *Journal of Personality and Social Psychology, 25,* 145–150.

Geen, R. G. (1981). Evaluation apprehension and social facilitation: A reply to Sanders. *Journal of Experimental Social Psychology, 17,* 252–256.

Geen, R. G., & Quanty, M. (1977). The catharsis of aggression: An evaluation of a hypothesis. In L. Berkowitz (Ed.), *Advances in Experimental Social Psychology* (Vol. 10). New York: Academic Press.

Geen, R. G., Rakosky, J. J., & Pigg, R. (1972). Awareness of arousal and its relation to aggression. *British*

Journal of Social and Clinical Psychology, 11, 115–121.

Gelman, E., Wang, P., Powell, W., & Smith, V. E. (1985, July 22). Hey America, Coke are it! *Newsweek, 106*(4), pp. 40–42.

Gerard, H. B. (1963). Emotional uncertainty and social comparsion. *Journal of Abnormal and Social Psychology, 66*, 568–573.

Gerard, H. B., & Mathewson, G. (1966). The effects of severity of initiation on liking for a group: A replication. *Journal of Experimental Social Psychology, 2*, 278–287.

Gerard, H. B., Wilhelmy, R. A., & Conolley, E. S. (1968). Conformity and group size. *Journal of Personality and Social Psychology, 8*, 79–82.

Gerbner, G., Gross, L., Morgan, M., & Signorielli, N. (1980). The "mainstreaming" of America: Violence profile No. 11. *Journal of Communication, 30*(3), 10–29.

Gergen, K. J. (1971). *The concept of self.* New York: Holt.

Gergen, K. J., & Taylor, M. G. (1969). Social expectancy and self-presentation in a status hierarchy. *Journal of Experimental Social Psychology, 5*, 79–92.

Gibb, C. A. (1969). Leadership. In G. Lindzey & E. Aronson (Eds.), *The handbook of social psychology* (2nd ed., Vol. 4). Reading, MA: Addison-Wesley.

Gibbons, F. X. (1978). Sexual standards and reaction to pornography: Enhancing behavioral consistency through self-focused attention. *Journal of Personality and Social Psychology, 36*, 976–987.

Gifford, R., & O'Connor, B. (1986). Nonverbal intimacy: Clarifying the role of seating distance and orientation. *Journal of Nonverbal Behavior, 10*, 207–214.

Gilbert, D. T., & Jones, E. E. (1986). Perceiver-induced constraint: Interpretations of self-generated reality. *Journal of Personality and Social Psychology, 50*, 269–280.

Gillig, P. M., & Greenwald, A. G. (1974). Is it time to lay the sleeper effect to rest? *Journal of Personality and Social Psychology, 29*, 132–139.

Ginosar, Z., & Trope, Y. (1980). The effects of base rates and individuating information on judgments about another person. *Journal of Experimental Social Psychology, 16*, 228–242.

Gintner, G., & Lindskold, S. (1975). Rate of participation and expertise as factors influencing leader choice. *Journal of Personality and Social Psychology, 32*, 1085–1089. © 1975 by the American Psychological Association.

Glass, D. C. (1977). *Behavior patterns, stress, and coronary disease.* Hillsdale, NJ: Erlbaum.

Glass, D. C., & Singer, J. E. (1972). *Urban stress.* New York: Academic Press.

Goethals, G. R. (1986). Fabricating and ignoring social reality: Self-serving estimates of consensus. In J. M. Olson, C. P. Herman, & M. P. Zanna (Eds.), *Relative deprivation and social comparison: The Ontario symposium* (Vol. 4, pp. 135–157). Hillsdale, NJ: Erlbaum.

Goethals, G. R., Allison, S. J., & Frost, M. (1979). Perceptions of the magnitude and diversity of social support. *Journal of Experimental Social Psychology, 15*, 570–581.

Goethals, G. R., Cooper, J., & Naficy, A. (1979). Role of foreseen, foreseeable, unforeseeable behavioral consequences in the arousal of cognitive dissonance. *Journal of Personality and Social Psychology, 37*,

1179–1185. © 1979 by the American Psychological Association. Adapted by permission of the authors.

Goethals, G. R., & Darley, J. M. (1977). Social comparison theory: An attributional approach. In J. M. Suls & R. L. Miller (Eds.), *Social comparison processes: Theoretical and empirical perspectives*. Washington, DC: Hemisphere/Halsted.

Goethals, G. R., & Darley, J. M. (1987). Social comparison theory: Self-evaluation and group life. In B. Mullen & G. R. Goethals (Eds.), *Theories of group behavior*. New York: Springer-Verlag.

Goethals, G. R., & Reckman, R. F. (1973). The perception of consistency in attitudes. *Journal of Experimental Social Psychology, 9*, 491–501.

Goethals, G. R., & Zanna, M. P. (1979). The role of social comparison in choice shifts. *Journal of Personality and Social Psychology, 37*, 1469–1476.

Goffman, E. (1955). On face work: An analysis of ritual elements in social interaction. *Psychiatry, 18*, 213–231.

Goffman, E. (1959). *The presentation of self in everyday life*. Garden City, NY: Doubleday, Anchor Books.

Goffman, E. (1967). *Interaction ritual.* New York: Anchor.

Goldsmith, H. H. (1983). Genetic influences on personality from infancy to adulthood. *Child Development, 54*, 331–355.

Goodstadt, M. (1971). Helping and refusal to help: A test of balance and reactance theories. *Journal of Experimental Social Psychology, 7*, 610–622.

Goranson, R. E., & Berkowitz, L. (1966). Reciprocity and responsibility reactions to prior help. *Journal of Personality and Social Psychology, 3*, 227–232.

Gorsuch, R. L., & Ortberg, J. (1983). Moral obligations and attitudes:

Their relation to behavioral intentions. *Journal of Personality and Social Psychology, 44*, 1025–1028.

Gouldner, A. (1960). The norm of reciprocity: A preliminary statement. *American Sociological Review, 25*, 161–178.

Greenberg, C., & Firestone, I. (1977). Compensatory responses to crowding: Effects of personal space intrusion and privacy reduction. *Journal of Personality and Social Psychology, 35*, 637–644.

Greenberg, J., & Musham, C. (1981). Avoiding and seeking self-focused attention. *Journal of Research in Personality, 15*, 191–200.

Greenberg, J., Pyszczynski, T., & Solomon, S. (1982). The self-serving attributional bias: Beyond self-presentation. *Journal of Experimental Social Psychology, 18*, 56–67.

Greenwald, A. G. (1980). The totalitarian ego: Fabrication and revision of personal history. *American Psychologist, 35*, 603–613.

Greenwald, A. G., & Pratkanis, A. R. (1984). The self. In R. S. Wyer, Jr., & T. K. Srull (Eds.), *Handbook of social cognition* (Vol. 3, pp. 129–178). Hillsdale, NJ: Erlbaum.

Greenwald, A. G., & Ronis, D. L. (1978). Twenty years of cognitive dissonance: Case study of the evolution of a theory. *Psychological Review, 85*, 53–57.

Griffitt, W. (1970). Environmental effects on interpersonal affective behavior: Ambient effective temperature and attraction. *Journal of Personality and Social Psychology, 15*, 240–244.

Griffitt, W., & Guay, P. (1969). "Object" evaluation and conditioned affect. *Journal of Experimental Research in Personality, 4*, 1–8.

Griffitt, W., Nelson, J., & Littlepage, G. (1972). Old age and response to agreement-disagreement. *Journal of Gerontology, 27,* 269–274.

Griffitt, W., & Veitch, R. (1974). Pre-acquaintance attitude similarity and attraction revisited: Ten days in a fall-out shelter. *Sociometry, 37,* 163–173.

Gross, A. E., Wallston, B. S., & Piliavin, I. M. (1975). Beneficiary attractiveness and costs as determinants of responses to routine requests for help. *Sociometry, 38,* 131–140.

Gross, E., & Latané, J. G. (1974). Receiving help, reciprocation, and interpersonal attraction. *Journal of Applied Social Psychology, 4,* 210–223.

Gruder, C. L. (1977). Choice of comparison persons in evaluating oneself. In J. M. Suls & R. L. Miller (Eds.), *Social comparison processes: Theoretical and empirical perspectives.* Washington, DC: Hemisphere/Halsted.

Gruder, C. L., Romer, D., & Korth, B. (1978). Dependency and fault as determinants of helping. *Journal of Experimental Social Psychology, 14,* 227–235.

Grush, J. E., & Yehl, J. G. (1979). Marital roles, sex differences and interpersonal attraction. *Journal of Personality and Social Psychology, 37,* 116–123.

Guerin, B., & Innes, J. (1982). Social facilitation and social monitoring: A new look at Zajonc's mere presence hypothesis. *British Journal of Social Psychology, 21,* 7–18.

Haas, D. F., & Deseran, F. A. (1981). Trust and symbolic exchange. *Social Psychology Quarterly, 44,* 3–13.

Haas, J., & Roberts, G. C. (1975). Effect of evaluative others upon learning and performance of a complex motor task. *Journal of Motor Behavior, 7,* 81–90.

Hackman, J. R., & Morris, C. G. (1975). Group tasks, group interaction process, and group performance effectiveness: A review and proposed integration. In L. Berkowitz (Ed.), *Advances in experimental social psychology* (Vol. 8). New York: Academic Press.

Hackman, J. R., Brousseau, K. R., & Wiess, J. A. (1976). The interaction of task design and group performance strategies in determining group effectiveness. *Organizational Behavior and Human Performance, 16,* 350–365.

Hakmiller, K. L. (1966). Threat as a determinant of downward comparison. *Journal of Experimental Social Psychology* (Suppl. 1), 32–39.

Hall, E. T. (1959). *The silent language.* New York: Fawcett.

Hall, E. T. (1966). *The hidden dimension.* New York: Doubleday.

Hall, J. A. (1984). *Nonverbal sex differences: Communication accuracy and expressive style.* Baltimore: Johns Hopkins Press.

Hall, J. A., & Taylor, S. E. (1976). When love is blind: Maintaining idealized images of one's spouse. *Human Relations, 29,* 751–761.

Halpin, A., & Winer, B. (1952). *The leadership behavior of the airplane commander.* Columbus, OH: The Ohio State University Research Foundation.

Hamblin, R. (1958). Leadership and crisis. *Sociometry, 21,* 322–335.

Hamilton, D. L. (1979). A cognitive attributional analysis of stereotyping. In L. Berkowitz (Ed.), *Advances in experimental social psychology* (Vol. 12, pp. 53–84). New York: Academic Press.

Hamilton, D. L., & Gifford, R. K. (1976). Illusory correlation in interpersonal perception: A cognitive basis of stereotypic judgments. *Journal of Experimental Social Psychology, 12,* 392–407.

Hamilton, D. L., Katz, L. B., & Leirer, V. O. (1980). Cognitive representation of personality impressions: Organizational processes in first impression formation. *Journal of Personality and Social Psychology, 39,* 1050–1063.

Hamilton, D. L., & Trollier, T. (in press). Stereotypes and stereotyping: An overview of the cognitive approach. In J. Dovidio & S. L. Gaertner (Eds.), *Prejudice, discrimination and racism: Theory and research.* New York: Academic Press.

Hamilton, D. L., & Zanna, M. P. (1974). Context effects in impression formation: Changes in connotative meaning. *Journal of Personality and Social Psychology, 29,* 649–654.

Hammock, T., & Brehm, J. W. (1966). The attractiveness of choice alternatives when freedom to choose is eliminated by a social agent. *Journal of Personality, 34,* 546–554.

Hamner, W. C. (1974). Effects of bargaining strategy and pressure to reach agreement in a stalemated negotiation. *Journal of Personality and Social Psychology, 30,* 458–467.

Hancock, R. D., & Sorrentino, R. M. (1980). The effects of expected future interaction and prior group support on the conformity process. *Journal of Experimental Social Psychology, 16,* 261–270.

Hansen, R. D., & Donoghue, J. M. (1977). The power of concensus: Information derived from one's own and other's behavior. *Journal of Personality and Social Psychology, 35*(5), 294–302.

Hardin, G. (1968). The tragedy of the commons. *Science, 162,* 1243–1248.

Hardy, R. C. (1976). A test of the poor leader: Member relations cells of the contingency model on elementary school children. *Child Development, 46,* 958–964.

Harkins, S. G., & Petty, R. E. (1981a). The effects of source magnification of cognitive effect on attitudes. An information-processing view. *Journal of Personality and Social Psychology, 40,* 401–413.

Harkins, S. G., & Petty, R. E. (1981b). The multiple source effect in persuasion: The effects of distraction. *Personality and Social Psychology Bulletin, 7,* 627–635.

Harkins, S. G., & Petty, R. E. (1983). Social context effects in persuasion: The effects of multiple sources and multiple targets. In P. Paulhus (Ed.), *Basic group processes* (pp. 149–175). New York: Springer-Verlag.

Harkins, S. G., & Petty, R. E. (1987). Information utility and the multiple source effect. *Journal of Personality and Social Psychology, 52,* 260–268.

Harris, M. B. (1974). Mediators between frustration and aggression in a field experiment. *Journal of Experimental Social Psychology, 10,* 561–571.

Harris, R. F., & Lindsay, D. (1972). *The state of cities.* New York: Praeger.

Harrison, A. A. (1977). Mere exposure. In L. Berkowitz (Ed.), *Advances in experimental social psychology* (Vol. 10). New York: Academic Press.

Harshberger, D. (1971). An investigation of a structural model of small group problem solving. *Human Relations, 24,* 43–63.

Harvey, J. H., Town, J. P., & Yarkin, K. C. (1981). How fundamental is "the fundamental attribution error?" *Journal of Personality and Social Psychology, 40,* 346–349.

Hass, R. G. (1981). Effects of source characteristics on cognitive responses and persuasion. In R. E. Petty, T. M. Ostrom, & T. C. Brock

(Eds.), *Cognitive responses in persuasion* (pp. 141–172). Hillsdale, NJ: Erlbaum.

Hass, R. G., & Grady, K. (1975). Temporal delay, type of forewarning, and resistance to influence. *Journal of Experimental Social Psychology, 11,* 459–469.

Hastie, R., Penrod, S. D., & Pennington, N. (1984). *Inside the jury.* Cambridge: Massachusetts Institute of Technology Press.

Hastorf, A., & Cantril, H. (1954). They saw a game. *Journal of Abnormal and Social Psychology, 49,* 129–134.

Hayduk, L. A. (1978). Personal space: An evaluative and orienting overview. *Psychological Bulletin, 85,* 117–134.

Hayduk, L. A. (1983). Personal space: Where we now stand. *Psychological Bulletin, 94,* 293–335.

Hediger, H. (1950). *Wild animals in captivity.* London: Butterworth.

Heider, F. (1944). Social perception and phenomenal causality. *Psychological Review, 51,* 358–374.

Heider, F. (1946). Attitudes and cognitive organization. *Journal of Psychology, 21,* 107–112.

Heider, F. (1958). *The psychology of interpersonal relations.* New York: Wiley.

Helmreich, R., Aronson, E., & LeFan, J. (1970). To err is humanizing—sometimes: Effects of self-esteem, competence and a prat-fall on interpersonal attraction. *Journal of Personality and Social Psychology, 16,* 259–264.

Henchy, T., & Glass, D. C. (1968). Evaluation apprehension and the social facilitation of dominant and subordinate responses. *Journal of Personality and Social Psychology, 10,* 446–454.

Hendrick, C., & Constantini, A. F. (1970). Effects of varying trait inconsistency and response requirements on the primacy effect in impression formation. *Journal of Personality and Social Psychology, 15,* 158–164.

Henley, N. M. (1977). *Body politics: Power, sex, and nonverbal communication.* Englewood Cliffs, NJ: Prentice-Hall.

Hess, E. H. (1965). The pupil responds to changes in attitude as well as to changes in illumination. *Scientific American, 212,* 46–54.

Hesselgren, S. (1975). *Man's perception of man-made environment.* Stroudsburg, PA: Dowden, Hutchinson, & Ross.

Heyerdahl, T. (1950). *Kon-Tiki.* Chicago: Rand McNally.

Higgins, E. T., & Bryant, S. L. (1982). Consensus information and the fundamental attribution error: The role of development and in-group versus out-group knowledge. *Journal of Personality and Social Psychology, 43,* 889–900.

Higgins, E. T., & McCann, C. D. (1984). Social encoding and subsequent attitudes, impressions, and memory: Context driven and motivational aspects of processing. *Journal of Personality and Social Psychology, 47,* 26–39.

Higgins, E. T., Rhodewalt, F., & Zanna, M. P. (1979). Dissonance motivation: Its nature, persistance, and reinstatement. *Journal of Experimental Social Psychology, 15,* 16–34.

Higgins, E. T., & Rholes, W. S. (1976). Impression formation and role fulfillment: A "holistic reference" approach. *Journal of Experimental Social Psychology, 12,* 422–435.

Higgins, E. T., & Rholes, W. S. (1978). "Saying is believing": Effects of message modification on memory and liking for the person described. *Journal of Experimental Social Psychology, 14,* 363–378.

Higgins, E. T., Rholes, W. S., & Jones, C. R. (1977). Category accessibility and impression formation. *Journal of Experimental Social Psychology, 13,* 141–154.

Hill, C. T., Rubin, Z., & Peplau, L. A. (1976). Breakups before marriage: The end of 103 affairs. *Journal of Social Issues, 32*(1), 147–168.

Hiltrop, J. M., & Rubin, J. Z. (1981). Position loss and image loss in bargaining. *Journal of Conflict Resolution, 25,* 521–534.

Hinkle, S. (1975). *Cognitive consistency effects on attitudes toward ingroup and outgroup products.* Unpublished doctoral dissertation, University of North Carolina, Chapel Hill.

Hinkle, S., & Schopler, J. (1986). Bias in the evaluation of in-group and out-group performance. In S. Worchel & W. Austin (Eds.), *Psychology of intergroup relations.* Chicago: Nelson-Hall.

Hiroto, D. S., & Seligman, M. E. P. (1975). Generality of learned helplessness in man. *Journal of Personality and Social Psychology, 31,* 311–327.

Hofling, C. K., Brotzman, E., Dalrymple, S., Graves, N., & Pierce, C. M. (1966). An experimental study in nurse-physician relationships. *The Journal of Nervous and Mental Disease, 143*(2), 171–180.

Hokanson, J. E., Burgess, M., & Cohen, M. F. (1963). Effect of displaced aggression on systolic blood pressure. *Journal of Abnormal and Social Psychology, 67,* 214–218.

Hokanson, J. E., & Shelter, S. (1961). The effect of overt aggression on physiological arousal level. *Journal of Abnormal and Social Psychology, 63,* 446–448.

Holahan, C. J. (1982). *Environmental psychology.* New York: Random House.

Hollander, E. P. (1958). Conformity, status and idiosyncrasy credit. *Psychological Review, 65,* 117–127.

Hollander, E. P. (1978). *Leadership dynamics: A practical guide to effective relationships.* New York: Free Press/Macmillan. Copyright © 1978 by The Free Press, a division of Macmillan Publishing Co., Inc.

Hollander, E. P. (1985). Leadership and power. In G. Lindzey & E. Aronson (Eds.), *The handbook of social psychology* (3rd ed. Vol. 2, pp. 485–537). New York: Random House.

Hollander, E. P., & Willis, R. H. (1964). An experimental study of three response modes in social influence situation. *Journal of Abnormal and Social Psychology, 69,* 150–156.

Horai, J., & Tedeschi, J. T. (1969). Effects of credibility and magnitude of punishment on compliance to threats. *Journal of Personality and Social Psychology, 12,* 164–169.

Horner, M. S. (1970). Femininity and successful achievement: A basic inconsistency. In J. Bardwick, E. L. Douvan, M. S. Horner, & D. Gutmann (Eds.), *Feminine personality and conflict.* Monterey, CA: Brooks/Cole.

Horner, M. S. (1972). Toward an understanding of achievement-related conflicts in women. *Journal of Social Issues, 28,* 157–175.

Houseknecht, R. (1977). Reference group support for voluntary childlessness. *Journal of Marriage and the Family, 39,* 285–292.

Hovland, C. I., Harvey, O., & Sherif, M. (1957). Assimilation and contrast effects in communication and attitude change. *Journal of Abnormal and Social Psychology, 55,* 242–252.

Hovland, C. I., Janis, I. L., & Kelley, H. H. (1953). *Communication and persuasion.* New Haven, CT: Yale University Press.

Hovland, C. I., Lumsdaine, A., & Shef-field, F. (1949). *Experiments on mass communications* (Studies in social psychology in World War II, Vol. 3, published by Social Science Research Council, 226). Princeton, NJ: Princeton University Press. Reprinted by permission of Princeton University Press.

Hovland, C. I., & Sears, R. R. (1940). Minor studies in aggression: VI. Correlation of lynchings with economic indices. *Journal of Psychology, 9,* 301–310.

Hovland, C. I., & Weiss, W. (1952). The influence of source credibility on communication effectiveness. *The Public Opinion Quarterly, 15,* 635–650.

Howard, D. (1972). *Territory in bird life.* New York: Dutton.

Howard, J. W., & Rothbart, M. (1980). Social categorization and memory for in-group and out-group behavior. *Journal of Personality and Social Psychology, 38,* 301–310.

Howard, M. (1982). *Eppie: The Story of Ann Landers.* New York: Putnam.

Howe, K. G., & Zanna, M. P. (1975). *Sex appropriateness of the task and achievement behavior.* Paper read at Eastern Psychological Association, New York.

Howells, L. T., & Becker, S. W. (1962). Seating arrangement and leadership emergence. *Journal of Abnormal and Social Psychology, 64,* 148–150.

Huesmann, L. R. (1982). Television violence and aggressive behavior. In D. Pearl & L. Bouthilet (Eds.), *Television and behavior: Ten years of scientific progress and implications for the 80's.* Washington, D.C.: U.S. Government Printing Office.

Hurwitz, J., Zander, A., & Hymoritch, B. (1960). Some effects of power on the relations among group mem-bers. In D. Cartwright & A. Zander (Eds.), *Group dynamics: Research and theory* (2nd ed.). Evanston, IL: Row, Peterson.

Huston, T. L. (1973). Ambiguity of acceptance, social desirability, and dating choice. *Journal of Experimental Social Psychology, 9,* 32–42.

Huston, T. L., & Levinger, G. (1978). Interpersonal attraction and relationships. *Annual Review of Psychology, 29,* 115–156.

Hyman, H. H., & Sheatsley, P. B. (1954). The authoritarian personality—A methodological critique. In R. Chrisite & M. Jahoda (Eds.), *Studies in the scope and method of "The authoritarian personality."* New York: Free Press.

Hymes, R. W. (1980). Political attitudes as social categories: A new look at selective memory. *Journal of Personality and Social Psychology, 51,* 233–241.

Imada, A. S., & Hakel, M. D. (1977). Influence of nonverbal communication and rater proximity on impressions and decisions in simulated employment interviews. *Journal of Applied Psychology, 62,* 295–300.

Insko, C. A. (1965). Verbal reinforcement of attitude. *Journal of Personality and Social Psychology, 2,* 621–623.

Insko, C. A., Thibaut, J., Moehle, D., Wilson, M., Diamond, W. D., Gilmore, R., Soloman, M. K., & Lipsitz, A. (1980). Social evolution and the emergence of leadership. *Journal of Personality and Social Psychology, 39,* 431–449.

Isen, A. M. (1970). Success, failure, attention and reactions to others: The warm glow of success. *Journal of Personality and Social Psychology, 15,* 294–301.

Isen, A. M., Clark, M., & Schwartz, M. F. (1976). Duration of the effect of good mood on helping: "Footprints on the sands of time." *Journal of Personality and Social Psychology, 34,* 385–393.

Isen, A. M., & Levin, P. F. (1972). The effect of feeling good on helping: Cookies and kindness. *Journal of Personality and Social Psychology, 21,* 284–388.

Isen, A. M., & Simmonds, S. F. (1978). The effect of feeling good on a helping task that is incompatible with good mood. *Social Psychology, 41,* 346– 349.

Isenberg, D. J. (1986). Group polarization: A critical review and meta-analysis. *Journal of Personality and Social Psychology, 50,* 1141–1151.

Ittelson, W. H., Proshansky, H. M., Rivlin, L. G., & Winkel, G. (1974). *An introduction to environmental psychology.* New York: Holt, Rinehart & Winston.

Jackson, J. M. (1987). Social impact theory. In B. Mullen & G. R. Goethals, *Theories of group behavior.* New York: Springer-Verlag.

Jackson, J. M., & Latané, B. (1981). All alone in front of all those people: Stage fright as a function of a number and type of co-performance and audience. *Journal of Personality and Social Psychology, 40,* 73–85.

Jacobs, R. C., & Campbell, D. T. (1961). The perpetuation of an arbitrary tradition through several generations of a laboratory misoculture. *Journal of Abnormal and Social Psychology, 62,* 649–658.

Jacobs, T. O. (1971). *Leadership and exchange in formal organizations.* Alexandria, VA: Human Resources Research Organization.

James, W. (1890). *Psychology.* New York: Holt.

Janis, I. L. (1972). *Victims of groupthink: A psychological study of foreign policy decisions and fiascoes.* Boston: Houghton Mifflin.

Janis, I. (1982). *Groupthink* (2nd ed.). Boston: Houghton Mifflin.

Janis, I. L., & Feshbach, S. (1953). Effects of fear-arousing communications. *Journal of Abnormal and Social Psychology, 48,* 78–92. © 1953 by the American Psychological Association.

Janis, I. L., Kaye, D., & Kirschner, P. (1965). Facilitating effects of "eating-while-reading" on responsiveness to persuasive communications. *Journal of Personality and Social Psychology, 1,* 181–186. © 1965 by the American Psychological Association. Adapted by permission of the authors.

Janis, I. L., & Terwilliger, R. F. (1962). An experimental study of psychological resistances to fear-arousing communications. *Journal of Applied Social Psychology, 65,* 403–410.

Jellison, J. M., & Green, J. (1981). A self-presentational approach to the fundamental attribution error: The norm of internality. *Journal of Personality and Social Psychology, 40,* 643–649.

Jensen, A. R. (1969). How much can we boost IQ and scholastic achievement? *Harvard Educational Review, 39,* 1–123.

Johnson, H. G., Ekman, P., & Friesen, W. V. (1975). Communicative body movements: American emblems. *Semiotica, 15,* 335–353.

Johnson, R. J., Feigenbaum, R., & Weiby, M. (1964). Some determinants and consequences of the teacher's perception of causation. *Journal of Educational Psychology, 55,* 237–246. © 1964 by the American Psychological Association.

Johnson v. Louisiana, 92 U.S. 1935 (1972).

Jones, E. E. (1964). *Ingratiation.* New York: Appleton-Century-Crofts. © 1964 by the Meredith Publishing

Company. Material reprinted by permission of Irvington Publishers, Inc.

Jones, E. E. (1965). Conformity as a tactic of ingratiation. *Science, 149,* 144–150.

Jones, E. E. (1979). The rocky road from acts to dispositions. *American Psychologist, 34,* 107–117.

Jones, E. E. (1985). Major developments in social psychology during the past five decades. In G. Lindzey & E. Aronson (Eds.), *Handbook of social psychology* (3rd ed., Vol. 1), pp. 1–46). New York: Random House.

Jones, E. E., & Archer, R. L. (1976). Are there special effects of personalistic self-disclosure? *Journal of Experimental Social Psychology, 12,* 180–193.

Jones, E. E., & Berglas, S. (1978). Control of attributions about the self through self-handicapping strategies: The appeal of alcohol and the role of underachievement. *Personality and Social Psychology Bulletin,* 4(2), 200–206.

Jones, E. E., & Davis, K. E. (1965). From acts to dispositions: The attribution process in person perception. In L. Berkowitz (Ed.), *Advances in experimental social psychology* (Vol. 2). New York: Academic Press.

Jones, E. E., Davis, K. E., & Gergen, K. (1961). Role playing variations and their informational value for person perception. *Journal of Abnormal and Social Psychology, 63,* 302–310. © 1961 by the American Psychological Association.

Jones, E. E., & Gerard, H. (1967). *Foundations of social psychology.* New York: Wiley.

Jones, E. E., Gergen, K. J., & Jones, R. G. (1964). Tactics of ingratiation among leaders and subordinates in a status hierarchy. *Psychological Monographs, 77* (3, whole no. 566).

Jones, E. E., & Gordon, E. M. (1972). Timing of self-disclosure and its effects on personal attraction. *Journal of Personality and Social Psychology, 24,* 358–365.

Jones, E. E., & Harris, V. A. (1967). The attribution of attitudes. *Journal of Experimental Psychology, 3,* 1–24. © 1967 by the American Psychological Association. Adapted by permission of the authors.

Jones, E. E., & Jones, R. G. (1964). Optimum conformity as an ingratiation tactic. *Journal of Personality, 32,* 436–458.

Jones, E. E., Jones, R. G., & Gergen, K. J. (1963). Some conditions affecting the evaluation of a conformist. *Journal of Personality, 31,* 270–288.

Jones, E. E., & McGillis, D. (1976). Correspondent inferences and the attribution cube: A comparative reappraisal. In J. H. Harvey, W. J. Ickes, & R. F. Kidd (Eds.), *New directions in attribution research* (Vol. 1). Hillsdale, NJ: Erlbaum.

Jones, E. E., & Nisbett, R. E. (1971). *The actor and the observer: Divergent perceptions of the causes of behavior.* Morristown, NJ: General Learning Press.

Jones, E. E., & Pittman, T. S. (1982). Toward a general theory of strategic self presentation. In J. Suls (Ed.), *Psychological perspectives on the self.* Hillsdale, NJ: Erlbaum.

Jones, E. E., Rhodewalt, F., Berglas, S., & Skelton, J. A. (1981). Effects of strategic self-presentation on subsequent self esteem. *Journal of Personality and Social Psychology, 41,* 407–421.

Jones, E. E., Rock, L., Shaver, K. G., Goethals, G. R., & Ward, L. M. (1968). Pattern of performance and ability attribution: An unexpected primacy effect. *Journal of Personality and Social Psychology, 10,* 317–340.

Jones, E. E., & Sigall, H. (1971). The bogus pipeline: A new paradigm for measuring affect and attitude. *Psychological Bulletin, 76,* 349–364.

Jones, E. E., Wood, G. C., & Quattrone, G. A. (1981). Perceived variability of personal characteristics in ingroups and out-groups: The role of knowledge and evaluation. *Personality and Social Psychology Bulletin, 7,* 523–528.

Jones, E. E., Worchel, S., Goethals, G. R., & Grumet, J. F. (1971). Prior expectancy and behavioral extremity as determinants of attitude attribution. *Journal of Experimental Social Psychology, 7,* 59–80.

Jones, E. E., & Wortman, C. (1973). *Ingratiation: An attributional approach.* Morristown, NJ: General Learning Press.

Jones, T. (1980). *Adrift.* New York: Avon. Reprinted with permission of Macmillan Publishing Company from *Adrift* by Tristan Jones. Copyright © 1980 by Tristan Jones.

Jones, R. A., & Brehm, J. W. (1970). Persuasiveness of one and two-sided communications as a function of awareness there are two sides. *Journal of Experimental Social Psychology, 6,* 47–56.

Jones, R. A., & Cooper, J. (1971). The mediation of experimenter effects. *Journal of Personality and Social Psychology, 20,* 71–74.

Jones, R. F. (1985, September 2). Warriors who will not stay down. *Sports Illustrated,* pp. 28–38.

Jourard, S. M. (1971). *The transparent self* (2nd ed.) New York: Van Nostrand Reinhold.

Julian, J. W., Regula, C. R., & Hollander, E. P. (1968). Effects of prior agreement from others on task con-

fidence and conformity. *Journal of Personality and Social Psychology, 9,* 171–178.

Kabanoff, B. (1981). A critique of leader match and its implication for leadership research. *Personnel Psychology, 34,* 749–764.

Kahn, A., & Tice, T. (1973). Returning a favor and retaliating harm: The effects of stated intentions and actual behavior. *Journal of Experimental Social Psychology, 9,* 43–56.

Kahneman, D., & Tversky, A. (1973). On the psychology of prediction. *Psychological Review, 80,* 237–251.

Kamin, L. J. (1974). *The science and politics of I.Q.* Hillsdale, NJ: Erlbaum.

Kandel, D. (1978). Homophily, selection and socialization in adolescent friendships. *American Journal of Sociology, 84,* 427–436.

Kane, T. K., Joseph, J. M., & Tedeschi, J. T. (1976). Person perception and the Berkowitz paradigm for the study of aggression. *Journal of Personality and Social Psychology, 33,* 663–673.

Kaplan, M. F. (1975). Information integration in social judgment: Interaction of judge and informational components. In M. Kaplan and S. Schwartz (Eds.), *Human judgment and decision processes.* New York: Academic Press.

Karlin, M., Coffman, J., & Walters, G. (1969). On the fading of social stereotypes: Studies in three generations of college students. *Journal of Personality and Social Psychology, 13,* 1–16.

Karuza, J., Jr., & Brickman, P. (1981). Preference for similarity in higher and lower status others. *Personality and Social Psychology Bulletin, 7,* 504–508.

Kassin, S. M. (1979). Concensus information, prediction and causal attribution: A review of the literature and issues. *Journal of Personality and Social Psychology, 37*, 1966–1981.

Kassin, S. M. (1985). Eyewitness identification: Retrospective self-awareness and the accuracy-confidence correlation. *Journal of Personality and Social Psychology, 49*, 878–893.

Katz, D., & Kahn, R. L. (1978). *The social psychology of organizations* (2nd ed.). New York: Wiley.

Katz, H., Cadoret, R., Hughes, K., & Abbey, D. (1965). Physiological correlates of acceptable and unacceptable attitude statements. *Psychological Reports, 17*, 78.

Katz, J., Glucksberg, S., & Krauss, I. (1960). Need satisfaction and Edwards PPS scores in married couples. *Journal of Consulting Psychology, 24*, 205–208.

Kelley, H. H. (1950). The warm-cold variable in first impressions of persons. *Journal of Personality, 18*, 431–439.

Kelley, H. H. (1952). Two functions of reference groups. In G. E. Swanson, T. M. Newcomb, & E. L. Hartley (Eds.), *Readings in social psychology* (2nd ed.). New York: Holt, Rinehart & Winston.

Kelley, H. H. (1966). A classroom study of the dilemmas in interpersonal negotiations. In K. Archibald (Ed.), *Strategic interaction and conflict*. Berkeley, CA: University of California, Institution of International Studies.

Kelley, H. H. (1967). Attribution theory in social psychology. In D. Levine (Ed.), *Nebraska Symposium on Motivation, 15*, 192–238.

Kelley, H. H. (1971). *Attribution in social interaction*. Morristown, NJ: General Learning Press.

Kelley, H. H. (1979). *Personal relationships: Their structures and processes*. Hillsdale, NJ: Erlbaum.

Kelley, H. H. (1982). Love and commitment. In H. H. Kelley, E. Berscheid, A. Christensen, J. Harvey, T. L. Huston, G. Levinger, & D. R. Peterson (Eds.), *The psychology of close relationships*. New York: Academic Press.

Kelley, H. H., & Stahelski, A. J. (1970a). Errors in perception of intentions in a mixed motive game. *Journal of Experimental Social Psychology, 6*, 379–400.

Kelley, H. H., & Stahelski, A. J. (1970b). Social interaction basis of cooperators and competitors' beliefs about others. *Journal of Personality and Social Psychology, 16*, 66–91(6). © 1970 by the American Psychological Association. Adapted by permission of the authors.

Kelley, H. H., & Thibaut, J. W. (1978). *Interpersonal relations: A theory of interdependence*. New York: Wiley Interscience.

Kellogg, R., & Baron, R. S. (1975). Attribution theory, insomnia, and the reverse placebo effect: A reversal of Storms and Nisbett's findings. *Journal of Personality and Social Psychology, 32*, 231–236.

Kelly, J. G., Ferson, J. E., & Holtzman, W. H. (1958). The measurement of attitudes toward the Negro in the South. *Journal of Social Psychology, 48*, 305–312.

Kelman, H. C. (1961). Processes of opinion change. *Public Opinion Quarterly, 25*, 57–78.

Kelman, H. C., & Hovland, C. I. (1953). "Reinstatement" of the communicator in delayed measurement of opinion change. *Journal of Abnormal and Social Psychology, 48*, 326–335. © 1953 by the American Psychological Association.

Kenny, D. A. (1985). Quantitative methods for social psychology. In G. Lindzey & E. Aronson (Eds.), *Handbook of social psychology* (3rd ed., Vol. 1, pp. 1–46). New York: Random House.

Kenrick, D. T., Dantchik, A., & MacFarlane, S. (1983). Personality, environment and criminal behavior. In W. S. Laufer & J. M. Day (Eds.), *Personality theory, moral development, and criminal behavior.* Lexington, MA: D. C. Heath.

Kenrick, D. T., & Trost, M. R. (1987). A biosocial model of heterosexual relationships. In K. Kelley (Ed.), *Males, females, and sexuality: Theory and research.* Albany, NY: SUNY Press.

Kerckhoff, A., & Davis, K. E. (1962). Value consensus and need complementarity in mate selection. *American Sociological Review, 27,* 295–303.

Kerman, S. (1979). Teacher expectations and student achievement. *Phi Delta Kappan, 60,* 716–718.

Kernis, M. H., & Wheeler, L. (1981). Beautiful friends and ugly strangers: Radiation and contrast effects in perception of same-sex pairs. *Personality and Social Psychology Bulletin, 7,* 224–231.

Kerr, N. L. (1983). Motivation loss in small groups: A social dilemma analysis. *Journal of Personality and Social Psychology, 45,* 819–828.

Kerr, N. L., & Brunn, S. (1983). Dependability of member effort and group motivation loss: Free-rider effects. *Journal of Personality and Social Psychology, 44,* 78–94.

Kerr, N., & MacCoun, R. (1985). The effects of jury size and polling method on the process and product of jury deliberation. *Journal of Personality and Social Psychology, 48,* 349–363.

Kiesler, C. A. (1969). Group pressure and conformity. In J. Mills (Ed.), *Experimental social psychology.* New York: Macmillan.

Kiesler, C. A., & Kiesler, S. B. (1969). *Conformity.* Reading, MA: Addison-Wesley.

Kiesler, C. A., Mathog, R., Pool, P., & Hovenstine, R. (1971). Commitment and the boomerang effect: A field study. Summarized in C. Kiesler (Ed.), *The psychology of commitment: Experiments linking behavior to belief* (pp. 74–85). New York: Academic Press.

Kiesler, C. A., & Munson, P. A. (1975). Attitudes and opinions. In M. R. Rosenzweig & L. W. Porter (Eds.), *Annual review of psychology, 26,* 415–456.

Kiesler, C. A., & Pallak, M. S. (1976). Arousal properties of dissonance manipulations. *Psychological Bulletin, 83,* 1014–1025.

Kiesler, S. B., & Baral, R. L. (1970). The search for a romantic partner: The effects of self-esteem and physical attractiveness on romantic behavior. In K. L. Gergen & D. Marlowe (Eds.), *Personality and social behavior.* Reading, MA: Addison-Wesley.

Kinder, D. R., & Sears, D. O. (1981). Prejudice and politics: Symbolic racism versus racial threats to the good life. *Journal of Personality and Social Psychology, 40,* 414–431.

King, M. L. (1980, March 11). Turned down thermostats turn off workers who face possible federal extension of the rule. *The Wall Street Journal.*

Kipnis, D. M. (1974). Inner direction, other direction and achievement motivation. *Human Development, 17,* 321–343.

Klein, A. L. (1976). Changes in leadership appraisal as a function of the stress of a simulated panic situation. *Journal of Personality and Social Psychology, 34*(6), 1143–1154.

Kleinke, C. L., & Kahn, M. L. (1980). Perceptions of self-disclosers: Effects of sex and physical attractiveness. *Journal of Personality, 48,* 190–205.

Kleinke, C. L., Staneski, R. A., & Weaver, P. (1972). Evaluation of a person who uses another person's name in ingratiating and noningratiating situations. *Journal of Experimental Social Psychology, 8,* 457–466.

Knowles, E. S. (1973). Boundaries around group interaction: The effect of group size and member status on boundary permeability. *Journal of Personality and Social Psychology, 26,* 327–331.

Knowles, E. S. (1983). Social physics and the effects of others: Tests of the effects of audience size and distance on social judgments and behavior. *Journal of Personality and Social Psychology, 45,* 1263–1279.

Knox, R. E., & Inkster, J. A. (1968). Postdecision dissonance at post time. *Journal of Personality and Social Psychology, 8*(4), 319–323.

Knox, R. E., & Safford, R. K. (1976). Group caution at the racetrack. *Journal of Experimental Social Psychology, 12,* 317–324.

Knudson, R. M., Sommers, A. A., & Golding, S. L. (1980). Interpersonal perception and mode of resolution in marital conflict. *Journal of Personality and Social Psychology, 38,* 751–763.

Koch, H. (1967). *The panic broadcast: Portrait of an event.* Boston: Little, Brown.

Kohn, H. (1981). *Who Killed Karen Silkwood?* New York: Summit Books.

Kohn, I., Frank, K., & Fox, A. S. (1975). *Defensible space modifications in rowhouse communities.* NSF Report.

Kolditz, T. A., & Arkin, R. M. (1982). An impression management interpretation of the self-handicapping strategy. *Journal of Personality and Social Psychology, 43,* 492–502.

Komorita, S. S., & Barth, J. M. (1985). Components of reward and social dilemmas. *Journal of Personality and Social Psychology, 48,* 364–373.

Komorita, S. S., & Brenner, A. (1968). Bargaining and concession making under bilateral monopoly. *Journal of Personality and Social Psychology, 9,* 15–20.

Komorita, S. S., & Chertkoff, J. M. (1973). A bargaining theory of coalition formation. *Psychological Review, 80,* 149–162.

Komorita, S. S., & Kravitz, D. A. (1983). Coalition formation: A social psychological approach. In P. Paulus (Ed.), *Basic group process* (pp. 179–204). New York: Springer-Verlag.

Komorita, S. S., & Miller, C. (1986). Bargaining strength as a function of coalition alternatives. *Journal of Personality and Social Psychology, 51,* 325–332.

Krebs, D. (1982). Altruism—A rational approach. In H. Eisenberg (Ed.), *The development of prosocial behavior.* New York: Academic Press.

Krech, D., Crutchfield, R., & Ballachey, E. (1962). *Individual in society: A textbook of social psychology.* New York: McGraw-Hill.

Kriss, M., Indenbaum, E., & Tesch, F. (1974). Message type and status of interactants as determinants of telephone helping behavior. *Journal of Personality and Social Psychology, 30,* 856–859.

Kuiper, N. A., & Rogers, T. B. (1979). Encoding of personal information: Self-other differences. *Journal of*

Personality and Social Psychology, 37, 499–514.

Kunst-Wilson, W. R., & Zajonc, R. B. (1980). Affective discrimination of stimuli that cannot be recognized. *Science, 207,* 557–558.

Kuo, Zing Yang. (1930). The genesis of the cat's responses to the rat. *Journal of Comparative Psychology, 11,* 1–35.

Laird, J. D. (1974). Self-attribution of emotion: The effects of expressive behavior on the quality of emotional experience. *Journal of Personality and Social Psychology, 29,* 475–486.

Landy, D., & Aronson, E. (1969). The influence of the character of the criminal and his victim on the decisions of simulated jurors. *Journal of Experimental Social Psychology, 5,* 141–152.

Landy, D., & Sigall, H. (1974). Beauty is talent: Task evaluation as a function of the performer's physical attractiveness. *Journal of Personality and Social Psychology, 29,* 299–304. © 1974 by the American Psychological Association. Adapted by permission of the authors.

Langer, E. J. (1978). Rethinking the role of thought in social interaction. In J. H. Harvey, W. Ickes, & R. E. Kidd (Eds.), *New directions in attribution research* (Vol. 2, pp. 35–58). Hillsdale, NJ: Erlbaum.

Langer, E. J. (1981). Old age: An artifact? In J. McGaush & S. Kiesler (Eds.), *Aging: Biology and behavior.* New York: Academic Press.

Langer, E. J., & Rodin, J. (1976). The effects of choice and enhanced personal responsibility for the aged: A field experiment in an institutional setting. *Journal of Personality and Social Psychology, 34,* 191–198.

LaPière, R. T. (1934). Attitudes vs. actions. *Social Forces, 13,* 230–237.

Lasswell, H. D. (1948). The structure and function of communication in society. In L. Bryson (Ed.), *Communication of ideas.* New York: Harper & Row.

Latané, B. (Ed.). (1966). Studies in social comparison. *Journal of Experimental Social Psychology,* (Suppl. 1).

Latané, B. (1981). The psychology of social impact. *American Psychologist, 36,* 343–356.

Latané, B., & Darley, J. M. (1970). *The unresponsive bystander: Why doesn't he help?* New York: Appleton-Century-Crofts.

Latané, B., Williams, K., & Harkens, S. (1979). Many hands make light the work: The causes and consequences of social loafing. *Journal of Personality and Social Psychology, 37,* 822–832.

Laughlin, P. R., & Earley, C. (1982). Social combination models, persuasive arguments theory, social comparison theory, and choice shift. *Journal of Personality and Social Psychology, 42,* 273–281.

Laughlin, P. R., & Futoran, G. (1985). Collective induction: Social combination and sequential transition. *Journal of Personality and Social Psychology, 48,* 608–613.

Lazarus, R. S. (1966). *Psychological stress and the coping process.* New York: McGraw-Hill.

Lazarus, R. S. (1982). Thoughts on the relations between emotions and cognition. *American Psychologist, 37,* 1019–1024.

Leary, T. (1957). Adapted from *Interpersonal diagnosis of personality.* New York: The Ronald Press Company, p. 65. Copyright © 1957, The Ronald Press Company, New York, and reproduced by permission.

Leavitt, H. J. (1951). Some effects of certain communication patterns on group performance. *Journal of Abnormal and Social Psychology, 46,* 38–50. © 1951 by the American Psychological Association.

LeBon, G. (1903). *The crowd* (Trans.). London: Allen & Unwin.

Lécuyer, R. (1976). Man's accommodation to space, man's accommodation of space. *Travail Humain, 39,* 195–206.

Lee, T. R. (1973). Psychology and living space. In R. M. Downs & D. Stea (Eds.), *Image and environment: Cognitive mapping and spatial behavior.* Chicago: Aldine.

Lefcourt, H. M. (1982). *Locus of control: Current trends in theory and research* (2nd ed.). Hillsdale, NJ: Erlbaum.

Leippe, M. R., & Elkin, R. A. (1987). Issue involvement and response involvement as determinants of persuasion. *Journal of Personality and Social Psychology, 52,* 269–278.

Lemyre, L., & Smith, P. (1985). Intergroup discrimination and self-esteem in minimal group paradigm. *Journal of Personality and Social Psychology, 49,* 660–670.

Lepper, M. R., Greene, D., & Nisbett, R. E. (1973). Undermining children's intrinsic interest with extrinsic reward: A test of the overjustification hypothesis. *Journal of Personality and Social Psychology, 28,* 129–137.

Lerner, M. J., & Agar, E. (1972). The consequences of perceived similarity: Attraction and rejection, approach and avoidance. *Journal of Experimental Research in Personality, 6,* 69–75.

Lerner, M. J., & Matthews, G. (1967). Reactions to suffering of others under conditions of indirect responsibility. *Journal of Personality and Social Psychology, 5,* 319–325.

Leung, K., & Lind, E. A. (1986). Procedural justice and culture: Effects of culture, gender, and investigator status on procedural preference. *Journal of Personality and Social Psychology, 50,* 1134–1140.

Leventhal, H., & Niles, P. (1965). Persistence of influence for varying duration of exposure to threat stimuli. *Psychological Reports, 16,* 223–233.

Leventhal, H., Singer, R., & Jones, S. (1965). The effects of fear and specificity of recommendation upon attitudes and behavior. *Journal of Personality and Social Psychology, 2,* 20–29.

Leventhal, H., Watts, J. C., & Pagano, R. (1967). Effects of fear and instructions on how to cope with danger. *Journal of Personality and Social Psychology, 6,* 313–321.

Levine, R., & Campbell, D. (1972). *Ethnocentrism: Theories of conflict, ethnic attitudes and group behavior.* New York: Wiley.

Levinger, G. (1976). A social psychological perspective on marital dissolution. *Journal of Social Issues, 32,* 21–47.

Levinger, G. (1980). Toward the analysis of close relationships. *Journal of Experimental Social Psychology, 16,* 510–544.

Levinger, G., & Senn, D. J. (1967). Disclosure of feelings in marriage. *Merril-Palmer Quarterly, 13,* 237–249.

Lewin, K. (1965). *A dynamic theory of personality.* New York: McGraw-Hill.

Lewin, K. (1943). Forces behind food habits and methods of change. *Bulletin of the National Research Council, 108,* 35–65.

Lewin, K. (1948). *Resolving social conflicts: Selected papers on group dynamics.* New York: Harper & Row.

Lewin, K., Lippitt, R., & White, R. (1939). Patterns of aggressive behavior in experimentally created social climates. *Journal of Social Psychology, 10,* 271–299.

Lieberman, M. A., Yalom, I. D., & Miles, M. B. (1973). *Encounter groups: First facts.* New York: Basic Books.

Likert, R. (1932). A technique for the measurement of attitudes. *Archives of Psychology, 140,* 1–55.

Lind, E. A., Kutz, S., Musante, L., Walker, L., & Thibaut, J. (1980). Procedural and outcome effects on reactions to adjudicated resolution of conflicts of interest. *Journal of Personality and Social Psychology, 39,* 643 653.

Linder, D. E., Cooper, J., & Jones, E. E. (1967). Decision freedom as a determinant of the role of incentive magnitude in attitude change. *Journal of Personality and Social Psychology, 6,* 245–254. © 1967 by the American Psychological Association. Adapted by permission of the authors.

Lindskold, S. (1976). *Power imbalance and the GRIT strategy.* Unpublished manuscript, Ohio University, Athens, OH.

Lindskold, S. (1986). GRIT: Reducing distrust through carefully introduced conciliation. In Worchel, S., & Austin, W. G. (Eds.), *The psychology of intergroup relations.* Chicago: Nelson-Hall.

Lindskold, S., & Aronoff, J. R. (1980). Conciliatory strategies and relative power. *Journal of Experimental Social Psychology, 16,* 187–198.

Link, S. M., & Pepler, R. D. (1970). Associated fluctuations in daily temperature, productivity and absenteeism. *ASHRAE Transactions, 76*(2), 326–337.

Linville, P. W. (1982). The complexity-extremity effect and age-based stereotyping. *Journal of Personality and Social Psychology, 42,* 193–211.

Linville, P. W., & Jones, E. E. (1980). Polarized appraisals of outgroup members. *Journal of Personality and Social Psychology, 38,* 689–703.

Little, K. B. (1968). Cultural variations in social schemata. *Journal of Personality and Social Psychology, 10,* 1–7.

Long, G. (1972). *Cohesiveness of high school baseball teams.* Unpublished master's thesis, Southern Illinois University, Carbondale, IL.

Long, G. (1984). Psychological tension and closeness to others: Stress and interpersonal distance preference. *Journal of Psychology, 117,* 143–146.

Lord, C. G., Lepper, M. R., & Mackie, D. (1984). Attitude prototypes as determinants of attitude-behavior consistency. *Journal of Personality and Social Psychology, 46,* 1254–1266.

Lord, C. G., Ross, L., & Lepper, M. R. (1979). Biased assimilation and attitude polarization: The effects of prior theories on subsequently discovered evidence. *Journal of Personality and Social Psychology, 37,* 2098–2109.

Lorenz, K. (1968). *On aggression.* New York: Harcourt, Brace & World.

Loretto, R., & Williams, D. (1974). Personality, behavioral and output variables in a small group task situation: An examination of consensual leader and nonleader differences. *Canadian Journal of Behavioral Science, 6,* 59–74.

Lothstein, L. (1972). Personal space in assault-prone male adolescent prisoners. *Dissertation Abstracts International, 338,* 1271.

Lott, A. J., & Lott, B. E. (1968). A learning theory approach to interpersonal attitudes. In A. G. Greenwald, T. C. Brock, & T. M. Ostrom (Eds.), *Psychological foundations of attitudes.* New York: Academic Press.

Lott, A. J., & Lott, B. E. (1974). The role of reward in the formation of positive interpersonal attitudes. In T. Huston (Ed.), *Foundations of interpersonal attraction.* New York: Academic Press.

Lott, B. E., & Lott, A. J. (1985). Learning theory in contemporary social psychology. In G. Lindzey & E. Aronson (Eds.), *Handbook of social psychology* (3rd ed., Vol. 1, pp. 1–46). New York: Random House.

Louis, J. C., & Yazijian, H. (1980). *The cola wars.* New York: Everest House.

Love, K., & Aiello, J. (1980). Using projective techniques to measure interaction distance. *Personality and Social Psychology Bulletin, 6,* 102–104.

Lowe, C. A., & Goldstein, J. W. (1970). Reciprocal liking and attribution of ability: Mediating effects of perceived intent and personal involvement. *Journal of Personality and Social Psychology, 16,* 291–298.

Luchins, A. (1957a). Experimental attempts to minimize the impact of first impression. In C. Hovland, W. Mandell, E. Campbell, T. Brock, A. Luchins, A. Cohen, W. McGuire, I. Janis, R. Feierabend, & N. Anderson (Eds.), *The order of presentation in persuasion.* New Haven, CT: Yale University Press.

Luchins, A. (1957b). Primacy-recency in impression formation. In C. Hovland, W. Mandell, E. Campbell, T. Brock, A. Luchins, A. Cohen, W. McGuire, I. Janis, R. Feierabend, & N. Anderson (Eds.), *The order of presentation in persuasion.* New Haven, CT: Yale University Press.

Lyle, J., & Hoffman, H. R. (1972). Explorations on patterns of television viewing by preschool-age children. In E. A. Rubenstein, G. A. Comstock, & J. P. Murray (Eds.), *Televi-sion and social behavior. Vol. 4. Television in day-to-day life patterns of use.* Washington, D.C.: U.S. Government Printing Office.

Lynch, J. G., Jr., & Cohen, J. (1978). The use of subjective expected utility theory as an aid to understanding variables that influence helping behavior. *Journal of Personality and Social Psychology, 36,* 1138–1151.

Lynch, K. (1960). *The image of the city.* Cambridge: Massachusetts Institute of Technology Press.

Lynn, M., & Oldenquist, A. (1986). Egoistic and nonegoistic motives in social dilemmas. *American Psychologist, 41,* 529–534.

Macaulay, J. (1970). A skill for charity. In J. Macaulay & L. Berkowitz (Eds.), *Altruism and helping behavior: Social psychological studies of some antecedents and consequences.* New York: Academic Press.

Maccoby, E. E., & Jacklin, C. N. (1980). Sex differences in aggression: A rejoinder and reprise. *Child Development, 51,* 964–980.

Mackie, D. M. (1986). Social identification effects in group polarization. *Journal of Personality and Social Psychology, 51,* 720–728.

Mackie, D. M., & Goethals, G. R. (1987). Individual and group goals. In C. Hendrick (Ed.), *Review of personality and social psychology.* Vol. 8. Newbury Park, CA: Sage.

Mackworth, N. H. (1961). Researchers on the measurement of human performance. In H. W. Sinaiki (Ed.), *Selected papers on human factors in the design and use of control systems.* New York: Dover.

MacNeil, M. K., & Sherif, M. (1976). Norm change over subject generations as a function of arbitrariness of prescribed norms. *Journal of Personality and Social Psychology, 34,* 762–768.

Maier, N., & Solem, A. (1952). The contribution of a discussion leader to the quality of group thinking: The effective use of minority opinions. *Human Relations, 5*, 277–288.

Maier, S. F., Seligman, M. E. P., & Soloman, R. L. (1969). Pavlovian fear conditioning and learned helplessness. In B. A. Campbell & R. M. Church (Eds.), *Punishment.* New York: Appleton-Century-Crofts.

Major, B. (1981). Gender patterns in touching behavior. In C. Mayo & N. Henley (Eds.), *Gender, androgyny, and nonverbal behavior.* New York: Springer-Verlag.

Major, B., McFarlin, D., & Gagnon, D. (1984). Overworked and underpaid: On the nature of gender differences in personal entitlement. *Journal of Personality and Social Personality, 4,* 1399–1412.

Malamuth, N. M. (1984). Aggression against women: Cultural and individual causes. In N. M. Malamuth and E. Donnerstein (Eds.), *Pornography and sexual aggression.* Orlando, FL: Academic Press.

Malamuth, N. M., & Check, J. V. P. (1981). The effects of mass media exposure on acceptance of violence against women: A field experiment. *Journal of Research in Personality, 15,* 436–446.

Malamuth, N., Haber, S., & Feshbach, S. (1980). Testing hypotheses regarding rape: Exposure to sexual violence, sex differences, and the "normality" of rapists. *Journal of Research in Personality, 14,* 121–127.

Mann, R. (1959). A review of the relationship between personality and performance in small groups. *Psychological Bulletin, 56,* 241–270. © 1959 by the American Psychological Association.

Mann, S. H. (1977). The use of social indicators in environmental planning. In I. Altman & J. R. Wohlwill (Eds.), *Human behavior and environment* (Vol. 2). New York: Plenum Press.

Markey, E. J. (1985). The politics of arms control: A matter of perception. *American Psychologist, 40,* 557–560.

Marks, G. (1984). Thinking one's abilities are unique and one's opinions are common. *Personality and Social Psychology Bulletin, 10,* 203–208.

Marks, G., Miller, N., & Maruyama, G. (1981). Effect of targets' physical attractiveness on assumptions of similarity. *Journal of Personality and Social Psychology, 41*(1), 198–206.

Markus, H. (1977). Self-schemata and processing information about the self. *Journal of Personality and Social Psychology, 35,* 63–78.

Markus, H. (1978). The effect of mere presence on social facilitation: An unobtrusive test. *Journal of Experimental Social Psychology, 14,* 389–397.

Markus, H. (1981). The drive for integration: Some comments. *Journal of Experimental Social Psychology, 17,* 257–261.

Markus, H., & Sentis, K. P. (1982). The self in social information processing. In J. Suls (Ed.), *Psychological perspectives on the self* (Vol. 1). Hillsdale, NJ: Erlbaum.

Markus, H., Smith, J., & Moreland, R. L. (1983). The role of the self in social perception: A cognitive analysis. Unpublished manuscript.

Markus, H., & Zajonc, R. (1985). The cognitive perspective in social psychology. In G. Lindzey & E. Aronson (Eds.), *The handbook of social psychology* (3rd ed., Vol. 1, pp. 137–230). New York: Random House.

Marshall, G. D., & Zimbardo, P. G. (1979). Affective consequences of inadequately explained physiological arousal. *Journal of Personality and Social Psychology, 37,* 970–988.

Maslach, C. (1974). Social and personal bases of individuation. *Journal of Personality and Social Psychology, 29,* 411–425.

Maslach, C. (1979). Negative emotional biasing of unexplained arousal. *Journal of Personality and Social Psychology, 37,* 953–969.

Maslach, C., Stapp, J., & Santee, R. (1985). Individuation: Conceptual analysis and assessment. *Journal of Personality and Social Psychology, 49,* 729–738.

Mathes, E. W., Adams, H. E., & Davies, R. M. (1985). Jealousy: Loss of relationship rewards, loss of self-esteem, depression, anxiety, and anger. *Journal of Personality and Social Psychology, 48,* 1552–1561.

Mathews, K. E., & Cannon, L. K. (1975). Environmental noise level as a determinant of helping behavior. *Journal of Personality and Social Psychology, 32,* 571–577.

Mathews, K., Cannon, L., & Alexander, K. (1974). The influence of level of empathy and ambient noise on body buffer zones. *Proceedings of American Psychological Association, 1,* 367–370.

Maychick, D. (1984). *Meryl Streep: The reluctant superstar.* New York: St. Martin's.

Mayo, C., & Henley, N. M. (Eds.). (1981). *Gender and nonverbal behavior.* New York: Springer-Verlag.

Mazis, M. B. (1975). Antipollution measures and psychological reactance theory: A field experiment. *Journal of Personality and Social Psychology, 31,* 654–660.

McArthur, L. Z. (1972). The how and what of why: Some determinants and consequences of causal attribution. *Journal of Personality and Social Psychology, 22,* 171–193.

McArthur, L. Z. (1976). The lesser influence of consensus than distinctiveness information on causal attributions: A test of the person-thing hypothesis. *Journal of Personality and Social Psychology, 33,* 733–742.

McArthur, L. Z., & Post, D. (1977). Figural emphasis and person perception. *Journal of Experimental Social Psychology, 13,* 520–535.

McBride, G., King, M. G., & James, J. W. (1965). Social proximity effects on galvanic skin responses in adult humans. *Journal of Psychology, 61,* 153–157.

McCain, G., Cox, V., Paulus, P., Luke, A., & Abadzi, H. (1985). The reduction of crowding in a school environment. *Journal of Applied Social Psychology, 15,* 503–515.

McCarrey, M. W., Peterson, L., Edwards, S., & von Kuniz, P. (1974). Landscape office attitudes: Reflections of perceived degree of control over transactions with the environment. *Journal of Applied Psychology, 59,* 401–403.

McCarty, D., Diamond, W., & Kaye, M. (1982). Alcohol, sexual arousal, and the transfer of excitation. *Journal of Personality and Social Psychology, 42(6),* 977–988.

McCauley, C., Stitt, C. F., Woods, K., & Lipton, D. (1973). Group shift to caution at the race track. *Journal of Experimental Social Psychology, 9,* 80–86.

McClintock, C., Stech, F., & Keil, L. (1983). The influence of communication on bargaining. In P. Paulus (Ed.), *Basic group process* (pp. 205–234). New York: Springer-Verlag.

McCollam, J. B., Burish, T. G., Maisto, S. A., & Sobell, M. B. (1980). Alcohol's effects on physiological arousal and self-reported affect and sensations. *Journal of Abnormal Psychology, 89,* 224–233.

McDougall, W. (1908). *An introduction to social psychology.* London: Methuen.

McGillicuddy, N., Pruitt, D., & Syna, H. (1984). Perceptions of firmness and strength in negotiation. *Personality and Social Psychology Bulletin, 10,* 402–409.

McGinniss, J. (1969). *The selling of the presidency, 1968.* Copyright 1969 by JoeMac Inc. Reprinted by permission of Simon & Schuster, Inc. Trident Press Division.

McGrath, J. (1984). *Groups: Interaction and performance.* Englewood Cliffs, NJ: Prentice-Hall.

McGrath, J. E., & Julian, J. W. (1963). Interaction process and task outcome in experimentally created negotiation groups. *Journal of Psychological Studies, 14,* 117–138.

McGuire, W. J. (1985). Attitudes and attitude change. In G. Lindzey & E. Aronson (Eds.), *The handbook of social psychology* (3rd ed., Vol. 2, pp. 233–346). New York: Random House.

McGuire, W. J., & McGuire, C. V. (1981). The spontaneous self-concept as affected by seasonal distinctiveness. In M. D. Lynch, A. Norem-Hebeisen, & K. J. Gergen (Eds.), *Self-concept: Advances in theory and research.* Cambridge, MA: Ballinger.

McGuire, W. J., McGuire, C. V., Child, P., & Fujioka, T. (1978). Salience of ethnicity in the spontaneous self-concept as a function of one's ethnic distinctiveness in the social environment. *Journal of Personality and Social Psychology, 36,* 511–520.

McGuire, W. J., & Padawer-Singer, A. (1976). Trait salience in the spontaneous self-concept. *Journal of Personality and Social Psychology, 33,* 743–754.

McGuire, W. J., & Papageorgis, D.

(1961). The relative efficacy of various types of prior belief-defense in producing immunity against persuasion. *Journal of Abnormal and Social Psychology, 62,* 317–337. © 1961 by the American Psychological Association. Adapted by permission of the authors.

McHarg, I. (1969). *Design with nature.* Garden City, NY: Natural History Press.

McHugh, M. C., Frieze, I. H., & Hanusa, B. H. (1982). Attributions and sex differences in achievement: Problems and new perspectives. *Sex Roles, 8,* 467–479.

Mead, G. H. (1934). *Mind, self and society.* Chicago: University of Chicago Press.

Megargee, E. I. (1969). Influence of sex roles on the manifestation of leadership. *Journal of Applied Psychology, 53,* 377–382.

Mehrabian, A. (1968). Relationship of attitudes to seated posture, orientation and distance. *Journal of Personality and Social Psychology, 10,* 26–30.

Mehrabian, A. (1972). *Nonverbal communication.* Chicago: Aldine-Atherton.

Mettee, D. R. (1971). Rejection of unexpected success as a function of the negative consequences of accepting success. *Journal of Personality and Social Psychology, 17,* 332–341.

Mettee, D. R., & Aronson, E. (1974). Affective reactions to appraisal from others. In T. L. Huston (Ed.), *Foundations of interpersonal attraction.* New York: Academic Press.

Meyer, J. P., & Pepper, S. (1977). Need, compatibility and marital adjustment in young married couples. *Journal of Personality and Social Psychology, 35,* 331–342.

Michenbaum, D. H., Bowers, K. S., & Ross, R. R. (1969). A behavioral analysis of teacher expectancy effects. *Journal of Personality and Social Psychology, 13,* 306–316.

Michener, H. A., & Burt, M. R. (1974). Legitimacy as a base of social influence. In J. Tedeschi (Ed.), *Perspectives on social power.* Chicago: Aldine.

Milgram, S. (1963). Behavioral study of obedience. *Journal of Abnormal and Social Psychology, 67,* 376. Copyright © 1963 by the American Psychological Association.

Milgram, S. (1965). Some conditions of obedience and disobedience to authority. *Human Relations, 18,* 57–76.

Milgram, S. (1970). The experience of living in cities. *Science, 167,* 1461–1468.

Milgram, S. (1974). *Obedience to authority.* New York: Harper & Row.

Milgram, S. (1977). *The individual in a social world.* Reading, MA: Addison-Wesley.

Milgram, S., Liberty, H. J., Toledo, R., & Wackenhut, T. (1986). Response to intrusion into waiting lines. *Journal of Personality and Social Psychology, 51,* 683–689.

Milgram, S., & Toch, H. (1968). Reply to the critics. *International Journal of Psychiatry, 6,* 294–295.

Miller, A. G. (1976). Constraint and target effects in the attribution of attitudes. *Journal of Experimental Social Psychology, 12,* 325–329.

Miller, C. T. (1982). The role of performance related similarity in social comparison of abilities: A test of the related attributes hypothesis. *Journal of Experimental Social Psychology, 18,* 513–523.

Miller, C. T. (1984). Self-schemas, gender, and social comparison: A clarification of the related attributes hypothesis. *Journal of Personality and Social Psychology, 46,* 1222–1229.

Miller, J. (1982). The effects of noise on people. *Journal of The Acoustical Society of America, 56,* 729–764.

Miller, N. E. (1948). Theory and experiments relating psychoanalytic displacement to stimulus-response generation. *Journal of Abnormal and Social Psychology, 43,* 155–178.

Miller, N. E., & Bugelski, R. (1948). Minor studies of aggression: II. The influence of frustrations imposed by the in-group on attitudes expressed toward the out-group. *Journal of Psychology, 25,* 437–453.

Miller, N., & Campbell, D. (1959). Recency and primacy in persuasion as a function of the timing of speeches and measurements. *Journal of Abnormal and Social Psychology, 59,* 1–9. © 1959 by the American Psychological Association. Adapted by permission of the authors.

Miller, N., Campbell, D., Twedt, H., & O'Connell, E. (1966). Similarity, contrast and complementarity in friendship choice. *Journal of Personality and Social Psychology, 3,* 3–12.

Miller, R. L., Brickman, P., & Bolen, D. (1975). Attribution versus persuasion as a means for modifying behavior. *Journal of Personality and Social Psychology, 31,* 430–441.

Mills, J., & Clark, M. S. (1982). Communal and exchange relationships. In L. Wheeler (Ed.), *Annual Review of Psychology, 33,* 121–144.

Milner, D. (1981). Racial prejudice. In J. Turner & H. Giles (Eds.), *Intergroup behavior.* Chicago: University of Chicago Press.

Minton, H. L. (1984). J. F. Brown's social psychology of the 1930's: A historical antecedent to the contemporary crisis in social psychology. *Personality and Social Psychology Bulletin, 10,* 7–30.

Moore, L. (1979). *The jury.* Cincinnati: W. H. Anderson.

Moreland, R. (1985). Social categorization and the assimilation of "new" group members. *Journal of Personality and Social Psychology, 48*, 1173–1190.

Moreland, R., & Levine, J. (1984). Role transition in small groups. In V. Allen & E. Van de Vhert (Eds.), *Role transitions: Explorations and explanations.* New York: Plenum Press.

Moreland, R. L., & Zajonc, R. B. (1979). Exposure effects may not depend on stimulus recognition. *Journal of Personality and Social Psychology, 37*, 1085–1089.

Moreland, R. L., & Zajonc, R. B. (1982). Exposure effects in person perception: Familiarity, similarity and attraction. *Journal of Experimental Social Psychology, 18*, 395–415.

Morgenthau, T., Smith, V. C., Josephs, N., & Leslie, C. (1985, June 24). Saying "No" to new Coke. *Newsweek*, pp. 32–33.

Morris, C. G., & Hackman, J. R. (1969). Behaviorial correlates of perceived leadership. *Journal of Personality and Social Psychology, 13*, 350–361.

Morris, W., & Miller, R. S. (1975). The effects of consensus-breaking and consensus-preempting partners on reduction of conformity. *Journal of Experimental Social Psychology, 11*, 215–223.

Morse, S. J., & Gergen, K. J. (1970). Social comparison, self-consistency and the concept of self. *Journal of Personality and Social Psychology, 16*, 149–156.

Moscovici, S. (1985). Social influence and conformity. In G. Lindzey & E. Aronson (Eds.), *The handbook of social psychology* (3rd ed., Vol. 2, pp. 347–412). New York: Random House.

Moscovici, S., & Mugny, G. (1983). Minority influence. In P. Paulus (Ed.), *Basic group process.* New York: Springer-Verlag.

Moscovici, S., & Personnaz, B. (1980). Studies in social influence vs. minority influence and conversion behavior in a perceptual look. *Journal of Experimental Social Psychology, 16*, 270–283.

Moss, M. K., & Page, R. A. (1972). Reinforcement and helping behavior. *Journal of Applied Social Psychology, 2*, 360–371. © 1972 by the American Psychological Association. Adapted by permission of the authors.

Moyer, K. E. (1971). *The physiology of hostility.* Chicago: Markham.

Muhleman, J. T., Bruker, C., & Ingram, C. M. (1976). The generosity shift. *Journal of Personality and Social Psychology, 34*, 344–351.

Mulder, M. (1981). On the quantity and quality of power and the Q.W.L. Paper presented at the International Conference on the Quality of Work Life, Toronto.

Mullen, B. (1983). Operationalizing the effect of the group on the individual: A self-attention perspective. *Journal of Experimental Social Psychology, 19*, 295–322.

Mullen, B. (1987). Self-attention theory. In B. Mullen & G. R. Goethals (Eds.), *Theories of group behavior.* New York: Springer-Verlag.

Mullen, B., Atkins, J. L., Champion, D. S., Edwards, C., Hardy, D., Story, J. E., and Vanderklok, M. (1985). The false consensus effect: A meta-analysis of 115 hypothesis tests. *Journal of Experimental Social Psychology, 21*, 262–283.

Mullen, B., & Goethals, G. R. (1987). *Theories of group behavior.* New York: Springer-Verlag.

Mullen, B., Johnson, D., & Drake, S. (1985). *Organizational productivity as a function of group composition: A self-attention perspective.* Unpublished manuscript, Syracuse University, Syracuse, NY.

Myer, T. (1972). The effect of sexually arousing and violent films on aggressive behavior. *Journal of Sex Research, 8,* 324–333.

Myers, A. (1982). Team competition, success, and adjustment of group members. *Journal of Abnormal and Social Psychology, 65,* 325–332.

Myers, D. G. (1982). Polarizing effects of social interaction. In H. Brandstatter, J. H. Davis, & G. Stocker-Kreichgauer (Eds.), *Group decision processes.* London: Academic Press.

Myers, D. G. (1983). *Social psychology.* New York: McGraw-Hill.

Myers, D. G., & Lamm, H. (1976). The group polarization phenomenon. *Psychological Bulletin, 83,* 602–627.

Nadler, A. (1986). Help seeking as a cultural phenomenon: Differences between city and kibbutz dwellers. *Journal of Personality and Social Psychology, 51,* 976–982.

Nahemow, L., & Lawton, M. P. (1975). Similarity and propinquity in friendship formation. *Journal of Personality and Social Psychology, 32,* 205–213.

Nelson, A. (1985). Psychological equivalence: Awareness and responsibility in our nuclear age. *American Psychologist, 40,* 549–556.

Nemeth, C. (1979). The role of an active minority in intergroup relations. In W. Austin & S. Worchel (Eds.), *The social psychology of intergroup relations.* Monterey, CA: Brooks/Cole.

Nemeth, C. (1981). Jury trials: Psychology and law. In L. Berkowitz (Ed.), *Advances in experimental social psychology* (Vol. 4, pp. 309–367). New York: Academic Press.

Nemeth, C. (1986). Differential contributions of majority and minority influence. *Psychological Review, 93,* 1–10, 23–32.

Newcomb, T. (1943). *Personality and social change.* Hinsdale, IL: Dryden.

Newcomb, T. A. (1947). Autistic hostility and social reality. *Human Relations, 1,* 69–86.

Newcomb, T. (1953). An approach to the study of communicative acts. *Psychological Review, 60,* 393–404. © 1953 by the American Psychological Association.

Newcomb, T. M. (1956). The prediction of interpersonal attraction. *American Psychologist, 11,* 575–586.

Newcomb, T. (1961). *The acquaintance process.* New York: Holt, Rinehart & Winston.

Newcomb, T. (1963). Persistence and repression of changed attitudes: Long-range studies. *Journal of Social Issues, 19,* 3–14.

Newcomb, T. M. (1968). Interpersonal balance. In R. P. Abelson (Ed.), *Theories of cognitive consistency: A sourcebook.* Chicago: Rand McNally.

Newcomb, T., Koenig, K., Flacks, R., & Warwick, D. (1967). *Persistence and change: Bennington College and its students after 25 years.* New York: Wiley.

Newman, O. (1972). *Defensible space.* New York: Macmillan.

Newman, O. (1975). *Design guidelines for creating defensible space.* Washington, DC: U.S. Government Printing Office.

Newtson, D. (1974). Dispositional inference from effects of actions: Effects chosen and effects foregone. *Journal of Experimental Social Psychology, 10,* 487–496.

Nisbett, R. E., & Borgida, E. (1975). Attribution and the psychology of prediction. *Journal of Personality and Social Psychology, 32*(5), 932–943.

Nisbett, R. E., Caputo, C., Legant, P., & Marecek, J. (1973). Behavior as seen by the actor and as seen by the observer. *Journal of Personality and Social Psychology, 27,* 154–164.

Nisbett, R. E., & Ross, L. (1980). *Human inference: Strategies and shortcomings of social judgment.* Englewood Cliffs, NJ: Prentice-Hall.

Noller, P. (1980). Misunderstandings in marital communication: A study of couples' nonverbal communication. *Journal of Personality and Social Psychology, 39,* 1135–1148.

Norman, R. (1976). When what is said is important: A comparison of expert and attractive sources. *Journal of Experimental Social Psychology, 12,* 294–300.

Nosanchuk, T. A. (1981). The way of the warrior: The effects of traditional martial arts training on aggressiveness. *Human Relations, 34,* 435–444.

Novak, D., & Lerner, M. (1968). Rejection as a consequence of perceived similarity. *Journal of Personality and Social Psychology, 9,* 147–152.

Olmstead, J. A., & Blake, R. R. (1955). The use of simulated groups to produce modifications in judgment. *Journal of Personality, 23,* 335–345.

Olszewski, D., Rotton, J., & Soler, E. (1978). Conversation, conglomerate noise and behavioral after-effects. Paper presented at Midwestern Psychological Association, Chicago.

Orne, M. T. (1962). On the social psychology of the psychological experiment: With particular reference to demand characteristics and their implications. *American Psychologist, 17,* 776–783.

Orne, M. T., & Evans, F. J. (1965). Social control in the psychological experiment: Antisocial behavior and hypnosis. *Journal of Personality and Social Psychology, 1,* 189–200.

Orne, M. T., & Holland, C. C. (1968). On the ecological validity of laboratory deceptions. *International Journal of Psychiatry, 6,* 282–293.

Orvis, B. R., Kelley, H. H., & Butler, D. (1976). Attributional conflict in young couples. In J. H. Harvey, W. J. Ickes & R. E. Kidd (Eds.), *New directions in attribution research* (Vol. 2). Hillsdale, NJ: Erlbaum.

Osgood, C. E. (1962). *An alternative to war or surrender.* Urbana: University of Illinois Press.

Osmond, H. (1957). Function as the basis of psychiatric ward design. *Mental Hospitals, 8,* 23–30.

Overmier, J. B., & Seligman, M. E. P. (1967). Effects of inescapable shock upon subsequent escape and avoidance learning. *Journal of Comparative and Physiological Psychology, 63,* 28–33.

Padawer-Singer, A. M., Singer, A. N., & Singer, R. L. (1977). Legal and social-psychological research in the effects of pretrial publicity on juries, numerical makeup of juries, non-unanimous verdict requirements. *Law & Psychology Review, 3,* 71–79.

Page, M., & Scheidt, R. J. (1971). The elusive weapons effect: Demand awareness, valuation apprehension, and slightly sophisticated subjects. *Journal of Personality and Social Psychology, 20,* 304–318.

Pallak, M. S., & Pittman, T. S. (1972). General motivational effects of dissonance arousal. *Journal of Personality and Social Psychology, 21,* 349–358.

Palmerino, M., Langer, E., & McGillis, D. (1984). Attitudes and attitude change: Mindlessness-mindfulness perspective. In R. Eiser (Ed.), *Attitudinal judgment* (pp. 179–197). New York: Springer-Verlag.

Papageorgis, D., & McGuire, W. J. (1961). The generality of immunity of persuasion produced by pre-exposure to weakened counter-arguments. *Journal of Abnormal and Social Psychology, 62,* 475–481.

Papastamov, S., & Mugny, G. (1985). Rigidity and minority influence: The influence of the social in social influence. In S. Moscovici, G. Mugny, & E. van Avermaet (Eds.), *Perspectives on minority influence.* Cambridge, Eng.: Cambridge University Press.

Park, R., & Rothbart, M. (1982). Perception of outgroup homogeneity and levels of social categorization: Memory for the subordinate attitudes of in-group and out-group members. *Journal of Personality and Social Psychology, 42,* 1051–1068.

Parke, R., Berkowitz, L., Leyens, J. P., West, S. G., & Sebastian, R. J. (1977). Some effects of violent and nonviolent movies on the behavior of juvenile delinquents. *Advances in experimental social psychology* (Vol. 10, pp. 139–169).

Patterson, A. H. (1978). Territorial behavior and fear of crime in the elderly. *Environmental Psychology and Nonverbal Behavior, 2(3),* 131–144.

Patterson, M. L. (1968). Spatial factors in social interaction. *Human Relations, 21,* 351–361.

Patterson, M. L. (1976). An arousal model of interpersonal intimacy. *Psychological Review, 83,* 235–245.

Patterson, M. L. (1977). Interpersonal distance, affect, and equilibrium theory. *Journal of Social Psychology, 101,* 205–214.

Paulhus, D. L., Shaffer, D. R., & Downing, L. L. (1977). Effects of making blood donor motives salient upon donor retention. *Personality and Social Psychology Bulletin, 3,* 99–102.

Pavlov, I. P. (1927). *Conditional reflexes: An investigation of the physiological activity of the cerebral cortex.* London: Oxford University Press.

Pearl, D., & Bouthilet, L. (Eds.) (1982). *Television and behavior: Ten years of scientific progress and implications for the 80's.* Washington, D.C.: U.S. Government Printing Office.

Pelton, L. H. (1974). *The psychology of nonviolence.* Elmsford, NY: Pergamon Press.

Pennington, D. F., Harary, F., & Bass, B. M. (1958). Some effects of decision and discussion on coalescence change and effectiveness. *Journal of Applied Psychology, 42,* 404–408.

Perrin, S., & Spencer, C. (1980). The Asch-effect: A child of its time? *Bulletin of the British Psychological Society, 32,* 405–406.

Pessin, J., & Husband, R. (1933). Effects of social stimulation on human maze learning. *Journal of Abnormal and Social Psychology, 28,* 148–154.

Pettigrew, T. F. (1958). The measurement and correlates of category width as a cognitive variable. *Journal of Personality, 26,* 532–544.

Pettigrew, T. F. (1959). Regional differences in anti-Negro prejudice. *Journal of Abnormal and Social Psychology, 59,* 28–36.

Petty, R. E., & Cacioppo, J. T. (1986). The elaboration likelihood model of persuasion. In L. Berkowitz (Ed.), *Advances in experimental social psychology* (Vol. 19, pp. 123–205). New York: Academic Press.

Petty, R. E., Cacioppo, J. T., & Goldman, R. (1981). Personal involvement as a determinant of argument-based persuasion. *Journal of Personality and Social Psychology, 41,* 847–855.

Petty, R. E., Cacioppo, J. T., & Heesacker, M. (1981). The use of rhetorical questions in persuasion.

Journal of Personality and Social Psychology, 40, 432–440.

Petty, R. E., Cacioppo, J. T., & Schuman, D. (1983). Central and peripheral routes to advertising effectiveness: The moderating role of involvement. *Journal of Consumer Research, 10,* 134–148.

Phares, E. J. (1984). *Introduction to personality.* Columbus, OH: Merrill.

Piaget, J. (1932). *The moral judgment of the child.* New York: Harcourt Brace Jovanovich.

Piliavin, I. M., Piliavin, J. A., & Rodin, J. (1975). Cost, diffusion, and the stigmatized victim. *Journal of Personality and Social Psychology, 32,* 429–438. © 1975 by the American Psychological Association. Adapted by permission of the authors.

Piliavin, J. A., Dovidio, J. F., Gaertner, S. L., & Clark, R. D., III. (1982). Responsive bystanders: The process of intervention. In V. J. Derlega & J. Grzelak (Eds.), *Cooperation and helping behavior: Theories and research.* New York: Academic Press.

Porter, L. W., & Lawler, E. E. (1968). *Managerial attitudes and performances.* Chicago: Dorsey Press.

Powell, M. C., & Fazio, R. H. (1984). Attitude accessibility as a function of repeated attitudinal expression. *Personality and Social Psychology Bulletin, 10,* 139–148.

Provins, K. A., & Bell, C. R. (1970). Effects of heat stress on the performance of two tasks running concurrently. *Journal of Experimental Psychology, 85,* 40–44.

Pruitt, D. G. (1965). Definition of the situation as a determinant of international action. In H. C. Kelman (Ed.), *International behavior.* New York: Holt, Rinehart & Winston.

Pruitt, D. G. (1976). Power and bargaining. In B. Seidenberg & A. Snadowsky, *Social psychology: An introduction.* New York: Free Press.

Pruitt, D. G., & Insko, C. A. (1980). Extension of the Kelley attribution model: The role of comparison-object consensus, target-object consensus, distinctiveness and consistency. *Journal of Personality and Social Psychology, 39,* 39–58.

Pruitt, D. G., & Johnson, D. F. (1970). Mediation as an aid to face saving in negotiation. *Journal of Personality and Social Psychology, 14,* 239–246.

Pryor, J. B., & Kriss, M. (1977). The cognitive dynamics of salience in the attribution process. *Journal of Personality and Social Psychology, 35,* 49–55.

Quattrone, G. A. (1985). On the congruity between internal states and action. *Psychological Bulletin, 98,* 3–40.

Quattrone, G. A. (1986). On the perception of a group's variability. In S. Worchel & W. G. Austin (Eds.), *Psychology of intergroup relations* (pp. 25–48). Chicago: Nelson-Hall.

Quattrone, G. A., & Jones, E. E. (1978). Selective self-disclosure with and without correspondent performance. *Journal of Experimental Social Psychology, 14,* 511–526.

Quattrone, G. A., & Jones, E. E. (1980). The perception of variability with in-groups and out-groups: Implications for the law of small numbers. *Journal of Personality and Social Psychology, 38,* 141–152.

Quigley-Fernandez, B., & Tedeschi, J. T. (1978). The bogus pipeline as lie detector: Two validity studies. *Journal of Personality and Social Psychology, 36,* 247–256.

Rabbie, J. M., & Bekkers, F. (1976). Threatened leadership and intergroup competition. *Nederlands Tijdschrift voor de Psychologie en haar Grensaebieden, 31,* 269–283.

Rabbie, J. M., Brehm, J. W., & Cohen, A. R. (1959). Verbalization and reactions to cognitive dissonance. *Journal of Personality, 27,* 407–417.

Rada, J. B., & Rogers, R. W. (1973, October). *Obedience to authority: Presence of authority and command strength.* Paper presented at the meeting of the Southwestern Psychological Association, New Orleans.

Raloff, J. (1982). Occupational noise— The subtle pollutant. *Science News, 121,* 347–350.

Rands, M., Levinger, G., & Mellinger, G. (1981). Patterns of conflict resolution and marital satisfaction. *Journal of Family Issues.*

Rankin, R. E., & Campbell, D. T. (1955). Galvanic skin response to Negro and white experimenters. *Journal of Applied Social Psychology, 51,* 30–33.

Rashke, R. (1981). *The Killing of Karen Silkwood.* Boston: Houghton Mifflin.

Raven, B. H. (1974). The comparative analysis of power and power preference. In J. Tedeschi (Ed.), *Perspectives on social power.* Chicago: Aldine.

Raven, B. H., Centers, R., & Rodrigues, A. (1969). *Social influence in the dyad: The basis of conjugal power* (Tech. Rep. 25, Nononr 233). Los Angeles: University of California at Los Angeles.

Raven, B. H., & French, J. R. (1958). Legitimate power, coercive power and observability in social influence. *Sociometry, 21,* 83–97.

Raven, B. H., & Kruglanski, A. (1970). Conflict and power. In P. Swingle (Ed.), *The structure of conflict.* New York: Academic Press.

Regan, D. T., & Fazio, R. (1977). On the consistency between attitudes and behavior: Look to the method of attitude formation. *Journal of Experimental Social Psychology, 13,* 28–45.

Reis, H. T., Nezlek, J., & Wheeler, L. (1980). Physical attractiveness in social interaction. *Journal of Personality and Social Psychology, 38,* 604–617.

Reizenstein, J. (1982). Hospital design and human behavior: A review of recent literature. In A. Baum & J. Singer (Eds.), *Advances in Environmental Psychology* (Vol. 4). Hillsdale, NJ: Erlbaum. Reprinted by permission of the publisher.

Rhodewalt, F., & Comer, R. (1982). Coronary-prone behavior and reactance: The attractiveness of an eliminated choice. *Personality and Social Psychology Bulletin, 8,* 152–158.

Rhodewalt, F., Saltzman, A. T., & Wittmer, J. (1982). *Self-handicapping among competitive athletes: The role of practice in self-esteem protection.* Unpublished manuscript, University of Utah, Salt Lake City.

Rholes, W. S., & Bailey, S. (1983). The effects of level of moral reasoning on consistency between moral attitudes and related behaviors. *Social Cognition, 2,* 32–48.

Rice, R. W., Bender, L. R., & Vitters, A. G. (1980). Leader sex, follower attitudes toward women, and leadership effectiveness: a laboratory study. *Organizational Behavior and Human Performance, 25,* 46–78.

Rice, R. W., & Kastenbaum, D. R. (1983). The contingency model of leadership: Some current issues. *Basic and Applied Social Psychology, 4,* 373–392.

Rice, R. W., Instone, D., & Adams, J. (1984). Leader sex, leader success, and leadership process: Two field studies. *Journal of Applied Psychology, 69,* 12–31.

Rickels, K., & Downing, R. (1967). Drug- and placebo-treated neurotic outpatients. *Archives of General Psychiatry, 16,* 369–372.

Riecken, H. W. (1958). The effect of

talkativeness on ability to influence group solutions of problems. *Sociometry, 21,* 309–321.

Riess, M., Rosenfeld, R., Melburg, V., & Tedeschi, J. T. (1981). Self-serving attributions: Biased private perceptions and distorted public descriptions. *Journal of Personality and Social Psychology, 41,* 224–231.

Rodin, J. (1976). Density, perceived choice and response to controllable and uncontrollable outcomes. *Journal of Experimental Social Psychology, 12,* 564–578.

Rodin, J., & Baum, A. (1978). Crowding and helplessness: Potential consequences of density and loss of control. In A. Baum & Y. Epstein (Eds.), *Human response to crowding.* Hillsdale, NJ: Erlbaum.

Rodin, J., & Langer, E. S. (1977). Long-term effects of a control-relevant intervention with the institutionalized aged. *Journal of Personality and Social Psychology, 35,* 897–902.

Rodin, J., Solomon, S., & Metcalf, J. (1978). Role of control in mediating perceptions of density. *Journal of Personality and Social Psychology, 36,* 988–999.

Roethlisberger, F., & Dickson, W. (1939). *Management and the worker.* Cambridge, MA: Harvard University Press.

Rogers, T. B. (1981). A model of the self as an aspect of human information processing. In N. Cantor & J. Kihlstrom (Eds.), *Personality, cognition, and social interaction* (pp. 193–214). Hillsdale, NJ: Erlbaum.

Rohles, F. J., Jr. (1981). Thermal comfort and strategies for energy conservation. *Journal of Social Issues, 37*(2), 132–149.

Rosch, E. (1978). Principles of categorization. In E. Rosch & B. B. Lloyd (Eds.), *Cognition and categorization.* Hillsdale, NJ: Erlbaum.

Rosen, S. (1984). Some paradoxical status implications of helping and being helped. In E. Staub et al. (Eds.), *Development and maintenance of prosocial behavior* (pp. 359–378). New York: Plenum.

Rosen, S., Bergman, M., Plestor, D., El-Mofty, A., & Salti, M. (1962). Presbycusis study of a relative noise-free population in the Sudan. *Annals of Otology, Rhinology, and Laryngology, 71,* 727–743.

Rosenbaum, L. L., & Rosenbaum, W. B. (1971). Morale and productivity consequences of group leadership style, stress, and type of task. *Journal of Applied Psychology, 55,* 343–348.

Rosenberg, M. (1965). When dissonance fails: On eliminating evaluation apprehension from attitude measurement. *Journal of Personality and Social Psychology, 1,* 28–42.

Rosenblatt, P. C., & Budd, L. B. (1977). Territoriality and privacy in married and unmarried couples. *Journal of Social Psychology, 41,* 421–428.

Rosenfield, D., Folger, R., & Adelman, H. F. (1980). When rewards reflect competence: A qualification of the overjustification effect. *Journal of Personality and Social Psychology, 39,* 368–376.

Rosenhan, D. L., Salovey, P., & Hargis, K. (1981). The joys of helping: Focus of attention mediates the impact of positive effect on altruism. *Journal of Personality and Social Psychology, 40,* 899–905.

Rosenthal, A. M. (1964). *Thirty-eight witnesses.* New York: McGraw-Hill.

Rosenthal, R., & Evans, J. (1968). Unpublished data, Harvard University.

Rosenthal, R., & Benowitz, L. I. (1985). Sensitivity to nonverbal communication in normal, psychiatric, and brain damaged samples. In P. D. Blanck, R. W. Buck, & R. Rosenthal

(Eds.), *Nonverbal communication in the clinical context*. University Park, PA: Penn State Press.

Rosenthal, R., & Fode, K. L. (1963). Psychology of the scientist: V. Three experiments in experimenter bias. *Psychological Reports, 12,* 491–511. Reprinted with permission of authors and publisher.

Rosenthal, R., & Jacobson, L. (1968). *Pygmalion in the classroom: Teacher expectation and pupils' intellectual development*. New York: Holt, Rinehart & Winston.

Ross, E. A. (1908). *Social psychology: An outline and a source book*. New York: Macmillan.

Ross, L. (1977). The intuitive psychologist and his shortcomings: Distortions in the attribution process. In L. Berkowitz (Ed.), *Advances in experimental social psychology* (Vol. 10). New York: Academic Press.

Ross, L., Greene, D., & House, P. (1977). The "false consensus effect": An egocentric bias in social perception and attribution processes. *Journal of Experimental Social Psychology, 13,* 279–301.

Ross, L., Bierbrauer, G., & Hoffman, S. (1976). The role of attribution processes in conformity and dissent: Revisiting the Asch situation. *American Psychologist, 31,* 148–157.

Ross, L., Rodin, J., & Zimbardo, P. (1969). Toward an attribution therapy: The reduction of fear through induced cognitive-emotional misattribution. *Journal of Personality and Social Psychology, 12,* 279–288.

Ross, M. (1981). Self-centered biases in attribution of responsibility-antecedents and consequences. In E. T. Higgens, C. P. Herman, & M. P. Zanna (Eds.), *Social cognition: The Ontario symposium* (Vol. 1). Hillsdale, NJ: Erlbaum.

Ross, M., & Fletcher, G. J. O. (1985). Attribution and social perception. In G. Lindzey & E. Aronson (Eds.), *The handbook of social psychology* (Vol. 2, 3rd ed.). New York: Random House.

Ross, M., & Olson, J. M. (1981). An expectancy-attribution model of the effects of placebos. *Psychological Review, 88,* 408–437.

Ross, M., & Sicoly, F. (1979). Egocentric biases in availability and attribution. *Journal of Personality and Social Psychology, 37,* 322–336.

Roth, S., & Kubal, L. (1975). Effects of noncontingent reinforcement on tasks of differing importance: Facilitation and learned helplessness. *Journal of Personality and Social Psychology, 32,* 680–691.

Rothbart, M., Dawes, R., & Park, B. (1984). Stereotyping and sampling biases in intergroup perception. In R. Eiser (Ed.), *Attitudinal judgment* (pp. 109–134). New York: Springer-Verlag.

Rotter, J. B. (1966). Generalized expectancies for internal vs. external reinforcement. *Psychological Monographs, 80*(1, Whole no. 609).

Rotter, J. B. (1971, June). External and internal control. *Psychology Today,* pp. 37–42, 58–59. Reprinted with permission from *Psychology Today* Magazine. Copyright © 1971 by the American Psychological Association.

Rotter, J. B. (1971). Generalized expectancies for interpersonal trust. *American Psychologist, 26,* 443–452.

Rowles, G. (1984). Aging in rural environments. In I. Altman, M. Lawton, & J. Wohlwill (Eds.), *Elderly people and the environment*. New York: Plenum Press.

Rowles, G., & Ohta, R. S. (Eds.) (1983). *Aging and milieu: Environmental per-*

spectives on growing old. New York: Academic Press.

Ruback, R., Dabbs, J., & Hopper, C. (1984). The process of brainstorming: An analysis with individual and group vocal parameters. *Journal of Personality and Social Psychology, 47,* 358–567.

Rubin, Z. (1970). Measurement of romantic love. *Journal of Personality and Social Psychology, 16,* 265–273.

Rubin, Z. (1973). *Liking and loving.* New York: Holt, Rinehart & Winston.

Rubin, Z., & Schenker, S. (1978). Friendship, proximity, and self-disclosure. *Journal of Personality, 46,* 1–22.

Ruble, D. N., & Feldman, N. S. (1976). Order of consensus, distinctiveness, and consistency information and causal attribution. *Journal of Personality and Social Psychology, 34,* 930–937.

Rule, B. G., & Nesdale, A. R. (1976). Emotional arousal and aggressive behavior. *Psychological Bulletin, 83,* 851–863.

Runge, T. E., & Archer, R. L. (1979). *Reactions to self-disclosure of public and private information.* Unpublished manuscript, University of Texas at Austin.

Rusboldt, C. E., & Zembrot, I. M. (1983). Responses to dissatisfaction in romantic involvement. *Journal of Experimental Social Psychology, 19,* 274–293.

Rushton, J. P., & Teachinan, G. (1978). The effects of positive reinforcement attributions and punishment on model-induced altruism in children. *Personality and Social Psychology Bulletin, 4,* 322–325.

Russell, D., & Jones, W. H. (1980). When superstition fails: Reactions to disconfirmation of personal beliefs. *Personality and Social Psychology Bulletin, 6,* 83–88.

Russell, D., Cutrona, C. E., Rose, J.,

& Yurko, K. (1984). Social emotional loneliness: An examination of Weiss' Typology of loneliness. *Journal of Personality and Social Psychology, 46,* 1313–1321.

Ryan, R. M. (1982). Control and information in the intrapersonal sphere: An extension of cognitive evaluation theory. *Journal of Personality and Social Psychology, 43,* 450–461.

Ryan, W. (1971). *Blaming the victim.* New York: Vintage Books.

Sabatelli, R. M., Buck, R., & Dreyer, A. (1982). Nonverbal communication accuracy in married couples: Relationship with marital complaints. *Journal of Personality and Social Psychology, 43,* 1088–1097.

Sagar, H. A., & Schofield, J. W. (1980). Racial behavioral cues in black and white children's perceptions of ambiguously aggressive acts. *Journal of Personality and Social Psychology, 39,* 590–598.

Saks, M. J. (1976). The limits of scientific jury selection: Ethical and empirical. *Jurimetrics Journal, 17,* 3–22.

Saks, M. J. (1977). *Jury verdicts.* Lexington, MA: D.C. Heath.

Saks, M. J., & Hastie, R. (1978). *Social psychology in court.* New York: Van Nostrand Reinhold.

Samuelson, C. D., & Messick, D. (1986). Inequities in access to and use of shared resources in social dilemmas. *Journal of Personality and Social Psychology, 51,* 960–967.

Sanders, G. S. (1981). Driven by distraction: An integrative review of social facilitation theory and research. *Journal of Experimental Social Psychology, 17,* 227–251.

Sanders, G. S., & Baron, R. S. (1975). The motivating effects of distraction on task performance. *Journal of Personality and Social Psychology, 32,* 956–963.

Sanders, G. S., & Baron, R. S. (1977). Is social comparison irrelevant for producing choice shifts? *Journal of Experimental and Social Psychology, 13*, 303–313.

Santee, R. T., & Maslach, C. (1982). To agree or not to agree: Personal dissent amid social pressure to conform. *Journal of Personality and Social Psychology, 42*, 690–701.

Savinar, J. (1975). The effect of ceiling height on personal space. *Man-Environment Systems, 5*, 321–324.

Scanzoni, J. (1979). Social exchange and behavioral interdependence. In R. Burgess & T. Huston (Eds.), *Social exchange in developing relationships.* New York: Academic Press.

Scarr, S., & McCartney, K. (1983). How people make their own environments: A theory of genotype → environment effects. *Child Development, 54*, 424–435.

Schachter, S. (1951). Deviation, rejection, and communication. *Journal of Abnormal and Social Psychology, 46*, 190–207.

Schachter, S. (1959). *The psychology of affiliation.* Stanford, CA: Stanford University Press.

Schachter, S. (1964). The interaction of cognitive and physiological determinants of emotional state. In L. Berkowitz (Ed.), *Advances in experimental social psychology* (Vol. 1). New York: Academic Press.

Schachter, S. (1971). *Emotion, obesity and crime.* New York: Academic Press.

Schachter, S., & Singer, J. (1962). Cognitive, social and physiological determinants of emotional state. *Psychological Review, 69*, 379–399. © 1962 by the American Psychological Association. Adapted by permission of the authors.

Schank, R. C., & Abelson, R. P. (1977). *Scripts, plans, goals and understanding: An inquiry into human knowledge structures.* Hillsdale, NJ: Erlbaum.

Scheier, M. F. (1980). Effects of private and public self-consciousness on the public expression of personal beliefs. *Journal of Personality and Social Psychology, 39*, 514–521.

Scheier, M. F., Buss, A. H., & Buss, D. M. (1978). Self-consciousness, self-report of aggressiveness, and aggression. *Journal of Research in Personality, 12*, 133–140.

Schlenker, B. R. (1980). *Impression management: The self-concept, social identity, and interpersonal relations.* Monterey, CA: Brooks/Cole.

Schlenker, B. R. (1982). Translating actions into attitudes: An identity-analytic approach to the explanation of social conduct. In L. Berkowitz (Ed.), *Advances in experimental social psychology* (Vol. 15). New York: Academic Press.

Schlenker, B. R., Helm, B., & Tedeschi, J. T. (1973). The effects of personality and situational variables on behavioral trust. *Journal of Personality and Social Psychology, 25*, 419–427.

Schlesinger, A. M., Jr. (1965). *The thousand days.* Boston: Houghton Mifflin.

Schmidt, D., & Keating, J. (1979). Human crowding and personal control: An integration of the research. *Psychological Bulletin, 86*, 680–700.

Schmutte, G. T., & Taylor, S. P. (1980). Physical aggression as a function of alcohol and pain feedback. *Journal of Social Psychology, 110*, 235–245.

Schneider, D. J., Hastorf, A. H., & Ellsworth, P. C. (1979). *Person perception* (2nd ed.). Reading, MA: Addison-Wesley.

Schneider, D. J., & Miller, R. S. (1975). The effects of enthusiasm and quality of arguments on attitude attribution. *Journal of Personality, 43,* 693–708.

Schneider, F. W., & Harsvick, C. L. (1977). Gaze and distance as a function of changes in interpersonal gaze. *Social Behavior and Personality, 5*(1), 49–53.

Schopler, J., & Bateson, N. (1962). A dependence interpretation of the effects of a severe initiation. *Journal of Personality, 30,* 633–649.

Schriesheim, C. A., & Kerr, S. (1977a). R.I.P. LPC: A response to Fiedler. In J. F. Hunt & L. L. Larson (Eds.), *Leadership: The cutting edge* (pp. 51–56). Carbondale: Southern Illinois University Press.

Schriesheim, C. A., & Kerr, S. (1977b). Theories and measures of leadership: A critical appraisal of current and future directions. In J. G. Hunt & L. L. Larson (Eds.), *Leadership: The cutting edge* (pp. 9–45). Carbondale: Southern Illinois University Press.

Schulz, R. (1976). The effects of control predictability on the physical and psychological well-being of the institutionalized aged. *Journal of Personality and Social Psychology, 33,* 563–573.

Schuman, H., & Kalton, G. (1985). Survey methods. In G. Lindzey & E. Aronson, (Eds.), *Handbook of social psychology* (3rd ed., Vol. 1, pp. 1–46). New York: Random House.

Schwartz, S. H. (1977). Normative influences on altruism. In L. Berkowitz (Ed.), *Advances in experimental social psychology* (Vol. 10). New York: Academic Press.

Schwartz, S. H., & Gottlieb, A. (1980). Bystander anonymity and reactions to emergencies. *Journal of Personality and Social Psychology, 39,* 418–430.

Sears, D., & McConahay, J. (1973). *The politics of violence: The new urban blacks and the Watts riot.* Boston: Houghton Mifflin.

Sears, R. R., Whiting, J. W. M., Nowlis, J., & Sears, P. S. (1953). Child rearing antecedents of aggression and dependency in young children. *Genetic Psychology Monographs, 47,* 135–234.

Secord, P. F., & Backman, C. W. (1974). *Social psychology* (2nd ed.). New York: McGraw-Hill.

Seeman, M., & Evans, J. W. (1962). Alienation and learning in a hospital setting. *American Sociological Review, 27,* 772–782.

Seligman, M. E. P. (1975). *Helplessness: On depression, development, and death.* San Francisco: W. H. Freeman.

Seligman, M. E. P., Abramson, L. Y., Semmel, A., & Von Baeyer, C. (1979). Depressive attributional style. *Journal of Abnormal Psychology, 88,* 242–247.

Senn, D. (1971). Attraction as a function of similarity-dissimilarity in task performance. *Journal of Personality and Social Psychology, 18,* 120–123.

Shaver, K. G. (1985). *The attribution of blame: Causality, responsibility, and blameworthiness.* New York: Springer-Verlag.

Shaw, J. I., & Condelli, L. (1986). Effects of outcome and basis of power on the powerholder-target relationship. *Personality and Social Psychology Bulletin, 12,* 236–246.

Shaw, M. (1932). A comparison of individuals and small groups in the rational solution of complex problems. *American Journal of Psychology, 44,* 491–504.

Shaw, M. E. (1954). Some effects of unequal distribution of information upon group performance in various communication nets. *Journal of Abnormal and Social Psychology, 49,* 547–553.

Shaw, M. E. (1964). Communication networks. In L. Berkowitz (Ed.), *Advances in experimental social psychology* (Vol. 1). New York: Academic Press.

Shaw, M. E. (1981). *Group dynamics: The psychology of small group behavior.* New York: McGraw-Hill.

Shaw, M. E., Rothschild, G., & Strickland, J. (1957). Decision process in communication networks. *Journal of Abnormal and Social Psychology, 54,* 323–330.

Sheppard, B. (1985). Justice is no simple matter: Case for elaborating our model of procedural fairness. *Journal of Personality and Social Psychology, 49,* 953–962.

Sherif, M. (1935). A study of some social factors in perception. *Archives of Psychology, 27*(187), 1–60.

Sherif, M., Harvey, O., White, B., Hood, W., & Sherif, C. (1961). *Intergroup conflict and cooperation: The Robber's Cove experiment.* Norman: University of Oklahoma, Institute of Group Relations.

Sherif, M., & Sherif, C. (1969). First and fourth group graphs (Starting with Individual), from Medians in groups of three subjects (p. 209). In M. Sherif & C. Sherif, *Social psychology.* Copyright © 1969 by Muzafer Sherif and Carolyn W. Sherif. By permission of Harper & Row, Publishers, Inc.

Sherif, M., & Sherif, C. (1979). Research on intergroup relations. In W. Austin & S. Worchel (Eds.), *The social psychology of intergroup relations.* Monterey, CA: Brooks/Cole.

Sherman, S. J., Presson, C. C., Chassin, L., Bensenberg, M., Corty, E., & Olshavsky, R. W. (1982). Smoking intentions in adolescents: Direct experience and predictability. *Personality and Social Psychology Bulletin, 8,* 376–383.

Shiflett, S. C. (1981). Is there a problem with the LPC score in leader match? *Personnel Psychology, 34,* 765–769.

Shinn, M., Rosario, M., Morch, H., & Chestnut, D. (1984). Coping with job stress and burnout in the human services. *Journal of Personality and Social Psychology, 46,* 877–891.

Shomer, R., Davis, A., & Kelley, H. (1966). Threats and the development of coordination: Further studies of the Deutsch and Krauss trucking game. *Journal of Personality and Social Psychology, 4,* 119–126.

Shotland, R. L., & Strau, M. K. (1976). Bystander response to an assault: When a man attacks a woman. *Journal of Personality and Social Psychology, 34,* 990–999.

Shribman, D. (1982, January 14). A deafening roar, then icy silence. *The New York Times,* pp. A1, B6.

Shribman, D. (1982, January 15). Deaths put at 78 in plane crash: Recovery effort starts in Potomac. *The New York Times,* pp. A1, D14.

Shure, G., Meeker, R., & Hansford, E. (1965). The effectiveness of pacifist strategies in bargaining games. *Journal of Conflict Resolution, 9,* 106–117.

Sigall, H., & Aronson, E. (1969). Liking for an evaluator as a function of her physical attractiveness and nature of the evaluations. *Journal of Experimental Social Psychology, 5,* 93–100.

Sigall, H., & Landy, D. (1973). Radiating beauty: Effects of attractive partner on person perception. *Journal of Social Psychology, 28,* 218–224.

Sigall, H., & Ostrove, N. (1975). Beautiful but dangerous: Effects of offender attractiveness and nature of the crime on juridic judgments. *Journal of Personality and Social Psychology, 31,* 410–414. © 1975 by the American Psychological Association. Adapted by permission of the authors.

Sigall, H., & Page, R. (1971). Current stereotypes: A little fading, a little faking. *Journal of Personality and Social Psychology, 18,* 247–255.

Simmel, G. (1955). *Conflict.* New York: Free Press.

Singer, J. L., Brush, C., & Lublin, S. (1965). Some aspects of deindividuation: Identification and conformity. *Journal of Experimental and Social Psychology, 1,* 356–378.

Singer, J. L. (1980). The power and limitations of television: A cognitive affective analysis. In P. H. Tannenbaum (Ed.), *The entertainment functions of television.* Hillsdale, NJ: Erlbaum.

Singer, J. L., & Singer, D. (1981). *Television, imagination, and aggression: A study of preschoolers.* Hillsdale, NJ: Erlbaum.

Sistrunk, F., & McDavid, J. W. (1971). Sex variables in conforming behavior. *Journal of Personality and Social Psychology, 17,* 200–207.

Sivacek, J., & Crano, W. D. (1982). Vested interest as a moderator of attitude-behavior consistency. *Journal of Personality and Social Psychology, 43,* 210–221.

Skinner, B. F. (1938). *The behavior of organisms.* New York: Appleton.

Skolnick, P. (1971). Reactions to personal evaluations: A failure to replicate. *Journal of Personality and Social Psychology, 18,* 62–67.

Smith, T. C. (1980). Arms race instability and war. *Journal of Conflict Resolution, 24,* 253–284.

Smith, T. W., Snyder, C. R., & Handelsman, M. M. (1982). On the self-serving function of an academic wooden leg: Test anxiety as a self-handicapping strategy. *Journal of Personality and Social Psychology, 42,* 314–321.

Smith, T. W., Snyder, C. R., & Perkins, S. C. (1983). The self serving function of hypochondrical complaints: Physical symptoms as self-handicapping strategies. *Journal of Personality and Social Psychology, 44,* 787–797.

Snow, R. (1969). Unfinished Pygmalion. *Contemporary Psychology, 14,* 197–199.

Snyder, C. R., & Fromkin, H. L. (1980). *Uniqueness: The human pursuit of difference.* New York: Plenum Press.

Snyder, C. R., Lassgard, M., & Ford, C. (1986). Distancing after group success and failure: Basking in reflected glory and cutting off reflected failure. *Journal of Personality and Social Psychology, 51,* 683–689.

Snyder, M. (1974). Self-monitoring of expressive behavior. *Journal of Personality and Social Psychology, 30,* 526–537.

Snyder, M. (1976). Attribution and behavior: Social perception and social causation. In J. H. Harvey, W. J. Ickes, & R. F. Kidd (Eds.), *New directions in attribution research* (Vol. 1). Hillsdale, NJ: Erlbaum.

Snyder, M. (1979). Self-monitoring processes. In L. Berkowitz (Ed.), *Advances in experimental social psychology,* (Vol. 12, pp. 85–128). New York: Academic Press.

Snyder, M., Berscheid, E., & Glick, P. (1985). Focusing on the exterior and the interior: Two investigations of the initiation of personal relationships. *Journal of Personality and Social Psychology, 48,* 1427–1439.

Snyder, M., & DeBono, K. G. (1985). Appeals to image and claims about quality: Understanding the psychology of advertising. *Journal of Personality and Social Psychology, 49,* 586–597.

Snyder, M., & Gangestad, S. (1982). Choosing social situations: Two investigations of self-monitoring processes. *Journal of Personality and Social Psychology, 43,* 123–135.

Snyder, M., & Kendzierski, D. (1982). Acting on one's attitudes: Procedures fot linking attitude and behavior. *Journal of Experimental Social Psychology, 18,* 165–183.

Snyder, M., & Swann, W. B., Jr. (1976). When actions reflect attitudes: The politics of impression management. *Journal of Personality and Social Psychology, 34,* 1034–1042.

Snyder, M., & Swann, W. B., Jr. (1978). Behavioral confirmation in social interaction: From social perception to social reality. *Journal of Experimental Social Psychology, 14,* 148–162.

Snyder, M. L., Schulz, R., & Jones, E. E. (1974). Expectancy and apparent duration as determinants of fatigue. *Journal of Personality and Social Psychology, 29,* 426–434.

Soloman, M. R., & Schopler, J. (1982). Self-consciousness and clothing. *Personality and Social Psychology Bulletin, 8,* 508–514.

Sommer, R. (1969). *Personal space: The behavioral basis of design.* Englewood Cliffs, NJ: Prentice-Hall.

Sommer, R., & Becker, F. D. (1969). Territorial defense and the good neighbor. *Journal of Personality and Social Psychology, 11,* 85–92. © 1969 by the American Psychological Association. Adapted by permission of the authors.

Sommer, R., & Ross, H. (1958). Social interaction on a geriatric ward. *International Journal of Social Psychiatry, 4,* 128–133.

Sorrentino, R. M., & Boutillier, R. G. (1975). The effect of quantity and quality of verbal interaction on ratings of leadership ability. *Journal of Experimental Social Psychology, 11,* 403–411.

Sorrentino, R. M., & Field, N. (1986). Emergent leadership over time: The functional value of positive motivation. *Journal of Personality and Social Psychology, 50,* 1091–1099.

Spence, K. W., Farber, I. E., & McFann, H. H. (1956). The relation of anxiety (drive) level to performance in competitional and noncompetitional paried-associated learning. *Journal of Experimental Psychology, 52,* 296–305.

Srull, T. K., & Brand, J. F. (1983). Memory for information about persona: The effect of encoding operations on subsequent retrieval. *Journal of Verbal Learning and Verbal Behavior, 22,* 219–230.

Staats, A. W., & Staats, C. K. (1958). Attitudes established by classical conditioning. *Journal of Abnormal and Social Psychology, 57,* 37–40. © 1958 by the American Psychological Association.

Stang, D. J. (1972). Conformity, ability, and self-esteem. *Representative Research in Social Psychology, 3,* 97–103.

Stasser, G., & Titus, W. (1985). Pooling of unshared information in group decision making: Biased information sampling during discussion. *Journal of Personality and Social Psychology, 48,* 1467–1478.

Staw, B. M. (1974). Attitudinal and behavioral consequences of changing a major organizational reward: A natural field experiment. *Journal of Personality and Social Psychology, 29,* 742–751.

Stech, F. J., & McClintock, C. G. (1981). Effects of communicating timing on duopoly bargaining outcomes. *Journal of Personality and Social Psychology, 40,* 664–674.

Steele, C. M., & Liu, T. J. (1981). Making the dissonance act unreflective of self: Dissonance avoidance and the expectancy of a value-affirming response. *Personality and Social Psychology Bulletin, 7,* 393–397.

Steele, C. M., & Liu, T. J. (1983). Dissonance process as self-affirmation. *Journal of Personality and Social Psychology, 45,* 5–19.

Steele, C. M., Southwick, L. L., & Critchlow, B. (1981). Dissonance and alcohol: Drinking your troubles away. *Journal of Personality and Social Psychology, 41,* 831–846.

Stein, A. H., & Friedrich, L. K. (1975). The impact of television on children and youth. In E. M. Hetherington (Ed.), *Review of Child Development Research.* Chicago: University of Chicago Press.

Steiner, I. D. (1972). *Group process and productivity.* New York: Academic Press.

Steiner, I. D. (1976). Task-performing groups. In J. Thibaut, J. Spence, & R. Carson (Eds.), *Contemporary trends in social psychology.* Morristown, NJ: General Learning Press.

Stephan, W. (1985). Intergroup relations. In G. Lindzey & E. Aronson (Eds.), *Handbook of social psychology* (3rd ed., Vol. 2, pp. 599–648). New York: Random House.

Stephan, F. F., & Mishler, E. G. (1952). The distribution of participation in small groups: An exponential approximation. *American Sociological Review, 17,* 598–608.

Sterling, B., & Gaertner, S. L. (1984). The attribution of arousal and emergency helping: A bi-directional process. *Journal of Experimental Social Psychology, 6,* 586–596.

Sternberg, R. J., & Grajek, S. (1984). The nature of love. *Journal of Personality and Social Psychology, 47,* 312–329.

Stewart, J. E. (1980). Defendant's attractiveness as a factor in the outcome of criminal trials: An observational study. *Journal of Applied Social Psychology, 10,* 348–361.

Stewart, R. (1965). Effects of continuous responding on the order effect in personality impression formation. *Journal of Personality and Social Psychology, 1,* 161–165.

Stogdill, R. (1948). Personal factors associated with leadership. *Journal of Psychology, 25,* 35–71.

Stokols, D. (1972). On the distinction between density and crowding: Some implications for future research. *Psychological Review, 79,* 275–278.

Stokols, D. (1978). A typology of crowding experiences. In A. Baum & Y. Epstein (Eds.), *Human response to crowding.* Hillsdale, NJ: Erlbaum.

Stoner, J. (1961). *A comparison of individual and group decisions, including risk.* Unpublished master's thesis, Massachusetts Institute of Technology, School of Industrial Management, Cambridge.

Storms, M. (1973). Videotape and the attribution process: Reversing actor's and observer's points of view. *Journal of Personality and Social Psychology, 27,* 165–175.

Storms, M., & Nisbett, R. E. (1970). Insomnia and the attribution process. *Journal of Personality and Social Psychology, 2,* 319–328. © 1970 the American Psychological Association. Adapted by permission of the authors.

Streufert, S., & Streufert, S. C. (1969). Effects of conceptual structure, failure and success on attribution of causality and interpersonal attitudes. *Journal of Personality and Social Psychology, 11,* 138–147.

Streufert, S., & Streufert, S. C. (1986). The development of internation conflict. In Worchel, S., & Austin, W. G. (Eds.), *The psychology of intergroup relations.* Chicago: Nelson-Hall.

Strickland, L. H. (1968). Changes in self-presentation in need for approval scores. *Perceptual and Motor Skills, 27,* 335–337.

Strom, P., & Buck, R. (1979). Staring and participants' sex: Physiological and subjective reactions. *Personality and Social Psychology Bulletin, 5,* 114–117.

Strube, R., & Werner, C. (1982). Interpersonal distance and personal space: A conceptual and methodological note. *Journal of Nonverbal Behavior, 6,* 163–170.

Stryker, S., & Statham, A. (1986). Symbolic interaction and role theory. In G. Lindzey & E. Aronson (Eds.), *The handbook of social psychology* (3rd ed.). New York: Random House.

Sullivan, H. (1950). *Interpersonal theory of psychiatry.* New York: W. W. Norton.

Suls, J., Gaes, G., & Gastorf, J. (1979). Evaluating a sex-related ability: Comparison with same-, opposite-, and combined-sex norms. *Journal of Research in Personality, 13,* 294–304.

Suls, J. M., & Miller, R. C. (Eds.). (1977). *Social comparison processes: Theoretical and empirical perspectives.* Washington, DC: Halsted-Wiley.

Sumner, W. (1906). *Folkways.* Boston: Ginn.

Sundstrom, E. (1978). Crowding as a sequential process: Review of research on the effects of population density on humans. In A. Baum & Y. Epstein (Eds.), *Human response to crowding.* Hillsdale, NJ: Erlbaum.

Swann, W. B., & Read, S. J. (1981). Self-verification processes: How we sustain our self-conceptions. *Journal of Experimental Social Psychology, 17,* 351–372.

Sweeney, P. D., Schaeffer, D., & Golin, S. (1982). Attributions about the self and others in depression. *Personality and Social Psychology Bulletin, 8,* 37–42.

Swingle, P. (1970). Exploitative behavior in non-zero-sum games. *Journal of Personality and Social Psychology, 16,* 121–132.

Swinth, R. L. (1976). A decision process model for predicting job preferences. *Journal of Applied Psychology, 61,* 242–245.

Tagiuri, R., Blake, R., & Bruner, J. (1953). Some determinants of the perception of positive and negative feelings in others. *Journal of Abnormal and Social Psychology, 48,* 585–592.

Tajfel, H. (1970). Experiments in intergroup discrimination. *Scientific American, 223*(2), 96–102.

Tajfel, H. (1972). Experiments in a vacuum. In J. Israel & H. Tajfel (Eds.), *The context of social psychology: A critical assessment* (European Monographs in Social Psychology, No. 2). London: Academic Press.

Tajfel, H. (1978). Intergroup behavior individualistic perspectives. In H. Tajfel & C. Fraser (Eds.), *Introducing social psychology.* Harmondsworth, Middlesex: Penguin.

Tajfel, H. (1979). Individuals and groups in social psychology. *British Journal of Social and Clinical Psychology, 18,* 183–190.

Tajfel, H. (1981). Social stereotypes and social groups. In J. C. Turner & H. Giles (Eds.), *Intergroup relations.* Chicago: University of Chicago Press.

Tajfel, H. (1982). *Social identity and intergroup relations.* Cambridge: Cambridge University Press.

Tajfel, H., & Turner, J. C. (1986). The social identity theory of intergroup behavior. In Worchel, S., & Austin, W. G. (Eds.), *The psychology of intergroup relations.* Chicago: Nelson-Hall.

Tajfel, H., Flament, C., Billig, M. G., & Bundy, F. F. (1971). Social categorization and intergroup behavior. *European Journal of Social Psychology, 1*, 149–177.

Tanford, S., & Penrod, S. (1984). Social influence model: A formal integration of research on majority and minority influence processes. *Psychological Bulletin, 95*, 189–225.

Tannenbaum, P. H., & Zillman, D. (1975). Emotional arousal in the facilitation of aggression through communication. In L. Berkowitz (Ed.), *Advances in experimental social psychology* (Vol. 8). New York: Academic Press.

Tapp, J. L. (1981). Psychologists and the law: Who needs whom? *Applied social psychology annual, 2*, 263–291.

Tarde, G. (1903). *The laws of imitation* (Trans.). New York: Holt.

Taylor, D. A., Gould, R. J., & Brounstein, P. J. (1981). Effects of personalistic self disclosure. *Personality and Social Psychology Bulletin, 7*, 487–492.

Taylor, M. (1979). Race, sex, and the expression of self-fulfilling prophecies in a laboratory teaching situation. *Journal of Personality and Social Psychology, 37*, 897–912.

Taylor, R. B., & Lanni, J. C. (1981). Territorial dominance: The influence of the resident advantage in triadic decision making. *Journal of Personality and Social Psychology, 41*(S), 909–915.

Taylor, S. E. (1975). On inferring one's own attitudes from one's behavior: Some delimiting conditions. *Journal of Personality and Social Psychology, 31*, 126–131.

Taylor, S. E. (1979). Hospital patient behavior: Reactance, helplessness, or control? *Journal of Social Issues, 35*(1), 156–184.

Taylor, S. E., & Fiske, S. T. (1975). Point of view and perceptions of causality. *Journal of Personality and Social Psychology, 32*, 439–445.

Taylor, S. E., & Fiske, S. T. (1978). Salience, attention and attribution: Top of the head phenomena. In L. Berkowitz (Ed.), *Advances in experimental social psychology* (Vol. 11). New York: Academic Press.

Taylor, S. E., Fiske, S. T., Etcoff, N. L., & Ruderman, A. J. (1978). Categorical bases of person memory and stereotyping. *Journal of Personality and Social Psychology, 36*, 778–793.

Taylor, S. P., & Gammon, C. B. (1975). Effects of type and dose of alcohol on human physical aggression. *Journal of Personality and Social Psychology, 32*, 169–175.

Taylor, S. P., Gammon, C. B., & Capasso, D. R. (1976). Aggression as a function of the interaction of alcohol and threat. *Journal of Personality and Social Psychology, 34*, 938–941.

Taylor, S. P., Vardaris, R. M., Rawitch, A. B., Gammon, C. B., & Cranston, J. W. (1976). The effects of alcohol and delta-p-tetrahydrocannibol on human physical aggression. *Aggressive Behavior, 2*, 153–162.

Tedeschi, J. T. (1974). *Perspectives on social power.* Chicago: Aldine.

Tedeschi, J. T. (1979). Frustration, fantasy, aggression, and the exercise of coercive power. *Perceptual and Motor Skills, 48*, 215–219.

Tedeschi, J. T. (Ed.). (1981). *Impression management theory and social psychological research.* New York: Academic Press.

Tedeschi, J. T., & Lindskold, S. (1976). *Social psychology.* New York: John Wiley & Sons.

Tedeschi, J. T., Schlenker, B. R., & Bonoma, T. V. (1971). Cognitive dissonance: Private ratiocination or public spectacle? *American Psychologist, 26,* 685–695.

Teger, A. (1980). *Too much invested to quit.* New York: Pergamon Press.

Tennen, H., & Eller, S. J. (1977). Attributional components of learned helplessness and facilitation. *Journal of Personality and Social Psychology, 35,* 265–271.

Terborg, J. R., Castore, C., & DeNinno, J. A. (1976). A longitudinal field investigation of the impact of group composition on group performance and cohesion. *Journal of Personality and Social Psychology, 34,* 782–790.

Terman, L. (1904). A preliminary study in the psychology and pedagogy of leadership. *Pedagogical Seminary, 4,* 413–451.

Tesser, A. (1984). Self-evaluation maintenance processes: Implications for relationships and development. In J. Masters & K. Yarkin (Eds.), *Boundary areas of psychology: Social and developmental.* New York: Academic Press.

Tesser, A. (1985). Some effects of self-evaluation maintenance cognition and action. In R. M. Sorrentino & E. T. Higgins (Eds.), *The handbook of motivation and cognition: Foundations of social behavior.* New York: Guilford Press.

Tesser, A., & Smith, J. (1980). Some effects of task relevance and friendship on helping: You don't always help the one you like. *Journal of Experimental Social Psychology, 16,* 582–590.

Thibaut, J. W. (1968). The development of contractual norms in bargaining replication and variation. *Journal of Conflict Resolution, 12,* 102–112.

Thibaut, J. W., & Kelley, H. H. (1959). *The social psychology of groups.* New York: Wiley.

Thibaut, J. W., & Riecken, H. R. (1955).

Some determinants and consequences of the perception of social causality. *Journal of Personality, 24,* 113–133.

Thibaut, J. W., & Walker, L. (1975). *Procedural justice: A psychological analysis.* Hillsdale, NJ: Erlbaum.

Thibaut, J. W., & Walker, L. (1978). A theory of procedure. *California Law Review, 66,* 541–566.

Thompson, W. C., Cowan, C. L., & Rosenhan, D. L. (1980). Focus of attention mediates the impact of negative effect on altruism. *Journal of Personality and Social Psychology, 39,* 291–300.

Thornton, B., Hogate, L., Moirs, K., Pinette, M., & Presby, W. (1986). Physiological evidence of an arousal-based motivational bias in the defensive attribution of responsibility. *Journal of Experimental Social Psychology, 22,* 148–162.

Thornton, J. W., & Jacobs, P. D. (1971). Learned helplessness in human subjects. *Journal of Experimental Psychology, 87*(3), 367–372.

Thurstone, L. L., & Chave, E. J. (1929). *The measurement of attitudes.* Chicago: University of Chicago Press.

Thurstone, L. L. (1946). Comment. *American Journal of Sociology, 52,* 39–40.

Tieger, T. (1980). On the biological basis of sex differences in aggression. *Child Development, 51,* 943–963.

Tilker, H. A. (1970). Socially responsible behavior as a function of observer responsibility and victim feedback. *Journal of Personality and Social Psychology, 4,* 95–100.

Time Magazine (1985, July 1). An attack on civilization, pp. 8–22.

Time Magazine (1985, July 8). At last, the agony is over, pp. 14–20.

Tobey, E. L., & Tunnell, G. (1981). Predicting our impressions on others:

Effects of self-consciousness and acting, a self-monitoring subscale. *Personality and Social Psychology Bulletin, 7,* 661–669.

Topf, M. (1983). Noise pollution in the hospital. *The New England Journal of Medicine, 309,* 53–54.

Topf, M. (1985). Personal and environmental predictors of patient disturbance due to hospital noise. *Journal of Applied Psychology, 70,* 22–28.

Torrance, E. P. (1954). The behavior of small groups under the stress of conditions of survival. *American Sociological Review, 19,* 751–755.

Touhey, J. C. (1972). Comparison of two dimensions of attitude similarity on heterosexual attraction. *Journal of Personality and Social Psychology, 23,* 8–10.

Travis, L. E. (1925) The effect of a small audience upon eye-hand coordination. *Journal of Abnormal and Social Psychology, 20,* 142–146.

Triandis, H. C. (1971). *Attitudes and attitude change.* New York: Wiley.

Triplett, N. (1897). The dynamogenic factors in pacemaking and competition. *American Journal of Psychology, 9,* 507–533.

Tuan, Y. F. (1977). *Space and place: The perspective of experience.* Minneapolis: University of Minnesota.

Tucker, J. A., Vucinish, R. E., & Sobell, M. B. (1981). Alcohol consumption as a self-handicapping strategy. *Journal of Abnormal Psychology, 90,* 220–230.

Turner, C. W., & Berkowitz, L. (1972). Identification with film aggressor (covert role taking) and reactions to film violence. *Journal of Personality and Social Psychology, 21,* 256–264.

Turner, J. C. (1982). Towards a cognitive redefinition of the social group. In H. Tajfel (Ed.), *Social identity and*

intergroup relations. Cambridge: Cambridge University Press.

Turner, J. C., & Brown, R. J. (1978). Social status, cognitive alternatives and intergroup relations. In H. Tajfel (Ed.), *Differentiation between social groups.* London: Academic Press.

Tversky, A., & Kahneman, D. (1973). Availability: A heuristic for judging frequency and probability. *Cognitive Psychology, 5,* 207–232.

Tyler, T. R. (1980). Impact of directly and indirectly experienced events: The origin of crime-related judgments and behaviors. *Journal of Personality and Social Psychology, 39,* 13–28.

Tyler, T. R., & Sears, D. O. (1977). Coming to like obnoxious people when we must live with them. *Journal of Personality and Social Psychology, 35,* 200–211.

U. S. Riot Commission. (1968). *Report of the national commission on civil disorders.* New York: Bantam Books.

Underwood, B., Berenson, J. F., Berenson, R. J., Cheng, K. K., Wilson, D., Kulik, J., Moore, B. S., & Wenzel, G. (1977). Attention, negative affect and altruism: An ecological validation. *Personality and Social Psychology Bulletin, 3,* 51–53.

Urruti, G., & Miller, C. E. (1984). Test of bargaining and equal access theories of coalition formation: Effects of experience, information about payoffs, and monetary stakes. *Journal of Personality and Social Psychology, 46,* 825–836.

Valins, S. (1966). Cognitive effects of false heart-rate feedback. *Journal of Personality and Social Psychology, 4,* 400–408.

Valins, S. (1972). Persistent effects of information about internal reactions: Ineffectiveness of debriefing. In H. London & R. E. Nisbett (Eds.), *The cognitive alteration of feeling states.* Chicago: Aldine.

Van Zelt, R. H. (1952). Sociometrically selected work teams increase production. *Personnel Psychology, 5,* 175–186.

Veitch, R., & Griffitt, W. (1976). Good news, bad news: Affective and interpersonal effects. *Journal of Applied Social Psychology, 6,* 69–75.

Videbeck, R. (1960). Self conception and the reaction of others. *Sociometry, 23,* 351–359.

Vogel, S. R. (1979). Dercurrant's comments symposium: Applications of androgyny to the theory and practice of psychotherapy. *Psychology of Women Quarterly, 3,* 255–258.

Von Baeyer, C. L., Sherk, D. L., & Zanna, M. P. (1981). Impression management in the job interview: When the female applicant meets the male (chauvinist) interviewer. *Personality and Social Psychology Bulletin, 7,* 45–51.

Wagner, R. (1985). Psychology and the threat of nuclear war. *American Psychologist, 40,* 531–535.

Wallace, M. (1980). Some persisting findings: A reply to Professor Wilde. *Journal of Conflict Resolution, 24,* 289–293.

Wallach, M., & Kogan, N. (1965). The roles of information, discussion, and consensus in group risk taking. *Journal of Experimental Social Psychology, 1,* 1–19.

Wallach, M., Kogan, N., & Bem, D. (1962). Group influence on individual risk taking. *Journal of Abnormal and Social Psychology, 65,* 75–86. © 1962 by the American Psychological Association. Adapted by permission of the authors.

Wallach, M., Kogan, N., & Bem, D. (1964). Diffusion of responsibility and level of risk taking in groups.

Journal of Abnormal and Social Psychology, 68, 263–274.

Walsh, R. H., Ferrel, M. Z., & Tolone, W. L. (1976). Selection of reference group, perceived permissiveness of reference group and personal permissiveness attitudes and behavior. *Journal of Marriage and the Family, 38,* 495–507.

Walster, E. (1966). Assignment of responsibility for an accident. *Journal of Personality and Social Psychology, 3,* 73–79.

Walster, E., Aronson, V., Abrahams, D., & Rottman, L. (1966). The importance of physical attractiveness in dating behavior. *Journal of Personality and Social Psychology, 4,* 508–516.

Walster, E., Berscheid, E., & Walster, G. W. (1976). New directions in equity research. In L. Berkowitz (Ed.), *Advances in experimental social psychology* (Vol. 9). New York: Academic Press.

Walster, E., Berscheid, E., & Walster, G. W. (1978). *Equity: Theory and research.* Boston: Allyn & Bacon.

Walster, E., & Festinger, L. (1962). The effectiveness of "overheard" persuasive communications. *Journal of Abnormal and Social Psychology, 65,* 395–402.

Walster, E., & Walster, G. W. (1963). Effect of expecting to be liked on choice of associates. *Journal of Abnormal and Social Psychology, 67,* 402–404.

Walster, E., & Walster, G. W. (1969). The matching hypothesis. *Journal of Personality and Social Psychology, 6,* 248–253.

Walster, E., & Walster, G. W. (1978). *Love.* Reading, MA: Addison-Wesley.

Walters, P. S., & Lindskold, S. (1982). *Intensity of conflict and response to conciliation.* Unpublished manuscript, Ohio University, Athens, OH.

Walters, R., & Willows, D. (1968). Imitation behavior of disturbed children following exposure to aggressive and nonaggressive models. *Child Development, 39,* 79–91.

Waterman, C. K. (1969). The facilitating and interfering effects of cognitive dissonance on simple and complex paired-associate learning tasks. *Journal of Experimental Social Psychology, 5,* 31–42.

Waterman, C. K., & Katkin, E. S. (1967). The energizing (dynamogenic) effect of cognitive dissonance on task performance. *Journal of Personality and Social Psychology, 6,* 126–131.

Waters, H. F., & Malamud, P. (1975, March 10). "Drop that gun, Captain Video." *Newsweek, 85*(10), 81–82.

Watson, R. I. (1973). Investigation into deindividuation using a cross-cultural survey technique. *Journal of Personality and Social Psychology, 25,* 342–345.

Weaver, W. (1970, October 25). Nixon repudiates obscenity reports as morally void. *The New York Times,* pp. 1, 71.

Webb, W., & Worchel, P. (1986). *Trust and distrust.* In Worchel, S., & Austin, W. G. (Eds.), *The psychology of intergroup relations.* Chicago: Nelson-Hall.

Webb, W., Worchel, S., Reichers, L., & Wayne, W. (1986). The influence of categorization on perceptions of growling. *Personality and Social Psychology Bulletin, 12,* 539–546.

Weber, M. (1946). The sociology of charismatic authority. Reprinted in H. H. Gerth & C. W. Mills (Trans. and Eds.), *From Max Weber: Essay in sociology.* (pp. 245–252). New York: Oxford University Press. (Originally published in 1921.)

Weiner, B. (1979). A theory of motivation for some classroom experiences. *Journal of Educational Psychology, 71,* 3–25.

Weiner, B., Frieze, I., Kukla, A., Reed, L., Rest, B., & Rosenbaum, R. M. (1971). *Perceiving the causes of success and failure.* Morristown, NJ: General Learning Press. © 1971 General Learning Corporation. Reprinted by permission.

Weiner, B., Frieze, I., Kukla, A., Reed, L., Rest, S., & Rosenbaum, R. M. (1972). Perceiving the causes of success and failure. In E. E. Jones, D. E. Kanouse, H. H. Kelley, R. E. Nisbett, S. Valins, & B. Weiner (Eds.), *Attribution: Perceiving the causes of behavior.* Morristown, NJ: General Learning Press.

Weiss, R. S. (1973). *Loneliness: The experience of emotional and social isolation.* Cambridge: Massachusetts Institute of Technology Press.

Weiss, R. S. (1974). The provisions of social relationships. In Z. Rubin (Ed.), *Doing unto others* (pp. 17–26). Englewood Cliffs, NJ: Prentice-Hall.

Wells, B. (1972). The psycho-social influence of building environment: Sociometric findings in large and small office spaces. In R. Gutman (Ed.), *People and buildings.* New York: Basic Books.

Wells, G. L., & Petty, R. E. (1980). The effects of overt head-movements on persuasion, compatibility, and incompatibility of responses. *Journal of Basic and Applied Social Psychology, 1,* 219–230.

Werner, G., & Latané, B. (1974). Interaction motivates attraction: Rats are fond of fondling. *Journal of Personality and Social Psychology, 29,* 328–334.

West, S. G., & Wicklund, R. A. (1980). *A primer of social psychological theories.* Monterey, CA: Brooks/Cole.

Westin, A. F. (1967). *Privacy and freedom.* New York: Atheneum.

Wexler, M. (1976). The behavioral sciences in medical education: A view from psychology. *American Psychologist, 31,* 275–283.

Wexner, L. B. (1954). The degree to which colors (hues) are associated with mood tones. *Journal of Applied Psychology, 38,* 432–435.

Wheeler, L. (1966). Toward a theory of behavioral contagion. *Psychological Review, 73,* 179–192.

Wheeler, L., & Koestner, R. (1984). Performance evaluation: On choosing to know the related attributes of others when we know their performance. *Journal of Experimental Social Psychology, 20,* 263–271.

Wheeler, L., Koestner, R., & Driver, R. E. (1982). Related attributes in the choice of comparison others: It's there, but it isn't all there is. *Journal of Experimental Social Psychology, 18,* 489–500.

Wheeler, L., Reis, H., & Nezlek, J. (1983). Loneliness, social interaction, and sex roles. *Journal of Personality and Social Psychology, 45,* 943–953.

Whitcher, S. J., & Fisher, J. D. (1979). Multidimensional reaction to therapeutic touch in a hospital setting. *Journal of Personality and Social Psychology, 37,* 87–96.

White, G. L. (1981). A model of romantic jealousy. *Motivation and Emotion, 5,* 295–310.

White, G. L., Fishbein, S., & Rutstein, J. (1981). Passionate love and the misattribution of arousal. *Journal of Personality and Social Psychology, 41,* 56–62.

White, M. (1975). Interpersonal distance as affected by room size, status, and sex. *Journal of Social Psychology, 95,* 241–249.

White, R. K. (1966). Misperception as a cause of two world wars. *Journal of Social Issues, 22*(3), 1–9.

Whyte, W., Jr. (1956). *The organization man.* New York: Simon & Schuster.

Wicker, A. (1969). Attitudes versus action: The relationship of verbal and overt behavioral responses to attitude objects. *The Journal of Social Issues, 25,* 1–78.

Wicker, A. W., Kirmeyer, S. L., Hanson, L., & Alexander, D. (1976). Effects of manning levels on subjective experiences, performance and verbal interactions in groups. *Organizational Behavior and Human Performance, 17,* 251–274.

Wicklund, R. A., & Brehm, J. W. (1976). *Perspectives on cognitive dissonance.* Hillsdale, NJ: Erlbaum.

Wicklund, R. A., Cooper, J., & Linder, D. E. (1976). Effects of expected effort on attitude change prior to exposure. *Journal of Experimental Social Psychology, 3,* 416–428.

Wicklund, R. A., & Frey, D. (1980). Self awareness theory: When the self makes a difference. In D. M. Wegner & R. R. Vallacher (Eds.), *The self in social psychology* (pp. 31–54). New York: Oxford University Press.

Wilder, D. A. (1977). Perception of groups, size of opposition, and social influence. *Journal of Experimental Social Psychology, 13,* 253–268.

Wilder, D. (1986). Cognitive factors affecting the success of intergroup contact. In Worchel, S., & Austin, W. G. (Eds.), *Psychology of intergroup relations.* Chicago: Nelson-Hall.

Wiley, R. (1982). One of few to hit 300. *Sports Illustrated, 57*(15), 69–72.

Williams, K., Harkins, S., & Latané, B. (1981). Identifiability as a deterrent to social loafing: Two cheering experiments. *Journal of Personality and Social Psychology, 40,* 303–311. © 1981 by the American Psychological Association. Adapted by permission of the authors.

Williams v. Florida, 399 U.S. 78 (1970).

Willis, R. H. (1965). Conformity, independence, and anticonformity. *Human Relations, 18,* 373–388.

Willis, R. H. (1972). Diamond model of social response. In W. S. Sahakian (Ed.), *Social psychology: Experimentation, theory, and research.* Scranton, PA: International Textbook.

Wills, T. A. (1981). Downward comparison principles in social psychology. *Psychological Bulletin, 90,* 245–271.

Wilson, C. E. (1974). The effect of medium on loss of information. *Journalism Quarterly, 51,* 111–115.

Wilson, G. D. (1966). Arousal properties of red versus green. *Perceptual and motor skills, 23,* 947–979.

Wilson, T. D., & Lassiter, G. D. (1982). Increasing intrinsic interest with superfluous extrinsic constraints. *Journal of Personality and Social Psychology, 42,* 811–819.

Wilson, T. D., & Linville, P. W. (1982). Improving the academic performance of college freshmen: Attribution therapy revisited. *Journal of Personality and Social Psychology, 42,* 367–376.

Winch, R. (1958). *Mate-selection: A study of complementary needs.* New York: Harper & Row.

Winkler, J., & Taylor, S. E. (1979). Preference, expectations, and attributional bias: Two field studies. *Journal of Applied Social Psychology, 2,* 183–197.

Wolfgang, M. E., & Fenacuti, F. (1967). *The subculture of violence.* London: Tavistock.

Won-Doornik, M. J. (1979). On getting to know you: The association between the stage of a relationship and the reciprocity of self-disclosure. *Journal of Experimental Social Psychology, 15,* 220–241.

Wood, W., & Eagly, A. II. (1981). Stages in the analysis of persuasive messages: The role of causal attributions and message comprehension. *Journal of Personality and Social Psychology, 40,* 246–259.

Worchel, S. (1974). The effect of three types of arbitrary thwarting on the instigation to aggression. *Journal of Personality, 42,* 300–318.

Worchel, S. (1978). The experience of crowding: An attributional analysis. In A. Baum & Y. Epstein, *Human response to crowding.* Hillsdale, NJ: Erlbaum.

Worchel, S. (1984). The darker side of helping: The social dynamics of helping and cooperation. In E. Staub, D. Bar-Tal, J. Karylowski, & J. Reykowski (Eds.), *The development and maintenance of prosocial behavior.* New York: Plenum Press.

Worchel, S. (1984). *A model of achieving group independence.* Paper presented at XXIII International Congress of Psychology, Acapulco, Mexico.

Worchel, S. (1986). The role of cooperation in reducing intergroup conflict. In Worchel, S., & Austin, W. G. (Eds.), *The psychology of intergroup relations* (pp. 153–176). Chicago: Nelson-Hall.

Worchel, S. (in press). The influence of contextual variables on interpersonal spacing. *Journal of Nonverbal Behavior.*

Worchel, S., & Andreoli, V. (1978). Facilitation of social interaction through deindividuation of the target. *Journal of Personality and Social Psychology, 36,* 549–557.

Worchel, S., Andreoli, V., & Folger, R. (1977). Intergroup cooperation and intergroup attraction: The effect of previous interaction and outcome of combined effort. *Journal of Experimental Social Psychology, 13,* 131–140.

Worchel, S., & Arnold, S. (1973). The effects of censorship and attractiveness of the censor on attitude change. *Journal of Experimental Social Psychology, 9,* 365–377.

Worchel, S., Arnold, S., & Baker, M. (1975). The effects of censorship on attitude change: The influence of censor and communication characteristics. *Journal of Applied Social Psychology, 5,* 227–239.

Worchel, S., & Austin, W. G. (Eds.). (1986). *The psychology of intergroup relations.* Chicago: Nelson-Hall.

Worchel, S., Axsom, D., Ferris, F., Samaha, G., & Schweitzer, S. (1978). Determinants of the effects of intergroup cooperation on intergroup attraction. *Journal of Conflict Resolution, 22,* 429–439.

Worchel, S., & Brehm, J. W. (1970). Effect of threats to attitudinal freedom as a function of agreement with the communicator. *Journal of Personality and Social Psychology, 14,* 18–22.

Worchel, S., & Brown, E. H. (1984). The role of plausability in influencing environmental attributions. *Journal of Experimental Social Psychology, 20,* 86–96.

Worchel, S., Lind, E., & Kaufman, K. (1975). Evaluations of group products as a function of expectations of group longevity, outcome of competition and publicity of evaluations. *Journal of Personality and Social Psychology, 31,* 1089–1097. © 1975 by the American Psychological Association. Adapted by permission of the authors.

Worchel, S., & Lollis, M. (1982). Reactions to territorial contamination as a function of culture. *Personality and Social Psychology Bulletin, 8,* 365–370. © 1982 by the Society for Personality and Social Psychology, Inc.

Worchel, S., & Norvell, N. (1980). Effect of perceived environmental conditions during cooperation on intergroup attraction. *Journal of Personality and Social Psychology, 38,* 764–772.

Worchel, S., & Sigall, H. (1976). There is no place like home, unless . . . *The ACC Basketball Handbook.* Charlotte, NC: VMI Publications.

Worchel, S., & Teddlie, C. (1976). The experience of crowding: A two-factor theory. *Journal of Personality and Social Psychology, 34,* 30–40.

Worchel, S., & Yohai, S. M. L. (1979). The role of attribution in the experience of crowding. *Journal of Experimental Social Psychology, 15,* 91–104. © 1978 by the American Psychological Association.

Word, C. H., Zanna, M. P., & Cooper, J. (1974). The nonverbal mediation of self-fulfilling prophecies in interracial interaction. *Journal of Experimental Social Psychology, 10,* 109–120.

Wortman, C. B., & Brehm, J. W. (1975). Responses to uncontrollable outcomes: An integration of reactance theory and the learned helplessness model. In L. Berkowitz (Ed.), *Advances in experimental social psychology* (Vol. 8, pp. 277–336). New York: Academic Press.

Wortman, C. B., & Dintzer, L. (1978). Is an attributional analysis of the learned helplessness phenomenon viable? A critique of the Abramson-Seligman-Teasdale reformulation. *Journal of Abnormal Psychology, 87,* 75–90.

Wright, P., & Crawford, A. (1971). Agreement and friendship: A close look and some second thoughts. *Representative Research in Social Psychology, 2,* 52–69.

Wrightsman, L. S. (1964). Measurement of philosophies of human nature. *Psychological Reports, 14,* 743–751.

Wrightsman, L. S. (1969). Wallace supporters and adherance to "law and order." *Journal of Personality and Social Psychology, 13,* 17–22.

Wyer, R. S. (1974). Changes in meaning and halo effects in personality impression information. *Journal of Personality and Social Psychology, 29,* 829–835.

Yancey, W. L. (1971). Architecture and social interaction: The case of a large-scale public housing project. *Environment and Behavior, 3,* 3–21.

Younger, J. C., Walker, L., & Arrowood, A. J. (1977). Post-decision dissonance at the fair. *Personality and Social Psychology Bulletin, 3,* 247–287. © 1977 by the American Psychological Association. Adapted by permission of the authors.

Youngs, G. A. (1986). Patterns of threat and punishment reciprocity in a conflict setting. *Journal of Personality and Social Psychology, 51,* 541–546.

Yukl, G. (1974). The effects of the opponent's initial offer, concession magnitude and concession frequency on bargaining behavior. *Journal of Personality and Social Psychology, 30,* 323–335.

Yukl, G. A., Malone, M. P., Hayslip, B., & Pamin, T. (1978). The effect of time pressure and issue settlement order on integrative bargaining. *Sociometry, 39,* 277–281.

Zajonc, R. B. (1965). Social facilitation. *Science, 149,* 269–274.

Zajonc, R. B. (1968). Attitudinal effects of mere exposure. *Journal of Personality and Social Psychology, 9,* 1–27.

Zajonc, R. B. (1972). *Animal social behavior.* Morristown, NJ: General Learning Press.

Zajonc, R. B. (1980). Compresence. In P. Paulus (Ed.), *Psychology of group influence.* Hillsdale, NJ: Erlbaum.

Zajonc, R. B., Markus, H., & Wilson, W. R. (1974). Exposure effects and associative learning. *Journal of Experimental Social Psychology, 10,* 248–262.

Zand, D. E. (1972). Trust and managerial problem-solving. *Administrative Science Quarterly, 17,* 229–239.

Zander, A. (1982). *Making groups effective.* San Francisco: Jossey-Bass.

Zanna, M. P., & Cooper, J. (1974). Dissonance and the pill: An attribution approach to studying the arousal properties of dissonance. *Journal of Personality and Social Psychology, 29,* 703–709. © 1974 by the American Psychological Association. Adapted by permission of the authors.

Zanna, M. P., & Cooper, J. (1976). Dissonance and the attribution process. In J. H. Harvey, W. J. Ickes, & R. F. Kidd (Eds.), *New directions in attribution research* (Vol. 1). Hillsdale, NJ: Erlbaum.

Zanna, M. P., & Fazio, R. H. (1982). The attitude-behavior relation: Moving toward a third generation of research. In M. P. Zanna, E. T. Higgins, & C. P. Herman (Eds.), *Consistency in social behavior: The Ontario symposium* (Vol. 2). Hillsdale, NJ: Erlbaum.

Zanna, M., Goethals, G. R., & Hill, J. (1975). Evaluating a sex-rated ability: Social comparison with similar others and standard setters. *Journal of Experimental Social Psychology, 11,* 86–93.

Zeichner, A., & Pihl, P. O. (1979). Effects of alcohol and behavior contingencies on human aggression. *Journal of Abnormal Psychology, 88,* 153–160.

Zelditch, M. (1955). Role differentiation in the nuclear family: A comparative study. In T. Parsons, R. Bales, et al., *Family, socialization and interaction process.* Glencoe, IL: Free Press.

Zillman, D. (1971). Excitation transfer in communication-mediated aggressive behavior. *Journal of Experimental Social Psychology, 7*, 419–434.

Zillman, D. (1978). *Hostility and aggression.* Hillsdale, NJ: Erlbaum.

Zillman, D. (1983). Transfer of excitation in emotional behavior. In J. T. Cacioppo & R. E. Petty (Eds.), *Social psychophysiology: A sourcebook.* New York: Guilford Press.

Zillman, D. (1984). *Connections between sex and aggression.* Hillsdale, NJ: Erlbaum.

Zillman, D., & Johnson, R. C. (1973). Maternal aggressiveness perpetuated by exposure to aggressive films and reduced by exposure to nonaggressive films. *Journal of Research in Personality, 7*, 261–276.

Zimbardo, P. (1965). The effect of effort and improvisation on self-persuasion produced by role playing. *Journal of Experimental Social Psychology, 1*, 103–120.

Zimbardo, P. (1970). The human choice: Individuation, reason and order versus individuation, impulse and chaos. Reprinted from the 1969 *Nebraska Symposium on Motivation.* Lincoln: University of Nebraska Press. Copyright © 1970 by the University of Nebraska Press, by permission.

Zimbardo, P., Weisenberg, M., Firestone, I., & Levy, B. (1965). Communicator effectiveness in producing public conformity and private attitude change. *Journal of Personality, 33*, 233–255.

Zimring, C., Weitzer, W., & Knight, R. C. (1982). Opportunity for control and the designed environment: The case of an institution for the developmentally disabled. In A. Baum & J. Singer (Eds.), *Advances in Environmental Psychology* (Vol. 4, pp. 170–210). Hillsdale, NJ: Erlbaum. Reprinted with permission.

Zuckerman, M., Amidon, M. D., Bishop, S. E., & Pomerantz, S. D. (1982). Face and tone of voice in the communication of deception. *Journal of Personality and Social Psychology, 43*, 347–357.

Zuckerman, M., DePaulo, B., & Rosenthal, R. (1981). Verbal and nonverbal communication of deception. In L. Berkowitz (Ed.), *Advances in experimental social psychology* (Vol. 14, pp. 1–59). New York: Academic Press.

Zukier, H. (1982). The role of the correlation and the dispersion of predictor variables in the use of nondiagnostic information. *Journal of Personality and Social Psychology, 43*, 1163–1175.

Zukier, H. & Pepitone, A. (1984). Social roles and strategies in prediction: Some determinants of the use of base-rate information. *Journal of Personality and Social Psychology, 47*, 349–360.

AUTHOR INDEX

SUBJECT INDEX

ABOUT THE AUTHORS

Stephen Worchel has been on the faculty at North Carolina Central University, the University of North Carolina, and the University of Virginia. He is presently Chair of the Department of Psychology at Texas A&M University. He received his B.A. degree from the University of Texas and his Ph.D. from Duke University. In 1979–80 he was a Senior Fulbright Research Fellow in Athens, Greece. Worchel has held editorial positions on the *Personality and Social Psychology Bulletin* and *Psychological Abstracts* and been a series editor for Van Nostrand Reinhold and Nelson-Hall publishing houses. He has written several books including *Psychology: Principles and Applications*; *Clinical Psychology: A Social Psychological Approach*; *Adjustment: Pathways to Personal Growth*; and *The Psychology of Intergroup Relations*. Worchel's recent research interests include interpersonal and intergroup conflict, group dynamics, and the influence of the environment on human behavior. Worchel believes that some of the most interesting applications of social psychology will involve an interdisciplinary approach. He is presently working with a team including investigators from business, engineering, and construction science on a research grant examining the factors that influence productivity, quality of work, and job satisfaction of construction groups.

Joel Cooper is currently chair of the Department of Psychology at Princeton University where he has been on the faculty since 1969. He received a B.A. degree from City College of New York and a Ph.D. from Duke University. In 1975 Cooper was Senior Fellow at the East-West Population Institute. He has served on the editorial boards of the *Journal of Personality*; *Journal of Experimental and Social Psychology*; and the *Social Psychology Quarterly*. He has contributed to many books and has written numerous articles in the field of social psychology. Cooper is working on research in attitude formation and change, cognitive consistency theories, and perception and evaluation of persons, among other areas.

George R. Goethals is Professor of Psychology and Acting Dean of the Faculty at Williams College in Williamstown, Massachusetts. He received his A.B. from Harvard and his Ph.D. from Duke University. He is on the Executive Committee of the Society of Experimental Social Psychology. Goethals' research interests are self-evaluation, social comparison, attribution, and person perception. He has served as Associate Editor of the *Journal of Experimental Social Psychology*. He is co-author of *Psychology* (with Crider, Kavanaugh, and Solomon) and co-editor of *Theories of Group Behavior* (with Mullen). Goethals escapes to the beaches of Martha's Vineyard or the high peaks of the Adirondacks whenever possible.

A NOTE ON THE TYPE

The text of this book was set in 10/12 Palatino using a film version of the face designed by Hermann Zapf that was first released in 1950 by Germany's Stempel Foundry. The face is named after Giovanni Battista Palatino, a famous penman of the sixteenth century. In its calligraphic quality, Palatino is reminiscent of the Italian Renaissance type designs, yet with its wide, open letters and unique proportions it still retains a modern feel. Palatino is considered one of the most important faces from one of Europe's most influential type designers.

Composed by Arkotype Inc., New York City.

Printed and bound by R. R. Donnelley & Sons, Crawfordsville, Indiana.